COMMUNICATION
FOR
MANAGERS
SIXTH EDITION

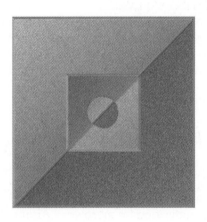

NORMAN B. SIGBAND
University of Southern California

ARTHUR H. BELL
McLaren School of Business
University of San Francisco

COLLEGE DIVISION South-Western Publishing Co.

Cincinnati Ohio

Acquisitions Editor: Jeanne R. Busemeyer
Production Editor: Sue Ellen Brown
Developmental Editor: Cinci Stowell
Marketing Manager: Scott D. Person
Cover Designer: Graphica
Internal Designer: Lesiak/Crampton Design
Production House: York Production Services

EH61FA
Copyright © 1994
by South-Western Publishing Co.
Cincinnati, Ohio

1 2 3 4 5 6 7 KI 9 8 7 6 5 4 3

Printed in the United States of America

Library of Congress Cataloging-in-Publication Data

Bell, Arthur H. (Arthur Henry),
    Communication for managers / Arthur H. Bell, Norman B. Sigband. —
6th ed.
        p.   cm.
    Previous ed. published under title: Communication for management
and business / Norman B. Sigband, Arthur H. Bell. 5th ed. ©1989.
    Includes bibliographical references and index.
    ISBN 0-538-83475-7 (alk. paper)
    1. Business communication.   I. Sigband, Norman B.   II. Sigband,
Norman B.   Communication for management and business.   III. Title.
HF5718.S53   1994
658.4'5—dc20   93-27425
                                                                                          CIP

I(T)P
International Thomson Publishing

South-Western Publishing Co. is an ITP Company. The ITP trademark is used
under license.

This book is printed on acid-free paper that meets Environmental Protection Agency standards for recycled paper.

The communication revolution, intercultural communication, ethics, collaborative communication, crisis communication, case-based instruction—these are some of the themes of increasing importance in business communication classes of the mid-1990s. The sixth edition of *Communication for Managers* offers several new chapters in these areas. At the same time, this edition maintains its commitment to managerial writing, speaking, and listening, with revised and updated examples and pedagogy.

The authors of this edition began their revision work by listening to the calls of instructors, students, practicing managers, and the American Assembly of Collegiate Schools of Business (AACSB) for applied communication studies as a significant part of business education at both the undergraduate and MBA levels. The thrust of these recommendations is for instruction that concentrates on the *how* of business communication: how ideas are generated and organized for writing and speaking, how new communication technologies are used to best advantage, and how communication styles adapt to audience and purpose in domestic and international settings. This edition responds to these needs by presenting a step-by-step guide, with many before-and-after examples, for achieving communication success.

New readings and cases provide opportunities to extend and apply communication insights. Selected materials from recent issues of the *Harvard Business Review, Business Week, Supervisory Management, Personnel Journal, Hispanic Business,* and other sources present viewpoints to supplement text perspectives. Cases focus on both traditional and emerging communication challenges in such areas as the health-care industry, mergers, multicultural work environments, and computer security. For some cases, video and film presentations are available.

The authors are especially grateful for the contributions of noted colleagues to this edition. Carol Shuherk, Academic Director of the MBA Program at the University of Southern California, wrote the *"Cultural Diversity in Communication"* features that appear frequently throughout the text. These penetrating and interesting essays give the reader a factual, added dimension to the on-going and important cultural changes in our society today. Tracy Dillon, Director of Business Writing at Portland State University, provided commentaries in the margins throughout the text. These not only give the reader quick summaries of key concepts but also emphasize the important principles discussed in the text. Dayle M. Smith, Associate Professor of Management at the University of San Francisco, compiled the Resource Guide. Used by instructors, the Guide will not only save countless hours of preparation time, but it will also provide suggestions on innovative and different ways of using the text materials in class, Ken Mitchell, Southeastern Louisiana State University, has reviewed and added to the end-of-chapter questions in a meaningful way.

Leaders from Johnson & Johnson, TRW, United Way, Methodist Hospital of Southern California and other major public and private organizations, appear at the beginning of each Part of the text. These individuals comment on their own communication experiences as well as the vital role communication plays in the manager's daily activities.

In a textbook in which so much is new, one essential design feature remains constant: the "three-books-in-one" concept that has seen *Communication for Managers* successfully into its sixth edition. In one volume, instructors and students have a textbook, casebook, and collection of readings.

In short, the sixth edition of *Communication for Managers* attempts to answer the call for a complete, progressive business communication textbook for the 1990s and beyond. In revising virtually every page for this edition, the authors and editors have been guided by one principle: prepare students for the future, not the past.

SUPPLEMENTS

The sixth edition is accompanied by a strong ancillary package:

- A *Resource Guide* with chapter summaries, quizzes, sample syllabi, a video/film directory, and sections on word-processing, desktop publishing, and computer graphics.
- A revised *Test Bank.*
- Computer ancillaries, including a classroom management system and diagnostic tools.
- Lecture transparencies, with examples of business documents as well as graphic aids.

We are especially indebted to knowledgable and well-recognized individuals in the field of management and business communications who have carefully reviewed the text and manuscript. Their suggestions and recommendations played a key role in the book's revision and added significantly to the value, content, and direction of this edition. Among those we wish to thank for their efforts are:

Jo Allen
East Carolina University
John D. Beard
Wayne State University
Bernadine P. Branchaw
Western Michigan University
Lillian H. Chaney
Memphis State University
William B. Chapel
Michigan Technological University
Daniel S. Cochran
Mississippi State University
Marian C. Crawford
University of Arkansas Little Rock
Karon L. Cunningham
Southwest Missouri State University
Nancy A. Dittman
Bloomsburg University

Robert D. Gieselman
University of Illinois Urbana-Champaign
Ridley J. Gros
Nicholls State University
Michael M. Harris
University of Missouri St. Louis
Janet E. Hildebrand
Texas Christian University
Thomas S. Hilton
Utah State University
Geraldine E. Hynes
University of Missouri St. Louis
Phillip V. Lewis
Abilene Christian University
Gail Lukasik
1111 Pine Tree, Libertyville, IL 60048

Donna W. Luse
Northeast Louisiana University
James S. O'Rourke IV
University of Notre Dame
Diana C. Reep
The University of Akron
Donald P. Rogers
Rollins College

William C. Sharbrough
The Citadel
Warren C. Weber
*California State Polytechnic
    University Pomona*
Marian K. Woodall
*Professional Business
    Communications Lake Oswego,
    OR*

In addition to the above, we are grateful to the following for helpful ideas and suggestions: Professors Jim Bennett of California State University at Northridge and Lois Bachman, Community College of Philadelphia; Dr. Edward Hesterlee, Mallinckrodt Corp.; Dr. Robert Hunter of Merck Human Health Division; Don Robinson, Executive District Manager of Merck Human Health Division; Davre Davidson, Chairman Emeritus, ARA Services.

Norm Sigband wants to express special thanks to Dean John A. Biles, Associate Deans Phillip R. Oppenheimer and Cynthia White, Faculty Affairs Director Patricia R. Brown, Management Development Director Philip J. Rapa, and Word Processing Specialists Jane Radaza and Elvie De Belen, all of the University of Southern California for their support in the revision, review and rewriting effort required.

Sincere appreciation is also extended to Elizabeth H. Wood, Head, Reference Section, Norris Medical Library, University of Southern California, for her major contributions to the Research Supplement in this book. Art Bell expresses deep-felt thanks to Dean Gary Williams, Associate Deans Eugene Muscat and Mary Smith, MBA Director Diane Dimeff, and professors Karl Bodecker, Kathleen Kane, and Dayle Smith of the McLaren School of Business, University of San Francisco, for their encouragement, conversations, and support.

The dedicated work and commitment at South-Western Publishing were, of course, vital in bringing this book to print. Among the many key people who were and are involved are Vice-President Jim Sitlington, a trusted mentor through many revisions of the book, Acquisitions Editor Jeanne R. Busemeyer, and Developmental Editor Cinci Stowell, who spent countless hours polishing and revising the author's effort, and Production Editor Sue Ellen Brown, who guided the book into print.

Once again, we want to acknowledge our families, from whom so much time was taken, for their support, encouragement and good humor.

For Norm Sigband, special thanks and love go to his wife, Joan, as well as his daughters, Robin Gotz, Shelley Wilkerson and Betsy Seamans; to his son-in-law, Glenn Gotz, and to two of the world's outstanding grandchildren, Tami and Laura.

And for Art Bell, deep-felt thanks go to his wife, Dayle, and children, Art and Lauren, for their love, support, and patience.

NORMAN B. SIGBAND
ARTHUR H. BELL

BRIEF CONTENTS

CONTENTS

P A R T   **5**
REPORTS AND PROPOSALS   350

16   THE RESEARCH PROCESS   352

17   VISUAL AIDS   391

P A R T   **6**

PROFESSIONAL SPEAKING AND LISTENING THAT WORKS   518

26 COMMUNICATION DURING CRISIS AND CHANGE   585

CASES FOR DISCUSSION   605

P A R T 1

A COMMUNICATION OVERVIEW

Devon Scheef is Manager of Organizational and Human Resource Development for TRW Information Systems and Services. She supervises the creation and administration of sales and management development programs for her company's account executives and managers.

TRW Information Systems & Services

500 City Parkway West
Orange, CA 92668
714.385.7000

Dear Future Manager:

It's my pleasure to tell you about my communication experiences at TRW. We're known as a company on the cutting edge of technology, and that holds true for communication technologies as well.

Probably the most important aspect of my position as Director of Training is communicating effectively to diverse audiences. These include employees just beginning their career with TRW, and veteran employees with decades of experience; secretarial workers in the company and senior management; and, clients and the general public. My staff and I are faced each day with decisions not only about what to say to these groups, but how to say it—and in what medium. Would a videotape be more memorable than a printed report or instructional manual? Would a fax have more impact than a mailed letter? Would e-mail seem to casual or an expressed letter too urgent or formal?

You're now involved in studying the communication topics that make or break a manager's effectiveness. I urge you to become deeply knowledgeable not only about the newest communication technologies but also about traditional communication values such as clarity, brevity, and organization. The ability to communicate well to various audiences has been important to my career success at TRW. I believe that what you're now learning about communication will be no less important to your professional future.

With best wishes for success,

Devon Scheef
Manager, Organization and Human Resource Development
TRW Information Systems and Services

THE PROCESS AND PROBLEMS OF COMMUNICATION

The greatest illusion in communication is to assume it always takes place effectively.

We are all deeply involved in the Information Age. In fact, it might be more accurate to say, as Alvin Toffler does in his book *Powershift* (1990), that we are in a communication revolution.

We are inundated with information. The daily newspaper that once was 12 pages long is now 210 pages; the single magazine delivered to our home weekly has been replaced by five magazines and many more catalogs, brochures, and booklets. Two or three movies or books were once released daily; now there are a dozen of each, plus a growing number of video and audio cassettes. In addition, fax machines, cellular phones, electronic mail, call forwarding, and a dozen other electronic devices assist us in our communication—and increase it. Only a generation ago, the giant computer functioned only in major corporations. Today, desk-top versions are common in the home (often with capacity equal to the very large earlier units), and dozens of computers operate in almost every organization in this country and abroad.

As many companies grow larger, mergers increase, and activities within organizations become specialized, even more communication is needed to keep the wheels turning. The business world depends on communication. For example, in just the past 2 to 3 years the fax machine has become an almost indispensable communication device.

Look at your own life. How do your academic activities compare with those of students 50 years ago? The routine of attending six lecture classes in a row has largely disappeared. You are frequently involved in discussion groups and in giving presentations in your classes. Social activities are much more oriented toward communication. Distances are shorter—traveling by car is easy and traveling by plane is far more common and often less expensive than it was 20 years ago. Consider how often you make local and long-distance phone calls.

But communicating more—at home, at work, at play—does not mean we are doing it better or even as well as we did 50 years ago. Yet, the importance of effective communication is recognized today as never before. In 1990 the University of Pennsylvania's Katz Graduate School of Business surveyed 300 corporations. One of the survey's objectives was to determine "the values and attitudes, strengths and weaknesses of recent MBA graduates." The leading response to the first item, "Please rate the following attributes on their importance to you in your recruitment/selection of MBAs," was "communication skills." In answer to the question, "Of the skills listed above (or others), which are the most important for an MBA to have when entering your organization?" the response "make written presentations" was second from the top with "oral presentations" following closely. Perhaps the most telling finding in this survey was the response to this question: "What one improvement would you suggest to business school deans concerning their MBA programs?" One of the most popular responses was "better written and oral communication skills."

A July 1991 article in *Fortune* magazine states that the Wharton School of Business (University of Pennsylvania) interviewed more than 1,000 recruiters, alumni, and executives. The survey found that MBAs were least skilled in dealing with people, leadership, teamwork, negotiating, communicating, and creativity. In 1989 the business school at the University of Chicago introduced a new MBA course covering leadership, negotiation, communication, self-awareness, and ethics.[1]

The addition of "communication" to the curriculum at the University of Chicago is being imitated in many other MBA programs throughout the country. Inclusion of communication in MBA programs reflects similar activities in other graduate programs as well as in executive and management development programs held nationwide. Businesspeople recognize that there is little value to competence in finance, planning, strategy, and a dozen other areas, if vital concepts cannot be communicated effectively to others.

COMMUNICATION AND THE ORGANIZATION

Formal channels of communication include written documents, meetings, and teleconferences.

In every organization, communication occurs constantly. If we walk from the third to the sixth floor of the Marquette Corporation, for example, we might observe the following activities: staff preparing reports, letters, memoranda, proposals, and studies; executives and managers participating in meetings, interviews, and presentations; other staff talking on the telephone, as part of a teleconference, and in negotiating situations. Almost every desk has a computer display terminal, and a printer is nearby. The work processing center is busy, electronic mail is flowing back and forth, and many other human and electronic communication activities are taking place through varied media.

These are *formal channels of communication.* When they do not satisfy an individual's need to know, that is, when they leave questions unanswered, that individual may turn to the *unofficial channels of communication.* For example, employees at the Marquette Corporation have heard that the West End work force may be cut and 300 employees transferred to the Merryville facility 40 miles north. Management has said nothing officially about this possibility. Understandably, employees are upset. The result? The grapevine, or the unofficial communication channel, takes over to explain the change. Any competent manager makes every effort to listen to the grapevine. In this case, the manager probably will distribute a memo to the concerned employees to clarify the situation.

Informal channels of communication are best thought of as the grapevine.

The examples of the Marquette Corporation are based on the behavioral theory of communication. In this chapter we discuss this theory and its implications. Later, in Chapter 3 (in connection with the office of the future), we will examine the mathematical theory. The similarities between the two theories will be easy to recognize by referring to the simple chart shown in Figure 1-1.

FIGURE 1–1 Flowchart Depicting the Process of Communication

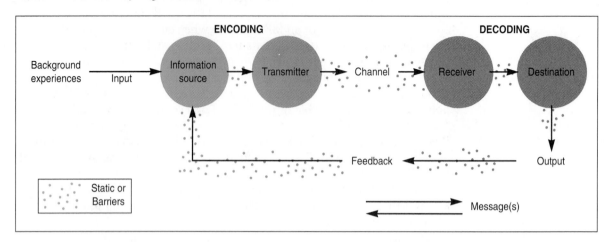

Let's begin our discussion by defining some terms:

Background experiences are bits of information in human or computer
    memory that are brought to ("input to") a communication or a message.
The *message* is made up of bits of information that can be transmitted.
Encoding is the selection and formulation of bits of information to be
    transmitted as a message in an understandable language.
The *transmitter* is the unit (person or machine) that sends the message to
    the decoder or receiver.
The *channel* is the means of conveying the message; it may be print,
    sound, touch, air, or another medium.
Decoding is the interpretation of the message by the receiver.
Feedback is the receiver's response, which gives the transmitter some
    indication of how the original message was received.
Input is stored information (in a brain or computer) composed of back-
    ground experiences. Input is used when communication takes place.
Output is the communication of information from the information source
    to the transmitter.

*Static prevents effective
communication by
interfering with the
sending or receiving
of the message.*

Often static occurs in the channels of communication. Static consists of barriers to effective communication that interfere with the sending or receiving of
the basic message. These barriers may be distractions, emotions, bias, or a dozen
others. (See discussion of barriers later in this chapter.)

Let us now look at two examples of communication: one machine, the other
human.

In a computer-assisted manufacturing assembly (CAM), an automobile line
may stop automatically because a car chassis is not properly balanced on the
conveyor mechanism. The instrument that is "tripped" because of the imbalance is the information source. The message it sends to the computer is selected
from various pieces of stored information such as "too heavy," "not balanced,"
or "backward." The information selected fits the situation and is encoded and
sent to the radio transmitter, which in turn transmits the message over a designated channel to a receiver. The message now goes to a computer to be
decoded. Because all the systems are programmed similarly, the message is
properly decoded "not balanced," and the conveyor mechanism automatically

stops. The instrument that was originally tripped is programmed to allow up to 4 seconds for the conveyor to stop. The halt of the conveyor is the feedback. Had the wrong feedback been received (no stop after 4 seconds), an alarm bell would have sounded and the next step in the program brought into play: termination of electric power to the conveyor belt.

A similar situation exists when manager Watkins says to staff assistant Butterfield, "Then, we're all set. You will submit a brief progress report tomorrow on the Jupiter Project to the executive vice president. I told him he would have it quite early." Here we have an encoder, decoder, message, and channel. There would seem to be no problem. However, in this case the experience and semantic backgrounds of the encoder and decoder are different. To the executive vice president and the manager, "quite early" means in the morning and before 9 A.M. To staff assistant Butterfield, who is not programmed the same way, "quite early" means before 2 P.M.

When the executive vice president receives "feedback" the next day, which is no report by 9 A.M., he calls manager Watkins and almost shouts, "You said 'quite early' but I still don't have it!" Watkins now recognizes that his experience (information source) was not the same as Butterfield's and feedback to Butterfield is necessary.

Because people are different, the meanings they attach to the same words and gestures may be different; the result is communication breakdown.

Thus, it is easy to see how barriers, noise, or static can cause breakdowns in human or machine communication. A related fact is also obvious: although computers can be programmed with similar bits of information to react similarly, people cannot. Because our experiences are different, we may attribute different meanings to the same verbal and nonverbal signals. When we do, communication (or decoding) between sender and receiver may suffer.

HUMAN OR BEHAVIORAL THEORY OF COMMUNICATION

The occurrences of verbal and nonverbal behavior in an organization are innumerable. Some communication specialists believe that almost all forms of behavior are really means of communication, and conversely, that all forms of communication reflect the behavior of individuals.

Theories of human communication focus on human perceptions.

People who are concerned with human communication do not focus on precisely what individuals say or write, but on how they *perceive and think about* the message. Experts in the behavioral sciences and related areas have contributed a great deal to the field of communication. For example, fundamental work on theories of human communication has been done by psychiatrist Jurgen Ruesch.[2] He identified several communication networks:

- The *intrapersonal* network is entirely within the individual and involves thinking and feeling.
- The *interpersonal* network links two or more persons.
- The *group* interaction network links groups of people. Because of the number of people involved, it is usually difficult to achieve effective communication with everybody.
- The *cultural* network is not related to a specific originator or receiver of the message. Certain symbols in society—modes of transportation, clothing, homes, morals, and the like—are part of a cultural network. It is almost impossible to correct or change a cultural network because of its powerful and pervasive nature.

Managers use communication to persuade, inform, and motivate.

In an effort to attain organizational goals, managers use communication to persuade, inform, and motivate people who play key roles in getting things done. Managers almost always get their jobs done through other people. They may be skilled controllers, production supervisors, or directors of engineering, but they need people to help them achieve their objectives. The only way a manager can get other people to do what he or she thinks should be done is through communication. Monetary rewards and fear may be effective motivators, but they rarely work on a long-term basis. Communication, which often fulfills basic social and egoistic needs, can and does work as a positive motivator. And spoken words of praise or recognition, or a look that reflects encouragement or approval, may be just as effective a means of communication as any written memorandum.

THE PROCESS OF HUMAN COMMUNICATION

The complex process of human communication involves senses, experiences, and feelings. It is more than just letters, reports, telephone calls, and interviews. Human communication is the action of people talking, listening, seeing, feeling, and reacting to each other, their experiences, and their environment.

Communication is an active process.

When one person speaks, writes, listens, or gestures to another, there is constant action and reaction between the two. In addition to interpreting the words we hear, we listen to and interpret voice inflections and interpret facial expressions, the drumming of fingers, the nervous tapping of a foot on the floor, and so forth. Our own internal stimuli—our emotions, feelings, experiences, interests, and other contributing factors—also cause us to perceive actions and words in specific ways.

When Mr. Able and Ms. Baker talk or write to each other, they are doing more than simply exchanging words. Let's listen to a conversation.

Able and Baker have been examining and discussing some construction plans for the past 3 hours. Baker leans back, stretches, and says to Able, "My head is so loaded with figures and statistics that it's going in circles. Besides, the air is hot in here; what do you say we go out to eat?" Baker has put some specific feelings into words (encoded them). Able, whose mind is still deeply involved with the building plans, listens (completely or partially) and must now understand (decode) Baker's message. But will he decode the message as Baker intended?

Baker is tired, not quite clear about the plans, and hungry. But Able is enthusiastic and wants to get the job done. As a matter of fact, he may be offended by Baker's apparent implication that he confused her. He may think that is why Baker's head is "going in circles." As for the "hot air" Baker mentions, Able's interpretation of that—in his mood—is unmistakable. Yet Baker made a simple, sincere statement whose meaning seemed obvious to her. Why, then, does Able suddenly seem angry and irritated with Baker's casual comment?

Able, of course, decoded or interpreted Baker's message on the basis of his feelings, experiences, thoughts, and perhaps even his desires; he interpreted not only Baker's words but also her gestures, actions, tone of voice, and their relationship. No matter that the interpretation may not be what Baker intended; as far as Able is concerned, it *is* what Baker intended.

The lesson here is frequently overlooked in the process of communication. We are often victims of the illusion that we have communicated effectively

Simply sending a message does not ensure that it will be received the way it was intended to be received.

when we have not. The apparent solution to this problem is to check the effectiveness of our communication (whether it is a statement, a memo, a report, a letter, or a speech) through feedback. But how valid is the feedback we receive?

In electronic communication, feedback is usually more reliable than it is in human communication. We press the power button and the screen lights up; we turn the switch and the motor begins; we release the lever and the 10-ton press begins to rise. Feedback is *immediate* and reliable.

Cybernetics is a branch of science that deals with feedback as an aspect of communication. It is further concerned with the theory of such systems as the nerve networks in animals, electronic pathways in computing machines, servo systems for the automatic control of machinery, and other information processing, transmission, and control systems.

In cybernetics, *feedback* refers to the ability of humans and some machines to detect an error or deviation from what is desired in an operation and to "feed back" that error to a control mechanism, which then makes the necessary correction. If a satellite destined for a point in space moves off course, the deviation is noted and fed back to the controlling mechanism for correction. A home thermostat records a temperature that is too low and feeds back a signal to the furnace, which then operates to make a correction. If a person's body temperature becomes lower than normal, that information is fed back to the nervous system and his or her physiological control mechanism makes the muscles shiver. Thus, a common feature of a control system is that the output produces an effect on the input. In communication engineering this effect is called feedback. A control-systems engineer refers to it as a closed-loop system.

The similarities of feedback in this technical concept to that in interpersonal communication are apparent. We even have a common expression, "Have you closed the loop?" This question asks whether the communicator (encoder) has secured a satisfactory response (feedback) from the receiver (decoder) and thus satisfactorily closed the loop and secured understanding.

Feedback refers to the receiver's response to our message, which in turn lets us know whether we have communicated successfully.

The popular meaning of the term *feedback* is the verbal or nonverbal response received from the individual to whom a message is directed. It may be a series of words; it may be a raised eyebrow, an angry expression, or a smile; it may be no response at all (which is a response indicating that the message was not heard, not understood, or not accepted). It is only through the feedback we receive that we can know whether we have communicated our ideas. Consider some examples:

- John asks his daughter to open the window and she does it, so John knows he has communicated successfully. However, if she opens the door, that incorrect response or feedback tells John that communication has broken down.
- A supervisor writes a memo to her manager about a new project. The manager does not fully understand the proposed project and asks the supervisor for more information. The manager's questions (or feedback) tell the supervisor how successful she was in presenting her ideas.
- A boss quickly explains a new procedure to her subordinate and concludes with, "Now, Mike, do you see how that works?" Almost invariably Mike will say, "Yes, I do."

Why do we so often say, "Yes, I understand," when we really do not? The answer is complex. Sometimes we really think we understand but we do not.

Feedback can be inaccurate when influenced by ego and emotion.

In most cases, however, our egos or our emotions force us to say, "Yes, I understand," when we really don't. Who wishes to be thought a fool? So the feedback is not accurate. Nevertheless, the receiver often accepts it as reliable. Perhaps this is also an ego problem. Who wants to hear that his or her communication was *not* clear?

On other occasions, we receive no feedback at all or receive it too late:

- Three weeks have passed since a report was submitted. McKenzie, the author of the report, learns that the company president needs additional information that was not included in the report. Yet when McKenzie offers to supply it, the president says, "I got it myself." Thus, the feedback came too late to be of value to McKenzie.
- A professor reads the final exam (the feedback) only to discover that 80 percent of the class didn't understand concept ABC. It is too late to bring them together to review it.

We can ensure that feedback is reliable only through thoughtful analysis and self-evaluation.

Feedback is often a dilemma. On the one hand, we say "We must check the feedback to determine how effectively we communicated." But on the other hand, we say, "Feedback may not be reliable." The answer seems to be that we must become sensitive to all the forms of feedback at our disposal. At times, we can *provide* feedback by self-evaluation and playing "devil's advocate" to our own ideas. In these ways we have a chance to make important adjustments before we sign the letter, initial the report, or sit down after a speech.

Unsparing openness to self-evaluation and self-improvement in communication takes courage, patience, and insight. Communicators at all levels, from the beginner to the expert, face the challenge of putting aside favorite notions and assumptions to really *hear* the other side of the story. That same openness must extend to nonhuman sources of information. Computers have a great deal to "tell" businesspeople: data printouts, statistical summaries, computer-managed logs, and even—with the advent of artificial intelligence—reasoned advice. "Computer anxiety," a somewhat natural response to a new and powerful technology, should not prevent anyone from hearing what computers have to say. Training programs and reading materials for the layperson can help allay any such anxiety.

As we communicate we must keep in mind the following four points about feedback received from the world around us:

1. It must be secured.
2. It may not be accurate.
3. It may come too late to correct the communication.
4. It can reach us by nonverbal and verbal ways (often both).

To assume that communication always takes place effectively may be the greatest illusion of all.

OBJECTIVES OF COMMUNICATION

We communicate for a purpose. Generally, there are three basic objectives in communication:

1. To be understood exactly as we intended
2. To secure the desired response to our message
3. To maintain favorable relations with those with whom we communicate

Whenever we communicate with others, *some* understanding (or misunderstanding) will take place. What we wish to ensure, however, is that the decoder understands the message as *we* understand the message. That is why the last three words in objective 1 are so important. As for objective 2, any response—positive, negative, or noncommittal—tells the encoder something. Of course, the encoder usually hopes the decoder's response (or feedback) will be positive. Finally, because we work, live, and exist in a world of associates, we hope to achieve objective 3.

For all types of communication, we should strive to be understood as we intended, secure the desired response, and maintain a favorable relationship with our audience.

An encoder can write or talk to a decoder and fail to achieve any of the objectives. Or it is possible to achieve the first objective but not the second or third. It is even possible to send a message in such a way as to secure objectives 1 and 2 but to antagonize the decoder and not achieve objective 3. Our goal in *all* types of communication, however, should be to attain all of these objectives.

BARRIERS TO COMMUNICATION

We must be able to identify barriers to successful communication in order to overcome them.

We have all had the experience of writing or speaking to others and then learning that the communication has not been effective: we did not achieve our communication objectives. Instead, barriers arose between sender and receiver. Perhaps it was bias on the part of one or emotions on the part of the other. Perhaps distractions impinged on both parties. Whatever the factors—and there are many—let's label them as barriers to effective communication. If we can identify the barrier or barriers in a communication situation and determine who is at fault (sender or receiver), we can work toward eliminating these obstacles.

NONVERBAL BARRIERS

It is no exaggeration to say that approximately 60 percent of our communication is nonverbal. The way we stand, walk, shrug our shoulders, furrow our brows, and shake our heads convey ideas to others. But we need not perform an action for nonverbal communication to take place. We also communicate by the clothes we wear, the car we drive, or the office we occupy. What is communicated may not be accurate, but ideas of some kind *are* communicated.

Sometimes a speaker's gestures or facial expressions contradict the apparent meaning of the message. Nonverbal signals then become barriers to successful communication.

Nonverbal external and internal stimuli play an important role in our interpretation of words. Sometimes these stimuli are so strong that we interpret them instead of the words directed to us. When these factors sway our understanding to a degree that does not harmonize at all with the meaning intended by the communicator, they become *barriers* to the clear interpretation of ideas. This, of course, is what happened to our friends Mr. Able and Ms. Baker. If we become more aware of what these barriers are, we may be able to cope with them better.

It's the encoder's responsibility to ensure that communication has taken place successfully. By knowing the barriers, the encoder can overcome them.

Perhaps a good analogy is the physician-patient relationship. It isn't enough for the physician to state, "The patient is sick." If the patient is to be cured, the physician must pinpoint the trouble and treat it appropriately. The same is true of the encoder who has failed to communicate effectively. That individual must determine the specific barrier(s) that caused the communication breakdown and then attempt to alleviate or eliminate it. If the encoder has some knowledge about the barriers that can occur, it will be easier for him or her to diagnose the case and remedy the problems.

CULTURAL DIVERSITY IN COMMUNICATION

**Cultural Diversity =
Communication
Complexity**

Carol Shuherk
*University of
Southern California*

Scholars generally agree that when it comes to communication, there are few truths (with a capital T) applicable to all human beings. We are too infinitely varied for that. One of the few, however, is the truth that the interpretation of any message depends on the perception of the person receiving it. The wider the gap in backgrounds and experience between communicators, the greater the chance the receiver's interpretation will differ from the sender's intent.

The cultural diversity in our world makes the communication process dramatically more complex. The increased focus on culture as a shaping force in the values, beliefs, and behavior of people has broadened our perspective of what cultures are—national and ethnic cultures, male and female cultures, the cultures of the disabled, of gays and lesbians, of religions, and of specific professions, to name a few. Bridging cultural boundaries is a major communication challenge for managers now and in the future.

Misunderstandings in communication can cause international business relationships to collapse; often the problem seems to stem from personal shortcomings. In fact, the source is often a difference in the cultural values and norms that dictate communication behavior. Consider two examples: An American manager working in Tokyo on a joint venture calls a meeting with his Japanese sponsors in the wake of several problems with the project. He explains in detail the reasons behind the problems and the impossibility of predicting these things in the planning process. He concludes by indicating willingness to take partial responsibility. The Japanese listen without comment. In subsequent conversations, he notices a distinct cooling in their attitude toward him and is unable to determine why. Another American, a negotiator for a manufacturing machine supplier, is invited to the home of his Middle Eastern counterpart in the final stages of negoti-

ating a contract to equip a new plant. While waiting for his host to complete a telephone call, he notices a woman and two small children outside in a central courtyard. Assuming she is his host's wife, he steps outside and introduces himself, remarking on her lovely home and family. Fully expecting the signed contract to arrive by mail shortly after, he is baffled when, in fact, it never comes.

In these two examples, the Americans unwittingly violated rules of communication. Japanese take the blame for problems that happen under their leadership. They do not explain, they do not justify, they simply say, "I am responsible." In fundamentalist Islamic nations strict taboos govern the interaction between men and women, and it is not appropriate to initiate conversation without introduction.

Back at home in the United States the cultural diversity of the American work force would not seem to present such pitfalls, bound as we are by a common language and shared national experience. In reality, it presents a peril of another kind. Often we've been exposed to people different from ourselves just enough to think we can make broad generalizations about how individuals will behave, based on their group identity as "Blacks," "Hispanics," "Indians," "Asians," or "Anglos." Stereotyping becomes a basis for interpreting the words and actions of groups outside our own and influences the ways we communicate with them.

Consider the employees of Chinese descent who sit quietly in staff meetings while around them their colleagues engage in lively debate over the pros and cons of a reorganization, or the Native American who responds to a manager's praise by looking downward and away, or the African-American male employee who, on being criticized for part of his work, provides no explanations but stares silently back at his manager. We might think we can explain these incidents quickly, based on general stereotypes of each group: Asians are quiet and shy, Native Americans are noncommunicative, and black men are hostile. In fact, Asian cultures teach to remain quiet as a demonstration of respect until asked by the person in charge to speak. Native American culture emphasizes the importance of the group, and individuals do not seek, nor desire, to be singled out. African-Americans, as a group, act more deliberately and study visual cues more than do most white males. The perspective based on stereotype turns out to hold a grain of truth but does not provide enough knowledge of an individual's cultural background to form a basis for interaction.

Further complicating the communication process is the increasing focus on cultural differences beyond national or ethnic identity. In her book, *You Just Don't Understand: Women and Men in Conversation,* author Deborah Tannen puts the communication differences between women and men in negotiation terms. As a source of differences, she points to differing value systems, the result of very different messages about what is important for males and females as they are growing up. Conditioned for membership in a culture that values action, reason, taking charge, and winning, male conversations are negotiations for control in which "people try to achieve and maintain the upper hand, protect themselves from other's attempts to put them down and push them around." Women, on the other hand, conditioned to a culture valuing nurturance, supportiveness, relationships, and intimacy, approach conversations as negotiations for closeness, in which "people try to seek and give confirmation and support, to reach consensus and protect themselves from other's attempts to push them away."

Nationalities, ethnic affiliations, gender . . . the list of different ways to view the world, from the lens of one particular group or another and from several groups at one time, can go on and on,

all with the potential to complicate the problems and the process of communication.

Communication gaps exist between groups who view the world of work itself from differing value systems. Professionals who work with ideas or for ideals, such as professors, journalists, architects, public officials, and the nonprofit sector, might be culturally labeled the "intelligentsia." They are expected to be liberal, independent, highly verbal, and creative. Their professional counterpoints are the members of "corporate culture," who are seen as team players, conformists, loyalists, and free-market conservatives. Huge communication gaps exist between those who labor under the effects of physical disability and those who do not. A former stock trader and beach volleyball champion who lost the use of his legs in a car accident notes that the major message members of the "physically whole" culture send to those who are disabled is, "You make me uncomfortable; I'd rather not deal with you." He comments that he never realized he had consistently sent that message himself until he saw his own past behavior reflected in the faces of people whose eyes dart toward and away from his withered legs and never directly into his eyes.

How can the process of communicating across cultures be managed to the mutual benefit of all? Is it necessary to become intimate with the values and the points of view of all these groups of people? That, obviously, would be impossible. The best strategy is to first appreciate that cultural differences enable people to bring different points of view to a business discussion that will broaden both analysis and strategy if effectively tapped. Second, focus on being responsive to the individuals involved, wholly apart from their cultural group identity. As a young architect, the child of a French-Canadian mother and an African-American/Creole father, put it, "I like it best when people relate to me as Debra."

Differences in perception of a situation may cause ineffective communication. Our previous experiences largely determine how we react to specific stimuli. Viewing the same thing, individuals of different ages, cultural backgrounds, and national origins often have different perceptions. They use their knowledge, their culture, and their experiences to interpret what they see. Not only does each of us see things differently, but when two of us hear a statement, we may also interpret (hear or perceive) it differently.

Let us look at Line Foreman Anderson, his supervisor, Assistant Plant Supervisor Benton, and Development Engineer Carleton. They have just finished lunch and are walking back to the shop area. Forty feet ahead of them are seven or eight production workers who work directly under Anderson and in Benton's department. As the three walk past, the circle of workers suddenly breaks into laughter and backslapping.

How did the foreman, assistant plant supervisor, and engineer each perceive this? Anderson, who has been having trouble securing cooperation from several of the workers, hears derisive and insulting laughter. Benton, who prides herself on "running a tight ship with high morale," hears good-natured steam being let off. Carleton, who works as an engineer with dozens of different shop groups from week to week, doesn't even hear the laughter, which has come at the precise instant when he has reached the high point of the story *he* is telling Anderson and Benton.

Consider the reaction of three employees to the sight of a large new machine being moved into the shop. Worker Fenton perceives it as a threat to his job—a replacement for his skills. Production Supervisor Gable views it as an asset that will help her achieve higher production levels and thus secure her bonus. Treasurer Holcomb perceives it as a further drain on the company's limited resources.

The point in both examples is that effective communication cannot take place among persons when each perceives something different. Because they visualize different situations, they *discuss* different situations.

Of course, we can't hope to perceive *every* situation as other people do, but if we make an honest effort to appreciate their points of view, we improve the possibility of achieving effective communication. It is important to understand that we don't have to *agree*. As a visual example of conflicting perceptions, notice how the shapes in Figure 1-2 can be perceived in different ways. (See page 20 for interpretations of Figure 1-2.)

Lack of interest in the subject matter, on the part of either the sender or receiver, can seriously deter the reception of ideas. There are several ways of arousing interest in readers and listeners. One way is to use an attention-catching opening or a statement so provocative or unexpected that the members of the audience must take notice. But such devices are, at best, short-term in their overall appeal. At the other extreme, it is possible to *order* people to be interested. "I'll expect that report to be completed and submitted by 4 P.M. *today*. If it isn't, don't bother to come in to work tomorrow!" Certainly a statement like that arouses the interest of the listener; in addition, of course, it arouses his or her animosity and antagonism, and the speaker has lost one of the objectives of good communication: maintaining favorable relationships.

The most effective way to secure the readers' or listeners' interest is to motivate them to *want* to pay attention. The best way to motivate is to build the message around the benefits the receivers will gain when they carry through on what the speaker or writer suggests. For example, to gain the interest of a

Differences in perception prevent successful communication unless one person is willing to see the situation from another's point of view.

Overcome lack of interest by convincing your audience that they will benefit from paying attention.

FIGURE 1–2 Perception Sketches

group of production supervisors, a plant manager may point out how production will rise if they follow his or her suggestions. In turn, the increase in production will result in higher pay or recognition. Because most of the supervisors are concerned with increased pay, they probably will be interested in the communication.

Lack of fundamental knowledge can be another barrier to the clear communication of ideas. How can you intelligently discuss a problem with those who do not have the background to understand what is being said? Certainly there will be a breakdown in communication if a nuclear physicist attempts to explain quantum mechanics to someone with only a high-school education. Conversely, it is conceivable that the speaker's or writer's knowledge of a subject is superficial. This also becomes a barrier, for it is always apparent when the instructor is, as the saying goes, only one chapter ahead of the class.

Before communicating, determine your audience's level of knowledge about the subject matter and avoid talking over their heads.

Sometimes the communicator, whose knowledge in a field is thorough, *assumes* that the receiver has adequate background or fundamental knowledge and then proceeds on the basis of this false premise. To overcome this barrier, determine how much knowledge of the subject the recipient of the message possesses before you speak or write. That is not always easy to do. As was indicated earlier, we usually depend on some type of verbal or nonverbal response to indicate understanding or lack of understanding, but the response from the recipient may not always be accurate.

The *emotions* of either the sender or the receiver can be another obstacle in communication. We have all been in situations in which the atmosphere became so emotionally charged that reasonable discussion broke down. When we have deep emotional reactions—love, hate, fear, anger—we find it almost impossible to communicate coherently anything but that emotion. The lesson here is obvious: calm down before you send or receive ideas.

Don't let your emotions become your message.

On the other hand, sometimes emotions can be a help in communicating. A person who is emotionally charged up or enthusiastic often finds this quality an asset in helping get a message across.

The *personalities* of those involved can be a barrier to communication. We are often so strongly influenced by the personality of the speaker or the writer that we may either accept or reject what is said without good reason. Personality is not confined to an individual, however. Sometimes an audience seems to react as if it were one person; many speakers will attest that a group was hostile, friendly, apathetic, or understanding. Of course, our recognition of the personalities of others is often tempered by our own. Perhaps when we feel that communication has broken down because of personality, we should first examine our own—difficult as this task is—and attempt to make changes that improve understanding.

Examine your own personality before blaming others for communication breakdowns.

The *appearance* of the communicator or the instrument used to communicate, such as a letter or report, can be another critical factor. A speaker whose jacket is awry, whose collar is askew, and whose general appearance is poor is not likely to arouse a favorable response in listeners. The same is true of a business letter or a report that is typed in heavy block paragraphs, is jammed on the page from side to side and from top to bottom, and has a jagged margin and messy erasures and, in the case of a report, few topic headings. The unkempt attire of a speaker or the careless and negligent appearance of a written message may be a serious barrier to the communication of ideas. The solution is simply correction of the fault. If the appearance of a report is poor, the business executive should have no compunction about sending it back to be retyped. The reader may be a thousand miles from the company, and his or her image of the firm may be based entirely on that sheet of paper.

An attractive appearance will elicit a favorable response.

Figure 1-3 shows a variety of barriers that may arise between the sender (encoder) and the receiver (decoder). Note that each person is pictured twice; that is to indicate still other barriers. For example, perhaps what the encoder formulated mentally is not what he articulated. Perhaps what the decoder heard was not interpreted as the encoder had intended. Could we even have three figures? What the encoder formulated mentally was not precisely what he articulated, and his nonverbal glances at his watch produced still a third message in the decoder's mind! Indeed, *effective* communication is difficult to achieve.

Prejudice can seriously impede the transmission of ideas. An unreasonable bias rejects ideas without consideration. Although we usually relate prejudice to race, religion, and color, most of us encounter it in many other ways. It may be a simple but strongly held viewpoint (or perception) on the part of the chief executive, or it may be the classic statement of the long-term employee: "Well, I've been here 28 years; we never tried it before, and I'm sure it won't work now."

Appealing to the audience's self-interest is the best way to overcome bias.

Of all the barriers to the clear communication of ideas, bias and prejudice are probably the most difficult to eliminate. The usual answer is education, but that is a lengthy and sometimes frustrating job. Perhaps a better way to overcome deep bias is to show people how they will benefit by following a specific course of action. People can adjust their prejudices surprisingly fast when their self-interest is at stake.

Make the message clear by eliminating sensory distractions.

Distractions can be a disturbing factor in communication. Clattering printers, noisy punch presses, inadequate illumination, hissing ventilation, or uncomfortable room temperature may be deterrents to the communication of ideas. It is most difficult for production-line workers to understand what the supervisor wants when they have to shout to one another over the noise of pounding machinery. Any upsetting factor on any of our senses—visual,

FIGURE 1–3 Barriers to Communication

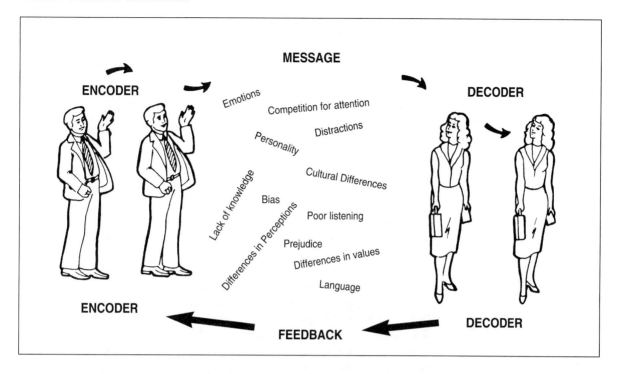

auditory, olfactory, or others—may prevent the clear transmission and reception of ideas.

Often *poor organization* of ideas is a serious barrier to communication. Even when ideas are presented clearly and logically, it is not always easy to assimilate them. The difficulties are compounded when thoughts are presented in a confused manner. No contractor lays a brick and no engineer positions a steel beam without first looking at the blueprint; a surgeon makes no move without examining the laboratory reports and the Xrays; an attorney would never file an important case without first drawing up a careful brief. Nevertheless, often we begin to write or speak without bothering to organize our thoughts.

Organize your thoughts coherently before attempting to communicate them.

Whether the organizational framework of our message is jotted down on a sheet of paper or carefully typed as a formal outline, we should not attempt to communicate without knowing precisely where we are going. If listeners or readers cannot follow us easily and logically, they will simply close their minds. A 3-minute oral presentation, a 15-line letter, a half-hour speech, or a 30-page report should all be planned before they are carried through. There is almost nothing we do, from an evening's recreation to the construction of a 20-story building, that we do not plan, except, all too often, speaking and writing.

Poor listening is one of the most serious barriers to the communication of ideas. Even though, we think of most communication in relation to reading, writing, and speaking, in fact, about 60 percent of our time is spent listening.

Poor listening is a natural result of the disparity in the time it takes to tell ideas and the time required to assimilate them. Most of us speak at the rate of about 140 words a minute, but we can assimilate approximately 500 words a minute. It is not surprising, therefore, that the listener's mind tends to wander as it moves further and further ahead of the speaker's ideas. Often listeners are

Make listening an active effort to understand the speaker's message and intent.

thinking of what they are going to say next, after the speaker has finished. In other cases, the listeners' preconceptions are screening out much of what the speaker is saying. Listening requires effort. If we try, we can learn to listen actively, to concentrate on what is being said, to hear the ideas beyond the words, and to appreciate the desires and needs of the speaker.

Effective managers listen actively in order to motivate workers.

Supervisors or executives *must* listen carefully: that's part of their job. They should know that it isn't necessary to agree with subordinates' statements or requests, but it is necessary to show that they understand and appreciate why the employees say what they say. Effective listening helps administrators control many of the activities under their jurisdiction.

The *competition for attention* in our society presents still another barrier. Because communication media bombard us throughout the day, we have, of necessity, become selective. Our grandparents may have lived with an eight-page newspaper, limited circle of friends, and static-filled radio receiver. In contrast, we live in a veritable torrent of sound and printed words. There are reports, technical journals, and a variety of newspapers and magazines to read (some on the computer screen), meetings to attend, friends to visit, television shows to watch, and so on. The result is that we become perceptually selective: we hear and do not listen; we see and do not assimilate. This wall of defense serves us to good advantage, for there is too much communication in our world for us to take in. We must choose—or have someone else choose for us.

Overcome an audience's defense against the bombardment of information they must deal with daily by making your message worth their time.

Because of our busy society, communicators must recognize that they are constantly competing for the attention of listeners or readers. They must make their messages so excellent, so clear, so concise, so interesting, and so compelling that the listeners or readers will *want* to assimilate them.

VERBAL BARRIERS

Language itself is probably the most common barrier to effective communication.[3] Among the problems in the use of language for communication are *differences in interpretation of statements.* We have all said things that we thought were perfectly clear and simple, only to have them completely misconstrued. Sometimes the cause is simply a misunderstanding. In other instances the speaker may have chosen a word that conveyed a meaning different from that intended. Although *fee, salary, wages, payment, stipend,* and *emolument* are listed in the dictionary as synonymous, each has a different connotation. Surgeons are not paid "wages" for an operation and a ditchdigger is not paid weekly "fees" for labor. As Mark Twain said, "There is as much difference between the right word and the almost-right word as between lightning and the lightning bug."

Then, too, a specific word may evoke different symbols in the minds of people whose backgrounds and experiences are different. What does the word *pig* conjure up in the mind of a steelworker or a farmer or a college student? What symbol does the word evoke when it is hurled in anger at a person?

Use words cautiously: the meaning you intend may not be the meaning your listener receives.

Languages uses words to convey ideas, facts, and feelings. Sometimes semantic problems arise in the interpretation of words because the meanings are not in the words but in the minds of the people who receive them. Meanings of concrete words do not vary too much from one person to another. For example, there is little possibility for confusion when we speak of *pencil* or *paper* or *book.* But as words become more abstract (*democracy, honesty, happiness*), they are more likely to be misunderstood. This is also true of words that carry emotional overtones in a specific society. What *liberal, radical, virtue, morality,* and *integrity* mean to the speaker or writer may not agree at all with the listener's or reader's concept of the same word.[4]

The stronger your vocabulary, the fuller your range of choices in expressing yourself clearly.

Another verbal barrier is *inadequate vocabulary.* If our stock of words is poor, forcing us to fumble as we attempt to express our ideas, our ability to communicate will be limited. It is important to build up our vocabularies so that we can express our ideas clearly, forcefully, and easily.

Errors redirect your audience's attention from your message to your mistakes. Clear messages are correct.

We should also make every effort to avoid *errors* in speaking and writing. Whether the error is in spelling, diction, grammar, or pronunciation, it immediately forces the reader or listener to focus on the mistake. Errors seem to jump out of a page or a statement. Errors should never be minimized or rationalized, regardless of how minor; efforts should focus on making language choices as correct as possible.

Communicate on your audience's level.

We should also remember to choose the *proper level* of language when communicating with others. To speak or write above the heads of the audience or down to them condescendingly is to invite misinterpretation, irritation, and confusion. A classic story illustrating this problem is that of the plumber who wrote to the Bureau of Standards in Washington stating that he used hydrochloric acid for cleaning out clogged drains. The bureau responded: "The efficacy of hydrochloric acid is indisputable, but the corrosive residue is incompatible with metallic permanence." The plumber replied that he was glad the bureau agreed with him. The bureau tried again, this time writing, "We cannot assume responsibility for the production of noxious and toxic residue with hydrochloric acid and suggest you use an alternative procedure." The plumber again replied that he was pleased that the bureau agreed with his findings. Finally, the bureau realized that it was not writing at this plumber's level. Thereupon the plumber received a note that said, "Don't use hydrochloric acid. It eats the hell out of pipes."

CONFLICT BETWEEN VERBAL AND NONVERBAL COMMUNICATION

An interesting fact about communication is that two messages may be transmitted simultaneously. Quite often a verbal message is conveyed with a nonverbal one. Someone may greet us with a great show of enthusiasm: "How are you? Good to see you. Come into my office and have a cup of coffee." The nonverbal communication, consisting of a surreptitious but pained glance at the clock, says something else. Another example is the employee who tries to sound relaxed and comfortable when he talks to the boss, while his tense posture tells a different story.

Nonverbal signals are more likely to reveal the sender's true feelings than are verbal ones.

Whenever the meaning of the nonverbal message conflicts with that of the verbal one, the receiver is most likely to find the nonverbal message more believable. The alert receiver is almost always able to determine when a problem exists. Most of us can discern the fearful person behind the good-humored, joke-telling facade. We somehow know quite well how dismally Karen and Mark's marriage is progressing, even though their exclamations of love for one another are voiced loudly and clearly. The nonverbal message is usually obvious, and if it does not agree with the verbal one, the receiver quickly and almost invariably recognizes the one that is true.

Most of the nonverbal messages that we receive come to us visually. We are quick to see the hurt in someone's eyes or another person's triumphant smile.

Communication—the interpretation of data by our senses—is a never-ending process.

We notice the twisting, nervous fingers in a lap and the confidence in the way a person walks. We also decode the message of a sudden, frightened tug at our arm when we are trying to cross a street in heavy traffic. What a wonderful message we decode when we walk into the comfort of a home where a Thanksgiving dinner is about to be served. The aromas of a roasting turkey, dressing, and pumpkin pie require no words to transmit a message. Any message—verbal or nonverbal, formal or informal—received and decoded by one of our senses is communication.

WRITING AND SPEAKING EXERCISES

1. Select friends or business associates who are members of two different minorities. Observe their nonverbal communication for 2 weeks. Prepare and present a report (oral or written) on the differences you have observed. Organize your report in the manner you feel is most logical.

2. Cut an advertisement out of a magazine or newspaper and submit it to your instructor with your analysis of the nonverbal communication that you think the advertiser intended to convey. Does the message extend beyond the obvious verbal communication?

3. Examine an office arrangement of a corporate headquarters. Discuss various aspects of nonverbal communication that are evident to you.

4. In small discussion groups, select three of the following quotations and have the spokesperson of each group read the quotation and the group's interpretation of it.
   (a) "To say that we know what a word means in advance of its use is nonsense."
   (b) "Meaning is relative to experience."
   (c) "Never mind what the words mean. What did the speaker mean?"
   (d) "Some companies believe management can exercise 'stop-go' control over information which employees receive."
   (e) "Speak in order that I may know you."
   (f) "Time talks; space speaks."
   (g) "Speakers are prisoners of their vocabularies."
   (h) "It's what and how you communicate or don't communicate that makes you what you are to others."
   (i) "Words in a communication can cause friendliness, humor, or happiness; used incorrectly, they can cause hatred, hostility, and even death."

5. Find a speaker (perhaps a political speaker or religious speaker) on television. Turn the volume off to observe his or her nonverbal messages. Make a list of your impressions of these messages. Then turn up the volume to see if the speaker's nonverbal messages concur with the verbal message. Write a short analysis of the similarities and differences between your nonverbal and verbal impressions.

Interpretation of two perception images in Figure 1-2, page 15. In the picture on the left, some people may see a greyhound looking backwards over its left shoulder. Others may see only disjointed lines. The picture on the right appears to be a series of spiral lines; however, the lines are all drawn as unconnected circles.

6. Choose two classmates who, together with you, have attended a presentation or lecture. List your own perceptions of what you have seen and heard (for example, "monotone voice"). Then ask your classmates to draw up a similar list (without showing it to you or one another). Finally, compare lists and write a brief analysis of how different people form different impressions of the same event.

7. This exercise should reflect a real situation in which you are now involved. Visualize a person with whom you do not communicate effectively. Now record the following on paper:
   (a) Identify the individual (spouse, boss, subordinate, friend, instructor, father, neighbor, mother-in-law, etc.).
   (b) State as specifically as possible the barrier(s) that make communication difficult. Also, note on whose part (encoder or decoder) the barrier(s) arise.
   (c) Indicate the possible solutions and the specific ways you intend to implement them.

8. Copy a quotation from a newspaper or magazine article and cite the source—a world leader, politician, public figure, business leader, or private citizen. Analyze the quotation from a semantic point of view in an attempt to substantiate events resulting from it.

9. What are the primary barriers to effective learning in your classes? What are your suggestions for removing them?

10. What are the primary barriers to increased productivity in your present place of employment? What are your suggestions for removing them?

11. Reproduce a comment, that you made to another individual in the past 2 to 3 days and his or her response (feedback)—one that did *not* address your statement. What barrier(s) do you feel caused the misinterpretation?

12. Repeat exercise 11 but now quote a statement from a newspaper or magazine article and the reaction or response (feedback) to it. Cite the barriers you think were responsible for the interpretation or misinterpretation.

CASES

Complete the following assignments from the Cases for Discussion section at the back of this book:

1. The Mark Teller Case—Assignments 1 and 2
2. The Barney Burton Case—Assignments 1 and 2

SUGGESTED RESOURCES

Eyo, Bassey A. "Innovative and Organizational Communication in Corporate America." *Bulletin of the Association for Business Communication* 55 (March 1992).

Fielden, John. "Why Can't Managers Communicate?" *Business* 39 (January-March 1989).

Foehrenbach, Julie, and Goldfarb, Steve. "Employee Communications in the 90s: Greater Expectations." *Communication World* 7, (May-June 1990).

Gayeski, Diane. "Rewiring Corporate Communication." *Communication World* 9 (March 1992).

Golen, S., and Burns, A. "Programmatic Research on Communication Barriers to Learning." *Journal of Business Communication* 25 (Spring 1988).

Kemper, Gary. "Managing Corporate Communication in Turbulent Times: Partnering with Human Resources." *Communication World* 9 (May-June 1992).

Klepack, Cathy. "Effective Employee Communications Leads to Higher Profits." *Bank Marketing* 22 (September 1990).

Sandler, Len. "How Managers Create Monsters." *Personnel Journal* 68 (November 1989).

Trimby, Madeline. "What Do You Really Mean?" *Management World* 17 (July-August 1988): 12–13.

Wilson, Donald O. "Diagonal Communication Links within Organizations." *The Journal of Business Communication* 29 (Spring 1992).

ENDNOTES

1. A. Deutschman, "The Trouble with MBAs," *Fortune* (July 1991).
2. J. Ruesch, "Psychiatry and the Challenge of Communication," *Psychiatry* 17 (1954).
3. See the movie, N. Sigband, *Communication: Barriers and Pathways,* 1992 (color, 20 minutes), Paramount Communications. Available from AIMS Media, Inc., 9710 DeSoto Ave., Chatsworth, CA 91311-4409.
4. A. L. Smith, "Bridging the Gap between Employees and Management," *Public Relations Journal* 46 (November 1990): 20–21.

2

COMMUNICATION
IN ORGANIZATIONS

There is no vacuum in communication. If something is going on, it will be communicated. If the formal channel is closed or unreceptive, the message will be communicated on the informal one.

An organization's success depends on how well its channels of communication work.

Whether in the public sector or the private one, organizations are complex. Obviously, the 6-person company is easier to manage than the 60,000-employee organization. But in both cases, communications are used to inform, to persuade, to compare, and to motivate. How effectively communication takes place, both internally and externally, will largely determine whether the organization achieves its goals.[1] Naturally, it is much easier to communicate and to manage in a small organization where the owner and the machine operator can quickly discuss a common problem. The task becomes more difficult when a single division numbers 5,700 employees. When the production-line employee has a problem that may affect the entire division, how long will it take for the message to be communicated up to the division manager? Or, conversely, how successful will the head of the division be if he or she must send a message down through seven levels?

Upward, downward, and lateral communications are essential.

Many factors are involved when a message is sent up or down, for it travels through several levels; for example, the lead person, supervisor, section head, department head, group leader, assistant division leader, and division manager. We need not contemplate what will happen to the accuracy of that original message, even under the best of conditions. What about the other obstacles it will encounter in its journey? It may be affected by such intangibles as empire building, social status, lack of time, and level of trust, as well as many of the barriers listed in Chapter 1. But as difficult as this task appears to be, communication *must* flow up, down, and laterally in an organization if it is to achieve its goals.

THE DIRECTIONS OF COMMUNICATION

Most organizational communication flows downward.

In most organizations, the largest percentage of vertical communication flows downward. Communications may be orders, directives, memos, policies, bulletins, or other types. Unfortunately, these are usually one-way communications, and they are based on the assumption by many managers that what is sent down is always received and understood. Infrequently, the manager requests a response. Here the difficulties of feedback may occur: the employee too often responds (upward communication) with what he or she believes the manager wishes to hear.

Downward communication can take several forms:

- Printed materials (bulletins, memos, orientation manuals, annual reports to employees, and policy manuals)
- Typed materials (memos, letters, and reports)
- Interview situations (appraisal, informative, counseling, and disciplinary)
- Presentations to groups
- Computer "bulletin boards" and message centers

Monitor feedback carefully to ensure that your downward communication was received as you intended it to be.

You, the manager, are cautioned to monitor carefully the feedback received from downward communication. If you assume that you have communicated effectively simply because you gave a speech, sent a memo, issued a report, distributed an employee manual, or held an interview, you may be making a serious mistake. Well-known management consultant Peter Drucker says flatly:

> For centuries managers have attempted communications "downward." This cannot work no matter how intelligently they try. It cannot work, first, because it focuses on what the manager wants to say. . . . All that can be communicated downwards are commands . . .[2]

Drucker states, however, that downward communication will work if the manager first permits communication to come up.

Managers must recognize that one-way communication may simply amount to whistling in the dark. For that reason, we will look carefully at ways to make downward communication work. One way, of course, is to secure effective upward communication first. The manager who listens carefully to upward communication from employees and assesses correctly what has been said will be better able to select the topics, the tone, and the time for effective *downward* communication.

DOWNWARD COMMUNICATION

One of the important needs of all people is the need to know. Employees want to know where the organization is going. Was the big contract secured or not? Why was the company's proposal to the Air Force rejected? Is there a reason for the drop in the stock's price? What about the rumor of a possible merger? How will a merger affect the work force? What were the results of the long-range planning meeting? And on and on.

More than ever before, employees in the 1990s want to know about the company's direction and capabilities.

Did employees 50 years ago make such demands for information? The answer is probably "no." At that time, employees certainly wanted to know about the company's plans and progress, but they were essentially concerned with their income. They were often content to "let the boss be boss." Today, by contrast, with well over 60 percent of our work force made up of two-income families, the physical need for more money is no longer the sole driving force. As a result, employees' social, egoistic, self-actualization, and information needs have become more demanding.

Certainly the need to know differs from employee to employee. For some, the job and everything associated with it is their life. For others, whose primary interests may be outside the job—in sports, church, or recreational activity—the job is simply a source to satisfy their economic need. This latter group is invariably a small part of any work force.

All employees need to know how to perform their specific jobs and how those jobs contribute to the company's success.

Employees' need to know can usually be divided into two categories. The first involves information about the job itself. All employees want to know what their tasks are, how they are to be performed, how they interrelate with other areas to achieve the organization's goals, where and when they are to be performed. Employees also want to know what their specific duties are, what freedom they have within those limits, and how their superiors view their performance.

A growing number of employees need to know how the company is performing and whether it is contributing to the well-being of society. By appealing to these concerns, the organization can build morale and productivity.

The second area concerns the employee's relationships with the organization and the organization's relationship with the world. Employees want to know, for example, what the firm's goals and objectives are; what its short- and long-range plans are; what the company's response will be to the union's new request and why; what the closing of the Belleville plant will mean to the overall work force; whether there is any truth to the rumor concerning a possible merger; how the firm has reacted to the various equal-opportunity rulings. The organization that does not recognize this second area of need to know, and does not build on it for its own benefit, surely will miss a good opportunity to improve morale and increase productivity.

More and more managers in contemporary organizations recognize the vital role of internal organizational communication. As a result, some have developed communications plans; others have structured communication policies.

FORMS OF DOWNWARD COMMUNICATION

Day-to-day jobs would not get done without effective downward communication.

There are several types of internal organizational communication. One type is basic because it consists of communication needed to get the job done each day: memos, directives, policies, orders, bulletins, interviews, meetings, presentations, and the like. These communications facilitate order processing and shipment, manufacturing and production, sales and services, income and expenditures, recruiting and hiring, and all the other daily activities needed to keep an operation in a healthy state.[3]

Downward communication that values employees ensures their cooperation and contribution.

Another important category of downward communication creates the feeling among employees that the company is *their* company. Communication on certain topics can set the climate for employees to accept and cooperate with orders, memos, directives, and policies. Some of these topics are listed here:

Wage and salary structures: How are they established and revised? How do they compare with industry standards?

Benefit program: What percentage of salary is for benefits? Who pays what percentage for what benefits? What are the retirement and educational opportunities?

Company products or subproducts: Who uses them and how? Are they used by consumers or manufacturers? Do they play a role in national defense? What countries buy them?

Company plans (long-range and short-range): Where does the company expect to be in 5, 10, and 15 years? What impact will those plans have on personnel numbers, product mix, and facility locations?

CULTURAL DIVERSITY IN COMMUNICATION

Organizational Communication and "Workforce 2000"

Carol Shuherk
University of Southern California

In June 1987, a study commissioned by the U.S. Department of Labor aimed at forecasting the work force of the next century was released by the Hudson Research Institute. The demographic data contained in "Workforce 2000: Work and Workers for the 21st Century" exploded any notion that the labor pool of the future could be predicted based on that of the past.

Traditionally, white, native-born males have formed the pool from which corporate America recruited and developed management talent. "Workforce 2000" predicts that dramatic change is underway. By the year 2000, the traditional source of corporate leadership will shrink to just 15 percent of the new entrants to the labor force. Just under 61 percent of all new workers will be women, and 29 percent will be people of color. Immigrant employment is also expected to surge. In summary, "Nonwhites, women and immigrants will make up more than five-sixths of the net additions to the workforce between now and the year 2000."

The report sparked a "taking stock" of the state of the work force in firms across the country, and for the most part, the current condition does not reflect the demographic trend. Another study, published around the same time by Korn Ferry International, an executive recruiting firm, found exactly 13 minorities and 29 women among the 1,360 executives in Fortune 1000 companies—barely 3 percent, even though women and minorities made up 51.4 percent of working Americans that year. The "new" labor force was inside the door, but it didn't appear to be going anywhere. Employee surveys, exit interviews, and complaints filed with the Equal Employment Opportunity Commission all indicated deep frustration with a system perceived to still present formidable barriers to the upward mobility of all but the traditional management talent pool.

In the wake of these studies, efforts to bring women and people of color into the management ranks have shifted in tone from moral obligation to business imperative, and future-minded firms began to examine the organizational systems, structures, and management practices that might be keeping some people from giving their best. Firms such as Digital Equipment, Xerox, Avon, Honeywell, 3M, U.S. West, and Motorola began to look for the internal obstacles to people's success and the ways and means to remove them.

Many of the problems are structural—a result of organizations being built around the work style and traditional needs of a white, male, managerial culture. In the traditional work setting, for example, there is no need for child care, because children are a personal issue handled privately by a spouse at home. But a more deeply felt problem, as voiced by the diverse workers, are managerial practices, the day-to-day assumptions, interactions, and decisions that affect the fabric of working life. These, too, are based in white, male culture and frequently ill-suited to women, Asians, African-Americans, Latinos and others.

Communication programs play a central role in adapting past practices to fit the new work force. In one form, they aim to surface the underlying attitudes and biases that may prevent managers from recognizing the potential in diversity. In another, they train managers in the interpersonal skills that allow diversity to be tapped. The first are called valuing diversity programs; the second are called managing diversity efforts.

Valuing Diversity Programs

Communication programs for valuing diversity seek attitude change. Their goal is to change the corporate culture by changing its members so that they appreciate individuality and avoid prejudgment. These programs bring managers together for frank conversations about normally taboo issues, such as racism and sexism at work and in society.

Led by a trained facilitator, they take various paths to recognition of personal biases.

The valuing diversity program at Digital Equipment started in the late 1970s as a way to defuse tensions over the firm's affirmative action and equal employment opportunity programs. Groups of eight to ten employees were encouraged to meet, on company time and with the assistance of a facilitator, to learn more about others who were different from themselves. As the groups came to know one another better, they became increasingly comfortable with revealing their feelings about each other's race and sex and individual peculiarities. Over the past 15 years, several hundred of these groups have taken root and have broadened their discussions to include age, physical ability, sexual orientation, smoking preference, and organizational roles. The result, according to the company's equal employment manager, is a more open, pluralistic environment in which women and people of color feel that their perspectives are understood.

Other valuing diversity programs take a more immediate and intense approach to "bias busting." In a class mixed to create a representatively diverse population, participants might work through an exercise titled "How I feel When I'm the 'Different' one." In a session at a large media company, an African-American reporter responded, "Most of the time I feel like a speck of pepper in a bowl of mashed potatoes." A white male editor offered, "Superior."

At U.S. West, a Denver-based telecommunications firm, managers in diversity seminars play the "labeling game." To demonstrate how everything from race to gender to life-style preference can affect how people are treated and how they behave, seminar leaders place a label on managers' foreheads without telling them what it says. Eerily, the labeled managers begin to take on the stereotypical traits of the groups they unwittingly represent. When managers

with the label "CEO" on their forehead are treated with deference, they begin to act more self-confident, directive, and outgoing. When managers with the label "militant feminist" see snickering or eyes rolled skyward in response to their presence, they become hostile and withdrawn. The exercise goes on to explore assumptions made about people based on their group membership. Repeatedly, participants realize that if people are in the same group, their assumptions about each other tend to be accurate, and when they aren't, they're not.

Diversity seminars that explore prejudice can grow tense. Another bias-busting exercise asks participants to share the way they believe they are viewed by other groups. Participants are frequently exposed to feelings similar to those heard by a U.S. Senate panel when it invited some distinguished African-Americans to answer that same question. "You see us as less than you are," said former Secretary of the Army Clifford L. Alexander, Jr. "You think we are not as smart, not as energetic, not as well suited to supervise you as you are to supervise us. . . ."

Combined with the difficulty of expressing deep-seated feelings of discrimination among women and people of color is the difficulty individual white males have in hearing anger directed at them as a group. They also fear that reverse discrimination is going to impede their careers. The point is not to place blame. The awareness-building workshops are intended as the first step to getting beyond stereotypes and valuing people as individuals.

Managing Diversity Programs

The managing diversity approach focuses less on underlying attitudes that affect communication than on management communication itself. The operating assumption is that strong people skills, together with cultural sensitivity, are the key to enabling managers to get beyond the obvious differences of race, gender, age, disability, life-style, and so on to learn from any employee what he or she needs to succeed at work.

In managing diversity programs, managers look at how the changed work force requires changes in downward and upward communication. For instance, say a manager simultaneously hires a white man and a Hispanic woman to do similar jobs. Traditional management practice holds that in order to avoid showing favoritism, both should be treated the same. But what if success in the positions requires the two new people to work successfully with and be able to influence line managers, most of whom are white men? The woman probably will not be as successful as quickly as the man, and so when the man starts doing his assignments faster, with higher quality and better information than the woman, he looks like a fast-track performer while she looks mediocre. In this case, the manager might need to personally introduce the woman to the line managers, promoting her to them as an expert in her area. He needs to coach her on how to deal with the line managers and emphasize that he is here to help if she runs into roadblocks, and that he expects she will. He also needs to explain clearly to the new male employee why he is doing this.

In most companies the managing diversity effort begins with an extensive bottom-up communication program. Honeywell began with the management practices index, which asked employees to rate their managers' skills at valuing them and enabling them to do their best work. Managers were given the results, provided opportunities to develop their skills, and, after a follow-up survey, held accountable for their people skills in their annual performance reviews.

At Pacific Gas and Electric, 100 line and staff employees became diversity trainers in a 6-day, 60-hour course. Nominees for the training were people who value diversity, think fast, handle conflict well, have strong communication skills, and enjoy good reputations in their business units. By the time the training was completed, they were ready to fan out across the company, delivering 8-hour seminars that examined the demographic shifts, distinguished between managing diversity and affirmative action, and helped managers to confront personal prejudices. In other firms, such as 3M and Motorola, task forces work to find ways to change structures and policies to better hire, develop, and retain a diverse work force. As a result, child and elder care, job sharing, and scheduling flexibility are increasingly part of business as usual in the United States.

Whatever their type of business, organizations of tomorrow will only fully realize the potential in their work force if they deal successfully with its diversity. The message from today's first-stage efforts seems clear: the traditional corporate mold, to which all employees were expected to conform, will have to give way to something more flexible, that is, adapted to the needs of its people. As it does, communication will be the vehicle for shaping the change—up, down, and across the organization.

Management-employee relationships: Are unions making any requests? How is management responding?

Social issues: What is the employee mix by gender and ethnic background? What company-community projects (educational, cultural, recreational) are in place? What do they cost, and are they successful? How is the company handling environmental issues such as waste disposal and pollution?

Company organization: How many plant locations, employees, and subsidiaries are part of the company? What is the organizational structure? How is the product line organized? What is the sales distribution process?

Research and development: What new areas are being investigated and why? What new products are being developed and what is their potential?

Rumors: What are the facts about current rumors?

Litigation: Is the company involved in lawsuits? If so, what are the likely results of litigation.

PRESENTING INFORMATION

"If you don't keep people informed, you get one of three things: rumor, apathy, or revolution."
—Thomas Jefferson

Management must establish a communication policy and create media to ensure that workers receive and understand important information.

Effective downward communication covering topics such as those just listed must be planned. Inserting occasional stories in the employee magazine concerning company dividends and plant relocation serves little purpose if they are lost among the items on retirements, new hires, and births.

Management must communicate seriously on significant issues. Its viewpoints must be presented consistently, clearly, and honestly. To do this, there must be a stated policy of communication and a series of communication media that are of such quality that they command attention and respect.

Managers today are exploring the relative effectiveness of computer information services, including electronic bulletin boards, for downward communication. Although most computers don't offer the advantages of photography, as found in a company publication, the electronic communication link allows employees to talk back to management and to each other. This feedback can take the simple form of answering a questionnaire or the more complex form of an employee roundtable discussion—all by computer.

POLICIES OF DOWNWARD COMMUNICATION

If management doesn't communicate significant information through formal channels, the grapevine will take over.

Effective communication policies ensure that managers keep workers informed.

In every organization, communications about a variety of activities are transmitted to employees in almost a constant flow. However, some firms do not share information about controversial or sensitive issues. Of course, not *all* information can be shared with *all* employees. Some situations are simply confidential.

When specific information cannot be communicated, managers can avoid many problems simply by telling employees that they understand their position and appreciate their desire to know, but, "It just isn't possible at this time. And here's the reason for not discussing the details." Such a frank admission is far more acceptable than some vague pronouncement that insults an employee's intelligence. Nothing will erode employee loyalty and diligence more rapidly than dishonesty or manipulation of information. If facts about an ongoing problem or activity are not supplied by management, employees will cultivate their own "facts."

The way to make sure that all managers communicate downward is to establish policies of communication for the organization. A carefully conceived set of policies lists the organization's overall communication goals. Among these might be the following:

- To inform concerned groups, such as employees, community members, customers, and vendors, of ongoing activities and/or problems that affect specific parties
- To indicate to employees company plans, directions, and goals

- To encourage, foster, and build a steady flow of two-way communication
- To communicate to employees, as quickly as possible, information about important events and situations
- To allocate sufficient funds and company time to implement company policies of communication

Beyond these overall corporate policies, other statements, none more than a few subpoints in depth, are needed for specific communication activities within the organization such as interviews, meetings, press releases, external written communications, and external oral presentations.

MEDIA FOR DOWNWARD COMMUNICATION

Management should make use of special media beyond routine, day-to-day communication to satisfy employees' need to know.

In addition to the memos, reports, directives, bulletins, orders, and other items that employees frequently receive and use in carrying out their day-to-day responsibilities, several other types of media are important. Among these are employee magazines, orientation manuals, handbooks, annual reports, letters to employees, and bulletin boards (including computer bulletin boards and message centers). If these are composed imaginatively and creatively, are completely honest, and recognize employees' need to know, they will increase productivity and improve morale. Such media can be used in attaining the following communication objectives:

- To inform employees about company activities, problems, expansion, markets, mergers, personnel, labor relations, profits, sales, market share, new products, diversification plans, and finance
- To emphasize the firm's dependence on the efforts, creativity, and loyalty of employees
- To discuss employees' responsibilities, achievements, and status in the firm
- To examine the variety of benefits that employees receive and to recognize the dollar value of such benefits as a significant segment of the employees' income
- To examine relevant social issues and responsibilities, government activities, and political affairs
- To examine company contributions to social welfare, cultural improvements, and educational advancements
- To inform employees' families of company contributions in an effort to build awareness and loyalty
- To examine in detail, from time to time, specific areas of company operations so that employees are informed of activities in areas other than their own
- To encourage employees to use company publications as a forum for expressing ideas

A firm's employee publications can attempt to achieve any or all of these objectives. (See Figure 2-1.) Certainly, messages can be emphasized most effectively if the organization issues many publications frequently. On the other hand, a company that can afford only a modest quarterly magazine can achieve similar goals if the publication is produced in a spirit of integrity and with a clear desire to fulfill the employees' need to know.

FIGURE 2–1   Magazines for Employees and Associates

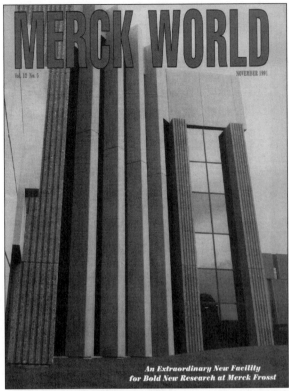

Reprinted by permission of Merck & Co., Inc.

Reprinted by permission of Marion Merrill Dow Inc.

Internal company magazines are becoming increasingly popular in businesses of all sizes.

Company magazines.   The number of organizational magazines published grows almost daily. Every organization of a few hundred or more employees publishes some type of internal magazine. In fact, a professional association comprises individuals in the field of communications who are editors, editorial or production assistants, graphic artists, photographers, and so on. The International Association of Business Communicators has more than 14,000 members who belong to chapters throughout the United States and Canada. Sister associations with huge active memberships exist in England, Europe, and Japan.

Many large organizations hire an employee-publications editor and an assistant or two, as well as a photographer and an artist. In smaller firms, these positions may be held by one individual, who has additional responsibilities in the personnel or industrial relations department. Other companies use a communications consulting firm or an advertising agency to design and write their employee publication.

Company magazines range from slick, sophisticated four-color publications printed on high-quality paper to modest eight-page affairs that have been run off on the office copier or have been created on a desktop publishing system. Most employee magazines follow one of these three formats:

1. Magazine format: The most popular of the three, the magazine usually includes several articles on various aspects of the concerned industry and news about contract awards and shipments, as well as listings of employee achievements, promotions, retirements, marriages, births, deaths, educational attainments, sports activities, and so forth.

FIGURE 2–2 Example of Tabloid-style Employee Publication

2. Tabloid format: The tabloid publication, usually about half the size of a newspaper, follows the format of a daily newspaper (Figure 2-2). It carries much of the same material as a magazine-type publication and often includes an extended classified ad section of items for sale, rides to share, personal notices, and so on.

3. Journal format: A journal usually includes either general articles or highly technical papers; usually, it lacks news of employee activities. Such periodicals are printed on high-grade paper and are illustrated with high-quality photographs or professional technical drawings. Examples of such magazines are Hughes Aircraft Company's *Vectors* (Figure 2-3) and Lockheed's *Lockheed Horizons*.

Recently, internal magazines have begun to emphasize journalistic stories about the company and its place in the community.

In recent years there has been a strong trend to omit much of the personal details (birthdays, retirements, marriage announcements, and the like) from the magazine and tabloid format to make room for more substantive topics. Company growth and decline, the securing or loss of contracts, legal issues, labor problems, social and community situations, and sales, production, and compensation discussions have become more common.

Probably no medium can better carry information to workers than employee magazines. Because their circulation probably exceeds that of all commercial

FIGURE 2–3 Example of Journal-type Company Publication

Reprinted with permission of VECTORS, a publication of Hughes Aircraft Company, Los Angeles, California

Employee magazines have tremendous persuasive potential.

magazines, they can be an immensely persuasive force—not only in the concerned industry, but in the nation as well.

Employee orientation manuals.   Every firm has many policies regarding such matters as work hours, promotions, vacations, days off, educational benefits, transfers, time off, and retirements. These policies, along with regulations on insurance plans and health benefits, constitute a formidable catalog of information. Although such matters may well be reviewed and discussed at a new employee orientation session, it is still vital to have them documented. Employee orientation manuals (Figure 2-4) basically serve three purposes:

Orientation manuals give new employees quick and conclusive answers to questions about company policies and procedures.

1. To provide an accurate, definitive source of information for all employees
2. To save time (employees need not crowd the personnel office with a constant series of questions: "Am I eligible for time off for . . . ?" "Does my policy cover elective surgery?" "Can I get paid for vacation time not used?")
3. To ensure that all employees receive the same answer to the same question

FIGURE 2–4 Example of an Employee Orientation Manual

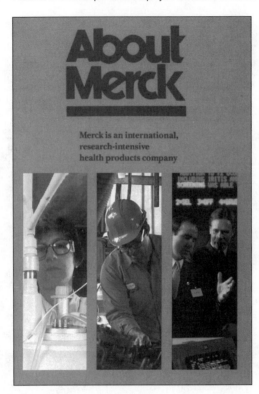

Reprinted by permission of
Merck & Co., Inc.

A typical organizational plan for an orientation manual might follow this sequence: a brief explanation of the company's history, a summation of its organizational philosophy, a listing of company policies, a rundown of short- and long-term goals, and a detailed section on benefits, procedures, and rules.

The orientation manual should be easy to use. The overall goals of the employee manual are to give each employee a feeling of unity with the company based on printed policies and philosophies and to permit every worker to find answers to questions quickly and easily. Therefore, the writing level and layout of the orientation manual should be determined with great care. Easy readability is of key importance. Illustrative material, including drawings, completed sample forms, and photographs, should be used generously. Sentences should be short and words selected carefully. Section dividers and topic headings can help employees find needed information easily. A second-language edition should be considered if the composition of the work force warrants this.

Some companies use a spiral binder or notebook for the employee manual. Whenever a change takes place, the company does not have to reprint and distribute a new booklet. Instead, a new page is printed and sent to employees with the appropriate instruction: "page 34 to be destroyed and the enclosed new page 34 to be inserted in your employee manual."

As the value of participative management is becoming more recognized, the terms *employee manual* or *employee orientation manual* are being replaced with *associates manual* or *associates reference guide.*

Annual reports to employees.   Some years ago, a small percentage of companies issued annual reports to employees. These were usually less expensive than the stockholders' report: black and white rather than color, fewer pages, inexpensive paper, and distribution from the workplace rather than by mail.

Most companies have replaced annual reports to employees with more frequent publications.

However, sometimes problems resulted. Employees asked questions about why they didn't receive the same report as shareholders, what was in the shareholders' report that wasn't in theirs, why they were being treated as second-class citizens, and so forth. In the long run, organizations consider it wiser to offer the corporate annual report to employees who wish a copy or to distribute an employee bulletin periodically. Most organizations now rely on employee publications and employee bulletins to communicate about ongoing company activities.

Videos make company communications more personal and strengthen employee loyalty.

Videos for employees.   Now that the cost of reproducing a video and packaging is inexpensive and most homes have a VCR attached to a TV set, many firms find it advantageous to provide employees with a video cassette. The advantages are impressive. The speaker is pictured and he or she can express emotions, feelings, and enthusiasm that no printed sheet can match. In addition to the employee, others may view the video. Thus, the corporation becomes involved with family members as well as the employee and a feeling of greater loyalty for the organization may be secured.

Because letters add a personal touch, they are gaining popularity as a way of communicating special information to employees.

Letters to employees.   More and more firms are writing letters to employees to communicate about vital issues, unusual problems, and other subjects. There are several reasons for the increased use of letters, not the least of which is the automated office. Computers can now be programmed to send the same letter—or four or five different ones—to the various levels of employees. Each letter can include an employee's name and address as well as a personal salutation. In addition, the letter has value because it is a personal message to the employee from, perhaps, the company president. The letter may be read by the employee's spouse; it may even be addressed to both. As such, it becomes an item for dinner-table discussion. What better way to build family loyalty to the firm?

The letter can cover wide-ranging subject matter, but it should not cover topics that can be discussed equally well in printed employee publications. A welcome to new employees; discussion of new products; explanation of a merger, an acquisition, or company profits; a commendation; labor problems (if such discussion is legal); and employee cutbacks are all likely topics for such a letter.

Letters to employees should be friendly and sincere.

Because personal letters addressed to employees usually come from the president or another high-ranking person, they should be worded especially carefully. The tone must be friendly and sincere—definitely not condescending, pompous, or dictatorial. All letters of this nature that are sent to employees' homes should, if at all possible, be personally signed in ink. Figure 2-5 is a good example of such a letter.

Pay envelope inserts.   An insert in the pay envelope, used judiciously, is a guaranteed communication device. A message printed on a card or small sheet of paper and attached to employees' paychecks is sure to receive attention. However, the message should be of some significance. If the communication is concerned with a routine topic or, even worse, something trivial, the insert will not be effective. Use such inserts on an occasional basis only. If every paycheck is accompanied by an insert (or two or three), employees will likely give them no attention or, at most, a cursory inspection.

When used infrequently, inserts in pay envelopes grab the employee's attention and effectively communicate significant information.

FIGURE 2–5 Example of Letter Sent to New Employees by Management

Date

Personal name
Address
City, state, zip code

Dear (employee's name):

Welcome to the Karton and Martin Company. We are sincerely happy to have you join our
_____ Division. Certainly the members of that Division, as well as the rest of us
at Karton and Martin, will do everything possible to make your stay with us challenging,
enjoyable, and happy in the years to come.

You are joining a family of 12,500 employees working in three plants in the Chicago area.
And as you know, we are not newcomers to the field of electronics. Our first office was
opened almost thirty years ago. Our growth has been steady and profitable. You are now part
of that team, and we will be happy to have you share our achievements in the years to come.

I'm happy to tell you that our salary plan is probably the highest in the industry. Added to
that, you will be able to take advantage of our profit-sharing plan, health benefits program,
insurance coverage, stock-buying privileges, paid vacations, and other benefits, which you
will learn about from your supervisor or at your orientation program.

But these are only some of the benefits you will receive as an employee of Karton and Martin.
There are paid holidays, time off for personal affairs, an excellent company medical system,
fine recreational programs, and wonderful people. I hope, too, that you won't hesitate to give
the company the benefit of your suggestions. We need your help and advice. Just walk in and
talk to your supervisor or me.

Good luck to you. We all join together in saying, "Welcome to Karton and Martin; may your
stay be a happy one."

Cordially yours,

Thomas Caxton

Thomas Caxton
President

A positive introduction welcomes the new employee and holds out the promise of ongoing employment.

Employee knows he or she has joined a winning team.

President Caxton explains how Karton and Martin will benefit the new employee.

President Caxton also encourages the employee to benefit the company.

The letter concludes warmly.

The same computer that generates paychecks is, in many cases, capable of printing short messages onto blank areas of the pay stub. Although such messages are certainly easier and less expensive to produce than messages hand-stuffed into envelopes, they may be read less and, therefore, may be less effective. Some companies have programmed their payroll computers to personalize a message on each check: "Frank, your check contains a bonus this month. Keep up the good work."

Employee bulletin boards. Traditional bulletin boards are among the least expensive of all organizational communication media and, if properly maintained, can be among the most effective sources of information. In most companies, they are used for a variety of purposes; the following are perhaps the most common:

Bulletin boards are inexpensive and effective tools for communication.

- To announce matters of general interest, such as approaching holidays, meetings, or recognition of outstanding employees
- To announce matters of specific interest, such as availability of discount tickets for recreational events, personal items for sale or wanted, or announcements of meetings of employee clubs
- To announce changes in company policies, rules, or regulations

All displayed notices should carry a stamped message of approval: "Okay for posting until May ___ , 19___." On the date indicated, that announcement should be removed. Nothing will halt readership of bulletin boards more quickly than outdated layers of announcements. Bulletin boards are effective communication devices only if they are supervised carefully. One person should be in charge of them to be sure that company policies are followed.

Bulletin boards should be carefully maintained and strategically located.

Bulletin boards should be placed strategically to secure maximum attention. Good locations are in cafeterias and locker rooms, near vending machines, and in the employee lounge or recreational room.

Companies are turning increasingly to electronic bulletin boards. These function just as traditional bulletin boards, but with the advantage that employees can access information from the nearest computer terminal. A "message queue" is displayed from which individual items can be retrieved one at a time. Many electronic bulletin boards allow any company employee to add a message. In this way, the bulletin board provides management not only with an information channel to employees, but also with a feedback device.

Electronic bulletin boards are gaining popularity in the automated workplace of the 1990s.

Management and supervisory bulletins. For management personnel, a controlled system of bulletins can be an excellent way to announce changes in policies, procedures, or regulations; to convey information; and to ensure that an important message is transmitted in the same way to all individuals at similar levels of authority. Figure 2-6 shows examples of such a bulletin.

Bulletins help prevent confusion within an organization by ensuring that all managers get the same message and pass it down consistently.

Bulletins may also assist a supervisor in communications with subordinates. If all supervisors at a specific level receive the same bulletin, they can pass down the same information. In this way, there is some assurance that all employees will receive essentially the same information at the same time. Such a procedure strengthens the supervisor's authority and emphasizes the position as a source of official information.

It is easy for a firm to become "bulletin happy," with announcements printed on six different colors of paper, emanating from a dozen offices, and spewing forth in a never-ending cascade. The remedy, as in the case of bulletin

FIGURE 2–6 Examples of Management/Supervisory Bulletin and Newsletter

Reprinted by permission of Marion Merrill Dow Inc.

Reprinted by permission of Merck & Co., Inc.

boards, is control. Bulletins or management letters should originate only with authorized persons in specific positions. Because bulletins may announce changes in or amendments to policies or procedures, they should be carefully numbered and dated. Three-hole punching allows them to be filed for future reference by the sender and receiver. Some companies give their bulletins added distinction by using different headings or colors to designate, for example, manufacturing, production, or engineering.

Many companies publish periodic reports for their retirees.

Publications to retirees, video reports and newsletters to employees.   With the numbers of articulate and influential retirees growing each year in the United States, more companies are publishing periodic reports for that group. News items usually include major changes in company operations, travel, recreational areas, news of retirements, and adjustments in company pension and health care programs.

Now that almost every home has a TV and a VCR, firms are issuing video reports from the president or division manager to employees. The advantage is that both the employee and family members hear the comments. Many executives hope that this direct approach will enhance not only the employee's loyalty to the organization but also that of family members.

Small companies can avoid costly publication expenses by developing in-house employee newsletters.

Companies with 200 to 400 employees usually cannot afford to publish a four-color, 16-page employee magazine. They can, however, achieve almost the same benefits with a monthly newsletter, which can be processed in-house from typing to printing. Given the advantages of desktop publishing, a creative employee can turn out an attractive, informative, and valuable employee communication.

LATERAL COMMUNICATION

Lateral or horizontal communication between departments may be inefficient because it is infrequent.

Of all the directions in which communications move in an organization, lateral, or horizontal, movement probably is the least efficient, because there is rarely pressure to communicate in that direction. It isn't vital that the marketing department know what is going on in production; and the transportation department need not know the details of research to carry on its own activities. Nevertheless, organizations do need a system for lateral communication simply to keep concerned personnel aware of companywide activities and to avoid expensive and needless duplication of effort.

Lateral communication must be controlled carefully. Department heads can easily bury each other in a blizzard of paper. One hope for ending the blizzard lies in *electronic mail.* In theory, messages can be sent and received on computer screens without the time-consuming and expensive routine of hand-delivered pieces of paper throughout the company. In fact, however, users of electronic mail have expressed surprise at just how much printer paper is still used for messages. Many managers still prefer to print out important messages—the so-called hard copy of the message—for easy transport and reference. Chapter 3 provides more discussion of electronic mail.

More perplexing is the electronic blizzard that has replaced the paper blizzard in many offices. Messages stack up one on another in the computer, all waiting to be read. "Where," one manager asked in frustration, "are they all coming from?" The answer lies in the technology of electronic mail itself. Once a sender generates a message on the screen, he or she can send it to an individual electronic mail box or to all electronic mail boxes in the company at the press of a key. The burden of photocopying and addressing no longer acts as a bottleneck to keep word-happy executives from publishing their opinions to all employees. Add to this, voice mail provided by telephone, and the communication load becomes heavier still.

Managers must use electronic mail judiciously to avoid a blizzard of irrelevant information.

The answer to the electronic blizzard lies in effective managerial decisions rather than in electronic mail itself. Management should determine who is to be informed of which department's activities, the amount of detail to be contained in such reporting, and the medium to be used. A knowledgeable corporate communication director can be of great help in making decisions about who should receive what.

Sometimes unexpected problems arise. Take, for example, an empire-building manager. This person usually has a predictable reaction to lateral communication: sending bulletins about department activities to almost everyone above, below, and at the same level to convey the idea of extreme productivity. The recipients, who know the source, discount the content of the announcements by about 50 percent. In addition, the empire builder requests almost all employees in the company to provide copies of their communications "so I may better support your activities." The result of all this is a desk covered with paper—a problem the effective communicator tries to avoid. The solution? A companywide communication policy combined with an alert director of communication can effectively curb the paper proclivities of the empire builder.

Department heads should apprise each other of their departments' activities through meetings and written records.

At the other end of the scale are department heads who communicate nothing on the mistaken assumption that knowledge is power, or "if they don't know what I'm doing, they may feel I'm indispensable." Realistically, any competent and successful manager is well aware of how important it is for department heads to be aware of each others' activities. He or she can accomplish good intracompany communication in two different but effective ways. First, supervisors can be called together periodically to give and receive information on current activities. This helps build a climate of cooperative participation. Intelligent supervisors appreciate knowing what is being achieved in related departments. Such knowledge often results in suggestions that lead to more efficient production, better economics, and more efficient use of personnel. Second, communication of information from one department to another can be accomplished through periodic reports, summaries, digests, or abstracts. Such methods are valuable in that a record exists for future reference.

Total quality management.   Because *total quality management (TQM)* is largely based on the team concept of employees working together and receiving and acting on customer and supplier suggestions, it is appropriate that it be discussed under lateral communication. The concept of TQM probably evolved from many sources, including the major work of W. Edwards Deming. Organizations in the United States have accepted the fact that to be competitive in the global marketplace, they must continuously improve the quality and efficiency of every process both within and outside the firm.

Total quality management involves employees at all levels in problem solving and decision making in order to promote quality customer service.

Total quality management empowers employees at every level to contribute significantly to new and better methods of internal process (production, manufacturing, warehousing, etc.) as well as external functions (customer and supplier services, delivery, sales, etc.). Employees are encouraged to turn the spotlight on problems and to be involved in not only designing but implementing solutions.

Total quality management is a business strategy of continuous process improvement to meet customer needs. It should grow out of an organization's mission statement and its strategic plans. To be successful, TQM should be based on management's vision and full support, performance standards, "ownership" by employees, input from throughout the organization, team work and team responsibility, and most importantly, communication to all employees, customers, and suppliers that is ongoing, consistent, honest, relevant, and clear.

Solid TQM programs depend on effective in-house and external communication.

Communication is vital if TQM is to succeed: effective and open internal communication—up, down, and laterally—and clear and open communication externally as well. Communication must be open externally if information, both negative and positive, is to flow back to the organization.

The basic theme of TQM thus revolves around securing *quality* in the total organization: products, customer service, manufacturing, production, finance, and all other areas. All employees are ultimately responsible for achieving the highest level of performance—thus, *total* quality management.

UPWARD COMMUNICATION

Upward communication can succeed only when management creates an atmosphere of trust.

For years organizations have struggled with the question of how to achieve successful and effective upward communication. Although there are such devices as suggestion boxes, forms to complete, group meetings, council meetings, and quality circle sessions, none is effective without an atmosphere of *trust*. It is difficult, however, to build a climate of trust between management and the work force. The problems are similar, regardless of the field, in all supervisor-subordinate relationships: owner and employees, senior engineer and technicians, doctor and nurses, and so on. Developing trust takes time, effort, and integrity. It is a fragile quality that can be destroyed through a single careless act. And when it must be rebuilt, an enormous amount of time and effort is required.

SUGGESTION SYSTEMS

Management should listen to and value employees' suggestions about the jobs they perform.

One of the most popular methods of securing upward communication is through some type of suggestion box. Based on the premise (usually accurate) that no one knows how to do the job better than the person doing it, management turned to workers for ideas as early as the late 1800s. However, it was during World War II that suggestion systems received their greatest impetus. Workers' suggestions for methods to secure increased productivity were sought and rewarded.

Many companies still solicit suggestions from workers. A monetary award usually is made when the idea is used; often the amount is equal to 10 percent of the first-year savings resulting from the suggestion. Companies have saved millions of dollars as a result of employee suggestions, and employees have benefited psychologically from participating in the company's efforts. Nevertheless, problems have caused many organizations to abandon their programs.

One problem is that many employees do not consider the awards adequate. Obviously, this attitude has an effect on the employee's morale and productivity and on those of fellow workers. There are always suggestions that have no merit and must be rejected, which create another problem. Employees often resent being turned down. Sending a token check to every employee who submits a suggestion would make a mockery of the entire program.

Another problem is the supervisor who resents a subordinate whose suggestion has been accepted. The supervisor may feel that the idea rightfully should have come to him or her first. Finally, management may prematurely implement some suggestions without careful consideration of the impact on employee morale, the potential for possible employee resentment, or even the possibility of union problems.

Despite the problems, managers in many firms conclude that suggestion systems are worthwhile because they do promote upward communication and often lead to improved production and procedures.

QUALITY CIRCLES

Quality circles enable managers and workers to exchange ideas in a nonthreatening setting.

The idea of quality circles took industry by storm in the 1970s and 1980s. The concept originated in Japan and continues to be deeply held in Japanese industrial culture. Basically, quality circles involve managers and workers sitting together and *listening* to each other's suggestions. There is neither pressure nor understanding that the ideas proposed will be implemented; they may or may not be. Discussion flourishes upward, downward, and laterally, usually with a minimum of negative evaluation, in the full spirit of participative interaction.

In the United States, organizations have had varied experiences with quality circles—ranging from success to dismal failure. When managers anticipate meetings in a negative or mechanical fashion, (e.g., "Well, it's the fourth Tuesday of the month. I guess I'll have to go to that quality circle and listen to those guys bitch."), the session is sure to fail. On the other hand, when managers feel that there is an opportunity to pick up new ideas and explain their point of view, the potential for success is much greater.

EMPLOYEE COUNCILS

Well-planned council meetings give management an opportunity to hear employee concerns that otherwise might remain unvoiced.

Employee councils are another valuable means of upward communication. Every company department or division elects a representative to serve on the council. All employee representatives meet with management representatives on a periodic basis, usually once each month. Employees present the questions and suggestions of their department members. Because representatives usually are speaking on behalf of anonymous members of their work groups, they do not hesitate to speak out.

For council meetings to succeed, several ground rules are essential:

1. Hold meetings in an informal setting, preferably after work hours, with food and beverages available.
2. Hold meetings not more than once each month. Almost any organization has more than enough topics to keep a monthly meeting lively. Also, some workers would have trouble clearing their calendars for more frequent sessions.
3. Choose a skilled meeting leader, one who is tactful, impersonal, and unbiased. He or she may well come from the work force rather than management. This person should serve as motivator, coordinator, or facilitator, not just "talker."
4. Select discussion topics carefully and draw up an agenda. Meetings should not be dominated by workers' complaints, management's problems, or trivia. Cultivate a positive mental attitude and allow the question of how we can improve to serve as a framework for discussion.
5. Allow the work group to decide how it wishes to select its representatives and build in a method for rotation of representatives.
6. Be sure a record of the meeting proceedings is available to all employees. For example, distribute a set of minutes, post bulletin board announcements, or play a videotape of the meeting during the noon hour in the cafeteria.

When someone complains, "Well, we tried those council sessions, but after five meetings there wasn't much left to talk about," hidden factors are probably involved. Perhaps the meeting was dominated by management, or trust was eroded or lost at an earlier session because of heavy criticism of an idea. Other possible reasons are faulty leadership, a poor agenda (or no agenda), and inadequate preparation.

OTHER MEANS OF UPWARD COMMUNICATION

Many other methods of securing upward communication are possible. Meetings are one common method: ROI (return on involvement) sessions, coffee sessions, the President's Quiet Hour, Let's Talk It Over, and so forth. Printed methods include forms headed "Spike That Rumor," "Open Line," (used at

Northrup), the Q and A Column (in the Southern California Edison employee newspaper), "Speak Up" (at IBM), and "Talk Up" (at Bank of America). In addition, organizations that support TQM must, of necessity, encourage upward communication as well as lateral and downward communication.

Preserving employees' anonymity ensures an atmosphere of trust.

Regardless of the method or format used, it is absolutely vital that managers respect anonymity and reinforce the quality of trust constantly.

THE INFORMAL CHANNEL OF COMMUNICATION

Employees at all levels depend on the grapevine to supplement or to replace information that is normally conveyed through formal channels of communication.

Another medium of communication in every organization is the grapevine. It is informal, follows no set pattern or direction, moves in and out of all communication networks, and is part of the social organization of employees. Defined briefly, the *grapevine* is the communication system of the informal organization. It is pervasive and exists at all levels of an organization, from top to bottom.

Managers have strong and conflicting opinions about the grapevine. Some managers view it as a positive force that acts as a safety valve for employees to blow off steam. It also fulfills a need to know on the part of some recipients and, in some cases, an ego need on the part of the message sender. Other managers perceive the grapevine as a problem: something that spreads rumors, upsets morale, undermines authority, initiates untruths, and most certainly challenges authority. Regardless of what managers think about the grapevine, one fact is certain: it is an integral part of the communication network of every organization. Therefore, you should be familiar with it and try to use it to your advantage.

The grapevine exists in every organization. Don't underestimate its importance and influence.

Unlike formal methods of communication, which proceed precisely and predictably in the organization (up, down, laterally, and almost always through "proper" channels), the grapevine jumps around. A message may begin with a supervisor on the second level, go to a line worker, be transmitted to the worker's brother-in-law who happens to be a division manager, hop to one of the organization's five vice presidents, and stop there. Or it may start in the office of the chief executive officer; the secretary transmits it to the division manager and it stops there . . . or goes on to a supervisor in the same car pool.

Liaison individuals keep information flowing through the grapevine, which stops with dead-enders and isolates.

A grapevine thrives primarily through a *liaison individual*. This person hears messages on the informal channel and passes them on to anyone who has a need to know or is simply curious. The liaison individual often receives some ego satisfaction from his or her role because of knowing while no one else does— "He (she) must have connections!" By contrast, *dead-enders* may hear messages, but because they have no interest in the topic, no need to know, and little desire for ego satisfaction, they do not pass them on. Finally, there are the *isolates*. At one time they may have been dead-enders, but because they apparently did not relay messages or perhaps did not even listen, they were removed from the informal communication network. They (the isolates) now hear nothing. (See Figure 2-7.)

WHY THE GRAPEVINE STARTS

Because the grapevine involves people and their complex needs, it can be difficult to explain and trace. Certainly it begins, however, in an effort to fill the vacuum created when the formal channel of communication is not working. People have a need to know, and they turn to the grapevine.

FIGURE 2–7 How the Grapevine Works

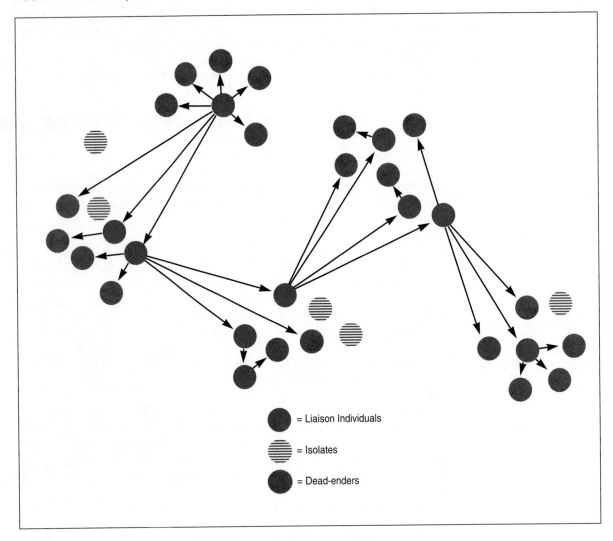

= Liaison Individuals

= Isolates

= Dead-enders

The grapevine functions when formal communication breaks down.

When changes occur in an organization (like terminations, plant closures, a dramatic drop in sales, elimination of products or departments, acquisitions, mergers, legal problems, social issues), employees want to know what is happening and how the change will affect them. If there is no response, an inadequate response, or an obviously false response on the formal channel, employees will turn to the informal channel. As long as their need to know exists, levels of fear, uncertainty, and frustration will continue to rise. At some point, employees' feelings will become antagonistic and even hostile. The grapevine—good, bad, or indifferent—will always exist to fill the information vacuum.

Management must remember that there is no such thing as a vacuum in communication; if the formal channel doesn't work, the informal one will take over. That is why this book repeatedly emphasizes the need to keep employees informed on the formal network. All channels—upward, downward, and lateral—must be open and available at all times.

CHARACTERISTICS OF THE GRAPEVINE

Many people have conducted research on the subject of the grapevine. As a result, a good deal is known about its functions and attributes. First, it is most active when change is taking place and when individuals' need to know or fear level is rising. Second, it is highly selective; some people hear everything on the grapevine; others hear absolutely nothing. Third, it operates more frequently in the work locale than in a social situation. Fourth, it travels rapidly. Finally, and most importantly, the grapevine is a normal part of the communication activities of an organization.

HANDLING THE GRAPEVINE[4]

Use formal channels to combat the grapevine's negative effects.

If the grapevine is a normal part of every organization, the obvious course of action for managers to take is as follows:

- Be aware of it; tune in.
- Listen to it; learn from it.
- Counteract false, malicious, or harmful facts by feedback through *formal* channels.

Listening to the grapevine. Managers must tune in to the grapevine, although doing so may not always be simple. A manager cannot ask an employee about the "latest rumor"; however, if a feeling of trust exists between a manager and his or her subordinates, the manager may ask, "What do you hear these days that I should know about?" A question like this is much better posed in an informal atmosphere rather than from behind a desk. If the manager wants to know what is on the informal channel, he or she should use that channel to inquire.

Only managers who actively listen to the grapevine can manipulate it to their advantage.

Other methods of tuning in mentioned earlier: "Spike That Rumor" forms, "Speak Up" and "Talk Up" forms, the "Rumor" column in the company newspaper, employee council meetings, and others. If the rumors are never voiced at council sessions or on any of the forms, managers may begin to wonder about the trust level between management and the work force.

Managers must respond to rumors in order to maintain openness and trust.

Responding to rumors. In most cases, a company responds to rumors through the formal channel. Some organizations accomplish this through a signed reply to each inquiry in the rumor column of the employee newspaper; a signed response note to the statement on a "Speak Up," "Talk Up," or "Spike That Rumor" form; an article in the company newspaper; or a meeting conducted by the company president. Other methods include managers meeting on a one-to-one basis with subordinates; an announcement on the intercom by a company officer; or a special bulletin or letter distributed to each employee or mailed to his or her home.

The critical factor, regardless of how it is accomplished, is to make a response.

WRITING AND SPEAKING EXERCISES

1. Draft what you feel would be an effective policy of communication for the college classroom. Include policies governing both in- and out-of-classroom communications between faculty members and students and between students and other students.

2. Some managers believe that the more communications they send to their subordinates, the better. Soon subordinates are receiving various kinds of written, verbal, and nonverbal data from the manager; receiving routine information from upper levels; exchanging all kinds of ideas horizontally; and attempting to keep in touch with the grapevine. These subordinates are excellent candidates for communication overload. Being specific, identify three things the manager can do to reduce the dangers of this phenomenon.

3. It is said that probably 80 percent of vertical communication in a company is downward and usually is quite ineffective. Make two specific suggestions to improve upward communication in most organizations.

4. Determine the date of publication of the employee publication (newspaper or magazine) for a nearby plant. Visit that organization the day after an issue is published and conduct a survey among white-collar and blue-collar workers as they leave. Your objective is to measure readership of the topics in the publication and determine if there are significant differences in reading interests among the two groups of employees.

5. Obtain two employee magazines. One should be from an organization of 10,000 or more employees and the other from a company of 3,000 or fewer employees. Present a short comparison of each noting the differences in content, tone, topics, and estimated expense of publication.

6. Think of a work group of which you have been a part. First, draw an organizational chart of that work group. Then make a diagram of the communication network of the group.

7. Imagine a magazine for a student organization to which you belong. What would be included? Create a specific list of regular features and suggestions for several special topics that would be of interest to readers.

8. Obtain employee newsletters or magazines from two different companies. Do an informal content analysis of each. How much space is devoted to personal news (such as retirements, marriages, and bowling scores) and how much to company business (such as profits, contracts, grants, goals, and competitors). In light of each company, its employees, and its products, which publication is more effective and why?

9. Interview an editor of an employee publication. Determine if he or she follows a specific policy of communication for the publication. What is it and who designed it?

10. Find a small group—a campus office, a secretarial pool, the executive meeting of a student group—where you will be able to study the communication flow. Observe and study how information is transmitted. Watch carefully for verbal and nonverbal communications. After observing the network in action, (1) prepare a written description of what you observed; (2) clearly identify the type of network you observed; (3) ask the leader of the group to describe the network from her or his perspective and compare the leader's analysis to yours.

11. There is probably a close correlation between how a person interacts with others on an interpersonal level and how he or she creates trust. Find a leader of a group, department, or organization who you feel has the trust of his or her subordinates. Observe how this person interacts with people. Identify the characteristics of this leader's managerial approach. Be as specific as possible.

12. List four different forms of downward communication.

13. Although most organizations have policies concerning personnel, benefits, compensation, financing, and other areas, few have policies on communication. Explain, in a paragraph or two, why you feel such policies should or should not be documented and distributed internally.
14. List several points in favor of employee suggestion systems and several problems that may result when such a system is used.
15. Describe several characteristics of the grapevine.
16. If management wishes to correct a false statement that is apparently circulating on the grapevine, what channel of communication (formal or informal) should be used? Why?

CASES

Complete the following assignments from the Case for Discussion section at the back of this book:

1. The Sun Fresh Case—Assignments 1 and 2
2. The Whose Perception Is Correct Case—Assignments 1 and 2
3. The Brooks-Martinez Case—Assignment 1

READINGS

See "The Case of the Team-Spirit Tailspin" in the Readings section at the back of this book.

SUGGESTED RESOURCES

Adam, E. E., Jr. "Quality Circle Performance." *Journal of Management* (March 1991).

Buch, K., and Spangler, R. "The Effects of Quality Circles on Performance and Promotion." *Human Relations* (June 1990).

Burnette, D., and Bousum, T. C. "Calculate Suggestion Program Savings." *Personnel Journal* (February 1989).

Fulk, Janet, and Boyd, Brian. "Emerging Theories of Communication in Organizations." *Journal of Management* 17 (June 1991).

Gonring, Matthew P. "The Communication Professional as Change Master." *Communication World* 7 (January 1990).

Honeycutt, A. "The Key to Effective Quality Circles." *Training and Development Journal* (May 1989).

Kanter, Rosabeth Moss. "A Walk on the Soft Side." *Harvard Business Review* 69 (November-December 1991).

Kelly, J. F., Jr. "Talk Eased Merger Stress for Great American Employees." *Personnel Journal* (October 1989).

Lawlor, E., and Mohrman, S. "Quality Circles: After the Honeymoon." *Organizational Dynamics* (Spring 1987).

McGoon, Cliff. "Skill Searching for Excellence." *Communication World* 6 (October 1989).

McGurrin, L. "Togetherness at the Suggestion Box." *New England Business* (May 1987).

Miller, T. R. "The Quality Circle Phenomenon: A Review and Appraisal," *SAM Advanced Management Journal* (Winter 1989).

Moore, M. "Employee Suggestion Systems Can Work." *CMA—The Management Accounting Magazine* (November 1988).

Pati, G. C., et al., "What Went Wrong with Quality Circles?" *Personnel Journal* (December 1987).

Pell, A. R. "Rumors." *Managers Magazine* (May 1991).

Rich, G. C. "Revamping Suggestion Systems Saves MDAC Million of Dollars." *Personnel Journal* (January 1987).

Sharon, Paul. "Communicating in the 1990's—Are We Ready?" *Communication World* 7 (May-June 1990).

Simmons, D. B. "How Does Your Grapevine Grow?" *Management World* (February 1986).

Simmons, D. B. "The Nature of the Organizational Grapevine." *Supervisory Management* (November 1985).

Smith, Alvie. "Bridging the Gap between Employees and Management." *Public Relations Journal* 46 (November 1990).

Temple, A. I., and Dale, B. G. "A Study of Quality Circles in White Collar Areas." *Management Decision* (May 1989).

Watanable, S. "The Japanese Quality Control Circle: Why it Works." *International Labor Review* (January-February 1991).

Whatley, A., and Hoffman, W. "Quality Circles Earn Union Respect." *Personnel Journal* (December 1987).

Whitworth, Brad. "Proof at Last." *Communication World* 7 (December 1990).

Zaremba, A. "Working with the Organizational Grapevine." *Personnel Journal* (July 1988).

ENDNOTES

1. G. M. Goldhaber, *Organizational Communication* (Dubuque, Iowa: W. C. Brown, 1986); G. Goldhaber and G. Barnett, eds., *Handbook of Organizational Communication* (Norwood, NJ: Ablex Pub. Corp., 1988); F. M. Jablin et al., *Handbook of Organizational Communication* (Newberry Park, Calif.: Sage Publications, 1987).

2. See P. Drucker, "What Communication Means" in *Management: Tasks, Responsibilities, Practices* by Peter F. Drucker, Harper & Row Publishers, Inc., and Heinemann Professional Publishing.

3. John S. Fielden, "Why Can't Managers Communicate?" *Business* 39 (January-March 1989): 41–43.

4. N. Sigband, *Communication: The Company Grapevine*, 1992 (color, 16 mm, 26 minutes), Paramount Communications. Available from AIMS Media, Inc., 9710 DeSoto Ave., Chatsworth, CA 91311-4409. This movie is based on The Sun Fresh Case in the Cases for Discussion section.

THE COMMUNICATION REVOLUTION

By the year 2000, getting information will be easy. But managing and interpreting information will remain a challenge.

The communication revolution continues to sweep through business and academic life. Business communicators during the 1980s, for example, saw the revolution transform the office. Typewriters were pushed aside for word processors. Bulky file cabinets gave way to data storage devices no bigger than a microwave oven. Coast-to-coast business meetings involved teleconferences, not transcontinental flights. In colleges, registration was by computer. For many students, access to a personal computer became a necessity for some accounting, finance, and communication courses.

Computers enhance the mind's ability to remember, to calculate, and to evaluate.

Consider the importance of the communication revolution in relation to other revolutions. The tool revolution—hammers, saws, combs, brushes, pens, scissors—extended the power of our *hands.* The transportation revolution—trains, planes, cars, bicycles—extended the power of our *feet.* The optical revolution—telescopes, microscopes, televisions—extended the power of our *eyes.* The auditory revolution—stereo, compact disks (CD), hearing aids—extended the power of our *ears.* The aesthetic revolution—trumpets, pianos, sculpture, painting, choreography—extended the power of our *emotions.* But one human power remained body-bound until the mid-twentieth century: the power to *think.* The communication revolution extends the power of *mind.*

Computers, the key to the communication revolution, amplify and augment ordinary intellectual abilities in several ways:

- Memory: Through the use of floppy, mini, and fixed-disk data storage devices, millions of bits of numeric, text, and graphic information can be saved in memory and almost instantly recalled by the computer.
- Calculation: The computer can perform thousands of arithmetic operations per second, vastly increasing the user's ability to measure, quantify, and calculate.
- Evaluation: Operating according to rules contained on software, the computer can perform quality control inspections on texts contained in its memory. Software such as RightWriter or Grammatik IV enables the computer to point out common writing errors and even offer suggested revisions.

- Artificial Intelligence: More sophisticated programs turn computers into expert systems that in effect imitate human intelligence. For example, computers now help doctors diagnose illnesses. Loaded with millions of items of medical data, the computer can assess symptoms provided to it by a physician and offer both diagnostic and therapeutic information.

BEGINNING OF THE ELECTRONIC COMMUNICATION REVOLUTION

In the history of electrical research, monumental minds like those of Michael Faraday and James Clark Maxwell noticed what thinkers of much earlier times had noticed: electrical impulses move faster than human legs or pigeon wings. For communicators, the goal seemed straightforward. A way had to be found to load words and images onto electrons instead of runners, bottles, pigeons, or ships.

That work occupied the best efforts of epic names in the history of communication—Thomas Edison, Alexander Graham Bell, Samuel Morse, Marchese Guglielmo Marconi—and less well known but important contributors like Philo T. Farnsworth (television), Lee De Forest (vacuum tube), and Heinrich Hertz (radio theory). They are the architects of a communication network without which the modern world would be inconceivable. These inventors literally helped create who we are and what we do.

Shannon and Weaver's A Mathematical Theory of Communication is a milestone in communication research.

Important communication theories flowed from the work of such early pioneers. Shortly after World War II, Claude E. Shannon and Warren Weaver published *A Mathematical Theory of Communication* (Urbana, Ill.: University of Illinois Press, 1949). This significant contribution to communication theory, largely developed by Shannon at the Bell Telephone Laboratories, examined the technical problems of transmitting a message from sender to receiver.

In Shannon and Weaver's model (Figure 3-1), the message begins with an *information source* (the sender), which is the mind of the speaker or writer. The speaker or writer chooses words and organizes them into sentences to encode a *message.* This message is transmitted as a *signal* (sound or light waves, or marks on paper). The signal is sent through a *channel,* but it can be garbled by *noise* (distractions, poor handwriting, static, and so forth). The *receiver* (person or machine) receives the message and decodes it into meaningful symbols. Finally, the receiver completes the communication process by sending *feedback* to the message sender. Feedback can be verbal ("I understand you") or nonverbal (as in the case of a smile or frown). Communication by computer follows the essential patterns described in the mathematical theory of communications.[2]

Throughout this century, the electronic revolution has favored the sender and has given the receiver little opportunity to provide feedback.

Some aspects of the electronics revolution have already stopped seeming new (much less revolutionary) to us. Radios, telephones, stereos, tape recorders, and even CD players and VCRs seem like standard furniture. They "belong," somehow, and we can't imagine life without them. These familiar appliances of the electronic communication revolution are largely one directional, however; they bring the world to our living rooms, but they do little to bring our living rooms to the world.

FIGURE 3–1 The Mathematical Theory of Communication

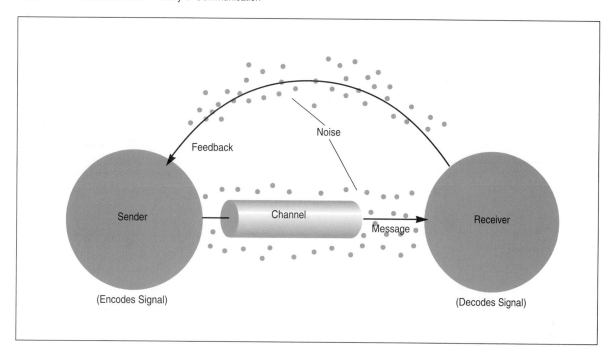

By the mid-twentieth century, average citizens still found their communication range to be severely restricted. True, the telephone could be used at any time to speak with another person almost anywhere. But what of printed messages? Was it necessary to own a publishing company or a newspaper to enjoy the full benefits of the electronic revolution? Placing printed messages in others' hands quickly, especially across great distances, was prohibitively expensive for an individual. Telegrams were reserved for life's most important occasions. Access to visual communication devices was equally restricted. The major television networks became the message senders, and the viewing audience settled for the role of message receiver.

The first to feel the discomfort of this relationship were American businesses. Most companies had something they wanted to say to their market. The biggest and wealthiest of these businesses wedged their way into a position of communication power by means of commercials. On radio and TV, and in magazines and newspapers, corporate giants began to play a shaping role in mass communication.

ELECTRONIC MEDIA AND BUSINESS USERS

During the past two decades of the twentieth century, smaller businesses and individuals began to feel the impact of what it means to be a message sender as well as a message receiver in the communication revolution. For costs that are already moderate and quickly becoming even lower, individuals and businesses can send oral and printed messages virtually anywhere on Earth—and beyond.

THE TELEPHONE

The modern telephone is an indispensable communication tool for businesspeople in the 1990s.

None of us needs instruction on how to use the household telephone. But telephone companies warn that we will have to pay attention to use the "new" phones effectively. These instruments have many innovative features to offer business, with more in the development stage.

First, the modern business telephone answers calls rather than postponing them. A caller either reaches you directly or is transferred to a line where you can be reached. If you cannot be reached, you can prerecord a message for callers (even leave individual messages for callers with prearranged access codes).

Second, a new phone helps you screen calls by displaying the caller's number before you answer. Callers' numbers can be sorted automatically by the telephone for later callback.

Third, business telephones can open both ends of the conversation to several speakers. By using conference microphones, one group of business people can talk freely with another individual or group. At the press of a button, the proceedings can be recorded for analysis later.

Fourth, modern phones help you reach your party. By means of a "camp-on" capability, the phone (not you) virtually stands in line when it receives a busy signal. You don't have to call back. Your intended party, meanwhile, receives a flashing "call waiting" signal. He or she knows you're waiting because your telephone number has already appeared on his or her telephone's display.

Most importantly, new telephones need not be plugged into the wall. Through the use of radio frequencies, cordless telephones can accompany you into meetings, on sales calls, and even (alas) on vacation. With the advent in the mid-1980s of cellular automobile telephones, businesspeople can be in touch with the office or clients while on the road.

Conference calls allow businesspeople to hold meetings from separate locations.

The conference call has been common in business communication for more than a decade. Speaking from separate locations, businesspeople hold joint discussions by interlinked telephone connections. Certain rules of the road have to be established in such calls to prevent confusion (Who is speaking now? What did she ask? Is it my turn to speak?). Participants quickly learn, however, to adapt personal communication styles to conference calling. They do not interpret silence as suspicion or reticence on the part of their listeners, as they certainly might in face-to-face conversation. Instead, they realize that moments of silence in conference calling may simply indicate courtesy; all speakers are waiting a moment to avoid inadvertent interruptions. As we will discuss later in this chapter, communication habits appropriate in conference calling go far in preparing managers for the world of teleconferencing (visual conference calling), which is currently sweeping the world.

The video telephone televises an image of the speaker while transmitting his or her voice.

In December 1991, AT&T unveiled its long-awaited video telephone, which presents the full-motion picture of each speaker on a small screen. Initial users have noticed a slightly jerky effect in the image shown on the screen. Unlike TV images, which are "refreshed" 30 times per second, the video telephone image makes do with only 10 image scans per second. The unveiling of the video telephone was delayed until fiber optic cables could be installed throughout the country. Such cables are capable of transmitting the complex data flow required by the video telephone. As businesspeople experiment with this new communication technology, they are weighing not only how the video telephone aids communication but also how it complicates communication. For example, the telephone sales call becomes more challenging when the salesperson's facial expressions, posture, physical form, dress, and background office environment are all exposed to the listener.

THE PERSONAL
COMPUTER

Though not as common as the telephone, the *personal computer (PC)* has by far passed the fad stage in large and small American businesses. Our discussion will not be concerned with uses such as processing data, handling payroll functions, running milling machines, and scheduling trains. Instead, we will focus on the five aspects of PCs that are critical to the business communicator.

PCs offer business communicators the convenience of word processing packages, which enable them to edit documents quickly and store them for later reference.

The PC as word processor.   By means of *software* (magnetically coded computer programs) such as WordStar, Multimate, WordPerfect, and others, the PC permits relatively easy entry into and manipulation of text. A business letter, for example, can be typed on the PC. Letter by letter, the words appear on the screen as you type, as much as they would appear on a piece of typing paper in a conventional typewriter. Unlike a typewriter, however, the PC lets you perform a variety of corrections at the press of a key. A misspelled word, for example, can easily be deleted or replaced. If the correct spelling contains more or fewer letters than the incorrect spelling, the lines of the letter—all of them, in the case of a longer document—automatically and instantly adjust to accommodate the new spacing.

Word processing software permits effortless insertion of lines, paragraphs, and whole pages. In addition, a search-and-replace function allows the person using the machine (the *user*) to select a particular word (let's say, *Brown*) that has been misspelled throughout a manuscript and a replacement word (*Braun*). At the press of a key, all occurrences of *Brown* in the manuscript are replaced by *Braun.* In addition, sophisticated spelling software enables the user to check all words in a document against a dictionary of words stored in computer memory—all in a matter of seconds. Progress is being made in the area of grammar as well, though the definitive grammar checker is years away.

Once a document has reached final form on the computer screen, it can be stored on a *disk* (either floppy or hard) for retrieval later. A disk costing no more than a few dollars can store 300 to 400 pages (with advances in technology increasing that amount each year). From the disk, the document can be printed out by a *dot-matrix printer* (at high speed but with low-quality print). *Laser printers* can produce text and graphics virtually identical in quality to the page of a book.

Materials become more useful when they can be broadcast onto a large screen for business meetings and conferences. Programs like Storyboard convert the PC to a well-equipped graphics laboratory, complete with colors, shapes, type fonts, and motion routines. With a little practice, even a beginner can create illustrative materials to accompany a business presentation or to be printed in a business document.

Desktop publishing packages enable even small businesses to produce professional-quality publications.

With a PC, appropriate software, and a laser printer, individuals can produce documents—brochures, newsletters, even whole books—previously possible only through traditional publishing techniques. Such *desktop publishing* has dramatically expanded the number and types of printed communications available within businesses and to the public. Of the estimated 26,000 different types of newsletters now published in the United States, most are produced on desktop publishing equipment.

What do you need for such an operation? Locate a reasonably powerful PC, with at least 640 K of memory and a hard drive with substantial memory. Choose desktop publishing software that can be run on the system. Two popular systems

Image Scanners and Optical Character Recognition

Scanners store images electronically for use in word processing documents.

OCR software scans and stores text as a word processing file.

For less than $1,000, personal computer users can acquire a high-quality stand-alone or handheld *scanner*. This device converts images such as photographs, charts, and logos to digital form so that they can be stored or manipulated on the computer and printed in 16 or more shades of gray. Using a scanner, a business writer can easily incorporate a product image or service flowchart into a letter, memo, or report. It is important to recognize, however, that such scanned images stored in the computer differ significantly from typical word processing files. A scanned image of a printed page, for example, would be reproducible on a computer printer only as a picture of that printed page. The words on the page could not be edited or searched by usual word processing means.

Optical character recognition (OCR) software allows computer users to edit scanned images of words as easily as word processing files. Through OCR software, the computer recognizes a wide variety of fonts (and even some handwriting) and records them as word processing files. A businessperson who has a scanner equipped with OCR software need not key in printed materials in order to edit them. He or she can simply "scan in" a printed draft of a report and begin editing it as a word processing file.

are Ventura Publisher (Xerox) and PageMaker (Aldus). Obtain a laser printer, such as Apple's LaserWriter or Hewlett-Packard's LaserJet. With practice, you can produce documents that, in format, type font, layout, and print quality, have a truly professional appearance.

PCs can be used to run inexpensive and effective training programs.

The PC as trainer.   Because it stores and presents information reliably and inexpensively, the PC is attracting growing attention as a trainer. The need for training, of course, can hardly be overstated in an era of significant change in the workplace. *Downsizing* has become a household word. Outmoded technologies and product lines are giving way to modern ones. Workers across the whole business spectrum must learn new concepts, skills, and applications—and they must learn them from someone or something.

The old training model relies on a human teacher with a limited number of students. Although public education continues to fund that model, American business is looking for a less labor-intensive and expensive way to communicate ideas, concepts, and skills. Videotape has some usefulness in this regard: a skilled teacher can record his or her training lesson, so it can be replayed numerous times in different company training locations around the country. Unfortunately, people do not learn effectively merely by watching. They must participate by making choices and learning both from their successes and failures. Videotape simply plays without regard to student responses.

The PC, however, can respond to student input. Especially when coupled with videotape, the computer can offer a high-quality, repeatable training experience. If a mid-level manager, for example, is learning negotiation skills, the computer can switch on a few minutes of videotaped negotiation. The tape can then pause for the computer to pose questions to the student. If the student's responses are correct, the computer can proceed with the lesson. If the responses show that the student misunderstood or misinterpreted the material presented, the computer can branch to a series of remedial lessons.

Although the creation of such programs takes time, money, and intelligence, they are cost-effective training tools once they are in place. PCs can play and replay training lessons without absenteeism, job burnout, mid-life crisis, union strikes, or any of the other overhead associated with human teaching.

Through computerized data storage and retrieval systems, PCs are replacing the cumbersome traditional means of filing information.

The PC as a file cabinet.   The storage and retrieval of business documents has long posed a human and financial burden. Staff members must complete the dreary task of hand-filing originals and copies of business documents. Expensive floor space—even entire rooms—must be devoted to bulky file cabinets.

The PC offers an appealing solution. Business documents that arrive by means of computer can be transferred immediately to a storage disk. Scanners can speed the work of transferring printed documents to computer disk without the laborious step of rekeying those documents. Filed on disk under descriptive headings, the documents can be recalled at any time to the screen for review or to a printer for hard copy production. The space required for storage is minimal. Literally hundreds of thousands of business pages can be stored on disks occupying no more space than a shoe box.

The risks inherent in a computer storage system must be mentioned. Paper documents can be destroyed by fire or flood, but otherwise they last rather well decade after decade. Documents stored on disk, by contrast, can be erased or ruined by serendipitous events: a magnet passed too close to the disk, a slight crease in the disk itself, or hot temperatures that distort the disk surface. For this reason, most businesses make a practice of backing up all data stored on disks. When information is irreplaceable, as in the case of bank records, the duplicate computer storage tapes or disks are kept in separate locations at all times, sometimes miles apart.

The risks seem minor, however, when the storage capacity of a computer is compared with that of file cabinets. In addition, the money that can be saved by *not* using space for filing cabinets can be substantial.

The PC and security.   As the computer becomes the main channel through which business sends, retrieves, and stores information, business leaders have every reason to question the machine's security mechanisms. How can a manager be sure that sensitive financial data entered into the office computer cannot be accessed by a 14-year-old "hacker" with a home computer and *modem* (an electronic link joining one computer to another)? Or worse, by a competitor?

Another concern for those who use and rely on data in large computer systems is the computer virus. A computer virus is an unauthorized program, often introduced by a saboteur or vandal, that destroys or alters data and computer functions. Similar to a biologic virus, a computer virus spreads from level to level (within the computer) impervious to an easy cure. Such destructive programs are responsible for millions of dollars in lost data.

Computers can be programmed to protect data from unauthorized users.

Any computer attached to other computers for communication purposes is subject to user commands. When such a command says, in effect, "reveal business data," the computer obeys. Computer specialists have, therefore, developed mathematical ways to make commands of authorized users *special* to the computer in a way that commands of nonauthorized users are not. By analogy, they give the authorized user a mathematical key to the locked portion of data within the computer.

Unfortunately, few keys have proved as foolproof as they were intended to be. Unlike physical keys, with notches carved into brass, the key to a computer is just a series of numbers—let's say, 39204939592. Intuitively, it would seem difficult, if not impossible, for anyone to guess that number and gain access to the protected data within the computer. But intuition fails us. A competitor or vandal bent on breaking into the protected data files can use the computer's vast speed to a criminal end; the "enemy" computer tries number combination after number combination, thousands every minute, until it happens upon the right number to break the electronic lock.

As newspapers and magazines feature stories of illegal entry into computer credit files, legal records, and so forth, businesspeople may be wary of revealing any sensitive business secrets to computers. Although such reticence is understandable, it can be overcome by knowledge. Businesses must take the lead in proving and publicizing the worth of reliable locking mechanisms. Only by such efforts can business communicators share the kind of confidence a bank manager feels after slamming shut the door of a vault.

By accessing databases through PCs, business-people can gather exhaustive information that they have neither the time nor money to find firsthand.

The PC and databases. Business decisions rely on knowledge, and knowledge can be expensive and time consuming to accumulate if it is gathered firsthand. An alternative is to access a business-related database by means of a PC. Such a *database*—in effect, a huge library of cross-referenced information—allows the user to enter "search" words relating to the business need at hand. For example, executives might need information on an issue in business law from the ABI/Inform database located in Louisville, Kentucky (see Chapter 15 for database lists and addresses). When a search word such as *libel* is entered, all articles pertaining to that term from more than 500 journals are available for review on the screen or on a printout. Brief synopses of articles help the executives pick the ones they need to read in full. A hard copy of these articles can be printed out on a long-distance basis from one computer to another. Without leaving their desks, the executives have visited one of the best business law libraries in the country.

There are literally hundreds of databases. Most of them store materials only in specific areas such as business, medicine, or finance.

Several communication companies now offer videotext service, a means of accessing printed information from database sources. These services allow the user to order individual pages, whole reports, or longer documents for review, research, or inclusion in published company materials. Users can preview materials on the computer screen before they decide if they want to have a hard copy printed. Much of videotext source material is uncopyrighted, so the user has a virtual encyclopedia from which to draw in preparing company proposals, reports, and publications.

A GLIMPSE AHEAD

In the business communication environment of the future, voice-driven computers will allow users to issue commands orally rather than by keystroke.

The memory capacity and computing power of PCs are growing phenomenally. With the advent of laser-disk storage of computer codes and images, new horizons are opening for computer training systems, self-contained databases (in effect, a library on your desk), and vastly expanded document storage systems. Two developments in particular already seem destined to affect computing in an especially powerful way. First, the *voice-driven computer* is no longer a dream or curiosity. At its heart is a voice chip that digitizes sound waves, making it possible to convert them to letters of the alphabet. Given the varieties of pitch, inflection, and accent in speech, the task of speech-print conversion involves powerful discriminatory powers on the part of the computer. Just imagine the possibilities: you sit at the computer and leisurely command business documents onto the screen. When you want to change a word or line, or when the computer has misprinted or misunderstood what you've said, you simply instruct the computer—orally—to make a few changes. When the document is done, you probably will find yourself saying, "Thank you." And no doubt the computers of the future will answer, "You're welcome."

Through the evolution of artificial intelligence, computers will be able to think and write for us.

The second and more compelling advance is *artificial intelligence.* The term means no more or less than it suggests: sophisticated programs enable computers to carry on intelligent processes. In short, computers simulate *thinking.*

What does a thinking machine do for you? This scenario may hit close to the mark: You tell the computer that you need a shipment of parts that was ordered weeks ago. The computer asks a few questions: Who is the supplier? Do you know why the shipment is late? Do you want to maintain a friendly tone? You answer the questions orally, as if you were talking to a business associate. The computer generates a letter for inspection. If the letter says what you want it to say, you instruct the computer to forward the message electronically to the supplier. If it needs correction, you mention particular lines and suggest improvement. Better yet, you "teach" the computer how to improve the incorrect lines so that next time a similar letter will be perfect the first time.

In an extension of this scene, an answer arrives from the supplier. The computer reads and understands the message. All you have to do is pose the question, "Computer, have we heard from the supplier yet?" You can then ask what the message was. Or you may choose to leave it up to the computer: "Did we get things straightened out?" The computer, after all, knows the production schedule, inventory, and shipping requirements. It is in a key position to assess whether the message from the supplier solves the problem.

More imaginative minds may want to drive the case a bit farther. Why ask a highly skilled computer anything? Why not let it generate a "hurry-up" letter every time parts are late (parts the computer ordered in the first place). Why not let it develop weekly or monthly reports that *it* can then analyze to see how business is going? And whom should it tell if things are going poorly? Certainly not the human manager. The manager has long since opted out of the complexity of computer-managed business. The report properly goes to a human specialist—a systems expert—who adjusts the program to bring better results.

Research into artificial intelligence is in progress at major academic centers around the world. Computers have already demonstrated their ability to master limited areas of understanding in English. Each month, that area of understanding grows, almost the way a child learns to speak. In time, computers will talk and write in an understandable way. They will master language word by word with ever-growing flexibility and naturalness. Then Milton's prophecy will be true: "We have lent out our minds."

TELECONFERENCING

Teleconferences allow businesspeople from around the world to meet without leaving the security of their individual headquarters.

In 1992, American business spent $30 billion in expenses related to flying business bodies around the world. In most cases, only business *minds* needed to travel.

A *teleconference* is an audio or audiovisual telephone call in which cameras and/or microphones in one meeting room transmit visual and/or auditory signals by satellite or ground line to another similarly equipped meeting room. With the assistance of trained technicians, geographically separated business-

CULTURAL
DIVERSITY IN
COMMUNICATION

**How Widespread
the Revolution?**

Carol Shuherk
University of
Southern California

The communication revolution has forged an electronic link between office and home, blurring the distinction between private and professional lives and changing the patterns of how Americans work. Desktop publishing systems, modem links to nationwide databases, electronic mail, and fax machines are widely available for private purchase in discount department stores as well as sophisticated consumer electronics centers. Without doubt, the technology of the communication revolution has been woven into the fabric of the American lifestyle.

Nevertheless, the slow growth of teleconferencing in American business shows that there is more to the adaption of technology than making it available. The chemistry between humans who are interacting and interaction in the cultural context that surrounds communicators and imbues their words with larger meaning are message elements not easily surrendered for the sake of "information expediency." Americans value innovation more than most other peoples around the world. So experience with teleconferencing should give food for thought to organizations planning to do business abroad. These organizations cannot assume that communication technology we view as "standard" will be considered good by businesses beyond our borders.

In the heady days of the late 1980s, the forces of democracy in Eastern Europe took encouragement daily from the satellite transmissions of CNN. They could see that their efforts were making news and that the force of world opinion was behind them. In the weeks before Tianamen Square, Chinese dissidents faxed their message to the world press,

providing first-person accounts of developing events without leaving a paper trail. But the use of communication technology by these people, revolutionaries themselves, may not be indicative of readiness throughout their cultures to embrace these electronic tools.

A 1987 report by the U.S. Bureau of the Census shows the following number of telephones per 100 citizens for the United States and our major trading partners across the globe:

United States	76.0
Western Europe	
France	60.8
Germany	62.1
Italy	44.8
Spain	36.3
Sweden	89.0
United Kingdom	52.4
Latin America	
Argentina	10.4
Brazil	8.4
Colombia	7.0
Ecuador	3.6
Mexico	9.1
Peru	3.2
Asia	
India	.5
Japan	55.5
Pakistan	.6
Philippines	1.5
Sri Lanka	.7
Thailand	1.5
Africa	
Egypt	2.4
Ghana	.6
Madagascar	.4
Nigeria	.3
South Africa	14.3
Zimbabwe	3.2

people can talk almost as naturally to one another as if they were in the same room.

Teleconferences offer many advantages over business travel: Participants avoid the stress of travel, including the time away from family and friends. Participants speak from their own turf, secure and confident. All the charts, models, and other visual supports that couldn't fit conveniently on a plane are avail-

Only Sweden, with 89.0 phones per 100 residents, has more telephones than the United States. While Western Europe and Japan approximate U.S. numbers, developing nations have up to 90 percent fewer. Mexico, our number two trading partner, has 9.1 telephones per 100 citizens compared to our 76.0. The Philippines has 1.5, and South Africa has 14.3.

It might be tempting to brush these numbers aside with the thought that they describe the situation in the general population and not in the business community, or that they simply reflect a state of underdevelopment that can be fixed with infusions of cash and equipment. In fact, far deeper assumptions about the essential nature of human communication and, from them, how to transact business relationships are almost certainly at work. As Vern Terpstra and Kenneth David note in their book, *The Cultural Environment of International Business,* "Existing sets of priorities defining what is good, proper, desirable, or important in a society may set limits on the kinds of technology that can successfully be introduced therein."

Looking at just a few aspects of culture, we can see big differences between American cultural values and those of most other nations that will have implications in regard to adoption of communication technology. In terms of language, we value explicit, direct communication. We emphasize content with meaning found in words themselves. Other cultures value implicit, indirect communication and place emphasis on context; meaning is found around the words. In terms of time and time consciousness, we have a linear, "exact time" consciousness. We value promptness and

equate time with money. Other cultures have a more "elastic" and relative time consciousness; they view time spent on enjoyment of relationships as time best spent. In terms of work habits and practices, we place great emphasis on the task at hand and view work as having intrinsic value. Other cultures place emphasis on relationships and view work as a necessity of life.

The perceived need for more efficient, high-speed tools of communication is certain to be different in business cultures other than our own. Likewise, the desirability of merging working and private lives to allow for receipt and transmission of business communication at home will be questioned in cultures outside our own.

For Americans planning to do business abroad, a sensitivity to culture and to the values placed on ways and means of communication therein is the first step in making appropriate technology choices. For those aiming to increase the use of communication technology in the cultures in which they do business, it will be useful to remember the difference between invention and innovation. Invention is the bringing together of previously unrelated ideas or objects. Innovation is the process of social communication of an invention. Managing this process is critical in the international transfer of any technology. It requires knowledge of the affected people and their social system and depends on persuasion based on local self-interest and perceived needs. Convincing people that what's good for us is also good for them requires a return to communication of the decidedly nontechnological kind!

able for display. Other personnel can attend the teleconference to lend support or participate.

For such reasons, major corporations like ARCO and Hughes Aircraft, as well as hotel chains like Hilton and Holiday Inn, have invested heavily in teleconferencing equipment. Although none of these companies has expressed outright regret at the investment, some have made reference to "learning the hard

Possible drawbacks to teleconferencing include the absence of social chemistry and misgivings about on-camera appearance, performance, and privacy.

way." They have discovered that teleconferencing is not a phenomenon that has gained quick or common acceptance.

The reasons for the slow growth of what seems like such a good idea are instructive. First, business conferences depend as much on social chemistry as on information sharing—and chemistry is created from posture, manners, asides, glances, chuckles, and all the other subtle signals of communication by which we learn to trust or distrust and like or dislike one another. Even business leaders skilled in personal contact are not automatic media presences like Dan Rather or Barbara Walters. Some businesspeople have difficulty trusting important negotiations to teleconferences because of unknowns: "What do I look like on camera?" "How will I know when to speak or when someone on the other end wants to speak?" "Can I look eye-to-eye with decision makers in the group?" Add to these concerns the justified worries of many businesspeople regarding privacy in their communications (see the feature titled "Tele-noia" on p. 61). Thousands of Americans have become involved in the hobbylike activity of "scanning," or electronically monitoring (and often recording) supposedly private communications from car phones, aircraft radios, teleconferences, and other transmissions. To date, few nonmilitary security measures have proven successful in limiting the access of such eavesdroppers to business and personal communications.

These issues cannot be resolved by improvements in teleconferencing hardware. Instead, people must be trained to use teleconferencing effectively. Business schools are now undertaking this task. We can look forward to the widespread use of a technology that comes close to total communication: teleconferencing relays not only voices but gestures, expressions, postures, and all other nonverbal signals.[3] Virtually all major corporations now make use of some form of teleconferencing, whether audio (as in the case of telephone conference calls) or audiovisual (ranging from a series of still photos to full-motion video). As transportation and conference site costs continue to rise, corporations large and small will no doubt turn increasingly to teleconferencing as a cost-effective solution for meetings of all types.

ELECTRONIC MAIL

As American business turns increasingly to interstate and international markets, the lag factor in mail delivery becomes more expensive. Major financial decisions, such as dividend changes, bond prices, or new borrowing, often are deferred pending written confirmation of new contracts and successful negotiations. Having such messages held up for even a few days in the channels of traditional mail can cost thousands of dollars in lost time and, too often, lost opportunities.

Electronic mail overcomes costly delays by sending written correspondence instantaneously through computer terminals and telephone lines.

Electronic mail provides almost instant written communication between computer terminals. A message sender in New York, for example, can type a message onto a computer screen, check it over for accuracy, and press a key for the "send" command. The message speeds by local telephone line to a mainframe computer in New York, which in turn races the message by satellite or ground lines to the message receiver in Los Angeles. There, the receiver can read the message on the terminal screen and print it out, if a hard copy is desired.

Mailgrams, Telex, TWX, and other electronic transmission systems from the 1960s and 1970s have already made a solid case for the advantages of fast,

Tele-noia: The Privacy Issue in Teleconferencing

The telephone has had almost a century to build its reputation as a relatively confidential medium for communication. The same mistrust that Granddad felt for "who might be listening in on the party line" is echoed by modern managers leery of teleconferencing. They point to newspaper stories of signal-stealing, ingenious hackers and backyard satellite dishes. When it comes to discussing personnel matters, tax planning, financial disclosures, product information, and personal career plans, many business leaders simply don't trust the teleconference.

Vendors have spent millions developing and publicizing encryption codes that supposedly make teleconference transmissions inviolable. But whether or not a particular code is breakable, *belief* is the issue. If managers believe that somewhere a hacker with a satellite dish is taking notes—perhaps for a competitor or a government regulator—teleconferencing will be reserved for only the most innocuous business transactions. Such tele-noia is reflected even in the architecture of teleconferencing centers. At ARCO, for example, the teleconferencing room was purposely designed to exclude even the equipment operators from any knowledge of what transpired within.

Add to such general mistrust the uneasiness many speakers feel when they talk room-to-room instead of person-to-person. No matter how broad the visual scan, speakers complain that they don't know the size or nature of their audience at the other end. Am I speaking to the face I see on the screen or a roomful of listeners? Will others enter the room while I'm speaking? Can others not on camera hear what I have to say? How can I adjust my words if I can't see their faces?

Excerpt from "Teleconferencing Comes of Age—Again" by Arthur H. Bell and Tom Housel from *T.H.E. Journal*, May 1986. Copyright ©1986 by Information Synergy Inc. Reprinted by permission.

These questions cause many teleconference speakers to think and speak without taking any risks. The wooden, empty statements that result please no one. The speaker feels awkward, the listener feels disappointed, and the business purpose is too often aborted.

accurate delivery of messages. Such systems were relatively expensive to the user, however, and hence were often reserved for urgent and emergency messages. The impact of a telegram or mailgram, therefore, depended in large part on its rarity: a mailgram each day would quickly cease to arouse special interest. Electronic mail, similarly, seems old hat to businesses already using services like Telenet and Western Union's EasyLink. The impact of such messages relies, as always, on fundamentals: the writer's ability to motivate readers through persuasive use of language.

Saving and filing electronic messages is easy. Each user has a file directory where hundreds of electronic messages can be filed under user-chosen guide words. A message from Ms. Smith of IBM, for example, might be stored under the guide word "Smith/IBM." The correspondence can be stored by just pressing a key and recalled to the monitor or printer just as quickly. In most cases, the physical tapes or disks holding the user's files do not reside in the user's building at all. Instead, they are given maximum security and protection at a specially designed computer center, often at a distant location. Physical distance makes little difference when transmissions take place at speeds approaching that of light.

Electronic bulletin boards provide an efficient, inexpensive means of communicating to many readers at once.

By the mid-1980s, several companies and government agencies provided electronic mail service on a fee basis. The most popular electronic mail service in the private sector is GTE's Telenet. In addition to its flexible and extensive set of commands for sending and receiving mail, the service features bulletin boards where companies or individuals can post information to be read by all (or selected) users of the system. Company announcements or training materials, for example, can be "published" and distributed electronically at far less cost and effort than traditional typesetting, printing, and physical distribution. Employees are simply told by memo, "Please read Bulletin #16 on Telenet before next Thursday's meeting." Employees can choose to read the material on the computer screen or print out a copy to take home.

In January 1982, the U.S. Postal Service inaugurated E-COM (Electronic Computer-Originated Mail). Major post offices around the country can receive messages entered from the computer terminals in their locale. The messages are then electronically transmitted to the post office of their destination. There, the message is printed out and placed in an envelope for delivery by traditional carrier.

In November 1984, Western Union placed its hat in the ring of electronic mail providers with EasyLink. For a fraction of the cost of a traditional telegram, computer users can send electronic messages to be delivered by Western Union either in electronic form—that is, directly to the receiving computer terminal— or as printed message packaged in a Western Union envelope. Businesses are finding this an attractive service for two reasons. First, Western Union provides compatibility between a great variety of different computers. An Apple in Pennsylvania can talk to an IBM personal computer in Michigan. Second, the Western Union name provides an identity and suggestion of urgency for messages delivered in envelopes.

At present, computer service companies such as CompuServe, Prodigy, and The Source provide the majority of electronic mail connections for individuals and, increasingly, for many companies. These systems have proven popular, especially for their user-friendly features: easy on-screen editing of messages, access to nationwide mailbox directories, and cost-effective sending and receiving options to minimize telephone expense.

Electronic mail may prove less effective than traditional business correspondence because it is often written in haste and lacks formal appearance.

While acknowledging the many conveniences of electronic mail, some users are quick to point out its problems. Some find that messages sent by electronic mail are taken less seriously than traditional business letters. Senders tend to dash off their thoughts in rough draft form, bypassing the review and correction often provided by associates or secretaries. Other users say they miss the pizzazz of traditional mail communication—classy black type on crisp, expensive stationery, with paragraphs and signature all calculated to amplify the persuasive effect of the message. "I miss signatures especially," says one executive. "I formed impressions of the individual I was dealing with by the way the name was signed."

But because electronic mail is fast and accurate, it is here to stay.

The future of electronic mail seems assured, if only because it provides two important factors to message transfer: speed and accuracy. Competition will encourage companies to provide more formatting capabilities for electronic messages—returning margins, paragraphing, and other graphic aspects of business messages. Company letterheads, too, may soon accompany printed messages. All of these refinements suggest that business messages are not and never have been mere words; instead, they are a combination of words and impressions gathered from the total effect of the written communication at hand.

An interesting footnote to the use of electronic mail involves business schools. In the last decades of the twentieth century, successful business schools find they have many more students then they anticipated. The problems arising from this situation are largely physical in nature, for example, not enough parking, classrooms, and eating facilities. Electronic mail offers an attractive, if partial, solution: students can often send assignments and questions to a professor and maintain contacts with fellow students by electronic messages from their homes. In some cases, professors post lecture notes and student assignments on electronic bulletin boards, all accessible by the college community. Such practical applications of electronic mail will surely increase in frequency and creativity as more and more colleges make owning a computer an entrance requirement.

FAX

Fax transmission is another popular, quick, and inexpensive communicative tool for modern business.

Facsimile (fax) transmission has become a standard communication link for American business. Virtually all Fortune 500 companies have at least one (and often many) fax number. Through telephone lines, a typical fax machine can transmit eight to ten pages per minute. Fax transmissions are comparable to photocopies; virtually every mark on the transmitted page is reproduced by the receiving fax machine. This capability allows businesses to use attractive letterheads in transmissions—a capability not possible with most electronic mail systems.

For shorter documents such as letters and memos, fax transmission is more economical than standard mailing, especially when envelope cost and preparation is added to postage costs. Many fax machines can store messages until off-peak hours and transmit them when telephone rates are lowest. Generally, rates for fax transmission are no more than rates for a telephone call of comparable length.

INTEGRATED OFFICE SYSTEMS

Integrated office systems overcome the problems associated with noncompatible interoffice equipment, thereby saving management valuable time and energy.

Despite the claims made in computer advertisements of the 1970s and 1980s, the computer and its peripheral devices were not immediate stars in many offices. The problem was compatibility. In many cases, the desktop computer could not access records in mainframe computer storage. The two computers simply spoke different languages. Additionally, companies had trouble achieving working relationships among electronic storage of documents, computer telephone information (who called? when? message?), photocopying equipment, and—most of all—graphic facilities.

Major computer companies like IBM, Xerox, and Wang took the lead in producing not just stand-alone equipment but whole office systems integrated to work harmoniously together. Achieving this sort of coordination among machines meant determining common specifications for hardware and software. The result is an office system that takes over many of the tedious chores of the business day. In a lawyer's office in Chicago, for example, the computer telephone rings. At the push of a button by the lawyer who answers the phone, the central computer receives a message from the phone that the call is to be billed at the rate of $2 per minute, with an invoice automatically sent to the client within 10 days. The computer, in turn, sends invoice information, complete with letterhead, to the laser printer, which prepares the invoice, along with an envelope complete with metered postage. The communication awaits only the lawyer's signature to go out of the door. If the client is served by electronic mail, of course, the process is even simpler: the computer sends an electronic billing directly and is paid, perhaps, by electronic transfer of funds.

At present, U.S. workers at all levels are heeding the call to "work smarter." To compete with European and Pacific Rim companies, the U.S. work force now relies increasingly on the time-saving advantages of integrated office systems. Earlier time-motion studies of U.S. managers showed significant "down" time per day for trivial tasks: standing at a photocopy machine waiting for 20 copies of a document, adding up figures by hand for purposes of billing or inventory, searching through bulky, ill-organized files to find a necessary document, and so forth. These frustrations of the business day not only interfere with creative, insightful management, they rob workers of energy. The integrated office system, as it continues to evolve, strives to put information and electronic assistants in the offices of each worker and manager.

THE BUSINESS RESPONSE TO THE COMMUNICATION REVOLUTION

As we look forward to communication techniques and technologies in the twenty-first century, what important changes can we foresee? Although the future always has a way of surprising us, the truth of the following basic propositions seems assured.

PROPOSITION 1:
WE WILL READ MORE

Each of us will read more in the new century. Writing will be a national and perhaps international obsession, due in large part to word processing. Word processing, as discussed earlier, simplifies the act of typing. Words, phrases, sentences, and whole paragraphs or pages can be transposed easily. Word processing also makes the composition process much less tedious.

The year 2000: technological revolutions in communication that ensure a deluge of written documents.

Word processing takes away the fear or dislike of typing. Experienced typists increase their typing speed (about 20 to 30 percent, some studies show), and workers who previously found typing too difficult or painstaking feel comfortable at the keyboard. Even hunt-and-peck typists find the combination of word processing software and a computer a forgiving and flexible production instrument.

The net effect of this capability is words, words, words. We can expect our business lives to be awash in documents of all kinds, each competing for our attention. As they compare their work in the 1990s with that in the 1980s, many executives claim to have twice as much to read now.

Voice-driven word processors will certainly not stem the tide of words. At first, the mere novelty of the process will cause a surge of print from office experimenters. After that, the ease we all feel in talking as compared with writing will ensure more documents, probably of greater length.

PROPOSITION 2: WE WILL REPRODUCE OUR WORDS MORE OFTEN

Not only will we produce more words, but the documents we create will be distributed much more globally than they are at present. Let's say, for example, that we have produced a three-page memo reporting production delays. If the memo must be duplicated by carbon copy, there is a good chance that we will send it to no more than four or five people (the maximum number of clear carbon copies on most typewriters). If, however, we have access to a photo-

The year 2000: a greater rate of reproduction and distribution of individual documents.

copying machine, we may send the document to many more people, even though the job entails collating, stapling, and addressing the various copies. Now imagine the same three-page document composed for electronic mail. A menu appears asking us where we want the memo distributed. One of our choices is "all authorized recipients," in this case all supervisors, managers, and directors. The temptation is overwhelming: at the press of a key, the document is on its way to over a hundred people. Some of them need to read the memo and others don't. We may reason that it's better to include too many readers than to leave someone out, isn't it? Words pour in to managers at an unprecedented rate. Everyone, it seems, has something to say through electronic mail, and copying the entire company is almost easier than picking out selected readers.

For documents that are not distributed by electronic mail, we will have high-speed, multitask copiers at our disposal. Laser printers and copiers reproduce the "image" of each page, rather than breaking it down letter-by-letter like a traditional typewriter. As a consequence, hundreds of original copies can be produced by a machine each minute. On many standard office copiers, documents can be automatically collated and stapled. Again, the effect? More documents for every manager to read, digest, and file.

PROPOSITION 3: WE WILL HAVE ACCESS TO MORE INFORMATION

The year 2000: easy availability of overwhelming amounts of research information.

More than 2,400 databases now serve the needs of business, medicine, law, engineering, and other fields. Taken together, these information services make available billions of printed pages from journals, reports, studies, books, and dissertations. In past years offices were not filled with such materials for good reason: the business library was across town, and research there was too costly in time and personal energy. A bottleneck of inconvenience prevented us from getting information we may have needed.

That bottleneck has been shattered by computer access to databases. From our computers, we can enter search words that within minutes bring to the screen pertinent information on virtually any topic relevant to business. The effect of this new availability? More words.

HOW WILL WE HANDLE MORE WORDS?

These three propositions clearly indicate the future: we will face vastly more printed words in our business lives. This phenomenon would matter less if the big chip—the one between our ears—kept pace with changes in all the microchips around us. More words don't matter if reading speeds and comprehension rates keep up.

Unfortunately, there is no evidence to suggest that we read any faster or comprehend more completely than businesspeople in previous decades. The implications are clear, if somewhat frightening. Something has to give as words pouring through microchips back up against a bottleneck impervious to technology: the human brain.

What will give, most likely, is the way we communicate. In the way we write, speak, and even think, we will make crucial adjustments necessitated by the new world of words. At the present time, the form of these adjustments can be observed only in part; therefore, the following descriptions of possible changes in communication are only hypothetical. Measure their accuracy against your own communication experiences as you contemplate a business career overflowing with words.

MORE VERBAL OR
ORAL CONTACT

To compete against the crush of printed materials, businesspeople must develop their speaking skills and communicate more frequently in person or by telephone.

Printed communication will lose effectiveness to the extent that it gets lost among piles of letters, memos, reports, and advertisements. On many important business matters, we will find ourselves making contact in person, by telephone, or by teleconference rather than by printed media. After initial business understandings have been reached, we may agree to confirm points in a backup letter or memo of some type.

This will have implications for business schools where the major communication emphasis is writing. Business majors will want to be prepared to do business by means of interpersonal conversations, group discussions, interviews, telephone and teleconferencing meetings, and other forums requiring practical oral skills.

EARLY MESSAGING

In his well-known video presentation, "Effective Writing," Joseph Florin demonstrates what a busy executive does with a pile of printed matter. There is the initial shuffle to see what looks interesting or important. Then there is the tentative selection of a few likely candidates for reading. After a glance here and there at how they begin, the "winners" are selected for serious attention. The rest remain unread, often for days or weeks, until they are filed or discarded.

What determines which document is chosen? Clear, early messages let the reader know what the writer plans to discuss and why. Too often that "headline" gets buried deep in memos, letters, and reports. Consider, for example, two opening paragraphs from a report. The first hides the central intent of the report; the second displays it early and openly.

DELAYED MESSAGING
The mission statement of the Office of Employee Safety within Entron Corporation requires that we review potential hazards within the company, and report on a quarterly basis to management. This report, though not our usual quarterly report, is felt to be justified by circumstances uncovered last week during routine maintenance of company air conditioning ducts. That maintenance was performed by Caudwell Associates and has now been completed.

EARLY MESSAGING
Carcinogenic asbestos fibers in Entron's air conditioning ducts pose a health threat to every employee. The Office of Employee Safety reached this conclusion after examining ducts exposed during recent servicing. This report describes our findings and makes recommendations.

Early messaging—placing a clear statement of purpose first—grabs the reader's attention.

Notice that readers are "caught" by the first line in the second example. They do not have to wade through boring preliminaries. *Early messaging* recognizes that each piece of writing has a short "window of opportunity" to catch the eye of the readers. If that moment—really a matter of only a few seconds—is lost due to irrelevant language, the document may go unread.

You can enhance your ability to produce early messages by emphasizing "Subject:" lines in memos and letters. Make these phrases attention getters as well as describers. Observe how a minor revision of a flat Subject line can breathe new life into the statement:

SUBJECT: *Upcoming Sales Convention* (descriptive but not urgent)
SUBJECT: *Your Role in the Upcoming Sales Convention*
(personalized to gain attention)

In longer works such as reports and proposals, the subject line is expanded into a succinct paragraph or two called the *executive summary.* This extended early message may be your only chance to attract the interest and the reading time of a busy executive. Use words early in your paragraphs that get to the heart of what the executive may care about in your longer document. For example, notice how the following short executive summary places emphasis on what matters most to the reader:

EXECUTIVE SUMMARY
Employees at VRC Corporation use virtually all of the sick time allotted to them each month. This practice costs the company more than half of its current profit margin. None of our competitors experiences a comparable rate of absenteeism.

Are VRC employees truly ill? The evidence suggests they are not (Section II). Only in four cases have employees been disciplined for taking unnecessary sick leave (Section IV). Three company policies should be changed to bring down the number of absentee hours due to the abuse of sick leave (Recommendations, Section VI).

The test for early messaging in any business document is simple: hand it to a business associate to peruse for five seconds. Then take it back and ask for impressions. If, in those five seconds, your associate has not at least glimpsed the central message and purpose of the document, your early message needs improvement.

INCREASED EMPHASIS
ON FORMAT

User-friendly formats invite the reader's eye to scan the page.

We form important judgments about business documents long before we read a single word. In the era of the communication revolution, first impressions will be crucial in determining whether a document gets our attention.

One way to attract the eye and mind is to format the document in a *user-friendly* way. This term comes from the language of computer manuals, in which computers are described, often inaccurately, as machines that are patient and forgiving to user errors and misunderstandings. In the case of documents, however, *user-friendly* has a more specific meaning: user-friendly formats don't scare the eye away.

Notice, for example, in this dense jungle of prose how the eye immediately decides, "Thanks, I'd rather not."

Heavy blocks of print unrelieved by white space prove uninviting to the eye. Even before the mind has a chance to consider what the words themselves have to communicate, the eye has already decided "too dense, too dark, too difficult." That predisposition influences how we read the words on the page. The task of reading such a dense block of print is comparable in many ways to remembering a long number: 411123456789101985775 1020. Notice how a bit of white space makes the number visually more approachable, and hence memorable: 411 12345678910 1985 775-1020. Use white space in the form of indentation, margination, and spacing to create visually interesting and attractive paragraphs and pages.

By contrast, the following paragraphs invite the eye's attention by their generous use of white space, indentation, and short paragraphs.

Heavy blocks of print are difficult to read. Even before the mind has a chance to consider what the words themselves have to communicate, the eye has already decided "too dense, too dark, too difficult."

That predisposition influences how we read the words on the page. For example:

- *Try to remember this long number: 41112345678910198577751020*
- *Now notice how a bit of white space makes the number visually more approachable and memorable:*

411 12345678910 1985 775-1020

Use white space in the form of indentation, margination, and spacing to create visually interesting and attractive paragraphs and pages.

Again, the test for adequate user-friendliness in documents is a human one. Hand the document to a business associate and ask, "How does it look?" Watch the person's eyes and expression for your answer. If the reader squints and frowns while looking over your document, you've missed your mark. Revise your format (easily done through word processing) so that there is more "breathing space" for the reader's eye and mind.

INCREASED USE OF GRAPHIC ENHANCEMENTS

Word processing and desktop publishing systems provide business communicators with important prestige cues.

In every era of business communication there have been "prestige cues" that indicate, at a glance, the relative importance of the document. In the 1970s, for example, letters typed with a fabric ribbon were considered more amateurish than letters typed with carbon ribbon (producing a booklike clarity in type). With advances in word processing in the 1980s, prestige cues changed. Then everyone seemed to have access to a letter-quality printer with carbon-ribbon type. The new cues had to do with the type itself: Could the writer justify (make even) both right and left margins? Could the writer emphasize some words through the use of boldface? Could the writer create large-letter headings? These changes raised the stakes in the game of looking professional. Popular word processing software like WordStar went through several revisions in an effort to provide more and more flexibility with type.

In the 1990s, document attractiveness surged forward again with the popularity of laser printers and desktop publishing. A wide variety of fonts, formats, and photoquality graphics were now possible in business documents.

The game, with its new set of cues, continues as we approach the twenty-first century. Now *all* business communicators seem to have access to word processing systems (and some to desktop publishing systems) for turning out attractive type in letters, reports, and proposals. The new prestige cues—the keys to who's ahead in the communication game—are the graphics within business documents.

Prestige cues include visuals from simple charts to full-color photographs that attract the reader's attention while conveying important information.

Software packages available for computers like the Apple Macintosh and the IBM PS/2 enable the user to create charts, graphs, maps, and photograph-like pictures for inclusion in business documents. Once created on the screen of the PC, these graphics can be placed anywhere in a business document and printed out by a printer with graphics capability. The graphics can be reduced or enlarged, rotated to any position, and, in many systems, printed out in a variety of selected colors. Once these graphics have been placed within the business document, they can be stored on disk for recall later. Thus, companies with a given product line can create a number of visuals depicting their products and place them in a visual library to be called up by any writer within the company who needs a handy illustration.

Far more than decoration, such graphic enhancements confirm the wisdom of the ancient saying, "A picture is worth a thousand words." Visual diagrams and representations attract the reader more powerfully than mere print, and they can reinforce central points in a lasting way.

To use these new prestige cues, familiarize yourself with a prominent graphics package as recommended by your college learning resource specialist or professor. You might also check with computer stores to find graphics software compatible with the PC and printer at your disposal. Now, test your response to a business page containing graphic enhancements (see Figure 3-2). In this case, the visual feature clarifies and focuses the printed message on the page. Graphic enhancements also act to relieve the tedium that often accompanies text-only reading.

THE RETURN OF FRIENDLINESS

Maintain a friendly tone to avoid the impersonality that often accompanies mechanized communication.

Will communication, as it grows faster and more mechanical due to new technologies, lose its human warmth? Will "It was great to see you, Frank" degenerate into "Per our recent meeting"? Just the opposite seems to be occurring. Perhaps because we fear a sterile, brave new world, we already seem to be conveying our personalities in communication carried electronically. Notice, for example, how the sample of electronic mail shown in Figure 3-3 manages to say, "Hey, there's a person behind this message—one you might like to know."

Formal it's not. But is it effective communication? Mary tells Bob exactly what she needs and when. In frank, friendly terms she explains the reason for the rush and seeks Bob's cooperation. In tone and substance, the message could be considered a written telephone call.

Shrewd communicators can use this tendency toward a more relaxed style to business advantage. Business relationships still depend to a remarkable degree on interpersonal chemistry and warmth—the key ingredients of trust. By striking a friendly but not presumptuous or brash tone, communicators can put their reader at ease, which is the best posture for persuasion. The act of communicating itself becomes easier as we let ourselves write in a friendly, open mode. Few of us find it easy to generate paragraph after paragraph of the business clichés we never use in ordinary speech: "regarding your . . . , thereby eliminating . . . , in full expectation of . . . , with all due respect." By letting ourselves write as though to a friend, we find words flowing more naturally and more persuasively. Often, we make a friend of our reader in business simply by treating him or her that way in words.

THE ADVENT OF SHARED WRITING

Historically, American businesspeople have considered writing a private form of self-expression. As such, criticism of one's style was tantamount to criticism of one's personality. That attitude—that a person's writing is private and personal—has roots that every business writer must understand, especially at a time when the attitude is changing dramatically. With the Romantic era of the nineteenth century came the idea that writing was based primarily on inspiration. Waiting for such inspiration came to be known as "writer's block"—that painful

FIGURE 3–2 Graphically Enhanced Page

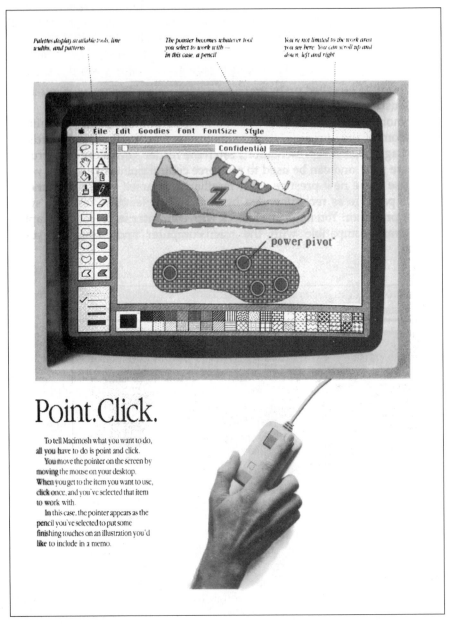

Courtesy Apple Computer, Inc.

staring at a blank sheet of paper. Poets like Byron talked of the "lava of the imagination" pouring forth into words.

Through our schooling, we are all heirs to such Romantic assumptions about where words come from. Once we have cast language onto paper, we adopt an almost parental attitude toward our choice of diction, phrasing, and even punctuation. Such protective attitudes may be appropriate for poets, but they are not well-suited to today's business communicators. Words in business are like nails in carpentry: items with which to get the job done. Business writers, especially in the fast-paced days of a communication revolution, put words

Remember that your words are merely tools for doing business. Let others help you use them effectively.

FIGURE 3–3 Electronic Mail Sample

```
EMS 3987 January 4, 19__
Storage Disk: 2238

We need the results of your marketing studies no
later than January 20, 19__, to complete
redesign of label and packaging for BerryTarts.
Contact us ASAP by EMS when you receive computer
runs, particularly for urban areas. By January
30, 19__, we will send preliminary redesigns to
you by FAX for your signoff. Thanks, Bob -- and
sorry for the rush. We're all under the gun to
beat the marketing effort of General Foods.
Happy New Year!

Mary Gilford
```

on paper with much the same attitude as builders frame houses. They welcome constructive comment by others, because the goal is to build good documents or houses, rather than to immortalize personal expression or inspiration. In short, the era of electronic communication emphasizes the *craft* of business communication—skills that workers are eager to share in the same way that craftspeople compare techniques. (See Chapter 8 on collaborative writing.)

This sharing attitude is already apparent in *communication quality circles* in American corporations. Writers within a work group circulate a document to test its effect on others in the group before releasing it for public scrutiny or company use. From their colleagues, business communicators get straightforward advice on what works and what doesn't. In this way, business employees are learning writing skills in a way they were never taught in school.

ADAPTING TO THE REVOLUTION

Anxieties tend to run high as the skills ensuring yesterday's job security are rendered nearly obsolete for tomorrow's technologies. Frustration also increases for some adults who are learning something completely new, often the first really new learning they've undertaken in years. Disappointment is rampant as new technologies hit expensive, time-wasting glitches—with the proverbial egg on the faces of those who recommended the new computer, new mail system, or new teleconference room. Jealousies occur as comparative youngsters are promoted into responsible positions (with big salaries) based on technological insight and skills.

These are the growing pains and signs of ferment in the communication revolution. Business communicators will do well to get used to them. Unlike past revolutions, this revolution in communication promises almost perpetual change and a dizzying onslaught of new possibilities. We now type our words into the computer; soon we will probably talk them in. By the year 2000 will we simply *think* our words into the computer? Will we establish our credibility as communicators with a card or code so we can concentrate on essential messaging? Will we develop special shorthand languages for rapid reading and writing?

The answers to these and questions we cannot even imagine are our not-so-distant inheritance. What an exciting time this is, to have something to say and to care about how it is said.

WRITING AND SPEAKING EXERCISES

1. Transcribe a typical discussion among your colleagues. Research Shannon and Weaver's model of communication. Analyze the discussion using their theory.

2. Review recent newspaper and magazine articles that discuss ethical and legal questions raised by developments in telephone technology. Write a memo summarizing your research.

3. Survey local businesses that use electronic mail or deal with other businesses that use it. In a short report, discuss the advantages and disadvantages of this technology based on responses to your survey.

4. Work with a knowledgeable individual on the subject of desktop publishing. Obtain several examples of materials produced in that manner. Present a report (oral or written) on the subject to your class or instructor indicating the value of this method of communication to small firms.

5. Investigate the topic of computer graphics. Make an oral presentation to your class on the value of using computer graphics in reports.

6. Discuss the following topic with at least one manager: What computer skills does his or her company desire in entry-level employees? Summarize your findings in a brief report to your class.

7. Discuss the following topic with one senior manager and one mid- or lower-level manager: What percentage of their time is spent at a computer installed in their office? What are typical computer tasks they perform there? Summarize your findings in a brief report to your class.

8. Each member of a group of four or five students should develop a short business document such as a memo or letter. Pass the rough drafts around the group for comments and suggestions. After you have seen one another's writing, discuss the usefulness of second and third opinions. What did you feel as others were criticizing what you had written?

9. Using a word processing program, make the changes in your document suggested by the group. Report to the group on your ease or difficulty in using the program. Compare the techniques you used with the steps you would have taken on a traditional typewriter to make the same corrections.

10. Identify five business occasions when instant messages via electronic mail would be vastly preferable to delivery by ordinary mail.

11. Take time to try out a word processing program on campus or at a computer store. Report your impressions to your class.

12. Interview three businesspeople who work with computers. Ask them to comment on the advantages and frustrations of their experiences.

13. Develop an oral or written presentation (as your instructor suggests) about the value of PCs for a business of your choice. If possible, aim your presentation at a traditional business that is not yet using computers.

14. Browse through at least two recent issues of a computing magazine such as *Byte* or *Personal Computing.* In the advertisements or articles, choose at least three technological devices *not* discussed in this chapter. Suggest a possible business application for each device.

READINGS

See "How to Use Electronic Mail Successfully" in the Readings section at the back of this book.

SUGGESTED RESOURCES

Becker, Susan K. "New Communication Technology: Helping or Hindering the Message?" *Employment Relations Today* 18 (Autumn 1991):303–312.

Begole, C. "Five Successful Alternatives to In-Person Meetings." *Working Woman* (October 1990):70–73.

Bentley, Trevor. "Electronic Mail." *Management Accounting* 69 (July-August 1991):10–14.

Burkitt, Alan. "A Video Vision." *Management Today* (September 1991): 123–124.

Finley, Michael. "Welcome to the Electronic Meeting." *Training* 28 (July 1991): 28–32.

Goode, Joanne, and Johnson, Maggie. "Putting Out the Flames: The Etiquette and Law of E-Mail." *Online* 15 (November 1991):61–65.

Sproull, Lee. *Connections: New Ways of Working in the Networked Organization.* Cambridge, Mass.: MIT Press, 1991.

Stevens, Mark. "The Right Connections." *D & B Reports* 39 (July-August 1991):40–44.

Taylor, Ron. "Videoconferencing—Building Ubiquity, Cutting Costs, and Communicating Easily." *Telecommunications* 25 (August 1991):46–48.

ENDNOTES

1. D. Wallenchinsky and Irving Wallace, *The Book of Lists,* 4th ed. (New York: William Morrow, 1990).

2. The mathematical theory of communication has been taken up, altered, and extended in the work of general system theorists like Anatol Rapoport and William J. Horvath, "Thoughts on Organization Theory," *General Systems* 4 (1959):87–91. Recent contributions are treated well in Walter J. Severin and James W. Tankard, Jr., *Communication Theory: Origins, Methods, Uses* (New York: Hastings House, 1979); Nancy Harper, *Human Communication Theory: The History of the Paradigm* (Rochelle Park, NJ: Hayden, 1979); Frank E. X. Dance, *Human Communication Theory: Comparative Essays* (New York: Harper and Row, 1982); E. M. Rogers, and M. Kincaid, *Communication Networks: Toward a New Paradigm for Research* (New York: The Free Press, 1981); and Janet Barnard,

"The Information Environments of New Managers," *Journal of the Association for Business Communication* 28(4):312–324.

3. See Arthur Bell and Thomas Housel, "Teleconferencing Comes of Age—Again," *T.H.E. Journal* (November 1986):24.

4

INTERCULTURAL COMMUNICATION FOR A GLOBAL ENVIRONMENT

To maintain a leadership position in any one developed country a business—whether large or small—increasingly has to attain and hold leadership positions in all developed markets worldwide. It has to be able to do research, to design, to develop, to engineer and to manufacture in any part of the developed world, and to export from any developed country to any other. It has to go transnational.[1]

Intercultural communication is thriving in the Information Age.

Intercultural communication is not new: people of different cultures have had to communicate with each other since the beginning of history. Now, however, as world events constantly bring diverse cultures closer together, the need for effective intercultural communication is much greater. Many other factors besides wars and subsequent alliances play a role in increasing communication among nations and the cultures they represent. Improvements in electronic communication permit excellent telephone, TV, radio, fax, and computer transmissions with the help of satellites in space. International banks and corporations cooperate to consummate "deals." Multinational corporations manufacture component parts in different nations and then combine them into a finished product in yet another country.

Recently, we have seen European nations move toward a one currency system and a common economic alliance. And most dramatic of all recent events has been the breakup of the Soviet Union and the progress of its component republics and neighboring states toward democracy. These factors plus improvements in air transportation, the economic dependence of nations on each other, common international health problems, and many other factors will surely have an enormous impact on redefining and improving intercultural communication across national boundaries.[2]

More and more, effective international communication is becoming the key to peace, understanding, and progress. Every day brings us newspaper accounts of Japanese automobile manufacturers opening additional plants in the United States. More investors from other nations are buying U.S. real estate. Japanese video game giant Nintendo became part owner of the Seattle

Mariners, and other Japanese firms have been buying rapidly into U.S. movie and record companies.

But as rapidly as foreign investments have expanded in the United States, even more quickly have U.S. companies moved abroad. General Electric's magnetic resonance imaging business and CAT scanners are first in the world. U.S. pharmaceutical companies supply worldwide a large percentage of medications for people and food supplements for animal feed. Disney theme parks thrive in Japan and France as they do in the United States. U.S. oil drilling and technical equipment firms operate around the globe, and our technical experts in many fields work in almost every nation.

Foreign investment in the United States mirrors U.S. investment abroad.

What makes all of this international exchange possible? The answers are complex; but undoubtedly, one factor is that the worldwide level of technology among developed countries is about equal. Or as Peter Drucker has said: "All developed countries are *equally* capable of doing everything, doing it equally well and doing it equally fast."[3]

A second factor is the ability of developed countries to share information almost instantaneously—information can be communicated anywhere, at any time, in fractions of minutes. The globe has become a village, and like a village, its citizens can communicate with one another quickly and easily. But if that is so, why do we encounter communication problems from one nation to another?

Although businesses in developed countries share the same information and technology, cultural differences can lead to communication breakdowns.

The answer is simple: worldwide we share much of the same information and technology, but not the same *cultures.* Werner Krause in Frankfurt may share the same detailed knowledge of computers as his Cleveland counterpart, Emily Westin, but he doesn't share the same culture. Their family, recreational, financial, and other values are different. Their values spring from their experiences, expectations, and habits—their cultures. The same types of cultural differences are true of Emily Westin and Togo Nakasone, or Ignacia Sanchez, or Mohammed Kassabian.

The same words and gestures may have different meanings in different cultures.

Technological advances in the past 100 to 200 years have spread and been adopted and refined worldwide. But cultures based on thousands of years of development are slow to change. And perhaps they should not change, for cultural differences among different societies give individual identity to each group. Persistent diversity of cultures has made the world an exciting place. But it has also created barriers that constitute a major challenge for communicators. Even with advances in transmission of information, when cultural differences prevent people from understanding words and actions the same way, communication can suffer. The key to remember when dealing with different cultures is that verbal and nonverbal communication may have different meanings to different cultures.

Some cultures do integrate fairly easily into other groups, but such integration is not usual. For example, the possibility that Asian cultures will be thoroughly understood and integrated into the Western culture—and vice versa—is slim indeed, at least for the few years left in this century.

The way to achieve better communication among the peoples of the world is through knowledge, appreciation, and understanding of cultural differences rather than through acceptance or integration. And that is what this chapter is all about: increasing your knowledge, understanding, and awareness of other cultures so that you may communicate more effectively with your business counterparts in this country and in the rest of the world.

CULTURES IN THE UNITED STATES

Have you noticed how cultural differences in the United States have become enormous, especially in the past ten years? Many major changes are taking place in urban centers such as Chicago, New York, St. Louis, Los Angeles, and Miami. Most immigrants to the United States go to urban centers because of economic opportunities such as jobs and the possibilities for opening businesses.

NATIONAL CHANGES

Immigrants account for much of the increase in the U.S. population over the past decade.

The growing number of non-English-speaking people in the United States will change the country's culture and business communication practices.

In 1990 the United States had a population of 248 million; just ten years before that, the number was 226 million. This amounts to a fraction less than a most impressive 10 percent increase in just ten years! A significant portion of those 22 million additional individuals are immigrants who enter the United States in an almost steady stream.

With the continued economic and political unrest in nations around the globe, the number of new arrivals is sure to increase in the coming ten years. Obviously, this flow of non-English-speaking individuals will have a major impact on communication patterns and cultural diversification in the United States.

Figure 4-1 illustrates the rather startling demographic changes in the United States in 1990 as compared with 1980. While whites increased 6 percent and blacks 13.2 percent, other groups soared. For example, the Eskimo, American Indian, Aleut group increased 37.9 percent in 1990 as compared with 1980; Asians or Pacific Islanders, 107.8 percent; Hispanic origin (of any race), 53 percent; and other races (a relatively small number), 45.1 percent! In actual numbers, the biggest increases in the U.S. population among races between 1980 and 1990 were among Asian or Pacific Islanders, which went from 3,500,000 to 7,274,000, and those of Hispanic origin, which rose to 22,354,000 from 14,609,000. Thus, of the 22-million increase in population in the United States in the 1980s, two groups (Asians and those of Hispanic origin) roughly accounted for 12 million, or more than 50 percent.

Asians and Hispanics accounted for more than 50 percent of the total U.S. population growth in the 1980s.

DEMOGRAPHIC CHANGES IN STATES AND URBAN CENTERS

The population of Asian or Pacific Islanders in the United States increased more than any other group in the 1980s.

The Hispanic population exhibited the next largest increase in the 1980s.

Urban centers in the United States experience the greatest cultural impact from new immigrants.

Asian or Pacific Islanders increased by at least 40 percent in all states except Hawaii, where that population is the majority. California's Asian and Pacific Islander population increased 127 percent: in fact, in 1990 California's population of that group was larger than the total population of 22 states! A majority of the Asian and Pacific Islander population in the United States live in three states: California, New York, and Hawaii.

California's Hispanic population increased sharply from 4,544,000 in 1980 to 7,688,000 in 1990, or by 69 percent. This increase exceeded the national Hispanic growth rate by 16 percentage points. California's Hispanic population in 1990 was larger than the total population of all but nine states. Three other states besides California (Texas, New York, and Florida) had Hispanic populations of more than 1 million.[4]

Although the demographic changes have been nationwide, the impact on existing cultures has been especially dramatic in major urban centers. This makes sense because the big cities offer the greatest opportunities for employment for those who speak little English, are not yet licensed in their professions (medicine, nursing, engineering, etc.), or are unskilled.

FIGURE 4-1 Percentage Change in Population by Race and Hispanic Origin for the United States: 1960 to 1990

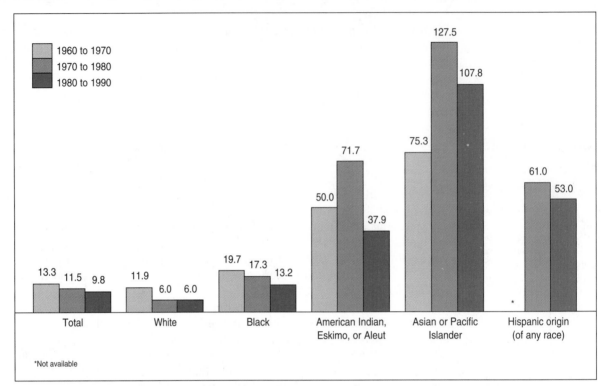

Source: Bureau of the Census, U.S. Dept. of Commerce, Economics & Statistics Administration, "1990 Census Profile: Race and Hispanic Origin," No. 2-June 1991, pp.3-7.

Communicating in the cultural melting pot of U.S. businesses and schools challenges natives and immigrants alike.

The impact of different cultures on U.S. culture is tremendous. The two arenas most affected are the workplace and the schools. In both of these areas, the newcomers change, but so do those who have been in the receiving culture for years. The immigrants' task is to adapt to not only the U.S. culture, but also the differences encountered among other immigrants. For the U.S. worker and U.S. student, the task is equally formidable. Communicating not only with Asians in general (as an example), but with Asians who speak different languages, practice different habits, and maintain different standards, according to whether their native country is Japan, China, Korea, Taiwan, the Philippines, or a dozen other nations is more than a little difficult.

Thus, every major urban center in the United States has as many cultural differences as may be found when any of the following cultures are contrasted with each other: Seoul, South Korea; Osaka, Japan; Riyadh, Saudi Arabia; Frankfurt, Germany; Helsinki, Finland; or Mexico City, Mexico. It is said people in Los Angeles need skills in 89 different dialects to communicate with every segment of that city's population.

The demand for intercultural communication has never been and never will be greater than it is in our time.

Because the rate of immigration cited cannot possibly continue in the United States for the next 75 to 100 years, the cultural differences will lessen. As the inflow decreases and the years pass, the homogeneity of our society will grow. Certainly by the year 2100, communications will be easier because of the melding. However, you and I are living in the 1990s. It is vital that we recognize that a vast variety of cultures *now* exist in our factories, offices, government bureaus, hospitals, and schools. We must deal with that diversity *now* with tact, diplomacy, efficiency, and most importantly, knowledge. Because of that need, the content of this chapter is especially important to every reader.[5]

CONTRASTS IN CULTURES

Avoid communication breakdowns by becoming aware of cultural differences.

Managers who travel to foreign countries to do business know that they will encounter even more variations in communication than they do in their plants and offices in the United States. Being aware of those variations and adapting to them can often make a most significant contribution to the success of a business transaction. Successful individuals, whether in business, industry, government, health care or other areas, know that in relationships with other cultures:

- there are no specific values or behaviors that are invariably "correct."
- that they must be flexible and accepting of differences in values, beliefs, standards, and mores.
- that it is important to be sensitive to verbal nuances and nonverbal behavior.
- that knowledge of religious, cultural, business, and social practices of other cultures is a necessity.
- that *within* a culture specific differences and values may exist.

THE PERCEPTION OF SPACE

Animals, both wild and domestic, guard their territory. Some animals use specific territories for mating and raising offspring. They return to the same place year after year until they die.

Territoriality also exists in nations, cultures, and even homes. To protect and define our territory we put up flags, fences, rows of bushes, signs, and so on. How many times have you seen students walk into a classroom for the first time, carefully select a seat, and occupy it every class period for the rest of the term? Interestingly enough, no other class member will take that seat.

Individuals base their perceptions of space on cultural norms.

Societal norms often govern "territory." The instructor occupies the space in front of the class; the students sit "out there." However, if the instructor wishes to communicate (nonverbally) that the rules have changed for today, he or she can rearrange the students' chairs into groups of six and move the instructor's chair to the side. The "rearranged" space communicates a message.

The concepts of primary, secondary, and public territories and personal space help us define our sense of place and status in the world.

Primary territories are items such as your bed, toothbrush, or comb; *secondary* territories include the chair you usually sit on at dinner or the desk in the chemistry class you usually occupy each day at 2 P.M. *Public* territories are places such as the library, parking lot, beach, or picnic area. But even here you can communicate a claimed space within the public territory by placing your books and jacket on the table in the library, unrolling your blanket on a spot of beach, painting your name or title on a parking space, or placing your food on a picnic table. *Personal* space is an area around you that expands or contracts because of the situation and/or cultural norms.

Culturally different perceptions of space can cause miscommunication.

If you do business with people from Mexico or Italy, you should expect them to occupy more of your personal space than would someone from Germany. Perhaps you have personally been involved, either here or abroad, with an Italian who is speaking with great excitement. He may be advancing, you may be retreating, and you both are puzzled. "Why is he moving into my space?" you wonder. "Why is he backing away from me as I address him? Does he disagree?" the puzzled Italian ponders. On the other hand, one source points out that the belief that Italians and Latin Americans are comfortable with little personal space and that North Americans are not may be nothing more than a generalization. Personal status or rank may play a more dominant role in space relationships.[6] Nevertheless, it is true that space is shared differently between a father and son or two men who are good friends in many Hispanic and Near Eastern cultures as compared with men in the United States.

Look at the designation of space in a U.S. corporation. The president, in splendid isolation, occupies a large office on the top floor with corner windows. French or Near Eastern managing directors sit among their subordinates so they can "see" all activities. Consider the Japanese home owner who often values a small home that is well proportioned and includes only the items needed for daily use; many home owners in the United States measure their home in thousands of square feet and fill it with furnishings that may never be used but are meant to communicate status.

The use of space by individuals in a culture or between cultures is not only a fascinating aspect of nonverbal communication study, but it is also a revealing one for the cross-cultural communicator. Think of how individuals react in a crowded elevator as compared with an elevator containing only four people; how the people density in a rock concert or prison yard may contribute to violence; and how space is viewed in the small but heavily populated nation of Japan as compared to the United States.

THE PERCEPTION OF TIME

Although most U.S. businesspeople believe punctuality reflects courtesy and respect, people from other cultures view time much differently.

Different cultures observe time differently. Time is of major importance to people in the United States. We are thoroughly time oriented: we "save time," "buy time," "make time," "spend time," "waste time," and "invest time." We are so time oriented that we become irritated when others don't observe time commitments the way we do.

The U.S. businessperson dealing with someone whose cultural orientation is different—whether here or abroad—must be aware of the possibility that that person may view time differently. The New York executive kept waiting for a half hour past the appointment time should not interpret the wait as an affront; it is "merely time." The businessperson in Latin America, the Near East, and some nations of Europe may have attitudes toward time that are quite different.

Industrialization increases a culture's obsession with time.

Change takes place in the perception of time by cultures as they move toward industrialization and become more Westernized. The Koreans, for example, have become more and more time conscious as they have become more industrialized.

MATERIAL ITEMS

Materialism may define success in one culture but give offense to another.

In the consuming culture of the United States, many individuals prize highly such material items as impressive cars, jewelry, furnishings, clothes, and so on. Large diamonds, coats, and Mercedes cars may be important items to communicate status in our society, but other cultures may look upon these items as ostentatious and even in poor taste.

Although jewelry has been a status symbol in most societies, the particular item varies. Diamonds and emeralds may only be colored stones of little value to some. On the other hand, a shell or animal tooth may be highly prized by others.

We usually perceive "big as better": a giant redwood, a large car and home, or a large precious stone. The Japanese, who find space limited in their nation, admire beautifully proportioned items that are small: a bonsai tree, a home, a garden, a carved netsuke, or an intricately worked piece of jade or ivory. Value is in the perception!

FRIENDSHIPS

Friendships develop slowly in many cultures.

Friendships and how they are viewed differ from culture to culture. Most people in the United States have moved from one city or state to another. Wherever we go, we usually make friends quickly and easily. New neighbors, church members, and work associates almost immediately become "Joe" or "Jenny." When we attempt the same approach in England, Germany, Japan, or Finland, we may frequently encounter communication barriers. They're not immediately "Nigel" or "Karin" or "Togo" and we aren't immediately "Jim" or "Jane" to them. They expect to be addressed as "Mr. Salisbury" or "Fräulein Baumann" or "Mr. Tamasaki," and they will call you "Mr. Stevenson" or "Ms. Wright."

Friendships develop slowly and carefully in many cultures. Neighbors in England or Germany may address one another quite formally for years if that is the preference of one or both parties. In many nations friendships are often based on loyalties, feuds, or physical encounters that span generations.

AGREEMENTS

The customs used to formalize agreements vary considerably across cultures.

To an average person in the United States, an agreement completed with a signed contract is almost sacred. To many people in the Near East, however, a contract is just "a piece of paper" that is dissolved when the paper is destroyed. But a handshake made after deliberate and thorough discussion over many cups of coffee, that is an agreement! Unfortunately, many U.S. construction firms that have embarked on major projects in the Near East have found that their contractual partners looked upon their carefully worded contracts as the *beginning* of negotiations, not the end. In recent years, however, the perceptions of the two cultures of what constitutes an agreement have come much closer together.

ETHICS

Accepted behavior in one culture may be considered unethical in another.

Ethical practices in one culture may be frowned on or even be illegal in another. Payment to an individual or a group to secure a contract for a product (with little or no reference to the quality of that product) would be termed a "bribe" in the United States. In another part of the world, such action is not illegal and is referred to as a "commission." Certain comments or even overt actions in a U.S. office between a man and a woman may be called "sexual harassment" and are unethical. In a business office in a Mediterranean nation, the same comments or actions may not be taken as seriously (that view is, however, rapidly changing).

What may be ethical and even an act of organizational or national heroism in one culture may be viewed as outright terrorism in another. Even though such an act may result in the loss of lives, different cultures view the act differently. Several major international incidents illustrate this disparity: the killing of Israeli athletes in the 1972 Olympics; the explosion that caused the death of more than 200 U.S. Marines in Beirut in 1983; the blowing up of the Pan American plane over Lockerbie, Scotland in 1988. To the Western world, these were all acts of terrorism; to many in the Near East, those responsible for the acts were considered heroes. To many in the United States, the pilots who dropped bombs on Iraq in the Gulf War were heroes; to the Iraqis, they were terrorists.

EATING CUSTOMS

Learn the eating customs of a foreign culture to avoid offending your host.

Customs in eating vary tremendously around the world. Who is served first, the men or women at the table? Or are women even present at an "important" meal? What about utensils—which ones should be used when, or are there none at all? What about liquor (never served in the Middle East)? Should you match your host toast for toast? Can you decline to drink? And be careful how you pass or reach for food at the meal. The left hand is never used in serving food in many of the Middle Eastern nations, for that is the hand usually reserved for "unclean" (toilet, for example) functions. Must you partake of the raw fish? It's best to learn of the customs beforehand so you are prepared.

MALE-FEMALE RELATIONSHIPS

Women still occupy subservient roles in many cultures.

Male-female relationships are a sensitive aspect of most cultures. When you are in the company of businessmen in the Near East do not discuss or even inquire about the health of his wife or 19-year-old daughter. Such an inquiry would be considered much too personal and forward. And where are the wives of Togo, Taki, and Mako as these three men prepare to serve as your hosts for an evening out in Tokyo? Don't ask. Wives rarely accompany their husbands at an evening "business" dinner.

What some cultures perceive as the "natural" subordination of women to men strikes many Americans as unfortunate and unjust. The political and moral issues involved come to a head when a U.S. businesswoman faces hard choices: can she do business in cultures that suppress women and, if so, how can she cope?

The answers to those difficult questions, of course, differ according to the culture and situation at hand. But three trends have emerged in recent years:

1. Businesswomen are visiting sexually hostile cultures in increasing numbers.
2. When businesswomen anticipate problems due to sexual assumptions, they prepare in advance by establishing their professional status with their foreign clients through correspondence, telephone conversation, and mutual acquaintances.
3. Women sometimes make initial business contacts in the company of male colleagues, who then withdraw as the business relationship develops.

American businesswomen may well set the example that leads to sexual equality in other cultures.

A favorite tenet of cultural relativism is that mores and customs are neither right or wrong, just different. But in the case of sexual discrimination, cultures like individuals can simply be wrongheaded. Attitudes change, however, as women assert themselves as professionals equally capable with men to do business. Attitudes also change as economically disadvantaged cultures observe that wealthy trading cultures respect women.

OTHER CONTRASTS

Awareness of potential differences in cultural interpretations can prevent misunderstandings and embarrassment.

There are many other areas where perceptions differ from one culture to another. An American man who brings his Berlin dinner hostess red roses (signifying romantic love) would probably arouse the hostility of his host. And white flowers (signifying mourning) might bring displeasure to a friend in Belgium.

Different cultures view odors differently. In the United States, people spend millions of dollars annually on deodorants and mouthwashes designed to eliminate body odors. In contrast, Arabs may breathe in each other's faces while speaking. Not to do so is to "deny one's breath" and is considered a grave insult.[7]

Eskimo, Maori, Samoans, and Philippine Islanders may rub noses or inhale as they place their noses against the cheeks of another.

Scents or odors are often associated with cultures, and these frequently come from diets. The scents are neither good nor bad, merely different. The U.S. manager traveling abroad must recognize that accepting or rejecting an individual because of an odor is unwise.

Paralanguage is behavior that interrupts, accompanies, or takes the place of speech. It may be a gesture, a movement of a hand, eyebrow, or face, or posture. Or it may be sound such as a grunt, whistle, or sigh. Paralanguage can even be a short or extended silence. The physician's "ummm" while staring intently at the lab report and the inward rush of breath as someone reads the bad or good news in a letter are examples of paralanguage that communicates a message. But we must be careful not to misinterpret. The long silence on the part of Japanese sellers is not a sign of rudeness or a ploy; they are attempting to examine the offer carefully from all points of view. The frequent nod of their heads as you speak to them probably means they understand you, but it may not mean they *agree* with you. Paralanguage varies from culture to culture.

COMMUNICATION IN DIFFERENT CULTURES

People take for granted that verbal language differs from culture to culture. When different cultures share the same language, certain words have quite different meanings. Many people are surprised to find that nonverbal language also varies across cultures. This section introduces some of these interesting differences.

NONVERBAL COMMUNICATION

Differences in nonverbal cues across cultures can create barriers to communication.

A great deal of communication in all cultures occurs nonverbally. Nonverbal cues can range from touching and smelling to gestures and body movement. The attitude in the United States toward the nonverbal area of touching is vastly different from that of many other cultures in the world. It is not unusual in Europe or the Middle East to see two men walking together with hands clasped or even encircling a shoulder. Such a sight would be as unusual here as seeing two men greet each other with a light kiss on each cheek—a relatively common sight in many nations.

Discussion between a manager and a subordinate in the United States may occur with each in a very relaxed posture in the former's office. They might be drinking coffee. If the manager is a man, he may have a foot hooked over an empty chair or planted on a nearby table top. Not so in the Middle East where crossed legs or facing the soles of your shoes toward another individual is a sign of rudeness. In so many nations, and certainly in much of Europe, the subordinate is almost "at attention" when briefly addressing a superior. And keeping your hands in your pockets as you speak to your German or Austrian boss is just not done.

In the United States we are sometimes concerned when the other person does not look us in the eye or seems visually evasive. Is there a lack of honesty or integrity here? In Japan, a businessman may interpret a lack of respect if another individual *does* look directly at him. We also have no hesitancy, when asked, to list our accomplishments. In Japan such a presentation would seem out of place and in bad taste. And it would not be wise for an American man-

CULTURAL DIVERSITY IN COMMUNICATION

Must We Be Experts in Every Culture?

Carol Shuherk
University of Southern California

Joking among strangers or new acquaintances makes Germans ill at ease. At meetings or in presentations, while an American or Briton might feel obliged to crack a joke or two, or an Italian or French person indulges in witticism, a German will remain consistently serious, neither using humor nor responding to it.

The most marked difference between business communication in Korea and the United States is the difference between American objectivity and Korean subjectivity. For businesspeople in the United States, relationships and personal feelings (both positive and negative) are to be set aside in favor of impartial and dispassionate logic. For Koreans, sincerity and commitment to individuals are the basis for business dealings. Business is transacted by two people, not the firms they represent.

Business meetings in Italy are usually unstructured and informal. They do not follow agendas, and participants may come and go as the meeting progresses. Anyone may speak at any time and eloquence, not status, is the key to earning an audience. Decisions implemented

THE ORGANIZATION DIMENSION

ORGANIC		SYSTEMATIC
Plans are based on hunches, intuition, and experience and are expressed in words.	Forecasting	Plans are based on analysis and expressed in numbers
Decisions evolve and are based on judgment.	Decision Making	Decisions are made and are based on fact.
Authority is based on trust; who you know matters most; accountability is vague.	Supervision	Authority is based on competence; accountability is clear.
Errors are blamed on people and lead to recrimination; criticism is personal.	Control	Errors are blamed on the system and lead to improvement; criticism is objective.
Communication is informal and people read between the lines (what does it mean?).	Communication	Communication goes through official channels and people read what is printed (what does it say?).
The right connections earn promotion; success depends on luck, and educational qualifications indicate breeding.	Reward	Competence earns promotion; success depends on skill; and educational qualifications indicate professionalism.
People strive for esteem, take pride in their status, and compete by outmaneuvering.	Motivation	People strive for achievement, take pride in professionalism, and compete by outperforming.
Rules are to be circumvented; informal associations and alliances are the real basis of the organization.	Style	Rules are to be obeyed; the organization chart shows reality.

later are likely to have no relationship to those made in the meeting.

In Vietnam, the boss is the boss—anytime, anywhere. In the United States, an executive away from the office can relax and pursue leisure however he or she chooses, but in Vietnam leisure must be pursued according to station in life. Executives would never eat in simple, little restaurants because the food is good; they must go only to first-rate, elegant restaurants.

Latin Americans tend to view all of life wholistically, and this perspective applies to business communication as well. Whereas a good conversation between U.S. businesspeople is one that is focused, task oriented, and concise, one between Latin Americans is more likely to touch on various topics, to consider each subject from all possible dimensions, and to move only indirectly toward a conclusion.

As these illustrations demonstrate, beliefs, value systems, and communication norms for business practice vary widely around the world. So how are people working in the global marketplace

THE LEADERSHIP DIMENSION

GROUP		INDIVIDUALISTIC
Planning is done by those responsible; everyone should know what the strategy is.	Forecasting	Planning is done by top management; only a few need to know the strategy.
Groups make decisions; consensus is paramount; everybody's opinion accounts for something.	Decision Making	Individuals make decisions; decisiveness is paramount; a superior's view always outweighs a subordinate's.
Authority must be constantly earned; leaders stay close to their followers and embody the will of the group.	Supervision	Authority must be demonstrated; leaders keep their distance and impose their will on the group.
Quality is a mutual concern and groups are accountable.	Control	Quality has to be enforced and individuals are accountable.
Communication moves in all directions; meetings are for information sharing and people should be good listeners.	Communication	Communication is downward; meetings are for briefing and people should be good communicators.
Teams strive for goals and are rewarded.	Reward	Individuals strive for achievement and are rewarded.
People work for the team, are self-motivated, and want harmony to predominate.	Motivation	People work for themselves, have to be directed, and thrive on competition.
Hierarchy, status, and subtitles are a convenience and modesty is prized.	Style	Hierarchy is essential and people should be assertive and confident.

to communicate effectively wherever they go? How does one know, from Tokyo to Rome, what is appropriate or not, what behavior will be understood as intended and what could cause a cross-cultural relationship to collapse? Is it necessary to become intimate with every culture in which a firm seeks to do business?

John Mole, an English author and consultant, writes in his book, *When in Rome . . . A Business Guide to Cultures and Customs in Europe,* that although the more you know about each country the better, you can use a simple system to make general assumptions about the differences in doing business in different nations. His work around the world for Mellon Bank—in the United States, Africa, the Middle East, and Europe—convinced him that there are two major factors in determining how people interact and in what ways interactions differ from company to company and culture to culture. The first is a set of beliefs about *organization* and the place of people within it. The ways work is organized, forecasting and planning processes, the techniques of gathering and disseminating information, and the measurement of results contribute to organization. The second is a set of beliefs about *leadership;* these beliefs involve the bases of authority, the ownership of power, the process of decision making, and so forth.

The organization dimension takes shape in a firm based on the extent to which the firm believed that a rational system should be imposed on human endeavor. Depending on how much systems are valued, the organization may range in type from loose and informal to highly structured and bureaucratic. Mole uses the terms *organic/systematic* to denote this range. The leadership dimension takes shape based on the extent to which a firm thinks that power is best used through groups or individuals. The forms of leadership may cover the spectrum from centralized and authoritarian to team based and egalitarian. Mole uses the terms *group/individualistic* to denote this range.

Both leadership and organization can be examined through eight factors: forecasting, decision-making, supervision, control, communication, reward, motivation, and style. A partial listing offers clues about how things are done. Within these two broad dimensions, Mole then plots the business cultures of various nations. The accompanying "Mole Map" shows nine countries. Mole is careful to note that these are generalizations about business organizations and leadership methods and that within national cultures and across industries similar differences can also be plotted.

The placement of the United States in the upper-right quadrant—high on

ager to praise one Japanese worker for an outstanding performance in the presence of his or her coworkers. It would be embarrassing because the Japanese want to be simply one of the group. "The nail that protrudes must be knocked down" say the Japanese.

LANGUAGE COMMUNICATION

"International English" is not "American English."

Fortunately for the United States, communities of the world are moving toward making English an international language. But "American English" is often not the same as "British English." And what happens to American English when it is translated into other languages can be disastrous.

Do you know that in England "bonnet" and "boot" are not items of clothes but refer to the hood and trunk, respectively, of an auto? "Dust bins" are refuse containers and a "scheme" may be a plan and not a conspiracy. "Satisfactory" to us is acceptable but to the British it may be interpreted from acceptable to

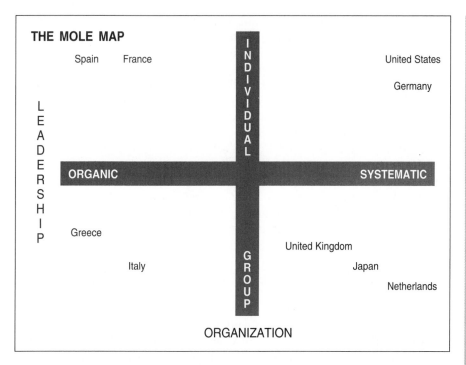

THE MOLE MAP

organizational structure and high on individualistic leadership compared with everybody else—runs counter to the way that we tend to view ourselves as compared with other nationalities individually. In fact, while informality and a casual approach are hallmarks of the U.S. communication style, when it comes to business organizations and the ways interaction flows within them, we more closely resemble the rigid hierarchy and authoritarianism of, say, the military than does any other nation. The following advice from this international business expert on conducting business abroad seems particularly important to U.S. businesspeople, who, it turns out, are more "different" from everyone else: (1) learn the language, verbal and nonverbal, and (2) do not jump to conclusions!

If the first impression we have of an international firm is that its organization is chaos and its leadership capricious, consider that to them, we may appear impenetrably bureaucratic and rigidly controlled.

excellent. An apartment is a "flat"; a Band-Aid is an "elastoplast"; a diaper is a "nappy"; a druggist a "chemist"; liquor is "spirits"; and what comes at the end of this sentence—what we call a period—is called a "full-stop."

Making an effort to learn the languages of other nations will help prevent miscommunication.

Phrases in U.S. reports and letters that are translated to other languages sometimes become incorrect and even humorous. The important point, however, is that delays, confusion, and misinterpretations often result. How can we solve such problems? Certainly, we must do a better job of learning the languages of the nations with which we do business. They certainly are learning more English. In many countries of Europe and Asia, several years of English are required in the educational programs of schoolchildren.

Nevertheless, the problems of semantics will continue to occur in English and in translations from English to another tongue. Some of the problems come from advertised products. A group of Hispanic ad agencies in Los Angeles have formed an organization called "Merito," subtitled "The Society for Excellence in Hispanic Advertising." The organization expects to become national to further its aim of eliminating "misunderstandings, bad translations, and bad advertising by non-Hispanics to the Hispanic market." One example cited by the group was the slogan of Braniff Airline: "travel on leather." The Spanish word for leather (*cuero*) also means naked. Thus, some Latin Americans interpreted the Braniff ad as "travel naked."[8] Other mistranslations (which often happen with colloquialisms) are "Come alive with Pepsi" which are turned into "Come out of the grave" in Germany and "Pepsi brings your ancestors back from the grave" in Asia, where "Body by Fisher" became "Corpse by Fisher." And the phrase "The spirit is willing but the flesh is weak" became in Russian "The ghost is ready but the meat is rotten."

Choose words carefully and ask for feedback to ensure that translations communicate correctly.

These are extreme examples. They illustrate, however, that U.S. managers must be especially careful of language. They should try to secure feedback or some type of response in an effort to monitor the accuracy of the translation.[9]

DO UNTO OTHERS AS THEY . . .

According to the Golden Rule, we should treat others as we would like to be treated. That assumes that we would all like to be treated similarly because we *are* similar. From a cultural point of view, we *are not* similar, and that often makes a profound difference in the verbal and nonverbal communication we send and receive in our interaction with individuals in other nations.

Let's look at the Golden Rule as it applies to just a few aspects of nonverbal communication. As stated earlier, men in some parts of Europe and the Middle East walk together with hands clasped and greet each other with a kiss on the cheek. Their wives follow several steps behind. These actions communicate a message. Would they communicate the same message if they occurred in the United States? You might argue that these are really just superficial factors in a culture, that "deep down" people are the same all over the world. But even at a less superficial level we find basic differences between cultures. We know, for instance, that different cultures have different ways of looking at the meaning of a contract, polygamy, or drinking alcohol.

Treat others as they would like to be treated in their cultures; as you would like to be treated in yours.

Of course, many cultures have customs that are decoded the same way by other cultures. But they also all have a multitude of differences, both superficial and at the core, that may be interpreted differently and that may create misunderstanding in attempts at cross-cultural communication. In other words, be wary of following the Golden Rule across cultures.

U.S. VALUES[10]

It is important for people in the United States to understand how their values contrast with those in other cultures. An appreciation of differences in values among cultures will permit us to better see how individuals from other cultures view us.

PERSONAL CONTROL OVER THE ENVIRONMENT

In the United States, people consider it normal and proper that human beings control nature. That may mean changing the size of a mountain, the type of weather, the direction in which a river flows, and perhaps even the genetic

Many cultures consider it wrong to change the environment. structure of living organisms. Most of the world's population think that such changes should not be made. They believe that fate controls certain decisions, which must be obeyed.

CHANGE

People in the United States usually feel change is good. Change is often associated with progress, development, growth, and advancement. Older cultures often consider change disruptive and destructive. Stability, tradition, and an ancient heritage are valued.

CONTROL OF TIME

As noted earlier in this chapter, time often controls people in the United States. Time is valuable and highly prized; not to observe time commitments is a sign of discourtesy. But people in many other cultures do not permit the clock to control their activities as we do.

EQUALITY

Still another U.S. value that differs significantly in many other cultures is the concept of equality. We say people have been created equal and we view equality as an important civic and social goal. But in most of the world, rank, status, and authority are viewed as part and parcel of everyday life. To many individuals in other cultures, knowing who they are and where they fit in the various strata of their society offers a sense of security.

INDIVIDUALISM AND PRIVACY

People in the United States feel strongly that they are individualists: "I'm a little special, a little different from others." Other cultures, where space is at a premium in homes, offices, and workplaces, and where large numbers of people are treated similarly, often do not appreciate our concept of individualism and need for privacy.

SELF-HELP

We take great pride in "making it" on our own. We accept inherited wealth, but give the individual little personal credit for wealth secured from a parent. The same view is not often the case in other cultures. The self-made man or woman is looked up to much more in the United States than he or she would be in many other nations.

COMPETITION AND FREE ENTERPRISE

We value competition and stress it as a desirable quality from the classroom to the sports field and the boardroom. But in societies that value cooperation, the intense competitiveness of the United States is not easy to comprehend. Almost every aspect of our culture fosters competitive values. Even our economic system is based on free enterprise. For millions of people in the world, however, competition is not easy to accept and may be viewed as a lack of cooperation.

FUTURE ORIENTATION

People in the United States constantly work, plan, and strive for a better future. We set long- and short-term goals; we devise strategies to improve the future whether it is economic, social, athletic, or medical. But much of the world may perceive an attempt to alter the future as futile and perhaps even sinful. "What will be, will be"—people must accept whatever happens.

ACTION AND WORK VALUES	We usually work hard—the day is planned and activities are scheduled weeks or even months in advance. We are often so involved in work that we become "workaholics." Many cultures don't share this constant attention to accomplishing productive labor; instead, spending a day strolling or meditating is considered important.
DIRECTNESS, OPENNESS, AND HONESTY	People from other countries often look upon us as being blunt, perhaps even unfeeling. But people in the United States often pride themselves on "telling it like it is." This direct approach is difficult to understand for an individual who comes from a society where saving face is important or one in which an indirect method is used for conveying bad news or an uncomplimentary evaluation. We seem to lose interest in people who hint at what they intend rather than stating the situation directly. Members of other cultures often lose trust in us *because* of our directness.[11]
THE VALUE OF PRACTICALITY AND EFFICIENCY	Most people in the United States look at situations and ask questions such as these: "Will it pay off?" "Can it be done in the time provided?" "Have we found the most efficient solution?" But in other cultures decisions are made in answer to such questions as "Is it aesthetically pleasing?" "Does it advance the arts?" "Will it increase knowledge?" "Will it prove enjoyable?"
MATERIALISM	Most people in other cultures perceive us as being more materialistic than we perceive ourselves. We usually feel that our appliances, cars, TVs, and computers are our just rewards for hard work. In contrast, many others see us as being obsessed with acquiring and maintaining "things."

INFORMALITY IN WRITING AND SPEAKING INTERNATIONALLY

Maintain formality when addressing unfamiliar international businesspeople.

Most cultures are more formal than the United States in both writing and speaking. U.S. businesspeople should be careful to use titles when addressing those in Europe and Asia, as well as those in most of the nations of the world. Unless you have a longstanding relationship with someone abroad and have already used his or her first name in casual conversation, always use a surname and/or title. (A German professional may even be addressed as "Herr Dr. Professor"—three titles!)

Use icebreakers in international correspondence.

Opening paragraphs of a letter in international correspondence are usually formal or introductory. Brief comments on the weather, a previous trip or association, or a noncontroversial international event or incident are quite appropriate as icebreakers. This is especially true in one-on-one relationships where a social event (dinner, visit to a museum, concert or play) precedes a discussion of business.[12]

Discussing problems directly may be considered insensitive and tactless.

Sensitive factors such as payments (or nonpayments), behavior of representatives, and errors or delays in shipping should be handled with sensitivity and tact. Certainly, those same topics might well be discussed (or written about) more directly between two U.S. businesspeople.

Cultural Values	In the United States	In some other cultures
	Personal control over the environment	Fate
	Change	Tradition
	Time and its control	Human interactions
	Equality	Hierarchy, rank, status
	Individualism and privacy	Welfare of the group
	Self-help	Birthright inheritance
	Competition	Cooperation
	Future orientation	Past orientation (tradition)
	Action and work orientation	"Being" orientation
	Directness, openness, honesty	Indirectness, ritual, "face"
	Practicality and efficiency	Idealism
	Materialism	Detachment

Remain polite.

In addressing audiences abroad, people from the United States should be careful to avoid terms that reflect superiority, power, or lack of concern. Off-color references or profanity and pejorative comments about competitors, nations, peoples, and customs are inappropriate anywhere.

It is true, however, that many international businesspeople are beginning to emulate the U.S. direct approach. Nevertheless, use this approach with caution, so as not to be labeled as discourteous or as an "Ugly American."

Take care with written format. White space is usually not as generous on letters and reports received from international contacts. Our signatures are usually quite legible; European and Japanese signatures frequently are not. We sometimes will designate a date as 5/9/93 or 5-9-93. Our international business counterpart would note the same date as 9/5/93. The solution: always write out the date (May 9, 1993) to avoid errors in interpretation or legal problems on either side.

Consider your international audience's cultural perceptions and expectations before communicating. Don't turn into the "Ugly American."

Although common sense should dictate what and how you write and speak to other nationals, still be careful. What is common sense to that person may not be to you. Always prepare carefully and check before speaking or writing.

CULTURES IN PERSPECTIVE

The term *foreign trade* may be a relic. There is international trade, but it is difficult to even determine what is foreign. Autos with Japanese-made bodies, German-made motors, and components from a dozen other countries as well as our own are assembled in the United States. Shall we call this a "foreign car"?

What are foreign products? When components are manufactured abroad on a U.S. license and then returned to this country to be integrated or assembled into an "American-made" product, how should it be designated—American-made or foreign-made? When we send components of a doll, toy, or electronic item to another nation for assembly and the finished goods return here for final packaging, how shall these products be designated?

These are problems better left to the U.S. Department of Commerce. What is important for U.S. managers to keep in mind when dealing with other cultures—either in this country or abroad—is that people from other cultures may perceive verbal and nonverbal factors in the environment differently than we do. While we can't expect them to always see our perceptions, we *must* always see theirs. Toward that end, more and more U.S. companies are carefully training employees in the ways of other cultures before sending them abroad.

We have become more aware of how other cultures view the United States. And, most important, we are now more sensitive to the needs and perceptions of individuals whose cultural background differs from ours, whether we travel abroad or interact with them in our daily activities in the United States. Education, international affairs, the print and electronic media, trade and other factors have contributed to making the world smaller.

WRITING AND SPEAKING EXERCISES

1. Present a written or oral report on the changes that have occurred in the social and economic cultures of the Russian republics. Compare conditions in the 1980s with what exists today.
2. Do you see common changes in nations such as Japan, Korea, and Taiwan (or Estonia, Latvia, and Lithuania) which seem to occur after industrialization and economic growth? Write a short report on these changes.
3. Interview three recent immigrants, each with a different national background, and determine which three U.S. cultural habits they find most irritating and which three most pleasing. Then ask the same questions of three second- or third-generation descendants from the same national groups. Did you find any agreement about which traits are pleasing and which are irritating? Write a short report, explaining your findings.
4. What specific cultural traits has the U.S. assimilated from other cultures? Why do you think the traits you have listed have been accepted? Develop your thoughts into a short report or oral presentation to the class.
5. Write a position paper arguing for or against the tendency of many ethnic groups to try to preserve their native culture, values, and language after immigrating to the United States.
6. Should employees in U.S. corporations located in major urban centers receive some training in cross-cultural habits and values? Write a short paper to recommend or not recommend such training.
7. Have the current opportunities for instantaneous communication among various cultures worldwide improved or worsened the effectiveness of international communication. Write a summary of your thoughts.
8. Research the subject of the changing perceptions and role of the Japanese wife in the 1990s. Make a presentation to your class (together with documentation) of your findings.
9. Explain in writing how time and space communicate differently in the U.S. culture under different circumstances. Give examples.

CASES

Complete the following assignment from the Cases for Discussion section at the back of this book:

1. When East Doesn't Meet West Case—Assignments 1 and 2
2. But Talking Isn't Working Case—Assignments 1 and 2

READINGS   See "Learning from Japan" in the Readings section at the back of this book.

SUGGESTED   Budd, John F., Jr. "Public Relations Faces Its Moment of Truth." *Public Rela-*
RESOURCES   *tions Review* 16 (Winter 1990).
                          Fine, Marlene. "New Voices in the Workplace: Research Directions in Multi-
                              cultural Communications." *The Journal of Business Communications* 28
                              (Summer 1991).
                          Knotts, Rose, and Hartman, Sandra. "Communication Skills in Cross-Cultural
                              Situations." *Supervisory Management* 36 (March 1991).
                          Limaye, M., and Victor, D. "Cross-cultural Business Communication
                              Research: State of the Art and Hypotheses for the 1990s." *The Journal of
                              Business Communication* 28 (Summer 1991).
                          Liss, Richard. "How Do You Develop Pan-European Communication? . . .
                              Very Carefully!" *Communication World* 7 (August 1990).
                          McIntyre, David. "When Your National language is Just Another Language."
                              Communication World 8 (May 1991).
                          Moran, Robert. "A Formula for Success in Multicultural Organizations."
                              International Management 43 (December 1988).
                          Palmer, George. "Transferred to Tokyo—A Guide to Etiquette in the Land of
                              the Rising Sun." *Multinational Business* (Winter 1990).
                          Pintak, Larry. "Shouts Heard Around the World: Communicating in the
                              Global Village." *Communication World* 8 (June-July 1991).

ENDNOTES   1. Peter Drucker, "The Transnational Economy," *The Wall Street Journal,* August
                              25, 1987.
                          2. Larry Pintak, "Shouts Heard Around the World: Communicating in the Global
                              Village," *Communication World* 8 (June-July 1991): 30-32.
                          3. Peter Drucker, "The Transnational Economy."
                          4. Bureau of the Census, *1990 Census Profile: Race and Hispanic Origin* (Washing-
                              ton, D.C.: U.S. Dept. of Commerce, Economics and Statistics Administration,
                              1991): no. 2:3–7.
                          5. *The Journal of Business Communication* 29 (Summer 1992). The entire issue is
                              devoted to intercultural communication.
                          6. L. A. Malandro and L. Barker, *Nonverbal Communication,* 2nd ed. Addison-
                              Wesley, 1988. This paperback is an outstanding source for a thorough discussion
                              of the differences in nonverbal communication among different cultures.
                          7. Malandro and Barker, *Nonverbal Communication.*
                          8. *The Los Angeles Business Journal,* September 7, 1987: 7.
                          9. George Palmer, "Transferred to Tokyo—A Guide to Etiquette in the Land of the
                              Rising Sun," *Multinational Business* (Winter 1990): 36–38.
                         10. This discussion is based on an intriguing and important paper titled "The Values
                              Americans Live By," by L. Robert Kohls, executive director, the Washington
                              International Center, Washington, D.C., 1984.
                         11. Rose Knotts and Sandra Hartman, "Communication Skills in Cross-Cultural Situ-
                              ations," *Supervisory Management* 36 (March 1981): 12.

12. The David M. Kennedy Center for International Studies at Brigham Young University publishes *Culturegrams* on 102 countries. These are revised annually and offer valuable insights into the habits, institutions, and cultures of the nations reviewed. The *Culturegrams* may be obtained by writing to Publication Services, 280 HRCB at Brigham Young University, Provo, Utah 84602.

5

ETHICAL ISSUES IN MANAGEMENT COMMUNICATION

I would rather be the man who bought the Brooklyn Bridge than the man who sold it.

—Will Rogers

Not a day goes by without the media reporting on some ethical issue. Newspapers, TV, and radio carry accounts of infractions of moral values or ethics. Respected (or formerly respected) individuals in industry, government, religion, education, and finance are involved in bribery, payoffs, immoral liaisons, economic high jinks, insider trading, industry-government collusion, and pure and simple fraud. Politicians have been turned out of office, high-ranking church officials imprisoned, CEOs indicted, financial giants jailed, government bureaucrats dismissed, and business managers disgraced— all for taking actions that were labeled "unethical."

But what is ethics or ethical behavior? Surely, it means doing the right thing, being honest and acting honestly, maintaining high moral standards, observing society's rules, working in the best interests of others, and dealing with associates justly and fairly.

In our society we would probably agree with all of these provisos. But let's stop, step back a bit, and think about the above definition. Ethical standards change over time: What is ethical in one generation may be unethical in another. What is legal in this century may be illegal in the next. Standards also change from one culture to another. What is ethical in a Western nation may well be unethical in a country in the Middle East. Standards for life support, fetal tissue use, marital relations, male-female relationships, levels of punishment, treatment of enemies and prisoners, terrorism, abortion, organ transplant, assisted suicide, and many other situations vary based on time, nations, moral values, perceptions, and cultures.

Because of these differences, the best we can do is to agree to restrict our discussion of ethics in management communication to Western culture and the

Ethics means doing the right thing, but what we consider "right" behavior in the United States today might be regarded as unethical in another time or place.

current time. And even with these restrictions, there may well be differences in interpretation.[1]

Let's look at an example of a difficult ethics issue. The Franklin Corporation's manufactured product is no longer selling. Although the company has tried many remedies, sales have dropped dramatically. The only answer, in fairness to the company and its thousands of stockholders, is to shut down most of the production lines. Therefore, the CEO has decided 2,000 of the 2,500 employees of Franklin will be terminated. Of course, this decision seems unfair to those 2,000 employees. The 500 other employees who will remain to produce the manufactured item for which there are still orders consider the decision fair, as do the firm's stockholders. However, the CEO has also decided to halt all production in 90 days and terminate the remaining 500 employees. Management does not want to tell the employees at this time, fearing that quality will go down and that the most competent of the 500 employees will leave immediately for other jobs.

Because the dynamics of most situations are complex, determining the ethical course of action can be difficult.

Not announcing the future termination to the 500 employees is fair to Franklin's stockholders but unfair to the employees. So what is the ethical CEO to do? And where do his or her loyalties lie? The stockholders have rights, as do the employees. How does the CEO solve the dilemma and still take ethical action?

In most cases, no single or obvious answers lead to the right or ethical course of action.

CORE VALUES IN MAKING ETHICAL DECISIONS

The communicator's motive determines whether the communication is unethical.

Although a decision may be viewed as ethical by one person and not by another, one principle probably does not vary: What is the communicator's (writer's or speaker's) motive or intent? If the communication is designed to deceive, it is dishonest and unethical. If the statement is accurate but somewhat circuitous in an effort to soften the blow of a rejection or refusal, it is not unethical. If the statement is incorrect because of an error or lack of knowledge, it is not unethical. The basic question of motive or intent governs the communication. A communication in itself is neither ethical nor unethical. The intent and motive of the communicator make the communication honest (ethical/moral) or dishonest (unethical/immoral).

Communicators who intentionally deceive their audiences behave unethically.

Here is an example. The Wagner Pharmaceutical Distribution Corporation sent each of its 780 retailers in the Eastern Division a letter indicating that the company will supply, free of charge, a neon sign valued at $400 stating "Prescription Department." This sign will be available to those retailers whose gross sales equal or exceed $75,000 in the quarter January 1 to March 31.

By March 25, all 150 signs have been designated for retailers who have met the requirements. Division Manager Williams has shipped those out with a personally signed letter of congratulations. However, the afternoon mail on March 31 brings orders from two additional retailers who now meet the requirements. If Williams orders two additional signs (instead of just the previous 150), the cost of each sign will increase from $400 to $675.

Williams decides to deceive. He writes the two retailers that their orders were not received until April 2 and "it would not be fair to our other customers to make an exception in your case." This message is clearly unethical.

If individuals and organizations establish a code of ethics or practice a series of core values, making ethical decisions becomes easier. In some cases, however, it is still difficult to decide where to assign loyalties. Consider the statements made to the employees of the Franklin Corporation. Should the CEO be loyal to the employees or to the stockholders? Where the CEO decides to place loyalty establishes the ethical course of action in this situation.

Nevertheless, observing a set of core values, such as the following ten,[2] makes it easier to make ethical choices.

1. *Caring:* Treat people compassionately. Do not use them just to attain, for example, your organization's goals. Base decisions on other people's goals as well as your organization's or your own.

2. *Honesty:* Be truthful; do not deceive or distort. "White lies" and withholding information, even when that information is not requested, are still a form of deception.

3. *Accountability:* Accept responsibility for and the consequences of your actions.

4. *Promise keeping:* Hold to your commitments even when they may later prove undesirable. Promises to stockholders in a corporate setting or to individuals in a social setting must be kept.

5. *Pursuit of excellence:* Strive to achieve at the highest level using all accepted avenues. Remember, however, that illegal means are not justified to attain goals. Many organizations stress the achievement of objectives but also emphasize that they should be attained only through accepted methods.

6. *Loyalty:* Be loyal — but to whom? This core value is difficult to apply. Loyalty to my aerospace company's management or to the U.S. taxpayer? Loyalty does not mean blind obedience. Loyalty to a supervisor, manager, or company is understandable, but not when that loyalty means following an immoral or illegal path.

7. *Fairness:* Treat people equitably. Do not take advantage of another's adversity or weakened position.

8. *Integrity:* Avoid conflict of interest situations and avoid taking a position in which you would benefit at the expense of someone else.

9. *Respect for others:* Respect the rights of others to privacy and self-determination. Be courteous, prompt, and open.

10. *Responsible citizenship:* Act in conformity with society's values and standards.

If a decision is to be interpreted as ethical, it must produce, in the long run, maximum good to all those involved and contribute to the general welfare.[3]

Unfortunately, it is possible to follow a code of values and still cause ill will and hostility because of the words chosen to convey the message. Here is an example. The New England Furniture Company has a specific policy printed on all its sales and billing materials that "returned merchandise must arrive within ten days of customer receipt." This policy is the same one established by the East Coast Furniture Association, of which the New England Furniture Company is a member. Waters Furniture Outlet returns $2,400 worth of dining room furniture 38 days after it received the original order. A tactless communication could say:

**CULTURAL
DIVERSITY IN
COMMUNICATION**

**Sexual Harassment:
Intent or Impact?**

Carol Shuherk
*University of
Southern California*

A nominee to the U.S. Supreme Court endures days of televised confirmation hearings before a Senate subcommittee after a former employee, now a law school professor, charges that she endured repeated sexual harassment while working for him at the Equal Employment Opportunity Commission. The Secretary of the U.S. Navy and three top admirals either resign or are relieved of their commands after an investigation reveals that sexual assaults on women aviators occurred at an annual convention of the Navy's "top guns" and that the official investigation was deliberately stymied by those assigned to conduct it.

These sensational cases in the early 1990s brought the touchy issue of sexual harassment to the center of the national stage. But they don't offer much assistance for practicing managers who need to be able to recognize and deal with sexual harassment at work. A close look at the issue reveals three important facts:

1. The problem is pervasive: 42 percent of all women surveyed by the U.S. Merit Systems Protection Board in 1988 reported that they had experienced some form of unwanted and uninvited sexual attention.
2. The 1972 amendment to the Civil Rights Act of 1964, which makes sexual harassment a violation of federal law, can be applied to protect men as well as women: in a 1989 California case (*Nelson* v. *Reisher*) a male social worker was awarded $1,500 by a district court because his female boss constantly criticized his work and sought to reprimand and harass him because she did not like working with a man.
3. The criteria for defining what constitutes sexual harassment places communication, between bosses and subordinates or between

coworkers, at the center of sexual harassment claims.

Federal law defines sexual harassment as "unwelcome sexual advances, requests for sexual favors, and other verbal or physical conduct of a sexual nature." Any one of these behaviors constitutes sexual harassment if one or more of the following criteria is met:

1. Submission to such conduct is made either implicitly or explicitly a term or condition of employment.
2. Submission to or rejection of such conduct by an individual is used as the basis for employment decisions affecting such individual.
3. Such conduct has the purpose or effect of unreasonably interfering with the individual's work performance or creating an intimidating, hostile, or offensive working environment.

The first two criteria are quite straightforward, in both the act and the enforcement. They involve people in positions of unequal status; one person has some control over another person's employment, and bribes, threats, or punishments are used by the harasser to try to gain sexual favors. Incidents of this type need only happen once to fall under the definition of sexual harassment. It is into the third category, however, that most (and the most difficulty to address) cases of sexual harassment fall. The third criterion requires that a repeated and pervasive pattern of offensive behavior — both verbal and nonverbal communication — be experienced by the receiver to establish "an intimidating, hostile, or offensive working environment." Examples of communication behavior found in court cases to constitute sexual harassment include the following:

VERBAL

Referring to an adult as a girl, hunk, doll, babe, or honey

Whistling at someone or making catcalls

Making sexual comments about a person's body

Turning work discussions to sexual topics

Telling sexual jokes or stories

Asking personal questions about social or sexual life

Making sexual comments about a person's clothing, anatomy or looks

Repeatedly asking out a person who is not interested

Making kissing sounds, howling, and smacking lips

Telling lies or spreading rumors about a person's sex life.

NONVERBAL

Looking a person up and down (elevator eyes)

Staring at someone

Blocking a person's path

Following a person

Giving personal gifts

Displaying sexually suggestive visuals

Making facial expressions such as winking, throwing kisses, or licking lips

Making sexual gestures with hands or through body movements

A central problem in managing sexual harassment cases stems from the wide variety of interpretations that any one of these behaviors might have, depending on the gender and the personalities of the people involved. Studies on the differences in perceptions of sexual harassment between men and women indicate five tendencies

1. Men tend to find sexual overtures from women at work to be flattering, whereas women find similar approaches from men to be insulting.
2. Men and women agree that certain blatant behavior such as assault or threat of termination constitute harassment, but women are more likely than men to consider more subtle behaviors such as provocative gestures and sexual teasing as harassment.
3. Men are more likely than women to blame women for being sexually harassed.
4. Men tend to think that behavior they describe themselves as sexual harassment will nonetheless be flattering to women.
5. Men tend to misinterpret women's friendliness as a sexual advance.

An additional complication is that what feels to one person like sexual harassment may truly feel harmless to another.

One way to confront the issue of whether your behavior is crossing the line from friendliness to sexual harassment is to ask yourself the following questions: Might the person I am dealing with perceive a difference in power between us? Is there equal participation between the person and me in personal areas of communication? Would I want a story about my behavior toward this person to appear on the evening news? Would I behave in the same way toward this person if my spouse or sweetheart were present? Would I feel comfortable if someone else were acting this way toward my spouse or sweetheart? If you answer any of these negatively, then the impact of your behavior may be other than you intend.

Dear Mr. Waters:

> *The items you returned on May 5, 199__ have been in your possession 38 days. Because this does not comply with our policy, your request for a $2,400 credit is hereby refused. The merchandise is being shipped to you today "freight collect."*

The writer's intent is not to deceive, but merely to explain. The explanation *is* true and the communication is ethical. However, its bluntness may well cause Mr. Waters to seek another source for furniture purchases.

Can the communication convey the same thought in a tactful manner and still be ethical? The answer is "most certainly."

Dear Mr. Waters:

> *As you know from your past relationship with us, we are always happy to cooperate with you and our other customers on returned merchandise.*

> *The items you returned on May 5 were logged in at your receiving dock on March 28. As you can see, the time period between receipt and return exceeds the ten-day return privilege established by the East Coast Furniture Association. Because we are members of that Association, we follow the ten-day policy.*

> *In fairness to our other customers and to the standards of the Association, we are sure you can appreciate our position in not complying with your request. We are returning the merchandise to you today with all freight charges prepaid by our company.*

> *Don't overlook, Mr. Waters, our summer sale for preferred customers beginning . . .*

This communication is also ethical. The decision is the same, but the more tactful tone may retain rather than lose a customer. The unethical action would be accepting the returned merchandise for credit in violation of a stated policy previously communicated to all customers.

ETHICS AND COMMUNICATION

Unethical words usually precede unethical deeds.

Unethical deeds such as embezzling, changing ledger accounts, or using an inferior component in a product are almost invariably preceded by words. Words set the stage that make the action possible. Let's look at ethical and unethical communications, both verbal and nonverbal, from the points of view of writing, speaking, visual aids, and computers.

ETHICS AND THE WRITTEN WORD

Writers intent on deception can manipulate the written word to mislead readers. By omitting or minimizing relevant information, writers can lead readers into erroneous conclusions, even when the information is essentially truthful. If the writers intend to mislead, then the message is unethical. For example, the Turner Company has manufactured an outstanding component part for years. Customers pick up the part and integrate it themselves into larger electronic units. As a result, Turner has never had the need for, nor has it developed, a complete shipping and delivery department.

Now, however, the Turner Company has a request for information about its component which may result in an extremely large and profitable order. The problem, however, is that the customer wants Turner to package and ship the components to its warehouse 2,500 miles away by specified deadlines. Mr. Turner spends some time in his response describing the component's reliability, manufacturing process, cost breakdown, product utilization, descriptions and quotations from satisfied customers, company and personnel history for the past 20 years, independent test results from evaluation agencies, and other details. The writing is persuasive, the charts and graphs impressive, and the price listings attractive. So far so good, but what about details on handling and delivery? Is it ethical for Mr. Turner to handle that issue in a short last paragraph that simply states, "Proper on-time delivery will be arranged." Mr. Turner believes he can make such arrangements, but he has not investigated, verified, or tested his belief. The answer is very probably that Turner is not acting ethically because his intent is to mislead.

Presenting relevant but unfavorable information about your company in such a way that readers will not notice it might be unethical.

As another example, a company prints an elaborate annual report that contains beautiful photos and impressive charts and sings the praises of all departments. Yet, a careful examination of the several pages of financial data in this 60-page report reveals that net earnings dropped $52 million from the previous year, which was reflected in a $1.17 return per common share as compared to $2.80 last year. Such a report practices deceptive if not unethical communication to shareholders. On the other hand, the report writer may say, "The information is there. Is it my fault if the reader didn't find it, or understand it, or ask for it?" Is the report writer's written communication ethical, unethical, or deceptive?

Business letters, advertisements, brochures, booklets, and reports can contain deceptive communication as well. We have all seen ads picturing a product and a beautiful woman, a happy child, an immaculate and attractive kitchen, and a handsome man. The ads don't say so, but they imply that you need only buy the product described and you will be as beautiful as the woman or as handsome as the man, and your child will be as healthy and happy as the one pictured and your kitchen will be immediately transformed into a model of beauty. Ethical communication? You decide.

What judgment would you make about the following common expression in letters and advertisements: "outstanding," "limited-time offer," "once-in-a-lifetime opportunity," "unusual value," "below manufacturer's price," "special purchase"? Of course, these words may be accurate. But if the limited time offer is for the first 5 days in the month and the ad appears every other month for a year, is the message ethical?

Statements such as "giant 25-inch screen" or a "huge 32-ounce box of cereal" can be misleading as well. Aren't 25 inches exactly 25 inches and 32 ounces simply 32 ounces? What does giant or huge mean, or are these words meant to misrepresent? Still another ploy sometimes used intentionally and unethically is the phrase "on the average." The differences among mean, median, and modal averages can be enormous. The following array lists seven salaries selected from among the 312 employees of the Kape Corp.:

EMPLOYEE NO.	SALARY
1	$295,000
3	212,000
48	35,000
101	34,000
162	33,000
275	29,000
301	29,000

Using words to misrepresent facts or mislead the reader's expectations is unethical.

If the intent is to deceive, the communicator will not cite the salary figures but simply say, "The average salary of a sample of salaries at the Kape Corp. is $95,285." The statement *is* true; the deception lies in the fact that the CEO's and president's salaries were included without stating that fact and that the *mean* average was selected. Had the statement reported the "modal average" (the figure occurring most frequently in the array), the sum would be $29,000; the median (the salary in the middle) would be $34,000. To simply say "on the average" may be correct but unethical if the intent is to deceive.

Words and pictures can change perception from negative to positive, from persuasive to neutral, from compliant to noncompliant. Where does persuasion end and manipulation begin? And how is the reader who accepts most messages without critical analysis protected? Is it ethical for the communicator to simply say *caveat emptor,* that is, let the buyer (the receiver of the communication) beware?

ETHICS AND THE SPOKEN WORD

When we read materials, we have the opportunity to analyze, weigh, evaluate, and even go back and review for accuracy. When we listen to others speak, however, most of us do not have the ability (nor the time) to retain and analyze everything that we hear. Ideas move rapidly in oral communication, and we frequently accept as true what is said and hurry on to the next statement the speaker makes. Thus, it may be easier to deceive through the spoken than the written word.

If we are to be ethical in our oral communication, we must make statements that can be scrutinized with the same care and depth as anything we write. The high pressure presentation made to those easily impressed is unethical. The "razzle-dazzle" team presentation designed to take attention away from critical, negative, or complex situations is also unethical.

Sometimes the communicator misleads by imparting information selectively to benefit the communicator but deceive the listener. Such communication can occur in both written and oral situations. For example, the speaker, Monica Miller, states that her firm, Miller and Associates is much more successful than two competitors, the Jason Company and the Jackson Corporation. Miller points out that her firm has more than 1,500 accounts, while Jason and Jackson only have 450 and 850, respectively. Furthermore, Miller sold 58,000 units in the previous year, while Jason sold 53,000 and Jackson sold 56,000.

Presenting information selectively may distort the facts.

What Miller did not say was that (1) her customers consistently buy in smaller quantities than do the customers of Jason and Jackson, and (2) she (Miller) has a return rate of close to 10 percent because of poor quality. Jason and Jackson rarely receive returns because of poor quality. Miller selected positive information to communicate about her firm and neglected the negative aspects (or complete information) concerning competitors.

An interview with a prospective employee can also present ethical issues. The applicant has submitted a resume that contains many writing errors. Yet, he is qualified technically, so you schedule an interview. His written test, taken just before the interview, illustrates his complete carelessness in spelling, punctuation, and sentence structure. If he were to send letters to your customers, they might associate his errors with the quality of your products.

What do you do in the interview? Should you tell him that you will file his application and if an opening occurs, you will call him? Should you indicate that if the candidate just selected doesn't work out, you will get in touch with him? Or should you tell him that his communication skills are unacceptable and for that reason you cannot possibly hire him? To make an ethical statement that is negative is never easy. Ethical decisions often require courage and are frequently difficult to communicate.

ETHICS AND NONVERBAL COMMUNICATION

Nonverbal signals can be manipulated unethically.

We do not usually assign the word *unethical* to nonverbal communication that we recognize as being inaccurate because frequently we want to be kind. "He just wanted to impress us . . ." "I think she wanted us to believe that expensive car was hers; actually it was rented, but what's the harm?" Nevertheless, nonverbal displays that attempt to convey a situation that does not really exist are unethical. When the intent of the communicator is to deceive, the action, even though harmless, is just as unethical as the action that deceives to benefit the communicator financially or to cause hardship to others.

As communicators in business, we must be careful not to practice unethical nonverbal communications ourselves and to alert others when we become aware of fraudulent situations around us. An example is the appliance on display that works perfectly for prospective customers hour after hour. What is not apparent is that the appliance has been carefully rewired, a stronger motor installed, and many of the plastic components have been replaced with brass substitutes. The appliances for sale in the sealed packages however, will probably malfunction on the fifth use.

Most of us have also encountered the look-alike logos of well-known products on inferior merchandise. The intent was to deceive, and at times we were taken in by this unethical simulation. Similarly, consider the investors who received a tour of very impressive, beautifully furnished headquarters offices. Model products were spotlighted in gleaming glass cases. But unknown to the investors, the production line, the employees, the materials, and the factory itself did not exist. Many hard-earned dollars were invested in this unethical and manipulative scheme.

The point of these examples is to recognize that much of our communication is nonverbal. When we use actions, artifacts, and possessions to deceive, we are being unethical. Unethical nonverbal communication is perhaps more difficult to avoid than unethical written or spoken communication because rationalization is so easy. All too often we say, "Oh what's the harm; I was only trying to create a good impression." If the intent was to deceive, the nonverbal communication was still unethical.

Selective omission can misrepresent the facts in charts and graphs.

Unethical communications can also take place with charts, graphs, and pictograms.[4] The bar chart in Figure 5-1 misrepresents through selective omission. We may assume that sales climbed steadily from 1984 to 1992. However, if we could examine the sales in years 1987, 1988, and 1989, which have been

FIGURE 5–1 Unethical Misrepresentation in a Bar Chart

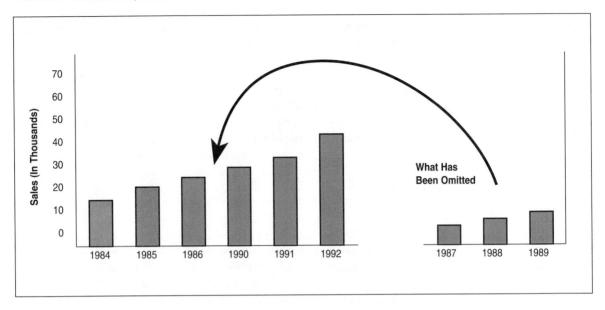

omitted (ostensibly to save space), we find quite a different story. Sales have not gone up consistently, and the presentation is surely unethical.

Distorting the visual depiction of otherwise accurate information might alter the message.

Distorting a visual representation is another way to convey a message that may be accurate (as is the bar chart with the omission), but is it ethical? The tops of the money bags in the pictogram in Figure 5-2 are at 30 or 60. However, the horizontal dimension in panels b and c has been widened to give the impression of a much larger sum. Compare panels b and c with panel a. The misrepresentation can be made even greater by removing the scale (0 to 60) on the left side of drawing.

Figure 5-3 shows another way to misrepresent using basically accurate information. The intent is to convey the effect of a dramatically rising sales line. To do that, the writer simply cut the bottom and top off the chart on the left and began the baseline at 40 in the chart on the right. Then the writer went to 80 and stopped. The result is a dazzling sales line.

ETHICS AND
THE COMPUTER

Computers have become a part of everyone's life in health, financial, social, and many other areas. Because our activities are so often influenced by computers, we need to determine if they play an ethical role in our lives. What constitutes *computer ethics*?

If someone manipulates a computer to alter a bank account or to change a grade, is that *computer* fraud, or has the computer simply been used to bring about fraud? The computer is an instrument (such as a gun) that assists in the commission of the fraud or crime. Is selling computers to nations that support terrorism or use the computer to manufacture nerve gas a violation of computer ethics? Are ethical issues involved in replacing workers with computer-guided robots or in placing computers in the workplace that may have a detrimental effect on users' vision.[5]

We may not really be able to determine what constitutes computer ethics. Perhaps the problem is one of semantics when we attempt to differentiate

FIGURE 5–2 Misrepresentation through Visual Distortion

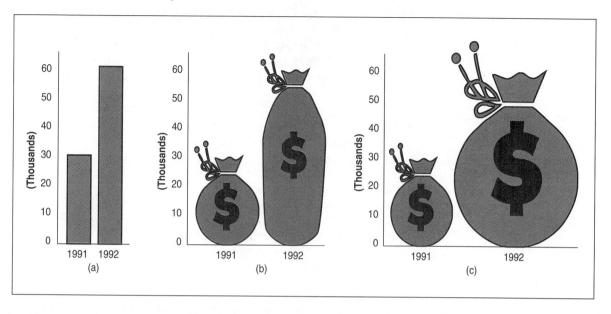

FIGURE 5–3 Misrepresentation Using Basically Accurate Information

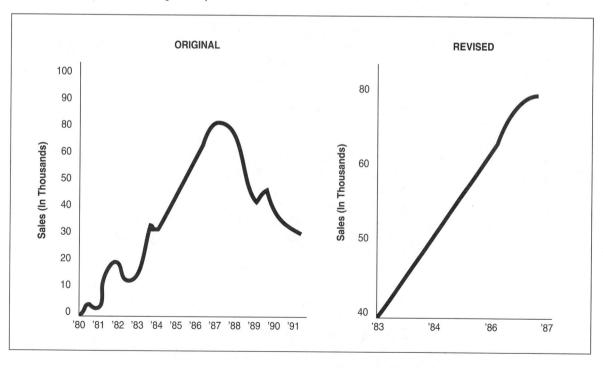

between using the computer (as a device) to bring about a violation of ethics (displacing workers or facilitating terrorism) or using the computer to change a situation for one person's gain and another's loss. Indeed, such a debate will accomplish little for our purposes here. What is more important is to recognize it is quite possible to accomplish unethical acts in business today through the use of the computer, just as it is through verbal and nonverbal communication.

Gotterbarn, in his article "Computer Ethics," states that using a computer to commit fraud is no more an example of "computer ethics" than using the newspaper to publish a harmful article is an example of "newspaper ethics." He feels that "ethics for computing professionals is not just another kind of ethics, but it is ethical values, rules, and judgments applied in a computing context based on professional standards and a concern for the user of the computer artifact.[6]

"Computer ethics" govern the development of helpful, nonharmful software.

To some, computer ethics is concerned with developing software that will do a specific job and "do no harm." Computer ethics, according to many in the field, involves the computer professional who represents himself or herself as having the skills to carry through computer assignments (developing software and computing artifacts) that will function properly and not harm the user or his or her activities.

Thus we come back to our earlier statements that there are often differing points of view on what constitutes an ethical decision where computers are involved. Perhaps the answer lies in answering the question of what is moral. And even here, the times, the circumstances, and the culture play a role.

CORPORATE CODES OF ETHICS

In deciding the ethical course of action, management must be competent, self-confident, and tough-minded. Decision makers should develop a code of ethics for employees and let their own actions set the example.

Several factors can make ethical decisions easier for the members of an organization. One of the most important is the character of the major decision makers. A second factor involves the statements and actions of the CEO and other top-level executives that reinforce the moral standards of the organization. Still another is the publication and employee discussion of the organization's code of ethics for business practices. Sometimes such a code is simply titled "What We Stand For," "Business Policies," or something similar. (An example of a code of ethics is pictured in Figure 5-4.)

In large organizations, ethics may be easier to preach than to practice.

Even with reinforcement, the practice of ethics in a large organization is difficult. Ethics, in many respects, is not as tangible, precise, or concrete as a company policy on when to grant a 3 percent customer discount or when an employee becomes eligible for a four-week vacation. Ethical standards and guidelines are not always clear when distances separate divisions from the organization's headquarters, when employees are made up of different ethnic groups, and when operations extend into nations where cultures are different. All of these factors make ethical decisions difficult.

Management's public actions reflect the organization's ethical integrity.

Despite these difficulties, employees need a set of standards for ethical practice and that is what company-wide publications such as "Ethical Principles" or "What Our Company Stands For" accomplish. Certainly, such printed statements reinforce the opinions and actions of an employee of high-moral standards. The determining factors in the long run, however, are the actions of the executive echelon in its relationships with government, customers, vendors, environmental agencies, community groups, and others in addition to what its marketing, advertising, and sales departments say in person and in print.

There are no more important individuals in reinforcing ethical practices than the CEOs. The CEOs' participation can't simply be what they say in the employees' booklet on ethics. They must display ethical leadership in their management decisions and in what they say as they discuss everyday affairs on the shop floor, at stockholders' meetings, and in the office setting.

FIGURE 5–4   A Code of Ethics: Ethics as a Practical Matter—A Message from David R. Whitwam, Chairman of the Board, Whirlpool Corporation

The question of ethics in business conduct has become one of the most serious challenges to the business community in modern times.

At Whirlpool, we share with millions of other Americans a deep concern over recent revelations of unethical and often illegal conduct on the part of some of this nation's most prominent business people and corporations.

The purpose of this message is not to pass judgment on any of these occurrences; each must and will be judged on its merits by those charged with that responsibility.

Rather this message is intended to place firmly on record the position of Whirlpool Corporation regarding business ethics and the conduct of every Whirlpool employee. It represents an irrevocable commitment to our customers and shareholders that our actions will be governed by the highest personal and professional standards in all activities relating to the operation of this business.

Over the years, circumstances have prompted us to develop a number of specific policies dealing with such critical elements of ethical business practice as **conflicts of interest, gifts, political activities, entertainment, and substantiation of claims.**

We also have a basic statement of ethics which places the ultimate responsibility for ethical behavior precisely where it belongs in any organization . . . on the shoulders of the person in charge:

"No employee of this company will ever be called upon to do anything in the line of duty that is morally, ethically or legally wrong.

"Furthermore, if in the operation of this complex enterprise, an employee should come upon circumstances of which he or she cannot be personally proud, it should be that person's duty to bring it to the attention of top management if unable to correct the matter in any other way."

Every Whirlpool manager carries the dual responsibility implicity in this policy statement, including the chairman of the board.

Our written policies deal with nearly all facets of business experience. We review, revise and recommunicate them to our managers on a regular basis . . . and we see that our managers carry on the communication throughout the company.

But as a practical matter, there is no way to assure ethical behavior with written policies or policy statements.

In the final analysis, "ethical behavior" must be an integral part of the organization, a way of life that is deeply ingrained in the collective corporate body.

I believe this condition exists at Whirlpool, and that it constitutes our greatest single assurance that this company's employees will conduct the affairs of this business in a manner consistent with the highest standards of ethical behavior.

At Whirlpool we have certain ways of doing things. They are commonly accepted practices, enforced not by edict, but rather by a mutual conviction that they will, in the long term, work in the best interest of our customers, our stockholders, the company and all its employees.

In any business enterprise, ethical behavior must be a tradition, a way of conducting one's affairs that is passed on from generation to generation of employees at all levels of the organization. It is the responsibility of management, starting at the very top, to both set the example by personal conduct and create an environment that not only encourages and rewards ethical behavior, but which also makes anything less totally unacceptable.

I believe this has been achieved at Whirlpool. The men who founded this company back in 1911 were individuals possessed of great integrity and honor. They fostered a tradition of ethical conduct in their business practices, and they perpetuated that tradition through careful selection of the people who would one day fall heir to leadership of the company.

The system works. Time and time again I have witnessed its efficacy. It shows no hospitality whatsoever to those not willing to abide by its standards, and unerringly identifies and purges them.

Unfortunately, the system is not automatically self-sustaining. It must be constantly reaffirmed by each new generation of leaders. In the position I now occupy, I view this as one of my most important responsibilities.

As this company grows, and as the pressures upon it increase, maintaining our tradition of ethical conduct becomes an increasingly difficult task. But I am confident it will be maintained, because it is necessary for continued growth, profitability and success.

Although the CEO and other executives must lead by example, written policies and procedures establish the organization's ethical climate.

The climate can be set by the company's printed word. Many such statements reflect an admirable tone and give employees a set of guidelines to assist them when making decisions on the job.

The "Code of Business Conduct" of Ashland Oil begins in general terms:

> Adherence to Law . . . employees will abide by the letter and the spirit of all applicable laws and regulations. . .
> Adherence to High Ethical Standards . . . employees will adhere to the highest ethical standards of conduct in all business activities . . .
> Responsible Citizenship . . . employees will act as responsible citizens . . .[7]

Ashland's ethics code then lists specific guidelines for accounting controls and reporting, relations with customers and suppliers, political participation, media relations, employee loyalty, security trading, confidentiality and other areas.

The Chrysler Corporation's "Code of Ethical Behavior" opens with a personal message from the CEO to the employees:

> This booklet is intended to reinforce Chrysler Corporation's commitment to operate at all times by the highest standard of ethical conduct. That's our policy because . . . it's the right way to conduct ourselves and, as responsible business people, it's the smart way.
> . . . if our ethical standards are perceived as lower than our product standards, then we will lose the support and confidence of our customers, our dealers, our suppliers, our shareholders, our governments and the communities in which we operate.
> And, maybe worst of all, we'll begin to lose the confidence of each other.
> The reputation of any company hangs by a thin thread. Even innocent mistakes can destroy that reputation. At Chrysler, we have to accept the responsibility to do the "right thing" every day.[8]

This booklet goes on to discuss specific areas such as, among others, report preparation, customer relations, and personal conduct. A most interesting portion of the Chrysler booklet (and unlike most ethical guides) is a checklist provided to assist the employee. Management suggest the following steps when employees face an ethical dilemma:

Analysis:
What are the facts? Who is responsible to act? What are the ethical and legal consequences of action? What and whose rights are involved? What is fair treatment in this case? What written guidelines or procedures apply?

Solution Development:
What solutions are available to me? Have I considered all the creative solutions which might permit me to reduce harm, maximize benefits, respect more rights, or be fair to more parties?

Select the Best Solution:
What are the potential consequences of my solution? . . . Are all parties treated fairly in my proposed decision?

Implementation:
Who should be consulted and informed? . . .

Follow-Up:
Was the decision implemented correctly? . . .

Such a checklist can be extremely helpful when an employee faces an ethical dilemma and isn't quite sure what direction to follow.

Management cannot assume that employees will automatically follow ethical codes. Ethical behavior must be nurtured and rewarded.

Nevertheless, issuing a booklet on ethical standards that carries a strong letter of endorsement from the CEO will not ensure ethical decision making on the part of every employee. An ethical climate is stimulated by the actual activities and statements of every executive. And an ethical climate requires time to develop at every level. There must be evidence of some reward system that results from ethical actions. The reward need not be monetary, but it should be a type of reward that all employees can appreciate. The worst scenario is the case of the company that has a printed statement on ethics but fires a whistle-blower who goes public with a legitimate complaint.

Ethical action is an individual choice, but management should devise ways of encouraging employees to act ethically.

At best, practicing ethical decision making is most difficult in a society with as many different values, cultures and standards as we have today in the United States.[9] Ethical behavior is an individual responsibility. Managers can reinforce employees' ethical behavior by constantly following ethical guidelines themselves. Various internal devices can further support ethical behavior. One article suggests (1) publishing an organizational newsletter with hypothetical dilemmas and how they might be resolved, (2) providing employees with a hotline and/or an ombudsperson who may be a member of the human resources department, (3) providing counselors, and (4) offering training programs covering ethics and ethical issues.[10]

WRITING AND SPEAKING EXERCISES

1. Select an article from your daily newspaper or *The Wall Street Journal* that is obviously concerned with the topic of ethics. Write a short paper evaluating the ethical consideration in the article and indicate if the situation can be interpreted from two different points of view based on ethical values.

2. Select a quotation from a news magazine or a newspaper. It may be a statement made by a politician, government representative, or business executive. Comment on the ethical implications of the quotation. On what specific theory of ethics is the quotation based?

3. Do you think the ten core values for making ethical decisions can be taught to students at the secondary level? If so, how would you do it?

4. Select an advertisement (from a magazine or newspaper) that you consider not completely ethical in either what it says, illustrates, or implies. Comment on the aspects of the advertisement that you feel are not completely ethical (or valid or truthful).

5. Comment on a quotation from an advertisement that is obviously meant to deceive (e.g., "an enormous gallon container" or "a huge 32-ounce package of Whizo Detergent"). Comment on the quotation in relation to the audience to which it is directed. Do you think the ad will be successful? Why or why not?

6. Have you ever faced a situation at school or at work that involved an ethical dilemma? How did you solve it? Comment on what aspects made it a dilemma for you.

7. Many corporations and nonprofit organizations published guidelines for ethical decision making for their employees in the period from 1970 to

1990, but few organizations distributed such material before 1960. Why do you think this change occurred?

8. Do you think federal and/or state governments should approve more legislation to enforce ethical policies? Defend your point of view.

CASES

Complete the following assignments from the Cases for Discussion section at the back of this book:

1. Bill Webster's Ethical Dilemma case — Assignments 1 and 2
2. Was This Really Fraud case — Assignments 1 and 2

READINGS

See "Handling Sexual Harassment in the Workplace" in the Readings section at the back of this book.

SUGGESTED RESOURCES

Carroll, A.B. "Principles of Business Ethics: Their Role in Decision Making and Initial Consensus." *Management Decision* 28 (August 1990).

Dillon, George C. "Does It Pay to Do the Right Thing?" *Across the Board*, 28 (July-August 1991).

Gandz, J. "Ethics Come Out of the Closet." *Business Quarterly*, 53 (Autumn 1988).

Green, F.B., and Hatch, E. "Involvement and Commitment in the Work Place: A New Ethic Evolving." *Advanced Management Journal*, 55 (Autumn 1990).

Ireland, Karin. "The Ethics Game." *Personnel Journal*, 70 (March 1991).

Jones, Thomas M. "Ethical Decision Making by Individuals in Organizations: An Issue-Contingent Model." *Academy of Management Review*, 16 (April 1991).

Kirrane, Diane E. "Managing Values: A Systematic Approach to Business Ethics." *Training and Development Journal*, 44 (November 1990).

Patrick, J., Wagley, R., and Von der Embse, T. "Structural Ethical Decision Making: Improving the Prospects of Managerial Success in Business." *Advanced Management Journal*, 56 (Winter 1991).

Pettit, J., Vaught B., and Pulley, K. "The Role of Communication in Organizations: Ethical Considerations." *The Journal of Business Communication*, 27 (Summer 1990).

Shostack, G.L. "Stand Up for Ethics." *Journal of Business Strategy*, 11 (May-June 1990).

Skeddle, Ronald. "Business Ethics: Dealing in the Gray Areas." *Financial Executive*, 6 (May-June 1990).

Vogel, David. "Business Ethics: New Perspectives and Old Problems." *California Management Review*, 33 (Summer 1991).

Webber, R. "Ethics Gap." *Chief Executive*, 58 (May 1990).

LEGAL CONSIDERATIONS

MANAGEMENT
COMMUNICATION
AND THE LAW

In choosing the method and medium for their communications, managers consider a variety of approaches: What will the audience find interesting? What will best convey the idea? What will prove persuasive? What can the company afford? Every manager must add another crucial question to that list of considerations: What is legal?

Virtually all managerial communications must be evaluated with an eye toward legal responsibilities and liabilities. Managers, after all, stand in an "agency relationship" with the company; that is, they are empowered to act for the company and to stand under the supervision of the company. For these reasons, the company must accept responsibility for the work-related actions and communications of its employees.

The agency relationship, in fact, is difficult to put aside, even when both the managers and companies involved wish to do so. Simply labeling an interview "off the record" or writing "confidential" on a memo does not put the communication beyond the reach of the courts. All managerial communications, including memos, phone records, files, and minutes of meetings, can be ordered into court as evidence under the power of subpoena (the court's legal demand for the submission of evidence).

Are such circumstances rare? Not at all. Hundreds of cases are brought each day against managers in communication-related charges, especially in these areas:

- Violation of equal opportunity legislation
- Failure to provide proper credit information or notification
- Violation of right-to-privacy laws
- Improper or discriminatory practices in hiring, supervising, and firing
- Inaccurate or misleading consumer information, including advertising, labeling, and warranties
- Suppression or destruction of information available under "sunshine" legislation

In these and other areas, managers must exercise the utmost care in what they communicate. When charges are brought against a company and its agents, what counts in court is not what managers mean to say or write but what in fact they *did* commit to paper or "publish" (make known) to third parties through conversation or oral presentation.

Consider, for example, the manager of a large mall in New York who communicated, by posted notice, that leaflets could not be distributed by nonmerchants on the mall premises. In this instance, an antinuclear group had tried to distribute protest and information leaflets in the mall corridors. Before the New York Court of Appeals, the manager lost his case. His letters, memos, and notices were brought forward by the plaintiff as evidence of an attempt to suppress freedom of speech. The court agreed, defining the mall as a "town center" where citizens have a right to speak out in oral and written forms.

Do such cases imply that managers should avoid communication altogether? No. To manage *means* to communicate, and managers spend as much as 90 percent of their business day in communication activities. But court precedents and common sense do suggest that managers educate themselves about the legal dimensions of every document or presentation in which they are involved. Throughout this text, therefore, we have provided information on the legal aspects of managerial communication in the following areas:

Business research and the law	p. 204
Reports and the law	p. 330
Employee communication and the law	p. 456
Credit, collection and the law	p. 602
Products, promotion and the law	p. 630

In each of these cases, the intent is not to provide legal advice for direct application in business life; only an attorney can provide specific guidance in such areas. Instead, each case alerts you to legal "hot spots" where common sense and legal precedents urge managers to exercise judgment and caution. The cost of being a careful communicator is low, especially when measured against the devastating financial, corporate, and personal consequences of legal action based on your communications.

ENDNOTES

1. David Vogel, "Business Ethics: New Perspectives on Old Problems," *California Management Review*, 33 (Summer 1991): 101–110.

2. These core values are discussed as guideposts for ethical decision making in Mary E. Guy, *Ethical Decision Making in Everyday Work Situations* (New York: Quorum Books, 1990).

3. George C. Dillon, "Does It Pay to Do the Right Thing?" *Across the Board* 28 (July-August 1991): 15.

4. Excellent discussions of this topic are illustrated in the classic book by Darrell Huff, *How to Lie with Statistics*.

5. An excellent article (though somewhat controversial) is D. Gotterbarn, "Computer Ethics," *Phi Kappa Phi Journal* (Summer 1991).

6. ibid.

7. Ashland Oil, Inc., "Code of Business Conduct."

8. Chrysler Corporation, "Code of Ethical Behavior."

9. John Donaldson and Peter Davis, "Business Ethics? Yes, But What Can It Do For The Bottom Line?" *Management Decision* 28 (November 1990): 29.

10. G. Edwards and K. Bennett, "Ethics and HR: Standards in Practice," *Personnel Administration*, (December 1987). Also for those readers interested in additional material on the topic of ethics, please see *The Journal of Business Communication*, (Summer 1990). The issue is devoted to articles dealing with ethics. Several additional articles may be found in *The Bulletin of the Association of Business Communication* (September 1990).

PART 2

BUSINESS WRITING THAT WORKS

DEBORAH GILLETTE is a Campaign Associate with United Way. She participates in the development and administration of charitable giving campaigns. Ms. Gillette is now completing her M.A. in Professional Writing at Old Dominion University.

United Way
of South Hampton Roads

Chesapeake • Norfolk • Portsmouth • Suffolk • Virginia Beach

Dear Future Manager:

For our community members to understand what we do at United Way of South Hampton Roads, we have to communicate with them often by letter and brochure. Whether we are informing the public of our company mission, the needs of local people, or more global concerns, we depend upon our written words to carry our message clearly and persuasively.

I've found my skills in persuasive communication an absolute job requirement in my career. I use these skills inside and outside my organization. Within the organization, I often must convince a co-worker or senior manager to consider my point of view or plan of action. Outside the company, I use skills in persuasion skills to encourage people to donate.

Your ability to communicate persuasively will no doubt be a strong asset in your career. I urge you to learn as much as you can now about written and oral persuasion. Those skills will pay significant dividends both to you and your employer.

Deborah J. Gillette

Deborah J. Gillette
Campaign Associate

6

THE WRITING PROCESS

Plan to communicate, **plan** your communication, and then **plan** what to say and how to say it.

It is important to consider business writing as a process, not as imitation. The imitation (or product) approach to business writing asserts that we learn to write primarily by imitating model documents. In effect, we copy until we can reproduce the model ourselves. By contrast, the process approach—the basis of this chapter—asserts that we learn to write well by following flexible but ordered stages of activity: planning, organizing, drafting, and revising/editing.

By thinking of writing as a process rather than a product, businesspeople will be better equipped to meet the growing challenges they face as communicators.

We believe that the process approach to writing will better fit your writing needs. If you learn this approach, you will be able to respond appropriately in a wide range of communication situations, many of them far beyond the limits of usual model documents. The process approach to writing equips you to be a creator of business messages, not simply an imitator. In so doing, you have the pleasure of expressing your own voice and style, when appropriate, in letters, memos, reports, and other documents. Let's begin with the planning and organizing stages of the writing process. In Chapter 7 we will look at the drafting and revising/editing stages.

INITIAL STEPS IN THE PLANNING PROCESS

Good planning and organizing are the keys to the success of a great many activities in our society. Without them, it would be impossible for a rocket to function properly, a building to be erected solidly, a surgical procedure to be carried through successfully, or a piece of oral or written communication to be presented effectively. Few activities, from baking a cake to going on a journey, take place without a plan or blueprint. Unfortunately, people often write or speak without following a plan.

Unplanned arguments tend to lose the reader's interest.

How often have you thrown down a magazine, slammed a book shut, snapped off a TV, or tapped someone on the shoulder with the comment, "Well, what's the point"? How often have you lost interest in an article, a report, or a speech because its theme or argument seemed to be going in circles? Perhaps the point got lost because the communication was not properly planned.

PLANNING

Planning helps the writer select and organize material so that the reader will understand it easily.

Business writers take time to plan their writing efforts for several reasons. First, planning helps the writer determine what details, evidence, and arguments to include. Second, a good working plan provides a writing agenda of sorts, giving the writer a step-by-step pattern to follow in writing the document. Last and of utmost importance, a clear, logical plan makes the document easy to read and understand.

Some business communicators make the mistake of skipping the planning step, reasoning that plans change anyway. Although it is true that plans do evolve as the document develops, writers should begin with at least a tentative outline.

But where do planning efforts start? Begin by answering five key questions:

1. What is the precise problem to be addressed in the report, proposal, memo, or letter?
2. What is the primary purpose of the communication?
3. Who is the reader?
4. In what ways should the topic be organized?
5. In what ways should the topic be limited?

The answers to these questions put the writer well on the way to developing a tentative plan for writing.

IDENTIFYING THE PROBLEM

Not every piece of communication deals with a problem, but a great many do. Whether the problem involves declining sales, an unusual increase in accounts receivable, or the rise in employee theft, you must identify the precise problem before you move to the next step.

Too often an executive notes that something is wrong in a particular area. In an effort to get to the bottom of the case and solve the problem, the executive may tell a subordinate, "Let me have a report on the situation." If the subordinate does not recognize the specific problem, the report may not solve the problem.

Let's look at two examples. Records indicate that employee pilferage is up 10 percent. If the boss asks for a report on that problem, the writer may try to explain the situation in an eight-page report by concentrating on inadequate security measures. However, that report will serve no purpose because the *real* problem is not inadequate security. It may be that pilferage is up because of what employees perceive as inadequate pay raises, poor management, or unfair promotion practices.

Identify the precise problem to avoid wasting time and effort.

The point is simply this: if the writer does not recognize the problem and focuses all efforts on a side issue, the resulting report will not contribute to solving the problem. As a result, the report was a waste of time and effort.

Let's consider another situation. Mr. George of Foremost Pharmaceuticals has just received a letter from one of the firm's retail accounts, Drayer's Drugs. Ms. Drayer asked Foremost to send one the free attractive signs, "Prescription Drugs," offered to Foremost accounts with $2,500 per month in sales.

Mr. George checks and finds that Drayer's sales have never exceeded $1,500 per month in the three years in which Drayer's Drugs has been making purchases from Foremost. Now, what is the problem? Is it the sign or is it retaining Ms. Drayer's sales?

If Mr. George decides the problem is simply the sign, he may refuse to give Ms. Drayer one and, as a result, lose her as a customer. If, on the other hand, Mr. George feels the problem is how to retain Ms. Drayer's goodwill and sales, he will write a different type of letter. Figures 6-1 and 6-2 show how the message can differ, depending on how the writer defines the problem.

Thus the first step in the planning process is recognition of the problem. Now you must determine the purpose of the written communication.

DECIDING ON THE PURPOSE

Determine your primary purpose and organize accordingly.

If we decide, in the preceding case of employee pilferage, that your purpose is to inform the reader, that would be one purpose of the report. On the other hand, your purpose could be to persuade the reader to purchase a new security system. It is possible that your purpose might be to compare method A of cutting employee pilferage with method B.

When you establish the primary purpose of a communication, its organizational pattern begins to fall into place. For example, a letter arrives from a customer asking for your firm's credit terms. Your purpose is simply to inform the customer of the credit terms, and you will organize your reply this way:

- Acknowledge letter requesting credit terms.
- Spell out credit terms in detail.
- Add a friendly closing.

However, if the customer is asking for credit and you discover that his or her asset-liability ratio is unsatisfactory, your purpose will be to persuade the customer to accept an alternative (e.g., COD instead of credit), and therefore you will organize your reply differently:

- Acknowledge letter requesting credit.
- Explain why it would be of benefit to the customer to improve his or her asset-liability ratio.
- Offer the option of COD, explaining its advantages. (The refusal to extend credit is implicit in the positive statements made here.)
- Add a friendly closing.

By following this plan, you need not say, "Therefore we cannot . . ." "We find it impossible . . . " or "We must refuse . . ." Under ordinary circumstances, if you first explain the reason for the refusal , a negative statement may be implied rather than stated, as illustrated in Figure 6-2.

IDENTIFYING THE READER

Your next basic question is, who is the prospective reader? The answer tells you at what *level* you should write. Should you present the discussion, charts, graphs, and related materials in a simple or a complex fashion?

Is the reader one of the people involved in financing this building project, a relatively uninterested shareholder who owns three shares of stock, or the consulting architect? Are you writing a release to the newspapers for publicity purposes or a detailed report to the board of directors? The style, level, and amount of detail will surely differ for each.

The *organizational plan* may also change according to who the reader is. In one case, a chronological approach, which is relatively easy to follow, may be better; in another case, a cause-and-effect order may be appropriate. More technical detail will be included in one organizational plan, and less in another;

FIGURE 6–1 Refusal Letter That Will *Lose* Goodwill

Foremost
Pharmaceuticals

July 28, 19__

Betty Draper
Draper's Drugs
1000 Cambert Place
Savannah, Georgia 31401

Dear Ms. Draper:

We received your letter requesting that we supply you with one of our free "Prescription Drugs" signs.

If you will check the letter you received announcing this offer, as well as our follow-up advertisements, you will note that only those retailers having sales over $2,500 per month are eligible. You do not fall into that category; in the past three years, your sales have never exceeded $1,500 per month.

Blunt and almost rude refusal

Therefore, your request must be refused.

Sincerely,

Phillip George

Phillip George
Customer Service

No attempt to retain goodwill

12200 Weston Road   Atlanta, Georgia 30341   (404) 110-2000

FIGURE 6–2 Refusal Letter Designed to *Retain* Goodwill and Customer Sales

Foremost
Pharmaceuticals

July 28, 19___

Betty Draper
Draper's Drugs
1000 Cambert Place
Savannah, Georgia 31401

Dear Ms. Draper:

Thank you for your letter of July 25. It is always a pleasure to hear from our long-term customers.

The sign you requested, "Prescription Drugs," was offered to our customers whose sales have exceeded $2,500 per month, as noted in our announcements.

I have personally checked your sales record and have found that although you are an excellent customer, your sales have been approximately $1,500 per month over the past three years. To be fair, we must apply the guidelines uniformly to all customers.

However, I do have a suggestion. Our quantity purchase cost for each sign is $52. If you would like one at that price, we will ship one to you, freight prepaid. Please call me collect, Ms. Draper, with your decision.

I'm also enclosing an advance copy of our "Fall Over-the-Counter Harvest of Values" announcement. Place your order prior to August 20 and take an extra 5 percent discount.

Sincerely,

Phillip George

Phillip George
Customer Service

12200 Weston Road　　　　Atlanta, Georgia 30341　　　　(404) 110-2000

Friendly opening

Explanation for refusal is brief.

Refusal is implied, not stated

Friendly alternative offered

Friendly close

**Getting to Know
Your Readers**

Use this checklist as a guide in assessing who your readers are and what they want from the document you are preparing.

What are the names of your readers? Can you find out? Should their names be included in the document?

Where are your readers from in the company or among its clientele? From what work units? What level of authority?

Do your readers know one another? Will they compare impressions after reading your document?

What instructions have been given to your readers with regard to your document? What are they supposed to do with the information you convey?

What subgroups make up your readership? Can you write to these sub-groups in the course of the document without losing the interest of your main audience?

What is the experience level (background) of your readership with regard to your topic?

What mind-set can you expect on the part of your readers as they begin reading your document? In what ways do you propose to change that mind-set?

What questions will occur to your readers in the course of reading your document? How can you address those questions?

Will a secondary or tertiary audience read your document after the primary audience reads it? Have you considered all of these audiences in the way you wrote the document?

---

complicated financial facts will be integral to one outline but not to another. Other variations may be reflected in the outline concerning visual aids, financial data, and the length and detail level of the narrative. In this way, the outline (and, therefore, the final paper) is designed with the reader in mind.

Your relationship with the reader influences your level of writing, your tone, your selection of data, and your arrangement of ideas.

The *tone* of the communication may also vary according to the identity of the reader. Is he or she someone with whom you have been doing business for 15 years or a new account who has just entered a second order with you? Is the reader one of your vendors with a total workforce of ten, or an impartial reader of proposals involving hundreds of millions of dollars that have been submitted to the U.S. Department of Defense?

Once you have defined your problem, purpose, and audience, record them on paper or in your computer file. At times, a purpose that seems logical initially loses its validity when you see it on paper or a computer screen.

Let's say, for example, that the company vice-president told you, "We have spent several hundred thousand dollars on scanning equipment for the checkout counters of our 16 stores. However, there is a problem: the equipment isn't being fully utilized. Look into this."

On the surface, the problem seems clear: The checkout clerks are not fully utilizing the scanning equipment. But further thought, as you begin to formulate and write down the purpose, reveals flaws in your assumption. *Why* isn't the scanning equipment being fully utilized? Is the problem that checkout clerks are simply ringing the items' cost on the register and *not using* the scanning equipment to read the universal price code? Is the problem that the scanning equipment is often "down" and *can't be used?* Is the scanning equipment not being fully utilized because some checkout clerks *don't know how to use* the equipment? Or is it possible that store managers are *not using the data* gathered by the scanners in relation to inventory control, pricing, and purchasing?

What if you accept the problem as simply, the scanning equipment is not fully utilized? If you now move to your *purpose,* "to determine why the checkout clerks are not fully utilizing the scanners," you may be way off base. It is quite possible that the checkout clerks *are* fully utilizing the scanning equipment, but the store managers are not! Although store managers can secure product turnover and inventory status from the scanners, it's possible that they are neglecting to do so. Or, perhaps it's headquarters personnel who are not fully utilizing the equipment.

Always make sure of the precise problem, purpose, and reader before moving ahead in the writing process.

Until the precise problem, purpose, and reader are identified, it is quite possible for a writer to move in the wrong direction and work for days or weeks on a topic that does little to solve the problem.

How can you avoid this type of well-intentioned but wasteful effort? One way is by clearly defining the variables and *discussing* them with the person for whom you are completing the work. When you reach an understanding, move into the next phase: the organizing stage.

ORGANIZING THE MATERIAL

Find the method of organizing that works best for you.

Writers use various methods to organize messages: Among them is the tried-and-true method commonly referred to as *outlining.* More recently, *clustering, storyboarding,* and *collaborative thinking* have gained followers. Any one of these methods can serve as the blueprint that will guide the construction of the finished document, whether it is a single-page business letter or a 40-page proposal. Our discussion begins with outlining.

The outline organizes your points in a logical order.

Outlining.   Outlining is a shorthand, time-saving method for visualizing and testing your final document. The points in an outline, listed in logical order, reflect the organizational pattern of your proposed written effort. Major items in the outline stand for major topics in your document; minor items, minor topics.

Say, for example, that your problem is to find ways to market your company's product to countries in the European Community. You may choose six major areas for examination:

1. Market acceptance	4. Method of distribution
2. Competition	5. Legal restrictions
3. Advertising and sales promotion	6. Cost of distribution

You may arrange these in a different order when you write the final paper, but you do know that they will be the major areas for analysis and investigation. They also become the major headings in your tentative working outline. Now you can begin to divide each one into subcategories:

1. Market acceptance	2. Competition
Households	From similar local products
The teenage market	Brand A
Institutional purchasers	Brand B
Governmental agencies	Brand C

From North American Products
    Brand AA
    Brand BB
    Brand CC
    Brand DD

3. Advertising and sales promotion
    To the consumer
        Newspaper
        Radio
        Television
        Direct mail
        Point of sales
        Miscellaneous
    To the distributor
        Trade publications
        Direct mail
        Salesforce
        Miscellaneous

You can further, if desired, subdivide the subpoints.

Begin organizing by identifying and subdividing your major topics.

The method of developing an organizational plan is very important. Always begin by listing your major topics for discussion and examination. After identifying these areas, develop each into subdivisions.

It is fairly simple to list the major points in an analysis. They are usually the specific questions that need to be answered. For example, assume you are faced with a problem of whether to manufacture new product X. There are several major questions:

- Do you have the facilities to manufacture it?
- Is there a market for it?
- What competition exists?
- What costs will be incurred?
- What advantages do you stand to gain?

You can determine your main points by asking critical questions.

Each of these questions can be easily reworded into a more succinct major topic heading; then the subpoints under each can be developed. Try another topic for presentation. This time assume that you are faced with the problem of whether to publish an employee magazine. First, list some of the primary questions to be answered: Will such a publication make a significant contribution to employee morale? What will the annual cost of such a venture be? What personnel must you secure to handle the project? What alternatives may accomplish similar ends? What are the experiences of similar industries in this area? Here again, you may now develop subtopics under each major topic. Always identify the major topics *before* subdividing.

Clustering.   *Clustering* is simply placing your main theme in the center of a sheet of paper or in the center of a large flip board sheet and through brainstorming, noting related topic areas, ideas, and suggestions around the core. If the thoughts seems to be key areas, note them in caps or in a distinctive color; if they are minor or simply contributing, note them in small letters or another color. Circle major topics.

Clustering allows you to brainstorm ideas freely while focusing on your central topic.

After noticing all logical (and perhaps a few illogical) ideas, step back and note several as major topic areas, some as subpoints under the key ideas, a few as minor factors under the subpoints, and some that should be discarded. List the remaining points and subpoint clusters in order of importance. Discard those that you do not plan to treat in the document.

Choose and organize main points from the clusters of ideas in the diagram.

Quite often the ideas clustered around the central topic will be in the form of questions to be answered, as shown in Figure 6-3. Of course you could add many more topics to the figure. Once you have included all necessary topics, you would draw connecting lines to all those related to the questions about, for example, government regulations, markets available, or methods of distribution. In turn, you would list these clusters in order of importance. Then you would discard those entries that you did not plan to consider in your document.

CRITICAL THINKING CONCEPTS

"That just doesn't make sense." We've all had occasion to say these words when we disagree with the logical design, or argument, at the heart of a written or oral communication. Critical thinking involves both the ability to detect flaws in the arguments of others and to avoid such flaws in our own arguments. Put more positively, critical thinking is the ability to connect separate ideas and facts into a logical, cogent series.

Of the many elements making up critical thinking, none is more important than the assumption that two diametrically opposed things (A and not-A) cannot be true simultaneously. This is the contradiction test. For example, if we assert that most people in the United States will have longer life spans in the coming decades, we cannot assert at the same time that there will be fewer senior citizens in the years ahead.

As obvious as that example appears, it reveals an important element in critical thinking: *all* components of an argument most be weighted against one another to test for possible contradictions. This intellectual task can be daunting, especially when we must deal with complex and convoluted arguments involving many assertions and types of evidences. In such cases, we must read or listen with great care to remember (and take notes on) the individual components of an argument that must be evaluated to determine the truth of the argument's conclusion.

1. Locate and discuss possible contradictions in the following portion of a political speech:

   As a newspaper editor in Indianapolis, I know that my paper receives far more letters opposing gun control than supporting it. Similarly, radio and television talk shows get many more calls from those who uphold the constitutional right to bear arms than from those against it. In voting for gun control, Congress is obviously not listening to the great majority of the American people. Is America no longer a democracy?

2. Locate and discuss possible contradictions in the following sales presentation:

   Our product, X-R7, can rid your yard of bothersome pests without harming the environment. One application kills flies, ticks, beetles, roaches, worms, ants, and bees. (Avoid using X-R7 on broad-leaf plants and on lawns used by household pets.)

FIGURE 6–3 Clustering as a Method of Organizing

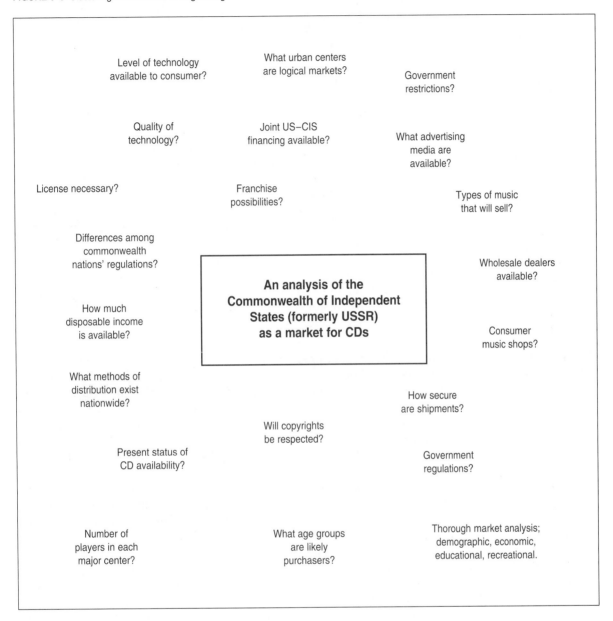

Storyboarding.   *Storyboarding* is often used in oral presentations or to brief conference participants. However, the method can profitably be used to organize a written presentation.

The method is simple. Place squares or rectangular boards or sheets of paper along a wall. Place specific ideas, sketches, photos and pictures on the boards. Then review, study and discuss them. At the same time, move them (where necessary) and place them in the order the topics should be covered in the presentation. Discard those not deemed essential.

Storyboarding has the further advantage of allowing the communicator to visualize as well as read the sketch or statement(s). This helps the writer or

Storyboards let you visualize your main ideas.

speaker in analysis as well as presentation. It is surprising how even crude sketches and heavy lettering can provoke new ideas, and how quickly the logical place for each idea can be recognized.

Collaborative thinking elicits a multitude of ideas from group participants.

Collaborative Thinking. *Collaborative thinking* is exactly what the term implies. The method is built on the maxim, "Two heads are better than one. " Two or more individuals, all familiar with and interested in the topic, assemble and contribute ideas. One person may act as a recorder. He or she uses flip charts or a board to record ideas suggested by those present. The recorder can use an outline form or clustering, or simply record ideas one after another, until the contributors "run dry." Then one or two individuals assign all or some of the topics to related areas and discard those deemed not essential.

Through clustering, storyboarding, and collaborative thinking, the writer escapes enslavement to a predetermined outline.

Clustering, storyboarding and collaborative thinking all reflect essentials of outlining: major points are recognized, minor points are designated under related heads, and unrelated or nonessential material is discarded. In addition, clustering, storyboarding and collaborative thinking permit easy visualization and easy movement of ideas from one section to another. Too often, when the inexperienced writer uses the outline method and places a heading under B which is a subpoint under II, he or she is reluctant to move it. These three alternative methods for organizing almost demand moving topics around.

LIMITING THE TOPIC AREAS

Before the investigator proceeds too far in analyzing and developing the organizational plan, boundaries and limits should be checked. In the report on marketing to the European Community, for instance, certainly there is no point in carrying out research in the areas of legal restrictions if the legal restrictions have already been determined and are part of company records. Or perhaps the legal restrictions are known to be minor and are not worth the time and effort to investigate. If an area need not be pursued, why expend time and energy on it?

The number and content of subtopics also must be limited. There is no need for in-depth coverage if it serves no purpose; it may even prove detrimental by giving readers more information than they want. If the concern is competition from similar products manufactured only in France, then do not get involved with those manufactured in North America or other countries in Europe.

Limit the scope of the subject and the number of subtopics.

Limitation of the subject area is vital if the communicator (or encoder) is to get to the heart of the precise area being investigated. It will also help prevent creative efforts from being dissipated. Suppose you are writing a report titled "The Advisability of Constructing a New Plant in Bennington, Ohio." Your major foundation blocks for investigation are:

Labor supply available	Community attitude
Physical plant	Availability of utilities
Market	Tax structure
Source of raw materials	Transportation facilities
Financing	

Now examine these major points to see if you can limit the study. If company records contain adequate material on the source of raw materials and community attitude, don't waste time on research; use what is already available.

The next step is to break down each of the remaining points into a logical series of subpoints. The number of subpoints will determine the depth of the analysis and usually the length of the presentation. If the prospective reader only wants to know if there are rail, air, water, and truck lines going into Bennington, that information can be covered in one paragraph:

> Transportation Lines into Bennington
> Rail
> Air
> Water
> Trucking

Your reader's needs determine the number of subtopics and their depth. If, however, the reader wants to know which transportation companies are involved, along with specific rates, schedules, guarantees, and history of performance, the result may be 20 pages of narrative, charts, and tables based on the following outline:

> Transportation Facilities
> Shipment of finished products
> Rail
> Santa Fe Railroad
> Mid-Continent Railroad
> Truck
> Commercial trucking firms
> Company trucks
> Leased trucks
> Air
> Commercial air freight
> Chartered air freight
> Comparative analysis
> Cost
> Rail
> Truck
> Air
> Shipment time
> Rail
> Truck
> Air
> Analyses of roads, air terminals, water, and rail facilities
> Roads
> Freeways, highways, major roads
> Secondary roads
> Access roads (to plant)
> Air terminals (75-mile radius)
> Passenger
> Freight
> Water Facilities
> Ports (import-export)
> Rivers (raw material; bulk products)

<pre>
        Rail Facilities
            Track spurs (on company property)
            Condition
            Ownership
        Terminals
            Railroad companies involved
            Accessibility
        Receiving and shipping points
    Employee transportation
        Public
            Commercial bus routes
            Rapid transit
        Private
            Individual automobiles
            Car pools
            Routes to and from residential areas
    Cost analysis
</pre>

If a reader wants one level of depth and receives another, the writer has organized the basic outline poorly. The solution is simple: plan and organize to specific needs and expectations of the prospective reader.

REVIEWING THE FIRST STEPS IN PLANNING AND ORGANIZING

Let's review quickly the initial steps of planning and organizing a written communication.

1. Problem: Our sales have declined. Is the problem due to the fact that we have a smaller segment of the market than our competitors? Is it the result of price increases? Is it a direct result of the change in the demographics of the area? Once we see the problem, we will plan accordingly. But we must first decide what the problem really is.
2. Purpose: Just what is the purpose? Is it to compare two systems? Is it to analyze a situation? Is it to cite information for record-keeping purposes? Is it to sell a course of action to a prospect? To explain a technical procedure to a reader? To defend and argue for the acceptance of a procedure?
3. Reader: Is the reader of the message a technically oriented engineer or a business-minded member of the board of directors? Is the reader a potential customer or a steady account?
4. Organization: Is your outline of the topics a logical one for this specific reader?
5. Limitation and scope: Has the topic been accurately limited on the basis of the reader's needs, desires, and level? Has the depth of the research and of the report, letter, or speech been properly determined?

Modify the outline to accommodate new ideas as you rethink your problem, purpose, organization, reader, and scope.

The tentative outline is developed as the writer carries through these steps. At no time should he or she hesitate to add to or delete from the outline or change its order to a more logical form. The outline is completely flexible and should be treated as a guide to be shaped, changed, and molded as the need arises.

DRAWING UP A TENTATIVE OUTLINE

As the writer begins research using primary and secondary sources, he or she may find that completing some of the points in the tentative outline is neither logical nor possible. Conversely, the writer may discover in the source material that certain areas were inadvertently omitted from the outline. And so the tentative outline is revised and polished. The writer cuts two points here and one there, and inserts a new item here and one there. The new, revised outline quite frequently will be quite different from the original outline.

VALUE OF AN OUTLINE

Always outline before writing.

Too often, writers may feel that drawing up an outline prior to the presentation of the report or speech is an extra and unnecessary step. Why, they may ask, go through the work? Why not just write the report or prepare the talk? The following pages describe several good reasons why all reports should begin with an outline.

The outline ... quickly identifies areas that should be developed or limited

Proportion. The length or depth of treatment of one part of the outline in comparison to the other sections can be easily evaluated. If a section is out of proportion—with either too much or too little data—it is easier to make the correction in the outline than in the finished presentation. The following example illustrates such an imbalance.

Employee Training at Allied Telephone
I. Employee Training in the Fairview Plant
   A. Executive training
   B. Engineering training
   C. Shop supervisory training
      1. Leadership classes for superintendents
      2. Foreman training
   D. Office personnel training
      1. Written communications
      2. Office equipment training
II. Employee Training at the Leance Plant
   A. Executive training
   B. Engineering training
      1. Electronic-control systems
      2. Engineering cost control
   C. Shop supervisory training
      1. Leadership classes for superintendents
      2. Foreman training
      3. Interpersonal relations
III. Employee Training at the Stone Plant
   A. Executive training
   B. Engineering training
      1. Engineering cost analysis
      2. Operations research
      3. Manufacturing processes
         a. Heat treatment of alloys
         b. Casting and molding
         c. Material joining

        d. Metal-surface treatment
        e. Material cleaning
      4. Computer use
        a. Analog and digital
        b. Computer codes
        c. Programming principles
    C. Shop supervisory training

In this numbered outline, point B under section III has been developed to an extent that is out of proportion to the other topics. If all of the material is needed, then perhaps a new major heading should be included; if all details are not necessary, they should be excised mercilessly. Section III will then be in better proportion to the other major headings.

. . . ensures logical development.

Logical development. If the outline is logical, the report will be logical. It is simple, for example, to move point B under section IV to another section of the outline if an analysis of the organization so indicates. Although word processing permits you to move sentences and paragraphs from page to page rather easily, the outline permits you to see, weigh, and evaluate proportion and placement of topics *before* you write the report. The following example illustrates how easy it is to make changes in the outline to secure a more logical plan:

    Employee Fringe Benefits
    I. Insurance Programs
      A. Hospitalization
      B. Major medical
      C. Life

    II. Pension Plan
      A. Company retirement program
      B. Social Security

    III. Miscellaneous
      A. Sick leave
      B. Annuity program (employee sponsored)
      C. Discount purchase of merchandise
      D. Long-term care coverage (employee sponsored)

. . . indicates whether the idea is complete.

Completeness. The communicator can use the outline to check on the completeness of the presentation. It is simple to evaluate an outline to determine if all necessary points have been covered; if they have not, additional items may be inserted easily.

. . . allows for evaluation of structure.

Order of development. The communicator can evaluate the order of development used. This point is closely related to logic, as discussed previously. There must be some method of logical development to any presentation: chronological, geographical, or cause and effect, for example. Here again, it is easier to check the outline and correct inconsistencies than it is to rework the finished version, even with the recent advances in word processing technology.

. . . saves time.

Time savings. An outline saves time. As the communicator evaluates the outline, he or she can quickly make additions, deletions, corrections, and revisions.

How much more effort is required—and how much more inconvenient it is—to take the same action on a finished document.

. . . assists with group writing.

Collaborative writing.   An outline allows the participation of other writers. As will be described in Chapter 8, many business writing projects are undertaken collaboratively by a writing team. For that team to work in a coordinated way, all members must agree on an organized outline. Parts of that outline can be distributed among group members for research and initial drafting.

In business, time is money. But some managers use that truism as an excuse for skipping the outlining step for documents. Consider the case of Gloria Simmons, new products manager for a computing company. Simmons hears a number of distressing messages from her subordinates:

- Key employees are thinking of quitting.
- A rumor is circulating that massive layoffs are coming.
- Someone has sabotaged one of the mainframe computers.
- Employees misunderstand the new flextime rules in the company.
- News is circulating that managers will soon receive substantial raises at a time when other employees will receive none.

Clearly, Simmons must communicate with her work force. But a quickly typed memo may do more harm than good. She takes time, therefore, to work out a tentative outline:

1. The truth about layoffs
2. Facts about flextime
3. Encouraging news about new company contracts (to counter, in an indirect way, the rumor that key employees are going to quit)
4. Facts about managerial raises

Simmons chooses not to deal with the sabotage issue in this memo, lest workers come to look on vandalism as a way of expressing displeasure. By following her outline, she is able to write a cogent, cohesive memo that goes far to allay anxieties and misunderstanding.

OUTLINE MECHANICS

Develop an outlining system that fits your personality.

How you design your outline is often a matter of personal preference. Some people prefer an elaborate numbering system of Roman numerals and letters all carefully arranged on clean, white stationery; others simply indent subordinate ideas under major headings on the back of an envelope. The mechanics of organizing are personal, and most of us eventually develop our own system.

Major sections should be noticeable at a glance.

Designate major and minor points.   Arrange the items in your outline so that a glance will reveal major areas, as opposed to minor ones. Think of the most important points as the key ideas and the subordinating ones as items of substantiating evidence.

The most frequently used numbering system is the *numeral-letter combination.* Roman numerals are used for major points, capital letters for subtopics, and Arabic numerals and lowercase letters for topics of lesser importance. If a further breakdown is necessary, parenthetical Arabic numerals and letters are used. Here is an example:

I. First Main Heading
  A. First subtopic under main heading
  B. Second subtopic under main heading
    1. First subtopic under B
    2. Second subtopic under B
      a. First subtopic under 2
      b. Second subtopic under 2
        (1) First subtopic under b
        (2) Second subtopic under b
          (a) First subtopic under (2)
          (b) Second subtopic under (2)
II. Second Main Heading

Engineers, as well as others in science and technology, favor the *decimal style.* This system is logical, easy to use, and affords a quick method for referring to specific points:

1. First Main Heading
  1.1 First subtopic under first main heading
  1.2 Second subtopic under first main heading
    1.21 First subtopic under 1.2
    1.22 Second subtopic under 1.2
      1.221 First subtopic under 1.22
      1.222 Second subtopic under 1.22
2. Second Main Heading
  2.1 First subtopic under second main heading
  2.2 Second subtopic under second main heading
    2.21 First subtopic under 2.2
    2.22 Second subtopic under 2.2

There are other methods of outlining, such as simple indentation and the use of specialized symbols. Any system that is accurate, permits easy analysis, and works for you is the one you should use.

Give equal treatment to ideas of equal importance.

Ensure parallel development.   In designing the outline, give items of equal importance similar levels of designation under major headings. Thus if "cost of materials" is an immediate subhead to Roman numeral I, it would not seem reasonable that under Roman numeral II "cost of materials" should slip to the level of a subtopic. Points of parallel interest should be listed at similar levels in the outline.

Be careful not to place a subordinate idea in the position of a main topic.

Avoid overlapping ideas.   If headings and subheadings are chosen properly, there should be little overlapping of ideas. The most common error of this sort lies in making a subordinate topic equal in placement to major topics. In a report on passenger safety in automobiles, for example, the major topics might be seat belts, air bags, and padded dash/steering wheel. The subordinate topic of quick-release seat-belt buckles should not be given equal placement with such major topics; instead it should be discussed under seat belts.

Develop your argument logically in order to maintain your persuasive edge.

Use a consistent and logical order of development.   Whether your communication is long or short, written or oral, simple or complex, you want your reader to understand and accept it. To achieve this goal, you must analyze the content of the message, the nature of the audience, and the purpose you hope to achieve. You go through these steps to secure the most logical order of development for your message. This attribute of logic is vital, for regardless of the excellence of your word choice, the clarity of your sentences, and the appearance of your communication, all will fail if the message lacks logic.

The critical businessperson may overlook a misplaced comma or a faulty phrase. But if the presentation lacks logic, the ideas become suspect, and the reader may simply tune out. You have certainly read such a presentation and noted at some point, "This doesn't follow; it's not logical; I can't accept it."

You cannot expect that everything you say or write will be accepted, but when something is rejected because you did not present it logically, then the fault is yours. Listed next are several methods to ensure the logical development of your communications.

Analysis breaks down a situation or pattern into its related elements.

Analysis and synthesis.   Before you design a plan for presentation, be sure you have recognized all of the important factors in the situation. For example, sales of your company's outdoor furniture products on the West Coast have declined dramatically. Let's analyze (identify the elements) to find out why the decline has taken place. The company does not have a West Coast distribution plant. A large market for patio furniture exists on the West Coast. Shipping your company's outdoor furniture from the Midwest is costly. Freight rates for shipping have risen steadily. Your company's West Coast customers have complained about high shipping costs. Surveys show your company's prices are not competitive with West Coast manufacturers of similar lines. . . . You began with a condition: decreased sales. You then analyzed the situation and attempted to identify the contributing factors.

Synthesis combines separate elements into a single pattern.

Or you may be confronted by a number of diverse elements that require synthesis (putting together) to form a logical whole or pattern. Production has declined rapidly since the early part of June. Employees have complained about the level of illumination in the production area. A new supervisor of the section took over in May. The safety equipment for the presses is slow and outdated. Compensation is on a piece-rate basis. The lead worker was discharged after she and the new boss had a severe argument on June 1. . . . These various facts can be related or synthesized with one another into the overall theme: Supervision, facilities, and compensation levels need to be reevaluated and improvements recommended.

Inductive development proceeds from the particular to the general.

Inductive development.   Inductive development proceeds from the particular or specific to the general. Here the writer cites details, specific events, and examples and finally arrives at a general conclusion. You might, for example, explain that the quality of the product was high, the price very competitive, the service excellent, and delivery fast, all of which resulted in a year of high sales.

Deductive development proceeds from the general to the particular.

Deductive development.   Deductive development proceeds from a general statement to particulars, details, and facts. You might begin by stating that a firm's primary activities depend on communication. From here you could point out how most external transactions are based on business letters; advertising in newspapers, radio, and TV; reports to government agencies; and proposals to potential customers. Internally, communication takes place through such media as news bulletins, company magazines, management memos, interdepartmental correspondence and reports, conferences, and meetings.

Chronological development presents details in the order they occurred over time.

Chronological development. In chronological development, a specific period of time is selected from which your discussion moves forward. Guiding phrases such as "In the past. . ." or "In the 1970s. . ." signal the first stage of such development. The middle stage comes next: "At present. . ." or "This year. . ." and so forth. Finally chronological development usually looks forward with sections beginning "Looking ahead. . ." or "In the future. . ." or "As we plan for the year 2000. . . ."

Use evidence when you argue that one event caused a later one to happen.

In chronological development, avoid this logical error: *post hoc, ergo propter hoc* (after this, therefore because of this). Just because one event happened in 1990 and another in 1991 does not mean that the first event caused the second event. A new manager, for example, may have been hired in 1990. Employee turnover in her division may have been exceptionally high in 1991. That fact does not automatically mean that the new manager caused the turnover. In using chronological development, do not be content merely to imply causality between events. Instead, use evidence and argument to show causal links.

Geographical development proceeds from one specific location to another.

Geographical development. In geographical development, begin at one location and then move to the next. If you are analyzing sales for a corporation with four district sales offices, plus sales headquarters in New York, it would seem logical to begin with a discussion of the activities of the New York office, then go on to an examination of the Chicago office; to Waterloo, Iowa; to Denver; and finally to Los Angeles. Or you might look at warehousing facilities in Camden, Fort Wayne, and Dallas before suggesting that the high speed loading dock be installed in the new warehouse in San Francisco.

CRITICAL THINKING CONCEPTS

One key to effective critical thinking in business lies in converting topic statements (The Price of Beans in China) to problem statements (Chinese Workers Threatened by Rising Bean Prices). The difference between the two statements may seem slight. But for the purposes of critical analysis, the difference is crucial.

Once stated as a problem, a statement can be evaluated by examining causes, effects, and remedies: What accounts for the rising bean prices? Who is responsible? Who is advantaged or disadvantaged? Who can do something about the situation? By contrast, a topic statement often seems to require only information (the facts) rather than critical analysis (why). Therefore, even if your report or presentation requires that you focus on a topic rather than a problem, it is usually worthwhile to temporarily convert the topic statement to a problem statement for the purposes of critical analysis.

1. Convert the following topic statements to problem statements: Housing Costs in New York City; Race Relations in Los Angeles; The Effects of High-Fat Diets; Changes in College Tuition.
2. For each of the problem statements you have created for question 1, suggest an outcome (or consequence) and at least one possible remedy.

Spatial development proceeds from one designated area to another.

Spatial development.   When the order of development moves from one logical space designation to another, it is called spatial development. In a plant, areas might be designated as administrative, manufacturing, packaging, storage, and shipping. If you were to examine the illumination levels (or safety hazards, or decorating schemes, or noise levels) in the entire plant, you would first discuss the aspect in one space (administrative, for example) and then discuss each of the others.

Directional development describes a step-by-step process.

Directional development.   A simple description of a process or product as it moves in a predetermined direction is called directional development. For example, a part must first be cleaned and sprayed. From there it goes to cutting and polishing. Then it is sent to inspection, after which it is sent to production, where diodes are attached. Again it is returned to inspection, after which it is sold and taken from stock. Those are the steps followed and the directions in which the item moves.

If you were to follow a state legislative bill from the time it was introduced in the House by a legislator, moving from committee A to committee B to the Senate to the executive branch to the governor, you would be describing the direction of movement of the bill.

Simple-to-complex development explains fundamentals before describing complexities.

Simple-to-complex development.   Simple-to-complex development is appropriate when you are faced with explaining a relatively involved situation to a reader who may not have a clear understanding of the fundamentals of the subject. If you begin with simple, easy-to-understand situations and gradually move to more complex areas of the same topic, the reader will be able to follow the explanation presented. If you wish to discuss a new automated production process, you might begin by explaining the fundamentals of a standard production process, then go on to the principles of a semiautomated situation, and finally to the complexity of a completely automated arrangement.

TYPES OF OUTLINES

Your thesis is your purpose.

The two most frequently used outline forms are the topic type and the sentence type. The paragraph outline is used infrequently. In addition to a list of items in topic, sentence, or paragraph form, the outline also has a title and often a thesis sentence. This thesis sentence should state clearly and concisely the purpose or objective of the message.

TOPIC OUTLINE

A topic outline allows you to list and revise ideas quickly.

Each entry in a *topic outline* consists of a few words or a short phrase. This type of outline has several advantages: the writers can jot down ideas quickly and need not bother with structuring each thought in a sentence. With a list of brief topics, the writer has little hesitation about adding several, dropping a few, moving one from one section to another of the outline, and making other revisions as the need arises.

A disadvantage of this type of outline is that it requires a good memory. When examining the two- and three-word headings weeks after writing them, the writer may have forgotten what the cryptic phrase "Losses—unexpected circumstances" refers to. Yet when the writer made that entry, he or she knew perfectly well what to discuss under that point. Here is an example of a topic outline:

A Survey of Fringe Benefits in Industry
  I. Insurance programs
      A. Life insurance programs
          1. Executive level
          2. Other employee level
      B. Hospitilization insurance
          1. Individual
          2. Family plans
      C. Major medical plans
          1. Company sponsored
          2. Insurance-company sponsored
      D. Surgical plans
          1. Individual
          2. Family plans
 II. Vacation and Holiday Plans
      A. Vacation Plans
          1. Standard vacation (specific period each year for all employees)
          2. Nonstandard vacation
          3. Time
              a. Weeks associated with years of company service
              b. Specific periods of time for different levels with no reference to length of service
      B. Paid holidays
          1. In conformity with union contracts
          2. As announced by the specific organization
      C. Extended leave periods (for research, travel, illness, etc.)
          1. With compensation
          2. Without compensation
III. Annuity and Pension Plans
      A. Government sponsored (Social Security)
      B. Annuity programs
          1. For executives
              a. Company-employee contributions
              b. Company contributions only
          2. For other employees
      C. Pension plans
          1. Company sponsored
          2. Company-employee sponsored
 IV. Profit-sharing Plans
      A. Broad coverage based on net earnings
      B. Limited employee participation

SENTENCE OUTLINE

A sentence outline conveys complete thoughts, but it should not be thought of as an early draft of the final document.

In a *sentence outline*, each entry is a complete sentence. This requires that writers structure their thoughts a little more carefully than with the topic outline. Ideas are stated completely, and the danger of forgetting what an entry refers to is considerably lessened. A major disadvantage of this style, however, is that it tempts writers to convert their sentence outlines into the document. The document is prepared through the simple expedient of connecting the sentences with a few transitional words or phrases. Of course, the results are poor. The writer of a sentence outline should remember that the outline must serve only as a guide to the writing assignment, not as an initial effort to be converted into the final document.

PARAGRAPH OUTLINE

A paragraph outline fully summarizes major ideas in paragraph form.

In planning an extensive report, a proposal, or a fairly detailed paper, it is sometimes wise to use a *paragraph outline.* In this instance writers use a paragraph to summarize a major idea, another paragraph for the next major idea, and so on. Once the broad portions of the entire report are broken down into individual paragraphs, these can then be subdivided (or outlined) into their component parts.

REAPING THE DIVIDENDS

Thoughtful planning ensures successful communication.

Planning pays dividends to both the writer and the reader. A working outline gives the writer an agenda to follow in creating a clear, organized document. That outline, as translated into headings and paragraph beginnings, serves the reader as a roadmap for following the writer's thoughts. The end result of such orderly sending and receiving is successful communication.

WRITING AND SPEAKING EXERCISES

1. Locate a text that discusses the writing process in terms somewhat different from this one. Outline the writing process chapter(s) in that text, in order to compare and contrast with the process as discussed in Chapter 6. Prepare a memo in which you highlight specific examples of both similarities and differences.
2. Discuss writing situations where inductive development is superior to deductive development. Is one method really better than the other? What specific factors should go into a writer's decision to choose a development method? Prepare a brief memo to a prospective writer addressing these questions.
3. As a member of a small group, research the topic of brainstorming. Choose one form of brainstorming, and prepare a short oral presentation for your class; explain how it relates to the discussion of the writing process in this chapter.
4. Find a current business article. Create an outline of its major and subordinate points. Write a paragraph in which you evaluate the organization and development of the article.
5. Time is probably the executive's most precious commodity. Preparing outlines takes time. As a cost-conscious manager, support or refute the need to develop outlines for communications in the organization.
6. Create an outline for a business document dealing with employee theft. Make sure the topic headings are parallel in form, as discussed in the chapter.
7. As a city planner, you are preparing a report on the growth of suburbs around your city. Outline your report, using directional development.

8. Writing, it has been said, involves selecting a target and the right arrows to hit the target. Explain the sense of this analogy with regard to business documents.

9. You are member of a student group in your academic department. To assist the department, your group wants to prepare a brochure that can be distributed to high-school seniors. The purpose of the brochure is to attract majors into the department. Outline the contents of the brochure.

10. A group of junior high students is intrigued with college students and wants to know about the typical day in the life of a collegian. Outline two presentations—one using the chronological scheme and the other using the geographical scheme.

11. You think your company should co-sponsor a rock music festival. Create two outlines of how you would present your ideas. One outline should be created for fellow employees, most of them under 35. The other should address senior managers, most of them over 55. Be prepared to discuss differences in the outlines based on readership.

12. Your institution is considering building an addition to the student center. You have studied the situation and think that the addition (which would primarily add recreational facilities like bowling, pool, and electronic games) is needed. Prepare an outline of a report that could be presented at a meeting of the student senate.
    (a) Prepare the first outline in an inductive manner.
    (b) Prepare the second outline in a deductive manner.

13. Find a display advertisement (a long ad, often boxed) in a newspaper or magazine. Read the ad with care. Develop an outline of the basic ideas, in their order of appearance. Write a brief critique of the success or failure of the advertisement in following a consistent topic design. Can you find a persuasive thread of argument through the entire ad? Where does it stray from that path? Submit the ad and completed assignment to your instructor.

14. Here are bits and pieces of an outline. Place them in a logical, persuasive order that you are willing to explain and defend. Rephrase any headings that seem clumsy or unclear.

    What Has Been Done to Date
    Recommendations
    Budgetary Considerations
    Definition of the Problem
    Conclusion
    We Should Analyze the Causes of the Problem
    Alternatives Need to be Examined

15. Identify a problem or situation that you understand well but that other members of your class will generally know little about.

    (a) Identify the problem.
    (b) Develop an outline that proceeds from the simple to the complex.

16. The following is an outline concerning the development of an employee communication program at a large corporation. The outline is not in parallel form. Shape it up!

I. The Need for Improved Employee Communications
   a. Our employees do not know their employer
   b. Progressive companies keep employees informed
II. Information = Productivity
   a. Knowledgeable employees work harder
   b. Pride and productivity
III. A Plan to Upgrade Our Employee Communication Efforts
   a. Bulletin boards will help
   b. Newspaper
   c. Meetings

17. Your instructor will assign one of the articles in the Readings section of this book. Draw up an outline of the article and submit it along with your brief evaluation of the organization of the article.

18. Select two students to work with and agree on a research topic. Below are suggested topics:

    Why the present U.S. health care system is unsound
    Why the term in office of elected officials should be (should not be) limited
    Why the cost of public higher education should (should not) be reduced

    Independently, make up a cluster with the chosen topic in the center and major and minor topics clustered around the center. Designate those that you consider most important with *I*, the next most important with an *A*, and the remaining topics (third in importance) with an *a*.

    Now come together as a group and critique each other's clusters as to the relevancy to the major topic of all subpoints listed as well as the logic of the level of importance assigned.

19. Select one of the three cluster outlines developed by your team for question 18 and convert it into a storyboard. In your storyboard arrangement be sure to include rough sketches for all illustrations, charts, tables, and graphs.

20. Using the storyboard your team created in question 19, give an oral presentation (as a team) on the topic selected.

21. Make up a new team of four students and do a collaborative thinking exercise on two of the following topics or two of your choice:

    Why business students need (do not need) liberal arts courses
    A solution to the illiteracy problem in the United States
    Why the United States should (should not) make a major financial commitment to the former Soviet republics
    How you can guard against information overload

SUGGESTED RESOURCES

Bailey, Edward P. *The Plain English Approach to Business Writing.* New York: Oxford University Press, 1990.

Boyd, D.R. et al. "Getting Your Message Across." *Management World* 17 (July/August 1988): 7–10.

Cross, M. "Aristotle and Business Writing: Why We Need to Teach Persuasion." *Bulletin of the Association for Business Communication* 54
(March 1991). No. 1.

Gilbert, J. "Watch Your Language." *Management Quarterly* 32
(Summer 1991).

Gonring, M. "The Communicator's Role in Leading Corporate Cultural
Change." *Communication World* 9 (February 1992).

Held, V. "Persuasive Business Writing, How to Make it Stick." *Canadian
Manager* 16 (Summer 1991).

Jackson, J., and Hall, B. "Some Ways to Perk-up Your Paperwork." *Supervisory Management* 36 (March 1991).

Larsen, E. "Producing Effective Writing in the Managerial Communication
Course." *Bulletin of the Association for Business Communication* 54
(March 1991).

Mandel, Barrett J. "Business Writing—Without Blood, Sweat, and Tears."
Working Woman (June 1990): 64–67.

Nisbet, M. "Write Right." *Canadian Banker* 98 (May/June 1991): 40–45.

Pollard, C. "Streamlining the Writing Process in Business Communication."
Bulletin of the Association for Business Communication 54 (June 1991).

Shea, G. "When Your Workplace is Divided by a Common Language."
Personnel 68 (July 1991): 14–20.

Suchan, J., and Colucci, R. "The High Cost of Bureaucratic Written Communication." *Business Horizons* 34 (March/April 1991): 68–73.

7

DRAFTING, REVISING, AND EDITING

The most valuable of all talent is that of never using two words when one will do.

—Thomas Jefferson

In this last decade of the twentieth century, managers at all levels need to know how to write fast and well. Many people depend on their clear, complete messaging. Subordinates need to know the whats, whens, hows, and whys of tasks assigned to them. Superiors need to know about progress, projections, and problems. Clients rely on unambiguous assurances, warranties, and guarantees. The public needs to know what the company does and what impact company actions have on social and environmental areas.

Managers owe good writing to their superiors, coworkers, subordinates, and clients.

The messages that answer these needs must often be *written,* in the form of memos, letters, reports, and proposals. No manager, therefore, can ignore his or her writing abilities with the excuse that "I'm great in person and on the phone." Nor can a manager throw together a few thoughts and ask a secretary to act as wordsmith. The reality in modern business is that no company can depend on a secretary to compose, edit, or rewrite messages signed by a manager. Managers today, whether they use a yellow pad or a computer, must be competent to communicate clearly, concisely, and accurately. They are the individuals who set the standard of communication for the organization to the world outside.

WRITING AND EDITING

Managers often act as editors.

Because written messages at all levels are crucial to company operations and image, managers often find themselves in the role of editor for company communications. They are responsible for final approval before a given document goes on to its intended audience. When assistant underwriters in commercial insurance draft letters to clients, for example, the unit manager, reads and approves the letters before they go out. In doing so, they examine the communication in several areas:

- Mission: Has the written communication responded successfully to its task? Have the client's questions been answered, complaints addressed, requests filled, and so forth?

- Company interest: Does the communication reflect well on the company in both form and content? Do all claims and assurances fall within company policy? Is any portion of the communication questionable from a legal or ethical point of view?
- Style: Does the written communication flow in a professional way? Has the writer used vocabulary, format, and sentence and paragraph length in effective and appropriate ways?
- Tone: Does the communication, read from the recipient's point of view, strike an appropriate and helpful tone? Has the writer communicated feelings that fit the occasion and business purpose of the communication?
- Accuracy: Down to the last apostrophe and comma, has the writer taken care to create a literate, careful document that reflects well on the company and assures understanding?

Managers must be able to identify, correct, and explain writing errors to ensure that subordinates meet and maintain company standards.

Busy managers form judgments about written communications evaluated by these standards. Managers can be glad they stopped ineffective and sloppy communications from going forward. But who has the time to rewrite poor communications? Usually not the managers. Yet, to hand the document back to unskilled writers may only recycle the problem. Faced with the "editing crunch," managers must be able to perform three editing functions quickly and accurately:

1. Spot writing problems
2. Make some corrections on the spot
3. Briefly describe errors for correction so that subordinates don't make the same errors over and over

The manager's writing abilities sets the example for subordinates.

Creating and maintaining high standards for written communication in the workplace is hard work on the part of the manager. But the effort is well repaid as subordinates begin to practice the same standards set by the manager. The alternative, simply letting poor writing go forward, backfires eventually on the bottom line, as clients, stockholders, and the public lose faith in a company that can't communicate accurately and clearly.

THE IMPORTANCE OF TONE

Effective written communications succeed in both rational and emotional ways. Skilled business writers convey and arouse feelings as well as communicate facts and ideas. We have all received written messages that sounded aloof, indifferent, or somewhat hostile. For example, an author whose book had sold well for a publisher for more than a decade finally received notice that the book would not be reprinted. The letter began, "Your book has failed to achieve the level of sales necessary for reprinting. . . ."

A thoughtless or insulting tone can damage business irreparably.

Errors in tone are often more serious than surface error, such as misspelling or an error in punctuation. An unattractive tone communicates an attitude that can undercut business relationships. In many cases, the tone communicated in a document is not intended by the writer. But that's precisely the point: writers must be in control of the tone they convey in the same way that they control the form and content of the document. Notice the difference in tone, for example, if the publisher's letter to the author had begun as follows: "Sales of your popular book have finally begun to wane to the point of no appreciable return for you or our company. You can, therefore, appreciate why a new reprint will not be published."

In the following sentences from a poorly written memo, you can feel the sarcasm between the lines—sarcasm that will undercut the message of the memo and the relationship between the sender and receiver.

AN UNNECESSARILY SARCASTIC TONE

I received your request for a personal leave day—your second in the last 60 days. It's always surprising to me how requests for personal days coincide with the opening of the fishing season. But I'll take you at your word that you need this day "for pressing personal matters." Your request is granted.

Far from feeling any gratitude for the day off, the reader of this message has every reason to feel personally insulted, The communication would have been much better if the writer had been more in control of feelings conveyed and aroused.

REVISION

I'm granting your request for a day of personal leave. Although the company doesn't want to pry into personal affairs, we appreciate as specific a reason as possible in requests for such leaves. Your cooperation helps us plan work loads and schedules for the good of all.

In both cases, the employee has been notified that a vague request for personal leave won't do in the future. But what a difference! The first communication left the reader angry, insulted, and demotivated for company tasks. The second memo has a much better chance of winning the employee's cooperation and loyalty.

THE WRITER'S JOB

One of the greatest hidden costs of business is *writer's block*—those agonizing periods when words just won't come. Based on an approximate hourly rate of $50 for managerial time, writer's block cost businesses literally millions of dollars in lost productivity each year.

Avoid costly writer's block by first carefully planning and then freely plunging into the writing task.

Why is writing so difficult at times? Motivated by friendship, most of us can generate personal letters very quickly. Motivated by anger, we can dash off complaints with equal speed. But faced with an extended letter, memo, report, or proposal to write, we may dawdle for minutes, hours, even days. In doing so, we consciously or unconsciously accept three mistaken myths about business writing:

1. The Just-Begin Myth: Business documents don't unfold top down like steps on a ladder. Don't begin by trying to write the first sentence, then the next, and so forth. Instead, plan your entire communication (see Chapter 6) before beginning the first draft.
2. The Easier-Tomorrow Myth: If writing is viewed as inspiration (which it's not), tomorrow always seems preferable to today for making a start. Recognize that whatever holds you back today will probably hold you back tomorrow. Make a start even if you don't feel like it.

3. The More-Research Myth: Reading what others have written is always a convenient retreat from the hard work of writing. Research, of course, can be crucial to the success of your argument. But don't allow the research activity to be an escape from your own production efforts.

Chapter 6 described a step-by-step method for identifying the problem, determining your purpose, limiting your topic, analyzing your audience, and outlining your material. Those steps are not simply preparation for writing but part of the writing process itself. If you view those first steps as part of the process you will be less tempted to skip over the planning work for the "real" writing that takes place in drafting. You will also avoid the pain of writer's block; by planning you've chosen a target and know which arrows to use to hit it.

THE FIRST DRAFT

Using your outline as a blueprint, draft your document. Then edit, revise, and rewrite as you work toward the final version.

Write your first draft rapidly. "Mistakes" can be repaired easily in the editing and revising stage of the writing process.

In a *first draft,* most of us do not say precisely and clearly what we mean, but there is a simple system you can use to achieve that final well-written communication. First, develop a satisfactory outline. Refer to it as you write a first draft. Then edit, revise, and rewrite until you are satisfied that your document says just what you mean it to say in the manner in which you mean to say it.

After you have gathered all the material, tabulated and interpreted the data, carefully checked the outline, and are confident that the document will achieve the stated purpose, you are ready to begin to write.

Write as rapidly as possible. The purpose at this stage is to get the thrust of your ideas on paper. Never mind the somewhat awkward sentence, the word that doesn't quite fit the situation, the obvious repetition, and the wordy paragraph. You will take care of these problems in the editing process. The most important step now is to make thoughts concrete by documenting them.

This stage should proceed rapidly, because you have finished the research, done your outline, and are familiar with the material. The detailed and logical outline serves as a guide, and you have filled cards with vital information waiting to be turned into sentences. All you need to do now is to write the first draft from the materials at hand.

EDITING AND REVISING

Revision is the most important and the most time-consuming stage of the writing process.

A primary purpose of an expository document is to present data, discussions, descriptions, conclusions, and recommendations as clearly and as accurately as possible. Faulty sentence structure, confusion in ideas, negligence in word choice, or any other carelessness in presentation that impedes the free flow of ideas should be corrected during the editing process.

People who have not done a great deal of writing may be somewhat surprised at how much work there is to do after completing the first draft. That first draft, as a matter of fact, is just the beginning. The serious job of rewriting must now be undertaken.

Sometime sentences must be completely reworked, paragraphs thoroughly revised, and entire sections reorganized. Many successful contemporary authors attest to the fact that the major portion of their time is spent not on the original composition, but in revising and rewriting (again and again) the initial draft (see "Editing Suggestions" later in this chapter).

One traditional roadblock to effective revision is the sensitive matter of disturbing a clean typed page. Many of us have the understandable, if unfortu-

Word processing makes revising easier.

nate, tendency to allow slipshod writing to remain uncorrected once it is typed. But word processing has removed that roadblock to revision. Using software such as WordPerfect, WordStar, MultiMate, or Microsoft Word, a business writer can easily change words, sentences, and whole paragraphs and pages without having to retype every word. In one popular system, for example, pressing two keys reformats a document from single spaced to double or triple spaced—certainly an improvement over complete retyping. When the document appears on the screen as the writer wishes it to look, it can be saved (i.e., stored) on a computer disk and printed out.

At the drafting stage, writers must not cling too tenaciously to each and every word, as if dealing with sacred script. Many of those words—whole paragraphs and pages at times—will have to be cut in the revision process. It is perhaps best to look at the rough draft as a jeweler looks at a diamond in the rough. Much will be cut away and polished before the intended gem emerges.

THE PARTS OF THE WHOLE

To communicate your ideas successfully, choose and arrange your word, sentences, and paragraphs properly.

When we communicate, we attempt to transmit ideas. We select words, order them into sentences, and connect the sentences to build paragraphs. The way we handle those three elements—words, sentences, and paragraphs—largely determines how effective we are in making ourselves understandable to others.

WORDS

It is estimated that the English language has well over half a million words in all their various forms. Many are compound words or words borrowed from other languages. Other entirely new words come from advances in the sciences, changes in the world of recreation, and the effects of unusual events, such as war.

Some words are suited for communicating ideas on a golf course, while others are preferable at a technical conference devoted to the use of transistors in new electronic components. Different levels of words, like different styles of dress, fit specific situations. You would not wear formal clothes to a baseball game or a T-shirt and slacks to a wedding. Similarly, you would not ordinarily use slang and jargon in an article for the *Harvard Business Review* or highly complex technical terms to explain lasers to third-graders.

Correct usage. If they are to communicate ideas effectively, words must be used carefully and correctly. There are two categories of commonly misused words: those that sound alike but have different meanings and those that are somewhat similar in sound or have the same root (see Appendix A).

Misspellings and incorrect word choices reflect a lack or professionalism.

Words that sound alike but are spelled differently and have different meanings (homonyms) are common in English: *where, wear, ware; bare, bare; would, wood; principle, principal;* and many others. Most people know what these words mean; the difficulty comes in spelling them. If, in a business letter, you write *principle* when you mean *principal,* the recipient will figure out what you mean, but he or she may feel that you are careless in communication and perhaps equally careless in how you handle an order or request.

Examples of the second group of misused words also abound: *uninterested, disinterested; imply, infer; credible, creditable; incredible, incredulous.* Judges should be *disinterested* in the cases being tried before them but surely not *unin-*

CULTURAL DIVERSITY IN COMMUNICATION

Revising Writing to Include Both Genders

Carol Shuherk
University of Southern California

The resurgence of the women's movement in the United States during the 1970s brought with it, for the first time, a focus on communication as it relates to gender. Sexist language, that which precasts men or women into roles based on sex alone, became a target for those seeking to bring equality to the ways we talk about the place of women and men in society.

How important is it to use nonsexist language? At the center of the debate is the traditional use of "man" terms, such as *mankind* and *modern man,* or male pronouns, *he* and *his,* to refer to both men and women when specific identity is unknown or if referring to people in general.

Those who argue for maintaining the current system claim that the traditional use of *he* and *man* to denote both sexes is widely understood and accepted to include both. They point out the clumsiness of using nonsexist language such as *congressperson* or the dual pronouns, *he or she.*

Those arguing for change cite studies showing that when male terms are used, listeners do not think of both men and women, but of men only. Furthermore, even if we accepted the claim that one term can adequately represent both sexes, taking it to its logical conclusion would prove female pronouns to be most appropriate because each—*she,female*—and *woman*—denotes one sex while literally including the other.

Converting to nonsexist communication, they say, will not produce awkward sentences if communicators select words thoughtfully. *Legislator, senator,* or *representative* can replace *congressman,* for example, as opposed to the awkward *congressperson.* In any case, the traditional use of male terms, particularly at work, no longer reflects reality. With women widely represented in business, in government, and in the military, speak-

ing or writing as if all were males renders the communicator inaccurate.

From a communication perspective, the basic rule that persuasion rests on audience analysis implies that a writer should know at least enough to be accurate about the sex of the reader. A business letter using the salutation "Dear Sir," when the intended recipient is a woman, is bound to have less impact than one that gets the gender right or is written to include both. Instead of the blanket "Dear Sir," business writers can find out the gender of the letter's recipient, and if that's not possible, use the dual salutation, "Dear Sir or Ms." or more simply, address the position: "Dear Staff Member," "Dear Sales Manager, " "Dear Search Committee Member," and so forth. All allow for the possibility that the designated reader may be a man or a woman.

To revise business writing so that it is accurate and inclusive of those being addressed or discussed, one general rule applies: Remove sexist expression while maintaining word patterns familiar to the reader. The most common and easy to revise expressions of sexism are found in pronouns and noun modifiers. The following guidelines suggest ways to get around them.

PRONOUNS

1. Use plurals
   INSTEAD OF: An accounting manager needs to update his staff annually on tax law.
   TRY: Accounting managers need to update their staff annually on tax law.
2. Use a variety of pronouns to avoid overuse of *he* or *she/his* or *her.*
   INSTEAD OF: Each programmer is responsible for his area. He reports to the information systems manager.

TRY: Each programmer is responsible for his or her area. This person reports to the information systems manager.

3. Use the second person *you* in place of the third person *he* where appropriate.

INSTEAD OF: A staff member should return his calls within 24 hours.

TRY: As a staff member, you should return all calls within 24 hours.

4. Revise to omit pronouns altogether or replace them with words like *the, a,* or *an*.

INSTEAD OF: The average employee prefers to receive his paycheck biweekly.

TRY: The average employee prefers a biweekly paycheck.

INSTEAD OF: Every collection agent signs her calls-placed sheet at day's end.

TRY: Every collection agent signs the calls-placed sheet at day's end.

NOUN MODIFIERS

Sexist noun modifiers cast the name of something as either male or female. This happens through use of gender-based word endings, occupational titles, and adjectives.

Word Endings

In the case of sex-based word endings, one term really will do to include both men and women as members of a particular area of endeavor. For each of the following terms, dictionary definitions are nonsexist, as in "Poet: one who writes poetry." To reserve the official definition's term for men while creating a subterm for women subtly suggests that the "real" doers of the activity are males.

Not	But
Poetess	Poet
Directress	Director
Actress	Actor
Executrix	Executor
Comedienne	Comedian

Occupational Titles

The use of the word *man* within certain professional titles implies that all who pursue those occupations are male. Some thought is require to convert them to titles that are inclusive.

Not	But
Policeman	Police officer
Fireman	Fire fighter
Mailman	Mail carrier
Men at work	Crew at work
Congressman	Legislator/ Senator/ Representative
Bellboy	Baggage handler
Stewardess/steward	Flight attendant

Adjectives

Adjectives become sexist when they are used to indicate the sex of the person in a particular profession. They can simply be dropped.

Not	But
Lady lawyer	Lawyer
Woman driver	Driver
Male hairstylist	Hairstylist
Woman superstar	Superstar

If revising for nonsexist language strikes you as tampering with the rules of English grammar and usage, keep in mind the concept that modern English is a living language; that is, it continually evolves to correspond to the changes in modern society. Even though the presence of English grammar handbooks and English language dictionaries suggests a fixed language system and a final authority on word usage, in fact, these books reflect rather than drive what is a dynamic and responsive human process. Multiple editions and revised versions are testimony to our language's ongoing adaptation!

terested. When I am speaking, I *imply* something; when you are listening, you *infer* something.

The writer or speaker who uses *disinterested* when *uninterested* is meant or *healthy* when *healthful* is meant not only lessens the exactness of the statement but also confuses the reader or listener and, in the long run, helps corrupt and weaken our language.

The carpenter who uses a screwdriver when a chisel is required will probably produce a less-than-perfect cabinet; when we use second-rate words (our tools), the ideas that we advance have less impact because they are not expressed as they should be.

A word's denotation is its literal definition; its connotation conveys emotional meaning.

Accuracy and precision.   Words have two distinct traits: they denote and connote. The *denotation* of a word is its factual meaning or definition. Its *connotation,* on the other hand, is the sum of thoughts and emotions it arouses or contains.

A word may have several denotations. The word *vessel,* for example, may refer to a component of the body's circulatory system, a container for liquids, or a waterborne vehicle. As a noun, *rest,* may mean repose, something used for support, a pause in music, or the remainder. Yet, there is little chance of confusion among these meanings; the context will make obvious which denotation the writer intended.

It is the connotations of words that create difficulties in communication. Everybody knows what *soldier* means; but consider the different emotions the word arouses in someone who has been recognized as a war hero and an individual who is a conscientious objector. What different feeling do you have about the words *fat, obese, roly-poly,* and *plump?* All have the same denotation. Makers of a diet food would never say it makes you *skinny;* they say it makes you *slim* or *slender.* Do you want a bar of soap that has a *smell,* a *scent,* a *perfume,* an *aroma,* or an *odor?* They all have the same denotation, but different connotations. The picture we wish to paint can be conveyed very accurately with the words we choose for our colors.

Knowing your reader helps you avoid bad connotations.

Attention to connotation is of primary importance in business communication. We have already seen its significance in advertising— and business letters and reports are a form of advertising—for yourself and your firm. Your letter is your image to the recipient. If it creates unpleasant feelings, it may be worse than no letter at all.

Remember *who* your readers or listeners are, and choose your words in light of their feelings, their educational level, their social status, and their needs.

SENTENCES

Writing that is clear and concise motivates and persuades others. Such writing is based on sentences that are well structured and cogent. In some material we read, sentences seem to flow into one another smoothly and effortlessly. Other material we must read and reread, for the prose seems choppy, difficult, and awkward.

Take a moment to consider that curious ability you have to feel the ebb and flow of pleasing writing. Where did you get it? Certainly not in formal classes on prose rhythm. Like a surfer on a wave, you have the ability to feel and flow along with the rise and fall of words, phrases, and sentences. You know when writing sounds abrupt and juvenile or long-winded and pedantic.

But *how* do you know? If English is your native language, you've trained your ear to the rhythms of English since you first learned to speak. That training became refined through your reading over the years and now is one of your best allies when it comes to writing. Even before you find the exact words, you have a feel for approximately how the next few words, phrases, or even sentences should go.

What factors contribute to a writer's style? How does the writer form sentences that flow rather than stumble? There are, of course, no simple answers, but there are some directions you can follow. To begin, you should be familiar with sentence structure and classification.

Make appropriate use of all sentence types: the declarative, interrogative, imperative, and exclamatory.

Types of sentences.   There are four primary kinds of sentences. The most common is the *declarative,* which is a positive or negative assertion. Other kinds are the *interrogative,* which asks a question; the *imperative,* which expresses a command or a wish; and the *exclamatory,* which ends with an exclamation point. All begin with a capital letter, end with the appropriate punctuation, and usually contain a subject and a verb.

Sentences may be simple, compound, complex, or compound-complex.

Sentences may be formed in several ways. A simple sentence consists of one independent clause; a compound sentence consists of two or more independent clauses. A complex sentence is composed of one independent and one or more subordinate clauses; and a compound-complex sentence is made up of two or more independent clauses and at least one subordinate clause.

Varying sentence structures makes for a lively style.

Variety of sentence structure.   One way to achieve interesting and clear writing is to vary sentence structure. Paragraphs composed entirely of compound sentences are monotonous and boring. Paragraphs constructed only of simply sentences are choppy and lacking in grace; however, the judicious use of a simple sentence can give writing force and impact. Complex sentences, because they are made up of independent and dependent clauses, clarify meaning and make for easier reading. Compound-complex sentences have inherent variety and bring vitality and interest to writing.

For variety within a sentence, use an occasional command, exhortation, exclamation, or question to replace the usual declarative sentence. Or why not modify the usual subject-verb sequence? Begin a sentence with a phrase or subordinate clause to give the details that lead in to the main idea of the independent clause.

Notice the differences in the examples that follow. Compare the abruptness and unnecessary overlapping of the simple sentences, and the monotony of the compound sentences, with the smoothness and variety of the sentences in the third example.

SIMPLE SENTENCES
Management in any large corporation depends on information. This information comes from many departments within a company. Sales, credit, production, research, advertising, and other departments forward information. This information is sent up to management. Often this information is in the form of reports. Each department presents information in these reports. The content of these reports must be accurate and complete. This is necessary because managers make decisions based on the content. Obviously they cannot make decisions if the reports do not contain adequate substantiating data. These data are usually statistical.

COMPOUND SENTENCES

Management in any large corporation depends on information, and this information comes from many departments within the company. Sales, credit, production, research, advertising, and other departments forward information, and this information is then sent up to management. Often this information is in the form of reports, and each department gathers this information. The content of these reports must be accurate and complete, and this is necessary because managers make decisions based on the content. Obviously, they cannot make decisions if the reports do not contain adequate substantiating data, and these data are usually statistical.

VARIETY OF SENTENCE TYPES

Management in any large corporation depends on the information it receives from the sales, credit, production, research, advertising and other departments. This information, which is sent up to management, is usually in the form of reports. The substantiating data (usually statistical) in these reports must be accurate and complete, for managers make decisions based on the facts provided.

Always write down your ideas freely; you can improve them later.

Revising sentences.   The best way to write, as the maxim goes, is to write. Let the sentences flow from your mind to the paper (or the computer). After you have written down a complete block of ideas, go back and revise the awkward and wordy sentences. As you become more critical of your own writing and more adept at revising sentences, you will find that your ability will improve steadily.

The following examples demonstrate what you can do when you make a serious attempt to edit and revise.

	FAULTY SENTENCE STRUCTURE	IMPROVED
Awkward complex sentence with two subjects; unclear reference (the word it*)*	Joe worked in his dad's store while attending school, and although he majored in management, I don't think he liked it.	Joe worked in his dad's store while attending school. He majored in management, but I don't think he liked the field.
Ambiguous reference	To fly efficiently, the pilot should check the plane after every flight.	If the plane is to fly efficiently, the pilot should check it after every flight.
Dangling modifier	Arriving home late, dinner was started immediately.	Because we arrived home late, we prepared dinner immediately.
Fragment; wordy; dangling modifier	Running down the sidewalk near the hospital which was a new modern building built to handle children's cases.	Maria ran down the sidewalk adjacent to the new children's hospital.
Sentence fragment	When I first started to play tennis with John, I found that my serve was quite good. Although I had not played for six years.	When I first started to play tennis with John, I found that my serve was quite good, even though I had not played for six years.

Wordy; run-on sentence	When I write a report, I find that it requires a good deal of concentrated effort and work, this is, as I think of it, necessary when I do any type of writing.	I find that a report, or any type of writing, requires a good deal of concentrated effort.
Wordy; lack of parallel construction	The annual report serves, by and large, two very important purposes today and the first of which is the presentation of financial information to stockholders and the second is to build company public relations in the business community at large.	The annual report serves two primary functions: the presentation of financial data to stockholders and the building of company public relations in the business community.
Wordy; hackneyed phrases	You will find enclosed, as per your basic request, the report which we have taken the liberty of forwarding to you.	The report that you requested is enclosed.

By reading your prose aloud, you can quickly identify awkward sentences in need of revision or replacement.

The experienced editor often evaluates a sentence by reading it aloud and listening. If it sounds awkward to the ear, it should probably be revised. Many people, when revising an awkward sentence, scratch out a word here and move a phrase there. The usual result of such minor surgery is some improvement but not a complete recovery. More often drastic surgery is necessary: delete the sentence and begin again.

Start sentences with important words.

Another valuable editing technique involves the first few words in each sentence. Are they important words that attract the reader, or are they mere fillers (e.g., "There is . . ." and "In the opinion of . . .")? Just as advertisers put product names first in slogans ("Coke is it!"), so business writers should put the words they care most about in the most prominent position of the sentence.

Search for the right word.

Yet another technique is to use the dictionary and thesaurus constantly; don't be satisfied with the almost-right word. Search until you find the word that conveys your intended thought precisely and gives your sentence the rhythm and tone you desire.

PARAGRAPHS

Each paragraph develops a single idea.

A paragraph is a group of related sentences. Each paragraph, though joined to the one before and the one following, develops an individual idea, whether or not that idea is explicitly stated. Thus, carefully constructed paragraphs serve the double purpose of joining and separating.

The expository paragraph provides information about the topic.

The *expository* paragraph tells about the topic. It is linked at top and bottom with other paragraphs, but it develops, explains, illustrates, or supports a particular point. It can do so by example, by definition of terms, by contrast and comparison, by analysis, by classification, or by narration.

The transitional paragraph directs the reader through the discourse.

The *transitional,* on the other hand, helps the reader follow from one thought to the next. "This is where we have been; that is where we're going."

When you rewrite a paper, be sure not only to choose the right words and put those words together into clear sentences, but to combine those sentences into logical, useful paragraphs.

Long paragraphs may prove too cumbersome to read, and short paragraphs may appear unorganized and choppy.

Be aware that readers judge your paragraphs at a glance, before they begin to read your actual words. Paragraphs that look huge and heavy on the page proclaim to the reader, "Hard work ahead! You're really going to have to plow through all these words to find meaning." Therefore, build in at-a-glance appeal when constructing paragraphs.

Can paragraphs be too short?

Yes, as these paragraphs are intended to show.

CRITICAL THINKING CONCEPTS

Perhaps the single greatest problem in business communication is this: what seems perfectly clear to the writer or speaker appears perfectly foggy to the audience. For example, read the following three sentences:

The company has lost two major government contracts.
The company must invest in marketing campaigns to attract new business.
The company will furlough 10 percent of its work force.

The writer may intend the first sentence as the *cause* for the second sentence. Furthermore, the writer may intend the first two sentences as the *cause* for the third sentence. But that intention exists only in the writer's mind, not in the words themselves. To the reader, these statements each stand on their own without apparent connection. The writer has failed to supply the logical links, or transitions, necessary for complete communication. By supplying logical transitions, the writer clarifies the intent:

Because the company has lost two major government contracts, it must invest heavily in marketing campaigns to attract new business. Until revenues increase, the company will furlough 10 percent of its work force.

Notice that logical transitions can be provided with a single word—*because, therefore, consequently,* and others—or a phrase, such as "until revenues increase." Professional business writers and speakers use such links to make sure the audience grasps the intended connection between separate thoughts.

1. Arrange the following statements in logical order. Then supply the logical transitions to make that order clear. Reword your final version as necessary for coherence.
   a. Male pattern baldness can be reversed by Hirsute Shampoo.
   b. Many men experience male pattern baldness.
   c. Loss of hair can cause anxiety and embarrassment for many men.
   d. Hirsute Shampoo should prove popular as a retail item.
2. For each of the following statements, use logical transition words (such as *consequently, therefore,* or *as a result*) to begin a second statement that stands in clear logical relation to the first.
   a. Only a small percentage of books published each year appear in retail bookstores.
   b. Much of the U.S. harvest of redwood is sold to the Japanese.
   c. More import cars than domestic cars were sold in the United States last year.

Do you notice that the eye and mind weary of putting together such disconnected pieces into one pattern of meaning?

Too many short, consecutive paragraphs can strike the reader as jumbled pieces of a puzzle. The reader may resent the fact that the writer never took time to put the pieces together.

QUALITIES OF WRITING STYLE

In a discussion of writing style, most authorities list the three standard qualities of rhetoric: *unity, coherence,* and *emphasis.* There are others, however, that deserve more than a passing glance: consideration for the reader, imagination, clarity, liveliness, and grace.

Style reflects personality.

A writer's style makes a work unique. One author's work may be lively, while others' may be dull, persuasive, or consistently entertaining. These qualities come from the heart of the composition and make up the rather indefinable quality labeled *style.*

Every business communication should have an effective style. Of course, few of us will approach the excitement of Hemingway, the cleverness of Agatha Christie, the intrigue of Edgar Allen Poe, the insight of Shakespeare, or the precision of Churchill. On the other hand, the writing need not be as dull as an inventory form or as uninspired as a page of stock quotations.

UNITY AND COHERENCE

Every paragraph should develop an idea; a group of paragraphs should move a single topic forward; and the sections of the communication should all contribute to the development of the specific topic with which the message is concerned.

In a unified paper, each separate idea supports or illustrates the main idea.

Irrelevant details not directly related to the core idea must be eliminated. Determine if the communication possesses this quality of "oneness" or unity. Each sentence, each paragraph, each section must march forward toward the objective you hope to achieve. If it does not, strike it out.

Coherence is the quality that connects ideas logically so that they can be read as a single, unified text.

Coherence results from ideas that are logically interconnected; ideas follow one another smoothly and are clear and easily comprehended. When transitional words, phrases, and sentences connect sentences and paragraphs, the whole body of material seems to move interestingly and coherently from one idea to another. Thoughts are not isolated but related to one another, and together they proceed logically toward a specific conclusion.

COURTESY AND CONSIDERATION

In any kind of communication, oral or written, business or personal, one of the prime requisites is consideration for the recipient. Courtesy and consideration require sensitivity and a little care.

Business communication involves more than common courtesy. Discourtesy or thoughtlessness might cause the loss of a good customer or a large sale. It might contribute to loss of prestige and status. It would almost surely mean a lessening of respect for and approval of you and your company.

Courteous writers consider their reader's needs before their own.

Consideration involves knowing your readers. If you know who they are, what they want, and why they want it, you can even refuse them without offending. Remember to write in terms of "you" rather than "I." Customers are interested in *their* requests or complaints, and you must be too.

The second ingredient for a courteous business letter or memo is "Please," "thank you," "I'm sorry," "I'm delighted." Liberal—but not excessive—use of these words will tell your reader you are polite and you care about them.

Interestingly, every significant study of electronic mail concludes that writers pour more personality, not less, into this new communication convenience. Perhaps because electronic mail robs us of the pleasantries of attractive letterhead, sharp type fonts, and flashy signatures, we attempt to compensate by including more personal warmth through our choice of words.

Skilled business writers know the value of person-to-person emotional contact. Communication may happen faster in the years ahead, but there is no sign that sincere human warmth has ceased to be important in the electronic revolution.

Choose words that your reader will understand.

The third ingredient in consideration goes back to knowing your readers. Use words and phrases and ideas that are on their level. If you talk over their heads, they will feel unhappy, insecure, and inferior. Arousing such feelings is no way to gain acceptance. If you talk beneath them, they will be insulted.

EMPHASIS

In some sections of a document, you may wish to motivate your reader to take specific action, or perhaps you may wish to focus attention on a particular section. You can reach these goals by using emphasis.

Emphasize an important idea . . . by giving it more space than other points

You can emphasize through a variety of methods. The method of *proportion* involves giving more space to a key point than to items of less importance. If you spend four pages discussing sales and only half a page on credit, production, and research, you will focus the reader's attention on sales.

Emphasis helps satisfy the reader's hunger for your point. Particularly in the middle of a hectic business day, your reader has no desire to wander through paragraphs in search of a key idea. Use every technique at your disposal, including choice of words, placement on the page, headings, and type style to make your point in an obvious way.

. . . by repeating it

Repetition of facts, ideas or words also helps. You may discuss an idea in the paper, present it factually in a table, and comment on it again in a further analysis.

. . . by placing it first

The thoughtful *placement* of ideas within the body of the writing can secure emphasis. Statements made in the early portion of the presentation, or at the beginning of a section, often receive special attention.

. . . by expressing it with attention-getting words

Attention-catching words or phrases highlight ideas. The use of dramatic words or alliterative phrases need not be limited to advertising writing: they can be used effectively in expository writing as well.

. . . by using attractive type fonts and visual devices

The use of *mechanical methods* has some value when you wish to emphasize a particular point: capitalizing words, underscoring phrases, using colored inks, or inserting cartoons, sketches, and photographs. In addition, an idea or thought can be set off by itself with a dramatic amount of white space around it.

Perhaps the most effective way to emphasize a point is through *excellent writing.* Your writing should be so effective, so clear, so persuasive that the reader will remember the ideas because of the quality of the writing and not just because of capitalized phrases or underscored ideas.

Martin Luther King, Jr., in his excellent and moving speech, "I Have a Dream," used repetition and word choice to emphasize:

I have a dream that one day this nation will rise up and live out the true meaning of its creed: 'We hold these truths to be self-evident; that all men are created equal.'

Frequent repetition of "I have a dream" impresses the phrases on readers or listeners.

I have a dream that one day on the red hills of Georgia the sons of former slaves and the sons of former slaveowners will . . .

I have a dream that one day even the state of Mississippi . . .

I have a dream that my four little children . . .

I have a dream that one day the state of Alabama . . .

I have a dream that every valley shall be exalted, every hill and mountain shall be made low . . .

In the conclusion of the same speech, King emphasized not only through repetition and word choice but also in the very rhythm of the phrases he selected:

The same principle of repetition is used with "Let freedom ring."

So let freedom ring from the prodigious hilltops of New Hampshire. Let freedom ring from the mighty mountains of New York. Let freedom ring from the heightening Alleghenies of Pennsylvania!

Let freedom ring from the snowcapped Rockies of Colorado!

Let freedom ring from the curvaceous peaks of California!

. . . let freedom ring from Stone Mountain of Georgia!

Let freedom ring from Lookout Mountain in Tennessee!

Let freedom ring from every hill and mole hill of Mississippi. From every mountainside, let freedom ring!

Notice the internal rhythm in the words selected.

When we let freedom ring, when we let it ring from every village and every hamlet, from every state and every city, we will be able to speed up that day when all God's children, black men and white men, Jews and Gentiles, Protestants and Catholics, will be able to join hands and sing in the words of the Negro spiritual, 'Free at last! Free at last! Thank God almighty, we are free at last!'[1]

Emphasis, as noted, can be accomplished in many different ways. Sometimes a word will do; at other times, humor is effective in making a statement memorable:

The word crush is so unusual in this context that it makes the statement emphatic.

I don't meet competition, I crush it.

—Charles Revson

Middle age is when your classmates are so grey and wrinkled and bald they don't recognize you.

—Bennett Cerf

Middle age is when you're sitting at home on Saturday night and the telephone rings and you hope it isn't for you.

—Ogden Nash

By far, the best way to emphasize ideas is through excellent writing.

Accomplishing emphasis through good writing is not easy. It requires analysis, time, and constant reference to the dictionary and thesaurus. But it is worth the effort, for effective writing makes an indelible impression in the reader's mind. The audience may recall a well-written statement for years, while they may forget an underlined sentence in a few minutes.

IMAGINATION

Imaginative writers view situations from their reader's point of view and never settle for second-best words.

Imagination is also important is business writing. Achieving it requires a sensitivity to words and a desire to find the exact words and combinations of words to impart not only facts but feelings. Prose that is a pleasure to read—emphatic phrases, clear and concise statements, ideas imaginatively presented—is more likely to achieve its purpose than writing that is dull, awkward, or pompous.

Writers with *imagination* not only put themselves in the place of the reader, but also look for the word, the analogy, the figure that best expresses what they want to say. They avoid clichés and ambiguities, worn-out similes, and irritating redundancies.

In an essay titled, "Imagination Helps Communication," the Royal Bank of Canada's monthly letter chose Shakespeare as an example of an imaginative writer:

> In 240 words of a single soliloquy of *Hamlet,* Shakespeare gives us these imaginative phrases, now part of our everyday language: to be or not to be, the law's delay, the insolence of office, the undiscover'd country from whose bourne no traveller returns, the slings and arrows of outrageous fortune, . . . there's the rub, shuffled off this mortal coil, conscience makes cowards of us all.[2]

EDITING SUGGESTIONS

Revise your document several times; focus on a new aspect of the discourse with each successive revision.

Review your first draft several times. In each review, focus your attention on a specific aspect of the writing. Step back, so to speak, from the document and determine if every sentence, every paragraph, and every section contributes to the theme and purpose. If any portion, whether a word or a paragraph, is irrelevant or unnecessary, cut it without compunction.

Writers, of course, are not always objective judges of which words should live and which should die in their work. By all means, reach out to colleagues for their *feedback* on your drafted document. Give your work to a friend you trust. Ask him or her to jot a question mark in the margin beside any sentence or paragraph that seems foggy, unnecessary, or misplaced. Then revise and clarify those passages. Your helper may even suggest specific changes.

Then check for *coherence.* Is there good transition between ideas? Do the sentences and paragraphs seem to be logically associated and connected? Do the sections flow easily and smoothly.

What about *clarity?* Does every sentence say precisely what you mean it to say? Do the words have the exact connotations intended? Does this phrase or that clause result in the proper picture in the reader's or listener's mind? No second-choice word or group of words is acceptable here. Use your dictionary or thesaurus to find the exact words—the words that will convey the precise idea, tone, and mood. Take every opportunity to use lively words, similes, metaphors, and other figures of speech that add vitality and color.

Check your *emphasis.* Did you emphasize the appropriate points? Did the methods of emphasis you chose achieve the intended impact?

Examine carefully all *statistical data* in your document. Would the use of charts or graphs make your presentation clearer and easier to read? Tables, charts, diagrams, and other visual aids must be used with restraint, but they are an important tool in communication. (See Chapter 17 for a detailed discussion of visuals and how they may be used most effectively.)

What does a piece of writing look like before and after editing? Figures 7-1 through 7-3 show parts of a report, a memo, and a letter in their first drafts and then after editing.

CRITICAL THINKING CONCEPTS

For all their power to enliven business writing and speaking, metaphor and analogy can also distort meaning when used carelessly. A metaphor is a figure of speech that identifies one thing as if it were another. In so doing, a metaphor attempts to explain the less known thing in terms of the more familiar thing. Consider, for example, the metaphor chosen by an employee who wants to compliment his boss on her strength, smooth manner, and aggressive skill in contract negotiation:

My boss is a shark when it comes to negotiating a contract.

The employee has tried to define the less known thing (the boss) in terms of the more familiar thing (the shark). But in so doing, the employee communicates more than he intends. The metaphor of a shark goes far beyond connotations of strength and skill to include viciousness, rapacity, and amorality. In short, the wrong metaphor has subverted what the employee intended to communicate.

An analogy is an extended metaphor that specifies more points of comparison between the less known thing and the more familiar thing. Analogies, too, must be carefully controlled, lest they distort the message they were intended to clarify. Notice the inadvertent distortion in the following analogy, which was intended by the writer to communicate the company's marketing philosophy.

Our marketing approach is basically a game of shuffleboard. The competition takes its best shot, placing products on the market as advantageously as it can. Then we take aim on those products, knock them out of play, and replace them with our own.

Although this analogy does express some aspects of the company's marketing strategies, it unfortunately connotes a level of leisure activity that movers and pushers in the company will probably find distasteful. Can you imagine a company executive huffing, "Me, a shuffleboard player? That's not how I think of myself at all!"

Business communicators must carefully evaluate their use of metaphors and analogies to guard against unintentional distortion and misimpression. Often, metaphors and analogies express ideas in a vivid, lively way. But used carelessly, they can inadvertently undercut the message intended by the writer or speaker.

1. Discuss the positive and negative impressions aroused by the following metaphors or analogies.
   a. This company plays to win.
   b. Our CEO thinks he's Attila the Hun.
   c. Being a member of our company family means caring for the welfare of each and every one of our new brothers and sisters.
2. Create a metaphor or analogy to express each of the following situations.
   a. Company profits show a sudden decrease.
   b. A supervisor manages in a way that you judge to be harsh and arbitrary.
   c. One of the company's most valuable employees decides to quit.

FIGURE 7–1A Page from a Short Report (Rough Draft in Need of Revision)

WESTERN MANAGEMENT SERVICES, INC.

In addition, I think it would be appropriate here to include some mention of how often employees have been absent during the first half of this year as compared to the first half of last year. (I am assuming the beginning of fiscal year as January 1.)

Overall, absenteeism was lower in some job categories and higher in others, with some categories about the same. For example, managers tended to come to work more often while programmers slipped a bit (though only by a day or two). In my opinion, the improvements we have seen in absenteeism, in those categories where improvement exists, is due to the company's new incentive programs, such as "Pay per Day," which, as you know, provides an extra 15 percent hourly pay for each sick/personal/legal day not taken during the year. Employees generally have responded favorably to this incentive. At least so I've heard in the lunchroom from time to time.

The only problem I can see with the incentive plan is that, at lower levels, that 15 percent really doesn't add up to much for low hourly wage employees, while upper level employees have much more to gain by coming to work as often as possible. We should discuss this and make changes.

The rough draft records a free flow of ideas.

FIGURE 7–1B Page from a Short Report (Revised)

WESTERN MANAGEMENT SERVICES, INC.

III. Absenteeism January 1 through June 30, 19__

At all employment levels, absenteeism dropped significantly (an average of 24 percent) when compared to the same period in 19__. Two employee surveys (summarized in Appendix A) attribute the drop to the company's new "Pay per Day" incentive plan.

By employment category, absenteeism occurred as follows:

	Ave. Days Absent	Ill	Personal	Legal	Misc.
Management I	4	2	1	1	
Management II	7	2	3	2	
Supervisor I	8	4	3	1	
Supervisor II	8	3	4		1
Foreperson	11	5	3	2	1
Group Leader	14	8	4	1	1
Technician	14	6	4	2	2
Programmer	17	11	5	1	

IV. Interpretation of Absenteeism Records

The company's "Pay per Day" incentive program offers proportionately higher incentives for upper management to avoid absenteeism than for rank-and-file employees. As a consequence, the categories of Foreperson through Programmer have shown less improvement (an average increase of only 7 percent) over comparable absenteeism records from 19__. At the Programmer level, in fact, absenteeism has actually been worse in 19__ than in 19__, by an average of 4 percent.

The revised report uses headings and a tables to organize ideas and to improve readability.

FIGURE 7–2A Memo (Rough Draft in Need of Revision)

Apex Reproductions, Inc.

To: Richard Hall
From: Sylvia Leaven
Subject: What have you been telling your clients???
Date: October 9, 19__

Apparently you have been telling your clients that we will give them a loaner copier if theirs breaks down during the warrantee period. This is not true, as you are well aware from your training classes in this company and my memos dated February 2 and March 16, 19__. The policy of this company is not to exceed or in any way elaborate upon the specific contractual provisos drawn up by our legal department and intended to accompany each respective product. This applies to all company personnel, from the president on down. Obviously we have to solve the problem you have created, and I need your input on how to best go about it. It is very important that we meet tomorrow morning.

Written in the heat of the moment, the rough draft might contain an inappropriate show of emotion.

The revised memo exhibits a more reasonable tone.

Apex Reproductions, Inc.

To: Richard Hall
From: Sylvia Leaven
Subject: Policy regarding verbal assurances
Date: October 9, 19__

This morning I spoke with three of your clients. All had purchased the #702 copier through you during the past year (see invoices attached) and all have a common compliant: they say you gave them verbal assurance that the company would provide loaner copiers of their copiers had to undergo warranteed repairs.

I will not prejudge the case by accepting the clients' version of this matter at face value. Let's meet at 9:30 a.m., October 10, in my office to discuss what was and wasn't said. Company policy, as you are aware, strictly prohibits employees at all levels from giving verbal assurances, warranties, or guarantees beyond the specific written language accompanying our products.

FIGURE 7–2B
Memo (Revised)

Please bring your notes and records of these transactions to our meeting. I'm anxious to resolve these misunderstandings quickly.

FIGURE 7–3A Letter (Rough Draft in Need of Revision)

Victor Financial Partners, Inc.
392 Liverpool Avenue
Miami, FL 33123
(305) 555-2839

January 7, 19__

Mr. Juan Gomez
3028 Henderson Drive
Fort Lauderdale, FL 33301

Dear Mr. Gomez:

You called last week to discuss possible investments that stand a good chance of providing significant return on investment, and I recommended a new offering we will have going beginning February 1, 19__, the Medinvest II limited partnership.

It involves buying a magnetic resonance unit and leasing it back to doctors. We think the lease arrangement when added to the tax benefits (see the new tax laws regarding depreciation of medical equipment) can provide a health return. We are putting some of our best clients into this investment because we view it as a "sure thing."

There is some literature enclosed about the investment. I can help you interpret it if you wish. Give me a call and we'll find a time to get together.

Don't delay, though, This investment is "hot."

Sincerely,

Robin J. Matthews

Robin J. Matthews

The rough draft may lack specific information and sound hurried or chatty.

FIGURE 7–3B Letter (Revised)

Victor Financial Partners, Inc.
392 Liverpool Avenue
Miami, FL 33123
(305) 555-2839

January 7, 19__

Mr. Juan Gomez
3028 Henderson Drive
Fort Lauderdale, FL 33301

Dear Mr. Gomez:

Thank you for your inquiry about the Medinvest II limited partnership we will offer beginning February 1, 19__.

As we discussed briefly by telephone, the Medinvest II program will create an investment team of 50 individuals for the acquisition of a General Electric Magnetic Resonance Unit, model #297. The purchase price to the partnership, less cash discount, will be $1.7 million. Medinvest partners will then lease the unit to physician groups in the greater Miami area.

Because of favorable tax treatment given to depreciable medical instruments, the general partner projects an annual return on investment of 24 percent, beginning with Year 2 and continuing through Year 7, at which time a lump sum distribution of additional accumulated capital will be made.

I have enclosed a Medinvest II Prospectus for your review. I would be pleased to discuss its major points with you at your convenience. May I ask you to give me a call when you're ready to meet?

Again, thank you for your interest in what we feel is an excellent investment.

Sincerely,

Robin J. Matthews

Robin J. Matthews
Vice President

The revised letter contains specific, relevant information, maintains a professional tone, and makes no unwarranted promises.

IMPROVING READABILITY

Over the years, various theories have been advanced on how to improve the readability of material. These theories have usually been accompanied by formulas for measuring readability, that is, how much difficulty the average reader has with any given material.

We can combine the advice of several reading theorists (Rudolph Flesch, Robert Gunning, and others) into five simple rules for making your writing more readable.

1. Keep sentences short. This advice does not mean that all sentences should be of the same length. Instead, occasional longer sentences should be balanced by shorter sentences. Overall, your typical sentence should appear attractively short and easy to the reader.
2. Say it simply. Prefer the common, straightforward expression to complex, encyclopedic language.
3. Strip away unnecessary words. Much business writing is padded, wordy, and pompous. Notice that a pared-down sentence is easier to read than an expanded version of the same content:

   DIRECT: *Please provide a remodeling estimate.*
   PADDED: *We would appreciate receiving from you an estimate of the costs we could expect to incur in the process of the remodeling we intend to carry out.*

4. Load your writing with active language. Readers like the strong, easy-to-grasp structure of sentences that include an active verb.

   ACTIVE: *Production dropped sharply.*
   PASSIVE: *A sharp drop in production was noted.*

5. Write to express, not impress. Egotism is always recognized for what it is. Throw out any long words, jargon, or pompous phrases that were included simply to impress the reader. Base your message on truthful, expressive language that gets right to the point.

Most of us have a good sense of when reading is easy and when it is difficult. Formulas also have been developed to determine the relative readability of a document. One popular formula is the Gunning Fog Index; it measures readability by the following computation:

- Find the average number of words per sentence. Use a sample of at least 100 words. Divide the total number of words by the number of sentences. This gives you average sentence length.
- Count the number of words of three syllables or more per 100 words. Don't count words that are capitalized, combinations of short easy words like *bookkeeper;* verbs that are made three syllables by adding *ed* or *es* (*created* or *trespasses*)

- Add the two factors and multiply by 0.4. This will give you the Fog Index. It corresponds, roughly, with the number of years of schooling a person would require to read a passage with ease and understanding.

Keep the readability level of your writing to between 10 and 12 on the Gunning Fog Index.

If material has an index of 8, it is at the eighth-grade level in the U.S. school system. An index score of 12 is equal to the senior level in high school. When the index reaches 16, the material is at a level where reading and comprehension are not easy. Over 20? Few readers will bother to plow through the material. A Gunning Fog Index of between 10 and 12 is quite safe for most readers of business materials.

Computer programs are now available that compute readability levels following procedures similar to the one described.

THE FINAL PRODUCT

Make the document visually attractive.

Now that you have completed the writing and editing of the final draft, check one more aspect of your document: the overall appearance.

TOPIC HEADINGS

Both the reader and the writer benefit from the use of topic and subtopic headings. They organize the document and make the argument easy to follow.

Is each new section properly headed? Will readers be required to search through the 15 pages on employee fringe benefits to find the section on sick-leave pay, or will they be able to find that section quickly because it is preceded by a heading? Assist your readers by using topic and subtopic headings. Choose the words for these headings carefully. Be sure the headings are concise and to the point.

For example, busy executives are delighted when they can skim through a report and see at a glance the major and minor areas discussed. They can quickly note the organizational pattern (or outline) the writer had in mind and thus appreciate the method of development and emphasis. With such knowledge, they can then select the specific sections that require detailed study.

Headings also assist the writer, because headings are a constant reminder to deal only with the topic noted. It is more difficult to digress when a guide of three or four words heads the section. Topic headings serve as road markers for both readers and writers.

WHITE SPACE

Use white space to improve visual appeal.

Don't spend a good deal of time and money on a report or letter and then economize on paper. The generous use of white space in the margins, between sections, above and below tables and charts, and on a title page adds to the appeal of a presentation.

The well-balanced page looks inviting; the material appears easy to read and assimilate. In contrast, a page with typing from the very top to the very bottom and only a half-inch margin on either side appears heavy and laborious to read.

APPENDIXES, CHARTS, SUPPLEMENTS .

Supplemental materials such as tables and charts should be placed so that they inform without distracting.

A technical paper may require various supporting documents. Inclusion of this material in the text may upset the continuity of the discussion, especially if the material is relevant but not vital to the topic. In such cases place the information in a footnote, if it is brief, or in an appendix if it is quite lengthy. Sometimes a complete set of supporting documents must accompany a study. These can be placed in an appendix.

You may want to include various supplements as part of the whole presentation to aid understanding. These may include sales promotion materials, statistics, and company records. Of course the table, graph, or supporting material should be placed in the text when it is vital to the ideas being presented.

These items are all valuable to include, but if they are not *vital* to the message, they should be attached as additions to the report proper. Nothing should interfere with the reader's understanding and assimilation of the core idea of the presentation.

BINDINGS, INTRODUCTORY PAGES, AND REPRODUCTION

Some type of binder is essential for an important study, research document, or report. A good binder helps the reader examine the communication, file it, or forward it to others. A firm that issues many reports may use a standard binder. Other companies may purchase anything from an inexpensive folder to an attractive spiral binder. In some cases, the quality of the binder is important.

Tastefully designed introductory pages, such as the title page, table of contents, and list of illustrations, enhance any presentation.

Today's laser printers can produce any number of attractive printouts with a selection of type fonts. But first, arrange your material attractively into pages using the capabilities of word processing or desktop publishing software. Photocopy machines are capable of fast mass reproduction, even in color.

Well-written and well-formatted documents make a positive and lasting impression on readers. Just as important is the impression the finished product makes on you, the writer. As you hold the completed work in your hands, you have every reason to feel proud of a creation—something valuable that did not exist before your hard work. Your confidence in your ability to produce such work makes your next writing task a more pleasant challenge. You know that you can do it; set about your work without crippling doubts and perpetual writer's block. In short, good writing pays double dividends: once to the business community that reads your work, and again to you, the writer.

WRITING AND SPEAKING EXERCISES

1. If you normally do not use a computer and word processing software when writing, try them for your next written assignment. Pay particular attention to the ways in which the writing process is easier, particularly revision and editing. Prepare a memo to someone unfamiliar with word processing; explaining the advantages and disadvantages (if any).
2. Contact members of the business community and discuss the importance of writing in their daily activities. Discover which strategies businesspeople use when drafting and revising. Compile your information into a short report.
3. As a member of a small group, develop a short letter to local business owners asking the questions addressed in question 2. After the group's first draft is written, each group member should revise and edit the letter individually. When all second drafts are completed, the group should compare and contrast the different versions of the letter to evaluate each in terms of effectiveness. Next, the group should produce a group final draft to make use of all the steps in the writing process.

Write a brief memo detailing exactly how the final draft differs from the first draft.

4. Obtain a recent business article and identify transitional paragraphs. Explain in writing how key words and synonyms for key words are used to make smooth transitions.

5. Rewrite the following paragraph. Add or subtract words as necessary to achieve sentence variety (in grammar, structure, rhythm, and length). Strive to make verbs active where appropriate.

Baudford Corporation is the object of a hostile bid by Wilson Enterprises. Baudford is a company that makes electrical connectors and cables. Wilson Enterprises is a firm that manufactures electrical switches and breakers. The takeover bid is being resisted by Baudford because Wilson Enterprises plans to replace top Baudford management. Baudford's past success is due to the skill and foresight of these men and women.

6. Rewrite the following flawed sentences; add or subtract words as necessary:

   (a) The multimillion-dollar transaction due in large part to Frank Williams' creative ideas for attracting investors.
   (b) Closing the Portland factory meant layoffs, most of the workers simply could not afford a month without pay.
   (c) The manager asking her to handle the Fitzpatrick account.
   (d) The employees left the building bundled in heavy overcoats.
   (e) Reputed to be a tough manager, the delivery boy said Ms. Foster actually told a joke from time to time.

7. The practice of reading documents aloud can help you discover stylistic problems. Choose one paragraph from your own writing. Read it aloud. Then explain in writing the possible areas for revision you discovered by your reading. Discuss why reading aloud uncovers problems that are difficult to spot by silent reading.

8. Look at one of your own pieces of writing in terms of unity, coherence, emphasis, reader consideration, clarity, liveliness, and grace. Then on a separate sheet of paper, describe your writing style. Submit both the original writing and your analysis.

9. Rewrite and combine the following sentences into one longer paragraph. Do not merely recopy the sentences. Instead, rearrange them as necessary into an organized, coherent paragraph. Add words if necessary.

We all remember the spirit of cooperation while Sandra Ortiz was chief executive officer. The best leaders have come from among the company's own ranks. She rose from quality control inspector to unit supervisor to vice president and finally CEO. The company has never experienced a significant downturn in profits while led by a leader from among its own. Because the employees knew that Sandra looked out for them, they worked hard for her.

10. Name and exemplify each of the three ingredients for achieving courtesy and consideration in business writing.

11. Throughout your education you are explicitly and implicitly encouraged to write in an impressive manner. "Simple" seems to be the antithesis of

modern education. But profit-making organizations don't have time for "impressive" missives. They need simple, straightforward communication. List and explain at least three recommendations you would make to students graduating from college as to how they should switch gears. Explain what they should do as they move into the workaday world, which will require letters, reports, memos, and other writing done simply rather than in a complex manner. Be specific in listing and explaining your recommendations.

12. Revise the following statements as necessary to improve clarity, conciseness, and style.

    (a) Terri promised David in June she would marry him.
    (b) One Zenith employee, Mark Webster, constructed a sail plane, "The Butterfly," with both sling and sail near his home in San Jose.
    (c) In order to lose weight, the doctor suggested to Pat that lunch not be skipped.
    (d) Recently I found that no food seems satisfactory to my dog which comes in a can.
    (e) Our basketball coach spoke about how to win the tournament on television.
    (f) Her future, full of questions, but also of hope and desire, and perhaps pain and disappointment, was never realized.
    (g) Kate exercised, such as jogging for 40 minutes, swimming 40 laps, doing pushups for 10 minutes, and jumping rope forever, on a daily basis.
    (h) Franco, noting the approach of the fire, the high winds, the lack of water, and his own physical incapacity, was frightened.
    (i) The winning of the games plus the increased salary which the players received brought the team full circle. This was, however, not what management desired.
    (j) The owner insisted that the color of the car be green. This irritated the dealer.

13. Read the following sentences carefully. If you find an error in punctuation, rewrite the sentence, inserting the correct punctuation.

    (a) The competition among automobile manufacturers has become intense, the solution, if there is a solution, is to offer higher quality and lower prices.
    (b) If you believe it will solve the problem and I have my serious doubts, why not attempt to pay the account, that should satisfy Tania even though it may not please her partner.
    (c) I released the emergency brake and then I put the car in gear.
    (d) You will find that a turbo-charged system will consistently save fuel, however that is not always the most important objective for the motorist.
    (e) I called Lee and learned he was not available today but I did determine that he would be at the party on Friday under any circumstances.
    (f) Sarah could not find her husband in the crowd, nevertheless she went directly to their seats and greeted her guests.
    (g) This situation, however, is different from the one which follows.

(h) I don't believe he will ever become a reliable and efficient parts manager, however, he does have the ability to become a competent personnel director.

(i) You may be correct about the mechanical features of foreign cars, however I do feel GM may match Nissan when styling is compared.

(j) I went to the class, which I always found interesting but Sandy stayed home to watch the final game in the series.

14. Each occupation has its own set of "jargon" words. List several items of jargon you had to learn in a past or present job. For each, write an equivalent expression you would use in communicating that item to an uninitiated reader.

15. The following text of a letter was intercepted from the word processing department before it left Hudson Restaurant Supply on its way to a prospective customer. Put yourself in the shoes of Hudson's general manager, who now reviews the letter. What changes would you recommend? More important, how would you go about educating the writer of the letter about better writing habits? (Only the body of the letter appears here.)

```
    You're giving your customers less than they deserve
if you're not buying from Hudson Restaurant Supply.
And you're probably wasting money as well.
    We can show you economical ways to begin serving a
quality product at your eating spot, not second-rate
fare. Our representative will be driving through your
part of town next Thursday or so. If his schedule per-
mits, he'll stop by to let you look over our product
line. You'll be impressed!
    We look forward to supplying all your restaurant
needs.
```

16. As a new employee at Midwest Agricultural Products, you've already gained a reputation as a good writer. Your supervisor asks you to lead a two-hour meeting on effective writing. What will you cover? Draw up a working agenda for your session; indicate the approximate amount of time you will devote to each topic.

17. The connotations of the words you choose can work either for or against you. Select three advertisements and show how connotations are used to build a positive image of the products.

18. The Maynard corporate president happened to see some correspondence various executives were sending to customers and vendors. The president labeled the materials rude, crude, and lacking completely in consideration. As assistant to the VP for administration, you have been charged with developing a brochure to present to all letter writers in the company. The brochure is tentatively titled, "Don't Be a Grouch—Be Courteous in Your Writing." You are to meet with the VP and the president next week and show them an outline of what will go in the brochure. Prepare the outline—and remember, the managers will probably need many examples.

SUGGESTED RESOURCES

Crow, Peter. "Plain English: What Counts Besides Readability?" *Journal of Business Communication* 25 (Winter 1988): 87–95.

Davidson, W. "Add Humor to Workplace Memos." *Personnel Journal* 71 (June 1992).

Davidson, Wilma. "Beat Page Fright." *Personnel Journal* 68 (September 1989): 36–38.

Ensman, Richard G. "Putting Your Pen to Paper." *Management World* 17 (July-August 1988): 10–13.

Forman, J. "Collaborative Business Writing." *The Journal of Business Communication* 28 (Summer 1991).

Gilbert, Joan. "Watch Your Language!" *Management Quarterly* 32 (Summer 1991): 28–32.

Gladis, S. "Talk It Out: How to Write Collaboratively." *Public Relations Quarterly* 36 (Summer 1991).

Hayes, R., and Hollman, K. "Some Practical Hints for CPAs." *The Ohio CPA Journal* 50 (September-October 1991).

Menelaides, S. "Writing Skills: What They're Looking For." *Journal of Accountancy* 172 (October 1991).

Morgan, M. "Patterns of Composing." *Technical Communication* 38 (November 1991).

Smeltzer, Larry R., and Gilsdorf, Jeanette W. "Revise Reports Rapidly." *Personnel Journal* 69 (October 1990): 38–42.

Woods, A. "Advice to Put Up With." *Communication World* 9 (March 1992).

Woods, A. "Tune in to Your Leading Linguistic Indicators." *Communication World* 9 (May-June 1992).

Zaslow, R. "Managers as Writing Coaches." *Training and Development Journal* 45 (July 1991).

ENDNOTES

1. Dr. Martin Luther King, Jr., winner of the 1964 Nobel Peace Prize, delivered this speech at the civil rights march in Washington, D.C. on August 28, 1963.
2. From the Royal Bank of Canada *Monthly Letter,* 41 (7). Reprinted with permission of the Royal Bank of Canada.

COLLABORATIVE WRITING

Working together involves patience, mutual respect, and shared goals.

Although people commonly distrust collaborative writing, some of the most important and successful business documents are written by teams.

"A camel is a horse designed by committee." "Too many cooks spoil the broth." Those two sayings communicate a common distrust for group work. Do you share that distrust? For too many business writers, a document written *collaboratively* (that is, in cooperation with others) ends up misproportioned in design and uneven in style. That needn't be the case. This chapter shows how collaborative writing, increasingly common across industries in the 1990s, can be good writing. Moreover, writing projects undertaken collaboratively are often more thoroughly researched, carefully designed, and efficiently written than similar projects taken on by a single writer.

To support those assertions, we will first investigate why many beginning business writers resist collaborative writing experiences. Next, we will discuss the importance, even necessity, of collaborative writing in modern business. Then we will describe the step-by-step stages in a collaborative writing process followed by many corporations. Finally, we will suggest practical techniques for leaders of collaborative writing groups.

RESISTANCE FACTORS IN COLLABORATIVE WRITING

To avoid the problems of group work, some writers prefer simply to do everyone else's work themselves.

"It's easier to just do it myself." During college or work experiences, we've all had occasion to say those words. You may recall a time, perhaps, when a professor assigned a term paper to be written by a group including you and three other students. Even though you were all friends, complications in the project seemed to spring up from the very beginning. You had difficulty finding a mutually agreeable time to get together. No one knew how to proceed or, just as bad, everyone wanted to proceed in a different direction. When the work got underway, some group members did too little and some did too much. Ill will occurred. Pieces of the term paper from individual writers didn't hold together neatly into a consistent document. Each of you wrote in a different style. Finally, perhaps, one or two of you simply took charge of the paper and did it yourselves. The group gave a collective sigh of relief to complete the project, but none of its members enjoyed the collaborative writing process.

The frustrations and reservations you may have already experienced with collaborative writing aren't unique to academic life. Business writers also face resistance factors to team writing. Some of them are described next.

LACK OF EXPERIENCE

Collaborative business writers often face the problem of having never written in groups before.

To date, most writing assignments completed in school are completed by individual writers working alone. Instructors have adopted this practice, in part, because they have to assign grades to individuals, not groups. Instructors also want to make sure that each student participates fully in the writing process. They worry that some writers will sit back and let others do the work in group writing assignments. In addition, the structure of most U.S. classrooms encourages individual writing and discourages group writing. Students usually sit at individual desks, not group work tables.

No wonder, then, that many business students enter the work force with little practice in effective collaborative writing.

LACK OF A COMMON MODEL

At the first meeting of an inexperienced writing team, it's not uncommon for each writer to insist upon his or her own way of beginning the writing process. Listen in, for example, on these voices at the initial meeting of one writing team:

RALPH: *I think we all know approximately what we want to say. Let's just start at the beginning and get the rough draft completed.*

MANUEL: *That won't work. Obviously, the first thing we have to do is make an outline. I always begin with an outline. Then we can divvy up parts and get this thing done.*

SUSAN: *How can we make an outline without any ideas? Shouldn't we have a few meetings to agree on basic ideas before we even think about writing?*

LINDA: *A few meetings! We've got a deadline for this project and we can't sit around talking. Let me try to write up the whole thing myself. Then you can all revise what I've done and put in any extra material you want. I'm a fast writer.*

When group members disagree about how to proceed with the writing process, the most dominant member usually wins but risks alienating the others.

It's easy to see that disagreements can quickly undermine the group's efforts and success. In such circumstances, the senior or most powerful member of the group usually has his or her way in the writing process. Grumbling, the rest of the writers give in. But none does his or her best work and some simply opt out of the process entirely.

LACK OF UNDERSTANDING ABOUT RELATING TO ONE ANOTHER

Successful group dynamics require members to share ideas and subordinate personal egos to the collective good.

Inevitably in the process of group writing, some group members will criticize and even discard the ideas or written work of other group members. Unless the group understands how to work through such disagreements, tempers will flare and work will grind to a halt. An important part of the writing process, therefore, involves successful group dynamics. On the one hand, the group should not fall into "groupthink," with members accepting all ideas for the sake of harmony. On the other hand, the group should not destroy itself by personal attacks, counterattacks, and hurt feelings. The group should seek the middle road where ideas and drafted work are evaluated fairly with a consensus view toward what's best for the project.

WHY COLLABORATIVE WRITING MATTERS IN BUSINESS

The struggles of a writing team to work together would matter less if business could get along without collaborative writing. But it can't, for five reasons.

First, participation in collaborative writing strengthens the work team. The value of collaborative writing lies not only in its end—the document completed on time—but in its means. Employees, often from different work units, learn to work together toward a common goal. They experience the value of sharing expertise and accepting feedback. In short, they build the team spirit so crucial for corporate success.

Collaborative writing projects give employees who do not normally work together a chance to build team spirit.

Second, collaborative writing is a political process as well as a work method. Few large U.S. corporations are pure dictatorships, with the CEO barking out strict orders for employees at all levels. Instead, many companies organize according to what Douglas Macgregor called "Theory Y" principles, including participative decision making and shared work goals. In this kind of business, a manager doesn't put an engineer, a technical writer, a personnel officer, and a computer specialist on the same writing team simply for the sake of their differing areas of expertise. Instead, the manager assembles the writing team to forge alliances and satisfy constituencies within the company. The engineering division, for example, may want to have its say in the document being written by the group; the inclusion of an engineer on the writing team assures that division that its interests will be represented.

Collaborative writing projects satisfy the various political agendas that exist throughout the company.

Thus, when a writing team succeeds in working productively, different sectors around the company reap political dividends. Seeing this example of effective interaction in the writing team, divisions within the company become more cooperative. The collaborative writing team is the tip of an iceberg that extends deep into the political structure of the company.

A third reason business needs collaborative writing is that it reduces risk factors. Few companies can afford the risks involved in turning over a major writing project to one individual. Even the most talented individual can be dead wrong at times. The company could face a disaster if an incorrect or one-sided report goes forward from one individual without the checks and balances of others. Another risk is the dependence of a major writing project on the continued employment, health, or work habits of one individual. The team approach to writing assures that the project will proceed, even if an individual on the team leaves the company or becomes ill.

Collaborative writing ensures that completion of a project does not depend solely on one person who may become unable to finish the job.

Collaborative writing incorporates more expertise—the fourth reason for its importance to business. No one person knows it all. Most important business documents must discuss more than one point of view and come to a balanced conclusion. For those points of view to emerge, they must be represented on the writing team. Using the collaborative approach to writing, a safety specialist's expertise can temper a design expert's enthusiasm for a new product. A technical writer's skills can convey in readable form the precision of a statistician.

Collaborative writing allows all areas of expertise within a company to be focused on a single subject.

The fifth reason collaborative writing is needed by business is that the process often makes the best use of company resources. When a contract is at stake or a government deadline looms, a company can't afford to have a solitary writer laboring for days or weeks on a project. The cost of assigning a team to work on the project is justified if the result is winning the contract, meeting the deadline, or satisfying the client. Choosing a team for the project presumes, of course, that the team members know how to work together to get the job done.

Efficient collaborative writing teams work much faster than a single writer can.

If they don't, one skilled writer-researcher might, indeed, do a better job than a disorganized, bickering group.

STEPS IN THE COLLABORATIVE WRITING PROCESS

Each team member must follow all the steps in the writing process.

The collaborative writing process follows the same general path as the writing process described for individual writers in Chapters 6 and 7: generate ideas, organize, draft, and revise/edit. But in collaborative writing, each of these important steps must be adapted to include the participation of the entire writing team. It won't do, in other words, to assign major parts of the writing process to individuals ("You think of the ideas, I'll do the writing") any more than two singers can divide the lyrics and the melody in a performance. What follows, therefore, is a step-by-step plan for involving *all* team writers in *all* stages of the writing process. These steps can be altered to suit varying business circumstances, as the needs of your purpose, audience, and resources dictate.

CRITICAL THINKING CONCEPTS

Perhaps the greatest watershed in Western critical thinking is the distinction between deductive and inductive analysis. Both are crucially important as logical structures for the arguments underlying written and oral communications.

In deductive analysis, all implications and conclusions flow from an established point of truth, or major premise. Deductive analysis proceeds by applying the major premise to specific instances. A corporate CEO, for example, may set forth the major premise that "this company must increase its international trade." All further discussion and action in the company flow from this premise. Subordinates work out in specific instances *how* the company can increase its international trade. There is always the possibility, of course, that the major premise is not true. In that case, all analyses of specific instances relating to the major premise will also be erroneous. Much philosophical and theological thought is based on deductive analysis.

Inductive analysis, by contrast, attempts to reach a final truth by evaluating individual items or incidents and only then arriving at a more general statement of truth. That final statement has value only insofar as it is supported by the combined evidence of the individual items. Moreover, that final generalization can be undercut or made meaningless by a small number of specific cases included in the sample or by a biased way of evaluating those cases. Much scientific thought is based on inductive analysis.

As an example of inductive analysis, a corporate CEO might ask employees to investigate sales trends for the company and its industry. Based on consideration of hundreds or even thousands of individual items of sales information, the CEO may eventually reach the conclusion that "this company must increase its international trade." This inductive conclusion is identical to the earlier deductive premise.

The actual words of the general truth do not reveal the inductive or deductive nature. Instead, it is the process by which the general truth is reached that determines whether inductive or deductive principles are at work.

1. Create a deductive argument to support this conclusion: A culturally diverse sales force is required for optimal retail sales.

2. Create an inductive argument to support this conclusion: Pets of all kinds should be barred from rooms in hotels and motels.

STEP 1: ASSEMBLE
A TEAM WITH
APPROPRIATE AND
COMPLEMENTARY
EXPERTISE

*When assembling a
writing team, consider
expertise, compatibility,
and complementary
personality types.*

Too often, teams are formed based on friendship, volunteers, or simply who's available. None of these methods guarantees a group of writers with complementary skills and expertise. As a manager in charge of assembling a writing team, consider both professional and personal qualities in deciding which writers belong together.

The purpose of and audience for a project determine what professional qualities various writers should bring to the team. For example, the writing of a flight training manual requires expertise from an experienced aviator, a training expert, an instructional writer, and probably a skilled illustrator. The writing of an annual report, by contrast, might well require one or more senior managers, a high-ranking financial officer, a professional writer, and others.

Equally important in assembling a writing team is assessment of the personal qualities of team members. Some managers use formal personality assessments (such as the Myers-Briggs Personality Type Indicator) to determine an employee's tendencies and habits of mind. By means of the Myers-Briggs instrument, a manager can measure the degree to which an employee is a thinker who prefers logical structure and planning; a feeler who cares most about human responses; a sensor who focuses primarily on applied, practical matters; or an intuitor who theorizes and speculates. Managers use such test results to build writing teams that include a full range of personality types. In so doing, managers reason that a team made up entirely of thinkers might produce a rational but cold and uninteresting document. A group composed entirely of intuitors, for all their philosophical brilliance, might never produce a document at all. In a group combining all types, however, members act to check and balance one another's excesses. A better product results.

Even if managers do not use personality assessment tests, they can try to combine complementary types on a writing team. They might put a detail-oriented worker, for example, on the team to balance the influence of a bright, but disorganized worker. A writer with a lively, journalistic style might be included to keep a statistician from burying the project in numbers.

STEP 2: MEET TO
DISCUSS WHAT, WHEN,
WHY, WHERE, HOW,
HOW MUCH, AND WHO

*Together, the group must
decide on the format and
purpose of the document.*

What are we writing? In the first meeting, each member of the team must help determine the answer to this question. Let's say, for example, that a senior manager assigns a writing team the task of writing a lengthy report on employee benefits. In this case, the writing team can decide the precise form of the document (in terms of length, organization, and format). From the beginning, all group members must reach agreement on the essential nature of the task: Is the report to be descriptive, giving the details of past, present, and future employee benefit plans? Or is the report also to be prescriptive, with recommendations for changing employee benefits in some way? Unless the group answers such initial questions, it cannot proceed productively to later stages in the writing process.

When? Just as college assignments usually come with a deadline, so business tasks are tightly constrained by time. The writing team must keep time constraints in mind when making decisions about the topic range and research

The group should base the scope of the project on the time available to complete it.

scope of the assigned project. Length alone cannot be used to accurately determine how much time a project will take. Projects with short page counts, in fact, sometimes take much longer than more wordy works. The French mathematician Pascal captured this reality in a memorable line to a friend: "I'm sorry I haven't written a shorter letter, but I didn't have time."

Each individual must understand the importance of the project.

Why?   It isn't enough for senior management to have a reason for doing projects. Each writer on the team must understand the business reasons and possible urgency of the writing task at hand. Team members who understand why they are writing a particular assignment have a much better chance of avoiding unnecessary digressions and redundant information.

The group must agree on mutually convenient meeting places and lines of communication.

Where?   The group must agree on the physical logistics of the writing process from the beginning. Where are team members physically located in the company? What communication links exist? Where will the group meet together? What research resources can they use? Where are these resources located?

The group should discuss the writing process itself so that all members agree on how to proceed.

How?   As we discussed earlier in the voices of Ralph, Manuel, Susan, and Linda, writers often come to the team with different approaches to the writing process. Therefore, they must discuss the process itself, with the goal of reaching consensus. For example, all group members could review the steps set forth in this text or another. Based on that review, the group could discuss and decide on its own the best way to accomplish the writing task.

From the outset, the group must recognize the financial limitations that may affect the scope of the project.

How much?   Money influences virtually every business decision. Writing, like all important business activities, costs the company money. (The salaries alone of four team members working for a week on a report could total $2,500 or more.) Instead of ignoring financial realities, the writing team should carefully assess how much the company wants to spend (in salaried time, research expenses, and support resources) to accomplish the writing task. Operating within a budget may mean trimming the team's development plans for the project. But it's better to deal with financial limitations from the beginning of a project instead of confronting them later, when the project languishes overextended, half-finished, and underfunded.

Unless one is already provided, the group must choose a leader.

Who?   In this last, crucial portion of a first meeting, the group designates a coordinator and perhaps other roles for team members. Sometimes, of course, the team coordinator is appointed in advance by senior management. If not, it's often better to wait until the end of an initial meeting to decide who will serve as coordinator. In discussing the what, when, why, and other questions, the group has had a chance to see each member in action. The group is then in a position to choose as coordinator the member most likely to keep the team on track, on time, on budget, and not on each other's nerves. The coordinator, in other words, needs to be a good manager of people as well as projects.

STEP 3: MEET IN PERSON OR ELECTRONICALLY TO GENERATE IDEAS

Most writing teams brainstorm their topics in face-to-face meetings. At these simultaneously intense but casual gatherings, writers try out ideas on one another. They listen, react, and avoid the temptation to settle on certain ideas in too early or fixed a way.

Especially when writers are separated by distance or schedule conflicts, they can, nevertheless, generate ideas and bounce them off one another by

Either in person or by computer link, group members need to brainstorm and share a multitude of ideas.

means of the many "groupware" programs now available for desktop computers. Groupware allows several users to display and arrange ideas on screen for mutual review and revision. Sitting at linked computers, team writers comment on one another's on-screen suggestions, highlight words and phrases, and rearrange items freely. The computer is especially advantageous for this purpose because all ideas entered can be stored and printed out for later use. By contrast, even the most careful human notetaker can overlook, misstate, or lose some contributions to the idea-generation process. To avoid such problems in face-to-face meetings, many writing teams tape record all idea-generation sessions. No matter what technology is used, each writer should leave idea-generation meetings with a clear, written record of the ideas proposed by group members.

The goal of idea generation is to produce not merely enough but more than enough useful ideas for the writing project. The writing team strives for as many and as far-ranging ideas as possible during idea generation. Winnowing those ideas (selecting some, discarding others) comes later, in the organization stage.

STEP 4: ORGANIZE IDEAS INTO A WORKING OUTLINE

Group members must agree on a working outline.

Some writing teams develop a working outline in a face-to-face meeting. Group members propose, challenge, argue, and compromise on each item in the growing outline until the full scheme lies before them. Other writing teams decide each member will form an organizational outline independently. Members then bring their outlines to a common meeting or share them by means of groupware. In either case, the group reviews the various organizational patterns and pieces together the best version—the working outline—from the versions offered.

STEP 5: EVALUATE THE WORKING OUTLINE WITH THE HELP OF STAKEHOLDERS

The group should get feedback about the outline before starting time-consuming research.

Before pursuing the hard work of research and writing that leads to the first draft, the group takes time to evaluate the working outline with care. What does the boss or other intended audience have to say about the outline? Does it satisfy the requirements and expectations of the company? Does the group have the talent, time, and resources to complete a project outlined in this way? Are all members clear about the meaning of each item in the outline and the relations between those items (i.e., the logic of the outline)?

STEP 6: DISCUSS AND UNDERTAKE THE RESEARCH PROCESS

Often, members of the team research different subtopics and combine their separate research results later.

As described fully in Chapter 16, writers investigate both primary and secondary materials to elucidate and support the bare assumptions on the working outline. The coordinator of the writing team probably assigns portions of the outline to each team member for research. Members bring back the results to a common meeting or, more likely, enter them into a computer database that all writers on the project can access. Such mutual access is necessary day-by-day during the project so that writers can learn of relevant materials uncovered by coworkers.

STEP 7: DISCUSS AND UNDERTAKE THE DRAFTING PROCESS

Some writing teams operate by gradual accumulation. Individual writers begin to draft small pieces of the project even during the research process. The team then decides which of those pieces fit well into the overall document and in what ways they should be expanded and connected.

Other writing teams require that each member turn over a carefully organized compilation of his or her research to one or two members who are responsible for actually drafting the document. In most cases, the drafters are the most proficient writers in the group—those with a special talent for style, clarity, and flow.

Rarely does a writing team compose each sentence of the first draft together. There are simply too many decisions to be made word-by-word in the drafting process for each writer to suggest and argue alternatives. Such discussion can be accomplished better at the revision stage.

Whether the early document grows piecemeal or is written by one individual who draws on the others' research, all team members should suggest improvements to the rough draft.

The first draft, once completed, should be regarded by all team members (especially those who actually wrote it) as an exceedingly tentative document. In the understandable excitement of nearing the end of the project, too many writing teams consider the words of the first draft as text cast in granite. A better approach is to distribute the first draft electronically so that each team member can work through it to note his or her suggested changes. (Several groupware products, including For Comment, allow several writers to make changes in a shared text without losing the original text or confusing one writer's changes with another's.)

STEP 8: EVALUATE THE FIRST DRAFT WITH THE HELP OF STAKEHOLDERS.

After the draft is formalized, the team seeks additional feedback from the intended audience.

All team members now carefully review the completed first draft. They look for qualities of logic, persuasion, appropriate support, style, and format (as discussed in Chapters 6 and 7).

And there's no better occasion than at this stage to see if the document suits its audience. If, for example, the project is being completed for senior management, the writing team may want to schedule a meeting to show them the first draft and talk through its major points. The team notes carefully all questions, criticism, and comments from stakeholders as part of the agenda for the revision process.

STEP 9: REVISE THE DRAFT FOR CONSISTENCY AND IMPACT

After revision, the document should be given a professional and attractive appearance.

No document is "right" until it is right for its audience. The team makes adjustments in logical development, persuasive argumentation, level of diction, paragraph length, tone, format, illustrations, and all other aspects of the project with one goal in mind: to carry out the intended purpose of the document.

To engage the audience in a suitable way, the team probably will decide to give the document a professional appearance by using desktop publishing software and perhaps by adding a bound cover. By all surveys, documents prepared with desktop publishing software score higher for credibility and attractiveness than do typed documents.

STEP 10: EDIT TO ACHIEVE ERROR-FREE TEXT

Finally, the document should be edited meticulously.

Revision differs from editing in the way that farming differs from gardening. The team's revision efforts focus on larger matters of placement and style; those matters often require reworking, rearrangement, or deletion. Editing, by contrast, takes a magnifying glass to each word, sentence, paragraph, and heading of the document. The team relies on successive editing by different pairs of eyes to catch every typo, misspelling, punctuation mistake, and other surface errors.

These ten steps define a path, but not the only path, for the development of a document by collaborative writing. If your writing group decides to skip one or more of the steps, take time to at least discuss what you're skipping and question if it might be important to the overall development of the writing project. It's fine to change a recipe, in other words, if you're sure you can bake a better cake that way.

CRITICAL THINKING CONCEPTS

What persuades an audience to believe what you write or say? In some cases, simply your reputation as an expert is sufficient to ensure acceptance of your message. When John Glenn, astronaut and Congressional representative speaks to an audience about space travel, the audience believes him because he has "been there."

In most cases, however, audiences require that writers or speakers provide substantiating evidence (in the form of statistics, authoritative references, examples, or anecdotes) to support their assertions. Such support is often more a matter of suggestion than actual proof.

Let's say, for example, that we want to support the assertion that "large urban areas have high crime rates." If we tell about frequent homicides in Washington, D.C. and muggings in New York City, we are providing *suggestion* to back up our assertion. Even though we have mentioned only generalized evidence from two large cities, our audience may well be persuaded to accept our assertion about big-city crime, especially if the audience is predisposed to agree with us on the topic.

But writers and speakers must be aware that such suggestion is far from definitive proof. In our original assertion, "large urban areas" include a hundred or more cities, not two or three. True proof for our assertion must provide evidence for crime rates in all or most of these cities. Furthermore, "high crime rates" presume a comparison of some sort. Proof requires that we specify the criteria or comparison points by which we are defining "high" crime rates. We might, for example, compare a recent statistical survey of crime reports in 100 urban areas with a similar survey of smaller towns and rural areas. Such evidence, although less lurid than examples and anecdotes of big-city crimes, provides a more substantial base of proof for our assertion. Statistical proof may be particularly valuable in persuading audiences disinclined to accept the writer's or speaker's assertion.

1. Assess the adequacy of proof in the following assertion:

   Working for the government provides much more job security than working in the private sector. Newspapers regularly report layoffs in private companies but rarely report layoffs for state or federal employees. According to the Bureau of Labor Statistics, 84 percent of all applicants for unemployment pay have lost private sector jobs, not government jobs.

2. Determine and discuss the kind of proof necessary to support the following assertion to a large group of personnel managers:

   A neat, flawless resume is of equal importance to grade point average and recommendation letters in determining whether to hire a candidate.

SUGGESTIONS FOR THE TEAM WRITING COORDINATOR

As coordinator, you have the difficult task of keeping the writing project moving forward with all members contributing to its development. Like a pilot, keep your eyes on the route ahead and your ears open for sounds of trouble. Here are several common distress signals from team members; these are the knotty problems that coordinators have to deal with in the team writing process.

As team coordinator, make sure that . . . each team member feels valued

"No one even listens to me." Your job as a coordinator is to make each team member feel valuable to the project and respected by team members. Inevitably, of course, some team members will contribute more than others. But the coordinator should do everything possible (including personal conferences and assigned duties) to prevent malaise, withdrawal, or resentment from disrupting the work of the team.

. . . other team members recognize and support your authority

"Who made you the boss?" Occasionally, a frustrated team member will directly challenge your role as coordinator. In such cases, let others in the group speak for you, or you can remind the complaining team member that you have the support of the other team members.

. . . team members understand and accept problems

"What are we waiting for?" In any process involving the work of several people, occasional delays will occur as one team member waits for another to complete his or her work. Make sure that your team understands both the inevitability of glitches in the team approach to document development and the importance of completing work on which others depend.

. . . criticism between members is positive and productive

"Where does he get off telling me I'm wrong!" We are all sensitive to negative criticism about the way we speak or write. That sensitivity carries over to the workplace, especially when one team member criticizes our work as "too wordy," "unclear," or "disorganized." We respond defensively—"do it yourself, then"—instead of understanding and possibly profiting from the interchange. As coordinator, emphasize that criticism is directed at the passage, not the person who wrote it. Conducting revision and editing sessions in a good-humored way goes far in alleviating the potential hostility that can develop when team members spar over language choices.

. . . team members understand why their contributions may have been altered.

"I don't understand your changes." Especially as deadlines approach, the coordinator and other lead members of the team may change the work of other members in a high-handed way. If a team member requests an explanation, it's important for the coordinator to provide one. Never simply say that a passage is "better my way." Doing so breeds ill will in the team and fails to teach preferable alternatives to the objecting team member.

COLLABORATIVE WRITING FOR THE FUTURE

Linking team writers by groupware is only a first step in the integration of writing into larger management and production processes. In so-called total quality (TQ) software systems, the collaborative work of writers is tied in with many other information and decision-making systems in the company. At IBM Decision Conference Centers, for example, collaborative writers use TQ software at their workstations to participate in electronic brainstorming, idea organization, audience analysis, drafting, revision, and editing. The collaborative writing component is but one part of a large-scale software program used for developing and evaluating new products.

Similarly, at Ford Motor Company software for collaborative writing has been integrated into a system known as quality function deployment (QFD). The process begins with a meeting of 8 to 12 participants who use a PC and a PC projection system. The group works together to build on screen what Ford calls a "house of quality"—a structured, visual plan to accomplish targeted business goals. The completed house of quality takes the form of graphics (showing at a glance the components of the plan) and explanatory text developed collaboratively.

Collaborative writing will be the rule rather than the exception in managerial communication throughout the next century.

As we near the next century, the image of a lonely writer working for days at a time in isolation from colleagues is fading. More and more common is the collaborative writer linked to others by personal contact and computer—a writer who's eager to learn what others think about his or her ideas and words and who has the electronic tools to find out quickly.

WRITING AND SPEAKING EXERCISES

The following questions require you to be involved in a collaborative writing situation as provided by your instructor. You will work toward the group production of a document (memo, letter, report, etc.).

1. As a separate part of your collaborative assignment, keep a diary of your experiences within your group. Focus particularly on conflicts and how successfully they were avoided or solved.
2. Isolate and identify all incidents of "groupthink" that took place during the writing process and speculate on the impact of groupthink on the final document (cite specific examples). Draft a letter to the members of your group and inform them of your observations.
3. Based on your experiences with this assignment, write a memo that discusses the contention that collaborative writing contains a political component.
4. Prepare a memo for your instructor in which you assess the impact of each of your fellow group members on the final document. Focus on the role of each person and the nature and extent of their contribution.
5. Compare, in as specific terms as possible, the writing process in the collaborative setting with the writing process you normally follow when producing written documents. Present your findings in a memo to your instructor.
6. Videotape one of your group's idea-generation meetings. After the meeting, have each group member jot down the main points stressed during the meeting. Later, meet as a group and review the tape of the meeting. Compare group members' notes about the meeting with the actual events recorded by the camera. What conclusion can you draw about the need to maintain careful documentation during idea-generation meetings? Draft a collaborative memo to your instructor that summarizes the group's conclusions.

7. During the collaborative writing assignment, did any member of the group show a negative attitude toward the assignment? If so, how did the group deal with this negativity? How might similar problems be avoided? Produce a plan to solve attitude problems that other students could follow when producing collaborative texts.

8. Response to this textbook's suggestions for the team writing coordinator. How effective are these suggestions? What would you add to the list? Integrate the ideas from the text with your own experiences. Be sure to list your suggestions in the order of their effectiveness.

9. *Critical thinking exercise:* Select at least three full-page magazine or newspaper advertisements for a product or service. Working together with two or three of your colleagues, discuss the means by which the advertisement attempts to support its assertions. Locate examples, if any, of inductive or deductive analysis. Determine the role of suggestion in relation to formal proof. Use the collaborative writing techniques described in the chapter to write a brief report to your class.

SUGGESTED RESOURCES

Bacon, Terry R. "Collaboration in a Pressure Cooker." *Bulletin of the Association for Business Communication* 53 (June 1990):4–8.

Beard, J.D., Rymer, J., and Williams, D.L. "An Assessment System for Collaborative-writing Groups: Theory and Empirical Evaluation." *Journal of Business and Technical Communication* 3(5):29–51.

Couture, B., and Rymer, J. "Interactive Writing on the Job: Definitions and Implications of Collaboration." In *Writing in the Business Professions,* edited by M. Kogan. Urbana, Ill. NCTE, 1989: 73–93.

Cross, G.A. "A Bakhtinian Exploration of Factors Affecting the Collaborative Writing of an Effective Letter of an Annual Report." *Research in the Teaching of English* 24(1990):173–203.

Forman, J. "The Discourse Communities and Group Writing Practices of Management Students." In *Worlds of Writing,* edited by C. Matalone. New York: Random House, 1989:247–254.

Forman, J., ed. *New Visions of Collaborative Writing.* Portsmouth, N.H.: Boynton/Cook, 1991.

Forman, J. "Collaborative Business Writing: A Burkean Perspective for Future Research." *Journal of Business Communication* 28 (Summer 1991):233–255.

Lunsford, A., and Ede, L. *Singular Texts/Plural Authors: Perspectives on Collaborative Writing.* Carbondale, Ill.: Southern Illinois Press, 1990.

PART 3

LETTERS

AND

MEMOS

HORACE B. WILLIAMS, Jr., Ph.D.

Dr. Williams is currently Director of Pharmacy at Methodist Hospi-

tal of Southern California and Adjunct Clinical Professor of Pharmacy

at the University of Southern California (USC) at Los Angeles.

At USC, Dr. Williams is a member of the Advisory Board of the Office

of Management Development in Health Care and team teaches the

bio-ethics course.

Dr. Williams has served as officers and on the boards of directors

of several professional organizations.

Dr. Williams holds the B.S. and M.S. degrees in pharmacy and a

Ph.D. in health care administration.

METHODIST HOSPITAL
300 WEST HUNTINGTON DRIVE, P.O. BOX 418
ARCADIA, CALIFORNIA 91066-0418
(818) 445-4441

September 25, 19___

S. Student
University of Excellence
PO Box 2000
Anywhere, USA 10001

Dear Student:

In the health care environment, it is extremely important to possess the skill to communicate concisely to a wide range of health care professionals. When carried through correctly, memos, letters and reports are excellent vehicles for communicating information, policy changes and decisions.

The hospital environment is an especially busy one with many diverse activities carried on at the same time. The health care worker's first priority is patient care and that care to be administered as quickly as possible. It is therefore absolutely necessary that communications in connection with that task be clear, concise, complete and courteous.

Health care professionals represent many diverse disciplines. Their education and experience vary tremendously and their job titles are probably more diverse than in any other professional field. Couple that with the many different ethnic groups represented in a hospital, and one quickly becomes aware of the tremendous importance of skillfully prepared communications.

Equal in importance to the communications carried on within the hospital or health care environment are the messages addressed *"outside"*. These include memos, letters, reports, proposals and a half dozen other types of communication sent to other health care professionals, various health care facilities, community groups, government agencies, educational institutions and others.

When one deals with an individual's health, the communications involved must be completed with special skill and diligence.

Sincerely,

Horace B. Williams, Jr.

Horace B. Williams, Jr., Ph.D.
Director of Pharmacy

9

Effective Memos

Data and information by themselves are not communication.

Probably the most common document written in contemporary business is the *memo* (short for *memorandum*). As described in this chapter, the memo serves a wide variety of routine and not-so-routine communication functions in the company. Office in-baskets are usually filled with information memos, policy and procedure memos, memos fixing responsibility, and longer memos explaining or analyzing business situations.

Memos are the most common business document and should be treated seriously.

Because memos are so common, business writers often treat them too casually. Unfortunately, it's still common in many companies to find hand-scrawled memos that were dashed off in a hurry and are virtually useless in their illegible state. Just as common is the "half-baked" memo—the one that presumes reader knowledge not contained in the memo itself.

Take, for example, this memo message: "I talked with the person you mentioned about that business opportunity. He repeated much of what he said to you and gave me a few new ideas." Such messages can frustrate a busy manager. To whom did the writer talk? What was the business opportunity? What did he repeat? What were the new ideas? Even though memos should be brief, that goal should never interfere with clear communication.

Business writers often forget that their memos, saved over time in files throughout the company, paint a picture of the writers' professionalism, for better or worse. Clear, succinct memos signify a clear-thinking, effective employee. Muddled, incomplete, incoherent, or illegible memos foretell an employee headed out the door.

MEMORANDUM BASICS

Memos provide a written record and thus help prevent misunderstandings.

Companies often urge their employees to write memos. One reason is to avoid the distortions and misunderstandings that occur when oral statements pass from one person to another. But there are several other reasons also:

- Memos make specific information a matter of record. Memos can be pulled from the file, referred to, and used as the basis for review and action or as a source material.
- Memos inform individuals of policies, procedures, and actions. Each recipient has the identical information presented in precisely the same way.

- Memos fix responsibility by naming specific individuals to take clearly defined actions.
- Memos record policies, decisions, and action items agreed to at a meeting, conference, or interview.
- Memos provide summaries of meetings for participants as well as for those who were absent.
- Memos confirm a decision, an agreement, or a policy previously agreed to by concerned individuals.

Regardless of length or subject matter, the memo's format generally does not vary. It almost always carries the word *MEMORANDUM* and a four-part heading: the recipient, the sender, the date and the subject.

```
                       MEMORANDUM
     To:      Robert Andrews, Vice President—Marketing
     From:    John Kane, Supervisor—Consumer Research
     Date:    June 27, 19__
     Subject: Budget allocation, Project 248
```

Memos should specify full names and titles of the writer and the audience.

Note that the full names and titles are given, rather than just first names, initials, or even complete names with no titles. As more and more pieces of business communication become a part of legal cases, the need for completeness becomes important. A company's liability may depend on what corporate position the memo writer held when the memo was written.

On many occasions, of course, an informal memo to a familiar coworker will not bear the sender's full name and business title. In fact, such formality could detract from the effectiveness and persuasive appeal of informal messaging. Note in Figure 9–1, for example, that Madeline Johnson chooses to attach her title, Manager, even though she is writing to warehouse personnel who may

Make the subject line brief yet complete.

FIGURE 9–1 Typical Short Memo

Use your title in a memo to maintain a formal relationship with your readers.

Dennison Furniture, Inc.

```
                        MEMORANDUM

     To:      Warehouse Personnel
     From:    Madeline Johnson, Manager
     Date:    April 6, 19__
     Subject: Water Damage to Furniture
```

During this period of heavy rains, report directly to my office even the slightest roof leakage. Showroom staff reports 12 furniture items sent from the warehouse with water damage in the past 30 days. If you will let me know right away about roof damage or other water problems, we can avoid costly damage to our merchandise.

CULTURAL
DIVERSITY IN
COMMUNICATION

The Memo: As Common
"There" As Here?

Carol Shuherk
*University of
Southern California*

We take memos for granted in our business organizations. Through memos, we communicate everything from routine staff promotions to major policy changes. For new employees in a U.S. firm the question is never, "Are memos written here?" but "What are the specific format requirements for memos in this company?"

When conducting business in another nation, however, it is not safe to assume that what is standard practice stateside is also common abroad. The use of memos as a means of communication varies widely in international business. In Germany, for example, writing a memo to confirm and elaborate on a management decision is not only appropriate, it is expected. Doing the same in Greece would invite pointed questioning of the writer's real intent and of the need for creating a permanent record. So how does a U.S. businessperson quickly discern the appropriate approach?

One way to find clues to the ways memos are used (or not used) in another nation's business culture is to take an overall look at communication patterns among the members of its firms. Memos are always a secondary communication tool; they reflect activities and decisions made by people at some earlier time.

A general rule of thumb is that in business cultures where formal hierarchy is important, where information and ideas are objectified, and where ability to influence depends heavily on command of facts, memos are used to deliver a reliably consistent message to those who need to act on decisions. In business cultures where informal contacts drive decision making, where ideas are owned by their originators, and where meetings are platforms for all to hear and be heard, whether genuinely knowledgeable or simply opinionated, memos are far less likely. In other words, where the emphasis is on clarity, facts, and procedural decision making, memos are common. Where relationships and informality dominate, memos are scarce. Yet, the very

topic of memo usage shows the risk in relying entirely on general rules for international business, because nation for nation, cultural idiosyncracies render the fit between rule and reality less than exact.

Germany, much like the United States, is a classic example of a business culture in which memos proliferate. Communication in German firms is marked by a top-down focus and deference to authority. Downward information is provided on a need-to-know basis; upward information is requested as needed. Meetings are held to provide briefings, ratify decisions, or coordinate action plans. Meetings are formal: they have an agenda and minutes and are dominated by the leader. More a mechanism to provide directions than an opportunity for those present to offer up opinions, meetings emphasize clarity and decisiveness rather than explanation and persuasion. Compliance, not consensus, is the goal, and people are expected to implement decisions regardless of how they feel about them. Memos delineating roles and responsibilities follow meetings.

The business cultures of France and the United Kingdom also rely heavily on memos, but they illustrate the subtle differences in operating philosophy that make reliance on blanket generalizations risky. Meetings in France appear to resemble those in Germany. Hot debate and collective decision making are not common; instead, briefing and coordination of action plans are the routine agenda. The difference is that unlike the German firms in which memos circulate after decision making to inform and direct action, in French firms memos circulate *before* decision making (in the form of short report memoranda or lengthier studies) for comment by those who will be expected to carry out the plan. These reports reflect only half of the total communication system in French firms—the formal process. Also important, and another divergence from the general rule, is the informal process–the dynamic network of personal relationships through which much business is conducted.

In the United Kingdom, the rule of formal, leader-dominated, command-and-control-style meetings as a feature of "memo-heavy" culture is shattered. Although memos are widely used, they appear to be used as a defense mechanism, to keep people informed by a leader frequently absent from his or her desk. In the U.K. business culture, meetings are crucial. Only the least important decisions are left to individuals to develop outside meetings. Everything else is formed, discussed, approved, and communicated through meetings. Although formal in the sense that they are preceded by an agenda, meetings are open forums in which new agenda items can be introduced and input from each person at the table is expected, whether or not they are prepared to speak. Memos may precede the meeting to allow participants to prepare. Whether or not they actually have prepared is not at issue once the meeting begins. So in the United Kingdom, we see elements of nonmemo business cultures, particularly in the give and take of meetings. The difference, as looking at a classic example of a nonmemo culture will show, is that in the United Kingdom open decision making and general ownership of information are valued.

In Italy memos are irrelevant. Personal alliances are the key to virtually all decision making in a business culture dominated by the concept of "family." Even though the level of interaction is high, the impression that decision making is being carried on by consensus is illusory. Meetings in an Italian firm are lengthy and dynamic, anyone may speak to any issue, and eloquence and passion are the keys to being persuasive. But the real goal of the decision makers in a meeting is to test the mood of others on a particular issue. And so the decisions agreed to, written, and planned for implementation may never happen. The actual course of action is planned separately and carried out by the leader's allies and subordinates, so the role of the memo as a summarizing or confirming document following the meeting is moot. While facts are important in Italian decision making, as they must be in any business, they are likely to be closely held by those who have them, the better to own and manage a desired course of action. Facts committed to paper are of a central focus: turnover figures, cash flows, gross profits, and so on.

In Greece memos are relied upon less as a means of organizational communication, but the business culture defies an easy fit with generalizations. Meetings look and sound a lot like those in Italy: dynamic and dominated by contrary opinions. They are, however, very different in their intent. Consensus is highly valued on virtually all issues, and Greeks will convene a separate meeting on a particular issue, until they reach consensus. Meetings range greatly in size and degree of formality; any conversation between affected parties constitutes a meeting, more or less, and the outcomes are a factor in the eventual decision. A unique feature of Greek culture that also has the effect of reducing reliance on written forms of communication in business is the existence of a separate written language, *katharevousa*. The difficulty of this written language has the effect of making letters and memos stilted and formal, which is not characteristic of Greek style.

Once again, this sampling of business cultures suggests that there is only one hard and fast rule for conducting business in the international marketplace: Learn as much as you can about the particular place you are going. Advance study and careful observation on arrival are the best means to ensure the correct writing approach!

be expected to know her position. In this case, Ms. Johnson reinforces the seriousness of her instructions by the inclusion of her title. In a less formal memo confirming a luncheon meeting with a coworker, Ms. Johnson probably would have omitted her title and, depending on her relationship with the coworker, may have simply used her first name.

The subject line should state the memo's topic as specifically as possible. A concise but complete subject line sets the stage for the reader. In some cases it may even eliminate the need for all or part of the introductory paragraph.

Because people throughout the company might read copies of a memo, be cautious when speaking your mind.

Memos can transmit more than information, policies, and summaries of meetings. Unfortunately, they can transmit attitudes that build barriers. Some managers send an inordinate number of interoffice memos; they fly from their desks like snowflakes in a storm. Often, such memos are hastily written and not even proofread. When a manager's attitude is, "Well, it's only a memo—nothing official. I'll just straighten this person out," trouble is likely to result.

Bear in mind that memos will probably be read not only by the designated receiver but by others in the company as well. The message receiver may show the memo or send copies of it to others in the organization. Eventually, the memo may find its way into a company file that is available for view by many employees. Speaking one's mind in a memo, therefore, must be undertaken with considerable care. Divulged confidences, personal remarks, and private judgments that seem innocuous to the designated receiver of the memo may become a source of pain and anger for other, unintended readers of the memo.

E-MAIL MEMOS

As companies seek to speed internal messaging and cut down on the paper glut, *electronic mail (e-mail) memos* are becoming commonplace. Chapter 3 describes e-mail in detail and gives examples of its use and misuse in U.S. business. In this chapter, we examine the kinds of information that are appropriate for e-mail transmission.

Use e-mail for quick memos that need not be saved.

Just as any other communication channel, e-mail has its limitations. E-mail is useful for messages with a short life span—those, in other words, that can be read quickly and do not need to be saved or filed. Here are two examples: "The staff meeting will be postponed until next Thursday at 2:00." "Please hand deliver your report to Nancy Trent when it is completed."

For more detailed messages that the reader may save for later reference, a traditional paper memo is often more efficient for all concerned. (Such a message sent by e-mail would probably be printed out by the message receiver anyway.) The distribution of paper copies of a detailed memo makes sense, especially if the memo is sent to several workers. Imagine the wasted time and simmering tempers in an office as many workers take time to print out the same e-mail memo.

A final caution regarding e-mail memos: Send them only to those who need to read them. The technology of e-mail transmission makes it seductively easy to send a message indiscriminately to many electronic mailboxes at once. Misuse of e-mail simply replaces the paper glut with the electronic glut, as system users try to sort out the mail that matters from irrelevant messages.

MEMOS TO FILE

The memo to file records information about a business event and is filed with related documents for future reference.

Businesspeople exchange information by telephone, e-mail, voice mail, fax, meetings, interviews, and in-person conversations. Because the information may be important to a transaction, procedure, project, or ongoing negotiation, it should be recorded in preservable form. Once documented, the information is less likely to be distorted, and it is available—in five days or five years—in exactly the same words. Often, businesspeople note such information in memo form and file it—thus the name, *memo to file* (see Figure 9–2). Sometimes a copy of the memo is sent to the other people involved.

INFORMATIONAL MEMOS

All memos are informational in nature, whether they are seeking information or presenting it. See Figures 9-3 and 9-4 for examples of information memos. Clearly written memos help to prevent distortion of information that often occurs when messages are spread solely by word of mouth.

Although memos can't be divided neatly into distinct types, two special uses of the memo are worth noting here: the policy memo and the follow-up memo.

THE POLICY MEMO

Many businesses use the *policy memo* to inform employees of significant company positions on personnel guidelines, procedures, public relations, and other matters (see Figure 9–5). Often, policy memos are labeled as such and sometimes appear on an identifying color or size of memo stationery. The clear label-

FIGURE 9–2 Memo to File (Note Preprinted Form)

MEMO TO FILE

❏ **Phone call to** Antonio Vasquez, Conway Industries   File No. _____

❏ **Phone call from** Rita Givings, VP   Date: _____

❏ Interview _____   Time: _____

❏ Meeting/Conference _____
Place _____

I assured Mr. Vasquez that this company would extend warranty on the #392 unit to June, 19__. Legal staff has been instructed to prepare an addendum to the present warranty agreement.

FIGURE 9–3   Information Memo

To: Marketing Department
From: Ronald Lions, Director of Advertising
Date: March 12, 19__
Subject: Theme for wallpaper media ads

After more than three weeks of meetings, the theme "Color My World" has been selected for the upcoming series of radio and television wallpaper advertisements.

A "walk-through" of the theme, as it applies to individual ads and products, has been set up in the executive lounge. Please take an hour during the next five days to get to know the exhibit.

Reserve March 26, 19__, 10:00 a.m. to noon, for a meeting with advertising and production staff members. The purpose of the meeting is to firm up our approach to the selected theme and to make specific plans for a multilevel marketing approach.

FIGURE 9–4   Informational Memo with Visual Aid

To: All District Sales Managers
From: Ellen Toshiba
             Vice President, Sales
Date: November 15, 19__
Subject: Sales, Mercury Program
             January-November, 19__

The following graph depicts the success of our Mercury Sales Force Incentive Program. You will receive specific data and figures for all items (by district) on December 20.

Effective use of graphic aids makes for brief yet clear memos.

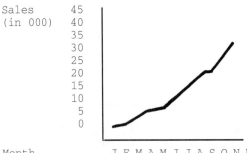

Congratulations, and keep up the great work!

FIGURE 9–5 Policy Memo

Memo

To: All Department Members
From: Tom Martin, Executive Vice President
Date: September 5, 19__
Subject: Change in Employee Appraisal Policy

Beginning on January 1, 19__, we will complete appraisals for all Class I, II, and III employees twice each year. Supervisors should submit forms to the Vice President of Human Resources between May 1 and May 15, and again between November 15 and November 30.

Employees with three months or less of service will be reviewed during the following period.

Continue to use forms 24 and 26.

Policy memos document changes in company policy and procedure and should be added to existing manuals for future reference.

ing of policy memos helps alert employees that these messages, because of their importance, should be set apart from the clutter of other memos received during the day. Because policy memos, taken together, eventually form a policy manual, many companies routinely issue such memos on three-hole-punched paper for easy insertion into each employee's or work unit's policy notebook.

THE FOLLOW-UP MEMO

As written records, memos clearly establish work responsibilities.

The *follow-up memo* (also known as the memo that fixes responsibility) is used to put in writing understandings and agreements reached in conversations, meetings, telephone calls, and other oral forms of communication. In its full form, the follow-up memo includes the time and place that the original agreement was reached as well as the nature of that agreement. Less formal follow-up memos may omit the reference to time and place or refer to it in passing (as in Figure 9–6). But whether formal or informal, the follow-up memo tries to state precisely what was agreed on, by whom, and what action or responsibility follows from that agreement.

LONGER MEMOS

Memos longer than one page are sometimes called memorandum reports.

Although most memos are quite brief, ranging from half a page to a full page, some may be as long as two or three pages. Longer memos are something less than a short report (because they lack the format and elements of a report), yet more extensive than a typical memo in the amount and depth of detail. Known as *memorandum* (or *memo) reports*, these extended memos use the traditional memo heading (*To: From: Date: Subject*:) and may include charts and graphs.

FIGURE 9–6   Memo Fixing Responsibility or Confirming an Agreement

```
To:       Shane Travella, Manager, Accounting Division
From:     Lani Worth, Vice President
Date:     May 7, 19__
Subject:  New Assignment to Forecast Newsletter

I'm glad we had a chance, on May 5, to discuss at
length your role as supervising editor for our new
executive newsletter, Forecast. You know how much a
steady stream of reliable financial information can
mean to our executive leadership in the company.

As agreed in our meeting, effective June 1 you will
be released from one-third of your present duties to
assume direct responsibility for production of this
biweekly in-house communication. We agreed, further,
that the first issue will appear no later than
August 1.

Thank you, Shane, for your enthusiasm in leading
this important new effort. I look forward to its
success.
```

Topic divisions within the memo report are typically marked by boldface or underlining rather than by the Roman numerals more common in short and formal reports.

In no case should the memo report appear simply as an unrelieved block of text spanning two or more pages. Readers should find the memo report just as readable (through use of white space, text placement, headings, and clear writing) as a briefer memo. Figure 9–7 exemplifies an in-house memo report. Note that the writer used underlined topic headings and numbered points to organize and emphasize a substantial amount of information. Figure 9–8 is a memo report for an external audience. In this case, the writer placed the memo on company letterhead. The same information could have been formatted as a traditional business letter. The writer preferred the memo form, however, because of its association with charts, graphs, and tables; use of brief, direct statements; and use of headings and numbered lists. In sending this memo to the reader, the writer may choose to accompany it with a brief cover letter conveying a less formal tone.

FIGURE 9–7   Memo Report (In-house Audience)

```
                     MEMORANDUM REPORT
To:        C.E. Johnsen, Executive Vice President
From:      T.E. Kerwin, Manager—Employee Communications
Date:      April 30, 19__
Subject:   Review of Employee Communication Activities

In response to your memo of April 25, 19__, here is a review of
our current employee communication activities.
```

Print

At the present time we issue three publications:
1. Framingham News
2. Management Review
3. Supervisor's Bulletin

Publications and Costs (as of January, 19__)

	No.Pub. Jan.19__	No.Pub. Jan.19__	Cost per Copy Jan.19__	Jan.19__
Farmington News	18,500	17,100	41¢	37¢
Management Review	600	570	12¢	11¢
Supervisor's Bulletin	1,500	1,400	9¢	8¢

In addition, from time to time we issue the following:
1. Employee Orientation Manual
2. Brochures describing new and/or ongoing benefits, such as
   hospitalization and insurance

Oral and interpersonal

1. Monthly Farmington Quality Circle (six representatives from
   the work force and six from management)
2. Annual president's report to all employees
3. Quarterly division managers' reports (to respective
   divisions only)

Personnel involved

The number of personnel assigned to the Employee Communications
Department has remained static over the past 24 months, even
though we have assumed three new major reponsibilities in that
period:
1. Inception of monthly Quality Circle meetings.
2. Inception of the Supervisor's Bulletin.
3. Assignment of one individual full-time to speech writing for
   Farmington officers. The department staff consists of
   1 Director
   4 Assistants to the Director
   2 Clerical Personnel

In-house memo reports, which deal with substantial data, are organized through headings and lists.

FIGURE 9–8   Memo Report (External Audience)

ZRM Electronics, Inc.
    751 MacLean Avenue
    Dallas, Texas 75223

October 21, 19__

To: Albert Hill, Manager
           Hill, Adams and Hill, Management Consultants
From: Roberta T. Black, Human Resources Director
           ZRM Electronics
Subject: Summary of Training Activities, 1991-1993

You indicated that it would be helpful to your firm to learn
about our training activities for employees from 1991 to
1993. The data that follow are a summary of those
activities.

Management Training
Managers were offered three specific courses. These were
well attended.

Course	Approximate No. Eligible	No. Enrolled	No. of Classes held
Supervision and Human Relations	260	65	3
Decision Making	260	50	3
Effective Written and Oral Communication	260	85	5

Engineering Training
Although a number of courses were offered to engineers, the
response was very weak. Perhaps the reason for this lies in
the engineering workload, which was very heavy due to military and space orders.

Course	Approximate No. Eligible	No. Enrolled	No. of Classes held
Cost Control for Engineers	350	45	3
Advances in Electronics	250	25	1
Engineering Reports	350	80	4

Writers sometimes choose the memo format to convey information to an external audience when the information requires graphic representation or headings and lists.

page 2

Clerical and Office Training
Response by clerical personnel to the training was consistently high. However, the company did not offer as many courses as could be filled because of the high turnover of employees in these categories.

Course	Approximate No. Eligible	No. Enrolled	No. of Classes held
Office Techniques and Management	425	150	6
Business Letters	300	110	6
Telephone and Filing Techniques	250	50	3

As you requested, we did not include shop training in this report. However, information is available.

Instruction
Instructors for all management-level training plus the engineering-reports classes were hired from outside the company. Most of the teachers were university professors or professional consultants.

All other courses were taught by company personnel.

Administration
All training was carried out under the direct supervision of the Human Resources Department. Mr. Asquith was specifically charged with coordinating and supervising recruitment, assignment, and class direction.

Concluding Comments
This report will give you some idea of our training activities. If you have any questions, please contact me. I am eager to work with you on long-range training plans.

R.T.B.

WRITING AND SPEAKING EXERCISES

1. What problems confront writers when the information they must communicate is negative? What steps should they take to ensure effective communication? Prepare a memo that addresses these concerns; offer specific recommendations to memo writers facing the task of delivering bad news.

2. As a normal part of your job, you are required to seek applicants for a newly created management position. The position requires six years of sales experience, excellent written and verbal communication skills, strong organizational skills, and some educational background in management. Company policy requires that the position be filled internally, if possible. Write a memo advertising the job opening.

3. After issuing the memo from question 2, you received 15 applications. However, you determined that none of these applicants fully met the job's requirements. Write a memo to your supervisor stating your position and asking for permission to extend the search for applicants beyond company employees.

4. A manager has verbally instructed you to take home an expensive piece of company word processing equipment so that you can complete a report. Write a memo to file in which you cover yourself against charges of taking company equipment without authorization and against liability for the equipment.

5. Write a policy memo to workers explaining why the company is not taking a day off for a nationally recognized holiday.

6. Below are three introductory paragraphs to memos. If each memo had a good subject line, the paragraphs would not be needed. For each of the following, write an appropriate subject line that would eliminate the need for the paragraph.

   (a) Following up on your request for a status report on the Baxter project, the following data and recommendations have been assembled.

   (b) The need for providing additional work space for our support staff is obvious. Following an extensive three-month study, we have determined an efficient and cost-effective means of gaining the needed space.

   (c) Beverly Beven has done an extraordinarily good job on projects that are actually beyond the scope of her job description. The purpose of this memo is to put her effort on record and inform you of her fine, cooperative spirit.

7. From time to time, we all want to establish policies for those around us. Take, for example, those influencing your living space: roommates, spouse, parents, landlord, or neighbors. Address a memo to one or more of these groups. In it, establish policies that, in your judgment, will lead to more harmonious relations.

8. Identify a problem on your campus that students have been discussing with the administration for years—but nothing seems to happen. Perhaps the problem is that oral messages can be forgotten or ignored rather easily. Write a memorandum report on the problem.

9. Choose one of your courses, perhaps the one you are taking in connection with this text. Write a memo from the professor to the students that

fixes responsibility for major class activities (grading, reports, assignments, attendance, and so forth).

10. One kind of memorandum report covers updates on important topics for superiors. Your boss has asked that any time you see an article germane to the operations of the firm, the Bailey Biscuit and Tea Company, you are to summarize the item in a memorandum report for her. Premised upon your major (be it accounting, marketing, finance, etc.), find a recent article that would apply to the firm. Summarize the article in a one-page memorandum report. On the back indicate your major.

11. "I wish I could remember . . . ." "There was an important point in that meeting I should have written down." How many ideas get lost because we forget them? One way to keep a record of good ideas is to write memos to file. Drawing on either a good idea you recently learned in class or an important point from a student group meeting, write a memo to file.

12. As vice president of marketing for a large corporation, you've been receiving paper by the bale from your employees—much of it in the form of unintelligible computer printouts. Write a memo addressed to all of your employees. Delineate the difference between data and communication. Emphasize that you want the latter in all future memos and reports.

13. Read the material below and edit it for content, clarity, conciseness, and organization. Submit your ideas in a memorandum report to John Farnsworth, vice president, marketing.

Your firm, Zimco, manufactures auto parts and equipment. Approximately three weeks ago, the head of your department—Marketing—called a meeting. The primary topic was "How Can We Motivate Our Dealers into A More Aggressive Sales Posture." You've come up with some ideas. You discussed them briefly with your boss and halfway through your comments he said, "Let's see a memo; then we can approve or disapprove your suggestions."

What you had in mind was a program of *cooperative advertising* (C.A.). Actually the theory behind C.A. is that both manufacturers and dealers will make a cost contribution to the premium item. Thus, each (the manufacturer and the dealer) has a stake in the program and usually greater commitment. The trick in C.A. is, of course, to require the dealer or distributor to make a financial contribution that is significant as well as attractive to him or her. However, the financial contribution should never be so large that it would cause the dealer to or distributor to decline to participate in the program. Finding the fine line between dealer participation and rejection is the most delicate task the manufacturer has in such a program.

Among your ideas is to offer all dealers custom-made all-wool navy blue blazers for salespersons. They would carry the individual company logo or crest and could be purchased by dealers for $40.00 each. A minimum purchase by a dealer would be 12 jackets. You've checked this out with Martin as well as Fairview Garment Manufacturers. The former would charge Zimco $58 per jacket and the latter, $60. Both require a minimum purchase of 400 jackets. You would also like to offer Zimco dealers a neon "Super Ride" sign that is extremely attractive and could be mounted in a dealer's window or in the dealership itself. Your thought is to provide the sign free to any dealer whose purchases of parts in the last quarter of this year is 120 percent or more of parts purchased in the last quarter of the previous year.

In addition, you wish to encourage dealers to purchase individual dealership radio time in their local towns and cities. You know that radio time is quite expensive, but you feel that it will pay. Your plan is to pay 100 percent of radio time cost over $500 per week which any dealer purchases. Thus, if a dealer purchases $600 one week, $750 the second week, $500 the third week, and $850 the fourth week of the month, Zimco will reimburse the dealer $700 for that month. The maximum monthly reimbursement would be limited to $1,000.

Incidentally, the crest on the jackets noted above is removable in the event the salesperson wished to use the garment as a sports jacket for leisure wear. As for the neon signs, they are extremely attractive and would cost $350 each if purchased from the sign division of Fordham Electric. Of course, this price is for an order of 200 signs minimum. If the request fell below that number, the price would go to $475 each.

Also, your rough figures indicate that a dealer's parts purchases for the quarter would have to increase about $20,000 over the previous quarter to pay for each sign, breakage, descriptive flyers to describe the program, transportation, and so on. But the signs are very attractive advertising items.

As for the radio time, you would limit that offer to the first quarter of 19__ only. And the monthly expenditure would be for station payments only. It would not include payments to script writers, singers, and so forth.

The benefits of your three suggestions are quire obvious. It has been proved that automobile dealers, television manufacturers, and heavy home appliance distributors (washers, dryers, etc.) increase sales 15 percent with sustained, minimum radio advertising offered to local communities.

Research by Fordham Electric has proved that neon signs are 20 percent more effective than regular nonelectric signs and 30 percent more effective than direct mail in securing prospective customer interest and attention in a product or service. As for jackets for sales personnel, the benefits are obvious. Sales personnel receive a $150 jacket for no cost or nominal cost. It is an attractive garment to add to their wardrobe. When the crest is worn, it increases esprit de corps, morale, and productivity.

Furthermore radio time increases listener awareness and identification of the dealership even if a sale does not result.

CASES

Complete the following assignments from the Cases for Discussion section at the back of this book:

1. The Mark Teller case—Assignment 3
2. The Jim Cantonelli case—Assignment 4
3. Hostile Takeover case—Assignment 3
4. Brooks-Martinez case—Assignment 3
5. When East Doesn't Meet West case—Assignment 3
6. The Sun Fresh case—Assignment 3
7. The Barney Burton case—Assignment 4
8. But Talking Isn't Working case—Assignment 4
9. Whose Perception Is Correct? case—Assignment 4
10. Bill Webster's Ethical Dilemma case—Assignment 4
11. Was This Really Fraud? case—Assignment 3

SUGGESTED
RESOURCES

Cross, Mary. *Persuasive Business Writing: Creating Better Letters, Memos, Reports, and More.* New York: American Management Association, 1987.

Fahner, Hal. "The 10 Commandments of Memo Writing." *Sales & Marketing Management* 142 (October 1990):85–87.

Gold, Rosalind. "'Reader-Friendly' Writing." *Supervisory Management* 34 (January 1989):39–43.

Straub, J.T. "Memos and Reports: Write Them Right the First Time." *Supervisory Management* 36 (July 1991):6–13.

Ware, R. "But the Good News Is." *Journal of Systems Management* 42 (July 1991):20–26.

Wueste, R.A. "Memos on the Loose! Stop Them Before They Get Started." *Management World* 17 (September—October 1988):40–47.

10

PRINCIPLES OF THE BUSINESS LETTER

Companies don't do business with companies; people do business with people. Make your writing sound like people talking.

Although letters vary widely in content and format, basic principles of effective communication govern their production.

What do all business letters have in common? Certainly not their content which can differ a great deal. In business, letters carry communication about a vast number of topics—personnel decisions, financial changes, product developments, sales appeals, regulatory compliance, and so forth. Even in form, business letters can look dissimilar, depending on their use of block, modified block, or other letter formats as described in Appendix B.

Basic principles, however, do underlie the writing of all business letters. In this chapter, we consider these principles. In Chapters 11 through 13 we will apply the principles to the most common kinds of business correspondence.

Computers and electronic communications have made a striking difference in our use of business letters. Many external messages are now being sent from computer to computer to computer printer to recipient, instead of being dictated, typed, and then mailed to the recipient. The computer-generated letter completed Monday afternoon in New York may arrive the next morning in California. If the companies involved have an electronic link, such as fax, the communication can arrive even more quickly. Computers and printers turn out hundreds of letters with the same content but with individualized addresses and salutations. In the best examples, there is no clue in the letter itself that it is, in fact, part of a mass mailing.

Even though the means of physically preparing and transmitting the business letter are changing, the basic principles of crafting a message remain the same. The business letter still represents people communicating with one another.

THE BUSINESS LETTER AND THE COMPANY IMAGE

Letters document business dealings, travel fast at low cost, and save time.

In most firms the business letter is the primary means of external communication for several reasons:

- A letter establishes a tangible record for later reference.
- A letter spans distances quickly at relatively low cost.

- A letter reduces the need for business travel to attend face-to-face meetings.
- A letter transacts routine business matters efficiently, often with the help of letter guides and forms.

For example, consider a large insurance company with millions of policyholders and thousands of agents from coast to coast. Questions about premiums, cancellations, medical bills, changes in beneficiaries, and a thousand other situations arise each day. Letters flow into the home office from a variety of sources. Replies go out on the company's letterhead and are written by hundreds of different employees, all contributing to the company's image.

When policyholder Mrs. Baxter of Three Forks, South Dakota, reads the letter she receives at her farm home, she forms a mental picture of the company. Mr. Smythe also forms an opinion of the company as he reads his letter in his apartment in a Chicago high-rise. The corporate officer who is considering the purchase of major policies for her company formulates impressions from the letters she receives. Each person—young or old, rich or poor, from the policyholder to the corporate officer—builds an image of the company on the basis of the letter he or she reads.

The quality of the letter reflects the company's professionalism.

If the letter is curt, the company appears abrupt. If the letter is trite, stereotyped, and dull, the company appears backward and stodgy. If the letter is discourteous or tactless, the company appears high-handed. If the letter is unattractive and sloppy, the company appears careless and negligent. On the other hand, if the letter is clear and concise, the firm seems well organized and competent. If the letter is courteous and friendly, the company seems concerned and helpful. If the letter is attractive and neat, the company seems efficient and accurate. Regardless of who wrote the letter, the message reflects the image of the company.

Companies that appreciate the importance of letters offer their employees training programs and devote entire departments to evaluating company correspondence.

The managements of many companies have set up training programs to improve the letter-writing abilities of their personnel. Some major corporations have departments whose primary functions are to evaluate company correspondence and to train employees in letter writing. One large insurance firm holds classes, reviews correspondence, issues bulletins, and at frequent intervals reminds its employees of the importance of effective correspondence.

Other strategies are possible. Some companies engage outside consultants for evaluation and training, and many firms subscribe to letter-improvement bulletins sent out periodically by companies specializing in this service. Most firms today are aware of the importance of good company correspondence and are attempting to raise their standards or keep them high. In recent years, the widespread use of electronic mail and fax transmission for letters has posed a special challenge. Because these technologies allow letters and other messages to be sent immediately after their composition, writers may not take time to weigh the impact of their communications—especially those written in the heat of emotion. Companies using e-mail and fax have noted a phenomenon called "flaming" among message senders. Blatant and ill-considered lines, such as "you're dead meat, buddy, if I don't get that report by 5 P.M.,"creep into e-mail messages and fax much more often than they ever appeared in traditional letters and memos.

The speed of e-mail and fax have led to "flaming," which occurs when writers communicate in the heat of the moment.

The most obvious explanation for flaming is the immediacy of transmission made possible by e-mail and fax. The writer no longer has the cooling-off period previously provided by the time it took to type the letter and envelope and then post it through company mail channels. E-mail or fax allow a message to be sent to the recipient (or many recipients on the electronic system) while the writer is still in the grip of strong emotion. An hour or day later, the writer may regret sending such a hasty and inappropriate message.

Companies are taking steps to educate employees about the legal and professional dangers of flaming. At TRW, for example, all employees receive training in the use of e-mail. At Cushman-Wakefield, a commercial real estate broker, *all* mail leaving the company passes through an approval process involving one or more managers.

MECHANICS AND FORM

In a previous era, managers often left matters of letter mechanics and form for secretaries to sort out. The manager's job in those days was to draft or dictate the message; the secretary's job was to polish and perfect it. With computers in managers' offices, however, matters of mechanics and form have again become the responsibility of the message composer. In some corporations, such as Hughes Aircraft, the widespread use of PCs by managers has removed secretaries almost entirely from the correspondence process. Managers now key in their own messages, send them by e-mail, or print them out for fax transmission or delivery by regular mail.

Readers judge your professionalism and competence on the basis of the writing mechanics and physical appearance of your correspondence.

If errors in mechanics or form occur on such correspondence, the professional image of the manager is at stake. Readers inside and outside the company form lasting impressions of a manager's ability to compose and polish correspondence. Their impressions either reflect well on the writer and the company or damage the image of both.

Accepted letter format varies from company to company.

What guidelines should managers follow in their efforts to create error-free correspondence? Almost all business writers agree to certain matters of mechanics (as contained in Appendices A and B). But specific details of business letter format can vary considerably from one company to another. One firm requires that its employees use block form; another prefers modified block. One organization recommends identifying initials of the sender and typist, and another company omits them entirely. The "correct" form is the one the firm requires. Many companies publish their own correspondence guides, which indicate company preference in letter layout, use of abbreviations, address style, signatures, and so on.

Communication technologies such as word processing have also influenced the mechanics of business correspondence. Most companies now prefer block style format, for example, because that style requires less time for keying in word processing software than does the indentation and tabular format of other letter styles.

PRINCIPLES OF COMMUNICATION

Although the mechanics of a business letter should be correct, an error in typing or the layout of a letter will not cost nearly as much goodwill as a tactless or sarcastic statement. Thus, it is knowledge of the *principles* of business writing that is most important.

TONE

A reader extends the tone of a single business letter to the entire company.

In written communications, *tone* is the total impression made by the words, topics, and level of formality. After reading a letter, a person may think, "The tone of Acme's message was extremely friendly," or "tactful," or "impersonal," or "very positive." Our impression of tone seems to depend on our reactions to the words used, the phrasing of sentences, and the order of ideas. The impressions we form of a letter's tone—friendly, formal, courteous, high-pressured—tend to extend to the company as a whole.

Naturalness. At one time business correspondence was stiff from use of trite phrases, obsolete and archaic references, and pompous statements. In contemporary business practice few letters contain such expressions. If you do sometimes tend to use trite expressions, drop them for more natural ones. You probably don't use expressions like the following in speaking, so why use them in writing?

> As in the above
> Advise
> As indicated
> As per
> At hand
> At early date
> Enclosed please find
> Esteemed order
> Hand you herewith
> Hereby acknowledge
> In accordance with

Natural words and expressions convey a friendly tone.

A letter filled with expressions like these conveys an impression of an impersonal and unfriendly company. Compare the two letters in Figure 10–1. Notice that the messages are similar but the tone is not. How would you feel toward the companies that mailed them? Letter 10-1a reflects sincerity, warmth, and a natural tone that builds goodwill. Letter 10-1b creates the impression of a company that is unfriendly and unconcerned about satisfying a customer.

Write conversationally to avoid a stiff or pompous tone.

Connecticut Life Insurance Company published a booklet for its employees titled *Speak When You Write*. Its pages were filled with suggestions on how to inject a natural, friendly tone into communications to increase goodwill. The key perhaps is in the title, which, of course, should not be taken too literally. If we did "write as we speak," our written communications would probably be wordy and repetitious. What the title really means is to write as *you sound* when you talk. Then your written communications will reflect the natural, friendly spontaneity of your spoken words. Among the suggestions contained in the booklet were the following three:

1. Talk out what you are trying to say before you write it out.
2. Speak to your reader in the same friendly tone (though not a chatty tone) that you would use for an in-person conversation.
3. Avoid diction that reminds the reader more of an encyclopedia or legal contract than a conversation.

Courtesy. In this hurried world, we sometimes overlook an opportunity to extend a little courtesy to those with whom we communicate. Letters often conclude with a phrase such as "Your merchandise was shipped on January 14."

FIGURE 10-1A An Unfriendly Business Letter and a Friendly Business Letter (compare with Figure 10-1b)

Farnsworth Corporation
Office and Stationery Supplies
2100 South Hampton Drive
Chicago, Illinois 60624

August 7, 19__

Mr. Henry Wineman
1717 Covington Drive
Roxbury, MA 02119

Dear Mr. Wineman:

Per our conversation Thursday last, this is to acknowledge receipt of your order dated August 1, 19__. In accordance with mutually agreed upon credit arrangements, we will expect your C.O.D. payment in the amount of $283.33 upon your receipt of merchandise.

We advise that said shipment should reach you on or before August 15. In the event of problems in this regard, do not hesitate to contact us.

Respectfully yours,

Robert Kevin

Robert Kevin
Vice President

Because of the trite phrases and the cold, formal tone, the reader may feel that the writer is unconcerned with the former's welfare.

Farnsworth Corporation
Office and Stationery Supplies
2100 South Hampton Drive
Chicago, Illinois 60624

August 7, 19__

Mr. Henry Wineman
1717 Covington Drive
Roxbury, MA 02119

Dear Mr. Wineman:

Thank you for your order of August 1, 19__. You should receive your shipment by August 15 C.O.D. Total charges due at that time will be $283.33.

We appreciate your confidence in our products and look forward to serving you.

Sincerely,

Robert Kevin

Robert Kevin
Vice President

FIGURE 10-1B
The use of personal pronouns and courtesy promote a feeling of personal concern.

Sincerity and courtesy build goodwill.

Consider adding a "Thank you very much," or "We appreciate your business," or "We were happy we could ship this equipment immediately, as you requested." When *thank you*, *please*, *I appreciated*, or similar expressions are used in a letter—and used sincerely—they help create goodwill.

Positive language.   Certain words and phrases evoke an unfavorable mental reaction, which the reader may associate with the product or service discussed in the writing. A department store does not display a sign saying, "Complaint Department," because these words would stimulate an unpleasant association. The label "Adjustment Bureau" or "Customer Service Department," on the other hand, makes the customer anticipate a positive experience.

What would be a customer's reaction to an order form with the statement, "To avoid errors and mistakes in shipping, complete the order form as directed"? The customer's immediate reaction is to picture the order delayed or lost and anticipate being billed for merchandise never received. It would be safer to tear up the order form and do business elsewhere. Because of such reactions, messages on most order forms aim to stimulate a positive image. Toward that end they may state, "Please complete the order form as requested for accurate and rapid shipment of merchandise." What is it about those two statements that triggers different reactions? It is the words themselves. Certain words and phrases in our culture, used in a specific context, induce unfavorable (negative) mental associations, whereas others evoke positive responses.

Positive word choice can prevent negative or hostile reactions.

NEGATIVE: *We hope you won't be dissatisfied with the new All-American line.*

POSITIVE: *We are sure you will be satisfied with the new All-American line.*

Under most conditions, avoid words that evoke a negative response. Words such as *trouble, dissatisfaction, complaint, neglect, errors* and *negligence* usually result in unfavorable mental associations for the product or service under discussion.

However, a negative tone is not always undesirable. It can be used for shock value when it is followed by a positive solution. Advertisers frequently use this device.

NEGATIVE PROBLEM: *Have you provided for your advancing years?*

POSITIVE SOLUTION: *Let us show you how enjoyable your retirement can be with Parker Protection.*

The negative tone used in this way can help sell many products: insurance, health items, and safety and personal hygiene products. Nevertheless, always handle the negative tone with care, for readers are more likely to remember (and associate with a product) the negative rather than pleasant, positive images. Perhaps for this reason, insurance today is *not* sold as "death benefits or protection from disaster"—all negative—but for "living comfort, peace of mind, and security"—all positive.

Tact.   In communication, tact is difficult to define. Generally, tact means saying the right thing at the right time in the right way. But when you are trying to write a tactful letter, what is the right thing to say? When is the right time? What is the right way? Clearly, the general definition of tact is not an adequate guide.

Like so many factors in communication, tact is intimately involved with words, their use, and their interpretation. The phrases, "You failed to include the order form," or "We were surprised you did not understand the directions," or "We received your letter in which you claimed we did not ship," are certainly tactless. However, are they tactless because of the *denotations* of the key words, "You failed," "We were surprised," or "You claimed," or their *connotations*? These phrases exemplify how important the personal interpretation of words can be. Words can assume special connotations in specific contexts and result in statements that are interpreted as tactless and discourteous.

Tact requires that you think about how your reader will interpret your words.

The solution to the problem is to avoid words or phrases that may antagonize or embarrass. You can point out others' errors without embarrassing them if you choose the right words.

> TACTLESS: *We received your letter in which you claim we did not send . . .*
> BETTER: *Thank you for your letter concerning our shipment of December 3.*

THE *YOU* ATTITUDE

Because of our nature and the society in which we live, our interests, activities, and goals usually center on ourselves. Most of us are impatient when *our* problem, *our* situations, *our* purchases are not examined from *our* point of view. We usually analyze and communicate about the situations in which we are involved from *our* position and with *our* perceptions. It is easy to forget that the other person also has a position, feelings, and reactions. Our decisions and actions seem logical to us, but do we ask ourselves how logical our actions are from the other person's viewpoint?

A *you* attitude consists of viewing a situation from the other person's point of view. It requires sensitivity, an appreciation of others, and respect. This interest must be sincere, for if it is not, the other person will perceive that it is false and resent it. The *you* attitude is most important when a difference of opinion exists. At such times it is vital to appreciate the other person's point of view, to be sensitive to his or her needs, and to communicate your appreciation of the situation.

Always consider the situation from your reader's view point.

The *you* attitude is not synonymous with *agreement*. It is possible to communicate a strong *you* attitude while disagreeing with the other person. The secretary who wants a new computer is more willing to accept a denial of that request if his or her employer first shows an understanding of *why* the secretary made the request for a new machine.

The letters in Figure 10–2 and 10–3 illustrate the difference between a *you* attitude and a *we* or *I* attitude. In Figure 10–2, Mr. Moreau is clearly concerned with his own profits and accomplishments. In Figure 10–3, however, he shows how his shop is there for Ms. March's convenience.

EFFECTIVE COMPOSITION

Let us now apply the principles of effective composition to business letters. As with all principles, these are easier to state than to apply. But each of the following qualities—completeness, good organization, conciseness, clarity, precision, accuracy, and attractiveness—is crucial to successful managerial correspondence.

FIGURE 10–2 "We"-centered Letter—Focusing Too Much on the Writer's Needs

Viva la France
Gourmet Specialties

29 Wilshire Blvd.
Los Angeles, CA 90017
(213) 555-8382

April 3, 19___

Ms. Wendy March
Owner
Wendy's Kitchen
3029 Reardon Drive
Beverly Hills, CA 90210

Dear Ms. March:

We are happy to announce the grand opening of Viva la France Gourmet Specialities, the single finest source for gourmet culinary items on the West Coast.

Our European-trained staff has painstakingly assembled a chef's paradise of hard-to-find spices, herbs, cooking implements, and recipe guides. Their efforts are directed by Pierre Raudanne, who for seven years was head chef at L'Oeuf in Paris. Mssr. Raudanne was trained at Cordon Bleu and has written more than 20 articles on French cooking and cuisine for international magazines.

At our grand opening, we will feature discount prices on many items, including the "French Starter Pack" of sauce recipes and spices. The owners, Mssrs. Goban and Fourier, will be on hand to lead the festivities.

We are proud to be the first and best source for gourmet items in Southern California.

Sincerely,

Francoise Moreau

Francoise Moreau
Manager

A we attitude stresses the company's abilities and may seem bragging in tone.

FIGURE 10–3 You-attitude Letter—Reader-oriented (Compare with Figure 10–2)

Viva la France
Gourmet Specialties

29 Wilshire Blvd.
Los Angeles, CA 90017
(213) 555-8382

April 3, 19___

Ms. Wendy March
Owner
Wendy's Kitchen
3029 Reardon Drive
Beverly Hills, CA 90210

Dear Ms. March:

You may have been driving to San Francisco or waiting weeks for delivery of your gourmet culinary needs. If so, celebrate with us the grand opening of Viva la France Gourmet Specialties, the single finest source for gourmet culinary items on the West Coast.

To meet your needs, our European-trained staff has painstakingly assembled a chef's paradise of hard-to-find spices, herbs, cooking implements, and recipe guides. Your expert-in-residence is Pierre Raudanne, who for seven years was head chef at L'Oeuf in Paris. Trained at Cordon Bleu and author of more than 20 articles on French cooking, Mssr. Raudanne looks forward to answering your every question about French cuisine.

To welcome you to a new, convenient source for gourmet items, we will offer discount prices at our grand opening on many items, including the "French Starter Pack" of sauce recipes and spices. The owners, Mssrs. Goban and Fourier, will be on hand to greet you.

You can look with confidence to Viva la France as your first and best source for gourmet items in Southern California.

Sincerely,

Francoise Moreau

Francoise Moreau
Manager

A you attitude stresses benefits to the client and portrays a helpful tone.

Completeness. When we inadvertently omit facts or ideas from a business letter, we tend to brush this off with a simple, "Oh, I forgot about *that*." The result, however, is not so simple. The recipient must write again and we, in turn, must reply again. Perhaps an isolated case causes no great harm, but if 10 percent of the letters a firm sends out are incomplete, and the company mails 3,000 letters a week, the cost of follow-up letters can be staggering. These unnecessary letters must be written, typed, and mailed. An additional expense involves the loss of goodwill and, quite possibly, customers.

Incomplete letters lose money and goodwill.

In other situations, the results are more difficult to measure. If, for example, Company Z writes to firms A, B, and C for information concerning cost, shipping dates, and guarantees on plastic widgets and receives complete replies from firms A and B but not from C, will Z write back to C? Not unless C's prices were significantly lower. Typically, Z will probably choose between A and B.

From time to time our letters will not cover everything the recipient wants. Nevertheless, we should be certain we don't omit important facts through carelessness. The key to writing complete letters is to organize the facts before you write.

Good organization. Before writing even the simplest letter, writers should know precisely what topics to cover. Some writers make notes in the margin or at the bottom of the letter to which they are replying. Others make notes on a piece of scratch paper or draw up an outline of their reply. Still others prefer to outline mentally. The method doesn't matter, as long as the writers have a guide to writing the reply letter. By checking the guide against the inquiry letter, the writers can ensure that the reply will be complete.

Organizing your ideas before you write ensures a complete message.

Conciseness. The recipient must read a business letter completely because it involves a business transaction. A letter that rambles on and on, with unending paragraphs, meaningless phrases, and unnecessary words, will irritate the reader.

Concise letters communicate thoroughly without wasting words.

Overall length is no sure guide to conciseness. A letter covering a third of a page may be short but wordy. On the other hand, a three-page letter may be concise. Strive to write business letters that do not waste words; write letters in which every phrase, clause, and statement says only what needs to be said.

WORDY: *I would ask your involvement in making a request to Mr. Rodriquez that, in anticipation of our meeting, he take the time to make a review of all records of sales for the fiscal year 1993.*

REVISED: *Please ask Mr. Rodriquez to review the 1993 sales figures prior to our meeting.*

Notice how meaning becomes clearer, understanding easier, and impact greater when unnecessary words are dropped and phrases are shortened.

Clarity. Unclear business communication always causes confusion. The sentence that can be interpreted in two different ways or can't be understood at all is most disturbing. How should the reader interpret this statement: "If the safety bracket for the 333 press has been completed, send it at once"? What should be shipped? The press? The bracket? Both?

Clarity of expression prevents confusion of ideas.

Check everything you write, whether a six-line memo or a three-page letter, for clarity. If you detect passages the reader might misinterpret, revise them.

Choose words that express your meaning precisely.

Precision. Statements can be clear, unified, and coherent yet not accurate and precise. If you mean "thoroughly examined," don't say "looked over"; if you mean "A proportional stratified sample was taken," don't write "A survey was made."

Because business communication is often the basis for making decisions, precision and accuracy in word choice are very important. One or two carelessly chosen words may convey a meaning far from the one desired.

> **VAGUE:** *Sales of the Kenwood Lumber Company have gone up during the past two or three years.*
>
> **PRECISE:** *Sales of the Kenwood Lumber Company increased by 4 percent in 1993 and 8 percent in 1992 over the gross sales figures of 1991.*

Accuracy. It is human nature to notice that something is awry. Readers notice errors in grammar or punctuation in a letter. Focusing on the errors, voluntarily or not, they will give less attention to the content of the message. As a result, some of the message is lost.

Accurate grammar and usage reflect your professionalism and attention to detail.

Because letters are often all the recipients know of a company, errors in basic English diminish their opinion of the firm. Management must be certain, therefore, that its correspondents have mastered not only tact, courtesy, clarity, and precision, but also the basic principles of English grammar. The author of written communication should proofread it carefully before placing it in a communication channel.

Attractiveness. The final principle of effective composition has little to do with effective statement of ideas, but everything to do with communication. Communication depends as much on the nonverbal message as it does on the verbal one. Your ideas may be brilliant and your statements clear, tactful, concise, accurate, and grammatical; but if they are thrown together haphazardly on paper, with no visual form or balance, the recipient may not even read them. If recipients do read such statements, it may be with a negative attitude.

Unattractive appearance may prevent your letters from being read.

Across industries, managers are increasingly taking control of document production and processing, including final editing and revisions of their own letters and memos. Consequently, these managers need to understand the importance of attractive margins, white space, balanced placement of text on the page, use of various type styles and sizes, paragraph length, and other elements that give business letters a truly professional appearance.

Form letters that repeat mistakes to multiple readers can seriously damage credibility.

A manager who lacks thorough knowledge of letter mechanics and word processing capabilities can inadvertently replicate his or her errors a thousandfold in composing form and guide letters for others. These letters, intended as models for other writers, too often are the least attractive letters sent by the company. (Consider, for example, form letters you may have received recently from banks, insurance companies, or the government.) The same electronic communication technologies that make quick revision possible also make the repetition of mistakes too easy for careless or uninformed writers.

**WRITING
AND SPEAKING
EXERCISES**

1. How do a firm's letters affect its image? Obtain letters from several well-known companies and note the ways in which corporate identity is established in written communication. Consider not only the written message, but the choice of letterhead, stationery, and letter style, as well as any other important variables. Be prepared to present your findings to the class in an oral presentation.

2. How have technologies (for example, the fax machine and electronic mail) affected the contemporary business writer? Specifically, can the instantaneous nature of e-mail and fax lead to communication that moves faster than a writer's judgment? Does rapid communication sometimes deteriorate into nasty or unexamined communication? Research this question and prepare a memo to your instructor that clarifies this issue.

3. Plan and distribute a survey to local businesses that use e-mail as a regular part of their business day. Determine their perceptions of advantages as well as disadvantages of the use of e-mail. Prepare a chart of your survey results.

4. The *you* attitude is easy to understand and often difficult to implement. For each of the following situations, write a first sentence for the letter clearly reflecting the *you* attitude.
   (a) A letter to a company that repaired your photocopy machine. Within three hours after the job was done, it broke down again; it's the fifth time this has happened.
   (b) A letter to the General Electric Company requesting a copy of its annual report.
   (c) A letter to the mayor asking if a street near campus can be closed on homecoming night for the annual bonfire.

5. Convert each of these *we*-centered statements to *you* statements.
   (a) I want your account so that I can demonstrate how experienced I am in property management.
   (b) My new store will open on May 17. Come see my fabulous collection of designer furniture, all personally selected by me to reflect the latest trends in contemporary interior design.
   (c) I appreciate the hospitality I received during my recent visit to the corporate offices of Henderson, Kay, and Co.
   (d) I am writing to provide notification that, according to my records, the September payment has not been received. I need that payment so that I can, in turn, make my own payments.

6. Convert each of the following statements from a negative tone to a positive tone.
   (a) You failed to obey the detailed instructions we provided with your glider kit.
   (b) We assume that you will not find fault with your Grass-All mower.
   (c) This company has no reason to doubt that our relationship will be free from unnecessary hassles and disappointments.
   (d) Please do not neglect to watch for unintentional errors when reviewing the manuscript.

7. Which of the popular business letter styles do your friends prefer? Conduct your own survey by showing two or more different formats of the

same letter to those surveyed. When they have made their choice, ask them to explain their preference. Sum up their reasons in a short report. Include statistics from the survey and your interpretation of them.

8. Gather at least four of your old reports or term papers. From them, glean a list of trite expressions you have a tendency to use. Beside each trite phrase, write a more adequate alternative.

9. Tone has a lot to do with word choice. Some words reflect a positive tone, while others reflect a negative tone. Illustrate the extreme by setting up a dozen matched pairs of words or phrases; make one list positive and the other negative. For example:

NEGATIVE TONE	POSITIVE TONE
cheap	inexpensive

10. Trite or archaic expressions may ruin your credibility before the reader gets past the first paragraph. The following sentences do not belong in any businessperson's correspondence. Revise appropriately.
    (a) As per your request, here is the summary of the *Marketing Research* article you wanted.
    (b) Hoping to hear from you in the near future, best wishes.
    (c) At your earliest convenience will you please return the draft memo so that it can be polished and distributed.
    (d) According to our records you have not returned *Communicating in Business* to the company library; may we hear from you at your earliest convenience?
    (e) Regarding your recent promotion, permit me to say how pleased Lin and I are for you; you deserved it and we wish you every success.

11. Find an advertisement that, in your opinion, exemplifies the appropriate use of the *you* perspective. Write an evaluation in which you suggest how this perspective influences those reading and viewing the ad.

12. Rewrite the following letter body so that it reflects the principles of tact discussed in this chapter.

    This will inform you that you have failed to qualify for scholarship aid for the coming academic term. Only students who demonstrated the ability to score 780 or higher on the Standard Qualification Index were considered for awards. If you have complaints about this decision, it is our duty to inform you of your right to appeal this negative response to the Complaint Committee of the Scholarship Board.

13. Describe a recent situation in which you used language that resulted in a response you did not anticipate. In other words, the connotation was inappropriate. Then indicate what you could have done to avoid the situation.

14. Incomplete letters create problems for both the sender and receiver. The problem can be remedied if the initiator of the communication ensures that all necessary information is included.
    You receive a telephone call summarized as follows:

    Janice Walberg of the International Association of Business Communicators wants to know if the hotel has one large meeting room (for 50 people), hotel rooms (35 singles), and banquet facilities for 50 people. Need this for the day and night of Wednesday, February 17, 19__.

Respond to his request as assistant manager of the Magnolia Hotel. Indicate on a separate sheet of paper the process you would go through to be sure you provide Walberg with complete information.

15. A university has a policy that first-year students must live on campus, in approved university housing, or with their parents or guardians. André Jackson lives in the town in which the university is located and resides with his parents. He receives the following letter (in part) from the university housing office:

Dear Mr. Jackson:

As you are residing in unapproved housing you are in violation of Section 1–c of the university housing regulations. See Mr. Pat Herman of our office before October 10, 19__, or your registration will be cancelled.

The letter has no *you* orientation, and the computer or personnel in the housing office have erred. However, now André is angry. How could the letter be written with more tact and not pronounce him guilty before hearing about the situation? Prepare a tactful letter that will not make innocent people angry with the organization.

16. For each of the following vague statements, write a brief paragraph discussing the problems that might ensue if these messages were actually sent.

(a) (from a vice president to a unit manager) I received your memo, and agree that we need to hire necessary help. Please proceed to do so.

(b) (from one employee to another) You and I are supposed to prepare something for next week's meeting. Let's get together sometime this week.

(c) (from an accountant to a manager) Monthly cash balances show some irregularities.

(d) (from a company president to vice presidents) I'll be on vacation for three weeks. Handle matters as best you can until I return.

SUGGESTED RESOURCES

Bacon, Mark S. "Persuasive Writing: Imitate the Prose of Pros." *Association Management* 40 (August 1988):164–168.

Basile, Frank. "Tips for Better Business Letters." *Journal of Property Management* 54 (January—February 1989):28–29.

Bell, Arthur H., and Kester, Cherie. *Effective Memos and Letters.* Hauppauge, N.Y.: Barron's, 1991.

Bredin, J. "Say It Simply." *Industry Week* 240 (July 15, 1991):19–20.

Fielden, J.S. "Meaning Is Shaped by Audience and Situation." *Personnel Journal* 67 (May 1988):107–110.

Lau, Barbara. "Adding Instant Readability Appeal to Your Business Correspondence." *Management Quarterly* 30 (Summer 1989):13–15.

Lundeen, H.K. "Are Your Words Working for You?" *Journal of Property Management* 54 (January—February 1989):26–28.

Shelby, A.N. "Applying the Strategic Choice Model to Motivational Appeals: A Theoretical Approach." *Journal of Business Communication* 28 (Summer 1991):187–212.

11

INQUIRY, REQUEST AND ORDER LETTERS

The right words are the greatest motivators of all.

T̲he most common business letters of all (and often the most overlooked) are inquiries, requests, and orders. Too often, these brief communications misfire because the writer has considered them "just routine." In doing so, the writer has forgotten to be concise, complete, courteous, and reader oriented.

The routine letters of business, however, are among the most important. Even the most simple business transaction usually requires requests for information, confirmation of orders, communications with regulatory agencies, and other routine written messages. These are the stitches that hold the fabric of business together.

MAKING INQUIRIES AND REQUESTS

Inquiries ask for information in reply to a question.

Essentially, an *inquiry* asks for information. A *request* goes further; for example, it asks for someone's services as a speaker, for endorsement of a product, or for a free sample. In short, a request requires action beyond a simple written reply.

Before you begin to write a letter of inquiry or request, determine exactly what your purpose is, that is, what information or action you want. Keep in mind that you and the recipient of your letter are both busy. In an outline, include all important points, pro and con.

State your purpose quickly.

Your inquiry may be simple and brief: Who is the distributor in our area? How quickly can a carload be shipped? Is a discount available? Or your inquiry may be complex and difficult: What would be involved in redecorating our offices? What kind of market is there for our product on the West Coast? What does the Affirmative Action Program mean to us? Regardless of the nature of the inquiry, the principle is the same—be complete, clear, and courteous. Get to the point immediately, particularly when the problem is complex. Your first sentence or two should state the subject, so that from the very beginning the receiver can identify the problem without wading through extraneous greetings and references. Responses will probably be more specific and direct if you ask in a specific and direct manner. Figures 11–1A and 11–1B (on pages 217 and 218) show examples of a poorly written and a well-written letter of inquiry.

Notice that both letters request information, but the effective letter will elicit exactly what Mr. Owens needs to know.

The effective letter of inquiry follows a general pattern:

1. Reason for inquiry in the first or second sentence
2. Explanation of circumstances, if necessary
3. Inquiry itself, with specific questions listed
4. Indication of the date by which a reply is needed
5. Assurance that information will be considered confidential (if applicable)

The well-written letter in Figure 11–1B meets these criteria, enabling the reader easily to understand what information the writer wants and to reply specifically.

Make answering easy for the reader.

The letter of inquiry should make it easy for the recipient to reply. You can do this by listing questions in an orderly fashion and by limiting the letter to essentials. It is unrealistic to ask so many questions that replying to the letter would require an unreasonable amount of time. If a problem is very complex, abstract, or detailed, set up a conference to discuss it. Finally, you may even wish to assist the recipient by including a self-addressed envelope.

Request letters follow the same pattern as inquiry letters. Because they are asking for a service rather than just an answer, they require some persuasion, and they should be written far in advance of the proposed date the service is to be performed. Like inquiry letters, request letters must be unmistakably clear. Respondents will probably hesitate to say "yes" to vague requests.

In Figure 11–2 (on page 219), notice the important role of persuasive language and argument in the request letter.

RESPONDING TO INQUIRIES AND REQUESTS: SAYING "YES"

When a major corporation places a double-page spread in a national magazine, it is not unusual for the advertisement to bring in a thousand inquiry letters: Where can I buy your television set? Is the model pictured in the lower left-hand corner available in walnut? What are the dimensions of the set pictured in the upper center of the page? What is the address of the dealer nearest my home?

Answer all routine inquiries completely, quickly, and courteously.

All inquiries should be answered, because each one represents a potential sale. In many situations, however, it would not be practical to answer each individually, so standard replies are prepared. These may be form letters, brochures, pamphlets, or even postcards. The form is relatively unimportant, provided the inquiry is answered completely and as quickly as possible. Furthermore, and perhaps most important, the reply—in whatever form—should express thanks for the inquiry and interest in serving the inquirer.

Sometimes letters of inquiry or request cannot be adequately answered with a form letter. A purchasing agent wants to know if a modification to an existing model is possible; a sales manager would like a price consideration on a quantity purchase; and a bookkeeper's inquiry concerns the handling of depreciation under unusual conditions. Such queries require individual replies.

State your answer early in your reply.

When you can answer an inquiry or grant a request, do so near the beginning of your letter. Don't leave the recipient in suspense. The letter in Figure 11–3 (on page 220) follows a general organizational pattern:

1. Introductory statement acknowledging the inquiry
2. Answer itself
3. List of the necessary information or reference to the source where it may be found
4. Constructive suggestion, if possible
5. Sales appeal (if applicable)
6. Friendly close

Whether granting or denying a request, give your reply as soon as possible.

Regardless of whether your reply to an inquiry or request is favorable or unfavorable, it is vital that the inquiry be answered promptly. If you can tell inquirers "yes," so much the better, but do not make them wait several days to receive a "no, we're sorry." If you communicate your decision immediately, they can then attempt further action. Or, if you cannot meet their wishes, they can turn elsewhere.

RESPONDING TO INQUIRIES AND REQUESTS: SAYING "NO"

We all prefer to say "yes" to inquiries and requests made of us, whether they come from clients or coworkers. They are pleased when we accommodate their wishes, and frankly we like to be thought of as agreeable people.

Develop your ability to say "no" firmly yet politely.

No manager succeeds for long, however, without the ability to say "no" firmly and politely. At times, you probably will have to say "no" to inquiries that touch upon sensitive company information. At other times, you'll have to say "no" to requests, however earnest, for favors that you cannot grant.

Here's a case in point. Mike Farring manages Victory Outdoor Signs, Inc., and supervises a large fleet of flatbed trucks. Marjorie Wilkes, director of a local charity, writes to Farring with the request shown in Figure 11–4 on page 221.

Put yourself in Farring's shoes. On the one hand, he feels that the charity does important work. On the other hand, his trucks must be available every day in June, the busy season, if the company is to meet its contracts. Farring decides to say "no." But should he invent an excuse—"insurance reasons," perhaps, or "broken-down trucks"?

Such excuses would lead Farring directly into trouble. If he refuses the request on insurance grounds, Wilkes may well offer to pay for a supplemental policy to cover the time the trucks are needed for the parade. Then what is Farring to say? If he refuses on the grounds of mechanical problems with the trucks, Wilkes may round up volunteer mechanics to fix the problem. Then what?

Farring decides to tell the truth politely and honestly. His letter is shown in Figure 11–5 on page 222.

You may ask, "But shouldn't he *solve* the problem described by Wilkes? Shouldn't he volunteer to rent three trucks for her?" Frankly, no. While he can choose to become involved in the Children's Charities project, *he is under no such obligation* merely because he received a request.

Even though Farring recognizes his freedom not to fulfill the request, he also knows that feelings are involved. Wilkes has made a sincere, well-intentioned

FIGURE 11–1A A Poorly Written Letter of Inquiry

Heavenly Mattress Corporation

383 Timber Drive
Portland, OR 97229
(503) 555-3831

May 6, 19___

Ms. Wilma Rudens
Vice President, Sales
Bennington Enterprises
989 Fifth Street
Seattle, WA 98121

Dear Ms. Rudens:

Because you market a line of steel bed frames, you are probably familiar with the Wendex frame. We have had bad luck with that frame. In fact, more than half of the complaints and returns we have had on our mattresses from our six discount warehouses have been due to frame collapses, not mattress flaws.

Needless to say, we want to do something about this problem, and so are writing to you since you are the major competitor, we understand, to the Wendex line.

Thank you for answering our questions as soon as possible.

Sincerely,

Ralph Owens

Ralph Owens
Quality Control Supervisor

Request is vague and incomplete.

FIGURE 11-1B Well-written Letter of Inquiry

Heavenly Mattress Corporation

383 Timber Drive
Portland, OR 97229
(503) 555-3831

Ms. Wilma Rudens
Vice President, Sales
Bennington Enterprises
989 Fifth Street
Seattle, WA 98121

Dear Ms. Rudens:

I am writing to ask your help with an expensive problem faced by this company: collapsing bed frames.

Since 1985, we have supplied Wendex Model #203 steel frames with our twin, full, double, queen, and king size mattress sets. Much to our dismay, 16 percent of these frames are returned to us for replacement within 24 months (our warranty period).

Therefore, we are looking for a more satisfactory frame. Specifically, we would appreciate your response to three questions:

1. Do you sell a frame comparable in price to the Wendex #203 but more stable in design and construction?

2. If so, is that frame available for all common mattress sizes?

3. Can you deliver in quantities of 100 frames directly to our six discount warehouses (addresses and map attached)? Please include an estimate of delivery costs.

We are eager to find a frame that matches the high quality we build into our mattress sets. Thank you for your early reply.

Sincerely,

Ralph Owens

Ralph Owens
Quality Control Supervisor

Specific questions help the receiver make a specific reply.

FIGURE 11–2   Request Letter Using Persuasive Language and Argument

Downtown Business Association

873 Central Street
Cleveland, OH 44104
(216) 555-8932

October 7, 19__

Professor Linda Forest
Marketing Department
School of Business
State University
Cleveland, OH 44136

Dear Professor Forest:

On behalf of the 120 members of the Downtown Business Association, I congratulate you on the recent publication of your book, *Selling in a Slow Economy*. Many of our members have read the book with great interest, as have I.

Your obvious expertise in sales psychology leads me to request a favor. In preparation for our annual convention (February 6–9), the Downtown Business Association is making plans for a panel discussion on sales techniques. We want to invite four successful sales managers to participate in this two-hour panel; we're able to pay a $500 honorarium to each participant. Can you suggest several sales managers who might be suitable for such a panel? Based on your recommendation, we will contact these people directly with complete details about participation.

Thank you, Professor Forest, for considering this request. Feel free to call me (555-8932) if you have any questions. Again, our best wishes for the success of your book.

Sincerely,

Paul Ortega

Paul Ortega
President, Downtown Business Assocation

FIGURE 11–3 Individualized Answer to an Inquiry

 Systems Planning Corporation
11394 N.W. 23rd Street   Washington D.C. 20071   (202) 555-7000

May 19, 19__

Ms. Donna Hayworth
Manager of Training
Energy Electronics Corp.
101 Sutter Street
San Francisco, CA 94150

Dear Ms. Hayworth:

We received your letter of May 15 in which you inquired about the recent training program conducted for our office personnel. I am happy to give you the information you requested.

The training was done by Communication Services, located here in Washington. We selected middle-management people whose job responsibilities require that they write many business letters and reports. The class was limited to 16 members and met for two hours each Tuesday afternoon, on company time. Twelve such sessions were held. Communication Services provided the instructor, text, and all handout material. Home assignments were given to the participants, and these were evaluated by the instructor and returned to the students.

We found the program to be valuable. Our employees enjoyed it and came away with many good ideas, which are clearly evident in their day-to-day writing assignments. We have scheduled a second class for this fall, and we know it will be as profitable as the one we just concluded.

If you wish any other information in this area, I shall be very happy to cooperate with you.

Yours truly,

Cathleen Campbell

Cathleen Campbell
Training Director

Present a positive answer as quickly as possible. Note how specific the reply is.

FIGURE 11–4 Request Eliciting Negative Reply

CHILDREN'S CHARITIES
302 Broad Street * Boise, Idaho 83702
(208) 555-2500

March 11, 19__

Mr. Mike Farring
Manager
Victory Outdoor Signs, Inc.
293 Seventh St.
Boise, ID 83710

Dear Mr. Farring:

A client of yours, Brad Jenning, suggested that I contact you to request a favor—a very worthwhile one.

Children's Charities wants to participate in the city's Summer Festival parade this June. We're seeking three flatbed trucks we can convert into floats for the parade. Mr. Jenning pointed out to me that your trucks would be ideal for this purpose.

Thank you, Mr. Farring, for considering this request. All of us at Children's Charities hope for your favorable response, and eagerly await your answer.

Sincerely,

Marjorie Wilkes

Marjorie Wilkes
Director

FIGURE 11–5   Brief Refusal Letter That Maintains Goodwill

VICTORY OUTDOOR SIGNS, INC.
293 SEVENTH STREET
BOISE, IDAHO 83710
(208) 555-1554

March 14, 19__

Ms. Marjorie Wilkes
Director
Children's Charities
302 Broad St.
Boise, ID 83702

Dear Ms. Wilkes:

We at Victory Outdoor Signs, Inc., have admired the fine work of Children's Charities at the annual Summer Festival parade for many years.

As it happens, Ms. Wilkes, we've already made contractual commitments during June for the equipment you request. We are, of course, obligated to fulfill those commitments to our customers as well as to our many employees who will be needed to complete our contracts. Not to do so would result in a hardship on both groups.

Although our equipment is already committed for the dates you specify, we can provide two volunteer drivers. If you can use their services, please let me know as soon as possible.

Thank you for thinking of us. We send you and your coworkers our best wishes for another successful Summer Festival.

Sincerely,

Mike Farring

Mike Farring
Manager

Honesty is the best policy when justifying refusals.

Explaining the reason for refusing the request and suggesting alternatives preserve goodwill.

request and deserves courtesy and, where possible, an explanation of the refusal. By appreciating the feelings involved, Farring can be sure that Wilkes will not consider him inconsiderate. Nor will she spread damaging rumors about his company's lack of civic involvement. Although Farring probably cannot prevent her momentary disappointment, he can at least buffer that disappointment by a courteous, explanatory response.

In summary, remind yourself that just as others have the right to make requests of you, so you have the right to turn down those requests in a polite and, if possible, constructive way. In usual business practice, soften the disappointment by following these three suggestions:

1. Provide a rational explanation (not an invented excuse).
2. Suggest alternatives where possible.
3. Express empathy in a way that will keep goodwill.

Read your refusal as if you received it. How does it make you feel?

The best guide for finding the right words in saying "no" is to place yourself in the other person's shoes. What would he or she feel? What explanation would be helpful without undercutting your refusal? What alternatives might be offered? By considering the other person's feelings, you will choose words that communicate your message without creating barriers to future business and communication.

PLACING ORDERS

Orders that include all relevant data avoid costly delays.

Because of the volume of orders, firms usually place orders using printed order blanks or purchase order forms rather than individual letters. Forms are more efficient and less costly. Whether you use a form or a letter, be certain to include most (or all) of the following data:

- Catalog number
- Quantity
- Description of merchandise (model number, size, color)
- Unit price; total price
- Precise identification of purchasing unit or purchaser
- Shipping address
- Shipping method (e.g., UPS, air express, truck)
- Payment method (COD, open account, check enclosed, etc.)
- Delivery date desired
- Miscellaneous information: order number, date of order, salesperson's name, information on substitutions, instructions for "back order"

The businessperson (or consumer) who writes a letter to place an order should be sure that it includes as much of the above data as possible. The objective is to receive the merchandise—not a reply requesting additional information.

RESPONDING TO ORDERS

In sending an order to your company, most clients probably feel that they have done you a favor. They look to you not only for prompt delivery of the order, but also for goodwill and gratitude. Therefore, orders provide an opportunity to encourage future business. Whether acknowledging orders, handling problem cases, or even refusing orders, your communications with clients can make or break future business relations.

Acknowledge receipt of an order that requires special handling.

Most business transactions between buyer and seller are routine. Merchandise is ordered on Monday and delivered on Wednesday. These are often stock items and few problems arise. If a portion of the order is not delivered on Wednesday, it will probably be sent out the following week.

When products are manufactured on the basis of special instructions or are to be delivered within a limited period of time, it is usually wise for the seller to acknowledge that the order has been received. This permits a formal understanding between buyer and seller so that possible future problems may be avoided. If the buyer requests a Black and Johnson Cutter, Model 304, to be delivered within 30 days, and he receives an acknowledgment of the facts of the purchase from the seller, he may then confidently assume that understanding exists. However, if he receives an acknowledgement from the seller indicating that a *Model 403* cutter is being prepared for shipment, he can call and correct the error immediately. Had the wrong cutter been shipped, both parties would have suffered. A simple acknowledgment can add to the efficiency of operations.

Although many acknowledgments can be made by means of a form or guide letter, some cannot. The distinction lies largely in whether the buyer is a steady customer or a new one.

Steady customers.   Firms that acknowledge orders from steady customers routinely use postcards, form letters, or duplicate invoices. The postcard contains only a brief message indicating that the order has been received, is being processed, and will be shipped shortly. Usually, the ordered items are not listed for customer verification.

The form letter functions like the postcard, but it seems slightly more courteous because it travels in a stamped envelope. Storing form letters on computer disk makes reproduction quick and easy.

The most efficient and least expensive means of acknowledgement is the duplicate invoice, which is sent to the buyer. It is typed at the same time as the invoice (along with other needed copies). This duplicate fulfills three functions. It informs the buyer that the order is being processed, it is an expression of courtesy, and it permits the buyer to check the specific details of the order.

Although orders from steady customers can be acknowledged with routine postcards, form letters, or duplicate invoices, and occasional personalized letter strengthens goodwill.

Every now and then a personal letter of acknowledgment should be sent to steady customers as an expression of pleasure in the business relationship (see Figure 11–6). Good customers like to know that they are not just taken for granted. This kind of unnecessary act helps build goodwill.

Send a personalized letter to a new customer: acknowledge receipt of the order quickly, explain policies and procedures courteously, and thank the client.

New customers.   Although it is impossible to respond personally to every order from steady customers, it is necessary to do so for new customers' first order. You want them to know that you truly appreciate adding their names to your customer list. This message also gives you an opportunity to delineate procedures and to clarify sale and payment terms.

The new-customer acknowledgment can be made up as a form letter, stored on computer disk, and individually printed out when the need arises. The readers should feel the red carpet has been rolled out for them, but the letter should not be so effusive as to sound insincere.

FIGURE 11–6   Personal Letter of Acknowledgment to a Steady Customer

Cross Timing Devices
1225 Lehigh Avenue   Boulder, Colorado 80303   (303) 555-6035

May 4, 19__

Mr. R. Stephan
Vice President
Brunswick Corp.
One Brunswick Plaza
Skokie, IL 60077

Dear Mr. Stephan:

I'm writing to let you know that your order #2983 for 120 men's watches (assortment B7) and 160 women's watches (assortment C2) was shipped May 3 via UPS to reach you no later than May 8.

Your purchases, which have been made so regularly during the past year, are always appreciated. Of course, we haven't written you an individual letter for each of the orders, but we want you to know that we will always make every effort to supply you with quality merchandise at the lowest possible prices.

If you have any special needs that we can fill, please give us an opportunity to assist you. We appreciate your confidence in us and shall try to earn it for many years to come.

Yours truly,

Emma Bartelli

Emma Bartelli
Customer Service Representative

New customers are primarily concerned with their orders, so the order should be mentioned first. Then other details may be given on the company's services, policies, and practices. For further verification of the order, a duplicate of the invoice may accompany the letter. The letter in Figure 11–7 is a good example of a new-customer acknowledgment.

ACKNOWLEDGING ORDERS WHEN THERE IS A PROBLEM

Not every order can be filled completely and efficiently. There are times when orders are incomplete or vague, or when the merchandise requested is not handled by the recipient of the order. Skillful communication can turn these potential problems into solutions that satisfy the customer.

Use tact when asking for information to clarity an incomplete order.

Incomplete orders.   Sometimes orders are incomplete or not clear. Don't guess at what the customer means, for if the wrong merchandise is shipped it will be returned, and ill will and expense will result. Either an individually typed letter (see Figure 11–8 on page 228) can be used, or a form letter with fill-in spaces can be stored on computer disk and adjusted as necessary to fit the situation. Notice the tactful and positive approach in Figure 11–8. The writer did not say, "You neglected," or "You forgot to list." She simply indicated the oversight and said as soon as the correct information was received, the merchandise would be shipped.

Merchandise not handled.   A customer may request merchandise your company does not handle. What do you do about this request? If you suggest a source of supply, you will create goodwill with the customer. Be aware, however, of some practical dangers. The source of supply recommended will probably make every effort to satisfy the customer, and it may be that you will lose the customer to the very source you suggested. On the other hand, business ethics almost demand that you make such recommendations.

Respond to orders for merchandise that you do not handle wisely so that you do not lose a potential customer.

A letter handling such a situation might follow the general outline suggested by Figure 11–9 on page 229. When the merchandise requested by a customer is peripherally related to the usual items handled and does not compete directly with an item in stock, it is a good deal easier to make a recommendation, as in Figure 11–10 on page 230. In some instances, a firm obtains the item (that it does not handle) from a supplier and forwards that item to its customer. This is a matter of courtesy, because usually the company makes no profit. Nevertheless a third party, who might be a competitor, is not introduced into the transaction.

REFUSING ORDERS

For a variety of reasons, orders must sometimes be refused, even when the merchandise is in stock and available for immediate shipment. A few such cases are listed here, and two sample letters are shown in Figures 11–11 and 11–12 on pages 231 and 232:

- The buyer is a poor credit risk.
- The buyer has exceeded his or her credit limit.
- Company regulations concerning a franchise or distributorship agreement would be violated.

FIGURE 11–7 Letter to a New Customer

Hobby Supplies, Inc.
492 Jason Street
New York, NY 10039
(202) 555-3923

June 1, 19__

Ms. Tory Williams
Manager
The Hobbyist
30 Cactus Drive
Palm Springs, CA 92264

Dear Ms. Williams:

We want to welcome you to the Hobby Supplies family of satisfied customers. At Hobby Supplies, we pride ourselves on immediate response to customer needs, including any problems or emergencies that may arise. Count on us to give you our best.

As specified in your credit contract, we will supply merchandise to you, to a credit limit of $10,000, provided payment is made within 30 days of receipt. If you pay within ten days of billing, a 3 percent cash rebate will be applied to your account. (Many of our customers accrue hundreds of dollars of savings through such prompt payment).

Jeff Thomas, your area representative, will call on you next Thursday to introduce himself and acquaint you with the full line at Hobby Supplies. His 24-hour message number is (714) 555-5935.

Thank you for your first order to Hobby Supplies. We are confident that you will be pleased with our products, prices, and service.

Sincerely,

Constance Yesterly

Constance Yesterly
Sales Director

FIGURE 11–8   Acknowledging an Incomplete Order

Western Home Products

878 Sheridan Road
Miami, Florida 33166
(305) 555-7656

March 20, 19__

Mr. Ken Conway
Conway's Home Center
1515 W. Portland Ave.
College Park, MD 20740

Dear Mr. Conway:

Thank you very much for your order of March 17, #204, which arrived today. All the merchandise that you requested is in stock and will be shipped via Florida Freight Lines.

You may recall that you listed four dozen American Beauty two-quart cooking containers. However, you did not indicate whether you prefer these with the copper or the stainless-steel bottoms. Please check your preference on the enclosed stamped card and send it to my attention. Your order will be processed and shipped immediately.

I am also enclosing a flyer on our new outdoor grill line. If you wish to order some of these fast-moving items, please indicate your choices on the same card.

Sincerely,

Midori Matsumi

Ms. Midori Matsumi
Customer Service

FIGURE 11–9   Acknowledging an Order for Merchandise Not Handled

Wilshire Office Products
388 Marine Drive
Los Angeles, CA 90099
(213) 555-8369

January 10, 19__

Ms. Jennifer Hart, Manager
Prime Time Corp.
Six North Forenbain Blvd.
Milwaukee, WI 53213

Dear Ms. Hart:

We have received your Order #202, dated January 7. All the merchandise, with one exception, will be on its way to you by this afternoon.

Although we handle all types of office supplies, we have never stocked the Arco Filing Cabinet. This is recognized as an excellent unit. However, our customers' needs at this level have always been fulfilled by the Apex Line, which we do stock. We can fill your order for Apex products immediately.

However, your request specifically lists your preference for the Arco cabinet. This cabinet may be purchased from the Dearborn Office Furniture Corporation, located in Chicago.

It has been a pleasure doing business with you, and we know that you will be satisfied for many years to come with the consistently high quality of merchandise we handle and the competitive prices we offer. Please call collect if you would like to purchase the Apex items.

Sincerely,

Cliff Van Art

Cliff Van Art
Sales Manager

Telling the customer where to find items you do not carry builds goodwill.

FIGURE 11–10   Recommending a Source for Merchandise Not Carried

Quality Auto-Parts

1500 West Fulton Street   Philadelphia, Pennsylvania 19102   (215) 555-0550

February 5, 19__

Ms. F.W. Flynn
Assistant Sales Manager
Powers Pontiac
150 S. Main Drive
Santa Monica, CA 90401

Dear Ms. Flynn:

Thank you for your recent note inquiring whether we handle automobile seat covers as well as our usual line of automobile accessories.

As you may know, we stock over 5,000 parts for cars. We have considered putting in a line of seat covers, safety belts, and so on but have not as yet.

Through our own experience, we have found that the Los Angeles Auto Seat Company is an excellent firm. The quality of its merchandise is high and the prices competitive. I recommend that you get in touch with the company. Ask specifically for Mr. Kameron, who has always given us excellent service.

Our latest parts catalog is enclosed. Check through it. We know you will find many items of interest.

Cordially yours,

Luis Perez

Luis Perez
Assistant Sales Manager

FIGURE 11-11 Refusing an order on the Basis of Poor Credit Risk

General Market Products, Inc.
2593 Container Drive
Huntington Beach,CA 92649
(714)555-3838

Mr. George Taylor
Manager
Taylor Mini-Markets, Inc.
1093 St. Louis Avenue
San Diego, CA 92107

Dear Mr. Taylor:

Thank you for applying for credit purchases from General Market Products.

Our credit agency, TRW, advises us that you qualify for a cash payment account at this time. If you have questions about specific reasons for their evaluation, please contact them directly at (800)555-3267.

As a cash customer, you will receive a 2 percent discount on all purchases. After a period of six months as a cash customer (or as soon as you clarify your credit status with TRW), we will be most happy to review your application for credit purchases.

Thank you for looking to General Market Products to serve your needs.

Sincerely,

Victoria Buenasto

Victoria Buenasto
Credit Manager

A direct, courteous explanation

A positive comment listing advantages

A tactfully worded explanation can take away the sting of refusal.

A direct, courteous explanation

FIGURE 11–12   Refusing an Order on the Basis of Violating Regulations

Cross Timing Devices
1225 Lehigh Avenue   Boulder, Colorado 80303   (303) 555-6035

May 25, 19__

Ms. Stacy Franklin
Franklin's Jewel Box
1010 S. Martin Drive
Washington, D.C. 20019

Dear Ms. Franklin:

We were happy to receive your request to stock our new Precision Watch Line.

Some months ago we visited Washington and at that time selected 12 jewelry outlets to handle the Precision Watch. Unfortunately, we did not get in touch with you. However, we did assure each of the dealers that Washington would have a maximum of 12 franchises. In fairness to these outlets, therefore, and in conformity with our agreement, we can open no others at this time.

If, however, one of these 12 does not wish to retain the franchise, we will get in touch with you immediately to determine your availability.

We certainly appreciate your interest in the Precision Line. We have enclosed our new catalog in the hope that you will find other nonfranchise items of interest to you.

Sincerely yours,

Steven Andrews

Steven Andrews
Manager

- Filling the order might be contrary to government regulations.
- Filling the order would be unprofitable because of the limited quantity ordered, distances to be shipped, or modifications requested.
- Only a limited supply is in stock, and this supply must be retained for steady accounts.

When refusing an order, use the you viewpoint and positive word choice to maintain goodwill and promote future business.

All of these cases should be handled tactfully, positively, and with a strong sales orientation. Figures 11–11 and 11–12 show two acknowledgment situations that can arise. The message communicated in each of these order refusals is conciliatory rather than confrontive or offensive. The writer says, in effect, "We're very much interested in doing business with you. We appreciate your order, but we need to restructure the order to make it work for both of us. Let's try doing it this way . . . "

The client, therefore, has no reason to feel insulted. He or she faces the reality that the company has necessary standards for business practice and is pleased to know that the company wants to make some arrangement work—if not now, then in the future. In all such cases, however, be sure of the reputation and reliability of the suppliers you are recommending. If the customer has a bad experience with a supplier you have suggested, the customer may blame you.

WRITING AND SPEAKING EXERCISES

1. Recently Sarah's Cafeteria removed your favorite item, Lemon-Cream Chocolate Pudding, from its menu. You have eaten at Sarah's for ten years, primarily because of this dessert. Write a letter requesting that Sarah return this culinary delight to the menu.
2. Joe Jones has ordered a 6-inch gate valve from your catalog. Unfortunately, that item has recently been deleted from your stock. Write a letter which explains this to Joe, and suggest that he order a 7-inch valve instead.
3. Write Joe's response to the letter from question 2, in which he requests specifications of the 7-inch valve. Specifically, he wants to know flow rate, unit cost, shipping weight, and country of origin. Furthermore, he is interested in obtaining a discount for large orders and wants to know the number necessary to qualify, as well as the amount of the discount.
4. Assume you're planning a trip to Europe with college friends. You have to get a passport—and in a hurry. Write a letter, as if to your local passport office, emphasizing your need for quick service. Try to build a persuasive message that not only tells your reader what you want, but motivates him or her to help you attain it.
5. Last semester a professor gave you a much lower grade than you expected or, you believe, deserved. Unfortunately, she has now left your college. Write a letter to the chair of her department, inquiring about what steps you can take to have your grade reviewed.
6. Visit or call three personnel directors. Determine from them if they have made changes in the past few years in their replies to requests for evaluations of previous employees. Have these changes been due in some respects to legal responsibilities and recent court cases? Be as specific as possible in your report on this topic.
7. Secure three actual refusal letters from three different companies. The

letters may refuse orders, credit, or job applicants. Report on the organization of each letter: discuss the placement of the refusal statement(s), the explanation, and the goodwill portion. Indicate strong and weak points of each according to your perception.

8. In the role of an office manager, write brief letters of refusal to each of these requests:

   (a) Our organization wishes to use your company cafeteria on May 6 from 2:30 to 5:30 p.m. for our "Feed the Homeless" project.

   (b) I understand that few of your secretaries practice shorthand anymore. As a retired teacher of shorthand, I will be happy to teach your people this valuable skill. My fees are quite reasonable.

   (c) The Eagle Troop would like to spend a day with your employees, matched one-on-one, to observe day-to-day operations of an actual business. We'll have approximately 140 youngsters on hand, most in their early teens.

9. In one of the business periodicals you read, you notice an ad concerning executive desk blotters. You can order them in a variety of sizes and colors of leather and with or without accessories such as letter openers and pencil holders. You want a blotter in green leather, about 30 by 20 inches, and you have no need for accessories. Order the item. The order form has been misplaced, so you will have to send a letter to the Barry Office Company, Box 3, Jefferson City, MO 65101.

10. You are chairperson of your school's Business Awareness Week. One of the activities during the week will be a series of speakers who have different perspectives on business. Write a letter of request to each individual. In some ways the letters can be the same, but they will have to be individualized also. The following is a list of the people you are going to ask to speak. Write the basic request letter.

    (a) Ms. Elizabeth McRoy, president, Onyx Inc. (one of your state's largest employers).

    (b) Dr. Raymond Jennings, director, Consumer Affairs Office, and assistant to the governor of your state.

    (c) Mr. Dennis Anthony, executive director of your city's Chamber of Commerce.

    (d) Mrs. Deloris Rayfield, an activist in community affairs and an outspoken critic of businesses and current business practices.

    (e) Mr. Harold Dykum, author of the book, *Businesses Rip You Off*.

    (f) Dr. Pilar Cortez, business professor who teaches business ethics at another college in your region.

    In making your request you should acknowledge that you have no funds to offer honorariums or to cover the expenses associated with their coming.

11. An item college graduates often need is a transcript of their college work. You work in the registrar's office and you see the hodgepodge of letters that arrive daily requesting transcripts. More than half the letters provide insufficient information to allow the desired response. In an attempt to make the process more efficient, you suggest that graduating seniors be given several order blanks for transcripts along with their diplomas. The registrar says, "Fine idea. Please develop the form."

    In developing the form, keep in mind that postage rates change periodically, some transcripts are needed for personal use and some are sent to potential employers, and you must ensure, because of privacy laws, that the request is valid.

12. You have received an advertisement for briefcases. The ad neglects to mention specific colors, referring simply to "a full range of popular shades." You want a light tan briefcase. Order the briefcase, making sure that the dealer does not send you the wrong shade of brown.

13. Write brief, constructive refusal letters to the following orders:

    (a) Please send 13 cases of Comstock Lubricant, your catalog #20301, no later than February 3. As a new company, we have not yet completed our banking arrangements; therefore, we will appreciate credit arrangements for the next 60 days or so.

    (b) We think your line of graduation jewelry will please our students. Before we order, however, we'd like to see actual samples. Please send several 18-karat class rings, bracelets, and chains for our inspection. We'll then let you know about the order.

    (c) You don't mention in your catalog if you sell on consignment. We assume, therefore, that you do. Please send 140 lamps and lighting accessories (see list attached) by May 6. This order must arrive in time for the grand opening of Western Lighting Showroom. We have high hopes for the success of our venture and count on your merchandise to make the grand opening a smash.

CASES

Complete the following assignments from the Cases for Discussion section at the back of this book:

1. The Barney Burton case—Assignment 5
2. But Talking Isn't Working case—Assignment 5

READINGS

See "Mishandled Inquiries Are Lost Opportunities" in the Readings section at the back of this book.

SUGGESTED RESOURCES

Bell, Arthur H. *The Complete Business Writer's Manual.* Englewood Cliffs, N.J.: Prentice-Hall, 1991.

Hemmings, Robert L. "Think Before You Write." *Fund Raising Management* 20 (February 1990):23–24.

Poe, Roy W. *The McGraw-Hill Handbook of Business Letters.* 2nd ed. New York: McGraw-Hill, 1988.

Thompson, Ann Raine. "Writing Effective Business Letters." *International Trade Forum* 24 (October—November 1988):22–29.

LEGAL CONSIDERATIONS

TERMS AND TITLES OF LAWS AND REGULATIONS OF IMPORTANCE TO THE MANAGER-COMMUNICATOR

Term or Title	Explanation
Agency	This area of law has evolved from common law and, in the context of the business or other organization, establishes that the principal (e.g., the employer) can employ people to act on the principal's behalf; establishes a communication link between the company and the manager
Antitrust acts	Legislation that has been passed concerning restraint of trade
Contract	An agreement between two or more people that will be recognized under the law
Decertification	A procedure available to union memberships that permits them to eliminate their collective agreement with their union
Defamation	Injury to an individual's person or character through communication of false information
EEOC	Equal Employment Opportunity Commission; can establish and monitor regulations concerning employer's hiring, promoting, training, and retirement practices
EPA	Environmental Protection Agency; can establish and monitor regulations concerning organization's influence on its surroundings via odor, noise, and sight
Equal protection of the laws	The constitutional principle that says people shall not be treated unfairly by reason of race, sex, creed, or national origin
ERISA	Employer Retirement Income Security Act; stipulates that employer shall communicate retirement program to employees in understandable language
Exempt (exempt employee)	Employee exempt from overtime pay, generally a manager
FTC	Federal Trade Commission; has authority to provide consumers with protection against "unfair methods of competition" (This can include how companies use language to communicate with customers.)
Garnishment	A legal proceeding wherein a creditor is permitted to hold property or some wages for satisfaction of a debt
Libel	A defamatory communication without legal justification
NLRB	National Labor Relations Board; can establish regulations concerning labor practices (regulations include communication activities

Nonexempt (nonexempt employee)	Employee not exempt from overtime; generally an employee paid by the hour and subject to overtime compensation (not a manager or supervisor)
SEC	Securities and Exchange Commission; created to oversee and regulate stock exchanges and those dealing with them. SEC can create rules and regulations on the relationship (communication) between the owner, manager, and other parties.
Subpoena	Order of the court to appear and testify; *subpoena duces tecum* (to appear with specific documentation)
Sunshine laws	Laws enacted to permit greater scrutiny—to let the "sun" shine in. Governments, as part of sunshine legislation, have been forced to open files and meetings to individuals and to the public. Therefore, this legislation has influenced communication.
UCC	Uniform Commercial Code; suggested language for uniform laws among the various states in such areas as contracts, sales, and letters of credit
UCCC	Uniform Consumer Credit Code; drafted federal legislation published for adoption by the states. Grants rights to consumer and regulates creditor.
Warranty	An assurance or guarantee that may be communicated explicitly or implicitly about a good; a kind of contract

12

Claim, Credit, and Collection Letters

Effective communication is the basis for credit relationships.

Consult an attorney before engaging in credit and collection correspondence.

Although claim, credit, and collection letters are often not the most pleasant business communications to compose, they are among the most important—and the most difficult. One initial word of caution: in all matters related to credit and collection law, seek the specific advice of a competent business attorney before delivering your correspondence to its recipient. The sample letters in this chapter may be relied upon as a *guide to style*, but they should *not* be used as a *legal guide*, especially because credit and collection law changes frequently.

CLAIMS

Business transactions do not always run smoothly. Regardless of how careful or efficient business organizations are, things go wrong from time to time. Merchandise may be shipped to an incorrect address or arrive in less than perfect condition. Badly needed articles may be delayed. Quality may not be at the level expected.

Complete, clear, and specific claim letters usually gain the requested adjustment.

When such situations arise, a claim letter is usually sent. Because most people in business recognize that errors do take place, a reasonable and properly written letter will bring the desired adjustment. Claims must be handled efficiently, for in just one year the amount of money involved can reach a significant level. One Los Angeles firm, for instance, found that many dollars were being drained away because of its poor claim procedures. A management consulting firm found that in one year the company had submitted $60,000 in claims to suppliers, shippers, and dealers. For that same time period the company had received only $8,000 in adjustments. Investigation disclosed that the claims entered had been incomplete and inaccurate and follow-ups almost nonexistent. The poor ratio of adjustments received to claims entered was the fault not of the firms to whom the results were submitted, but of the company itself.

In an attempt to improve the adjustment record, the firm initiated a training program for the people concerned with claims. Once they began writing complete, clear, and specific claim letters, the dollar amount of adjustments rose dramatically. In the year after the initial survey, adjustments received increased an estimated $30,000 as a result of improved communication.

There are various levels of claim problems. If a transaction does not go precisely as requested and the problem is a matter of correcting a very understandable situation, you make a *routine* claim. If, however, the situation has several facets and there is a question as to who is responsible, you enter a *nonroutine* claim.

ROUTINE CLAIM LETTERS

Routine claims deal with minor problems that are an inevitable part of normal business dealings.

Routine claim letters are usually associated with relatively minor problems. When the wrong quantity, size, color, or model has been shipped or an error has been made in pricing, discount privileges, or other routine matters, all that is necessary is a clear, specific, concise claim letter listing the facts of the situation. In Figure 12–1 the writer says clearly that, except for three watches, the delivery was satisfactory. He does not say, "You mispacked the watches," (personal statement criticizing an individual), but "Because of mispacking." He mentions the demand for the product and assumes his claim is completely valid and will be taken care of immediately (positive tone).

Because mistakes do happen in order filling, shipping, and billing, some firms use form letters for routine claims (blank spaces are completed for the specific situation).

NONROUTINE CLAIM LETTERS

Nonroutine claims result when the buyer and seller disagree as to who is at fault.

When an error occurs, often the facts are not obvious. The buyer may feel that $140 is due because the damage took place before receipt of the merchandise. The seller, however, may contend that the merchandise left the premises in perfect condition. Or perhaps the buyer maintains that a case of merchandise was not received, although the seller insists that it was. Situations like these require nonroutine claim letters. They are nonroutine because there is a difference of opinion as to who is at fault. Sometimes the adjustments are in favor of the seller; sometimes they favor the buyer. One thing is certain: the seller does not relish receiving a claim letter, nor does the buyer like to write one.

A claim letter should elicit a definite answer, whether favorable or unfavorable.

The claim letter should be so well written that it will result in a specific answer. Buyers hope that answer will be a "yes, we will credit your account." If, however, buyers cannot secure an affirmative reply, they should strive for one that suggests a compromise. If they can secure neither, then they must look for an answer that says "no." Of course, the "no" is not satisfactory, but at least it tells them where they stand. They may now take their business elsewhere if they are unhappy or accept the "no." A follow-up to a "no" will depend on the strength and size of the claim. In any situation the claimant should make every effort to avoid eliciting a reply that conveys no definite answer. Such a response is merely a brush-off or a delaying action. It goes something like this:

> *We will look into it; may we suggest that you do the same. Please be assured that this will be settled to our mutual satisfaction. Now let me call your attention to a special we are running . . .*

This type of letter is no better than none at all. Time has been wasted, and as the days and weeks go by without an adjustment, the strength and immediacy of the claim decline.

Claim letters *can* be written so that they result in a definite answer. Follow this outline to compose an effective claim letter:

FIGURE 12–1   Routine Claim Letter

RANDALL FINE WATCHES
47 Main Street
Phoenix, AZ 85044
(602) 555-3819

September 18, 19__

Ms. Linda Ortiz
Customer Relations
Grenell Watch Company
80 West Sixth Street
Cincinnati, OH 45202

Dear Ms. Ortiz:

Thank you for delivering our order of August 1 in time for our "Back to School" watch
sale.

Three watches included in the shipment, however, were damaged in transit, apparently
because of mispacking. The boxes for these watches were not taped shut (your usual
practice), and during shipment, the watches fell to the bottom of the shipping container.

I've enclosed the damaged watches. Note the abrasions on the bands and faces.

Please replace these watches by UPS one-day service so we can fill standing orders
quickly. Please call immediately if you anticipate a delay.

Sincerely,

Tim Watson

Tim Watson
Owner

*Effective claim
letters are
matter-of-fact
rather than
angry and
accusing.*

1. Introductory statement referring precisely and specifically to the transaction
2. Specific description of the loss or damage incurred
3. Specific statement of the adjustment desired
4. Statement that will motivate favorable action
5. Friendly close

When buyers are certain that their claim is correct from every point of view, and that the adjustment they are requesting is honest in every respect, then they should check their letter to be sure that the tone is positive (not accusing), the statements specific, and the details precise. On the other hand, if the buyers are not sure who is at fault or how the damage or loss occurred, they can only honestly request that both parties do what is necessary to reach an equitable solution.

If a buyer's letter reflects a tone of uncertainty, the recipient may seize on that tone to delay making an adjustment. In the following examples the revised phrases have a more positive tone:

ORIGINAL: *We believe the damage took place . . .*
REVISED: *The damage took place . . .*

ORIGINAL: *We think you did not include . . .*
REVISED: *. . . was not included.*

Just as the tone should be positive, so too should the statements of loss or damage be specific and precise. Note the contrast between the original and revised versions of these sentences:

ORIGINAL: *We suffered a considerable loss.*
REVISED: *Our loss was $58.12.*

ORIGINAL: *The damage was quite extensive and we believe that . . .*
REVISED: *The damage amounted to $114.52.*

Positive specific claims guarantee specific replies.

Sometimes the writer, in an effort to be courteous, is not as positive and as specific as possible, lest his or her statements be interpreted as pushy. Although it is important to be courteous, uncertainty or vagueness may give the adjustor an opportunity to send a response that will result in delay and unnecessary correspondence. A claim letter outlined as suggested, with a positive tone and specific statements usually elicits a definite answer.

Notice in Figure 12–2 how precisely the writer presents that facts and how positive the tone of the letter is. The writer seems certain the recipient will not question the claim. The contrasting letter in Figure 12–3, however, enables the reader to send back an equivocal reply. It offers many opportunities for the recipient to legitimately delay taking specific action. The word *probably* in the last paragraph will surely result in a letter asking for further investigation. Then, too, the writer did not indicate whether the table had been left in protective wrappings while stored, and she neglected to point out what adjustment she would consider equitable. Should the table be replaced or refinished? Also, she made no reference to former business associations that might help motivate a favorable response. When this writer receives a reply that only suggests further investigation, she will have no one to blame but herself.

FIGURE 12–2   Well-organized Claim Letter

Hank's Hardware
300 Main Street
Virginia Beach, Virginia 23451
(804) 555-9700

May 15, 19__

Ms. Roberta Fox, Sales Manager
Summer Fun Furniture Co.
101 South Felly Drive
Chicago, IL 60604

Dear Ms. Fox:

On March 15 we received our order #207 from you. You may recall that the order
included a large quantity of lawn furniture, barbecue accessories, and outdoor cookware.

If you will check our original purchase order, you will find that we requested six dozen
sets of your Patio Grill Sets. Three dozen were to be sent in the regular style at $2.50 each
and the remainder in the deluxe style at $3.50 per set.

As we started to display this merchandise, we found that you inadvertently sent us five
dozen of the regular and only one dozen of the deluxe. However, we were billed according to our original purchase order. Please credit our account for the $24 which is due to us.

Since this is the first claim that we have submitted in three years of satisfactory business
relations with you, we know you will handle it as we request. In the future we shall check
the markings on each package to avoid such a situation.

Sincerely yours,

Frank Fale

Frank Fale
Vice President

*In a claim
letter, tell the
reader exactly
what action to
take.*

FIGURE 12–3   Poorly Written Claim Letter

Kalamazoo Plastics
Industrial Park, No. 10
Kalamazoo, Michigan 49001
(616) 555-2929

July 10, 19__

Mr. William Wolf, Vice President
Wolf Brothers Furniture
101 Star Street
Glen Ellyn, IL 60521

Dear Mr. Wolf:

On March 28 your truck delivered the Empire Conference Table which we ordered February 2.

Because our executive office facilities were not yet completely decorated at the time of delivery (as we had hoped they would be), the table was stored in our warehouse. Two days ago the decorating of the conference room was completed and the table was brought in. It was at that time we noticed a deep scratch running across the top of the table.

You may be sure we were very upset, for we feel that the damage probably occurred prior to our receiving this piece of furniture. We do hope that you will want to make the proper adjustment in this case and we look forward to hearing from you at your convenience.

Yours truly,

Kimberly Lally

Kimberly Lally

The claim is so vague that the recipient could hardly make an adjustment even if he were so inclined. Note also that a specific adjustment is not requested, nor is a due date for action given.

MAKING ADJUSTMENTS: CLAIM GRANTED

The number of items most firms handle now is greater than it was a generation ago. Billing procedures are more complex. Inventory controls are more detailed. Handling and shipping of merchandise require more attention. In fact, the current process of getting goods from source to consumer requires more steps now than it did in the past. Because there are more factors involved, there are greater possibilities for error. Most businesspeople recognize that errors do occur, so their claims or adjustments are tempered with patience.

Handling claims quickly and courteously reflects positively on the company and maintains goodwill.

Intelligent managers are aware that a claim can bring attention to an internal area needing improvement or change. In addition, they accept most claims as legitimate and fair. Furthermore, managers recognize that the people who submit claims are customers, and the firm's business depends on satisfying customers. Thus it is important to handle claims quickly and courteously so that the firm is perceived as fair. Nevertheless, the firm must neither gain a reputation of accepting any claim, nor a reputation of refusing all claims.

Give the buyer the benefit of the doubt.

Most claims are legitimate, and it is on this basis that firms usually establish a fairly generous adjustment policy. If there is a question as to who is at fault, companies usually give the benefit of the doubt to the buyer to encourage future business.

An adjustment policy is often governed by whatever is accepted in the trade. For example, furniture manufacturers have agreed on a standard return privilege, and appliance manufacturers have set down an industrywide repair policy.

The way in which the adjustment is made can build or erode goodwill. An adjustment given grudgingly usually will do more harm than one that is refused but carefully and courteously explained.

BUYER AT FAULT

Not infrequently in business, buyers submit unjustified claims. Someone has run a machine over its rated capacity and now requests a replacement. A customer returns furniture after the ten-day return period has passed or orders merchandise at a special price long after the last date announced for the sale. When a company grants such claims, it is purely for the purpose of building goodwill.

When you are building goodwill by granting a claim in which the buyer is at fault, make sure the buyer realizes that he or she was at fault.

If the buyer is at fault and the claim is granted, structure the letter so that an explanation precedes the favorable adjustment (see Figure 12–4). Usually good news should be given immediately in a business letter, but this is not true when granting a claim in which the buyer is at fault. If the adjustment letter immediately grants a claim, the buyer may not read further to learn that he or she was at fault. Even when the buyer does read the entire letter, the psychological impact of the explanation may be lost. A courteous, straightforward explanation *before* the grant is made should point out that the buyer was at fault. In most cases the following organization is recommended:

1. Statement referring to the specific transaction
2. Statement explaining tactfully how the buyer is at fault
3. Statement granting the claim graciously
4. Sales appeal, if appropriate
5. Friendly close

The tone should be direct, courteous, and openhanded.

FIGURE 12–4   Granting a Claim—Buyer at Fault

All-Company
203 Sperry Road • Madison, Wisconsin 53714
(608) 555-0400

July 10, 19__

Mr. Meyer Milton
Plant Manager
Summer and Summer Co.
14 South Lansing Boulevard
Ann Arbor, MI 48109

Dear Mr. Milton:

We received your letter of July 5 in which you requested that we pick up the American 1/3 h.p. motor and replace it with a 3/4 h.p. unit.

We were sorry to learn that the 1/3 h.p. motor which we sold you on June 15 did not prove satisfactory. In your letter, however, you indicated that it was used to power a Jackson-Smith Industrial Saw, model #208. We checked this with our chief engineer because we want to furnish our customers with the best and most efficient materials available.

He found that the manufacturer of this saw recommends that a 3/4 to 1 h.p. unit be used with this particular model. Apparently this was overlooked by the people in your shop and our 1/3 h.p. unit was used. Of course, we realize that incidents such as this occur, and we are sending out the larger motor you requested. However, for your satisfaction and the most efficient operation of equipment in the future, we strongly suggest that the manufacturer's recommendations be checked and followed.

The new motor should be delivered to your warehouse no later than August 10. At that time our driver can pick up the original unit. If we can assist you in any way in the future, Mr. Milton, please call us.

Sincerely,

Frank Ferragamo

Frank Ferragamo
Vice President

The customer is tactfully told he is at fault *before* the grant is made. If the grant were made first, he might stop reading and thus never become aware of his error.

POOR:	*While the circumstances of this breakdown are suspicious at best, we are giving you the benefit of the doubt in making an adjustment.*
REVISED:	*We are pleased to make the adjustment under these circumstances.*
POOR:	*In our view, your demands are clearly without foundation. But to put an end to the matter, we are granting your claim and crediting your account in the amount you requested.*
REVISED:	*We understand your side of the story in this unfortunate incident and have credited your account as you request.*

SELLER AT FAULT

When the buyer at fault requests an adjustment, the seller may grant the claim, refuse it, or offer a compromise. When the seller is at fault, however, there is no alternative: the claim must be granted.

Correcting errors before they result in claims builds immeasurable goodwill.

Before receiving a claim.   At times the seller is not aware that a mistake has been made until a claim is made. But when the seller determines shortly after a shipment that something is wrong, he or she should attempt to correct the error before the buyer asks for an adjustment. The seller may discover that a particular lot of merchandise has not been manufactured properly after the merchandise is on its way to the customer. Or the seller may receive a justified complaint from only one of several buyers. In any of these situations, all buyers who have been shipped faulty merchandise should be notified and offered a proper adjustment. The seller who makes an adjustment before receiving claims and complaints will secure an amount of goodwill no advertising can purchase. Adjustments made under these circumstances are the mark of a reliable firm, and the reputation gained by such action is invaluable.

Take care not to lose your client's goodwill when you are answering a claim in which you were at fault.

Answering claims.   The letter granting a claim when the seller is at fault is a difficult one to write. The seller must indicate that an error has been made, but in such a way that buyers will not lose confidence and take their business elsewhere.

What makes this such a difficult assignment is the fact that people act like people. Although most of us will readily admit that we made errors, we cannot understand how those from whom we purchase can make such "dumb and completely inexplicable mistakes." Thus, when a seller does make an error, the consumer often enters a claim, accepts the adjustment, and then does business elsewhere. At the wholesale level, however, the businessperson usually recognizes that mistakes do happen and accepts the adjustment in good faith.

What is the proper order of points in the letter acknowledging the seller is at fault and granting the claim? If the message opens with a grant, the item of major interest, the reader may never continue to the explanation of how the situation occurred. To reverse the order, though, is problematic. After all, the buyer is primarily interested in whether he or she is going to receive a credit and is not very much concerned with the fact that the computers suddenly went down. In most cases the situation and prospective reader should determine the order of the letter.

Indeed, some question whether an explanation should be included at all. A detailed discussion of what went wrong and why may only compound the situation and erase what little confidence the customer has in the company.

Perhaps the best thing to do when your company is at fault is to open by saying that you made a mistake, are making an adjustment, and will do your best to see that a similar case does not occur in the future. Follow this organizational pattern for an adjustment letter when the seller is at fault:

1. Opening referring to the situation and making a grant
2. Explanation of how the incident occurred, if such an explanation sounds reasonable. If it will only magnify a careless error, it should be omitted.
3. Attempt to regain the customer's confidence
4. Sales appeal, if it seems appropriate
5. Friendly close

The letter in Figure 12–5 alludes to several possible explanations that will probably help make the situation more understandable to the buyer.

THIRD PARTY AT FAULT

In most transactions between buyer and seller, a third party is involved: a shipper, carrier, broker, or storage agent. If loss or damage occurred while merchandise was in the hands of a third party, the seller normally replies with a courteous letter that extends assistance to the buyer. If some of the seller's accounts are small retail merchants, the seller may even offer to process the claim for them (see Figure 12–6 on page 249). Be aware that it is costly for the seller to get involved in a claim in which he or she has no legal responsibility. Nevertheless, the goodwill that may accrue in such circumstances will be well worth the effort expended.

OTHER ADJUSTMENT SITUATIONS

There are times when both parties are at fault, in other cases the fault is not known, and sometimes the problem is the result of a misunderstanding. Each of these situations, and other comparable ones, must be handled on its own merits and in conformity with the adjustment policy of the seller.

Regardless of the circumstances, all such adjustment letters should carry a strong sales and goodwill message (see Figure 12–7 on page 250). Sometimes a claim can be adjusted by "educating" the customer, for example, through courteous instructions for handling the product (see Figure 12–8 on page 251).

UNFAVORABLE RESPONSES: CLAIM NOT GRANTED

As suggested in our discussion of inquiries and requests (Chapter 11), saying "no" is never easy. Yet you sometimes must turn down claims and demands. The task is made more difficult when the person you must refuse is someone whose goodwill you value highly: a spouse, a child, a sibling, a friend, a customer, a subordinate, or an associate. Nobody enjoys being told "no."

A complete, tactful, and accurate denial might maintain the client's goodwill.

Requests can be refused in a manner that maintains goodwill and arouses a minimum of antagonism. In Figures 12–9 on page 252 and 12–10 on page 253 the explanation and refusal are presented as courteously and tactfully as possible. In both of these letters the explanation is complete and accurate. After each implied refusal, a positive offer or suggestion is made. Notice that there are no statements that might arouse negative or unpleasant associations. Once the refusal is made, even if only by implication, it is not referred to again, and there are no apologies.

FIGURE 12–5   Granting a Claim—Seller at Fault

Benson Mirrors, Inc.

509 West Ninth Avenue
Tucson, AZ 85701
(602) 555-6800

September 6, 19___

Ms. Vera Olin
8723 Sunset Drive
Tucson, AZ 85745

Dear Ms. Olin:

While we never enjoy hearing that a valued customer has experienced problems, we do thank you for your letter of September 4. The problem you describe--a Benson mirror losing its silvering--is rare indeed. We will replace the mirror at no cost and, we hope, no inconvenience to you.

Show that you appreciate your customer's views by verbalizing them.

To help us understand and correct this unusual occurrence, we would appreciate your answers to three questions:

1. Was the mirror in contact with solvent or solvent fumes, such as nail-polish remover?
2. Was the mirror exposed to hot afternoon sun over a prolonged period of time?
3. Was the mirror exposed to sustained moisture?

Your answers to these questions will help us make sure that Benson mirrors remain the finest on the market.

End a claim letter by looking forward to positive relations.

Please call us soon to make arrangements for installation of your new mirror.

Sincerely,

Brett Felson

Brett Felson
Sales Manager

FIGURE 12–6   Granting a Claim—Third Party at Fault

EKKO

ELECTRIC COMPANY
404 NORTH FOURTH STREET
DANVILLE, CALIFORNIA 94526
(415) 555-5987

September 15, 19__

Mr. Roger Canterbury
Canterbury Corp.
15 South Foremost Street
Clovis, CA 93610

Dear Mr. Canterbury:

We were sorry to hear that several of the lamps included in order #705, which we shipped via Rapid Freight Lines, did not arrive in satisfactory condition.

As you know, this carrier, like all others, inspects merchandise before accepting it. We have their receipt indicating that this order was turned over to them in excellent condition.

For this reason you will probably want to get in touch with Rapid Freight as quickly as possible and enter a claim for the four damaged lamps. I have enclosed two blank copies of Interstate Commerce Commission Form 202, which you can complete and forward to the carrier.

Set the record straight when a third party is at fault.

If I can assist you in any other way, Mr. Canterbury, please let me know.

Sincerely,

Hedda Hill

Hedda Hill
Manager

FIGURE 12–7 Making an Adjustment Graciously

Bakers
Fashions
Inc.
102 Main Street
Racine, Wisconsin 53402
(414) 555-2371

October 10, 19___

Mr. Kermit Dayton
Dayton Family Shoes
100 South Main Street
Douglasville, GA 30134

Dear Mr. Dayton:

You're correct. Your order #506 did call for six dozen Women's Casual Line footwear. Why we sent you 16 dozen (and billed you for this number) is a mystery we can't solve.

You may return them, of course. In fact, we will be happy to pick them up when we deliver your latest order, which is scheduled to arrive in your store one week from today.

May I suggest, however, that you seriously consider retaining the extra ten dozen. This line is moving far beyond our expectations, and we think you will find this merchandise to be a fast-selling item. Our advertising on this item is now in full swing, and a double-page spread will appear in the June issue of the Women's Shopping Guide. We know that this, plus the high quality of this footwear, will help increase your sales.

Naturally, we will save shipping and bookkeeping costs if you elect to retain all the original shipment. For your cooperation, you may deduct 5 percent from the bill that covers this merchandise. Please call me collect, extension 205, and let me know if this proposal is satisfactory to you.

Yours truly,

Mija Choi

Mija Choi
Vice President

An opening with a you *attitude establishes a positive tone.*

A soft sell might persuade the customer to follow your advice.

FIGURE 12–8   "Educational" Claim Adjustment

Nathan Polishes, Inc.

698 Pirate Cove Drive
Wilmington, VT 05363
(802) 555-2966

December 7, 19__

Mr. Peter Marshall
Owner
Marshall Antiques
77 Coast Highway
Beaufort, SC 29902

Dear Mr. Marshall:

We were sorry to hear from you that our #7900 finish stripper did not meet your expectations. We enclose a refund.

You mentioned in your letter that the stripper was applied to furniture "out behind your shop." It is possible that outdoor temperature and moisture conditions reduced the effectiveness of the stripper. (You'll note on the application instructions packaged with the stripper that it "should not be applied when temperature falls below 55 degrees or when humidity exceeds 70 percent.")

Because our #7900 is rated regularly by independent laboratories as the best stripper on the market, we hope you'll give it another try. For our part, we'll test the partially used can you returned to make sure it meets our high standards.

Sincerely,

Brenda Nelson

Brenda Nelson
Products Manager

The friendly tone of this explanation should build goodwill.

FIGURE 12–9 Claim Not Granted

F

Fayetteville Department Store
1900 E. Lake Avenue
Fayetteville, Arkansas 72701
(501) 555-9444

April 19, 19__

Mrs. Bernice Hardy
2025 South Robins Drive
Fayetteville, AR 72703

Dear Mrs. Hardy:

When we received your letter of April 15 and the package containing our Beach Fun bathing suit, we were concerned to learn that your daughter did not find the suit satisfactory and wished to exchange it for a different model. Under ordinary circumstances we do everything possible to please our customers in the matter of adjustments, for we recognize how important you are to the Beach Fun Company.

The bathing suit presents a problem, however, for in keeping with the statutes of this state, garments of this type may not be restocked after they have been sold. I am sure that you were not aware of this regulation, but because of it we cannot send the model you requested in exchange.

The suit you sent to us is being returned along with the addresses of several dealers who handle the Beach Fun line in your area. We know that you will find all the latest styles and fashions in beach wear on display in our dealers' stores.

Cordially yours,

Jose Rojas

Jose. Rojas
Customer Service

A polite explanation justifies a refusal while maintaining goodwill.

FIGURE 12–10   Claim Not Granted

F
F   **FOREMAN'S FINE FURNITURE**
F   1933 Cally Road
       Lewisburg, West Virginia 24901
       (304) 555-9545

December 7, 19__

Mr. Sam Stark
Stark Fashion Furniture
201 Center Street
Long Beach, CA 90810

Dear Mr. Stark:

We received your letter of December 3 concerning your request for credit to your account of $28.50. You may be sure that we want you to receive the full benefit of the discounts due you.

As you are probably aware, the discount policy throughout the furniture field permits a 2 percent reduction when bills are paid within ten days of date of invoice. The amount, which represents our saving in billing and handling, is passed on to our customers.

We checked your July and August orders (with which this $28.50 discount is concerned) and found that they were inadvertently paid 18 (#209), 16 (#402), and 22 (#991) days after the discount period. This oversight in handling bills payable sometimes occurs and has certainly happened to us. Nevertheless, in fairness to our other accounts, we cannot agree to your request.

Use impersonal statements to describe faults.

We think you will feel as we do that this action is equitable. However, if some special circumstances are involved in your case, we will be very happy to review the facts.

I have enclosed our new brochure on the Patio Aluminum line of outdoor furniture. Our preferred customers may take a 10 percent discount from the prices listed, from now through the end of the month. Why not indicate your needs on the enclosed order form and return it so that we an ship you a quantity of this high-quality, excellent-markup line of furniture?

Sincerely yours,

Fred Feldman

Fred Feldman
Credit Manager

The writer gives the reason for the refusal, tactfully implies the refusal, and makes a suggestion in a way that encourages the reader to accept it. Follow this basic plan in organizing a communication (a letter, an interview, or a telephone conversation) that contains an unfavorable reply:

1. Introductory statement acknowledging the reader's problem
2. Explanation of the situation making the refusal necessary
3. Refusal, implied or expressly stated
4. Constructive suggestion
5. Sales appeal, if applicable
6. Friendly close

CREDIT COMMUNICATIONS

Credit accounts for 65 percent of retail and 85 percent of wholesale and manufacturers' sales.

Our wallets bulge with plastic credit cards that can be used to finance almost everything from gasoline to license plates. Around us we see credit-financed skyscrapers, expanding factories, and plants with many additions. Credit enables businesses to carry inventories larger than their cash resources ordinarily permit. They are thus in a position to make more sales. Although estimates vary, about 65 percent of retail sales and 85 percent of wholesale and manufacturers' sales are conducted on credit.

Capital, character, conditions, and capacity determine a client's creditworthiness.

Credit is an estimate of the ability of an individual or a company to pay debts at a later date. This ability is estimated by the credit manager on a careful analysis of several credit factors: cash reserves, credit history, and sales trends.

ROLE OF THE CREDIT MANAGER

Effective credit managers balance liberal and conservative approaches to protect company resources without alienating potential clients.

Even the most honest individual may not always be able to meet his or her obligations. An oversight, a difficult business situation, or hard times may cause delay in paying bills. The credit manager must watch every step of the credit process to ensure maximum benefits to the company as well as to the credit user.

The credit manager's judgments have a profound effect on the progress of the firm. If credit is granted too liberally, company resources can be overextended. An overly conservative credit policy can lose sales. Competitors will surely secure the rejected accounts.

Management must recognize the need for a thorough, progressive, carefully administered, and carefully controlled credit system. In the credit system the credit manager plays the dominant role, often through letters and reports. The purposes for which letters are written include these six:

1. Acknowledging requests for credit
2. Acknowledging receipt of credit data
3. Requesting credit information from applicants' references
4. Sending credit information in response to requests from other credit managers
5. Granting credit
6. Refusing credit

ACKNOWLEDGING A REQUEST FOR CREDIT

Companies often encourage their customers to open charge accounts. The customer who has a credit line with a firm will usually buy more from that company.

FIGURE 12–11 Acknowledging a Request for Credit

Dear Mr. Phelps:

Acknowledgment and directions

Thank you for your interest in a credit account at Foster Wholesale Plumbing. Please fill out the enclosed credit application and return it to me as soon as possible.

No commitment—positive or negative—is made.

In the meantime, we will be happy to fill your cash orders at a 2 percent discount. I have enclosed our current catalog, with several pages marked for your special attention.

Again, our thanks for your interest in a business relationship with Foster Wholesale Plumbing.

Acknowledge a customer's request for credit quickly and courteously.

When a customer asks that a credit account be opened, the acknowledgment should be swift and courteous. Note the optimistic and positive tone in Figure 12–11. For example, the statement "We will be happy to fill your cash orders at a 2 percent discount . . . " is much better than "After your credit rating is approved . . . "

Acknowledging Receipt of Credit Information

Sometimes 15 to 30 days may be required to secure the information needed to make a decision. In such cases, let the applicant know that the request for credit is being processed (see Figure 12–12). Such a letter is especially necessary if an unusual delay is anticipated.

Requesting Credit Information

Inquiries about an applicant's credit history should be easy to answer.

When you request information about an individual or a company that has applied for credit, you are basically sending out an inquiry letter. Such a letter must be easy to answer. To achieve this reduce the letter to a few courteous statements with room provided for fill-ins (see Figure 12–13 on page 257), or attach a form to a brief cover letter. Most organizations also use credit-rating services or credit bureaus to determine whether the applicant should be approved.

Supplying Credit Information

Supplying negative credit information requires careful legal consideration.

Credit managers are routinely asked to send information about their accounts to other businesses. Usually, fulfilling this request requires little more than completing and signing a form. At other times the request is broad, and the manager is asked to send background credit data. A brief letter, such as the one in Figure 12–14 on page 258, is often satisfactory. When a negative evaluation is necessary, statements should be qualified and opinions stated tactfully. In sending replies of this nature, some companies omit the name of the firm on which the evaluation is made. A reference, instead, is made to the date of the inquiry.

FIGURE 12–12   Text of a Letter Acknowledging Receipt of Credit Information

---

Dear Mr. Phelps:

Thank you for returning your completed credit application so promptly. We have begun our evaluation process and, as promised, will contact you with our response no later than December 17.

Our area representative, Jeff Fields, would like to stop by your store to introduce himself and to acquaint you with several exciting promotions we're conducting. He will call first to arrange a convenient time for you.

We look forward to serving your needs for wholesale plumbing items.

GRANTING CREDIT

When granting credit, explain policies and procedures.

It is always easy to tell people, "Yes, you can have what you requested." But the credit letter should also attempt to build sales and goodwill. In addition to granting credit, the letter should set down the terms of credit in a clear and specific manner to ensure prompt and correct payment and to avoid misunderstandings (and ill will) later concerning due dates, discount privileges, and related factors. The letter on page 259 follows the usual pattern in letters of this nature:

1. Friendly opening
2. Credit acceptance (this may be part of the opening)
3. Clear and specific statement concerning company credit policies and practices (or reference to a booklet describing these in detail)
4. Friendly close

If possible, these letters should be individually typed and signed. It isn't necessary to make each one different. They can be stored on computer disk as form letters and personalized by including the recipient's name and some personal reference.

REFUSING CREDIT

When refusing credit, first explain the reason for denial . . .

It is always difficult to say "no" to an applicant, especially when an evaluation of the applicant's legal or business circumstances is involved. The organizational pattern for this type of letter is similar to that of all refusal correspondence. The key is to explain the reason for the negative action before denying the request for credit.

At times, the credit manager will find that the information received about a consumer is so negative that to explain or mention it as a basis for the refusal might arouse antagonism. How can you point out that you've checked and found an applicant to have a consistently delinquent account and, therefore, to be an overall poor risk? In such instances it is wisest not to explain but simply to refuse tactfully. This will avoid embarrassing the applicant and perhaps retain his or her goodwill. A refusal letter to a consumer requires extra tact, for a private individual may not be as understanding or as objective about a refusal as a company accountant or executive.

. . . unless the explanation would cause the customer to be embarrassed.

FIGURE 12–13   Requesting Credit Information on a Consumer Application

Freeport Menswear
2700 Main Street
Cincinnati, OH 45202
(513) 555-0100

September 5, 19___

Ms. Sally Frame
Credit Manager
Holbrooke and Holbrooke
141 South Marquette Drive
Studio City, CA 91604

CREDIT APPLICANT:
Mr. Robert Forester

Dear Ms. Frame:

The above-named individual has applied for a retail credit account with us. Your comments on this person's financial responsibility, credit reputation, and payment record with you will prove very valuable to us. The information you send will be kept confidential. A stamped envelope is enclosed for your convenience. Thank you.

When did applicant have an account with you?
_____

What item(s) was purchased? _____

His high credit was $_____

His payments were _____   _____   _____
                        prompt   slow   delinquent

Does this person have an open account with you now?   _____   _____
                                                          Yes   No

Other Comments: _____
_____
_____

Sincerely,

Ramon Cruz

Ramon Cruz
Credit Manager

FIGURE 12–14   Text of a Letter Supplying Credit Information

Dear Ms. Johnson:

As you requested, we are supplying confidential credit information on National Yacht Design, Inc.

Account Status:	Active, paid to date, since 1990
Credit Limit:	$10,000
Payment Record:	80 percent of payments within 30 days, 10 percent within 60 days, 10 percent within 90 days

Please contact us if we can be of help in any way.

With business clients, the usual refusal pattern is followed almost invariably. As in the case of individual applicants, it is important to project a sincere *you* attitude. (Recall that the *you* attitude emphasizes the reader's interests and viewpoints.) You must explain your refusal and yet retain their goodwill. Just one or two poorly chosen words can turn your explanation into a lecture that is perceived as antagonistic.

Examine the letter in Figure 12–16. It offers a brief explanation of the refusal, a suggestion on how the business relationship can still be maintained, and the hope that credit will be granted in the future. Notice the *you* attitude (the frequent references to "you" and "your"), the invitation for discount purchases, the offer to reconsider a later application, and the statement of appreciation that concludes the letter. In each of these instances, the presumed interests of the reader take precedence over the interests of the writer.

Maintain a you attitude, because the client you refuse today may be a major account tomorrow.

The credit denial letter must be well written, for the applicant you refuse today may be a desirable credit account in five years. Securing and maintaining goodwill are essential.

COLLECTION LETTERS

Companies save time, money, and the goodwill of their clients when they succeed in collecting past-due accounts by letter instead of by legal means or collection agencies. The art of composing an effective series of collection letters, however, requires insight into the debtor's attitudes and considerable skill in persuasive argumentation.

Risk classifications indicate the client's ability and desire to pay.

Delinquent consumer accounts require different types of communications from those used for the wholesale or commercial account. The collection letter sent to the "good risk" differs in content from the one sent to the "poor risk." Because time is short and workloads heavy, companies formulate standard collection letters, which can be adapted to different situations. Perhaps that is why collection letters are not particularly successful: they lack the individual, personal approach.

FIGURE 12–15 Text of a Letter Granting Credit to a Commercial Applicant

A positive opening

Details of billing

Dear Mr. Phelps:

Welcome to the Foster Wholesale Plumbing list of preferred credit customers.

Your account number is 39823, with a present credit ceiling of $5,000. We look forward to raising that limit as our business relationship grows.

You will find credit order forms enclosed, preprinted with our account number and delivery address. Please check these with care. If you wish to make changes, call our order hot-line, at (800) 555-3829.

Thank you for doing business with Foster Wholesale Plumbing. We will do our best to meet your needs.

FIGURE 12–16 Text of a Letter Refusing a Commercial Credit Applicant

At times the explanation for refusal is such that the applicant will only be embarrassed by the facts. However, by stating what *can* be done you also indicate what *cannot* be done.

Dear Ms. Thompson:

Thank you for applying for a credit account with XYZ Landscape Products.

Your credit information was carefully evaluated by the Commercial Credit unit at TRW. Based on their report, we cannot extend the credit you request at this time. If you wish to know details of their evaluation, please contact them directly at (800) 555-2812.

We hope you will continue to take advantage of the 2 percent discount given on cash sales. Certainly, we will be pleased to reconsider a credit application when your credit circumstances have changed.

Thank you for looking to XYZ Landscape Products for the best buys in plants and plant supplies.

Yet, how can firms possibly send personal, individually typed letters to each of 5,700 delinquent retail or wholesale accounts, who owe anywhere from $2 to $2,000 each? The merge functions of word processing programs (which can be used to insert names and phrases into form letters) allow companies to generate large varieties of collection letters. Each letter is an individually *printed* (not written) letter bearing the debtor's name and account information. Figure 12–17 is a typical collection letter.

STEPS IN THE COLLECTION SERIES

In dealing with delinquent accounts most corporations divide their collection procedure into three steps: form reminders, personal letters, and, finally, collection agencies or court action.

The reminder.   Shortly after a bill has become past due, most firms send out a reminder. The assumption is that the payment merely has been overlooked.

Reminders that assume the overdue bill was merely overlooked are often effective.

One form of reminder is a colored sticker pasted on a duplicate invoice, bearing a message such as "Past Due—Please Remit Today," "This Bill Is Now Due and Payable," "Perhaps You've Overlooked," or "Don't Forget Us." Sometimes a rubber stamp is used. Reminders are also printed on cards, small sheets of stationery, and even rolls of tape (in different colors to indicate different levels of urgency), which can be cut off and attached to the invoice.

Some firms have found that the most effective type of reminder is a short, sincere note written on the face of the invoice. When this is signed by the company president, treasurer, or controller, the delinquents are likely to feel the personal touch very strongly. In many cases they react favorably to this type of appeal.

The personal letter.   Sometimes more than a reminder is necessary. A personal letter (or two or three) usually will produce payment or explanation. People generally respond when they are treated like people rather than like numbers.

Using a collection agency or legal action is a last resort.

The collection agency or legal action.   If a series of personal letters to a debtor does not result in payment, a company may decide to turn the account over to an agency or legal firm for collection. This action should be a last resort, because it is not good for the debtor or for the creditor.

VARIABLES IN COLLECTION LETTERS

The collection letter you send depends on the client's risk classification.

Before sending a collection letter, you should know whether the client has been classified as a good, fair, or poor risk and what further evaluations have been made. On the basis of the classification, several factors in the collection actions will vary.

Tone of the letter.   Like all other aspects of the collection letter, its tone must help to achieve one goal: the successful collection of the overdue amount. Obviously, a sarcastic or harsh tone will have just the opposite effect. By arousing

An angry or impolite tone might delay payment.

anger and resentment in the debtor, a mischosen tone may actually delay eventual resolution of the debt. Therefore, make the tone of a collection letter civil and respectful, no matter what the debtor's credit history or circumstances.

Type of appeal.   The type of appeal may vary. Some appeals (see "Appeals to Motivate Payment") are more adaptable to the good-risk than to the poor-risk client. For example, an appeal to fear or self-interest may be wiser with the poor risk than an appeal to pride.

FIGURE 12-17   Text of a Typical Collection Letter

An appeal to self-interest and
avoidance of future trouble

Dear Mr. Donnelson:

Your account is overdue, with a current amount due of $285.

We request immediate payment. Won't you take a moment right now to write a check for $285 and mail it in the enclosed envelope?

Your payment must be received no later than January 16 to avoid additional fees and possible legal action against you. Thank you.

Number of letters.   Normally, more letters are sent to the good risk than to the poor risk before drastic action is instituted. Whereas the good risk may receive from four to seven letters, the poor risk may get two to four. The poor risk may well be delinquent to several firms and subject to many pressures. If you send seven letters before taking action, it may be too late to recover anything.

Time between letters.   The person who has been in business for 20 years, has adequate capital, and has been classified as a good risk will certainly be given *more time between* collection letters than the poor risk.

Time before action.   Time before action may vary according to type of risk. The poor risk's account will be turned over to a collection agency or lawyer more quickly than the good risk's delinquent bill. Here again, if you are too lenient with the poor risk, you may find yourself arranging a court date only to find that the delinquent has paid off as much as possible—and has left town.

**APPEALS TO
MOTIVATE PAYMENT**

To collect successfully, explain why the client's best interests are served by paying you before other collectors.

Individuals or companies do not owe money to a creditor because they want to. Rather they are in trouble, and they probably owe several creditors besides you. They had to decide what to do with their limited funds. They can choose to pay the other debts, buy more merchandise for their business, increase advertising in order to build up sales, or pay you. A simple appeal, "Send it to me," may not be very effective when weighed against the demands they are receiving from others. You must show them why they should pay you now—why it is to their benefit to do so. In these situations the collection correspondent can employ the *you* attitude very effectively.

Appeals vary in strength, but they are all designed to make debtors want to pay their bills or to send an explanation of why they can't pay at present and what their plans are to pay later. The appeal may be to ethics and fair play, to maintaining a good credit reputation, to self-interest, to the saving of time and trouble, to status, to fear of court action, or to a combination of these motives.

FIGURE 12–18A   Collection Letters Using Various Appeals

Fair play

Dear Ms. Tumkosit:

It has now been _____ days since your account for $ _____ has been marked
"Past Due." We are puzzled and can only assume that you have inadvertently
overlooked this bill.

We certainly cooperated in filling your requests promptly for quality furniture
at competitive prices. They say "Turn about is fair play." Therefore, won't you
pay this bill today?

I've enclosed a stamped envelope for your convenience. Please return it with
your check for $_____.

B.

Dear Ms. Tumkosit:

The head of our accounting department has just been in to see me about your
delinquent account of $_____.

I must say I was surprised. There must be a very good reason for your nonpayment. Why don't you pick up a pen and jot a note on the reverse side of this
letter telling me what the problem is? We want to help in any way we can.

For some time you have been one of our valued customers and you have
enjoyed a fine credit reputation. Surely, we both want you to retain that credit
rating. Please help me to help you by sending me a check today for $_____
or an explanation for the nonpayment of your bill.

Reputation

Firms frequently use more than one of these appeals in their collection letters. However, the effective letter (or series of letters) always emphasizes the
benefits to the debtor of paying the bill. The letters in Figure 12–18 are typical
of those sent to collect from past-due accounts. Notice that few, if any, collection letters bother with a sales appeal unless the letter is the first or second in
a series. The primary purpose is to secure money due, and any discussion that
clouds that central message should be eliminated.

**COLLECTION
FORM LETTERS**

For large corporations, the cost of writing and sending personal letters to all
delinquent accounts is prohibitive, even with the help of word processing software. Furthermore, personal letters are not necessary in most situations, because

Action/reputation

Dear Ms. Tumkosit:

We are at a loss to understand why you have taken no action to pay or reduce your bill of $_____ which is now _____ days past due.

We have written you several times and have received no response. You can appreciate our position, for we must now think of turning your account over to the National Furniture Wholesalers Association for collection.

We do want to avoid this for it means that your name is published and distributed industrywide as a delinquent account. Obviously, such an announcement does your credit rating almost irreparable damage.

We have no recourse except to forward your name to the Association within 15 days or by _____, 19__. Please help us avoid such action by mailing us your check for $_____, or a substantial part of this sum, prior to the date indicated.

C.

Dear Ms. Tumkosit:

After several reminders and letters concerning your past-due bill of $_____, we are now forced to consider taking drastic steps to collect. This means turning your account over to our attorneys for court action.

This action is not desirable for either of us. For you it means the payment of not only the sum due but considerable court costs. In addition, think of the time and trouble involved.

Why not save yourself all this difficulty by sending us your check for $_____? If we do not hear from you by _____, your account will be turned over to McAlister, Kelley, and McAlister for legal action.

Legal action

D.

a short, courteous form letter will motivate most people to pay. Many companies, therefore, use form collection letters.

Inexpensive form letters are the most common form of collection correspondence.

Word processing programs allow form letters with blank spaces to be filled in with the proper date and amount due by means of the merge function. Today, word processing makes it easy and inexpensive to store, retrieve, and add personal touches to a previously recorded letter. The result is a personalized yet inexpensive "form" letter.

**WRITING
AND SPEAKING
EXERCISES**

1. As part of a group, prepare an oral presentation in which you discuss the question of anger and the business letter. Are there situations when anger is an appropriate part of claim, credit, and collection letters? If so, when, and if not, what can angry businesspeople do to restrict their anger from their correspondence? Your group may choose to use secondary research when exploring this topic.

2. Prepare a memo for people who write collection letters to help them understand goals of a collection series.

3. Bill Smith, a long-time client, is 60 days behind in his payment to you. Bill has never been a credit problem before, and you value his business, but you require all customers to pay their bills on time. You have written two polite requests for payment, but so far you have heard nothing from Bill. Write a letter that attempts to retain Bill's goodwill but emphasizes the importance of settling his account.

4. Saying "no" to someone's request for credit can cause disappointment. Describe specific says you can lessen that disappointment in your credit communications.

5. You can assume that your reader will be pleased when you say "yes" to his or her request for credit. What other messages in your letter can be conveyed to advantage at this time of good feelings?

6. Mr. Henderson bought an expensive television from you two years ago on a three-year credit agreement. The television, now beyond its warranty, has broken. By telephone, Henderson has angrily told you that he won't make any more payments until you provide him "with a brand new TV to replace this lemon." Describe the collection steps you would take. Write three collection letters for various stages of the collection process.

7. In working through your in-basket, you handle the following claims. Write two adjustments, two refusals, and two requests for additional information in processing the following six items:

   (a) Ms. Marta Owens requests a full refund for her toaster purchased nine months ago (your warranty was for 60 days). She has enclosed a piece of burnt toast and tells you "to pick up your toaster anytime after giving me my money back."

   (b) Brentwood Leather insists on a 15 percent rebate on the commercial stitching machine they purchased last month. The machine went on sale at your store nine days after they paid full price. As a steady customer, the company thinks it deserves the sale price.

   (c) Victor Ortiz encloses an electric razor purchased from you three weeks ago. He simply states that it does not run and he wants his money refunded. It appears to you that the razor has been dropped into water, but you cannot be sure.

   (d) Queen Lake Bakery writes to complain that your model #293 mixer is not strong enough to mix bread dough. The bakery purchased nine mixers from you last month and wants to return all nine for a complete refund. The letter asks you how you wish the mixers to be sent.

   (e) Frank Collins writes to demand a refund for a fishing reel he purchased five months ago (under 60-day warranty). He claims that the connection holding the reel to the fishing rod was defective. A large fish on his line yanked the whole reel out to sea. Naturally, Collins has not included the reel; it lies "about 400 feet down in the ocean," he estimates.

(f) Pacific Packing claims that your plastic carpet protectors are sticky to the touch when temperatures rise above 90 degrees. The firm purchased $3,800 worth of protectors in the past two months and wants to know what you plan to do about the problem.

8. Describe how word processing can speed up and personalize the collection-letter series.

9. Your company manufactures all kinds of stickers—from mailing labels to holiday stickers. Westmont Furs sometimes has a bill-collecting problem and wants you to develop a message that can be placed on a small sticker. The sticker will be attached to the past-due bill and sent to the customer. Generally, caution is the rule in using gimmicks, but in this case Westmont thinks the idea is most appropriate. Design three stickers for Westmont from which they can select one to use.

10. As the new owner-manager of Louie's Furniture, you are attempting to build business and establish a loyal clientele. You took over the established business from a previous owner, and you retained some of that owner's customers. However, you have altered the product line in the store and are upgrading the lines you carry.

    During the six months that you have operated the store, about 90 percent of your business is cash. You recognize that people who have charge accounts are more likely to visit and make purchases at a store than those who do not. In an attempt to build a loyal clientele, you want to send a letter to all customers who have made a cash purchase in excess of $100 or have made three or more purchases in the last year, regardless of the amount spent.

    Develop a letter you can send to these people, encouraging them to open a charge account today at Louie's Furniture.

11. As manager of Jack and Jill's Clothing in Carbonville, a university town, you have a segmented market: the established local population and the more transient college student. Your clothing line appeals to both, and your sales during the year are almost evenly divided between these two groups.

    Almost all of the steady customers in the local, established customer group have charge accounts with you (your own charge system), and you rarely have any problem in collecting the amount due. Because of your success, a few years ago you started to let apparently creditworthy college students also open charge accounts. It has been a disaster. Your accountant told you to take immediate action to remedy the accounts receivable. Finally, you had to write off those losses, and at the same time you established the policy of no credit to nonresident college students.

    In your store you have brochures available to people who want to apply for credit. Frequently a nonresident college student will submit one of the brochures requesting credit. Develop a form response that you can send to the student making this request. You know you have to keep credit available to members of the established community, or you run the danger of driving those people away.

12. Write a three-part series of collection letters to Olney Electrical Supply, a company that purchased $2,782 worth of office furniture on credit from your company. The company agreed to pay $182 each month for 24 months. Forty days have passed since the sale and you have not received any payment.

13. Today has not been your day.
    (a) The side chair you ordered for your office arrived. However, instead of being trimmed in green leather as ordered, it was in red.
    (b) At home, you find that the custom-made shirts you ordered with your initials monogrammed arrived—JRW. The only problem is, your initials are RJW.
    (c) For years you have ordered items from the MAIL-IT catalog and have been satisfied. But today, the white caulking substitute (a product to improve the look of bathroom tile caulking) arrived, and you feel that the advertisement in the MAIL-IT brochure misrepresented the product.

    For each of these situations, write a claim letter. Keep in mind that you want to be fair and firm. Also, indicate what kind of settlement will be satisfactory to you.

14. Choose a brand of automobile. Assume a breakdown has occurred and you cannot get satisfactory service from your local dealer. Write a claim letter to the automobile factory representative. Describe your problem clearly, as well as the steps you have already taken to resolve the problem. Make your request clear and specific.

15. In the role of a factory customer representative, respond favorably to the claim letter described in problem 14. Do so without compromising the integrity of your dealerships.

16. Again in the role of a factory customer representative, respond negatively to the claim letter described in problem 14. Explain the grounds for your refusal. Offer the customer constructive alternatives to resolve the problem.

SUGGESTED RESOURCES

Bures, Alan. "How to Resolve Conflicts." *USA Today* (August 1991):120–127.

Hilton, Chad. "The Mixed Message: Recognizing and Eliminating This Enemy of Clear Writing." *Bulletin of the Association for Business Communication* 51 (March 1988):18–20.

Murray, E. "A Key Question: What Did He Say?" *Purchasing* 11 (September 1991):24–25.

Pollock, T. "Keep Emotional Opposition Out of Your Words." *Supervision* 52 (June 1991):25–26.

Ware, R. "Communication Problems." *Journal of Systems Management* 42 (September 1991):20–24.

LEGAL CONSIDERATIONS
CREDIT, COLLECTION, AND THE LAW

Debtors are viewed as disadvantaged and, therefore, particularly vulnerable by the law. As such, they are protected against unfair pressure or manipulative tactics from those to whom they owe money.

The Truth-in-Lending Act of 1969 (Title I of the Consumer Credit Protection Act) ensures that people gaining credit are fully and accurately informed of the details of their credit agreement. Regulation Z directs advertisers of credit to specify the terms clearly and conspicuously. The Truth-in-Lending Act also outlines garnishment procedures. For instance, an employer cannot fire an employee because wages have been garnished for any single debt.

The Equal Credit Opportunity Act of 1974 (Title VII of the Consumer Credit Protection Act) prohibits discrimination in the granting of credit on the basis of marital status, color, race, sex, national origin, or age. The law requires that any refusal of credit be in writing. Previously common questions concerning plans for children are prohibited. Married women seeking their own credit can no longer be asked to gain the cosignature of their spouse. As an extension of this act, auto dealers, real estate brokers, and other who arrange for credit must comply with the same federal antidiscrimination rules that apply to lenders.

The Fair Credit Billing Act of 1974 ensures speedy attention to the customers' complaints about bills. The act requires the credit grantor to communicate certain kinds of information to clients on a regular basis. The bill must be sent at least 14 days prior to the payment due date so that the client can avoid a finance charge. When the client inquires in writing about a bill within 60 days of receiving it, the creditor has 30 days to acknowledge it.

The Fair Debt Collection Practices Act of 1978 (Title VIII of the Consumer Credit Protection Act) prohibits unreasonable means of collecting debts. The false suggestion or implication of a lawsuit cannot be made. In specified situations, the creditor may be prohibited from contacting the debtor's employer or telephoning the debtor or relatives.

This act was passed because of unscrupulous actions on the part of some creditors and their agents. Communications regarding debt may not be initiated in a harassing manner, and the communications must not create false impressions or cause the recipient to become physically ill. To settle Federal Trade Commission charges that they illegally harassed debtors, Universal Collection Bureau, Inc. and six of its affiliated companies agreed to pay $90,000 in civil penalties. The firms were accused of falsely representing that customers who did not pay debts would be arrested, of using obscene language on the phone, and of telling other people that the consumer was in debt.

The passage of several recent state and federal acts have broad implications for the evaluation of credit and collection of debt. The Americans with Disabilities Act (1990) ensures that disabled citizens have legal protection against various types of discrimination, including credit discrimination. The Immigration Reform and Control Act (1987) contains regulations and protections regarding the use of citizenship as a criterion for hiring or for credit. The Age Discrimination in Employment Act (1988) puts strict curbs on age considerations in these areas. Privacy legislation enacted in the late 1980s and early 1990s in New York prohibits many inquiries into an individual's background, even criminal convictions. Under current Illinois law, a dishonorable discharge from military service cannot be used in credit evaluations. The District of Columbia similarly bars discrimination on the basis of "sexual orientation, family responsibilities, physical handicap, or political affiliation."

13

SALES, GOODWILL AND OTHER LETTERS

Every letter you write should be a sales letter.

W riting the letter that sells a product or service can be an adventure. Doing a good job requires vivid imagination, skill in the concepts of written communication, and the sales ability to create desire through words.

Imagination lets you see situations from your reader's viewpoint and choose your words accordingly.

Writers must possess the *imagination* to project themselves into the readers' position and recognize their hopes, needs, and desires. This is not easy, for our world revolves around *our* needs, *our* hopes, *our* desires. Writers of sales letters must *become* the people to whom they are attempting to sell; they must see, appreciate, understand, and feel the readers' needs.

Imagination is necessary to recognize new needs, new uses, and new reasons for a product. Imagination is needed also to select the words that will build a compelling picture of the product in the readers' mind.

Skillfully composed sales letters persuade readers.

Skill in composition is required in every written communication, but especially in the sales letter. The organization of the letter must be logical and smooth. Persuasive points must be constructed unobtrusively from the introduction to the final statement, which motivates the purchase of the product or service. Sentences must be so clear that they flow effortlessly from one idea to another. Readers should never be required to stop and reread to understand a statement.

Word choice must be accurate and precise so that it evokes the exact response desired. The words should be selected so that they will elicit only one response. The total composition must also be concise. Most readers will not read through three pages if the message can be contained in one.

Descriptive words build desire for the product.

Sales correspondents must combine imaginative abilities with communication skills to *build desire;* their words must persuade readers. It can't be just a "white or blue shirt." It must be a "highly styled, classic shirt, fashioned in luxurious silk and available in Wedgwood Blue or Snow White." A better picture than "a modern office desk" is a "contemporary-styled desk in rich oiled walnut or burnished rosewood to enhance your present office decor and provide your staff with an efficient, convenient, and attractive work area."

INITIAL STEPS FOR THE SALES LETTER

Sales writers benefit by performing several steps before writing letters:

1. Conduct a product analysis.
2. Understand the market analysis.
3. Review the needs of the prospect.
4. Select the attribute(s) of the product that will fulfill the need.
5. Plan the presentation.

PRODUCT ANALYSIS

Writers who know the product and the competition anticipate customer concerns.

Writers of sales letters must know their product thoroughly if they hope to sell it. They must know how it is made, what its components are, where the raw materials came from, what research has gone into it, what it will do, who it will do it, and many other factors. They must also know a good deal about competing products. Only then will they be qualified to do a good job of selling. Such detailed information not only permits writers of sales letters to talk knowledgeably about the product or service, but it also adds two vital selling factors to presentations: (1) sincerity and belief in the product, (2) the ability to anticipate almost any question or objection the prospect might raise.

A product analysis may be conducted in many ways. Sales writers may visit the manufacturer and interview those engaged in making the product. They may gather information about quality and sources of raw materials, production techniques, quality control standards, method of operation, performance levels, design and appearance, distinguishing features, repair and service facilities, and prices and terms. These are just some of the areas about which information can be secured. Some writers make the areas examined headings on a chart and enter data under each head. The completed chart provides them an excellent resource from which to draw information for sales letters and promotion pieces.

MARKET ANALYSIS

Market analysis using primary and secondary sources helps determine if a product will sell.

Most companies bring out new products only after sophisticated market analysis. Sales writers do not conduct the market analysis themselves, but they need to know what the analysts have discovered.

Thousands—sometimes millions—of dollars are invested in producing a product. Before spending such huge sums, companies want to determine if a profitable market exists. Market analysis helps them determine several factors about the market:

- Potential number of buyers
- Present sales and acceptance of competitive products
- Present buying habits and geographical concentrations of potential buyers
- Likes, drives, and status symbols of potential buyers
- What the potential buyer wants in the product
- Buyer's buying power
- Conditions and terms under which the buyer will act
- Short- and long-range selling potential of the product
- Possible tie-ins with other products

Information about these factors and others can be secured from a variety of sources. Company records, earlier market studies on similar products, government statistics on buying habits, and journal articles that discuss sales potential in various fields are only some of the easily available *secondary* sources. *Primary* sources of information are also extremely valuable. Interviews and questionnaire surveys of a sample of potential buyers are used frequently. Another valuable primary source is unobtrusive observation, at the very moment of selection, of just how or why a buyer decides to purchase one product instead of another. Discussions with people who have had years of experience in the field—manufacturers, advertising executives, and sales representatives—are also helpful.

NEEDS OF THE BUYER

Successful products fulfill buyers' physical, social, and egoistic needs.

Market analysis indicates which group or groups in the population can be expected to become buyers. The characteristics of these specific groups must then be examined to determine group needs and drives, along with what appeals should be used to motivate members of the group.

Psychologists say that most daily activities revolve around our efforts to fulfill our needs. Our needs are usually divided into three categories: physical, social, and egoistic. In U.S. society our physical needs—food, shelter, warmth, and so on—are usually met, and thus we concentrate on our social and egoistic needs. Our social needs include our desire to give and receive affection, to affiliate with others, and to take care of others and be taken care of (nurturance).

Unlike social needs, which concern our relationship with others, egoistic needs involve our relationship with ourselves. These needs may be filled by achieving recognition for something we have done, acquiring status symbols such as expensive cars or luxurious homes, occupying a position of authority, and so on. Most of us have the following egoistic needs:

Love	Efficiency	Approval from others
Security	A position of authority	Respect
Social distinction	More time	Prestige
Comfort	Good Health	Good food
Pleasure	Warmth	

Specialists in consumer motivation have produced various lists of human drives, or motives, which include from fifty to several hundred items. Many of these wants are offshoots to those just listed and overlap each other. All of these wants must be taken into account, for *consumers usually buy on the basis of the need that the product will fulfill rather than the product itself.*

The buyer of an expensive automobile may be purchasing prestige and respect rather than transportation. A person may want status and position from a mink coat rather than comfort and warmth. In owning a foreign sports car, instead of simple transportation, a person may be looking for individuality, nonconformity, and distinctiveness. A teenager may be purchasing beauty and popularity rather than just cosmetics, soap, or clothes. In the timeworn phrase: "Sell the sizzle—not the steak."

MAJOR APPEAL

A product's major appeal sets it apart from competitors and fulfills buyers' needs.

Select one or two outstanding attributes of the product or service offered—the *major appeal*—and emphasize these in the sales message. Choose the characteristics that will help fulfill the real or imagined needs of the prospect.

Narrowing the appeal is necessary for two reasons. First, customers don't have the time or inclination to weigh ten wonderful attributes of the product.

They ask, "Why is it better than the other cars, computers, shavers, or televisions on the market? Give me a short, quick answer, and I'll decide for myself whether to purchase your product."

Second, the seller is interested in showing how his or her product surpasses competing items. When the seller emphasizes one or two product attributes absent from competing products, attention is drawn to so-called superior features rather than to common attributes. This major appeal is always based on the needs of the prospect.

To see how this works in practice, suppose we have just been asked to sell prospects on the idea of coming to our appliance store to purchase the new Arctic Refrigerator-Freezer for $895. We are to mail 50,000 letters to prospects in the greater Chicago area to induce them to visit our downtown location.

Our refrigerator-freezer has many outstanding attributes, but our prospects are not interested in all of them. Furthermore, their needs vary. Some of them live in $180,000 to $350,000 homes in the suburbs, while others live in densely populated city neighborhoods. Incomes vary from $12,000 per year to $150,000. The sizes of families range from two to ten. All of these people are excellent prospects, but their needs and buying motives vary. We must, therefore, try to adapt our appeals to our prospects' needs.

In one letter (directed to upper-income areas), our major appeal may be an automatic ice cube maker, contemporary styling, or a new temperature-controlled butter keeper or vegetable crisper. To another group (perhaps suburban or rural), we emphasize the frost-free freezer. For the low-income group, we may focus on price, installment buying, time-payment plans, and trade-in deals. In the letter sent to neighborhoods with large families, we may underscore Arctic's storage capacity and efficiency. The refrigerator-freezer and its price never change, but the major appeal does.

Look through newspapers and magazines and note how advertisements for the same car, the same soap, the same cigarette, and many other items change from one publication to another. The various messages appeal to the needs of the various buying segments. The same variation appears in sales letters.

A product's major appeal changes according to the needs of buyers.
The major appeal for a sales letter must be based on market analysis and market segmentation. In selling to consumers, appeals may be based in emotion—status, prestige, beauty, securing an attractive mate, and so on. In letters sent to wholesalers, the central appeal is more practical—emphasizing profits, business efficiency, and rapid turnover.

PLAN OF THE LETTER

Many of those who work in sales communication contend that the most effective sales letter has four parts:

1. *Interest:* Because of the tremendous competition for the attention of the prospect, we must write a sales letter that almost instantly secures the reader's attention and holds it.
2. *Description:* Once interest has been secured, we must explain how the product or service will fulfill the prospect's needs and result in benefits.
3. *Proof:* Because the marketplace gives the prospect an opportunity to select from competing products and services, we must prove that ours is superior and should be selected.
4. *Action:* Because the payoff for both seller and buyer is in the sale, we must request the action that will complete the transaction.

Interest, description, proof, and action characterize effective sales letters.

Every sales communication should be checked for IDPA: interest, description, proof, and action.

Arousing interest.   Many types of devices can awaken a prospect's interest. How clever, tricky, or unusual they should be depends on who the reader is and the nature of the product or service.

In all cases, avoid the attention-catching device that is a tasteless gimmick. Also, don't choose a device so unusual that the reader's interest focuses on the attention-catching device rather than on the item to be sold.

Arouse reader interest by including a product sample.

Sample of the product.   Although sampling can be a rather costly way of attracting attention, it is one of the most effective. Who can discard a free swatch of cloth, slice of plastic, piece of metal, or square of rubber without first carefully examining it? Some companies have even had their letters printed on a sample of their product (wood, plastic, cardboard).

When prospective buyers can see, feel, bend, tear, taste, or smell the actual item, they are more likely to read the sales letter accompanying the sample.

Provide a photo or drawing of the product.

Photographs or sketches.   Some items are too big or in some way not adaptable for a sample. A good photograph permits the prospect to see the product and integrate it into the word picture formulated in the letter.

Consider a promotional gimmick or gadget.

Gimmicks and gadgets.   Some sales letters include objects intended to stimulate the reader's interest or provide an additional bit of advertising. These may be reproductions of the product, a useful tool or desk implement bearing advertising, or some other item related to the product or service offered. For example, *Time* magazine regularly includes a miniature pencil with its subscription sales letters.

Different openings to attract attention.   Unusual messages, type sizes, and word arrangements can be used to attract attention. Consider these six:

1. Unusual offer
   Let me send you six weeks of Sports Fisherman *for free.*
   *A genuine ruby can be yours—absolutely free—for responding to this
     letter.*

2. Surprising statement
   Most cookware lasts only 18 months.
   Teenagers control more money than America's 20 richest people.

3. Inside address opening
   Just How Often
   Have You Said "No"
   When You Should Have Said "Yes"?

4. Vital facts about the product
   *What drinking water passes the American Medical Association test
     for purity? Only one . . .*

5. Story opening
   *In 1879, Erich Andrews' first ride down Slippery Jack Mountain was
     accidental. A mining cart got away from him and slid more than*

2,000 feet down the snow-covered hillside. Erich would laugh today to see thousands of avid skiers taking the same route . . .

6. Reference to prospect's problem
   Face it: you don't have time to jump in the car, wait in line, then search for change every time you need a photocopy.

Notice in several of these openings that the reference is personal: *you.* This approach immediately involves the reader and can be accomplished with most openings.

Whatever opening you choose, remain positive and appeal to readers' needs.

Openings of sales letters should be positive to awaken in the prospect favorable associations with the product or service. Also, openings should always relate to the sales item. Readers are usually irritated when their interest has been awakened by a device that has nothing to do with the product.

Describing the product or service.   Now that we have aroused the prospect's interest, we must describe the product carefully and show how its purchase will be beneficial. Not only must we describe the product so the reader can almost see and feel it, but we must do this in a way that he or she *desires* it. In our description, we must answer these questions: "What does it look like?" "How is it made?"

Describe the product benefits immediately after arousing reader interest.

The Torata-1000 laptop computer weighs a mere 6 pounds. It slides easily into a standard briefcase or its own carrying case. Powered by battery, the T-1000 goes anywhere—airplane, train, car, or park—with many hours of use before a few minutes of quick, easy recharging. The tilt-up screen features a full 24 lines of text in crisp, clear detail. All external components are formed from the same impact-resistant material used for jet cockpits.

Although we shouldn't inundate the reader with details, there should be enough so that he or she can visualize the product or service. Desktop publishing (as discussed in Chapter 3) allows us to include product or service pictures, charts, graphs, and other visual aids within the sales letter. Visually enhanced letters often save the expense of producing a brochure to accompany the letter. In all such letters, the details in the pictures and in the text should support the central appeal of the letter.

The graphics capabilities of most desktop publishing systems allow you to describe a product thoroughly and attractively.

But even as the prospect reads, silent questions are asked: "What will it do for me?" "How will I benefit?" These questions must be answered early in the letter if we are to hold the reader's attention: how the product or service will provide profit, prestige, comfort, security, love, beauty, economy, health, or some other desired factor to the potential buyer.

Working at the computer would be much easier if it weren't for the noise, the clutter, the interruptions—in short, if it weren't at the office.
   Bring the computer home—the Torata-1000 laptop computer. Or take it with you to the library or park. Relax under a tree as you propose a merger. Spread a blanket on the sand to finish an important report. The Torata-1000 helps you escape the hassle factors and get down to work.

In describing the product and explaining the benefits, be specific, positive, and detailed in reference to the primary selling appeal. It isn't necessary to describe the product first and then show the benefits. The order can be reversed, or the two steps can be integrated.

Use proof to support your claims about product benefits.

Proving the point.   Potential buyers can be skeptical: "Sounds great, but I don't believe it will do all that. Prove it!" If we expect the prospect to make the purchase, then we must prove it.

The type of proof we select will depend in large part on who the prospect is and the nature of the product. One person will be impressed by a testimonial from a movie star, but another will only shrug. Here are some of the common types of proof:

SAMPLES:

Carefully examine the enclosed swatches of cloth—cloth that is used to tailor America's finest suits. Note the silk-like quality of the Italian sharkskin, the beauty of the English tweeds, the design of the American worsted silks, and the attractiveness of the smartly styled gabardines. Each can be hand-tailored to . . .

GUARANTEE:

And you will be happy to know that your National Stove is backed by a full five-year guarantee on parts and service. Plus, it has the National Homemakers' Seal of Approval.

FREE TRIAL:

Therefore, with no obligation or risk on your part, we will be happy to send you the next six issues of National Affairs. *After you have read a few copies of this vital national news magazine . . .*

NAMES OF PREVIOUS PURCHASES:

After your firm has received its Executive Conference Table, you will find it as useful and as attractive as have International Harvester, General Motors, Western Electric, and many other major corporations.

TESTIMONIALS:

"There can be no doubt," said Martel plant superintendent Bill Peterson in a recent letter to us, "that Kelley Safety Equipment is directly responsible for our safest year on record."

"The National Briefcase," wrote Mr. Harry Berg of Hughes Aircraft, "has carried a multitude of papers and books for me and looks as attractive and impressive today as the day I purchased it almost ten years ago."

"OUTSIDE" AGENCY RECORDS:

Conclusive tests conducted by the chemistry department of Central Illinois University during the winter of 19__ indicated that every one of the Teltax cans of paint examined contained . . . . These samples of Teltax were purchased at random throughout Illinois, Michigan, and Indiana. Surely . . .

The United States Testing Company, Inc., carefully evaluated each of our new lines and found . . .

MONEY-BACK GUARANTEE:

We are so sure you will find the new Arctic Frozen Fruit line so tasty that we promise to refund the price you have paid for any item that does not meet with your complete satisfaction. All you need to do is . . .

Analyze your readers'
needs to determine
which proof will overcome
their skepticism.

The proof in the sales letter should be restrained, specific, and well documented. It should overcome any doubts the prospect has, and it should convince people that the product or service will be of value.

Although proof is normally placed after the description, it need not be. Sometimes the proof can be so startling and dramatic as to serve the twofold purpose of arousing interest and convincing the prospect to make the purchase.

Dear Ms. Bertonelli:

You're considering the purchase of a Selway Solar Heater, and you're in good company. The system has already been installed at the corporate headquarters of IBM, Prudential, Santa Fe, TRW, Zenith, Standard Oil, and General Electric.

Action for sales. We have aroused the interest of our prospects through a well-written opening; we have made them want to possess the product or service through our description of it; and we have proved to them that it will give full value. Now the prospects must take the crucial step; they must buy the product or service. But most people hesitate. For this reason, the "buy" section of the sales letter should use an appeal sufficiently strong to move prospects to action (see Figure 13–1)—immediate action. The longer they delay, the less likely they are to act favorably.

Convince your reader to
follow your recommended
course of action.

The action need not be the purchase of a product. It may simply involve "purchasing" the next step. It may be sending for a brochure, agreeing to see a sales representative, accepting a demonstration, or setting up an appointment.

The type and tone of the approach to use in the action section depends on the prospect. Sometimes incentives are offered to potential buyers so that they will act quickly (see Figure 13–2): premiums, special prices, special deals for a limited time, limited availability.

Telling prospects what to do and how to do it also helps set them in motion: "Cut out the coupon." "Sign and mail." "Check the box, sign, and mail." "Include 50 cents, add your signature, and mail."

COVER LETTER AND ENCLOSURE

Brief sales letters are
the most effective. Use
them to introduce
enclosures containing
lengthy product
descriptions.

Sales letters usually cover one page, although in some cases a sales letter of several pages can be successful. Most experts, however, when faced with the need for a long, involved presentation, prefer to use a variation of the one-page sales letter. This variation usually consists of a letter accompanied by a brochure. Prospects usually do not object to reading an attractively designed and well-written enclosure if it is concerned with a product they are seriously considering buying. They do, however, object to wading through six typed pages of a sales letter. That is why most people in the direct mail business prefer the cover letter and enclosure to the detailed sales letter.

Authorities in the direct mail business recommend a cover letter of one of two forms: (1) a general letter designed to arouse interest and motivate the reader to turn to the enclosure (see Figure 13–3), or (2) a short sales letter following the IDPA formula—interest, description, proof, and action (see Figure 13–4). Each section is so brief that the letter must be supplemented by the enclosure.

The design, color, layout, and text of the enclosure can be as imaginative as the writer wishes. Naturally, decisions are governed by the prospect group

FIGURE 13–1 Letter Than Gets Action

HAIBAB CARPET OUTLET

17 Railway Center
Oakland, CA 94619
(510) 555-4232

January 7, 19__

Ms. Virginia Fellows
Box 889
San Francisco, CA 94120

Dear Ms. Fellows:

We like to let our regular customers know about special sales before our ads hit the newspapers.

Beginning January 12, at 8:00 a.m., we will feature a 24-hour 30 percent off sale on all wall-to-wall carpeting, including the newest designer patterns and tufted wools. We have over 900 colors and patterns to choose from, at truly incredible savings.

Who's invited? Only a select handful of our best customers—including you—as well as San Francisco's finest interior designers and office-space architects. To make your shopping even more pleasant, we're hosting a champagne brunch buffet.

Where? The one stop for carpet bargains: 17 Railway Center, just behind the Broadway department store on Market Street.

We look forward to greeting you, one of our favorite customers, on January 12.

Sincerely,

Mora Haibab

Mora Haibab
Owner

Appeals to egoistic needs arouse interest and persuade readers to act.

FIGURE 13–2   Action Letter with Incentive

EKKO
Electric Company
404 North Fourth Street
Danville, California 94526
(415) 555-5987

April 16, 19__

Mr. Pat Harper
Harper's Home Center
4040 W. Walnut Grove
Philadelphia, PA 19174

Dear Mr. Harper:

Enjoy a full 22 percent margin when you sell a set of Palmer Patio Lights at the nationally advertised price of $6.95 per unit!

Palmer Patio Lights consist of a string of eight colored lights wired at 5-foot intervals and attached to a heavy-duty outdoor extension cord 40 feet long. There are three styles from which to choose, and you will find your customers buying one of each as they change the motif of their outdoor gatherings. The Party Line is especially popular, with the Hawaiian Luau and Wild West running close behind.

All units are approved by the Underwriters' Laboratories and sold with a money-back guarantee. You can order them in dozen lots, either in cartons of four sets of the each of the three lines or packed twelve of a type to a carton.

The enclosed folder describes the Palmer Patio Lights in more detail, lists prices, and tells you how you can get three free sets for yourself when you order before June 1. Order today. You'll be happy you did.

Sincerely yours,

Kelly Kanowski

Ms. Kelly Kanowski
Vice President

Catch the reader's attention.

Describe product benefits.

Give proof.

Offer incentives to move the reader to action.

FIGURE 13–3 Cover Letter Arousing Interest

Closet Systems, Inc.
2891 Trent Avenue
Cambridge, MA 02139
(617) 555-9425

May 9, 19__

Mr. Tom Briggs
3892 Emerson Place
Cambridge, MA 02141

Dear Mr. Briggs:

Go ahead—it will take just a few seconds to throw away the attached brochure.

Or, you could take the next three minutes to read it.

What do you have to gain? Freedom from clutter, wrinkled clothes, misplaced belts, lost ties. Hours of new-found time each month—time made possible by a new, organized approach to personal living.

But the choice is yours. We hope you'll read on.

Sincerely,

Rachel Barker

Rachel Barker
Director

An imaginative approach motivates buyers to read more.

FIGURE 13–4   Cover Letter Incorporating the Four Parts—Interest, Description, Proof, and Action

Western Home Products

878 Sheridan Road
Miami, Florida 33166
(305) 555-7656

May 7, 19__

Ms. Kayla Miller
155 West Beverly Drive
Glenview, IL 60025

Dear Ms. Miller:

ENJOY--

Cool days and pleasant nights during the warmest, most uncomfortable weather Chicago has to offer.

Yes, that's what an Arctic Central Air-Conditioning System can give you at an amazingly low price.

The unit occupies very little space in your yard and may be placed behind shrubs. Its operation is whisper-quiet, thoroughly efficient, and almost completely maintenance-free.

Cool, refreshing air flows through the present ducts in your home and provides comfortable days and restful nights.

Our expert engineers will make a scientific survey to determine the exact size unit your home requires. Then with no inconvenience to you, the Arctic System will be installed in one afternoon.

You may be sure you will be as satisfied as the 9,400 Chicago-area home owners who purchased a unit last year. The Arctic System has been approved by the American Home Builders' Association and carries our five-year guarantee on parts and service.

Examine the enclosed brochure and then return the postcard to us. One of our expert engineers will stop by to see you—no obligation, of course—to show you how easy and inexpensive it is to own an Arctic Air-Conditioning System.

Sincerely yours,

Phil Phorest

Phil Phorest
Sales Manager

Make the enclosure attractive and appeal to the prospects' needs.

and budgetary concerns. The enclosure directed to a businessperson will be more conservative than that sent to a teenager. With modern high-speed printing devices, which reproduce photographs and color art with remarkable fidelity, the only limitations on the sales writer are money and imagination.

MAILING LISTS

The best sales letter will not sell if it does not reach a potential buyer, so special attention must always be given to mailing lists. Competent sales writers review relevant lists of names periodically. Some of the questions they ask follow:

1. Is each name spelled correctly?
2. Is every person a good prospect for the product or service?
3. Do all people listed have several common attributes?
4. Is the list divided—by geographical location, economic level, and other characteristics? (When a long list is divided this way, or in other ways, different appeals can be used in different sales letters selling the same product.)
5. Have all the names of people who have moved, died, or expressed no interest in the product been removed?
6. Have names of new accounts, customers, and prospects been added?

Develop a mailing list of dependable customers.

Most firms develop their own mailing lists, usually made up of the names of customers. A list of this type is valuable because these people have already established a friendly relationship with the firm and are willing to buy through the mail.

Every firm expands sales by seeking new names. One way of obtaining names is from a mailing-list firm. Thousands of lists are available, covering almost every conceivable category—clock manufacturers, sculptors, female World War II veterans, compact-car dealers, and bell collectors, to name a few. College students are subdivided into many categories for example, male, female, in universities or in community colleges, at denominational or public schools, by major fields, and by ethnic group. If the mailing-list firm does not have a list in a desired field, it will compile one.

Always be sure that a firm keeps its lists up-to-date. There is no point in buying a list of names of people who have moved, died, or changed jobs.

Expand your mailing list by buying names from a mailing-list firm or by consulting other merchants, clubs, public lists, and directories.

It isn't always necessary to buy a mailing list. Company records are another excellent source of names. Lists may also be rented or borrowed from other merchants. Organizations—professional, social, or business—sometimes provide membership lists. Public rosters offer good sources: tax rolls, vital statistic listings, auto registrations, and voter lists. Hundreds of different directories are available, not only telephone and city directories, but directories of lawyers, doctors, manufacturers of aircraft components or auto parts, shippers, clothing dealers, building contractors, and many other categories of professions and businesses. Such lists provide names, addresses, and vital facts of business operations. For a list of directories and other reference sources, see Chapter 16.

Some businesses compile mailing lists by offering a prize to prospects who complete a name and address card. Thus, there are many ways to complete, design, or obtain mailing lists.

GOODWILL LETTERS

Goodwill letters containing a strong sales pitch are insincere and might damage customer relations.

The goodwill letter is similar to the sales letter, but instead of selling a product or service, it sells friendliness, sincerity, and good relationships. It is the letter that doesn't *have* to be sent but *is*. It is the business letter whose purpose is to build goodwill—not to sell, inquire, or adjust.

Many businesspeople think the goodwill letter is nonsense, but they are wrong. Human nature calls for appreciation!

For a goodwill letter to be successful, it must be sincere. It is not the place for a strong sales pitch. Occasionally, a goodwill letter will be used to sell the idea of resuming business relations when an association has ended. The recipient will feel irritated, however, if the apparent goodwill letter turns out to have the ulterior purpose of trying to make a sale.

Some firms feel they are sending out goodwill letters when they mail form letters addressed to "Dear Customer" or "Dear Occupant." They are like the people who don't have time to write personal letters and instead spend a great deal of time selecting ready-made greeting cards. How much more effective is the short, sincere, individually written letter, whether it comes from a company or from a private person!

USE OF THE GOODWILL LETTER

Companies send goodwill letters to maintain existing clients and to win back lost clients.

Businesspeople find numerous situations in which to use goodwill letters, but two categories predominate:

1. Letters that extend good wishes or thanks (These letters are usually sent to steady customers and are sometimes mailed in conjunction with a national holiday.)
2. Letters that attempt to build goodwill with customers who have terminated or reduced their business relations

To the steady customer.   Steady customers are often taken for granted; they become account numbers. Firms give them special attention only when they stop buying. By that time, it is probably too late. The best time to thank customers is when their orders are coming in consistently.

To the new customer.   Perhaps a sales representative has been working for some time to get an account. That first order has just been shipped. Now is the time to let the new customer know that not only the salesperson but the company president appreciates the business (see Figures 13–5 and 13–6).

To the absent customer.   Businesses survey their accounts periodically to identify inactive customers. Some were excellent accounts; others, mediocre. But they all added to the company's profit margin. A goodwill letter seeks to reestablish the business relationship.

To the "incomplete" customer.   A surprising number of customers may purchase only part of their needs from the company. Perhaps they aren't aware of the extensiveness of the firm's line or maybe they are satisfied with another source of supply.

A goodwill letter might bring in almost all of their business with only a minimal increase in the cost of selling.

FIGURE 13–5 Goodwill Letter

**ROYAL
BLUE
POOLS**

31 West Plains Drive
Dubuque, Iowa 52001
(319) 555-4500

June 3, 19___

Mr. Samuel Nolan
3829 S. Bend Road
Hinton, Iowa 51024

Dear Mr. Nolan:

We're writing to thank you for the opportunity to build your new pool and to wish you
many enjoyable years of carefree swimming.

Open sincerely.

Over the years, Royal Blue Pools has built a reputation for skill and value by giving customers what they deserve: the best possible work for the best possible price. As a result,
more than half of our business is now by word of mouth, as satisfied customers tell their
friends and neighbors they got a great deal at Royal Blue Pools.

Remember that we're here to answer any questions you have as you learn to use your new
pool. Call us anytime. Again, thank you for trusting your pool project to Royal Blue
Pools.

*Remind your
reader of
customer
benefits.*

Sincerely,

Brad Ash

Brad Ashmont
Marketing Director

FIGURE 13–6 Goodwill Letter to a New Customer

**Vermont
Office Supply
Company**

114 N. Vermont Avenue   San Diego, California 92103   (619) 555-5226

March 10, 19___

Mrs. B. Melton, President
Melton Office Supplies
500 East Grant Avenue
Burbank, CA 91506

Dear Mrs. Melton:

Welcome to Vermont Office Supply. We are delighted to have you as one of our customers, and you may be sure we will do everything possible to merit your business and goodwill.

Our activities have always revolved around the wishes and demands of our customers. You come first. If you have some special desires or requests on shipments, merchandise, account payments, or product modifications, let us know. We will work with you.

Each month our sales representative will bring you window fliers and display materials. Our salesperson also will be happy to make arrangements for you to obtain our special counter and floor display cases or schedule traveling demonstration units for your showroom.

Mrs. Melton, we are delighted to serve you, and we want you to know that we will work with you . . . from president to stock clerk. Just tell us how, and we'll jump into action.

Sincerely yours,

Betty Clayton

Betty Clayton
Vice President

Appeal to the reader's need to feel valued.

Use the reader's name to add a personal touch.

EVALUATION OF THE
GOODWILL PROGRAM
A goodwill letter program may not produce immediate, tangible results. Be patient; a goodwill program requires a long-range point of view.

Check the goodwill letter before it goes out. Does it carry a personal pen-and-ink signature? Does it look neat and attractive? Is the letter always sent by first-class mail? Does it have a friendly tone and a *you* attitude? Above all, is it honest and sincere?

MISCELLANEOUS LETTER SITUATIONS

Letters serve a variety of purposes in addition to those we have just discussed: to tell someone that he or she has received a promotion, to send a congratulatory message, to comment on a job well done, and to convey condolence. For most of these situations (and many others), greeting card companies have developed mass-produced messages. But how well do they achieve their objectives?

Martha Martinson was elected president of the 900-member Belleville City Cancer Prevention Association three days ago. Today she received seven "congratulations on your election" cards. Two are cute, two are clever, and three extol her virtues. Each is signed by a good friend. She notes that price codes indicate they cost from $1.25 to $1.50 each. Mrs. Martinson also received the brief note shown in Figure 13–7. Which of the eight messages will she most likely remember? Chances are it will be the note from Betty Anderson, and Ms. Anderson undoubtedly spent less time on her message than did the others who had to visit card shops and make selections.

FIGURE 13–7   Personal Letter of Congratulations

Personal notes build goodwill more effectively than do mass-produced messages.

Dear Martha,

The "old gang" at Western Electric read with pride (but not surprise) about your election to the presidency of the Belleville City Cancer Prevention Association. Our sincere congratulations!

During your years with us, you consistently demonstrated the difference that commitment and hard work can make. We're sure you'll bring that same energy to your new responsibilities.

We're proud of you, Martha, and hope to see you soon.

Sincerely,

Betty Anderson

Betty Anderson

FIGURE 13–8   Condolence Letter

Dear Bob,

I learned of Pauline's tragic accident late last night. My thoughts and prayers are with you.

She brightened the lives of all who knew her. I particularly recall her comment before dinner when we got together for Christmas Eve last year: "Let's live the best we can today. That's the best we can do."

Call me anytime, Bob. I'll be in touch soon.

My very best wishes,

Richard Pilson

Richard Pilson

CONGRATULATORY LETTERS

Many situations call for congratulatory letters. All congratulatory letters should follow the same basic principles: they should be brief, deal with the primary topic only, and carry a positive, conversational tone.

LETTERS OF CONDOLENCE

The letter of condolence is difficult to write. One person may be grateful for a brief, sincere note; another would appreciate a longer message. Perhaps the best advice is to remember to whom you are writing and write from the heart (see Figure 13–8).

WRITING AND SPEAKING EXERCISES

1. Interview someone familiar with direct mail advertising. Seek his or her advice about how to construct a successful sales letter and share the insights in a memo to your instructor.
2. After reading "Legal Considerations" at the end of this chapter, choose any of the listed federal laws, executive orders, or Supreme Court decisions as a basis for further research. Present the results of this research in a memo written to your fellow students.
3. You want to market a new line of matched luggage. Develop a list of six consumer needs. For each, determine what qualities in the luggage to emphasize in your sales appeal. Use your list to write a direct mail letter.
4. As a manager of a growing computer firm, you're always on the lookout to hire talented workers. Write a congratulatory letter to an old college

roommate for the publication of her book, *Understanding Computer Networks.* Indicate (with some subtlety) that you would like to discuss job possibilities with her. Conclude your letter by trying to arrange a meeting.

5. As director of promotion for your service fraternity, you want to notify various civic clubs, social agencies, retiree groups, and so on, that your organization will donate time to assist them in their community activities. Explain how you can develop a mailing list so you can send an informative letter to these organizations.

6. Your company has moved to an industrial park that contains 23 other businesses. Write a goodwill letter that lets those companies know who you are and what you do.

7. Write the opening paragraph of a sales letter (not the entire letter) for each of the following items advertised by direct mail:
   (a) A new computer magazine
   (b) A set of gourmet kitchen knives
   (c) A subscription to a book club
   (d) A time-sharing arrangement for condominium rentals in vacation areas
   (e) A watch that needs batteries only once every five years
   (f) A set of encyclopedias directed toward junior-high and high-school students

8. Enclosures can help get the message across. Enclosures also potentially increase the cost of your mailing because of their weight. Your college wants to send a first-class letter to the top merit scholars in your state. The letter will include a one-page communication from the college president and an enclosure. Write the president's letter and select the enclosure. Keep the total weight of the mailing to under 1 ounce. If your college does not have an appropriate item to use as an enclosure, design your own.

9. Identify a product that has been on the market for less than six months. Following the suggestions presented in the chapter, briefly analyze the market for this product. Decide whether the product will survive or fail in the marketplace. Explain your rationale in some detail.

10. *From backpacks to briefcases.* Trends change, and the Albright Company has determined that whereas college students have been "packing" backpacks for a number of years, the trend is going to shift from that means of lugging things around campus to the briefcase. In line with this market analysis, Albright has developed an attractive briefcase, which is very lightweight, sturdy, and virtually mar-proof. It is expandable, so it can carry almost everything students have carried in their backpacks. Also, the case is a neat item for simply carrying some paper, pencils, and one text.

   Albright does not sell its products in retail outlets but via mail. Its customers have traditionally been "older"—several years removed from the college-age population. Therefore the direct-mail approach will need to be carefully thought out to target the college market. Here are the problems, and you may work on all or some of them as assigned:
   (a) Analyze the product.
   (b) Analyze the market.
   (c) Specify the needs of the potential buyers.

(d) Identify the major appeal.

(e) Concerning the appeal, does it change by (a) male vs. female student, (2) graduate student vs. undergraduate student, (3) major—liberal arts vs. business?

(f) What are two different ways in which the Albright Company can develop reliable mailing lists? Keep in mind that college students are traditionally very transient.

(g) What can be enclosed with the letter? How can the enclosure be designed to appeal to women, men, and people of different races?

(h) Should some gimmick be used, and how will college students relate to a gimmick? Name a potential gimmick and determine if it should be used. Test the gimmick on some students to see if it will help or hinder the sales letter.

(i) Write a letter that you think would be successful in getting orders from college students.

11. As a key wordsmith within your business organization, you've been selected to lead a one-day seminar on effective sales writing for company writers. What topics would you cover? In which order? What "recipes" would you offer (or would you offer recipes at all)? Create a one-page description (as if for circulation to employees) of your seminar.

12. A former college roommate, now graduated, writes to you with "an idea that just can't fail." She has access to men's and women's belts at good prices. She want you to join her in a direct mail effort to sell the product. Write a letter to your former roommate in which you objectively analyze both the pros and cons of the idea. (Feel free to make up any financial information you require).

CASES

Complete the following assignments from the Cases for Discussion section at the back of this book:

1. The Mark Teller case—Assignment 4
2. The Jim Cantonelli case—Assignments 4b and 5
3. Hostile Takeover case—Assignment 6
4. Brooks-Martinez case—Assignment 4
5. When East Doesn't Meet West case—Assignments 4a, 4b, and 4c
6. Bill Webster's Ethical Dilemma case—Assignment 5

SUGGESTED RESOURCES

Austerman, Donald. "Writing Sales Letters That Really Sing." *Sales & Marketing Management* 141 (February 1989):40–44.

Cone, Paul. "How to Sell in Writing." *Sales & Marketing* 143 (November 1991):71–76.

Harris, Denton. "Your Letters Can Build Business." *Agency Sales Magazine* 21 (February 1991):24–28.

Held, Vera N. "Persuasive Business Writing: How to Make It Stick." *Canadian Manager* 16 (July 1991):18–19.

Lynton, Linda. "The Fine Art of Writing a Sales Letter." *Sales & Marketing Management* 140 (August 1988):51–53.

Mounce, Harold. "Leadership Through Communications: You Can't Go Wrong If You Can Write." *American Salesman* 33 (November 1988):16–20.

Rudin, Sherwood. "Banishing Writer's Block from Letters, Reports, and Memos." *Personnel* 64 (April 1987):46–53.

Thomsett, Michael C. *Winning Numbers: How to Use Business Facts and Figures to Make Your Point and Get Ahead.* New York: AMACOM, 1990.

Wayman, Dave. "How to Write 'Killer' Sales Letters." *American Salesman* 35 (January 1990):6–9.

LEGAL CONSIDERATIONS
PRODUCTS, PROMOTION, AND THE LAW

The claims companies make for their products and services have legal consequences. To limit the company's liabilities in such communications, managers must first understand the uses and abuses of letterhead stationery. Messages on letterhead should involve business matters only. Discussions of an individual's personal, political, or religious activities or preferences should not appear on company stationery. The letterhead signifies the organization's concurrence with the message, regardless of any statement to the contrary. In other words, the letterhead establishes the "agency" relationship between the writer and the company. To avoid exposure to the company and potential legal entanglements, many executives keep personal stationery at the office.

To reinforce the agency relationship, many writers add the company name beneath their personal signature. Note, however, that omitting the company name does not dissolve the agency relationship when the message is written on letterhead.

Contracts can occur in ordinary memos, letters, and even college catalogs, as construed by many state laws. A contract relates some kind of promise that the law will recognize. That "promise" can be stated in sales language, as in the promotional promise to "service what we sell." It is not always necessary for the person to whom the offer is made to communicate in return. If, for example, a bank offers "$1,000 for information leading to the arrest of the person who robbed the bank . . . ," the person claiming the reward need not have accepted the contract in advance.

Warranties communicate that the product or service will do certain things. The language of such warranties must be in simple, easily understood language, according to a 1975 law. The law does not require that products come with warranties. But for items costing more than $15 and accompanied by warranty, the language and terms of the warranty must meet specified criteria, such as specifying whether the warranty is "full" or "limited." If under full warranty, the product must be repaired or replaced by the seller within a reasonable time without charge if there is a defect. A limited warranty describes what the seller does and does not promise to do, and must be conspicuously displayed so that buyers are not misled.

The Fair Packaging and Labeling Act of 1966 permits the Federal Trade Commission (FTC) and the Food and Drug Administration (FDA) to specify what kinds of language can be used on packages, and to develop standards for package sizes. Also known as the Truth-in-Packaging Act, this legislation has gone far toward ensuring that labels accurately describe the product contained within the package. Recent amendments and court interpretations of this act have dealt with the question of accuracy in the use of such words as *light, natural,* and *organic* in food advertising. Federal courts opposed auto manufacturers' claims that cars were "made in America" when, in fact, most of the parts were produced abroad. The FDA battled with the makers of vitamins and food supplements over allegedly unsubstantiated health claims made for their products. In all such cases, the goal of the courts is to ensure the fair, accurate use of language for the protection of the consumer.

Major Federal Legislation, Executives Orders, and Supreme Court Decisions Relating to Managerial Communications

Item	Action	Approx. Date	Manager-Communication Implication(s)
1	Sherman Act	1890	Prohibits business from conspiring or communicating to restrain trade.
2	Clayton Act	1914	Prohibits price-discrimination practices, tying contracts, and exclusive dealing contracts. It is important that company communications do not imply such entanglements.
3	Federal Trade Commission Act Amended, Wheeler-Lea Act, and subsequently amended	1914 1938	Prohibits unfair trade, establishes FTC; establishes regulations concerning false advertising; regulates language used in describing products.
4	National Labor Relations Act (Wagner Act)	1935	Directs business to communicate with unionized employees over wages, pay rates, working hours, and conditions of employment; business felt it limited their right to speak regarding unionization. Creates NLRB.
5	Fair Labor Standards Act Equal Pay Act	1938 1963	Established the 40-hour week; Act has been amended many times; the equal pay stipulation makes it illegal to pay women less than men doing the same work with equivalent skills; communications are to reflect such.
6	Labor-Management Relations Act (Taft-Hartley Act)	1947	Permits business greater speech rights: Sec. 8C, "that expressing of any views, argument, or the dissemination thereof, whether in written, printed, graphic, or visual form, shall not constitute or be evidence of an unfair labor practice . . . if such expression contains no threat of reprisal or force or promise of benefit."
7	Civil Rights Act, Title VII Amended by the Equal Employment Opportunity Act	1964 1972	Prohibits discrimination in employment, hiring, upgrading, pay, and benefits on the basis of race, color, religion, national origin, and sex; creates EEOC, which can establish regulations for affirmative action programs for government vendors.

Item	Action	Approx. Date	Manager-Communication Implication(s)
8	Freedom of Information Act	1966	Permits individuals to have greater access to government files; as amended in 1974, allows for speedier access. Allows competitors to have access to what firms report to the government.
9	Fair Packaging and Labeling Act (Truth-in-Packaging Act)	1966	Permits the FTC and the FDA to establish standards for regulating what language can be used on packages; also promotes the voluntary development of standards for package sizes.
10	Executive Order 11375 (L. B. Johnson)	1967	CEO should issue a written statement declaring the organization will not discriminate on the basis of race, creed, or national origin plus physical handicap. The EEO policy must be communicated to recruiters, subcontractors, unions, and employees.
11	Age Discrimination in Employment Act	1967	Prohibits discrimination against persons between 40 and 69 in hiring, discharge, retirement, pay, and conditions of employment. Communications should not refer to employees' or potential employees' age.
12	Consumer Credit Protection Act (CCPA)	1968	The original legislation, periodically amended, dealt with unscrupulous practices on the part of creditors.
	Truth-in-Lending Act (part of CCPA)	1969	Concerns complete disclosure of credit terms; also specifies that careful and clear wording shall be used in lending agreement.
13	Clean Air Act[1] (Amends 1967 Air Quality Act)	1970	Empowers Environmental Protection Agency (EPA) to set air quality standards to protect public health.
14	Fair Credit Reporting Act (FCRA)	1970	Protects credit standing and reputation of individual; businesses are to be correct in communicating credit information and are to correct errors.
15	39 U.S. Code (Concerning U.S. Mails)	1971	Sets restrictions on mailing of sexually oriented advertisements in the mail; establishes procedures for people to not receive such by having name removed from certain mailing lists. It is communicator's responsibility to not communicate with those requesting to be eliminated from list.
16	Noise Control Act[1]	1972	Empowers EPA to establish noise emission standards.

Item	Action	Approx. Date	Manager-Communication Implication(s)
17	Warranty Legislation; UCC-Sec. 2:312–18 (periodically amended)	1972	The uniform Common Code is *not* federal legislation, but is an attempt to gain common statutes among the states. This particular section establishes seller's responsibilities for express or implied warranties.
18	Vocational Rehabilitation Act	1973	Stipulates equal opportunity for handicapped; communications shall not reflect discrimination on this basis.
19	Family Education Rights and Privacy Act	1974	Permits parents and students over 18 to have access to their files held by public schools and colleges; the legislation has altered the use and nature of recommendation letters.
20	Privacy Act	1974	Concerns governmental information and how individuals can update information in government files; for managers in governmental agencies, limits their exchange of information among agencies.
21	Fair Credit Billing Act	1974	Establishes methods by which creditor must communicate with customer; establishes time limits for various kinds of communication creditor may send to customers.
22	Employer Retirement Income Security Act (ERISA)	1974	Stipulates that each employee must receive retirement fund information in easily understood language.
23	Equal Credit Opportunity Act	1974	Eliminates discrimination in credit on basis of standard discriminatory acts; also requires creditor to state in writing why credit was denied.
24	The Consumer Protection Warranty Act and Federal Trade Commission Improvement Act (Magnuson-Moss Warranty Act)	1975	Establishes that warranties must use language that is free of ambiguous terms, exemptions, and disclaimers.
25	Fair Debt Collection Practices Act	1978	Places limits on methods and substance of communication from creditor to debtor.
26	U.S. Copyright Law (Amendment of 1909 Law)	1978	Protects publishers for a limited amount of time from others publishing their materials; the new statutes limit the use of photocopying and prohibit the reproduction of consumable items.
27	U.S. Supreme Court. *First National Bank of Boston et al.* v. *Bellotti, Etc. et al.*	1978	Banks can communicate to public via advertising and executive speech, for example, on a referendum issue. Establishes that corporations can communicate.
28	U.S. Supreme Court. *Consolidated Edison Company of New York, Inc.* v. *Public Service Commission of New York*	1980	Establishes right for public utility company to communicate to customers with bill insert on controversial issue; the company need not grant envelope space to opposing groups.

Item	Action	Approx. Date	Manager-Communication Implication(s)
29	U.S. Supreme Court. *Central Hudson Gas & Electric Corp.* v. *Public Service Commission of New York*	1980	Establishes right for a public utility to communicate a point of view that is not consistent with a national goal.
30	Job Training Partnership Act	1982	Establishes government/private sector programs for job training; sets forth employee rights of trainees.
31	Comprehensive Immigration Reform and Control Act	1986	Sets forth communication rights and communication channels for immigrants.
32	Comprehensive Equality Banking Act	1987	Extends description of depositor rights and reasonable expectations in business relations with banks.
33	Food, Drug, and Cosmetic Act	1988	Defines patent standards and regulatory supervision for certain products.
34	The Americans with Disabilities Act	1990	Prohibits discrimination in hiring and other areas against disabled persons.

[1]Noise and smoke communicate nonverbally. Since the early 1970s there have been various federal and state bills designed to regulate these potentially harmful nonverbal communications—smog, noise, and waste disposal.

PART 4

CAREER COMMUNICATION

Sandy Poulos is Manager of Organizational Development for Lucky Stores, Inc., a large California-based supermarket chain. She has responsibility for training and development programs for 45,000 employees. In particular, she specializes in developing the communication skills of her company's managers.

Stores, Inc.
Southern California Division

6565 Knott Ave.
Buena Park, CA 90620-1158
714/739-2200

Dear Future Manager:

I'm the Manager of Organizational Development for Lucky Stores, Inc., a subsidiary of American Stores Company. We're one of the largest chains in the retail food industry with 429 stores and 45,000 associates.

Let me explain the importance of effective communication at Lucky. Virtually every aspect of our work involves sending and receiving clear messages in some form. Store managers communicate with one another and with their employees. Senior administrators in the company keep open channels of communiation with staff, regulatory agencies, store managers, and, through advertising, with the general public. My group has responsibility for communicating effective training and development programs at virtually all levels in the company.

No wonder, then, that Lucky values a person's communication abilities in the hiring process. In this company, no one is exempt from the necessity to communicate clearly and professionally as a member of the Lucky team. No matter if you're an accountant, a senior manager, a buyer or a courtesy clerk, your communication abilities will be vital to your career success at Lucky.

I suspect most companies look for highly developed communication abilities in those they select for employment. Therefore, I suggest that you highlight your communication skills on your resume and in your employment interviews. Those skills may well be your "plus" over other candidates competing for the same job.

Sincerely,

Sandy Poulos

Sandy Poulos
Manager of Organizational Development
Lucky Stores, Inc.

14

CAREER PLANNING

The search for a satisfying career begins by finding yourself.

Too often, students preparing to enter business feel a letdown if their first few applications do not land a job. What was the purpose of all those years of education? Doesn't the world care about my abilities? These questions are natural for someone who has worked long and hard to achieve career goals.

But such questions are also counterproductive if they tempt you to focus on what you can't get, can't do, or can't be. No matter what you deserve, what you get is often a matter of what you make happen. Your career probably will not fall into your lap; instead, it will be shaped by the calls you make, letters you write, and interviews in which you participate. Especially at the end of a strenuous senior year or MBA program, you must dig deep to find the energy for crucial job-seeking activities. If you do not pursue these activities, even the best academic and business preparation may be wasted.

Learning to plan your career through appropriate communication techniques pays dividends throughout your work life. Many employed people you know are happy with their positions and find each working day an enjoyable adventure. But many others are not happy, and there are some who thoroughly dislike their assignments. In addition, some people have no strong feelings one way or another about their daily labors and are neither challenged by their jobs nor working at their full potential. Often, they are earning far less than they should be.

Too many people in our society remain in jobs for too many years— unhappy and dissatisfied. Competent and hardworking people who are unhappy with their position or insufficiently challenged should not hesitate to look for a new one.

The search for a different job may have useful results. Job hunters may learn that their current position is the best available in the present job market. If so, they may accept their job and salary and thus overcome the urge to "do better." Or they may find more satisfying or satisfactory jobs.

What we say in this chapter and Chapter 15 will apply equally to the person seeking a first position as well as to the individual seeking a better job.

SOURCES FOR FINDING JOBS

Job seekers have a wide variety of sources for locating suitable employment. These include traditional services, such as the college placement office or employment agency, as well as less traditional sources, such as the professional contacts of instructors and friends. The most successful job seekers don't hesitate to open all of these doors to career opportunities.

COLLEGE PLACEMENT OFFICE

College placement offices offer knowledgeable counselors who can help match your qualifications with a prospective employer's needs.

For college students, there is probably no agency as effective, as well prepared, and as inexpensive as the college placement office. College placement officers are experienced in various phases of personnel testing, counseling, and evaluation. They are also usually well acquainted with the human resources directors and companies' personnel needs in that geographical area. Because of this background, placement directors sometimes make suggestions concerning job opportunities that may never have occurred to the job seeker. However, their primary function is to match employers' needs with students' abilities.

Many career placement offices host corporate recruiters who visit the campus to search for competent personnel. Recruiters select dates prior to campus visits. The placement office then schedules prospective graduates for interviews with recruiters. Recruiters usually interview a student once or twice on campus. Those who "pass" are then scheduled for subsequent interviews at company offices.

Wise students will take full advantage of the resources of their school placement office. Services may include testing, evaluation, and reference materials such as annual reports, company history brochures, and company product bulletins. Many schools maintain libraries of videotapes of corporate personnel explaining their firms' policies, philosophies, and broad plans. Students who view such tapes before being interviewed find them extremely valuable.

Rely on other sources if your college's placement office has not assisted job seekers.

The frequency and intensity with which employers seek new employees through college placement offices waxes and wanes with the economic times. In addition, some colleges attract few recruiters because of size, location, or reputation. In such cases, the job seeker should rely upon other sources discussed in this chapter, including networking through professional associations, instructors, and friends.

EMPLOYMENT AGENCIES AND PLACEMENT SERVICES

Employment agencies match you with a firm for a fee.

Employment agencies are good sources for positions. Many specialize in specific technical fields: engineering, business, computers, and so on. Agencies often act as intermediaries, bringing the prospect together with a firm looking for specific skills. These agencies charge fees for their services. Sometimes the employing company pays the fee; sometimes the new employee pays it. The percentage paid may vary from agency to agency, but it is often based on the new employee's first year's salary.

It is in the employment agency's best interest to place an applicant at the highest salary possible. At times, however, in an effort to make the match as quickly as possible, an agency may place you with a firm that can't or won't use you to your best advantage.

Many agencies will offer to write your resume, based on their "years of experience." This, of course, entails an *additional fee.* Be wary. No one should be

Write your own resume, even if you consult an employment agency.

able to write a better resume for you than you. The material in this book should give you all the information and examples you need to be an outstanding resume writer. The reason you should prepare your own resume has nothing to do with rugged independence. In an interview situation, you must respond to questions based on the content of your resume. More than one job seeker with an agency-prepared resume has stumbled badly over interview gaffes such as this one:

> *Mr. Wilkins, I see on your resume that you have extensive experience as a nautical safety specialist.*

> *I . . . uh . . . . that is, well, I was really a lifeguard for two summers.*

Too often, a resume prepared by someone other than the job applicant is filled with overstatements, half-statements, and general hype that only subverts the job seeker's effort to establish credibility with interviewers.

Determine fees and methods of payment before committing yourself to an employment agency.

Be careful when dealing with an employment agency. Make sure you receive satisfactory answers to the following questions: What is the fee? Who is responsible for payment? What arrangements are made on the fee if the employer and employee agree after the first month that the match is not a good one? Are there counseling fees or interview fees?

Employment agencies serve a valuable function, but use them with care. Do not sign anything before carefully reading the document and having *all* questions answered. Be sure to ask questions. As in every field, some employment agencies' principles of ethics and integrity leave much to be desired.

EXECUTIVE SEARCH FIRMS

Executive search firms place highly specialized workers and high-level administrators.

Executive search firms are common today. Some specialize in specific jobs or administrative levels, and others handle placement in executive positions that pay well into the six-figure category.

Individuals with years of experience often use search firms. Like employment agencies, executive placement services usually charge a fee. Many keep in close touch with corporations to find out about new openings. Keeping up with job openings permits the search firm to immediately call one of its clients whose attributes seem to match the company's job description.

PROFESSIONAL ASSOCIATIONS

Professional societies offer excellent networking opportunities.

Local, state, and national organizations usually have their own placement services. Professional and semiprofessional associations of people in accounting, advertising, engineering, health care, office management, computer programming, marketing, finance, real estate, and most other business-related areas maintain flourishing placement services. In addition, they usually have corporate speakers at their monthly meetings who can provide good leads. Also, the members themselves are often aware of openings. If you are in the job market or about to enter, join and attend the meetings of the professional society in your field of interest.

INSTRUCTORS AND FRIENDS

Most college instructors who are active as consultants in their field have many contacts in companies that operate in their areas of specialization. Get acquainted with these professors; let them know you're in the job market. If you have distinguished yourself in their classes or in your school, they will usually be happy to recommend you. The same is true of your own personal

Friends, relatives, and professors can provide job leads and recommendations.

friends or even friends of your parents. Sometimes a phone call will do wonders when a respected professional makes it on your behalf.

Contacts with instructors and friends are known collectively as *networking.* Although the networking process may seem more casual than working through a placement office or employment agency, pursue it with energy and persistence. "People who know people" continue to be a rich source of job opportunities.

ADVERTISEMENTS

Personnel ads in newspapers, magazines, and professional journals are an obvious source of job leads. Responding to an ad necessitates writing and mailing a resume. The task of selecting the right ad to reply to will be discussed later in this chapter. Chapter 15 will discuss resume writing.

STEPS PRECEDING THE JOB SEARCH

Planning your job search ensures success.

As with any important assignment, reading, self-analysis, careful planning and research should precede the job search. To determine the kind of job you want and to review others' ideas on careers, career planning, and the job search, begin by spending at least several evenings reading. A few suggestions appear at the end of this chapter.

Of particular interest is *The National Job Bank 1993* (Boston: Bob Adams, Inc.). This volume contains thousands of job descriptions for a wide variety of companies in all regions of the United States. Entries specify the nature of the company's business, the positions for which it typically hires, the background required for applicants, and up-to-date contact information for making application. Other job-seeking guides, including guides for international employment, are listed at the end of this chapter.

Obviously, you don't want to become mired down in reading about careers and opportunities and never get to the job search. Nevertheless, people in the job market should do *some* reading to determine whether their goals need some change in direction.

ANALYZING YOURSELF

Analyze your capabilities to determine what you have to offer.

After reading, begin a self-analysis to determine what you have to offer a prospective employer. What professional attributes do you possess? What are your specific capabilities? How expert are you in finance or accounting? Do you enjoy working with others? How fluent are you in a foreign language? Can you handle business programs on the computer? Do you like to assume responsibilities? What is your level of initiative? Do you work well with others? How effectively do you supervise others or take orders from others? What are your strengths? What are your weaknesses?

One of the best ways to get to know yourself in preparation for interviewing is to write out, then talk out, your answers to the following questions:

TEN WINDOWS TO WHO YOU ARE AND WHAT YOU WANT
1. How would you describe your personality?
2. What kind of people do you enjoy working with?
3. List three work-related activities you take pleasure in and three work-related activities you dislike.

4. Are you motivated more by praise or criticism? Why?
5. How much of your personal life are you willing to give in commitment to a job?
6. Do you seek work that contributes in an overt way to the development and well being of society?
7. How important is money to you? What aspects of your life are you
   willing to sacrifice for financial gain?
8. How quickly do you want to "climb the ladder" within a company?
9. How patient are you with repetitive tasks? To what degree do you
   require variety and excitement in your job?
10. Where do you want to find yourself in ten years? How do you plan
    to get there?

In addition to doing self-analysis, visit the campus counseling center and placement office. The people in these offices can usually give you excellent advice on your areas of competence, the potential of many fields, salary levels, and related information.

Your self-analysis should include written plans for the long-term and short-term future. Keep in mind that there are only 24 hours in the day; your planning, therefore, should include separate sections to cover career, personal, family, recreational, financial, and other concerns that are vital to you. The point is, if you don't know where you want to go, you won't get there! Or you may arrive somewhere, but not at the time in your life or at the level you desire.

Learn as much as you can about the job and yourself to determine whether you would be happy taking the position.

The more you learn about a job in an interview and the more you know about your own desires and capabilities, the more easily you can determine whether a position is one you can work in most efficiently and enjoyably.

UNDERSTANDING WHAT EMPLOYERS WANT

Companies make an investment when they hire an individual, so naturally they expect a fair return on their investment. Here are some of the attributes employers often seek.

Loyalty.   Do you value the attribute of loyalty? Employers look at your length of employment in previous jobs; what you have to say about previous supervisors, companies, and teachers; and other evidence of your ability to follow through.

Cooperativeness.   How well do you get along with others? Do you work well with colleagues, especially in difficult situations? Do you handle stress well, especially in group work?

Industriousness and commitment.   Are you a hard worker? An employer tries to measure this attribute by looking at accomplishments, grades, part-time work assignments while attending school, the quality of the application letter, and other items.

Ability to communicate.   In the modern world the ability to communicate effectively in writing and speaking is critical. Have you served as an officer in an organization? Have any of your writings been published? How well do you come across in the interview? Do you have experience in speaking before groups?

Wide interests.   Do you have interests in art, music, world affairs, books? Will you be able to carry on intelligent conversations with clients in social as well as business settings?

Ambition and drive.   How far do you want to go? Companies often seek applicants who wish to move to management positions. Companies know that employees who wish to reach the top will surely benefit the organization as a result of their efforts and ambition. In addition, if an employee wants to secure an advanced degree while working, that fact in itself is evidence of his or her ambition.

Organization and punctuality.   Are you organized and punctual? Your organization and planning skills are evident in your short- and long-term career plans, the quality of your resume, and the level of preparation made for the interview.

Good appearance.   How would you dress for an interview? Firms want you to look neat and well groomed, as evidenced by your clothes, hair, and posture.

RESEARCHING THE JOB AND THE JOB MARKET

What specific job do you want to do in the coming years?

Perhaps the first area to check in the steps preceding the actual job search is the specific job. If your abilities permit you to apply in two or more areas, which specific type of job has the best potential in the years ahead? Should you concentrate on computers or inventory control or cost accounting or auditing or personnel management if you have the ability and knowledge in each of these areas? Of course, opportunities that become available within a company in the years ahead will also determine your career path. But you can help shape your future by making specific choices early in your career.

What opportunities exist in your field?

The second area to check is the job market itself. Examine the classified ad section of local as well as out-of-town newspapers. Read the job-opportunities section of professional journals. Examine the list of jobs available at your college placement office. Have interviews with company recruiters who visit your school. Read the job-opportunity bulletins sent out by government agencies and corporations. Take suggestions from your college professors, friends, associates. Check out such books as *The College Placement Annual* and others listed at the end of this chapter. Finally, send letters of application to firms in your field and take advantage of the resulting interviews.

Which companies offer the greatest stability and growth opportunities?

What about companies in which employment is available? This is a third area to research. What is the future of each firm? What are the objectives of the firms? Do they or will they participate in leading-edge technology? What are their earning records? What are their plans for expansion and diversification? What do the records reflect in financial and personnel growth? Is there a possibility that the firms will merge or be taken over? What facts can you learn from their annual reports? What do knowledgeable people think about a particular firm? Does the company have a reputation for retaining its personnel for long periods or is there frequent turnover? Check *The Wall Street Journal,* the Fortune 500 list, *Dun's Review,* and individual company annual reports, which you will find in most libraries.

Because your success is intimately associated with that of your employer, make every effort to take a position with a firm that seems to have a bright and dependable future.

CULTURAL
DIVERSITY IN
COMMUNICATION

Career Paths for Women:
Still a Rocky Road?

Carol Shuherk

University of
Southern California

"Students in college today think the battle has been won; or they're not aware there was one." So began the remarks of broadcast journalist Marlene Sanders, first panelist to speak at a 1989 conference on women's careers in the media at the University of Southern California. The other panelists, including a former CBS president, syndicated columnist Ellen Goodman, and author Betty Friedan, concurred: the massive influx of women into the work force in the past 25 years has led many to conclude that female advancement in a traditionally male world is a problem solved. In truth, the facts show that while the presence of women in the work force is unmistakable, their progress on the career ladder is still disproportionate to men's. Just 3 of every 100 top executives are women. Female vice presidents earn 42 percent less than men in similar jobs. Overall, women make 72 cents for every dollar a man makes (ten years ago it was 64 cents), and 79 percent of Fortune 500 chief executives admit that there are "identifiable barriers" to women getting to the top.

What is to blame and how do female careerists surmount the obstacles? The roots of the problem run deep. Of the executives who see barriers, 81 percent said they were due to societywide stereotypes and preconceptions about the "proper" role of women and men in society. These preconceptions are rooted in socializing processes that start in infancy and continue through adulthood. They encourage nurturing, supporting, and relationship building in females and autonomy, independence, and personal power building in males. Their outcomes are reflected in workplace practices and the behavior of individual men and women.

In the workplace, formative experiences translate into assumptions about what women want from their careers as well as what they must do to reach their goals. In a 1990 Department of Labor study on gender discrimination in the executive suite, male decision makers in many of the companies studied assumed that a woman with children wouldn't be interested in a high-profile transfer or change of assignment because of the longer hours the job would require. In another recent survey of Fortune 100 executives, 90 percent of those responding saw women in senior management as most likely to be in human resources roles. Fewer than 10 percent thought women likely to be in plant management or production roles. But willingness to transfer, to take on risky and high-profile assignments, or to succeed in a line position are necessary for upward mobility.

Attempting to chart a path by which women might pursue their career of choice, organizational sociologists Ann Morrison, Randall White, and Ellen Van Velson asked 98 Fortune 100 executives to describe the qualities and characteristics that hurt or helped people succeed in their firms. Four sets of *contradictory* expectations, blending traditional male and traditional female behavior emerged from their interviews. First, on the one hand, women must be willing to take risks; on the other, all their work must be consistently near perfect. Women must be willing to take on new assignments, to push past their current areas of expertise, to take chances. At the same time, they are expected to be extremely competent in everything they do—often more competent than men in the same job. When they are not, their failures are twice as likely to be attributed to their gender than to personal limitations.

Second, women are expected to be tough but not macho. Ability to make decisions, call the shots, take a stand, and stay cool under pressure are necessary to success, but at the same time, the desire for women to act "like women" is strong. In the words of one executive, successful women had to be "tough, yet demure."

Third, successful women needed to be very ambitious but not expect equal treatment. Those who were given a chance to fill a high-level position were expected to put the job first and family second. Their drive to succeed was a crucial factor in their selection. At the same time, women had to accept, for the time being anyway, that having the same title as men in the company did not mean equal treatment. Salary differentials are the most obvious example. Even with a Harvard MBA and comparable experience, women are paid considerably less than men at the same level.

Fourth, women are expected to take responsibility but follow other's advice. On the one hand, senior executives want women to know what they want and go for it. On the other, senior executives seem to expect women to accept whatever advice and opportunities they provide. Knowing clearly what she needs in order to sort through and sometimes reject what she doesn't, combined with the ability to leave superiors feeling good about their advice or offers being rejected, are crucial to success.

These conflicting expectations form the basis of what's come to be called the "glass ceiling," a web of unspoken rules of the workplace that dramatically affect the career progress of women. But the socialization that leads to discriminatory business practice has also been shown to cause individual women to be at odds with themselves in the pursuit of their goals. By the time they accept their first career position, women's confidence to pursue success has been eroded in comparison to men's. This can be reflected in how they present themselves at work. The way in which they talk about their careers may not reflect what they actually feel inside.

Studies conducted in the United States and Britain throughout the 1980s concluded that the climate in co-ed classrooms from first-grade through college is one that steadily undermines self-esteem for women and has significant implications for their behavior later in the workplace. Compared with girls, boys are five times more likely to receive the most attention from teachers, eight times more likely to speak out and be responded to in class, and two times more likely to be praised by teachers.

A 1989 *Wall Street Journal* story about these findings linked them to another study begun at the University of Illinois in 1981. That study measured the self-confidence of 80 high-school valedictorians, salutatorians, and honor students and found that, at graduation, 23 percent of the men and 21 percent of the women believed they were "far above average" in intelligence. As college sophomores, only 4 percent of the women felt far above average, and 22 percent of the men rated themselves that way. By their senior year, none of the women reported feeling far above average while 25 percent of the men said they thought they were.

An author of one of the studies of classroom interaction, David Sadker of American University, concluded from all of this: "In the workplace women are less likely to present themselves as effective managers. A lot of it deals with passive roles they assume in school." Yet another study, this one conducted in the workplace by two Harvard researchers, appears to agree. Margaret Hennig and Anne Jardim asked men and women in a variety of professions three questions about themselves as careerists. The results made two things clear: There is very little difference between career men and women in their aspirations and their desire to obtain them. But there can be immense differences in how men and woman speak about themselves as achievers.

Each participant in the study was asked to respond to three questions: How did you get the specific job you have today? Where do you want to be in five years? What will be the single most critical factor in your getting there? There were no differences in the types of answers men and women gave to the second question about career goals five years down the road; responses included

CULTURAL DIVERSITY IN COMMUNICATION

things like "in senior management," "completing my master's degree," "in my own business," and "starting a family," equally from both sexes. In contrast, there was a significant difference in the way men and women talked about themselves when asked how they got to where they were and what it would take to reach the five-year goal.

Hennig and Jardim described women's responses to "how did you get here?" as a sense of passivity: a syndrome characterized by "it just happened to me" or "somebody did it for me/pushed me to do it." Specific responses included: "I was good at my work and it just happened," "I was just lucky—someone left at a critical point and they asked me to take over," "I had a boss who believed I could do it," and "I didn't want to do it, but my boss was relentless so I finally gave in."

Their answers to "how will you get there?" could be clustered into two separate categories under the general heading of an "individual struggle" view of what it takes to reach one's goals. Many of the

women's responses pointed to having to improve individual capabilities: consistently harder work, outstanding performance, higher job competence, further training, or more formal education. Or they pointed to personal factors: developing greater self-confidence, becoming more aggressive, learning to let go and delegate more to other people on staff, or finding the time to get a backup person.

How did men's responses differ? In the first place, men talked actively and gave themselves the credit for being where they are today. Secondly, when they spoke of what it will take to reach their goals, they talked about acting on the system they are a part of. They said they will make what they want known to the people who matter and that they will win the support of bosses, peers, and subordinates. They spoke of needing to know as much as possible about the political system, of planning to be visible, of taking risks and making sure people see them as the person right for the job.

It appears that the major difference

EVALUATING JOB ADVERTISEMENTS

Job advertisements provide a quick way to identify openings.

If you are not familiar with advertisements that list openings, begin reading them. Announcements appear in professional journals, the classified sections of major urban newspapers, and in *The Wall Street Journal* and *Barrons.* In addition, the sports or financial sections of major newspapers often carry large ads (3 by 4 inches, 4 by 5 inches), known as display ads, listing professional job openings. This type of ad also appears in financial newspapers, such as *The Wall Street Journal.*

Read job ads critically. *Blind ads,* like the one shown here, are often placed by a reputable company that does not want to expose its name or specific career openings in a widely published advertisement. As the name suggests, a blind ad shields the company from revealing too much about its hiring needs in a public way. Quality Care Hospital, for example, may choose to place a blind ad expressing its urgent need for cardiac care nurses rather than attaching its name openly to such an ad.

BLIND AD
Goal-oriented manager wanted for attractive salary-commission position with major East Coast clothes wholesaler. Extensive travel commitments, including bimonthly trips to Europe. Mail resume, including salary history, to Box 5836, Philadelphia Register. *An Equal Opportunity Employer.*

between the men and women managers in Hennig and Jardim's study was mind-set. As the studies in the classroom suggested, women have either been socialized to be more self-effacing or their natural self-confidence has been eroded over time. One way to characterize the differing mind-set regarding the third question is to say that men seem to be more in tune to the informal as well as the formal system in organizations. The two different mind-sets can result in patterns of communication that propel men and impede women in the career-long process of self-presentation and influence seeking.

Clearly, serious career women must be alert. They must watch how they say what they say about themselves, and they must watch for the unconscious (and often conscious) effects of stereotyping and preconceptions that color the perceptions others have of them. It might be tempting to brush off the studies in the classrooms and the workplace as "dated." That was the eighties; we are in the nineties! Things *are* changing and for the better. But a couple of points to remember: Anybody who is reading this book today was a student in grade school, high school, maybe even college, literally one of the people at the desks, when the researchers were in the back of the room observing the student-teacher interaction. And it took ten years for women's salaries as compared to men's to go up 8 cents, from 64 cents to 72 cents for every dollar earned by men. At that rate, it will be 2027 before women's and men's salaries reach parity. By that time, most people reading this book will be near the end of their careers.

But don't be discouraged. The knowledge gleaned from studies of women and the workplace equips women to anticipate and plan for the challenges of the workplace as they go forward in their careers. And the communication patterns that diminish a woman's standing as an action-oriented and politically astute professional can be altered through awareness and practice.

Companies and individuals misuse blind ads at times to make an opportunity seem greater than it is. For example, the "company" placing the blind ad may be no more than an individual with a business idea. He or she may actually be trying to attract investors or commission-only salespeople by means of the ad. Exercise caution and judgment in evaluating the opportunities described in blind ads.

The ad that you *should* reply to, big or small, is the same one that other ambitious, intelligent people will find attractive—one with a contact name. The ad shown next is typical of those found in the classified columns. Display ads usually list advanced qualifications, higher salary, ability to handle responsibility, and several years of experience.

AD WITH CONTACT NAME

Top-performing licensed real estate agents wanted for outstanding opportunity. Eight agents will be selected for sole sales authority, Lake Regents residential developments #4 and #5. Current agents earning in excess of six figures. Best benefits package in the industry. Contact J. Blake, Box 4093.

Don't waste your time applying for a position for which you do not qualify.

Evaluate how your own qualifications match those listed in the ad. Choose only ads that are appropriate for you. If the ad calls for "10 to 12 years of experience as a corporate controller" and you are a 22-year-old recent graduate, don't waste your time or theirs by responding.

PERSONAL JOB APPLICATIONS

Two forms of application letters are available to the job-seeker. The *one-part job search letter,* which is our primary focus in the remainder of this chapter, contains elements calculated to arouse interest, describe abilities, support assertions, and win an invitation to interview. In this way, the one-part job search letter combines the elements of the second form of application (discussed in Chapter 15), the two-part application. The two-part application consists of a cover letter and a resume.

Mid-level managers and executives use one-part job search letters to introduce themselves in a personal narrative before providing a complete resume.

In the 1990s, the one-part job search letter is used less than the cover letter and resume combination. Nevertheless, the one-part option is useful when the job seeker wants to narrate his or her abilities and experience in a more complete way than is common in the briefer cover letter. Many mid-level managers and executives use the one-part application letter and at a later stage in the hiring process submit a complete resume.

Specific details give credibility to claims made in your resume.

Human resources directors and recruiters increasingly report that "facts" in some resumes are false and that statements concerning education and experience are often open to question. In writing your cover letter and resume, remember to be as specific as possible. In addition to listing information such as degrees received, places of employment, and military service, specific dates, addresses, names of individuals, and other items that will lend credibility to what you've said are easily verifiable.

Keep in mind that the job search letter is a type of sales letter: instead of selling a product or service, you are selling yourself in a quiet yet forceful manner. Naturally, there is always an internal struggle about how to sound acceptably modest while impressing the potential employer with personal achievements. The line is a fine one, but you can achieve it with care, concern, and attention to the details of good writing.

Basically, application letters can be categorized in two ways: the *solicited letter,* in which you are replying to an advertisement or a job-opening announcement, and the *unsolicited letter,* in which you send an inquiry asking about job openings and requesting an interview.

Solicited application letters respond to an advertised opening and face stiff competition.

An unsolicited letter inquiring about possible openings requires follow-up measures to ensure that an application is considered seriously.

If you reply to an ad or announcement, you know an opening exists. An interesting and inviting ad that prompts you to write will probably bring letters from many other applicants. You don't face this level of competition when you mail an unsolicited letter, but the company may have no immediate opening for you. Job seekers must face the fact, of course, that many if not most unsolicited letters bring no response at all from potential employers. In some cases, the letters are kept in case a job opening develops. Often, however, the letters are simply discarded. But don't be discouraged about sending unsolicited letters; instead, follow up your letters with, for example, phone calls to determine if a job opening exists.

LETTER ORGANIZATION

A sales letter attempts to sell a product or service, but in job letters, writers attempt to "sell" the best possible picture of themselves. The job application letter can be divided into several sections: (1) it attempts to *arouse the reader's interest* in the job seeker, (2) it *describes the background* that makes the appli-

*Successful job application
letters follow sales
strategies: they arouse
interest, describe and
prove qualifications, and
persuade the reader.*

cant eligible for the job, (3) it *continues with proof* for the statements made by citing degrees, places of former employment, and references, and (4) it concludes with a *request for an interview* (or the sale itself). The amount of detail and the general approach differ, depending on whether the letter is a cover letter to a resume or a job search letter.

AROUSING INTEREST

Prospective employers are not usually impressed with cute or clever openings, nor are they intrigued with the stereotyped statement, "this is in reply to your ad." Avoid openings such as the following, which revolve around the writer and are dull:

> *On June 5 I shall receive my degree from Central College and then will be ready to take a professional position with your firm.*

> *This is in reply to your ad which appeared in the June 27 issue of the* Times.

> *After many years of study and application, I have reached my goal and am now available to consider the position you have available.*

*Effective openings
concisely describe the
benefits you can offer
potential employers.*

In contrast, the openings that follow are concisely worded, give the reader a quick overview of the applicant's qualifications, and indicate how the company can benefit from the applicant's abilities. The employer's attention is aroused when the applicant indicates major attributes and how they will help the company. This is the time for the writer to use the *you* attitude sincerely and effectively.

> *We have a common interest; you seek a college graduate with a strong technical sales background and I seek a company with a fast-track opening for a proven sales performer in the technical area.*

> *A college degree in accounting, a CPA certificate, and three years of experience working directly under a corporate controller qualify me for the accounting associate position you described in yesterday's Sunday* Sun.

> *My ability to key-enter data accurately, speak intelligently to customers and clients, come up with an original idea occasionally, and be pleasant and good-humored are surely the attributes you would like in the administrative assistant for whom you advertised. I have these qualities plus many others. Here are some details.*

These openings are fresh, original, and indicate how the applicant's abilities will help the firm. (For some jobs, such as advertising and copywriting positions, it might be advisable to inject an attention-getting statement, an intriguing sentence, or a startling and clever paragraph.) The opening statement also affords a good opportunity to give your reader a capsule account of your primary selling points: experience, education, special abilities, and the like.

DESCRIBING ABILITIES

In the one-part letter of application, make clear and specific statements describing your education, experience, leadership abilities, and awards. In the two-part letter application, generally allude to these accomplishments in the cover letter and list them specifically in the resume.

Write the description to match the job's requirements or the ad's demands. If the job description emphasizes experience and you possess it, state your experience in detail. If education is vital or leadership qualities are important, then emphasize those qualities. The sample letters in Figures 14–1 and 14–2 (pages 310–313) illustrate different methods for handling these situations. Figure 14–1 is a job-search letter that focuses the reader's attention on general descriptions of experience and education. Figure 14–2, by contrast, emphasizes specific positions and responsibilities held in the past. The first letter would probably be most useful to a person in the early years of a career; the second letter relates to more experienced applicants.

Cover letters direct the reader to specific information contained in the accompanying resume.

When your resume accompanies the job search letter, use the letter to pique the reader's interest through highlights of your academic or work experience. In short, give the reader something to look for when he or she turns to your resume. Here is such a highlight statement from a brief job search letter.

> *Ms. Victors, you may be particularly interested in my internship with IBM during the summer of 19__. As described more fully in my resume, that position gave me hands-on experience in computer marketing.*

When Ms. Victors turns to the resume, she will not be merely perusing it. Instead, she will be *looking* for something—in this case, the IBM experience. When she finds it, she will experience a double satisfaction: the pleasure of simply finding what she was looking for and the pleasure of recognizing the applicant's accomplishments. When a reader feels satisfaction, the writer has achieved an important goal.

PROVING STATEMENTS

In the one-part application letter, be sure to state specifically your references, degrees, and former employers (all proof of your abilities). However, in the cover letter of a two-part application, only refer to these elements, leaving them for detailed discussion in the resume.

Whether detailing your qualifications in a one-part letter or in a resume, give specific evidence to support your claims.

In listing degrees you will indicate your specific areas of study. When noting previous employment, describe briefly your duties and responsibilities so that the prospective employer has some idea of what you can do. Also describe any activities that illustrate leadership qualities: offices held, meetings conducted, articles written, conferences attended. Remember to list volunteer work in civic or charitable organizations. Human resource managers report they are looking for individuals with volunteer experience. Such background indicates the use of valuable skills that are easily transferable to the job market.

GETTING THE INTERVIEW— THE REQUEST FOR ACTION

In both the cover letter for the resume and in the one-part letter of application, use the final statements to request an interview and suggest ways to arrange one. The final statement should *not* be a simple "If you are interested, please call me" or "If you have any questions, I shall be pleased to answer them."

End by appealing for an interview.

Your request for an interview should be emphatic and positive. It should also clearly state that you want the interview so that you can tell the prospective employer about your attributes in greater detail. One possible strategy is to imply that the information in the letter is only part of the story (as it can only be) and that you want the interview to expand, add, and clarify details.

May I have an interview so that we can discuss in greater detail my education, experience, and other qualifications for the position? I can be reached . . .

I would appreciate an opportunity to meet with you so that I can explain more completely how my experience, education, and ability to work hard and take responsibility all qualify me for the job. Please call or write . . .

I would like to meet with you so that I can give you a more complete picture of how a degree in accounting, six years of responsible work as assistant to the controller, and a desire to work hard can benefit the Cantrel Corporation.

KEY POINTS TO REMEMBER

Human resource directors consider several factors important for all job seekers:

- The job applicant's initial contact should be in writing.
- Letters of application are highly desirable to companies even if there are no job openings at present.
- A satisfactory tone, good grammar, proper spelling, typing (not handwriting), and neatness are absolutely essential attributes.
- Three references should be included. The types of people listed are of major importance to the human resources directors. Typically, one or more past employers and a university professor (who knows your work in your major) are listed.

Be positive and thorough as you seek the right job opportunity for you.

Perhaps the most important factor in seeking a full-time job or in making a career change is to go about the task optimistically and systematically. Positions are available and if you use the correct procedure, you will be successful. But first, it is absolutely vital to determine what you want and what you have to offer. Next, what does the market want? Once you know these facts, then match your interests and abilities with the qualities the companies want. Be careful not to shoot too high or too low.

Approach the task as you would a campaign. Don't be content with responding to one ad or applying to one company. If you use an unsolicited resume approach, select 10 to 20 prospective companies and mail letters to all simultaneously. If you are answering ads, respond to all those you have carefully selected. In that way, if you receive five invitations for interviews, you can schedule them all within a few days, select the best job, and make a commitment.

If you send only one letter and wait a week for a reply, and then another letter and wait a week, you may stretch your job search out for months.

Above all, *work* at finding the job that will challenge and reward you. Companies are always looking for hard-working, qualified individuals. You *can* secure the job you want and for which you are qualified if you expend the effort in a logical and well-organized manner.

FIGURE 14–1   One-part Job Search Letter

4150 North Wescott Lane
Kalamazoo, MI 49008

June 27, 19__

Personnel Director
Brunswick Corporation
One Brunswick Square
Skokie, IL 60076

Dear Director:

My college background, two years of part-time experience as an accounting clerk, three years of work in corporate training, and a keen desire to work in the field of human resource development qualify me to fill the position described in the *Midwest Accounting Journal.*

The position of associate director of training, as described in your ad, is exactly the job I had in mind.

<u>Experience</u>

During my last two years in college and for two summers I worked as an accounting clerk for Price Waterhouse. After graduation from the School of Business of Western Michigan University, I joined the Management Training Department of Michigan Central Electronics Corporation. As a training specialist, I schedule and coordinate training programs for middle-management-level employees.

I am still with Michigan and would not leave except for the limited opportunities for advancement in the training area which currently exist.

<u>Education</u>

In 19__ I received my bachelor of science degree from the School of Business of Western Michigan University. My major area of study was marketing, with a minor in finance. I also served as teaching assistant in finance at Western Michigan.

Next year I hope to enroll in an evening master's degree program in organizational design and development.

Many job seekers just beginning their careers prefer to give a general idea of their experience and expertise.

<u>Memberships</u>

I am an active member of the Academy of Management, the Finance Association, and the American Society for Training and Development (ASTD).

<u>References</u>

Dr. Manuel Ortega
School of Business
Western Michigan University
Lansing, MI 39010

Joan T. Morrison,
Vice President
Human Resources Department
Central Electronics Corporation
Industry Square
Milwaukee, WI 53203

Robert Kelbourne, Manager
Price Waterhouse
234 South Michigan Avenue
Chicago, IL 60604

Roberta Clark, Senior Accountant
Price Waterhouse
234 South Michigan Avenue
Chicago, IL 60604

Because of my background, I am sure I can do an outstanding job for Brunswick. I am familiar with your fine products and am eager to join your team. Please call me at (301) 555-4211. I am available for an interview at your convenience.

Sincerely,

Marilyn Berman

Marilyn Berman

First-time job seekers benefit from listing personal references who can support their general claims.

FIGURE 14–2   One-part Job Search Letter

1020 West Sunset Drive
Burbank, CA 91509
(714) 238-9722
August 18, 19__

Ms. Maria Rodriguez
Director of Operations
Elton Electronics Organization
2000 Phoenix Square
Phoenix, AZ 85044

Dear Ms. Rodriguez

According to the *Phoenix Sun,* Elton Electronics is rapidly expanding after being selected as a subcontractor for the DOD X-51 Missile System. Although I have been employed by Lockheed California for several years, I would be very interested in applying my electronics knowledge in your firm. A job with your firm would permit me to move to Arizona where I have family and friends.

I have detailed below some of my assignments as an introduction to my background.

ELECTRONICS ENGINEER
From 1980 to 1984 I was employed by Motorola in Chicago as an electronics engineer with special application to mobile car telephones. In this capacity I helped develop a new monitoring system for which a patent was issued to the company.

MANAGER, ELECTRONIC TRANSMISSION SYSTEMS
In 1984 I moved to California, where I secured employment with a division of Hughes Aircraft. In just eight months I was made manager of a radar development group which worked on ADA software for U.S. naval vessels. I left Hughes in 1988 to accept an invitation from IBM in New York.

ENGINEER AIR TO AIR GUIDANCE SYSTEMS
From 1988 to 1991 I was at IBM involved with management information systems as they applied to guidance controls. My responsibilities included supervising several technicians and six engineers. Our program was completed successfully and manufacturing begun. Several applications of the original work were spun off and applied to related projects.

Experienced candidates may opt for the one-part job search letter that lists specific positions and responsibilities.

SENIOR ENGINEER, ADVANCED PRODUCTS

In 1991 I accepted an offer from the Lockheed California Company and moved to California. As a senior engineer, I supervise a department charged with specific project development on highly classified work.

In all the positions listed above, 1980 to the present, evaluations of my competence, work habits, and personal attributes have been either "excellent" or "superior."

EDUCATION

I received both undergraduate and graduate degrees in electrical engineering from the University of Illinois. Attendance at numerous seminars has permitted me to keep abreast of my field.

From time to time I have also taught in evening divisions of universities in a conscious effort to keep up-to-date.

PUBLICATIONS

Since 1989 I have published five papers in various journals. In addition, I have appeared as a speaker in the annual conventions of the Western States Aeronautical Engineers Association in 1990 and 1992.

REFERENCES

These will be furnished in detail on request.

I will be happy to fly to Phoenix for an interview or meet with you if you are in the Southern California area. I am eager to move to Phoenix and associate myself with a firm of your high caliber.

Sincerely,

Marcus Clark

Marcus Clark

**WRITING
AND SPEAKING
EXERCISES**

1. Find a job ad for an entry-level position in your chosen field. Write a two-part letter applying for that position. Exchange letters with a classmate, and after a careful reading, discuss strengths and weaknesses of the application. Revise your first attempt to reflect your discussion.

2. Prepare a memo to your instructor explaining the nature and extent of the changes to the letter written for exercise 1. What specific issues did you discuss, what revisions did your classmate suggest, and how do you see the second draft as superior to the first? Turn in copies of both drafts of your letter with the completed memo.

3. Prepare a short oral presentation that details the career planning options available at your campus. Remember to include campus clubs and organizations, library resources, internship programs, and counseling services, as well as the local placement office. You may choose to work with other students on this project.

4. Talk to at least five recent job applicants to determine what interview questions they found most difficult to answer. List those questions and write your own response to each.

5. Visit an employment agency to inquire about its fees and policies. Write a report detailing what the agency does for an applicant, what the applicant's obligations are, and any other pertinent information.

6. Prove it! List five elements of proof you could cite in your application letter and resume to support the contention that you are qualified for the job you want.

7. Read the job ads critically. For the profession you want to join, obtain three employment notices. Select ads that differ in the way they describe the job and its responsibilities and compensation. Critically analyze each ad. Identify which job of the three is best for you and write a summary explaining why.

8. What are the advantages of using the free placement bureau on the college campus? Write to the director of one campus placement bureau and ask him or her to identify the primary benefits of using on-campus service. Your instructor will coordinate this assignment so each student writes to a different director.

9. The admissions office of your college has advertised the position of recruitment counselor in the campus newspaper. The ad specifies that the graduating student must do a considerable amount of traveling to recruit students for your college. The position requires many on-campus public relations activities. Resumes are to be sent to Dr. Margaret Westlund, director of admissions.

   You have a fine resume, but you know that for this sales-oriented job you need to develop a good cover letter. Develop a four-paragraph letter in which each paragraph accomplishes one of the purposes of the job letter as discussed in this chapter. Be prepared to discuss how you accomplished the various goals of the "sales" letter in this application.

10. You want to contact an employment agency for help in securing your first full-time job. However, you are unsure how such agencies work, especially when it comes to the payment of fees. Using the telephone book for a major metropolitan area, identify three employment agencies.

Write to each agency to discover how it handles fees for its clients. Keep writing to agencies until you obtain at least one answer. Be prepared to discuss in class the topic of fees for clients of employment agencies.

11. The job market climate sometimes changes rapidly. This can be discouraging for a college student who spends years preparing for a particular profession and then, at graduation time, finds that the market has turned sour. With some planning and careful observation, you can avoid such problems and stay on top of the employment market.

    Identify a specific job in the profession you want to pursue. In correct bibliographical form, list the following: (1) two books published within the past two years that provide you with information relative to your specific job hunt; (2) two articles published in bulletins or journals (published within the past year) that provide specific projections for your profession; and (3) two items from newspapers or current periodicals (published within the past six months) that provide a current update on the prospects of your profession.

    Based on your research, do the following in a short report: (1) describe the job outlook for the profession you want to enter; and (2) explain how the outlook will influence your job hunt strategy.

12. Interview a human resources director of a corporation. What does he or she want to see in job application letters and resumes? What mistakes do applicants often make? What hints can he or she give you for the job application process? Write a summary of the results of your interview for your instructor.

13. Revise each of the following one-part application letters (only the letter body appears). In your revision, strive to be clear, enthusiastic, specific, and thorough. You will no doubt want to add details and topics not supplied in these flawed samples.

    (a) As you may have read in the newspaper, Western University will be holding its graduation for business majors on June 7, 19__. I am one of those graduating (major in finance) and, of course, I'm trying to find a job. That's what this letter is about.

    I would describe myself as hardworking, intelligent, and sociable. Once I take on a task you can be sure it will be done on time and in a competent fashion. My past job experiences and university work have proven that.

    The job I'm particularly interested in is the one you advertised last week in the classified section. You didn't mention much about the benefits in the advertisement, so please send me information on that topic as soon as possible.

    If you want me to come in for an interview, please keep in mind that I can't come on Mondays, Tuesdays, or Thursdays due to classes that I'm finishing up at Western. I understand that you hire a lot of Western graduates and I hope you'll hire me.

    (b) It has come to my attention that you seek an entry-level employee recently matriculated from a major university with a business-related degree.

Without presuming to know your specific requirements, I can with some assurance say that I am such
a person. Barring unforeseen complications in my
current classwork, I shall be granted the
undergraduate degree in marketing from Bingham
State University on the seventh of June, 19__.
While my extensive academic references summarize my
academic career in some detail, I may mention here
that my grade point average qualified me for the
dean's list all but one semester (the lapse due to
what I still consider a blatant case of professor-
ial incompetence).

As you may surmise from this correspondence, I
believe I can bring a certain lustre and panache to
your organization—the touch of class, if you will,
that distinguishes true corporate enterprise from
mere business.

Should you wish to speak personally before concluding our arrangements for this position, I shall
make every effort to find a place for you on my
calendar. You may contact me directly at 290-3923
or leave a message with my mother at 382-3894.

READINGS   See "Finding Solid Ground in a Shaky Job Market" in the Readings section at the back of this book.

SUGGESTED RESOURCES

Bell, Arthur M. *International Careers.* Boston: Bob Adams, Inc. 1991.

Bloomsberg, Gerri, and Holden, Margaret. *The Women's Job Search Handbook: With Issues and Insights into the Workplace.* Charlotte, VT.: Williamson Publishing, 1991.

Boe, Anne, and Youngs, Bettie B. *Is Your "Net" Working? A Complete Guide to Building Contacts and Career Visibility.* New York: John Wiley & Sons, 1989.

Dawson, Kenneth M., and Dawson, Sheryl N. *Job Search: The Total System.* New York: John Wiley & Sons, 1988.

Half, Robert. *How to Get a Better Job in This Crazy World.* New York: Plume, 1990.

Sandroff, Ronni. "How to Get the Job You Really Want." *Working Woman* (April 1989):111–118.

Van Camp, Ann J. "How to Find a Job Online." *Online* 12 (July 1988):26–34.

Books about occupations and careers

Career Planning Handbooks: A Guide to Career Fields and Opportunities. Washington, D.C.: U.S. Civil Service Commission, U.S. Government Printing Office.

Dictionary of Occupational Titles. Washington, D.C.: U.S. Department of Labor, U.S. Government Printing Office. Describes skills and characteristics for 23,000 occupations.

Occupational Outlook Handbook. Washington, D.C.: U.S. Bureau of Labor Statistics, U.S. Government Printing Office. Lists employment opportunities in various fields.

Career Information Service. Box 51, Madison Square Station, New York, NY.

Career. Career Inc., 15 West 45th Street, New York, NY. Lists employment opportunities in leading organizations.

Directories and guides

College Placement Annual. College Placement Council, 35 East Elizabeth Street, Bethlehem, PA. Contains a listing of almost 2,000 organizations, their addresses, contacts, and related information.

College Placement Directory. Industrial Research Service, Dover, NH. Some 1,500 business firms are described, with their addresses, types of graduates desired, and so forth. Like the *Annual,* it has an occupational and geographical index.

Foreign Operations. Foreign Operations, Inc. New Haven, CT. Lists overseas employment opportunities.

Dun and Bradstreet Middle Market Directory. List names, addresses, and phones of about 23,000 firms.

Dun and Bradstreet Million Dollar Directory. Similar to above but for firms of over $1 million net worth.

Fortune Magazine's Directory of Largest Corporations. Published in four parts.

Poor's Register of Directors and Executives; U.S. and Canada. Standard and Poor's Corporation, 345 Hudson Street, New York, NY. Lists 27,000 firms, addresses, principal products, and key officers.

Thomas' Register of American Manufacturers. Thomas Publishing, 461 Eighth Avenue, New York, NY.

LEGAL CONSIDERATIONS

Title VII and EEOC legislation makes one point: job selection should be a fair process unencumbered by prejudice. For example, a country that proclaims all human beings equal should not endure a system of hiring that, as a basis of selection, asks women how they plan to take care of their children during the day but does not ask the same question of men. Nor should dark-skinned applicants automatically be screened from consideration because "they won't mix well with our clientele."

Race or Color

The strict prohibition in federal and state legislation against discrimination on the basis of race or color has several corollaries that are obvious. Candidates should not be asked to affix pictures of themselves to applications. Such pictures, of course, would tend to reveal race and/or color, and they could be used to screen minority candidates out of contention for positions.

Similarly, an applicant (of any race or color) cannot legally be asked to state personal views on civil rights, to name his or her birthplace or that of relatives, or to list membership in organizations that may tend to reveal race or national origin. Birth certificates, naturalization papers, baptismal records, and the like cannot be required prior to employment because they would tend to answer questions deemed illegal by EEOC or Title IV law.

In their efforts to be fair to protected minority groups, some interviewers have stumbled into unexpected pitfalls, as an Ohio company discovered in 1990. Company interviewers, who had been trained in what to ask and not to ask, nevertheless routinely noted "black" or "Mexican-American" in the margins of application materials and interview forms for minority applicants. These notes were intended, the interviewers said, as reminders to follow all applicable Title VII and EEOC regulations in interviewing these candidates. However, one minority applicant who was turned down for a job took the company to court, charging discrimination. Key evidence in his successful lawsuit (at great expense to the company) was his employment application on which interviewers had written notes pertaining to his race.

Citizenship

As of May 1987, it became illegal for employers to consider citizenship in hiring decisions. But with the passage of the Immigration Reform and Control Act in that same month, it is now also unlawful knowingly to hire or continue to employ unauthorized aliens.

What's an employer to do? A safe course is to ask applicants if they have the legal right to be employed in this country. After the selection process, employers can (and now must) secure and examine documents establishing the identity of the candidate and his or her legal right to work in the United States. If the candidate's preemployment claims to legal work status prove bogus, the employer can terminate employment.

Family and Marital Status

Interviews should not ask if a candidate is single, married, divorced, or separated. Federal law interprets such questions as prejudicial to certain minority groups, for example, women. Such prohibitions are intended to prevent employers from making adverse judgments about a person's private life.

Sex and Sexual Preference

The list of jobs that legally are "for men only" or "for women only" gets shorter and shorter each year. Men are nurses and women drive tractors. Courts consider all the following questions to be sexually discriminatory:

- Inquiries regarding the original name of an applicant whose name has been changed by court order
- Questions concerning child care, future plans for children, pregnancy, or status as principal wage earner in the family
- Questions regarding attitudes or biases of the applicant's spouse
- Questions regarding the applicant's views on women's liberation issues
- Inquiries about how long an applicant plans to work

Handicaps and Health-related Issues

The Rehabilitation Act of 1973 and the Americans with Disabilities Act of 1990 have clearly indicated that the key for employers in this area of questioning is to keep the cart behind the horse: job-related requirements should be described, and only then should the candidate be asked if he or she has any physical handicap, illness, or condition that might prevent satisfactory performance on the job. Employers must be willing to make what these acts term "reasonable accommodation" to assist physically or mentally handicapped employees in the performance of job duties. Such accommodation may include changing the physical structure of the workplace and providing necessary aids.

Age

In many job categories (including airline attendants, sales positions, and others) employers have tended to favor the under-30 applicant. The young applicant can be hired for less and can be expected to serve the company longer. The Age Discrimination in Employment Act puts strict curbs on such age prejudice. Applicants cannot be asked to state their age, except to determine if they meet legal age requirements in the state (usually 18 or 21). Questions that imply the age of the applicant ("When did you graduate from college?") are similarly prohibited.

Future Employment Law

Like ripples circling out from a stone thrown into a pond, the implications of federal and state employment legislation continue to challenge managers, interviewers, and applicants. Amendments and new laws affecting selection procedures appear every few weeks. Employers, therefore, are well advised to keep in touch with legal counsel on hiring procedures, read widely in journals and magazines (e.g., *Personnel, Personnel Administrator, Fortune, Personnel Journal,* and *Forbes),* and develop companywide programs that meet the intent of federal and state legislation in a proactive way, rather than reacting to complaints and lawsuits.

Based on information contained in The Complete Manager's Guide to Interviewing by Arthur H. Bell (Business One Irwin, 1990).

15

SUCCESSFUL APPLICATIONS, RESUMES, AND INTERVIEWS

Prospective employers ask this key question: "What can you contribute to my organization?"

W hat is the most important business document you've ever written? When asked that question, Roger Wyse, a remarkably successful aerospace manager, didn't name a particular memo, letter, proposal, or report. "The document that has meant the most in my career rise," Wyse said, "has been my resume."

The resume summarizes you.

This short document sums up "you" in a page or two. Because it is so vital to your job-seeking and job-changing efforts, the resume deserves your best effort. The resume also has uses beyond the job search. It serves as a substantiating document when you submit an article or a paper for publication, when you file for office, or when you apply for credit. People who ask you to lead a committee, give a speech, or be a member of a panel will find your resume helpful.

As your goals and qualifications change, revise your resume.

Look on your resume as something that grows with you. Write it early in your career and then revise and update it as your career progresses, your goals change, and your background becomes richer. The style, format, and layout of resumes change with the times, and yours should change also.

This chapter discusses, in order, the resume, the cover letter to the resume, the combined cover letter and resume, the job interview situation, and job-related letters of various types. Examine all the materials carefully and use them as a basis for your own efforts. Although you would not want to *copy* a cover letter, resume, or job acceptance letter, you surely can derive ideas from the samples shown. The samples can assist you in building your own job-related communications—both resumes and solicited and unsolicited letters of application.

Looking at the resume first forces you to summarize your major strengths and weaknesses as they apply to the job search. Once you have listed your attributes, volunteer work, references, honors, and so forth, you can see which areas to emphasize and which to handle with care.

Making up the resume *before* the cover letter is like preparing an outline *prior* to writing a report or essay. It tells you what to emphasize in what depth and in which order in the cover letter.

THE RESUME

Creating a resume helps you identify your strengths and weaknesses and provides an outline for application letters.

Prepare your resume so it can stand alone, without a cover letter. In some situations, for example, prior to giving a speech or when you are asked to serve on a committee, not all the items of information on the resume may apply. Nevertheless, their presence does not detract from the effect of the resume.

LENGTH

Effective resumes are brief but do not omit vital details.

Perhaps the best answer to the question of length is the one Abraham Lincoln supposedly gave when asked, "How long should a thoroughbred horse's legs be?" He replied, "Long enough to reach the ground." The resume should be long enough to cover the subject and no longer. A common admonition is to keep the resume to one page. This is good advice if all the facts needed fit easily on a single page. But to omit important and persuasive information just to adhere to this limit is foolish. If prospective employers are going to make an investment of thousands of dollars in employees, they won't mind reading a second page. As a matter of fact, more details are better than fewer. If you choose to list three or four impressive references, it is almost impossible to keep your resume to one page. Include all information necessary in your resume. Make sure it is clear, concise, complete, and attractive. Use the number of pages the result requires.

If you encounter a rigid one-page requirement, and your resume is somewhat longer than a page, type it on a large sheet of paper (17 by 22 inches) and then reduce it so it fits comfortably on an 8 1/2 - by 11-inch sheet of paper. Most office copiers are capable of reducing (or enlarging) materials. Once reduced, the items are still perfectly legible and balanced nicely on the page.

Many kinds of printers provide a variety of type sizes. If you have access to one of these, simply produce your resume in a type size large enough for easy reading yet small enough to be condensed to one page.

CONTENT

Most resumes cover the following areas, although not always in this order:

- Name, address, and phone number
- Career objective(s)
- Major qualifications
- Education
- Experience
- Awards, honors, organizations
- Personal data
- References

Career objectives.   In your career objective, you may wish to specify both your short-term and long-range goals. Be careful to do so tactfully, so that you do not sound brash or insensitive.

An immediate association with a firm as a junior accountant. Eventually, I hope to become a vice president of finance where I can make a significant contribution to the growth of a progressive organization.

The career objective reflects what you offer to the company rather than what you demand from the company.

Note the strong use of the *you* attitude. The applicant wishes to contribute to the firm. The statement does not say, "I expect to increase *my* knowledge," or "I'm looking for a firm that will reward *me* very well financially for my efforts."

It is proper and acceptable to indicate that you wish to rise to vice president, operations, a controller's position, or a top management position in a high-tech organization. Most prospective employers are delighted to hire ambitious people. They know that a person who wishes to become a vice president of marketing will probably work hard to attain that goal and, in the process, carry the firm forward.

A word of caution is in order, however. Be sure that the career objective section is worded in such a way that attaining your goals will also be beneficial to the organization (*you* attitude).

You may decide to omit the career objective from the resume if you include it in your cover letter or if you are using your resume for a more general application. (Figure 15–2, which appears later in the chapter, illustrates a resume that does not include career objectives.)

Summarize your major qualifications in a few lines.

Major qualifications.   State your major qualifications briefly—in two to four lines. This statement is essentially a short summary of your major selling points. Don't trumpet your qualifications, but do list them; no one else will do it for you.

> *A degree in accounting, two years of part-time plus one year of full-time experience with a major accounting firm, and a recently acquired CPA certificate.*

> *Collegiate background in marketing, on-the-job consumer research experience, creative abilities in problem solving, and proven ability to work with others are some of the qualifications I can offer your firm.*

Although the section on major qualifications can be useful as a type of executive summary for the resume, some companies and instructors prefer that it be omitted. In this case, the resume begins directly with education in the base of a *chronological resume* and experience (or work experience) in the case of a

The chronological resume lists most recent experiences first and works backward in time. The functional resume emphasizes abilities acquired over time but does not present information chronologically.

functional resume.

A chronological resume, as you will see later in this chapter, lists educational and work experiences according to chronology, usually proceeding backward in time. Typically, the chronological resume begins with information about education, and proceeds to work experiences. A functional resume dispenses with chronological order and focuses instead on what the applicant can do. This type of resume usually beings with job abilities (supported by job experience) or job titles with accompanying responsibilities.

List your area of greatest strength first when arranging summaries of education and experience.

Education and experience.   The sections on education and experience will doubtless take up most of the space in your resume. How you handle them is critical, because they are vital to "selling" you to a potential employer. If your major selling point is education, list that first after major qualifications. If experience is your strong point, then that should be first. In both education and experience, list your most recent school and job first, and then work backward chronologically. An exception is to list first a job or education that ties in closely with the position for which you are applying.

In listing experience, describe the positions with an eye to easy readability as well as visual attractiveness. A good format might look something like this:

Baxter and Robinson, Certified Public Accountants
101 South Webster Avenue
Eugene, Oregon 97401
Dates: January 19__ to May 19__ (part-time)
Duties: Worked with T.L. Baxter, CPA, as an assistant. Primary involvement was
  with corporate tax returns and audits.

Western Lumber Corporation
1540 West Franklin Boulevard
Eugene, Oregon 97402
Dates: June 19__ to present
Duties: Senior accountant in charge of accounts payable, receivable, and all tax mat-
  ters. A staff of five report directly to me.

If you have held a variety of part- and full-time jobs while attending college
and several of them have no association with your present field, it is probably
best to list them as a group:

Date: 19__ to __
Held several part- and full-time jobs while attending college. The income paid for
all educational expenses.

In listing education, again start with the most recent and work backward.
There is little point in listing secondary education unless it is directly related
to the field. Note colleges, universities, degrees and dates received, and major
and minor field(s) of study. Whether courses should be listed is debatable. In
the fields of accounting and finance, such a list serves a good purpose, but avoid
meaningless designations like "Accounting 421 or Finance 250." It is more helpful to be informative—"Cost Accounting; Advanced and Corporate Finance,"
for example. If you have attended seminars, executive programs, and other special training sessions associated with your field, list those also. Again, be aware
of readability. Use white space and indentations to separate schools and internal listings.

Detail special achievements at work and school.   In both experience and education, be certain to note special attainments.
If you are fluent in another language, if you were promoted to manager within
a year, if you were self-supporting throughout your college career, or if the spotlight shone on you in any special way at school or at work, say so! If you feel
that the listing section of the resume is not the right place, add your accomplishments adroitly into the cover letter. Of course, describe them with mod-
esty and discretion.

Honors, awards, and associations.   This section, usually brief, lists educational,
work, and civic honors and awards. Also note professional association memberships, published papers, and presentations made at professional meetings.

Personal data.   Companies are constrained by Title VII and EEOC guidelines
If you choose to share personal data, list only your job-related qualities; avoid sensitive material such as age, race, and religion.   to consider only job-related qualifications in the evaluation of job candidates.
You may choose, therefore, to omit the section on personal data (or personal
information, personal background, personal characteristics) from the resume.
If you decide to include it, do not give information about your age, race, marital status, religion, or other matters explicitly defined as out-of-bounds in the
hiring process. You may want to use this section to convey your work habits
(a self-starter), reliability (detail oriented), and interpersonal abilities (skilled
in working with the public).

The Ethics of Preparing a Resume

In 1988, *The Christian Science Monitor* reported a House subcommittee finding that one of every three Americans lies about job credentials. These prevarications on application forms and resumes take many forms: exaggerating job titles or responsibilities, inflating grade point averages and academic awards, overstating or making up association memberships and recognitions, lengthening the duration of jobs, and fabricating performance information.

Are those who perpetuate such unethical practices caught by their prospective employers? The answer is "sometimes." In its 1991 report on employment trends, the Northwestern University Lindquist-Endicott Report surveyed 320 companies regarding their hiring procedures. Barely half of the surveyed companies reviewed an applicant's college transcripts, and fewer than half (44 percent) considered faculty references.[1] These findings support an earlier survey of the Society for Human Resource Management which found that fewer than half of companies (43 percent) check personal references and that only a small number (13 percent) check credit references.[2] Both surveys concluded that an applicant's representations regarding education, employment history, and work skills frequently go unverified.

For the opportunist, such data may seem an invitation to fabricate favorable information on the resume. The odds, after all, appear to be against getting caught. More ethically minded job seekers resist this temptation for at least two reasons. The first reason is personal, rising from the core of one's moral being: "I don't lie because I don't lie; my definition of myself includes the concept of integrity." The second reason is social: "If my actions were to become standard behavior for all, what sort of world would result? Would I approve such a world for myself or others? If not, I can't participate in actions that contribute to that degeneration."

1. "What Personal Offices Really Stress in Hiring," *The Wall Street Journal,* March 6, 1991:B1.
2. Joe A. Cox et al., "A Look Behind Corporate Doors," *Personnel Administrator* (March 1989):56–59.

List only those references who are prepared to support your claims about job qualifications.

References. Many people prefer simply to say, "References will be furnished on request." This is a common practice of individuals who presently hold jobs but are looking for a change. The reason is obvious: although most firms do not usually contact a reference before checking with the applicant, some do. It is very embarrassing to have your boss asked about your qualifications when you don't want your current company to know you are in the job market! Even a note asking that references not be contacted before an interview with you can be overlooked or ignored.

If you have no reason *not* to list references, do so. An impressive series of names and titles can only be of value to you. A basic rule is to list a minimum of three and a maximum of four references: two related to work, one academic, and one personal. Prospective employers rely primarily on what a work reference has to say about you. To a lesser extent, employers perceive academic references as reliable.

RESUMES WITHOUT COVER LETTERS

Many occasions call for a resume without a cover letter. You may see an attractive advertisement in your professional journal or your newspaper that lists a phone number rather than a mailing address. You call and chat with the appropriate person, who suggests, "Well, let's get together. If Wednesday at three is good for you, please come in, and bring a copy of your resume." Or you may

Because you might need a resume for situations other than the job search, keep copies at hand.

be asked by a city or university official to serve on a panel or committee. Your resume may be needed for the record or for administrative approval. Because you need a resume quite often, keep a quantity on file. As you gain experience and background, you are likely to rewrite your resume several times.

Notice that resumes without cover letters, as shown in Figures 15–1 and 15–2, do not differ in form from resumes with cover letters, as shown later in the chapter. These examples of resumes without cover letters are provided simply to enrich your view of various resume arrangements, including use of fonts, patterns of margins, and handling of educational and work details.

THE COVER LETTER TO THE RESUME

Use the cover letter to highlight experiences of special interest to the employer.

Always adapt your cover letter to the advertisement you are answering or company to which you are applying. If an ad places heavy emphasis on experience, the cover letter should focus on that. If "excellent interpersonal skills" are required, the cover letter should emphasize that. In other words, determine what attribute the prospective employer feels is vital, search your own abilities to see if you can match it, and then focus on that as a key sales point. When the reader finishes your letter, there should be no doubt about your superior abilities in one or two specific areas.

In addition to emphasizing your primary selling point, the cover letter should arouse interest, reflect enthusiasm, and motivate the reader to reach eagerly for your resume. Write your letter from the reader's point of view. Explain how your education, your experience, your background, and your enthusiasm will benefit the organization to which you are applying.

Effective cover letters tell what you can do for the company, emphasize your selling point, and secure an interview.

Although there are no rules about content, a good cover letter usually consists of a minimum of three brief paragraphs, each of which attempts to accomplish a specific objective.

The first paragraph summarizes your major attributes and how you can help the organization:

Two years of part-time accounting experience, a bachelor of science degree in accounting, and a desire to work hard make me feel I can make a significant contribution to your firm in the job you advertised.

The second paragraph should emphasize your key attribute or selling point:

My experience as the assistant controller of a major corporation for four years and the owner of a twelve-employee CPA firm for three years qualify me for the position you described. In my work experience I was responsible . . .

The third paragraph, sometimes referred to as the action paragraph, functions to secure an action or a response:

I feel it would be mutually beneficial if we could meet for an interview at your convenience. At that time I can tell you in greater detail about my education and experience and how they can be put to work for your firm. At the same time, I can add details in supplementary areas in which you are interested. You can reach me at (201) 555-2888.

The cover letter could have more than three paragraphs; the areas covered in these paragraphs are just described are a minimum. On the other hand, the cover letter should seldom be more than one page.

FIGURE 15–1   Sample Resume without Cover Letter

RAMON A. RODRIGUEZ
1717 West Park Lane
Austin, Texas 78701
(512) 555-2242

JOB OBJECTIVE

A position with a large corporation in the area of finance with special attention to acquisitions and mergers. A long-range position of finance director is desired.

MAJOR QUALIFICATIONS

Bachelor and Master of Business Administration degrees in corporate finance and three years' experience with petroleum corporations in engineering and financial management.

EDUCATION

University of Texas at Austin, MBA degree, June 19___, major in corporate finance
Courses included corporate financial management, financial accounting, long-range corporate planning, strategy, policy, mergers and acquisitions, and related topics. In-depth research carried through on major corporate takeovers, 19___ to 19___.

University of Texas at Austin, Bachelor's degree, June 19___, major in corporate finance
Major area of study was petroleum engineering. Internship with Mobil Corporation plus scholarship for junior and senior years.

EXPERIENCE

Baker Corporation, Dallas, 19___ to 19___
Field engineer primarily working as a liaison to various corporate field units on drilling operations: bit selection, core drilling, sand use, and safety procedures.

Mobil Corporation, Houston, 19___ to 19___
Division of Financial Management. Responsibility for audit and controls of all foreign expenditure, foreign payroll of U.S. citizens, and foreign tax analysis. Supervised staff of eight.

HONORS, AWARDS, AND ASSOCIATIONS

Young Business Leader's Award, 19___, presented by Dallas Rotary Club
President, Texas Entrepreneurs Society, 19___ to present

PERSONAL BACKGROUND

Ongoing interest in national and international business affairs, music, and outdoor sports. Have traveled extensively in Europe and the Near East. Willing to relocate.

References available on request.

FIGURE 15–2 Sample Resume without Cover Letter

Mary C. Van Geem
4141 South Viceroy Avenue
Philadelphia, PA 19102
(215) 555-7113

QUALIFICATIONS

Six valuable years of experience in retail communication products, with both a small privately owned chain and a large corporate chain. Direct, firsthand knowledge of all phases of the business, including marketing, ordering, stocking, merchandising, customer relations, and overall store management. Formal education in mass communications, advertising, and broadcast sales was obtained concurrently with work experience.

EDUCATION

Franklin Junior College (Philadelphia)
September 19__ to June 19__
Associate of Arts Degree—General Education
Satisfied all lower-division requirements in preparation for upper-division courses on university level.

University of Pennsylvania
September 19__ to June 19__
Bachelor of Arts Degree—Communication Studies
Communications courses stressed theoretical analysis of mass- and interpersonal-communications techniques; advertising, public relations, and a particular emphasis on the print and broadcast media.

Radio Advertising Sales Workshop (Philadelphia)
Graduated August 19__
Course dealt with all aspects of modern commercial broadcasting, including sales presentations, marketing research, prospecting, merchandising, copywriting, and competitive advertising media.

EMPLOYMENT EXPERIENCES

ViTech Communication, Inc.
June 19__ to Present, Store Manager
Primary responsibilities include supervising personnel and effectively serving customers on a personal basis at second largest store in chain.

July 19__ to June 19__, Assistant Manager
Primary responsibilities included supervising the stocking of store merchandise and effectively dealing with customers on a personal basis in a retail situation.

Radio Shack
June 19__ to August 19__, Assistant Manager
Responsibilities included writing and transmitting merchandise orders, managing store personnel on second shift.

PERSONAL CHARACTERISTICS

Effective communicator with customers and all levels of management.
Dedicated professional with a strong desire to excel in challenging and rewarding field.
Good planner and organizer who knows the value of proper research and preparation.

REFERENCES

Excellent references available on request.

Most importantly—the cover letter should show a strong *you* attitude throughout. Emphasize how you can contribute to the organization. See, "A Checklist for the Job Letter," the next section in this chapter. Figures 15–3 and 15–4 are examples of effective cover letters.

COMBINING THE COVER LETTER AND RESUME

Above all, the resume and application letter must be attractive and professional.

Prepare the cover letter and resume on high-quality bond paper. Use an off-white or light-beige stock. Use a top-quality typewriter or, a letter-quality computer printer. Where appropriate, you can format with boldface type and bullets to highlight key items. Use the same type style for the resume and cover letter. Spacing, white areas, and margins should contribute to the attractiveness and clarity of the pages. Check and recheck the content for accuracy in spelling, grammar, and punctuation. The letter and resume should be perfect.

Experiment with type fonts and sizes and page formats to create visual appeal.

Examine Figure 15–5 through 15–7 (pages 331-337) carefully, noting styles and approaches. In particular, notice the alternatives you have for type fonts, page arrangement, patterns of margination and indentation, capitalization, and highlighting (by bullets, underlining, and boldface). Some styles will appeal to you more than others. In addition, some styles will suit the details of your specific education and work record better than others. Experiment with your resume in several forms before deciding upon its final form for use in job applications. Consider showing alternative forms of your resume to your instructor, your present or previous employer, and to your colleagues to get their opinions on which form best represents you.

A CHECKLIST FOR THE JOB LETTER

After you have finished your cover letter and resume, check them carefully for the following attributes:

Attractiveness.   When the prospective employer reads your letter and resume, you want him or her to say, "This is obviously a well-organized, conscientious individual. The letter has excellent balance, logical organization, and easy readability. The applicant took care in its preparation."

Accurate.   Human resources directors, without exception, expect college graduates' letters and resumes to be free of errors. All that is required to achieve that is careful editing. As one employment supervisor stated,

> There are few more important letters an individual will ever write than the job application letter. It should be perfect. We can understand when a letter from a shop supervisor exhibits an error or two, but not when the message comes from a college-trained man or woman. After all, if he or she is careless in a letter, what can we expect in his or her handling of our ledgers?

So check your letter carefully, and make sure it is clear, concise, complete, and correct.

Reader orientation.   Have you attempted to point out how the *company* will benefit from your skill, service, and ambition? Human resources directors are

FIGURE 15–3 Sample Cover Letter to a Resume

2105 West Lexington Avenue
Norman, OK 73003
(405) 555-6543
April 15, 19__

Ms. Roberta Peterson, Personnel Director
Western Refining Corporation
One Oklahoma Square
Oklahoma City, OK 73101

Dear Ms. Peterson:

I enjoyed our discussion on campus earlier this month. You may recall that I told you that with my degree in accounting (to be awarded next month), my two years of part-time experience in the field, and my strong desire to be affiliated with WRC, I know I can make significant contributions to the firm in the years ahead.

My undergraduate work in accounting at the University of Oklahoma was concentrated in taxation, which was the area you and I discussed. During my last two years of college, I worked part-time and summers for Meister and Feister, CPAs, in a variety of accounting assignments. This experience gave me the confidence I need to handle competently the assignments I will encounter at WRC.

I look forward to having a formal interview with you, Ms. Peterson. I am sure you have questions. In turn I want to add to the details you will find on the attached resume. Please let me know when it will be convenient for us to meet. I can be reached at the phone number listed above.

Sincerely,

Suzanne Garro

Suzanne Garro

Enc

The cover letter highlights your major qualifications, education, and experience before appealing for an interview.

FIGURE 15-4   Sample Cover Letter to a Resume

5800 West Franklin Boulevard
Indianapolis, IN 46204
(317) 555-2410
September 10, 19__

Ms. Glenda Owens
Personnel Director
Elliot Systems, Inc.
1500 Kellogg Square
Indianapolis, IN 46201

Dear Ms. Owens:

I enjoyed meeting your Western Region manager, Paul Kane, at the Computer World
meeting last week. He suggested that I contact you to express my interest in joining Elliot
Systems, Inc. With my degrees in decision systems from Indiana University, extensive
work experience in computer applications, and a strong desire to take on professional
challenges, I know I can make a strong contribution to your company. Given your reputation in the field, I'm also aware of how much you have to offer me.

As manager of information systems for my present organization, I am responsible for
inventory control, billing, payroll, taxation, and many other areas. I have converted our
accounting system to computer. I find directing a staff of 12 to be enjoyable, challenging,
and rewarding.

I am eager to meet with you to discuss employment possibilities. Please contact me at the
address and phone number above. I look forward to hearing from you.

Sincerely,

Stanton Murphy

Stanton Murphy

Enc

FIGURE 15-5A   Cover Letter to Resume in Figure 15-5B

1011 Fourth Street, Apt. 115
Santa Monica, CA 90403
(213) 555-2163 (home)
(213) 555-7061 (work)
July 14, 19__

Box 242, Terminal Annex
The Wall Street Journal
Los Angeles, CA 90067

Dear Human Resources Director:

Your very attractive advertisement in yesterday's *The Wall Street Journal* seemed made to order for me. Your needs are for an assistant manager for your Vienna subsidiary. The individual you want should have "thorough background in financial management, good marketing skills, and fluency in German." I feel that I score at the top in all three areas.

My experience and educational background have given me excellent training in financial management and marketing. For two years, as an employee of a well-known PR firm, I was almost totally involved in marketing entertainers. Also, financial management was my MBA area of concentration. My fluency in German is first-rate. For two years I attended graduate classes at the University of Heidelberg. From 1987 to 1991 I compiled, summarized, and translated materials from German for researchers at the well-known think tank, The Rand Corporation.

The attached resume will provide some facts for you. However, I'm sure you will want to learn more about me as an individual. I certainly want to know more about your organization. Please call me at one of the numbers listed above so we may arrange a time for an interview to be held at your convenience.

Sincerely yours,

Bonnie Swihart

Bonnie Swihart

Enc

Use the cover letter to amplify information that the resume briefly mentions but that your reader will find of special interest.

FIGURE 15–5B   Chronological Resume Accompanying Cover Letter in Figure 15–5A

BONNIE JEAN SWIHART
1011 Fourth Street, Apt. 115
Santa Monica, CA 90403
(213) 555-2163 (Home)
(213) 555-7061 (Work)

EDUCATION

MBA, University of Southern California
May 1993
Emphasis: financial management
Fellowship award, 1992 to 1993.

MA, University of California at Los Angeles
December 1991
German language and literature
Teaching associate for German 1, 2 and 3.

University of Heidelberg, Germany
September 1985 to May 1987
Graduate studies in German language and literature at the
Germanische Fakultaet and the Dolmetscher Institute.

BA, Scripps College, Claremont, CA
June, 1978
Major: German

EXPERIENCE

University of Southern California
September 1992 to present
Instructor for business communications,
School of Business Administration
Prepared and administered all coursework for undergraduate
class designed to develop skills in public speaking and writing
for business purposes.

The Rand Corporation, Santa Monica, CA
June 1987 to December 1991
Researcher for Dr. Michael Mihalka and Mr. Alex Alexiev.
Responsible for compiling, summarizing, and translating material
for research projects. Topics include: German and British
national security policy in the 1930s; East German involvement
in Third World countries; German occupation of Soviet territories
during World War II. Translations of texts from German into
English. Private tutorial in German for seven Rand analysts.

BONNIE JEAN SWIHART

EXPERIENCE
(continued)

Hanson & Schwam, Public Relations, Los Angeles, CA
August 1983 to June 1985
Administrative assistant to the vice president, Corporate
Division. Performed all activities relating to the service of
corporate clients in the entertainment industry.

R.W. Thom & Co., Beverly Hills, CA
July 1981 to August 1983
Personal lines underwriter for the insurance agency. Managed
all personal insurance accounts for the agency; responsible for
all duties related to coverage of home owner's, auto, and
personal liability insurance.

Bishop Amat High School, La Puente, CA
September 1978 to June 1981
Teacher of German, English, and business courses. Prepared,
administered and evaluated all coursework. Business courses
taught: business law, business procedures, and typing.

AWARDS

California State Scholarship

Scholarship to the University of California Summer Program at
the Eberhard-Karls Universitaet Tuebingen, Germany, 1992.

Fellowship, University of Southern California, Graduate School
of Business Administration, 1992 to 1993.

LANGUAGES

German; fully fluent.
English; native language, two years of teaching and tutorial.
French; reading, three years of undergraduate coursework.

ORGANIZATIONS

Foreign Trade Association of Southern California
Member, USC Professional Business Women's Association

REFERENCES

Dr. Michael Mihalka, Political Science Department, The Rand
Corporation

Mr. David Wisely, V.P., Corporate Division, Hanson & Schwam
Public Relations

Prof. Norman Sigband, Business Communications Department,
University of Southern California.

*Because the
advertised job
calls for
relocation,
the resume
develops
specific details
to the writer's
advantage.*

FIGURE 15–6A   Cover Letter to Resume in Figure 15–6B

5151 W. Wabash Avenue
Boston, MA 02104
(617) 555-8642
August 4, 19___

Box 101, Museum Annex
Boston Globe
Globe Square
Boston, MA 02101

Dear Sir or Madam:

This morning's *Boston Globe* carried your ad for "an office manager to supervise a staff of 12 of a growing consumer financial corporation." My previous experience as an office manager for an export firm, knowledge of office procedures and equipment, and a college education in business and administrative management are all qualities that should serve you well.

My educational background includes work in administrative management, computer science, and seminars in office automation, word processing, office management, and related areas. I have worked as an office manager for an exporter of electronic components. For three years, I built the office practices and procedures of this growing organization. In addition, I installed a computer system for billing, inventory, and payroll. I left this position to complete my BA.

My background in administration, consumer behavior, and research seems to dovetail very well with your requirements. I know I can do the kind of job for you that will consistently show up in your asset column. I look forward to an interview with you where I can cite in much more detail how my qualifications will benefit your organization. Please call me at the phone number listed above so we may arrange a time for an interview.

Sincerely yours,

Ito Tanaka

Ito Tanaka

One focal paragraph smoothly summarizes relevant education and work experience.

FIGURE 15–6B   Functional Resume Accompanying Cover Letter in Figure 15–6A

ITO TANAKA
5151 W. Wabash Avenue
Boston, MA 02104
(617) 555-8642

career objectives

To secure a position as office manager where my skills can help advance the organization. My long-range plan is to rise to an officer position in the area of finance or consumer relations.

major qualifications

Several years' experience in office management, educational background in finance and consumer education, and a desire to work hard as a conscientious team member.

experience

Electronics Exports, Inc.
1000 W. Western Avenue
Boston, MA 02102
　　Dates: Jan. 19__ to June 19__
　　Duties: In charge of staff with responsibility for billing, payroll, and all overseas documentation. Established a computer system and word processing, hired and trained specialized personnel, and brought system to working efficiency.

Marston and Kelly, Electronics
5222 N. Franklin Avenue
Boston, MA 02102
　　Dates: Jan. 19__ to Oct. 19__
　　Duties: In charge of consumer sales, education, and adjustment department. Created all form letters for sales adjustments and acknowledgements. Established an ongoing consumer contact system and completed research for a direct mail campaign.

French and French Shoe Outlet
1000 W. Main Street
Newton Highlands, MA 02109
　　Dates: Feb. 19__ to Oct. 19__
　　Duties: Floor clerk in women's shoe department. Leading sales figures for any clerk in 19__.

The accompanying resume uses generous white space to create an uncluttered look.

education

Boston University
School of Business
Bachelor's degree in management, 19__

Major Courses

Marketing I and II	Computer Sciences I and II
Consumer Behavior	Management Communication
Advertising	Financial Management
Administrative Management I and II	International Trade

Seminars, 19__ to 19__

Topic Areas

Word Processing Methods	Computer Billing
Office Management	Export-Import Documentation
Human Resource Management	Management Communication
Financial Management	

honors, awards, organizations

Blue Key (Business School Honors Organization)
President, Administrative Management Association, Boston Chapter, 19__
Employee of the Month, City of Boston, May 19__
American Finance Association
Boston Chamber of Commerce
Toastmasters

references

Available on request

FIGURE 15-7 Cover Letter

4721 Wilshire Blvd.
Los Angeles, CA 90027
(213) 555-7247
October 19, 19___

Search Committee
Director of Management Education
School of Business Administration
University of Southern California
Los Angeles, CA 90089-1421.AA/EOE

Dear Committee Members:

I am applying for the position of Associate Dean/Executive Director of Management Education based on lengthy experience, significant educational background, and the recommendation of Dr. Norman Sigband, with whom I have been associated. Thirteen years' work in universities and several years as a management development consultant, have given me the experience to qualify as an excellent candidate for the position:

- Proven ability to successfully direct a management development organization
- Academic credentials appropriate for a leading university
- Talent and proven record for innovation and creativity
- Sensitivity to change that maintains leading-edge curricula
- A confident, diplomatic style that moves easily among various cultures and levels of management

Bullets allow you to list attributes that your reader can take in at a glance.

I am currently working as consultant in management development to California Edison, a leading electric utility. My responsibilities include training and development services for fifteen line organizations.

Please call me at the number shown above to arrange an interview. I look forward to meeting with you to share my vision for management education at the University of Southern California.

Yours truly,

Linda William, Ph.D.

Linda William, Ph.D.

not particularly concerned with how the firm will give *you* experience, provide *you* with interesting and challenging situations, and offer *you* promotions and pay increases. They are interested in learning how your education and experience can be used to advance the firm.

> *My degree in accounting and two years of part-time experience with Merril and Maxwell, CPAs, should prove valuable to your company.*

> *If your company can use a professionally trained advertising person who has loads of energy and ambition, plus three years of experience, I'm the one who can make a contribution to your firm's progress.*

Detail.   Generalizing about what you have done in the past and can do in the future usually makes little impact on the reader. We live in a world of specialization; in professional areas especially, employers like to know precisely what the job seeker can do for them.

Specific details bring your letter to life.

It isn't enough to indicate that your degree is in business administration. What was your major? There is too much left to the imagination with, "I held a management position for two years with Croxton and Croxton." "I was the office manager of Croxton and Croxton's Southfield division," or "human resources assistant in charge in training" is better. On the other hand, be careful not to give the reader the impression (unless you sincerely mean to) that you would only be happy doing inventory control or could do only payroll accounting. Indicate a middle ground.

Enthusiasm and personality.   Your cover letter should reflect your enthusiasm and your personality. There is nothing deadlier than a flat recitation of facts, figures, dates, and company and school names. Make sure your letter comes alive. There's nothing wrong with stating, "I really enjoy working with people," or "All my life I've dreamed of the day when I could assume responsibility as Chris Martin, CPA." Let the real you shine through your letter with a well-placed phrase or two.

Show personality and enthusiasm in your letter.

Originality and honesty.   Never copy a paragraph, and certainly not a complete letter, from another source. Find examples of clever letters and use them for *ideas* if you wish, but be aware that human resources directors have read them all many times. Honesty is critical. Stretching the truth, inventing a job, or falsely claiming to have taken a course will only return eventually to haunt you. Use good judgment to avoid a nasty surprise—termination—when letters of confirmation begin to roll in.

Copying a form letter gives little chance of distinguishing yourself from the competition. Be original and state your qualifications honestly.

THE JOB INTERVIEW

The letter of application rarely results in a job offer. The purpose of the letter is to obtain an interview. Write the letter that way—with the objective of securing an interview, not a job.

To get a job offer, you must first sell yourself at the interview. Spend much time and care on that phase as on the preparation, planning, and writing of the letter. The half hour spent talking to the prospective employer is vital. You must give evidence of a pleasant personality, ability to communicate, knowledge of your area, your objectives, the information you have about the company, your

Preparing for the interview helps you present yourself confidently and comfortably.

level of courtesy, and your familiarity with topics of professional, political, and cultural interest. To get across all this information requires preparation.

New York Life Insurance Company issued an excellent booklet titled *Making the Most of Your Job Interview*. It begins with the statement:

> The employment interview is one of the most important events in a person's experience, because the 20 or 30 minutes spent with an interviewer may determine the entire future course of one's life.
>
> Yet interviewers are continually amazed at the number of applicants who drift into job interviews without any apparent preparation and only the vaguest idea of what they are going to say. Their manner says, "Well, here we are." And that's often the end of it, in more ways than one.

Some people, although they undoubtedly do not intend to do so, create an impression of indifference by acting too casually. At the other extreme, applicants work themselves into such a nervous state that when they arrive they are able to answer only in monosyllables. You can avoid these marks of inexperience by knowing what is expected of you and by making a few preparations before the interview.

PREPARING FOR THE INTERVIEW

Anticipate the interviewer's questions.

To prepare for your job interview, think of at least 20 questions the interviewer is likely to ask and rehearse how you will answer them. Examine the following list of typical questions asked by human resources recruiters. How would you answer them?

What are your vocational plans?

In what school activities have you participated? Why? Which did you enjoy most? Why?

What type of position interests you most?

Why do you think you might like to work for our company?

What jobs have you held? How were they obtained and why did you leave?

What courses did you like best? least? Why?

Why did you choose your particular field of work?

What percentage of your college expenses did you earn? How?

How did you spend your vacation while in school?

What do you know about our company?

Do you feel that you have received a good general training?

What qualifications do you have that make you think you'll be successful in your field?

What extracurricular office have you held?

What are your ideas on salary?

If you were starting college all over again, what courses would you take?

How much money do you hope to earn at 30? 35?

Do you think your extracurricular activities were worth the time you devoted to them? Why?

What do you think determines a person's progress in a good company?

What personal characteristics are necessary for success in your chosen field?

Why do you think you would like this particular type of job?

Do you prefer working with others or by yourself?

Are you primarily interested in making money or do you feel that service to humanity is your prime concern?

Can you take instructions without feeling upset?

Understanding Sexual Harassment

Charges of sexual harassment during preemployment interviews and in work situations have been made at all levels of U.S. business and government, from the smallest company to the Supreme Court. It is important for men and women to understand the law with regard to sexual harassment—for their own sakes and for the welfare of those with whom they work.

The EEOC guidelines define sexual harassment in these terms: Unwelcome sexual advances, requests for sexual favors and other verbal or physical conduct of a sexual nature constitute sexual harassment with (1) submission to such conduct is made either explicitly or implicitly a term or condition of an individual's employment, (2) submission to or rejection of such conduct by individual is used as the basis for employment decisions affecting such individual, or (3) such conduct has the purpose or effect of unreasonably interfering with an individual's work performance or creating an intimidating, hostile, or offensive working environment. Employers have a double responsibility according to the EEOC: (1) for notifying all employees, especially supervisors, of the nature and illegality of sexual harassment in the workplace, and (2) for any sexual harassment on the part of employees when the employer knew about or should have known about such behavior. (Refer to Chapter 5 for more discussion of sexual harassment).

What kind of boss do you prefer?
How did previous employers treat you?
What have you learned from some of the jobs you have held?
Can you get recommendations from previous employers?
What interests you about our product or service?
Have you ever changed your major while in college? Why?
When did you choose your college major?
Do you feel you have done the best scholastic work of which you are
    capable?
How did you happen to go to college?
What do you know about opportunities in the field in which you are
    trained?
Which of your college years was the most difficult? Why?
Did you enjoy your four years at your university? Why or why not?
What job in our company would you choose if you were entirely free to
    do so?
What types of books have you read?
Have you plans for graduate work?
What types of people seem to rub you the wrong way?
Have you ever tutored an undergraduate?
What jobs have you enjoyed the most? the least? Why?
What are your special abilities?
What job in our company would be your goal?
Would you prefer a large or small company? Why?
What have you done that shows initiative and willingness to work?
Do you like routine work? Do you like regular hours?
What size city do you prefer?
What is your major weakness?
Define cooperation.

Do you demand attention?

Do you have an analytical mind?

Are you eager to please?

Do you like to travel?

Do you mind overtime work?

What kind of work interests you?

What are the disadvantages of your chosen field?

Are you interested in research?

Even a quick survey of these questions shows the importance of preparation. Try to answer the first three questions now. How well did you do?

"Tell me about yourself," is the type of question designed to get you to talk. What you say and how you say it will give the interviewer a measure of your personality, your perception of yourself, and others' perceptions of you.

Questions regarding what kind of job you seek point out the importance of selecting a major area or two for which you feel qualified. The applicant who says, "I just want a job" or "I can do anything," makes the interviewer think, "That person can probably do nothing." So determine what you can do and want to do. Then assemble all the facts that substantiate your choice: education, experience, personal attributes, goals, desires, and so forth.

Showing that you have researched the company reveals your desire to join the team.

"What do you know about our company?" is a favorite question designed to test your interest in the firm and desire to become affiliated with it. If you show considerable knowledge of the company, the interviewer will assume your desire to join it is considerable too. Obtain information on the company's products, plant location, number of employees, financial past and present, its growth picture, its past and present position in the market, and other factors. Background data can be secured from sources such as the following: the company's annual report and 10K form (a financial disclosure report required by the Securities Exchange Commission); Thomas' Register of American Manufacturers; and government booklets (for federal departments, bureaus, and divisions). Learn the names of the company president and find out about recent acquisitions, mergers, or take-over efforts. In short, do your homework before the interview.

Speak concisely and make an attractive, professional appearance.

Take care not to ramble if asked about foreign policy, national affairs, or your profession. Make your comments concise and in good taste. If you are asked about instructors or former employers, remember that the interview is not the place for disparaging others. But be frank and honest in all replies.

Dressing neatly, having good posture, and speaking clearly, correctly, and completely are all crucial in the interview. Ask yourself these questions: How do I come across in interviews? Do I talk too much? too little? Am I a good listener? How good is my eye contact? You certainly know *what* to do. If you don't do it, figure out how to change.

Plan to find an opportunity during the interview to tell about your major achievements or important qualities:

My job in the bookstore helped me to pay almost 80 percent of my college expenses.

My knowledge of Spanish will enable me to carry on correspondence and routine business activities with your Latin American accounts.

I received a General Bank and Trust Company scholarship as a freshman and maintained the high grade point average required to hold it for all four years.

Ask your interviewer thoughtful questions about the company and your duties.

Also plan to ask several carefully worded questions. These may concern opportunities within the firm, compensation in addition to the base salary (hospitalization, annuity funds, tuition-refund plans, stock option programs, profit sharing), plans for company expansion and diversification, job duties, travel requirements, advancement policies, and so forth.

> Can you tell me what a typical day would be like?
> What are the major responsibilities of this position?
> Can you explain the typical career pattern of someone entering in this position?
> Can I progress at my own speed or is advancement structured?
> How frequently do you relocate professional employees?
> Does this firm recommend taking evening classes during the first year?
> What is the firm's policy with regard to paying for educational tuition and fees?
> How often are performance reviews given?
> Is it possible to transfer from one division to another?
> Does this firm promote within the ranks?
> How much responsibility is given after one year?
> How much exposure and contact with management is there?
> What are the commonly experienced satisfactions and frustrations of this job?
> Is it possible to move through the training program faster than average?
> How much freedom is given and how much discipline is required of new employees?

Asking questions promotes discussion that can put you at ease.

The answers to such questions may determine which job you choose. Furthermore, a two-way discussion gives you an opportunity to relax as the interviewer speaks. And it may open up important new avenues for discussion. But be tactful in framing your questions.

Don't say, for example, "What are the vacation privileges?" (The interviewer may think that you don't have the job yet and you already want to go on vacation. The question is important, however, so think it through. You'll probably come up with something like, "Can you tell me about the firm's employee benefit package?" The same is true of advancement. It's a reasonable topic, but don't ask, "When do I get promoted?" Instead, ask something like, "On the basis of hard work and merit, does the firm have specific policies on advancement?"

Be prepared to deal with a job offer during the interview. If you aren't prepared to accept it at that moment, don't stall or accept it with some mental reservation. Say directly that you have other interviews scheduled and that you want to defer a decision, for the benefit of the company as well as yourself. Interviewers are usually reasonable people; they will accept an honest approach.

THE INTERVIEWER'S POINT OF VIEW

The interviewer is looking for the most qualified person for the job. How that is determined is largely a function of his or her own perceptions, values, and training. Some interviewers use a *structured* format, almost following a checklist of questions. In fact, some interviewers score answers, adding up the points at the end of the interview!

Others use an *unstructured* approach in which topics and subjects change rapidly according to the interests of each party. The interviewer is as interested

The interviewer might take a structured or unstructured approach and conduct a stress or a behavior-based interview. Be prepared for whatever happens.

in learning about the interviewee's personality, attitude, and values as much as about experience and education.

The somewhat unusual *stress* interview is designed to keep the interviewee under a degree of tension through relentlessly pointed, barbed, personal, and even somewhat antagonistic questions. The goal is to see how the interviewee responds under stressful conditions. One manager, who uses a free flow of ideas, asks questions designed to determine these characteristics (Hinda Smith, Southern District Manager of Critikon, personal communication, October 10, 1992):

How applicants feel about the job for which they are applying. (Is the area vital? challenging? fun?)

How they feel about people.

How they feel about themselves. (Their level of confidence and competence.)

What they feel are their major strengths and weaknesses.

What they consider their personal values.

One of the most recent forms of the selection interview is the *behavior-based interview*. It focuses exclusively on what the candidate has done, is doing, or would do in the future. This form of interviewing does not probe for attitudes or opinions; instead, it elicits specific information about the candidate's actions. Here, for example, are two behavior-based questions:

Tell me about a past client you wouldn't do business with again. Explain why.

Describe a sales experience that involved misunderstandings or anger. How did you handle the situation?

Keep in mind that the interview is a vital step in the job-seeking process. Expend lavish amounts of time to prepare for it. Role-playing the interview situation with a qualified person is a good idea. Because of its importance in your future, the interview deserves your full attention, careful preparation, and maximum effort.

THE FOLLOW-UP LETTER TO THE INTERVIEW

Send a follow-up note of thanks to indicate your ongoing interest in the position.

Normally you would not send a follow-up letter as a result of an initial, brief, exploratory interview. If you have been interviewed at length and you are very interested in the position, however, send a follow-up note. Such a note will put your name in front of the interviewer again and reinforce your interest in the position.

Make your written follow-up to the interview (see Figures 15-8 through 15-10) concise, sincere, and courteous. Its purpose is to thank the interviewer for the time and effort expended in talking to you and to review briefly your own qualifications. Perhaps the most important quality of the letter is honesty. If you include obviously insincere statements or overly enthusiastic praise, it will surely fail. Mail your note the same day or the day following the interview.

FIGURE 15–8   Text of a Follow-up Letter

May 27, 19___

Dear Mr. Cates:

Thank you very much for the time you spent with me this morning. I found your discussion of the Fairmont Company most interesting, and the opening you described was very challenging.

You will recall that I received my commerce degree from California State last year, acquired a CPA certificate a few months ago, and have been employed for one year as a junior accountant with Continental Aerospace Company.

I would certainly like an opportunity to work more extensively in an electronic data processing position such as the one you described. I do hope you will call me at 555-4622 for further discussion.

Sincerely yours,

Roy Yakamoto

FIGURE 15–9   Text of a Letter Declining a Job Offer

June 27, 19___

Dear Mr. Berman:

Thank you most sincerely for the time you and Ms. Cannon spent with me during our discussions of the past two weeks.

I was certainly impressed with the operations of your organization and the potential opportunities the company affords its employees. However, the position does require rather extensive travel and, as I indicated, this is something I would like to avoid.

On that basis, I have accepted a position with a local firm in the same capacity we discussed.

Sincerely yours,

Stephanie Anderson

FIGURE 15–10 Text of a Letter of Resignation

September 15, 19__

Dear Mr. Kelly:

Doing marketing research for the past two years under your direction has been a rewarding, enjoyable, and challenging experience. I found all my academic background put to good use and the freedom to innovate (which you encouraged) a delightful situation.

Recently, however, I have been asked to head the marketing division of a consumer products company. The opportunity is really too good to turn down.

Therefore, I am resigning my position here, effective October 6. If you feel that time is not convenient, I am sure alternative arrangements can be made.

Sincerely yours,

Manual Ortega

DECLINING A JOB OFFER

Declining a job offer tactfully in writing helps maintain goodwill.

At some time you may find yourself in the enviable position of having more than one job offer. Don't be tempted to call the interviewer's secretary and state, "Please tell Mr. Martin that I can't take the junior accountant's job after all, but I sure appreciate his asking me." Instead, write a carefully worded, courteous note (see Figure 15–9). It can build goodwill, while a telephone message will not.

LETTERS OF RESIGNATION

Letters of resignation record the facts surrounding an employee's departure and are helpful when future employers seek background information.

Always resign from a position tactfully and courteously. Set down the facts in a letter to keep the record straight. A letter in your file enables the firm to give you a reference years later. Such a letter may also assist those in the company who may not know you, but who must deal with a request for information about you. In a potentially difficult situation, as in the case of Figure 15–10), a direct factual approach is usually the best.

**WRITING
AND SPEAKING
EXERCISES**

1. Is it reasonable to compare the resume and cover letter to a sales letter? Explore, in a written document, their similarities and differences.
2. Interview someone who is responsible for hiring at a local business. Prepare a short report, in memo format, that identifies what that person perceives as typical problems exhibited by interviewees. What advice, if any, does your source offer to the potential employee?
3. Use a computer and desktop publishing software to produce several versions of your resume. Analyze, in writing, perceived differences in the impact of your resume produced by changes in type, format, use of white space, and so forth. How important do you think these differences are to a potential reader?
4. Many books offer guidance, much of it conflicting, on how to produce a winning resume. Find a recent book that describes resumes different in style and content from those described in this text. Discuss in writing the advantages or disadvantages of these alternate styles.
5. The resume is closely identified with the job search. However, the resume can serve purposes that have nothing to do with seeking employment.
   (a) Identify the profession you plan to enter.
   (b) For that profession, describe two situations in which it would be beneficial to have an up-to-date resume.
6. Ask two or three of your classmates to form a mock interview panel. In advance, tell them the job for which you are applying. They should interview you for 20 to 30 minutes, using interview questions contained in this chapter in addition to their own. After the interview, complete the following tasks:
   (a) Write down your own assessment of your performance. What did you do well? What needed improvement? Which questions were especially easy or difficult?
   (b) Ask each of the panel members to list three things you did well and three things which you should work on.
   (c) Listen as the panel discusses your interview and decides whether to offer you the job. After you have heard what they have to say, write down the points that seemed especially important to the panel in reaching its decision.
7. Distribute your resume to five people. Ask them to circle three items on the resume that they would use as the basis for interview questions. After you have collected your resumes, draw some conclusions about the success with which you designed your resume with interviews in mind. In what specific ways can you highlight material so the interviewer will ask you about it?
8. Stating the career objective in specific and realistic terms is often one of the more difficult parts of the resume to construct.
   (a) Write a career objective that addresses only your short-term goal.
   (b) Write a career objective that combines your short- and long-term goals.
9. The resume should be an honest representation of your abilities and qualifications. However, if one of your personal characteristics is a

liability, you should not list it on the resume. Give some examples of items that a person might leave off of a resume but be willing to address in an interview.

10. Imagine that you have just been interviewed for a job. Write the following letters:
    (a) Thank-you letter for the interview
    (b) Letter accepting a job offer
    (c) Letter declining a job offer

11. The chapter discusses an ongoing controversy in business communication literature—the length of a resume. Prepare two resumes for yourself, one of them one-page long and the other two pages. Submit both resumes, along with your critical analysis of each to your instructor. Your analysis should clearly state which resume you plan to use in your actual job search. Specifically address the issue of resume length.

12. College bulletin boards, daily newspapers, and the Yellow Pages regularly advertise resume preparation services. Call three such services to learn what, in addition to typing, they offer their clients. Specifically, inquire about what they claim to do for you that you cannot do for yourself. Write down their claims and your response to those claims. End your analysis by indicating whether you would use a resume preparation service. Submit this paper to your instructor as a completed memo.

13. An interviewee must be well prepared before the employment interview. The chapter indicates a variety of sources for obtaining information needed for the interview.
    (a) Name a specific organization with which you might reasonably interview.
    (b) Name a job you might consider in the organization.
    (c) List three specific questions you would probably ask the interviewer.
    (d) Cite five places where you could secure information about the organization. Briefly indicate the kinds of information listed in each.

14. During the past several years, a number of articles have appeared in the press about dishonest resumes. Evidently, some people take more than literary freedom with what they include in their resumes. Some resumes contain incorrect information about colleges attended, degrees earned, positions held, employment responsibilities, and the like.

    As a resume writer who wants to be completely honest, what can you do in your resume and cover letter that will suggest that all facts presented are valid and verifiable?

15. Revise each of the following unsatisfactory letter bodies, using the checklist in this chapter.

    THANK-YOU LETTER
    Just a note to say thanks. Let me know if anything comes of our discussion. I sure hope you'll see fit to hire me. You can call me day or night at 555-6832.

    LETTER DECLINING A JOB OFFER
    I'm very sorry to tell you that I cannot accept the offer made to me in your recent letter.
    Thank you, however, for considering me for the position.

LETTER OF RESIGNATION
Effective May 5, 19__, I resign. My desk and files will be cleaned out by 5 p.m. on that date. I request that all necessary forms be sent to me immediately.

SUGGESTED RESOURCES

Bostwick, Burdette E. *Resume Writing: A Comprehensive How-to-do-it Guide.* 4th ed. New York: John Wiley & Sons, 1990.

Duffy, Cathleen A. "Resumes Can Float or Sink Job Hunters' Chances." *Computerworld* 25 (July 1, 1991):67.

Dulek, Ronald E., and Suchan, James A. "Application Letters: A Neglected Area in the Job Search." *Business Horizons* 31 (November-December 1988):70–75.

Grossman, Jack H. "How to Sell Yourself: A Guide for Interviewing Effectively." *SAM Advanced Management Journal* 56 (Spring 1991):33–36.

Hochheiser, Robert. *Throw Away Your Resume.* 2nd ed. New York: Barron's, 1990.

Holton, E. *The MBA'S Guide to Career Planning: Everything You Need to Know to Get a Great Job the MBA Way.* Princeton, N.J.: Peterson's Guides, 1989.

Macdougall, Neil. "An Employer Ranks Resumes." *CMA Magazine* 64 (September 1990):35–38.

Rosen, Elizabeth Anne. "Writing Your Own Resume." *Management Solutions* 33 (August 1988):40–45.

Ruhl, Janet. "Taking the Job Hunt On-Line." *Computerworld* (October 9, 1989):102.

PART **5**

REPORTS AND PROPOSALS

Hinda M. Smith is Southeastern Division Manager for Vascular Access Products. She manages a nine representative sales force in seven states for Critikon, Inc.

CRITIKON
a *Johnson & Johnson* company

Dear Future Manager:

There's a widespread misconception that some managers, particularly those in sales, seldom use their professional writing skills. I want to dispel that notion.

Even though I spend a considerable portion of my business life making or observing presentations, attending or leading meetings, and communicating by telephone, I nevertheless rely upon my writing skills for a wide variety of communication tasks, including reports, proposals, letters, and memos. These written messages are the ones that reach both my co-workers and clients with the greatest initial impact and long-term influence.

If I were to give one bit of advice to future managers, it would be this: use your college experience to learn crisp, clear writing skills. They will serve you well in your career.

Sincerely,

Hinda M. Smith
Division Manager
Critikon, Inc.
A Johnson & Johnson Company

16

THE RESEARCH PROCESS

Investigate what was done yesterday if you wish to contribute to advances tomorrow.

Information gives managers the power to succeed.

This well-known axiom is certainly true: Knowledge (or information) is power. Adequate information permits us to eradicate a disease, solve a complex construction problem, develop a space station, construct an Earth-orbiting satellite, surpass a business competitor, or defeat a battlefield enemy. Access to information often spells the difference between success and failure.

Computer-assisted research is today's state-of-the-art.

As we shall see in this chapter, ways of storing, accessing, controlling, and distributing information are changing in revolutionary ways. Today, most major indexes and many directories and sources of factual information are available through computers, either online or through compact disk read-only memory (CD-ROM). How these formats differ will be described later in this chapter. The essential process for gathering and using information, however, is as old as Aristotle. We have all gathered and applied information, in one form or another, since we were children.

Consider, for example, how we negotiated our first allowance from our parents. First, we considered the problem: no money for the convenience store. Then we defined our objective: to get money legally. We went on to analyze our audience, those loving but tight-fisted parents. In the light of that analysis, we narrowed our central purpose to a workable range: $10 per week. Finally, we put our developing idea (our hypothesis) to the test, paying particular attention to feedback ("We'll think about it . . . ") and revising our hypothesis accordingly.

Successful researchers identify their problem, define their objective, analyze their audience, specify their purpose, seek feedback to their hypothesis, and revise.

This basic process of topic formation and information gathering underlies even the most complex research projects in business. Luckily, we do not have to reinvent the wheel in our search for available information on our topic. Once we know where we are going and why, we can try to find out what others have discovered about our subject or about related areas. There is really no point in duplicating work that others have already completed. When we have reviewed the work of others—referred to as *secondary research*—we can break new ground through *primary research*.

SECONDARY SOURCES

Consult secondary sources to see how others have solved similar problems.

Let's say we have a problem to solve. The company president wonders if retailers and consumers would prefer to stock and purchase frozen vegetables contained in colorful, attractive packages or labeled plastic bags. The retailer likes the packages, which are easy to handle and pack and present a more attractive appearance. On the other hand, the profit margin is greater with the plastic bag. The consumer may think the packaged product is of higher quality; however, the plastic bag is costs less. Both the level of profit and sales are involved in addition to retailer support and customer satisfaction. Which choice should we make?

Many *similar* problems have been described in various books, magazine articles, reports, and research studies. Of course, they are not necessarily concerned with the precise topic of vegetable packaging, but they consider related aspects. The material they present can guide and shape our thinking. For example, in researching the vegetable packaging question, we would find several reports on how consumers and retailers reacted to paper vs. plastic bags for carrying home groceries, how consumers reacted to the use of scanners vs. cash registers, how consumers reacted when full-service gasoline stations changed to self-service, and how motorists responded when plastic versions of many previously manufactured metal parts began appearing on their automobiles. These reports could serve as a foundation for further research. Never ignore existing knowledge. Search secondary sources and build on the information of others.

Secondary sources can be divided into several general categories: (1) books; (2) periodicals, newspapers, and other serials; (3) government documents; (4) business or trade directories; and (5) miscellaneous sources. In this chapter we discuss all of these categories in general. A listing of useful reference guides in each category, plus suggestions on how to use the computer in research, appears at the end of the chapter.

BOOKS

Books will always be a source of current as well as classic ideas.

Because the time required to turn manuscripts into books in now sometimes a matter of weeks instead of months, researchers have no reason to view recently published books as out of date for research purposes. In many cases, the lag time between completion of a manuscript for a book and for a journal or magazine article is comparable. Even older books often contain classic studies or background material vital to current research efforts.

Using card catalogs.   Most research in a library begins with consulting the card catalog for books on a specific topic. Title, subject, and cross-reference entries are checked. The advent of electronic card catalogs has greatly reduced the time involved in locating desired sources. The computer has made it possible not only to locate sources of information quickly, but also to find related sources and abstracted summaries of books and articles.

Using library stacks.   Library stacks enable a researcher to browse through actual studies instead of making research judgments based only on information in the card catalog or in a published abstract. Such browsing often pays the additional dividend of turning up new avenues for investigation and new sources for evidence. The stacks contain back issues of magazines and journals in addition to books.

PERIODICALS,
NEWSPAPERS, AND
OTHER SERIALS

Periodicals and newspapers are rich sources of information for those conducting research. With the assistance of the computer, materials can be accessed from dozens of reference sources quickly, easily, and inexpensively.

Use periodical indexes to track down useful articles.

Using periodicals.   Sometimes you will be given a hint by a helpful friend who says, "I read a great article on your topic a couple of months ago. I think it was in *Business Week,* but maybe it was in *Forbes—Fortune.* I don't remember the exact title, but it was really good, and you should use it. I think you'll be able to find it. I'm sure it wasn't more than six months ago that I saw it." Where do you begin? Preferably not by thumbing through stacks of *Business Week, Fortune,* and *Forbes.* Instead, use one of several excellent periodical indexes that cover fields of business and social sciences. To discover which of these indexes will best suit your particular needs, check the list of periodicals indexed in each. Indexes containing abstracts may be of special interest because of their descriptive notes, but they usually do not cover all articles in a journal.

Newspapers contain vast information on various subjects and are conveniently indexed.

Using newspapers.   Newspapers carry tremendous quantities of valuable information of all types: statistical, political, financial, and so forth. But how do you get at it? Again, the answer is to use an index. Some newspapers, such as the *Wall Street Journal, The Christian Science Monitor,* and *The New York Times,* have their own indexes. These papers are also indexed collectively in the *National Newspaper Index.*

Using other serials.   Each year thousands of excellent reports, bulletins, brochures, and studies are issued by universities, foundations, corporations, cultural and social institutions, and professional societies and organizations. Even though there is no *one* index to this information, some useful guides are published.

GOVERNMENT
DOCUMENTS AND
STATISTICAL SOURCES

Many government documents provide vital information to business researchers.

More than two hundred government departments, bureaus, ministries, agencies, and committees issue a wide variety of technical reports, pamphlets, bibliographies, periodicals, translations of foreign documents, and other publications each year. In fact, the U.S. government is probably the world's largest publisher. Many of its publications are extremely sophisticated and of very high quality. Much of this literature is important to businesspeople and researchers, so appropriate reference guides can be of great assistance.

Through diligent research, you can use complex statistical sources to find information.

Statistics are vital to business. In addition to the U.S. government, there are many other compilers and publishers of statistical information. If you are not familiar with the more specialized sources, turn to the comprehensive statistical compilations. These usually refer the user to appropriate specialized sources. Fortunately, excellent statistical reference guides and indexes are published to point the way through the maze of available data.

BUSINESS OR
TRADE DIRECTORIES

Business or trade directories describe companies and identify business professionals.

In addition to listing the names and addresses of individual companies and products, business or trade directories carry a wide variety of information on organizations and individuals. Businesspeople use these directories for many purposes: to identify company officers or directors, to identify competitors in a particular area, to verify company names, and so forth. Many directories are published annually, with supplements appearing throughout the year. Job seekers sometimes find background information in company directories that is useful during employment interviews. Almost every field, from automotive products to wholesale jewelry, has its own directory of national and international listings.

MISCELLANEOUS SOURCES OF INFORMATION

The rapid development of international business has made information about political, economic, and social differences among nations very important. Use the reference guides and indexes to international data to develop a global perspective.

Additional sources of information such as atlases, annuals, and yearbooks contribute to the wealth of reference materials. At some time, you may consult them all.

THE COMPUTER AS A RESEARCH AID

Computers store literally billions of pages of business information in memory structures called databases. By telling a computer which databases to search for information on a given topic, you can save yourself many hours of manual research. In addition, you are likely to discover articles and studies that you may not have found in your company or university library. Several business-related databases are listed at the end of this chapter.

USING DESCRIPTOR TERMS

With a computer and modem, researchers can directly access databases without actually visiting a library.

Because of the value of computerized sources of information, the "visual library," or "library without walls," is approaching reality. This library is one that exists *only* in electronic format. Users obtain facts, figures, and full texts online through a microcomputer connection and the many national and international networks available. Almost all of the major indexes are now online and on CD-ROM. The Internet and BITNET systems make texts, library catalogs, bibliographic indexes, and factual information available to anyone with a modem. When the U.S. government implements the National Research and Education Network (NREN), the "visual library" could become a reality.

Online and CD-ROM sources are accessible through a library or individually. Individuals or corporations can open an account with a database vendor or purchase CD-ROM equipment. Libraries routinely teach their users to search in both formats and may make the necessary hardware and software available in the library.

Use descriptor terms to access articles on a specific subject.

To begin a computer search, you must first specify *descriptor terms* which the computer uses as guides. If, for example, you were investigating new plant construction, you would ask the computer to search for articles classified under "plant construction," "relocation," "labor availability," "city tax structure," and so on. The computer searches its databases and provides a list of articles on these subjects. Usually included in each listing are the title of the article, author's name, journal name, date of publication, and a brief abstract of the paper itself (see Figure 16–1).

The computer can rapidly search a variety of databases. Among the advantages of computerized literature searches are the following:

FIGURE 16–1   Printout Page from a Computerized Database Search

Article title

Authors' names

Abstract or article summary

Journal title, issue number, and
volume, article pages

```
Document 49
UI  10504862
Title of Article
1   Communication skills in cross-cultural
    situations.
Author
1   Knotts, Rose
2   Hartman, Sandra J.
Abstract
1   Supervisors should develop communication skills
    for dealing with cross-cultural situations.
    Slang, very formal language, and occupational
    vernacular should be avoided. Supervisors can
    ensure that they do not speak too quickly by
    asking listeners for frequent feedback. Employ-
    ees do not have to learn foreign idioms, but
    they should conduct some basic research on for-
    eign languages to avoid misunderstandings.
    Japanese employees, for instance, often use the
    word 'yes' during conversations, but 'yes' only
    means that the speaker has heard what has been
    said, not that the speaker agrees. Supervisors
    should help their employees become aware of the
    importance of simple and direct cross-cultural
    communications.
SO  Supervisory Management
    (March 1991) v36 n3 p12(1)
```

The computer search is fast, thorough, timely, and convenient. You can even obtain a copy of an article from a journal not available in your library.

- Speed: A computerized literature search, usually completed in a library, can save enormous amounts of time. Contrast a ten-minute computer search with hours spent searching through card catalogs, indexes, and old magazines and journals.
- Thoroughness: The computerized search ensures that you will discover *all* issues of relevant journals, periodicals, or other sources. Your manual search, by contrast, may be frustrating because of missing volumes.
- Timeliness: A printed index is compiled from the online database. Thus, citations are available from the computer at least a month before the published index is available.
- Convenience: There is no need to take notes on available sources. A computer printout lists the title, author, name of journal, date of publication, and an abstract of the article as well as other information.
- Document delivery service: You can obtain a copy of most articles cited (for a fee). This rapid service is especially valuable if a particular journal is not available in your library.

CD-ROM

*One CD-ROM can hold
150,000 pages worth
of information.*

A CD-ROM resembles a music compact disk except that it contains data, not music. It is a sandwich of polycarbonate and aluminum with an acrylic or lacquer coating. Although it appears smooth, the working side of the disk is pitted. A laser beam from the CD-ROM drive, or player, reads the pits and converts what it reads into information. Each CD-ROM can hold 650 megabytes—about the equivalent of 1,500 floppy diskettes or more than 150,000 typed pages. An entire encyclopedia, or a database, can fit on one little disk.

Nearly two hundred business and management information sources are available on CD-ROM, including major online sources such as ABI/Inform, the Business and Company ProFile, the Business Periodicals Index, PAIS International, Predicasts, Standard and Poor's Stock Reports, and telephone directories and company catalogs from around the world.

The advantage of CD-ROM over dial-up online systems is that once the disk is purchased, there are no "connect time" or royalty charges. Searchers can take their time; they can even leave the system permanently booted up and ready to search. Online systems are updated more often, but CD-ROM subscribers usually receive updated disks weekly or monthly.

CD-ROM can be incorporated into local-area and wide-area computer networks for multiple users. The searching software can be loaded behind a menu shell so that users are unaware of the mechanics. All the users need to know is that the search system is ready to be used.

PRIMARY SOURCES

In today's busy world, most of us depend on newspapers, radio, and television to tell us what's going on. They in turn, get much of their information through the questions their personnel ask. "Interviews with key government officials in Washington," begins one story. "A survey of workers at the Danbury plant," runs another. A politician is disposed of with the words, "A nationwide poll showed that Throttlebottom ranked far down in the public's preference."

*Documents, personal
observations, and
interviews are primary
sources because the
information in them
is discovered and
interpreted first hand.*

Information obtained by asking questions is one kind of *primary information*. Other kinds of primary data include company records, diaries, original reports, letters, lab experiments, notes, and personal observation.

The data secured from primary sources are considered "raw" because they have not been subjected to interpretation and analysis by others. The researcher may well be the first person to analyze, evaluate, and interpret the information. For example, a company conducts primary research to find out whether its new product should be packaged in the red carton or the green one, whether the new plant should be built in Topeka or Kansas City, or whether to advertise on TV or radio. Companies devote substantial resources to answer such questions.

THE POPULATION, OR UNIVERSE

*A population or universe, is
the group whose members
have interest in and
knowledge and opinions
about a research topic.*

In carrying through research on a specific topic, you often need the opinions of individuals who are concerned with that topic. These people may be accountants, teachers, lawyers, retail clerks, airplane pilots, electricians, physicians, plumbers, or a combination of several different groups. Whatever segments of society you select, there will be a commonality among them: interest, knowledge, and/or opinions on the topic of your research. These people, whether 10,000 or 100,000 are your *population,* or *universe.*

CULTURAL DIVERSITY IN COMMUNICATION

In a Diverse Marketplace, Primary Research is Primary!

Carol Shuherk
University of Southern California

Do you remember the Frito Bandito or recall the days when Aunt Jemima wore a bandana? Did you ever eat at a nation-wide chain restaurant called Sambo's? If not, it may be because the ethnic groups these advertising symbols represented pressured their makers to change or remove them before you were an active consumer.

The increasing diversity of U.S. culture makes primary research more important than ever. Whether a company is interested in increasing productivity in its diverse work force or attracting diverse buyers to its products, no assumptions about how most people will respond are safe. The evolution of advertising communication in this country offers a telling illustration of the business imperatives of "going to the source" before making product or personnel decisions in a culturally diverse society.

Before the 1960s, product advertising communicated mostly an "us and them" image of the diverse population in the United States. "Us" was the largely Anglo, largely male, members of the business community and buying public. "Them" were the various groups represented by advertisers in cultural stereotypes: lively Latins, thrifty Scots, fruit-peddling Italians, pig-tailed Chinese,

and subservient African-Americans.

When U.S. minorities found their political voice in the civil rights movement, they also began to gain the ear of an advertising industry that was just embracing the concept of market segments: African-American, Asians, teenagers, women, and so forth. Frito-Lay dropped the Frito-Bandito from its corn chip promotions in 1971, after complaints from Hispanic groups that they found it demeaning. Quaker Foods, bowing to pressure from African-Americans, transformed Aunt Jemima's image from servant mammy to a African-American homemaker. And in 1982, the California-based Sambo's went out of business after a nationwide boycott of its stores.

In 1990, African-Americans represented a $218 billion market; Hispanic markets were estimated at $134 billion and Asians, $35 billion. Thirty years of trying to tap these markets had taught advertisers that speaking directly to those potential customers (through in-house specialists, surveys, and focus groups) was fundamental to shaping effective advertising campaigns. The learning process was sometimes costly.

Most advertiser' first attempts to reach ethnic groups involved direct translation of slogans or simple substitution of

A population is usually too numerous to survey. However, if you carefully select a *portion* of that population, or a *sample,* that is representative of that universe, you can assume that their opinions will approximate those of the universe.

SELECTING THE SAMPLE

The survey sample should reflect a cross-section of a population or universe.

When you make a survey to find out what large numbers of people are thinking or feeling, don't try to approach everybody. To survey everybody would be too expensive and perhaps impossible. Instead, take a sample of the people whose opinions you are interested in. If the sample is carefully selected so that it is representative of the group (or universe) as a whole, surprisingly accurate results can be obtained from a very small sample.

The important point is that the sample should be a reliable cross-section of the group you're studying. If it isn't, your results will not be valid. A statistician or market analyst can tell you best how to go about selecting the sample. For some purposes, a random sample may be the answer. Other cases are more suited to a stratified, cluster, double, selective, or area sample.

people of color for whites in print or broadcast ads. The occasionally disastrous results of direct translations have become industry legends, for example, the Coors beer slogan "Get loose with Coors" translated into Spanish as "Get the runs with Coors."

More subtle, but equally important in gaining consumer acceptance of a company's products, is the awareness that cultural values are more persuasive than visual depictions of a product in minority hands. Quaker Foods made this discovery belatedly after a campaign for its convenience products failed with the Hispanic market. Subsequent focus groups revealed that convenience is not a value in Hispanic culture, so premixed cakes or instant oat cereals held little appeal.

As marketing research into the diversity of the U.S. population increased, so did the complexity of the data it produced. Some surveys and focus groups revealed that virtually all U.S. citizens, including immigrants and minorities, want to see themselves enjoying the essential "American Dream" of good jobs, material comfort, and enjoyable leisure activity. On the other hand, their complex and varied mix of social values and their particular history in this country make them sensitive to just how these things are por-

trayed. Although African-Americans prefer to see African-American people pursuing leisure activities on the billboards in predominantly African-American areas, they do not want leisure consistently depicted as consumption of alcohol or tobacco products.

Ultimately, primary marketing research yields a basic truth about all persuasive communication: it must be tailored for each product and every target group. Even within cultural groups, age, income, education, and other differences may require a change in approach. While some things have universal appeal—response to Bill Cosby as a celebrity promoter for various products appears to be color-blind and age-irrelevant- most are not. Research told Pepsi-Co. that Michael Jackson couldn't sell Pepsi to African-Americans aged 25 to 40 (they think his reported plastic surgeries and reclusive life-style indicate he's "selling out") but that virtually all teenagers, the elderly, and the Japanese would respond to him as a Pepsi representative.

In a world where information proliferates and access to good information determines power, in the marketplace and within the firm, developing skills in primary research can mean finding the competitive edge.

Perhaps the most popular samples are *random* and *stratified.* In a truly *random sample,* every item in the universe has an equal chance of being selected. One way to accomplish a random sample is to put everyone's name or every item's number into a hat and then draw out a predetermined number. Each person or item has an equal chance of being selected. In actual practice, researchers use a table of random numbers, thereby bypassing the chore of drawing designations from a hat.

A *stratified sample* is one in which the universe has been segmented into homogeneous groups first: lawyers, physicians, nurses, professors, engineers, and chemists, for example. If each of these groups is made up of different numbers and you draw ten from each group, your stratified sample is *nonproportional.* However, if you draw a number from each group that represents, say, 15 percent of the total of each group, your sample is a *proportional stratified sample.* Other types of samples are explained in more detail in most basic statistics books.

In almost every instance, an increase in the sample size selected will increase the degree or percentage of the universe that sample represents. That

Weigh the increase in validity against additional survey costs to decide if surpassing the plateau of validity is worthwhile.

level is usually referred to as the level of reliability or *validity* of the sample in its representation of the universe. A plateau of validity is attained with a specific sample size beyond which the degree of validity does not increase significantly. And although the cost of continued sampling increases, the level of validity rises very slowly after the plateau level has been established. Thus a sample of 5,000 may provide, say, a validity level of 90 percent. If you include an *additional* 5,000 in your sample, the validity level may only rise to 92 percent. You must now determine whether the added expenditure from further surveying is worth the increase in validity from 90 to 92 percent. If you are assessing consumer response to blue vs. white packaging, a 90 percent validity level is fine. On the other hand, if you are checking an antiviral serum to be injected into millions of children, you probably want to feel 99.999 percent confident that results are correct. In such a case, the added cost is worthwhile.

CONDUCTING THE SURVEY

Even with a good sample and a well-planned questionnaire, a survey may fail if it is not conducted properly. Respondents to a survey are doing you a favor, and they should be treated accordingly. If the survey is an interview type, it is especially important for you as the interviewer to be courteous, alert, and perceptive. At times, respondents may offer a verbal reply that does not agree with the respondent's nonverbal communication delivered at the same time. In such an instance, ask a follow-up question or note the response as being questionable.

TYPES OF SURVEYS

Questions are not difficult to ask; the problem is getting reliable and truthful answers. Several methods are popular for securing information from people. Basically, they all involve asking questions or presenting situations, securing reactions, and then determining how the respondents will behave in a practical situation based on their responses to the survey. Sometimes the conclusions sound like this: "Of those interviewed, 53 percent preferred the smaller package, 26 percent preferred the larger, and 21 percent had no preference." Among the methods used are mail questionnaires, personal interviews, telephone interviews, unstructured or depth interviews, and observation. The first three use a series of questions to secure information. Nevertheless, each is very different from the others and has its own advantages and disadvantages.

Mail questionnaires are relatively inexpensive, considering the potential number and wide distribution of respondents.

Mail questionnaires.   Chief among the advantages of the *mail questionnaire* are its low cost per response and the ease of securing responses from a wide geographical area. Also, respondents can be assured of anonymity, which helps increase the proportion of questionnaires returned. Securing answers from hard-to-see people (such as company presidents) is easier with a mail questionnaire. In addition, there is no possibility of interviewer bias, which can influence the responses.

Unfortunately, researchers cannot be certain that mail questionnaires reflect an accurate cross-section of the population.

But there are disadvantages to the mail survey. It must be relatively brief, or people won't bother with it. People who feel strongly—pro or con—are the most likely to respond. Thus, the survey results may not accurately reflect the attitudes of those lacking strong opinions. It is also difficult to know whether the intended respondent personally completed the questionnaire or gave it to some member of the office staff or family to do so. Many respondents fail to answer a mail questionnaire because of the effort involved. For these reasons, researchers are never quite certain whether those who reply are really representative of the target population.

Personal interviews. Perhaps the biggest disadvantage to the *personal interview* technique is its cost. Hiring competent interviewers is costly. Even when professional interviewers are affordable, there is a risk that the interviewer's bias may influence responses. Securing data through interviews is time consuming in comparison with mail surveys. Also, people often don't have the time or inclination to talk to an interviewer.

Even though personal interviews can be costly and time consuming, they do elicit in-depth responses and target representative population samples.

On the other hand, interviewers can delve into specifics more than is usually possible by mail. They can also obtain answers to questions in sensitive areas (income tax, sex, politics, religion) and elicit a reply where a mail survey may fail. Because interviewers can choose their respondents to a certain extent, their surveys usually include more representative samples.

Telephone interviews. The *telephone interview* has several major limitations. Questions must be brief and generally limited to not more than three or four. Questions requiring discussion or even careful thought cannot usually be included, nor can any that are concerned with personal relationships. Not every telephone call leads to an interview. On the other hand, telephone interviews are inexpensive, almost anyone can be called regardless of his or her position, and simple information (gender, make of auto, marital status, number of children, vocation, etc.), can be secured quickly and easily.

Telephone interviews should be brief and avoid lengthy or in-depth discussion.

Depth or unstructured interviews. Respondents don't always answer questions truthfully. Because of societal conventions and individual inhibitions, they often answer questions as they think the interviewer wants them answered. They don't want to admit that they hate their boss, dislike baseball, or find certain television programs entertaining. They may not lie, but they evade. Naturally, if the replies are not honest, the survey results cannot be valid.

Depth interviewing encourages respondents to express their true feelings.

Some experts believe that if people talk to a skilled interviewer about a topic freely and easily, their true feelings will become apparent, regardless of the conventions of society. This is the theory of *depth interviewing:* to set up a climate for the respondents so that they will talk freely and frankly about the topic. For example, "Tell me how you select the candidate for whom you vote" may produce some key information, even though the answer lasts five minutes and contains a great deal of irrelevant material.

Personal observation. Information can often be obtained simply by *personal observation.* Researchers watch how a shopper chooses one breakfast food from among 30 or whether a conference with a friend is necessary before choosing a T-shirt. Observers also collect data by watching traffic patterns, counting shoppers, noting people's restaurant habits, and so on.

Through personal observation, researchers gain information simply by watching people.

DESIGNING THE QUESTIONNAIRE

Whatever type of survey you use, the most important point is to ask the right questions. Nothing is easier to design than a poor questionnaire, and nothing is more difficult than designing a good once. But following a few rules will increase your chances of success.

Almost every detail of a questionnaire is important, even the title and introductory comments. To call a questionnaire "Executive Survey" may appeal to

Poorly designed questionnaires will fail to elicit an adequate number of valid responses.

the respondent's ego. The title "Confidential Analysis Among Our Retailers" encourages a sense of close relations between researcher and respondent. At times, a carefully worded introductory sentence or two, appealing to the respondents' professional knowledge or responsibility, their loyalty, or even their sense of humor, may motivate them to complete the survey.

The precise wording of the questions can be a significant factor in the percentage of returns, Some suggestions follow.[1]

Arrange questions logically.

List questions in logical order.   There is no point in asking respondents in question 3 what flavor icing they prefer on cakes, and then asking in question 6 if they ever eat cake. If the questionnaire does not seem logical to the respondents, they may discard it.

Place easy questions first and more difficult questions last.

Provide easy-to-answer questions early in the questionnaire.   Respondents who have gone easily through the first eight questions may be reluctant to discard the questionnaire when they encounter difficulty on question 9. If this suggestion conflicts with the preceding one about following a logical order, do what is most advantageous under the circumstances.

Use effective transitions.

Create smooth transitions between questions.   Smooth transitions and parallel wording help respondents move easily from one question to the next.

Each question should address a single topic.

Word each question so that it is concerned with one topic only.   If respondents are faced with giving two answers to one question—and only one space is provided—they may discard the form. Or, if they do answer, their responses may not give a clear indication of their preferences. Consider, for example, this question: "Would you like movies on commercial air flights at a small extra charge?" If respondents answer "no," does it mean they wouldn't like movies even if they were free? If they would like movies on long flights but not on short ones, how do they answer? If they don't want movies at all, whether there is an extra charge or not, how do they respond?

Make it easy for respondents to answer the questions and return the questionnaire.

Design the questionnaire so that it looks (and is) easy to answer.   Arrange questions so that respondents see clearly where to indicate their replies. There should be plenty of white space, and the numbering should be easy to follow. Choose words carefully so that everyone will understand. Provide an addressed, stamped envelope in which to return the questionnaire.

Avoid connotative words.

Avoid words that may elicit a biased or emotional response or carry an undesirable connotation.   These are usually abstract words (happiness, morality, democracy, communism) or words relating to politics, sex, religion, and race.

Strive for clarity.

Eliminate ambiguity; clarity is of the utmost importance.   A question like "What type of soup do you prefer?" can cause difficulty. One respondent will answer "hot," another "Campbell's," a third "beef noodle," a fourth "frozen," and a fifth "inexpensive." One way of handling this problem is to provide a list of alternative answers from which to choose.

Avoid leading questions.

Avoid questions that "lead" respondents to specific answers.   A bias will enter into most respondents' answers if you ask questions such as these: "Do you prefer General Motors cars?" "Do you usually purchase the best seats when attending a play?" "Do you always drink moderately?" "Do you prefer imported wines?" Here again, it helps if you give respondents a list of choices.

Don't expect the respondent to work hard at figuring out an answer.

Do not expect respondents to search their memories or perform computations. You can't expect an accurate answer to "In what year did you take your first jet trip?" Not many people will bother to compute the answer to "How much does your family spend each year on movies?" Questions such as these will cause respondents to toss the questionnaire into the wastebasket.

Don't get personal.

Avoid personal questions if possible. People dislike being asked questions about their political or religious affiliation, sex habits, income, or age. A promise of anonymity may help, but it is better to avoid these issues if possible.

Don't require the respondent to skip questions.

Don't ask skip-and-jump questions. People are likely to give up in despair when confronted with "If you answered yes to question 4, skip questions 7 and 8 and go directly to question 9, unless you live in New York, in which case do not answer question 9."

Don't require respondents to interpret your questions.

Avoid questions with blanket meanings. Some words are open to a variety of interpretations. For example, the word *often* in the question, "Do you often take your spouse out to dinner?" may mean once a month to some respondents and once a week to others.

Figure 16–2 is an example of a mail questionnaire. Evaluate the questions in regard to quality, wording, and order in which they are presented. Note the different kinds of questions. A *check* question requires only that respondents make a mark to choose from among predefined alternatives. A *scale* question asks respondents to locate their opinion on a continuum of possible responses. *Open-end* questions allow respondents to generate answers without predefined limitations.

Figures 16–3 through 16–5 are examples of other questionnaire formats. They show alternative ways of arranging the questions. To measure attitudes or feelings, a *semantic differential* is often used, as in the format of Figure 16–2. A semantic differential format permits respondents to choose among answers ranging from one extreme to another. Somewhat similar to a semantic differential is a *scaled question,* which asks respondents to indicate their reactions to a question from a list of choices going from low to high. Because most respondents do not see things as black or white but perhaps somewhere in between, the scale gives them an opportunity to make a choice somewhere between extremes on the scale. On one end of a line may be 1 and "poor" and on the other end 10 and the word "outstanding." In between are numbers from 2 to 9 and "good," "very good," and "excellent." Respondents mark their preferences at the appropriate point. Other lines may have "never" at one end to "frequently" on the other, or "never purchase" and "frequently purchase" or "not comfortable" to "very comfortable." A check mark somewhere on the line indicates the respondents' feelings in reference to the question.

Answers from all respondents can then be charted and correlated to show how groups differ in the strength of their feelings.

DIRECT-MAIL SURVEYS.   Some of the advantages and disadvantages of mail questionnaires have been mentioned. Such questionnaires are probably used by more researchers, and

FIGURE 16–2   Typical Mail Questionnaire with Check, Scale, and Open-ended Questions

▲ APEX
  AIRCRAFT
  CORPORATION

1. What is your present position in this organization? *(Check or fill in one.)*
   Manager   _____
   Supervisor   _____
   Nonsupervisor   _____
   Other   _____

2. How long have you worked for this company?_____ years

   How many years in your present capacity? _____ years

3. What is your age?

4. How much formal education do you have?

   Below high school_____
   Completed high school _____
   1–4 years of college_____
   More than 4 years of college_____

5. List below the names of seminars, management development programs,
   and other special courses or training you have had in the previous ten
   years.

   _____
   _____

6. In general, how well are you kept informed about things you need to know
   to do your job?

Poorly Informed		Barely Informed		Adequately Informed		Well Informed	

7. When you receive an assignment from your immediate superior, how
   frequently are the instructions adequate?

Never		Seldom		Often		Always	

   Please return no later than February 28

Check questions define respondent's choices

Scale questions let the respondent visualize a range of feelings about a topic.

FIGURE 16-2 continued

8. Do people at your level in the organization keep their superiors informed of their problems and needs?

Never		Seldom		Often		Always	

9. How often do you feel that your superior is sincere, rather than manipulative, in his or her dealings with you?

Never		Seldom		Often		Always	

10. Does your immediate superior show respect for you as an individual?

No Respect		Some Respect		Enough Respect		Full Respect	

11. Does your immediate superior's behavior give you the feeling that he or she has complete confidence in your ability and capacity?

Never		Seldom		Often		Always	

12. Does your immediate superior give you candid and sincere criticism on your job performance?

Never Does		Seldom Does		Often Does		Always Does	

13. Do people at your level communicate to their superiors frankly and honestly?

Never		Seldom		Often		Always	

Please return no later than February 28

FIGURE 16-2 continued

14. Is it your feeling that subordinates in your company communicate to you and others at your level frankly and honestly?

Never			Seldom			Often			Always		

15. In meetings and conferences, do you feel that you are permitted to participate in a way that your contributions are actually considered?

Never Permitted			Seldom Permitted			Often Permitted			Always Permitted		

Open-ended questions invite a free flow of ideas in responses to brief prompts about a topic.

16. Put a check under the face that expresses how you feel about communication in general in your company.

17. Do top managers and executives in your company communicate to each other frankly and honestly?

Never			Seldom			Often			Always		

18. The space below is for your overall comments concerning communication in your company—its completeness and honesty up, down, and laterally. How relevant is it? How quickly is it conveyed? What impact does it have on the overall climate?

_____

_____

_____

_____

_____

Please return no later than February 28

FIGURE 16–3 Example of a Check-type Questionnaire

HUGHESNEWS

Hughesnews readership survey
We have questions. You have the answers.

For more than 40 years, the Hughesnews has been publishing articles and news items for and about employees, the products they produce, and the services they perform. This survey will help us find out how well we have been doing our job and whether there are things we could be doing better.

Please check the boxes or fill in your answers in the spaces provided. The small numbers alongside and above the possible answers are for computer tabulation only, so ignore them.

We do not want to know your name but we do ask that you fill in the few "personal" questions at the end of the survey, which will enable us to learn how particular segments of our readership

(age groups, company organization, etc.) feel about the Hughesnews.

To return the questionnaire, tear out this page, fold it in half and then in thirds along the dotted lines (instructions on back of page.)

Send the questionnaire to us by company mail. If you do not have access to the company mail distribution system, you may send it through the U.S. Postal Service.

Remember, the more people we hear from, the more we will know about how to make the Hughesnews as useful and informative as possible. Help us reach those who may not be reading the paper regularly—encourage them to participate, too.

1. The Hughesnews is published every other Friday. Do you feel this is too often, not often enough or about right?
   - Too often ....( )1
   - Not often enough ....( )2
   - About right ....( )3

2. Is the Hughesnews readily available to you every two weeks?
   - Yes ....( )1
   - No (please explain and include your closest Hughesnews pickup point .( )2

3. How often do you pick up a Hughesnews?
   - Most issues ....( )1
   - Occasionally ....( )2
   - Rarely ....( )3

4. How much of the paper do you usually read?
   - All of it...........................( )1
   - Most of it ....( )2
   - About half of it ....( )3
   - Selected articles ....( )4
   - Very little, just glance at it ....( )5

5. Who, besides yourself, usually reads your copy of Hughesnews? Please check all that apply.
   - Family ....( )1
   - Friends............................( )2
   - Other employees ....( )3
   - No one ....( )4

6. Is your overall opinion of Hughesnews favorable, unfavorable or neutral?
   - Favorable...........................( )1
   - Unfavorable.........................( )2
   - Neutral..............................( )3

7. Listed below are groups of words and phrases. In each group, please check the one response that comes closest to expressing your opinion of the Hughesnews in general or that applies to its stories.

   - 11-1( ) Informative
     2( ) Not informative
   - 12-1( ) Educational
     2( ) Not educational
   - 13-1( ) Employee-centered
     2( ) Mouthpiece for management
     3( ) Balanced
   - 14-1( ) Believable
     2( ) Not believable
   - 15-1( ) Objective
     2( ) Slanted
   - 16-1( ) Complete
     2( ) Missing information
   - 17-1( ) Useful
     2( ) Useless
   - 18-1( ) Candid
     2( ) Doesn't tell me everything I'd like to know

   - 19-1( ) Thorough
     2( ) Superficial
   - 20-1( ) Willing to speak on any issue
     2( ) Unwilling to speak on some issues
   - 21-1( ) Accurate
     2( ) Not accurate
   - 22-1( ) Interesting
     2( ) Dull
   - 23-1( ) Story length too long
     2( ) Story length too short
     3( ) Stories are the right length
   - 24-1( ) Well written
     2( ) Poorly written
   - 25-1( ) Too technical
     2( ) Over-simplified
     3( ) Right amount of detail
   - 26-1( ) Clear
     2( ) Confusing

8. Hughesnews covers a number of different subjects. Please indicate your interest in the subjects listed below.

	Very -1	Somewhat -2	Not usually -3	Not at all -4
Program or product-related stories	( )	( )	( )	( )27
Heir Fare	( )	( )	( )	( )28
Anniversaries	( )	( )	( )	( )29
Announcements (such as HEA events)	( )	( )	( )	( )30
Classified ads	( )	( )	( )	( )31
Leisure Life	( )	( )	( )	( )32
Stories about employees' activities on the job	( )	( )	( )	( )33
Stories about employees' activities off the job	( )	( )	( )	( )34
Who's News at Hughes	( )	( )	( )	( )35
Patents awards	( )	( )	( )	( )36
Management's industry-related activities (speeches, appearance before Congress, etc)	( )	( )	( )	( )37
Information about Employee Benefits	( )	( )	( )	( )38
Graduations from company-sponsored classes	( )	( )	( )	( )39
Award presentations	( )	( )	( )	( )40
Savings Plan Unit Values	( )	( )	( )	( )41
Credit Union stories	( )	( )	( )	( )42
Employee sports activities	( )	( )	( )	( )43
In Memoriam	( )	( )	( )	( )44

9. Are you interested primarily in reading about the activities of your Group (GSG, RSG, etc) or organization (Support Systems, Research Labs, subsidiary), your Division, or the entire company? Check only one of these.
   - Group or organization.........( )1
   - Division...........................( )2
   - Entire company ....( )3

10. How well does the Hughesnews usually satisfy this interest?
    - Very well..........................( )1
    - Fairly well ....( )2
    - Not very well ....( )3
    - Poorly..............................( )4

11. What types of articles or stories would you like to see *added* to the Hughesnews? Check as many as you like and feel free to write in other suggestions.
    - Editorials from management ....( )1
    - Question and answer column ....( )2
    - Industry news...( )3
    - Inteviews with management about industry or company problems ....( )4
    - Letters from employees...( )5
    - Stories about our competitors...( )6
    - Other suggestions ....( )7

12. We want your comments. Please see reverse side of this page.

(More on back of page)

FIGURE 16–4   Example of a Fill-in and Check Questionnaire (One Page of Six)

II. FUTURE DIRECTIONS FOR RESEARCH

24) In your opinion, what are the most important emerging or neglected research areas in business communication that should be explored in the future? In the space below, please describe up to three research areas needing to be investigated.

A. _____

_____

B. _____

_____

C. _____

_____

Please rank your responses as to importance (1 = most important, etc.):

Response #A_____   Response #B_____   Response #C_____

25) Listed below are several <u>possible</u> research areas for business communication. Please circle a number from 1 to 7 to indicate how important you feel it is that research be conducted in each area.

		Not at all Important					Very Important	
a)	Active Listening	1	2	3	4	5	6	7
b)	Assessment of Business Writing	1	2	3	4	5	6	7
c)	Business Writing Process	1	2	3	4	5	6	7
d)	Collaborative Writing Processes	1	2	3	4	5	6	7
e)	Communication and Organizational Performance	1	2	3	4	5	6	7
f)	Communication Ethics	1	2	3	4	5	6	7
g)	Computers and the Writing Process	1	2	3	4	5	6	7
h)	Conflict Management	1	2	3	4	5	6	7
i)	Construction of Theories and Models	1	2	3	4	5	6	7
j)	Cross-national Communication	1	2	3	4	5	6	7
k)	Cross-cultural Communication	1	2	3	4	5	6	7
l)	Discourse Communities in Business	1	2	3	4	5	6	7
m)	Document Design	1	2	3	4	5	6	7
n)	Effective Business Presentations	1	2	3	4	5	6	7

Source: Reprinted by permission of Professors John D. Beard and David L. Williams.

FIGURE 16–5   Example of a Questionnaire Cover Letter with an Incentive

<table>
<tr><td colspan="2">

☆ **WESTERN STATES** ☆
UNIVERSITY

P.O. Box 7727
Seattle, WA 98102   **BOOKSTORE**   (206) 555-7277

</td></tr>
</table>

April 5, 19__

Dear Faculty Member:

Your bookstore is here to serve you and your students. In an effort to continue that policy, we need your help.

As you are probably aware, a new addition to the bookstore is presently being constructed. Because we wish to use the new space as productively as possible, we need your opinions as to the new types of merchandise we should stock and display.

Please take a few minutes to complete the enclosed questionnaire, telling us which product lines you feel you and your students would most likely patronize. A return envelope is enclosed for your reply. Because we need to place our merchandise order early, may we have your response no later than May 7, 19__?

We certainly appreciate your cooperation, and we do hope you will use the enclosed booklet of three coupons for a free issue of *Time, Newsweek,* or *U.S. News and World Reports* anytime in May, June, or July. Any store cashier will be happy to take care of you.

Sincerely yours,

Kim Kelly

Kim Kelly
Bookstore Manager

Enclosure

Request information by showing that you value the reader's contribution.

State your purpose clearly.

Make returning the questionnaire easy and politely give the reader a deadline.

Offer an incentive for participating.

FIGURE 16–5 continued

☆ WESTERN STATES UNIVERSITY ☆
Bookstore

Page 1 of 2

	I would probably purchase.	I would probably *not* purchase.	Students would probably purchase.	Students would probably *not* purchase.
1. Daily local newspapers				
2. Paperback fiction books				
3. Paperback nonfiction books				
4. Audio tapes of rock music				
5. Audio tapes of "oldies" music				
6. Audio tapes of classical music				
7. Small appliances (electric shavers, coffee makers, heating pads, etc.)				
8. Prescription drug products				

9. I suggest the bookstore stock and sell _____

_____

10. My spouse __ does, __ does not, make purchases at the university bookstore.

11. I would find it a convenience if I could charge merchandise and receive a monthly bill for bookstore purchases. _____ Agree, _____ Disagree

12. I feel the entire bookstore should be designated as a "nonsmoking" area. _____ Agree, _____ Disagree

(GO TO NEXT PAGE, PLEASE)

Please return no later than May 7, 19__

Note that the tone throughout this letter seems to suggest, "We are interested in your welfare."

certainly are better known to the public, than any of the other survey methods. To obtain the best results, not only the should questionnaire be well done, but also the accompanying letter.

The cover letter.   In a direct-mail survey, the quality of the cover letter strongly influences whether respondents return completed questionnaires. A well-written cover letter may motivate them to answer the questions carefully and return the questionnaire promptly.

An attractive, professional cover letter creates a positive impression and causes the reader to take the questionnaire seriously.

There are many reasons why people do not return a questionnaire, and there is no way to design a survey instrument that will ensure a 100 percent response. People who receive questionnaires may have no interest in the topic, they may be busy, or perhaps their employer does not permit completion of surveys. These are all understandable reasons for not completing a questionnaire. But why do so many people simply discard questionnaires without considering completing them? The answer may lie in a poor cover letter: one that is writer-centered, pompous, too demanding, or lacking an explanation of the survey's purpose. The recommendations below will help increase the percentage of responses.

Briefly state the purpose of the questionnaire and the benefit of responding.

Keep the cover letter brief.   Go over the draft deleting every extra word and phrase. Readers are busy. State what you want, why you want it, how they will benefit from giving it to you, and then stop. With rare exceptions, the cover letter should never be longer than one page (see Figure 16–6).

Show respondents the importance of participating in the survey.   We all want to be needed, and we like to know that we are making a contribution. Tell respondents what the survey aims to accomplish and why it is important. Couple this with the role of the respondents in the survey, so that they will want to help you.

> *Because you are a scientist working in the area of biotechnology products, we know you will be interested in contributing your knowledge by answering the enclosed questionnaire. The information received from this survey of 649 of your professional associates and you will be published in* The Journal of Pharmaceutical Research *and will benefit the entire field of biotechnology.*

Show respondents how they will benefit from completing the questionnaire (the you *attitude).*   Explain the situation honestly. Perhaps you are trying to develop an improved delivery or packaging program which will eventually produce a better product for the respondents. Or perhaps you want to improve your use of computers, so as to lower your costs and pass the savings on to consumers.

Inject a personal tone.   Research substantiates the value of making the cover letter seem personal. For example, add a handwritten signature or a handwritten postscript (it may be necessary to simulate this if a large mailing is planned), use the respondents' names in the salutation and/or body of the letter, and give the letter a conversational tone. Avoid obsolete phrases.

> *P.S.: Because you and others in this carefully selected sample have been long-time customers of Webster's Fashions, we are especially interested, Ms. Fenton, in your response to the enclosed questionnaire.*

Mention a due date for returning the questionnaire. Most of us tend to put things off. If we are asked to do something by a certain date, however, most of us will do it. Always give the due date in both the cover letter and the questionnaire.

> *So that we can begin our new, faster delivery service to you as quickly as possible, please return the completed questionnaire no later than August 3.*

Where possible, assure respondents of confidentiality or anonymity. If you feel that questionnaires will be discarded because potential respondents do not wish to divulge confidential information, or because they fear the embarrassment of being identified, take precautions. Sometimes a simple statement will significantly increase returns:

> *You may be sure that all the information you include will be kept completely confidential.*

> *Of course we don't want you to sign the questionnaire; we are interested only in your answers.*

Offer to send respondents the results of the survey—if that won't be too expensive or won't divulge findings you want to keep confidential. Most respondents are interested in or working in the field with which the study is concerned. If you tell respondents you will send them a copy of your findings, you may encourage them to complete the questionnaire. You can maintain their anonymity by including a postcard, addressed to you, which the respondents may return separately from the questionnaire. Or you can suggest that they "write to the address above anytime after December 3 for a copy of the survey."

In the sample letters shown in Figures 16–6 through 16–9; notice that most of the recommendations just described were followed.

Rewards encourage responses.

Motivating the prospective respondent. Research directors have found that giving prospective respondents a "reward" usually significantly increases the percentage of completed questionnaires returned. A coupon that may be traded for a package of the company's product, a ballpoint pen, or a crisp dollar bill ("to be passed on to your favorite charity") are some of the devices used (see Figure 16–7). Interestingly, a study showed that a promised contribution of one dollar to "your favorite charity" drew a higher response than a promise of the same amount to the respondent.[2]

Sometimes attachments to the cover letters can save the researchers a significant amount of money overall. Let's say that 5,000 questionnaires are sent out, each of which costs 60 cents (printing, folding, postage, and such). If 400 completed questionnaires are received, the cost per completed questionnaire will be $7.50. If, on the other hand, 2,000 are mailed, each of which has an enclosure (cost per questionnaire: 60 cents plus 25 cents) and 550 are received, the unit cost will drop to about $3 including the expense of the coin. Thus if premiums can significantly increase the percentage of response, they can result in a less-expensive survey. However, they should always be used with caution. Some prospective respondents may consider them unethical. Also, there is the danger that respondents who accept the coin or coupon may answer the questionnaire as they think the researcher desires, rather than as they honestly feel.

FIGURE 16–6 Cover Letter to Questionnaire

University of
New Orleans
SHAPING OUR FUTURE

Department of Management

New Orleans   August 12, 19__

Louisiana 70148

(504) 555-6481

Norman B. Sigband
3109 Dona Susana Drive
Studio City, CA 91604

Dear Norman:

You have been identified as a coauthor of one or more articles published in the ABC Journal or Bulletin during the last seven-year period. Because you have coauthorship experience, will you please take a few minutes to respond to the enclosed questionnaire? Your opinions and insight are valuable to a current study of collaboration among business communication professionals.

As you know, collaboration has become a central theme in business communication. In response to a need for team skills among workers entering the work force, collaborative assignments are currently being promoted among all disciplines, including business communication. Collaboration offers some distinct advantages to the academician as well, and the incidence of collaborative research seems to be on the rise across disciplines.

The contribution of this research will be the development of a profile of the typical business communication coauthor and the pooling of information about collaboration that may be of value to other business communication authors and researchers. Findings will be presented at the ABC annual convention in Honolulu, November 27 through December 1, 19__.

Therefore, will you please take a few moments to complete and return the questionnaire by August 30, 19__; the anonymity of your response is assured.

Sincerely,

Debbie D. DuFrene
Beverly H. Nelson

Enclosure

FIGURE 16–7   Cover Letter to Questionnaire with Incentive to Increase Response Rate

▲▲▲▲▲▲▲▲
FIELD FRESH
FOOD PRODUCTS

92000 INDUSTRY CENTER
COVINGTON, LA 70432
1-555-229-3500

QUALITY SINCE 1920

Dear Consumer:

For 70 years, Field Fresh has brought quality canned fruits and vegetables to your food-mart's shelves. In all that time, we have provided the consumer with high-quality products at competitive prices.

Next year, we will enter the fresh-frozen food market with a line of products. To meet your specific needs as to (1) product, (2) package size, and (3) price, we need your help.

Please complete the enclosed short questionnaire to tell us your preferences. We want to fill your needs to the best of our ability. We wish to offer exactly what you want, in the sizes you want, and at prices you feel are attractive.

Because we have selected a relatively small sample of consumers, your reply is especially important. Please complete and return the questionnaire in the stamped envelope enclosed prior to September 15.

Thank you so much for your cooperation.

Sincerely yours,

Janet Jensen
Marketing Research Director

P.S.: For your returned questionnaire, Field Fresh will donate a case of canned fruit to your local shelter for the homeless.

FIGURE 16–8   Cover Letter with Incentive

Simmons Market Research Bureau, Inc.

April 25, 19__

Dear Survey Member:

Please help make our 21st annual TV and radio study a success. Your experience will help us to better understand viewing and listening habits in all parts of the United States.

Whether you watch TV or listen to radio a little or a lot, we need to hear from you. You have been selected to represent people like yourself. This was done according to scientific research procedures and we are not permitted to make substitutions. Your cooperation is, therefore, most important to the success of the study and will be most appreciated. Please be assured that all the information you provide is used only in a statistical form.

The TV diary and the radio diary we mentioned in the letter we sent you about ten days ago are enclosed.

We have only a limited time to complete our 19__ study and so we are asking participants to keep their TV diary for specific two-week periods. Kindly start your diary on *Monday, May 2* and go through *Sunday, May 15.*

Please note that we are interested only in the programs you yourself watch in your own home. If on a particular day you did not watch TV, there's a place to tell us. Please answer the questions on the cover page. As an aid, some instructions are printed in the TV diary.

On each of the two days printed in your radio diary please fill in all the listening you do. We would like to know about your listening to, or hearing a radio played, in your own home, in a car or anywhere else.

On *Monday, May 16* please mail us your completed TV diary and your completed radio diary in the enclosed pre-addressed return envelope. No stamp is necessary.

Thank you for your help,

Frank Stanton

Frank Stanton
President

FS:npd
Enclosures

P.S. Within four weeks after receiving your completed TV and radio diaries, we will mail your
$5 check for your thoughtfulness. Meanwhile, please accept this $1 bill as a token of our
appreciation.

SMRB 219 East 42 Street, New York, NY 10017 (212) 555-1414

FIGURE 16–9   Cover Letter to Questionnaire Appealing to Respondents' Sense of Altruism

42nd and Dewey Avenue
Omaha, NE

**University
of Nebraska
Medical Center**

College of Pharmacy
Department of Pharmacy Practice

Dear Pharmacy Educator:

Impairment due to substance abuse can devastate many lives, including faculty members. Unfortunately, efforts to prevent and treat impairment in pharmacy faculty members suffer from a lack of relevant data. To meet this need, researchers from the University of Nebraska College of Pharmacy, in cooperation with the American Association of Colleges of Pharmacy,* are surveying pharmacy faculty nationwide to identify attitudes and patterns of faculty alcohol and drug usage. We are asking your help in this effort and hope you will take 15 to 20 minutes to complete and return the enclosed questionnaire. We hope you will find it interesting and thought provoking.

Please review the "Informed Consent Form" and complete and mail the number-encoded postcard to indicate your decision regarding participation. **Participants are asked to list responses to the questionnaire on the computerized answer sheet as instructed, and return this (separate from the number-encoded card) in the postage-paid envelope.** If you wish to provide comments to supplement your responses, please do so on the enclosed comments sheet and enclose it in the return envelope with the answer sheet. Responses are anonymous; please do not indicate your name or address on any material you are returning.

Your cooperation is voluntary. However, we hope that as a pharmacy educator, you will respond frankly and as completely as possible. Your participation is important since a high response rate is necessary to ensure the validity of any population-based research.

Thank you for your cooperation.

Sincerely,

Jeffrey N. Baldwin, Pharm.D.
Associate Professor

*Funded through an AACP GAPS Grant, 1988–1989.

University of Nebraska-Lincoln   University of Nebraska at Omaha   University of Nebraska Medical Center

**WRITING
AND SPEAKING
EXERCISES**

1. Visit a reference librarian and discuss research strategies and opportunities available at your campus. Prepare a short written report to share the results of your research with others.

2. Conduct a survey of students on your campus to determine the level of their knowledge about research strategies and opportunities available at your campus library. Compare the results obtained in your survey with the information contained in the report written for question 1. What conclusions do you reach about the degree and accuracy of student knowledge with regard to research assistance at your school's library? Prepare a memo to your reference librarian, explaining your conclusions.

3. Working in a group of three to five members, research more fully the legal considerations of business research and the law. Choose any one of the considerations presented in the "Legal Consideration" section, which follows these exercises. Prepare an oral presentation that describes the results of your group's research.

4. Write survey questions that will produce the type of response specified.
   (a) Structured responses: a question on soft drink preferences; a question on sleeping garments; a question on automobile colors.
   (b) Unstructured responses: a question on clerk friendliness; a question on company image; a question on customer loyalty.

5. For each of the following topics, suggest three sources you would use in beginning your search for useful information. Make use of the list of sources that appears in the supplement to this chapter.
   (a) Financial information about a major corporation
   (b) Recent books on economic theory
   (c) U.S. government publications on agriculture

6. Define and give examples of a "descriptor term" used in computer searches.

7. Certain words should be avoided in questionnaires. In addition to the examples cited in the text, list six words you would recommend banning from questionnaires.

8. Assume that most students on your campus are apathetic about student government and its role. Develop a cover letter that will accompany a mail questionnaire aimed at determining why the students are uninterested in their government.

9. Secure a questionnaire, preferably one that is not more than two pages long. Evaluate it thoroughly, basing your judgments, in part, on the standards for questionnaires described in this chapter. You may wish to organize your comments along the lines of 1) design and content of questions, 2) logic of organization, and 3) the format of the questionnaire.

10. Evaluate each question posed in (a) through (i) below and state whether or not it should appear in a questionnaire. Defend your choice of keeping or discarding the question.
    (a) Do you often purchase items other than gas and oil at service stations?
    (b) How much money did you make last year?
    (c) Consider the following attitudes toward movie theatres:
        A. too expensive   B. too crowded
        C. too dirty   D. too little parking

Which of the following attitudes reflects your own?

A and B are true	B and C are true	A, B, C are true
B only is true	C and D are true	A, B, D are true
C only is true	A and C are true	A, C, D are true
D only is true	A and D are true	B, C, D are true
A and B are true	B and D are true	A, B, C, D are true

(d) Express in writing your viewpoint on the harassment and domination of women in business.

(e) Would you favor a greater choice in yogurt flavors, even if it meant a slightly higher price?

(f) Do you usually select fruit that has not been artificially ripened?

(g) To begin this questionnaire, we want to know if you consider the automobile you now own, or one you have owned in the recent past (within the past five years), to be something more than mere transportation for you or members of your family who must commute to work or school.

(h) If you responded with numbers 1 or 4 to question 3, proceed to Section II. If you responded with either numbers 2 or 3, do not go on to Section II, but instead turn the page to Section III and continue with question 4 on that page.

(i) How many times have you attended a movie in the past three years? How many times have you listened to a compact disk in the past six months? How many times have you listened to a radio broadcast of music for more than 30 minutes in the past two years?

11. Asking a question such as the following one, "What type of soup do you prefer?" can result in a wide variety of answers. Take the intent of the inquiry and develop a question that will result in uniform and useful data.

12. A former professor has hired you to aid in some research. For the course the professor teaches, students are required to do a considerable amount of studying in the college library. However, the professor is not pleased with student performance. Your job is to use observation research to determine how students are studying. Then you are to make recommendations on what can be done to improve student performance. In some detail, explain how you will implement the research.

13. Develop a short questionnaire to assess preferences in ice cream. Do respondents favor cones or paper cups? What flavors? What brands? With what frequency do they buy? Administer the questionnaire to a specific demographic sample of 25 people. Tabulate your results.

14. Collect as much information as possible on computer-assisted database searches available through your college. What must the researcher provide? How much does it cost? How long will it take? What does the researcher eventually receive? Draw up a short guide to computer-aided research for use by your classmates.

READINGS

See "The Knowledge-Creating Company" in the Readings section at the back of this book.

SUGGESTED RESOURCES

Duhan, D., and Wilson, R. "Prenotification and Industrial Survey Response." *Industrial Marketing Management.* (May 1990).

Hubbard, R., and Little, E. "Cash Prizes and Mail Survey Response Rates: A Threshold Analysis. *Journal of the Academy of Marketing Science.* 16, (Fall 1988).

Klein, E. "What You Can—and Can't—Learn from Focus Groups." *D and B Reports.* 37, (July-August 1989).

Miller, R. "The Design and Implementation of Employee Opinion Surveys." *Employment Relations Today.* (Winter 1989).

Murphy, P., Dalenberg, D.R., and Daley, J. "Improving Survey Responses with Postcards." *Industrial Marketing Management.* 19, (November 1990).

Roberson, M.T., and Sundstrom, E. "Questionnaire Design, Response Rates and Response Favorableness in an Employee Attitude Questionnaire." *Journal of Applied Psychology. 75, (June 1990).*

LEGAL CONSIDERATIONS

BUSINESS RESEARCH AND THE LAW

Legislation protecting individual's rights to privacy and fair treatment govern managerial communication about customers and employees.

To what information do you have a legal right? The answer to that question differs dramatically depending on whether you seek data from private or public sources.

Privately Held Information

The Fair Credit Reporting Act of 1970 (Title VI of the Consumer Credit Protection Act) restricts access to information about your financial and employment history. Credit reporting agencies are required by this legislation to tell you the names and addresses of those to whom information is reported. Any organization reporting secondhand information or making subjective statements about your credit has the legal responsibility under Title VI to

- provide protection from false information.
- inform you of communication regarding your credit.
- allow access to you to your own credit information.

The Equal Credit Opportunity Act (ECOA), as amended in 1988, prohibits discriminatory use of information relating to a person's sex, marital status, race, color, religion, or national origin. In addition, ECOA legislation restricts the use of information regarding public assistance received by credit applicants or rights they have exercised under the Federal Consumer Credit Protection Act.

Libel and slander laws further constrain the release of subjective judgments about people's actions and characters, even in such areas as recommendation letters. If an employee asks for a letter of recommendation from you, remember that you may be subject to suit if, in the employee's view, your letter misrepresents his or her abilities or character. Specific damages to be awarded to the employee could be substantial wages supposedly lost as a result of your letter.

Because of such cases, fewer negative recommendation letters are written today than in previous decades. Instead, managers choose a "code language" of less-than-enthusiastic but nonactionable euphemisms. Words like "capable," "diligent," and "steady" can be used to describe an unmotivated low performer. Managers sometimes decline the request for a recommendation letter altogether, or ask that a waiver be signed by the employee, foregoing his or her right to see your letter.

Your ability to seek information from private sources, therefore, is often a matter of law, not simply what the private source will permit.

Publicly Held Information

Legislation ensuring the public's right to know requires public institutions to disclose sensitive information.

Much more legislation guides the handling of information by public institutions. The Freedom of Information Act of 1966 permits individuals greater access to records maintained by the federal government. As amended in 1974, the legislation defines what kind of information the government must release and in what time frame the delivery of information must occur.

One result of "sunshine" legislation such as the Privacy Act of 1974 and the Family Education Rights and Privacy Act of 1974 has been the discovery of many sensitive business secrets. The many forms and registrations that must be filed by companies large and small are now, in large part, available for public scrutiny—including the eyes of competitors. One difficult task for security-conscious managers is how to meet governmental filing requirements without giving away valuable or sensitive company secrets.

As a case in point, until 1980 the reprimands, orders, and instructions of bank regulators to banks under their scrutiny were hidden from the public. But late in that year the Consumers Union, acting under the Freedom of Information Act, successfully sued three bank regulators for release of consent agreements and cease-and-desist orders to banks. For the first time, consumers were able to read and evaluate those agencies' orders and to make their banking decisions accordingly.

The cumulative result of such legislation and court action has been the elimination of most "secret files" from government agencies. Managers of those agencies are now forced to make a regular review of what kinds of information they hold on file. Private sector managers, at the same time, have become more cautious about information they release to such "transparent" government files. An ongoing struggle continues between the need for "sunshine" freedom of information vs. the understandable desire of companies to protect their product and marketing secrets.

For state and federal agencies, the degree to which files and facilities must be made available to the public was defined in the Equal Access Act (1984) and further interpreted by the Supreme Court on June 4, 1990. Later that month, on June 21, the Supreme Court ruled that editorial statements in print media, television, and radio were not automatically exempted by the First Amendment from libel lawsuits.

ENDNOTES

1. Richard E. Miller, "The Design and Implementation of Employee Opinion Surveys," *Employment Relations Today* (Winter 1989):315.
2. R. Hubbard and E. L. Little, "Cash Prizes and Mail Survey Response Rates: A Threshold Analysis," *Journal of the Academy of Marketing Science* (Fall 1988):42–43.

A RESEARCH SUPPLEMENT*

The pages that follow include general comments on each secondary source category and a basic listing of useful reference guides. Because the scope of business research is often global, a section on guides to international information has also been included. Most titles in this listing are available online and/or on CD-ROM.

GUIDES TO BOOKS AND BOOK REVIEWS

GUIDES TO BOOKS

Books in Print. New York, R. R. Bowker Co. 1948 to present.
   Issued annually, this guide lists books currently in print (with a few exceptions such as Bibles) in the United States. Entries include author, title, price, and publisher. Author, title, and publisher indexes appear in separate volumes. *Books in Print Supplement* (beginning in 1973) appears midyear between annual issues. *Books in Print Online* includes reviews.

Business and Economics Books and Serials in Print. New York, R. R. Bowker Co. 1990.
   This comprehensive bibliography of books and serials provides access to more than 50,000 books and 7,500 periodicals in all areas of business and economics. Full bibliographic data and thorough author and/or title and subject indexing are provided for each entry. *Books in Print* and *Subject Guide to Books in Print* also list these same books along with other volumes on nonbusiness topics.

Cumulative Book Index: A World List of Books in the English Language. Bronx, N.Y., H. W. Wilson Co. 1928 to present.
   Issued monthly (except August) and cumulated at intervals with eventual permanent cumulations, this index lists books published in the English language throughout the world. Entries are arranged by author, title, and subject. Each cumulation includes a list of publishers.

National Union Catalog. Washington, D.C., Library of Congress, Card Division. 1942 to present.
   Printed monthly with cumulations quarterly, annually, and every five years, this catalog includes works cataloged by the Library of Congress and by other major North American libraries. Entries are indexed by author. Coverage has varied through the years.

Subject Guide to Books in Print. New York, R. R. Bowker Co. 1957 to present.
   Books currently in print in the United States, as listed in *Books in Print,* are presented annually under Library of Congress subject headings.

GUIDES TO BOOK REVIEWS

Book Review Digest. Bronx, N.Y., H. W. Wilson Co. 1905 to present.
   Issued monthly (except February and July) and cumulated annually, this publication lists books reviewed in more than 80 periodicals. Arranged

---

*The authors are indebted to Elizabeth H. Wood, MSLS, Head, Reference section, Norris Medical Library, University of Southern California, for her review, editing, and additions to this research supplement.

by author, entries include quotations from a few reviews and citations to others. Subject and title indexes are included.

Book Review Index. Detroit, Mich., Gale Research Inc. 1965 to present. Issued bimonthly and cumulated annually, this index covers more than 380 periodicals in a wide range of disciplines. Citations are listed under the author reviewed with full title index in each issue. *Book Review Index 1969–1979: A Master Cumulation* provides access in a single alphabetical sequence to 11 years of material.

Current Book Review Citations. Bronx, N.Y., H. W. Wilson Co. 1976 to present. Published monthly and cumulated annually, this comprehensive index includes more than 1,200 book-reviewing periodicals and subject periodicals in all major fields including business, the humanities, and the sciences. Entries are arranged by author and indexed by title.

GUIDES TO PERIODICALS, NEWSPAPERS, AND OTHER SERIALS

GENERAL GUIDES

Gale Directory of Publications and Broadcast Media. Detroit, Mich., Gale Research Inc. 1990 to present.
Issued annually with a semiannual *Update,* this descendant of the *Ayer Directory* covers 36,000 newspapers, periodicals, radio and television stations, and cable systems in the United States and Canada. It is organized by state or province and city. Entries for newspapers and periodicals include circulation statistics, rates, names of publishers, size of page, and so forth. Entries for radio and television stations include format, owner, operating hours, wattage, and rates. There are many indexes and a comprehensive collection of maps showing locations of the publications and media.

National Directory of Newsletters. Robert C. Thomas, ed. Detroit, Mich., Gale Research Inc. 1978–91.
Issued in four parts, each part contains about 750 entries with vital information about newsletters issued on a regular basis by businesses, associations, societies, clubs, government agencies, and other groups.

Standard Periodical Directory. New York, Oxbridge Communications, Inc. 1964 to present.
Issued annually, this classified directory provides subject access to more than 66,680 U.S. and Canadian periodicals. Entries, which include subscription rate, circulation, and basic advertising rate, are indexed alphabetically.

PERIODICAL INDEXES

Business Periodicals Index. Bronx, N.Y., H. W. Wilson Co. 1958 to present. Issued monthly (except August) and cumulated annually, this basic subject index for the business field covers about 275 periodicals in all business-related fields such as finance, labor relations, insurance, management, and advertising. For materials prior to 1958, use the *Industrial Arts Index.*

Engineering Index Monthly and Author Index. New York, Engineering Index, Inc. 1896 to present.
This monthly index (formerly *Engineering Index*) provides abstracting and indexing services for the world's engineering literature. Data from

technical magazines, government bureaus, and research laboratories are recorded as well as abstracts of reports, book reviews, and articles. This index is available online as *Compendex.*

F&S Index United States. Cleveland, Ohio, Predicasts, Inc. 1960 to present.
Issued weekly and cumulated monthly, quarterly, and annually, this index provides a brief summary of articles from about 1,200 published sources reporting U.S. business and technical events. It is a companion index to *F & S Index International* and *F & S Index Europe.* Entries are arranged in two parts: part one, by SIC number or product; and part two, by company. Major articles are designated by a black spot preceding the journal title. This index is available online from *Predicasts.*

Index of Economic Articles. Homewood, Ill., Richard D. Irwin, Inc. 1965 to present.
This index (formerly *Index of Economic Journals*) lists articles in English for more than 140 principal economic journals of various countries. Coverage varies: vol. 1, 1886–1924; vol. 2, 1925–1939; vol. 3, 1940–1949; vol. 4, 1950–1954; vol. 5, 1955–1959; vol. 6, 1960–1963; vol. 6A, 1960–1963 Collective Volumes; vol. 7, 1964–1965; vol. 7A, 1964–1965. Collective Volumes; and vol. 8, 1966. Frequency is annual after 1966. Arranged by a detailed classification scheme, citations are full and precise with an author index in each volume. Beginning with vol. 6A, coverage includes collective volumes such as Festschriften, conference reports and papers, and collected essays.

Ulrich's International Periodicals Directory. New York, R. R. Bowker, Co. 1965 to present.
Issued annually with quarterly updates, this comprehensive directory to 126,000 of the world's journals is organized by subject and indexed by title. Entries include full subscription information, editors, circulation, where the title is indexed, and descriptive details.

Readers' Guide to Periodical Literature. Bronx, N.Y., H. W. Wilson Co. 1900 to present.
Issued semimonthly (except monthly in February, July, and August), this index provides author and subject access to about 190 popular periodicals. This valuable guide contains references to articles in a broad range of fields.

Social Science Index. Bronx, N.Y., H. W. Wilson Co. 1974 to present.
Issued quarterly and cumulated annually, this index (which supersedes in part, the *Social Science and Humanities Index*) provides author and subject access to articles in more than 275 journals. Subject areas covered include anthropology, area studies, economics, environmental science, geography, law and criminology, planning and public administration, political science, psychology, sociology, and related topics. An author listing of citations to book reviews follows the main body of the index.

MORE SPECIALIZED INDEXES

Accountants' Index. New York, American Institute of Certified Public Accountants. 1920 to present.
Issued quarterly and cumulated annually, this index provides author, title, and subject access to English-language journals, books, and govern-

ment documents in accounting and related fields. Frequency of earlier volumes varies.

Index to Legal Periodicals. Bronx, N.Y., H. W. Wilson Co. 1908 to present.
Published monthly and cumulated annually, this index covers 417 major legal periodicals in all areas of jurisprudence. This three-part index includes a subject and author index, a table of cases, and a book-review index.

Management Contents. Northbrook, Ill., Management Contents, Inc. 1975 to present.
Issued biweekly, this guide reproduces the tables of contents from about 285 of the best U.S. and foreign business journals, proceedings, and transactions.

Social Sciences Citation Index. Philadelphia, Pa., Institute for Scientific Information. 1972 to present.
Issued three times a year with the third issue cumulating the year, this international, multidisciplinary index covers more than 1,500 journals and 200 books in the social, behavioral, and related sciences. It enables the user to identify related writings by indication of sources in which a known work by a given author has been cited. The "Permuterm Subject Index" provides subject access. Available online as *Social Sci-search.*

NEWSPAPER INDEXES

Gale Directory of Publications and Broadcast Media. Detroit, Mich., Gale Research Inc. 1990 to present.
Issued annually with a semiannual *Update,* this descendant of the *Ayer Directory* covers some 36,000 newspapers, periodicals, radio and television stations, and cable systems in the United States and Canada. It is organized by state or province and city. Entries for newspapers and periodicals include circulation statistics, rates, names of publishers, size of page, and so forth. Entries for radio and television stations include format, owner, operating hours, wattage, and rates. There are many indexes and a comprehensive collection of map showing locations of the publications and media (also listed on page 382).

National Newspaper Index. Foster City, Calif., Information Access Company (IAC). 1979 to present.
This online index to five major national newspapers covers world affairs, politics, business, and other subjects. Sources are *The New York Times,* the eastern and western editions of *The Wall Street Journal,* the national edition of *The Christian Science Monitor,* the final edition of the *Washington Post,* and the home edition of *The Los Angeles Times.*

*Newsearch.*Foster City, Calif., Information Access Company (IAC). Most recent two to six weeks.
More than 2,000 publications are included in this online indexing and abstracting service. Each month, as new items are added, older material is transferred to one of several IAC databases such Computer Database, Legal Resource Index, Magazine Index, Management Contents, National Newspaper Index, Newswire ASAP, and *Trade & Industry Index.*

Newspaper Abstracts. Ann Arbor, Mich., University Microfilms International. 1984 to present.
More than 20 major newspapers, regional, national, and international, are indexed with abstracts in this online service. Subjects include

current events, business and economic trends, and political and governmental issues.

GUIDES TO GOVERNMENT DOCUMENTS

GENERAL GUIDES

Andriot, John L., ed. *Guide to U.S. Government Publications,* McLean, Va., Documents Index. 1973 to present.

This annotated guide (formerly *Guide to U.S. Government Serials and Periodicals*) lists publications of the various U.S. government agencies. Volume 1 lists those publications in existence as of January 1, 1975; volume 2 covers publications of abolished agencies and discontinued publications; volume 3 contains a detailed description of the SuDoc classification scheme and agency chronology.

Monthly Catalog of United States Government Publications. Washington, D.C., Superintendent of Documents. 1895 to present.

This monthly index to public documents is issued by the U.S. Government Printing Office (GPO), the world's largest publisher. This index is organized by subject and indexed by title keywords. There is an annual *Series Supplement.* Order numbers are provided.

U.S. CATALOGS, INDEXES, AND BIBLIOGRAPHIES

CIS/Index. Washington, D.C., Congressional Information Service, Inc. 1970 to present.

Published monthly and cumulated quarterly and annually, this source provides access to U.S. congressional publications and legislation. Coverage includes both depository and nondepository committee hearings and prints; House and Senate reports, documents, and special publications; and Senate executive reports and documents. Issued in two parts; part one is an index of briefly annotated entries corresponding to full document descriptions in part two.

Federal Index. Cleveland, Ohio, Predicasts, Inc. 1977 to present.

Issued annually, this index is divided into three sections allowing subject access by government agency, by government function, or by affected industries, persons, institutions, or countries. Coverage includes more than 60,000 key articles appearing in the *Congressional Record,* and *Federal Register,* and the *Weekly Compilation of Presidential Documents.* Entries include government agency involved, action taken or proposed, citation to U.S. Code, code of *Federal Register,* and so on, and journal abbreviation, date, and page reference. Available online on the *Predicasts Terminal System.*

Selected United States Government Publications. U.S. Superintendent of Documents. Washington, D.C., Government Printing Office.

Issued monthly, this annotated guide lists new publications for sale by the U.S. Government Printing Office as well as important older publications still in stock.

GUIDES TO U.S. STATISTICAL SOURCES

GENERAL GUIDES
AND INDEXES

American Statistics Index. Washington, D.C., Congressional Information
Service, Inc. 1974 to present.
Published monthly and cumulated quarterly and annually, this comprehensive guide provides access to data in more than 7,000 statistical
publications of the U.S. government. Coverage includes every type of
U.S. government document, regardless of depository status, whether
issued by the U.S. Government Printing Office or an individual agency.
This index is published in two parts: part one is an index of briefly
annotated entries corresponding to full document descriptions in part
two. This is a companion service to *Statistical Reference Index.*
Statistical Reference Index. Washington, D.C., Congressional Information
Service, Inc. 1980 to present.
Published monthly and cumulated quarterly and annually, this companion service to *American Statistics Index* includes significant statistical
publications from more than 1,000 non-U.S. government associations
and institutes. Topics covered include business, industry, finance, and
economic and social conditions. The index is published in two parts:
part one is an index of briefly annotated entries corresponding to full
document descriptions in part two.

COMPREHENSIVE
STATISTICAL
COMPILATIONS

Standard & Poor's Statistical Service. New York, Standard & Poor's Corp.
1941 to present.
Issued monthly and cumulated annually, this service provides statistical
time series in the following areas: banking and finance, production and
labor prices indexes; income and trade; building and building materials;
transportation and communications; electric power and fuels; metals;
autos, rubber, and tires; textiles; chemicals; paper; agricultural products;
and securities prices.
Statistical Abstract of the United States. U.S. Bureau of the Census. Washington, D.C., Government Printing Office. 1978 to present.
Issued annually, this guide serves both as the prime source for U.S.
industrial, social, political, and economic statistics and as a bibliographic guide. The majority of tables are national in scope, providing
one or two years of consecutive annual data. Source notes are given
at the foot of each table. The "Guide to Sources and Statistics" section
lists important statistical publications by subject including a descriptive list of recent census publications. The *Statistical History of the
United States from Times to the Present* (New York: Basic Books, 1976)
serves as a historical supplement to *Statistical Abstract.*

BASIC SPECIALIZED
COMPILATIONS

Business Statistics. U.S. Bureau of Economic Analysis. Washington, D.C.,
Government Printing Office. 1951 to present.
Issued as a supplement to *Survey of Current Business,* this publication
provides a historical record of the more than 2,500 statistical series
appearing in the *Survey.* Tables give annual averages, beginning with
1947, and monthly figures for the most recent five years. Sources,
references, and explanatory notes are included.

Handbook of Labor Statistics. U.S. Bureau of Labor Statistics. Washington, D.C., Government Printing Office. 1924–26 to present.
This compendium of major BLS statistics provides figures for as many years as they have been compiled. Statistics given include those for the labor force, employment, unemployment, productivity, prices and living conditions, and foreign labor statistics.

GUIDES TO DIRECTORIES

GENERAL GUIDES

Guide to American Directories. New York, B. Klein Publications. 1960 to present.
Arranged by subject, this directory includes more than 6,000 major industrial and professional directories. Entries include description and price and are indexed alphabetically. Industrial directories are listed under the "Manufacturers" heading.

BASIC U.S. COMPANY DIRECTORIES

Directory of American Firms Operating in Foreign Countries. New York, Simon & Schuster. 1907 to present.
Dun & Bradstreet, Inc. Million Dollar Directory. New York, Dun & Bradstreet, Inc. 1959 to present.
Issued annually, this three-volume directory lists over 120,000 U.S. companies with an indicated worth of $500,000 to $1 million or more. Volume 1 covers 49,000 of the top companies ranked by net worth; volumes 2 and 3 cover the remaining companies (many of them privately held). Entries include names of officers and directors, products or services, SIC number, approximate sales, and number of employees. Each volume contains a complete alphabetical index to all companies in the set. Entries within each volume are also indexed by geographical location and by industry.
National Minority Business Information System: A National Directory of Minority- and Women-Owned Firms. Emeryville, Calif., Source Publications. 1981 to present.
Reference Book of Corporate Managements. New York, Dun & Bradstreet. 1980 to present.
Standard & Poor's Register of Corporations, Directors and Executives. New York, Standard & Poor's Corp. 1928 to present.
This three-volume directory lists more than 37,000 U.S., Canadian, and major international corporations. Volume 1 is an alphabetical listing with information on officers, products or line of business, stock exchange listing, SIC number, sales range, and number of employees. Volume 2 lists executives and directors with a brief profile on each. Volume 3 contains an index of companies by SIC and by location, a list of companies and a list of executives added for the first time, and an obituary section.
Thomas Register of American Manufacturers and Thomas Register Catalog File. New York, Thomas Publishing Company. 1905/06 to present.
This multivolume work has three parts: a subject index of products and manufactured goods, company profiles, and company catalogs.
Try Us. National Minority Business Directory. Minneapolis, Minn., National Minority Business Campaign. 1975 to present.

COMPUTERIZED INFORMATION SYSTEMS/DATABASES

Computerized information systems place mountains of information at your fingertips. You or your library can subscribe to various online database sources to secure continuously updated news reports, stock quotations, bond listings, and other data. You can also get a list of most articles available on a topic you are researching. In other words, you can eliminate most of the tedious hours spent in manual research by using computerized databases. Think of the database as a computerized library organized in such a way that many users may secure what they wish quickly and easily.

In using a database, choose your *key words,* or *descriptors,* carefully. They are terms for which the computer searches. Select descriptors that are as specific as possible. For example, "international communications," would serve you better than "intercultural communication" if you were interested in business communication rather than aspects of verbal and nonverbal communication in various cultures.

Many databases have their own thesauri of descriptors. Using thesaurus terms rather than your own words makes searching more effective and efficient. Your reference librarian can help you select descriptor terms for your computer search.

Some database services such as a Dialog and BRS were designed to be used primarily by research specialists working in business, professional, and educational institutions. Online databases can be classified into three types:

Bibliographic databases direct you to articles, books, and other reference sources on a specific topic. You may search for items by using key words, dates, and authors' names. Summaries or abstracts (see Figure 16–1) of the sources cited are often available online. Some services also provide a copy of the full printed text for a fee. Dialog provides such a service.

Full-text databases place on your computer screen a full-text copy of an article or news story. Several databases having this capability are available from LEXIS, NEXIS, Dow Jones News Retrieval (DJNR), and NewsNet.

Source databases provide information on stockmarket quotations, airline schedules, physical and chemical properties of various items, and miscellaneous topics.

Various databases have been designed for professional use. Among these are LEXIS for lawyers, MEDLARS for medical specialists, and Data Resources, Inc. and DJNR for businesspeople. Dialog and BRS are vendors who provide access to a variety of databases such as Dow Jones, MEDLARS, and others. The number of databases is growing.

DATABASE SERVICES

The following are just a few of the more frequently used services:

BRS Information Technologies Maxwell Online
800 Westpark Drive
McLean, VA 22102
  Over 80 databases covering physical and social sciences, business, education, medicine
Data Resources, Inc. (DRI)
29 Hartwell Avenue
Lexington, MA 02173

Over 100 economic and financial databases, including demographic and stock market data.

Dialog Information Retrieval Service
3460 Hillview Avenue
Palo Alto, CA 94304-1396

Over 200 scientific, technological, general news, and business databases; abstracts and some full texts available

Dow Jones New Retrieval
P.O. Box 300
Princeton, NJ 08540

Full-text news from *The Wall Street Journal* and Dow Jones sources; emphasis on business and finance

LEXIS
Mead Data Control
9393 Springboro Pike
P.O. Box 933
Dayton, OH 45401

Federal and state laws, tax codes, specialty law

NEXIS
Mead Data Control
9393 Springboro Pike
P.O. Box 933
Dayton, OH 45401

Full-text articles from over 120 newspapers, magazines, and periodicals; NAARS is a database of annual reports and proxy statements

MEDLARS
National Library of Medicine
8600 Rockville Pike
Bethesda, MD 20209

Biomedical databases referencing international medical literature

GUIDES TO DATABASES AND INFORMATION SYSTEMS AND SERVICES

You can keep track of the hundreds of databases that are available with the following guides. They describe each database and indicate how it may be accessed.

Directory of Online Databases. Santa Monica, Calif., Cuadra Associates, Inc. 1979 to present.

Issued quarterly, this directory includes over 5,000 online bibliographic and nonbibliographic databases. Entries for databases include producer name, organization through which it is available, type and amount of information, geographical and chronological coverage, and frequency of updating. Entries are indexed by subject, database name, producer name, and online organization name.

Computer-readable Databases. 5th ed. Detroit, Mich., Gale Research Inc. 1989.

Encyclopedia of Information Systems and Services. Anthony T. Kruzas, ed. Detroit, Mich., Gale Research Inc. 1971 to present.

Issued biennially, this international guide includes about 2,000 organizations, including many in countries other than the United States. Types of organizations include computerized databases, SDI services, database publishers, clearing houses and information centers, library information networks, data collection and analysis centers, micrographic systems and services, and consulting research and coordinating agencies. Arranged alphabetically by organization or service and indexed in multiple ways, entries include description of system or service, input or data sources, microform or computer applications and services, and computer and information-processing equipment. The supplements are called *New Information Systems and Services.*

BUSINESS REFERENCE GUIDES

There are several guides to business reference sources. One that is recommended is *Business Information: How to Find and Use it,* 2nd ed. Oryx Press, Sparks, Nev., 1992. Your reference librarian can direct you to others.

17

VISUAL AIDS

Be alert to words that confuse and figures that lie.

A picture is worth a thousand words. For many readers in the 1990s a good visual aid can't be replaced by *any* number of words. As we find ourselves swamped in paper, primarily as a result of word processing technology, we look forward to easy-to-understand graphics in business communications. In fact, many of us give preference to visually enhanced documents.

Visual aids clarify complicated material and are a mainstay of effective communication in the 1990s.

Graphic representation tells a story directly. A well-designed chart, graph, or table can often convey a complex relationship more quickly and easily than can words. Have you ever tried to read a memo citing many different sums of money, tons of production, yearly changes in costs, or percentage differentials? You may plow through such a discussion several times without fully understanding it. Finally, you may resort to making a table or chart of your own that presents the numbers in a more meaningful way. How much better it would have been if the writer had supplied that visual aid in the first place!

COMPUTER GRAPHICS

Years ago, the computer was almost a status symbol for large corporations. Now it is a necessity for virtually every organization, large and small. The computer stores, retrieves, and outputs information not only on inventory, sales, payroll, and financial transactions, but on many other activities as well. Reports and more reports are generated by the computer, and the number continues to increase almost overwhelmingly. One reason for this increase is the refinement of laser technology, which has greatly increased the speed of the computer printer.

Overall, business has experienced a tremendous increase of available data. In many organizations the flow of information has become a flood. Reports seem to multiply and grow daily. They are filled with statistical data and information, but they are rarely read completely.

Computer graphics programs easily convert data into visual aids.

One advance in computer technology has improved the communication of computer-generated data. That innovation is computer graphics. Computer software now has the capability of automatically converting volumes of data into easy-to-assimilate visual aids. These graphic representations are made by six-color pen plotters, electrostatic plotters, graphic-colored cathode-ray-tube terminals (CRTs), and digitizing boards. Pie charts, organizational charts, bar

FIGURE 17–1   Examples of Computer-generated Graphics

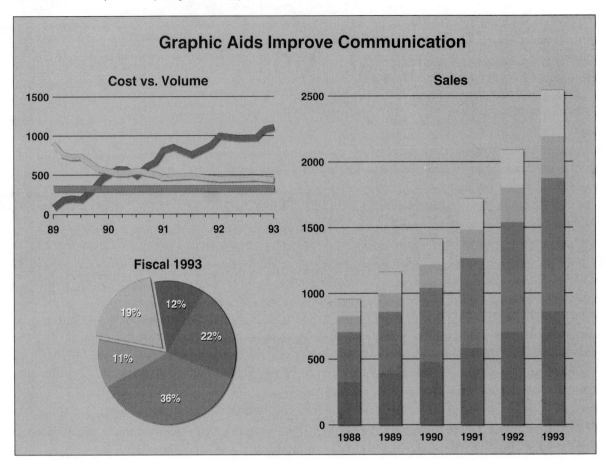

charts, and three-dimensional representations of almost anything, in virtually any color, can be produced through the use of computer graphics. Figure 17–1 shows examples of computer-generated graphics.

VALUE OF COMPUTER GRAPHICS

Graphics programs convert volumes of data into understandable form and help in the design and manufacture of new products.

The value of computer graphics cannot be overstated. Computers can convert enormous quantities of data into a graphic presentation that is not only easy to comprehend but also saves a great deal of time in decision making. Pages of data can be represented in a simple visual aid (see Figure 17–2).

Computer-assisted design and computer-assisted manufacturing (CAD/CAM) help engineers and product designers manufacture new items. Advertising art, architectural units, newspaper layouts, clothing patterns, auto designs—almost anything—can be drawn with computer assistance. Designers revise their work until the desired results are achieved. Then the designs are used by the computer system as it implements the final product.

HOW COMPUTER GRAPHICS WORK

The combination of *laser printers* and sophisticated software has enhanced the graphic capabilities of computers. The user who has a software package such as Harvard Professional Graphics, ChartMaster, or another, keys in data (number of units sold, performance levels over time, etc.). The software dis-

FIGURE 17–2   Computer-generated Graphic Representation of Statistical Information (Originals in Four Colors)

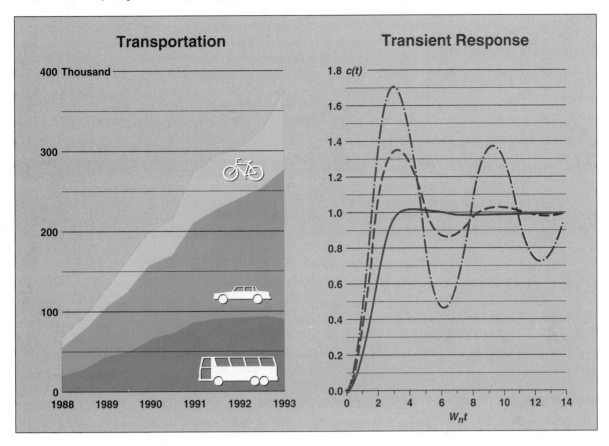

Software allows the user to experiment with and alternate graphic displays.

plays a menu of choices for the user. Typically, data can be displayed as a map, pie chart, bar chart, line graph, or combination graph in a variety of content-coded colors. The user can review several visual displays of the same data to determine which will best suit the intended use. Once the desired visual aid is selected, it can be printed out on a laser printer or stored within the computer for inclusion later within a document.

Another type of computer-generated visual aid relies on the *pen plotter* as the output device. The pen plotter can create large graphic images. Here's how it works.

Computer programs reduce data to a series of X- and Y-coordinates. The first XY-coordinate is the starting point, and the second coordinate becomes the ending point. The pen starts at the first point and draws a straight line until it reaches the second coordinate. This process continues until all data are plotted. Some lines are so short that when they are put together, they result in a circle. Different sets of XY-coordinates may be selected for different colors.

Pen plotters produce quality charts in a fraction of the time freehand drawing requires.

Six-pen as well as two-pen plotters are available, together with a wide range of graphics software. These plotters draw on paper (as large as 11 by 17 inches) or transparent film. They can draw up to 15 inches per second, and a top-quality chart can be produced in three to four minutes. Compare that with the time needed for freehand drawing! With the advent of *flat-screen monitors* (those with displays less than an inch thick), it will be possible to create computer graphics on the screen and then actually place the screen on a copying machine to transfer the image from the screen to paper.

Animated drawings help manufacturers visualize experimental products.

Animation has also become a part of computer graphics. Once a shape has been defined mathematically within the computer so that it can be rendered in three dimensions, that shape can be made to "move" through space on the screen as directed by the computer operator. In this way, a manufacturer, designer, or an engineer is able to view an animated portrayal of the product before it actually exists in a prototype model.

SELECTING GRAPHIC AIDS

Use graphics only when needed and never merely to impress.

Graphic aids should not be used only for cosmetic reasons. Their purpose is to clarify the data being presented. If they have no instructional function, they will only confuse the reader. At times, confusion is a deliberate goal; that is, some graphic aids are intended to misrepresent data. Refer to Chapter 5 for an extended discussion of this unethical practice.

DEFINING THE READER

Choose graphic aids that the reader will understand.

As in all phases of report writing, writers must consider the reader before choosing graphic aids. If a report is directed to a group of aerospace engineers, the charts, graphs, and tables used can be complex. But a logarithmic chart, for example, would not be appropriate in an annual report to stockholders. An illustration fulfills its purpose only if the reader finds it clear, informative, and easy to understand.

CHOOSING THE BEST GRAPHIC AID

Choose graphics imaginatively.

Report writers must also ask themselves this question: "What type of chart or table will best tell my story?" Some writers get in the habit of using a table for one type of representation and a bar chart for another; they adapt this pattern to almost every situation. They know the graphic aids well and can use them effectively, but they run the risk of not stretching their imaginations enough to determine if there might be a better way to present the data. If the readers are interested in *trends,* for example, a series of bars or a line graph may be useful. If, however, they are concerned with specifics and precise data, a table may be most appropriate.

DESIGNING THE CONTENT

Report writers must not only determine which type of graphic aid best presents their data, but they must also decide how complex or simple it should be in reference to the data and the reader. One reader is comfortable with five different information designations on one chart, for example, solid, broken, dotted, dashed, and dot-dash lines. Another reader requires five separate charts, because he or she doesn't have the interest, motivation, or background to analyze a single, complex visual aid.

AN EXAMPLE OF CHOICE AND DESIGN

Which is the best visual aid to represent the data contained in the following report paragraphs?

Twelve of our Star-Economy gasoline stations in the Chicago area were selected to check the effectiveness of the two display stands in generating sales. For purposes of the survey, the stations were designated with numbers from 1 to 12 (see Appendix A for number and address of each station).

The test was conducted from June 5 to June 10, and the total sales for three items were recorded: "Road Safety Flares, package of 4," Unit 201; "All-Purpose Med Kit," Unit 404; and "All-Purpose Wrench Kit," Unit 605.

Two different cases were used to display these three items for sale. Six of the cases were our regular 5-foot walnut with chrome-trim affairs, while the other six were newly manufactured by the Greeley Company. These were only 2-feet wide, constructed of heavy cardboard, and equipped with a continuously flashing red and yellow electric blinker. Stations 1, 4, 5, 7, 9, and 10 received the 5-foot case, and stations 2, 3, 6, 8, 11, and 12 the 2-foot case with blinkers.

Total sales of the three items during the six-day test period (Monday through Saturday) were as follows: Stores 1, 2, 3, and 4 sold 350, 820, 870, and 440 respectively. In stores 5, 6, 7, and 8 sales were recorded at 375, 950, 475, and 675 units. Sales of the same units in store 9 were 550; store 10, 525; store 11, 1150; store 12, 1050. It would certainly appear that there is a correlation between sales and type of display case. This correlation was also apparent in a similar survey conducted in Detroit early this year.

On the basis of the data given, you must decide whether to present *trends* in sales, *specific sales figures,* a combination of both, or a "picture" of the information (represented as a pictogram, a visual aid combining representational art with quantitative measures, which is discussed later in this chapter).

A quick review of the data tells you that the key is to be found in the question, "Which display case resulted in more sales?" Not, "Which station(s) had the greatest sales?" If you were to present the data as in Figure 17–3 you would not communicate very effectively. If you group the data by type of display case, as in Figure 17–4, however, the reader will see immediately what is important.

DESIGNING TABLES, GRAPHS, AND CHARTS

Understandable graphics give the message at a glance.

No matter what the graphic aid, three principles apply to its design:

1. Major points must be apparent to the reader in the first few seconds of viewing. A reader should not have to pore over a graphic aid to figure out what it means.
2. Colors, perspective, and other highlighting techniques should support the major points of a graphic aid. Attractiveness in and of itself is not an adequate rationale for graphic enhancement.
3. The complexity of the graphic aid should be determined by the abilities of the audience. A simple graph such as one in a newspaper may be appropriate for general readers but inappropriate for scientists.

Tables summarize data in rows and columns.

Designing tables.   As shown in Figure 17–5, a table is a summation of data according to column and row (or line) headings. In tables containing extensive data, the use of shading, boxing, or other highlighting techniques helps the reader locate the major points intended by the writer.

FIGURE 17–3   Poor Presentations of Identical Data in Tabular, Graph and Chart Form

Sales of Units 201, 404, and 605, June 5–10

Example 1

Station No.	Total Sales
1	350
2	820
3	870
4	440
5	385
6	950
7	475
8	675
9	550
10	525
11	1150
12	1050

Reflects specific data, though not effectively presented

Example 2

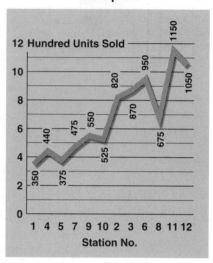

Reflects data

Example 3

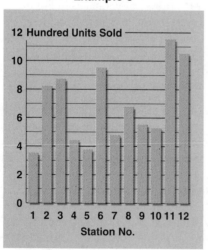

Reflects trend but difficult to assimilate

Example 4

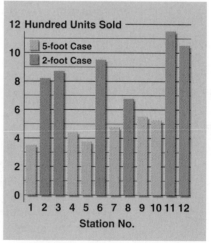

Reflects trend but is confusing

FIGURE 17–4   Satisfactory Presentations of Identical Data in Graph, Tabular, and Chart Form

Example 5

Station No.	5-foot Display Case	2-foot Display Case (Blinker)
1	350	
2		820
3		870
4	440	
5	375	
6		950
7	475	
8		675
9	550	
10	525	
11		1150
12		1050

Reflects specific data

Example 6

Station No.	5-foot Display Case	2-foot Display Case (Blinker)
1	350	
4	440	820
5	375	870
7	475	
9	550	
10	525	
2		820
3		870
6		950
8		675
11		1150
12		1050

Reflects specific data; distinguishes types

Example 7

Station No.	5-foot Display Case	Station No.	2-foot Display Case (Blinker)
1	350	2	820
4	440	3	870
5	375	6	950
7	475	8	675
9	550	11	1150
10	525	12	1050

Reflects specific data; well organized

Example 8

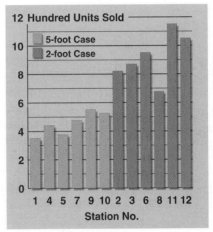

Reflects trend; well organized

Example 9

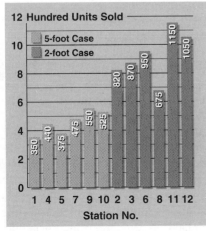

Reflects trend and cites specific data

Example 10

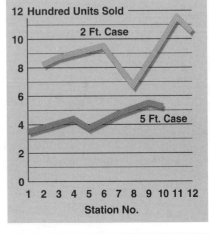

Reflects trend; subject to misinterpretation

FIGURE 17–5 Parts of a Table

TABLE 1 Title

Subhead	Multicolumn Head		Single-column Head	Single-column Head
	Subhead	Subhead[1]		
Line head	20	40	18	16
Line head				
Subhead	4	6	4	3
Subhead	3	4	2	5
Totals	27	50	24	24

Source: (footnote containing source of data in table)

[1]One or more superscripted numbers (or, alternately, single and double asterisks) are used to provide explanation or commentary on data items.

FIGURE 17–6 Parts of a Graph or Chart

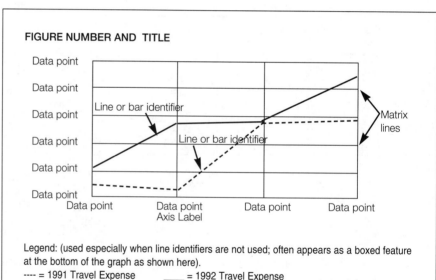

FIGURE NUMBER AND TITLE

Legend: (used especially when line identifiers are not used; often appears as a boxed feature at the bottom of the graph as shown here).
---- = 1991 Travel Expense ____ = 1992 Travel Expense

Source: (a footnote containing the source of data contained in the graph)

Designing graphs and charts. As shown in Figure 17–6, the parts of a graph or chart include the graph or chart title (often stated as a figure title), labels for the X- and Y-axes, labels for data points, and line or bar identifiers. (Sometimes a legend shows what different types or colors of lines represent). Matrix lines make the graph or chart easily interpretable for readers, so long as the lines do not clutter or obscure the graphic aid. Graphs and charts should not be over-complicated by too many lines or bars. As a general rule, use no more than three graph lines on a single graph. If your purpose and data require more lines, present them in separate but related graphs.

TABLES

What would your reaction be to the following paragraph encountered in a sales report for a large auto dealership?

January 1993 proved to be one of the best months ever. We sold 275 Cheetah pickups as compared to 250 in January 1991, amounting to a 10 percent increase. The popular GRS series saw a 5 percent jump in sales, with 220 in 1993 and 210 in 1991. Due to rising gasoline costs, the larger Deluxe line decreased slightly in sales (a 5 percent decrease), with 380 sold in 1993 and 400 in 1991.

Now compare the example above with the table in Figure 17–7. Can there be any question that a table is far superior to a series of sentences in communicating quantitative ideas? In addition, tables have many other advantages:

- Materials can be listed concisely.
- Reference to specific facts can be made quickly.
- Comparisons between and among statistics can be made easily.
- The reader can comprehend and assimilate quantitative data in tables much more quickly than if the same information were presented in paragraph form.

Follow this checklist whenever you construct a table:

- Head each vertical column clearly and concisely.
- Assign a number and a title to each table. Use subtitles, if necessary, to further clarify or explain.
- Place comparative data on a horizontal plane from left to right (the usual direction of the eyes in reading).
- Give fractions in decimals.
- Use standard terms throughout the table (yards, meters, and fathoms should be converted to a standard unit of measure and explained in a footnote).
- Design tables so that reading and understanding are easy by using rules carefully, white space generously, and titles clearly.

FIGURE 17–7   Statistical Table

AUTOMOBILE SALES

	January 1993	January 1992	Percentage Change
Cheetah	275	250	+10%
GRS	220	210	+5
Deluxe	380	400	–5

CHARTS AND GRAPHS

Charts and graphs show trends.

Charts, graphs, pictograms, and sketches present information dramatically and skillfully. With a glance at a bar or line chart, the reader can determine the trend of an activity. For example, have sales increased? declined? remained stationary? Has the gross national product gone up? If readers see a tiny money bag next to a bigger one, they will have their answer immediately.

Charts and pictograms do not contain the quantity of specific data found in a table, but then, their purpose is different. Trends, rather than precise data, are their concern.

PIE, OR CIRCLE, CHARTS

In pie charts, which give percentage breakdowns, the segmented pieces should be proportional to the percentage they represent.

The *pie chart* (also called *circle chart*) is one of the most commonly used visual aids. It is easy to interpret, does not require extensive artwork, and communicates its basic ideas with clarity and simplicity. Although each segment represents a different percentage, the total comes to 100 percent. The pie chart can be presented in a variety of ways. Some firms use a picture of their product to represent their "pie" and divide it into appropriate segments to represent cost of materials, salaries, depreciation, and so on. One electric company used a pie chart reflecting percentage and amounts to depict its distribution of revenue. See Figure 17–8.

A pie chart may contain all sorts of things, including falsehoods. Beware of the pie whose segments are labeled only in words, with no percentage figures. And be skeptical of the pie that has segments numbered consecutively

FIGURE 17–8   Pie (Circle) Chart

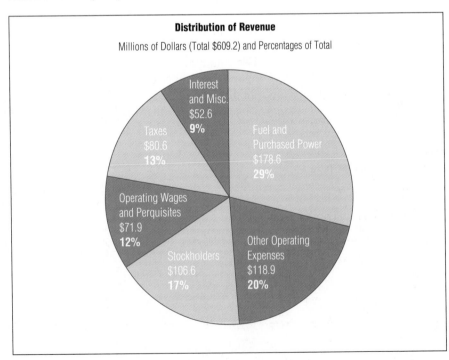

and explained at the bottom of the page. One of the most common ploys in the game of "lying with statistics" is the pie (or product) chart with out-of-proportion segments. Each segment in the pie chart should be identified and should show the percentage it represents.

BAR CHARTS

Bar charts reflect changes in quantity over time.

The *bar chart* is constructed so that each point is located in reference to two variables: one a quantity—money, temperature, or volume—usually indicated along the vertical axis; and the other a time, distance, load (etc.) factor, most frequently indicated along the horizontal axis (see Figure 17–9). Bar charts may be presented either vertically (often called *column charts*) or horizontally; the

FIGURE 17–9   Bar Charts—Vertical and Horizontal Formats

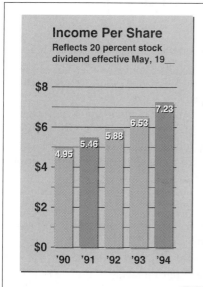
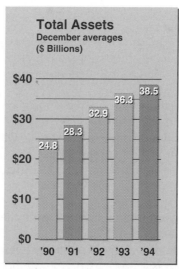
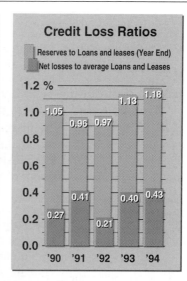

length of the bar normally indicates quantity. Ordinarily, the variation in bars should be only in length. A bar changed in length *and* width, to designate *two* variables, produces confusion in interpretation.

Various visual techniques make the bar chart more interesting: bars in a second color, shading, projective drawing, or sketches of the company's products in a stylized column form.

One valid criticism of the bar chart is that it does not reflect quantities with precision. When the reader's eye moves from the top or end of the bar to the scale axis, it is impossible to determine the *exact* quantity designation. However, this weakness can be overcome by placing figures within the bars or at the top of each bar.

The *segmented bar chart* is a variation on the pie chart. A single bar represents the total data. However, it is split into segments that are in proportion to the quantities designated (see Figure 17–10). Here also, the bar may be horizontal, vertical, or designed to duplicate the company's product.

CURVE CHARTS

Curve charts show trends over time.

The *curve chart,* sometimes referred to as a *line chart* or *line graph,* enables the reader to quickly and easily see trends over periods of time. It is easy to construct: once you have plotted various items on the chart, simply connect the points with a curved line.

A further advantage of the curve chart is the great quantity of information that may be depicted on one chart. It is relatively simple to place multiple curves on one drawing to depict related data. Of course, each curve must be slightly different (through the use of dashes, dots, and other graphic elements), so the reader can easily tell them apart (see Figure 17–11).

BAND CHARTS AND COMPONENT BAR CHARTS

Band and component bar charts show trends through shading instead of curves.

The *band chart* is similar to the multiple-curve chart except that it has shadings (see Figure 17–12). Each shaded section (usually beginning at the bottom with a dark color and moving up to lighter colors) represents a quantity. The same pattern is followed with the *component bar chart* (see Figure 17–13).

Use these charts only to give an impression of general relationships. If you wish to give exact relationships or precise data, use some other visual aid.

FIGURE 17–10   Segmented Bar Chart—Vertical Format

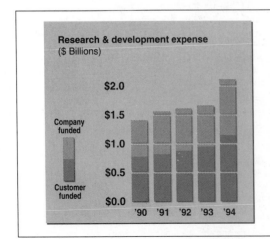
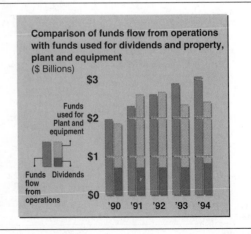

FIGURE 17–11 Curve Chart with Multiple Curves

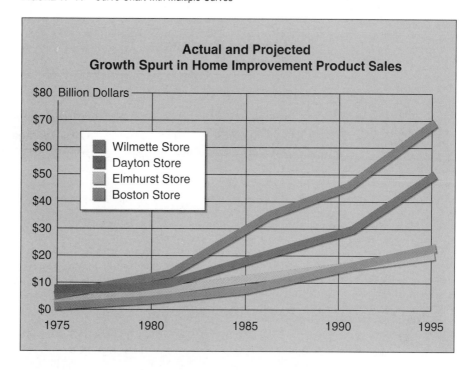

FIGURE 17–12 Band Chart

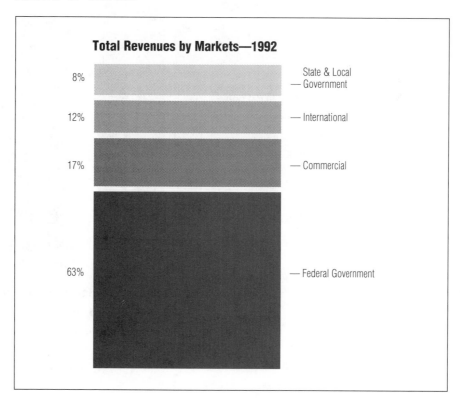

FIGURE 17–13   Component Bar Chart

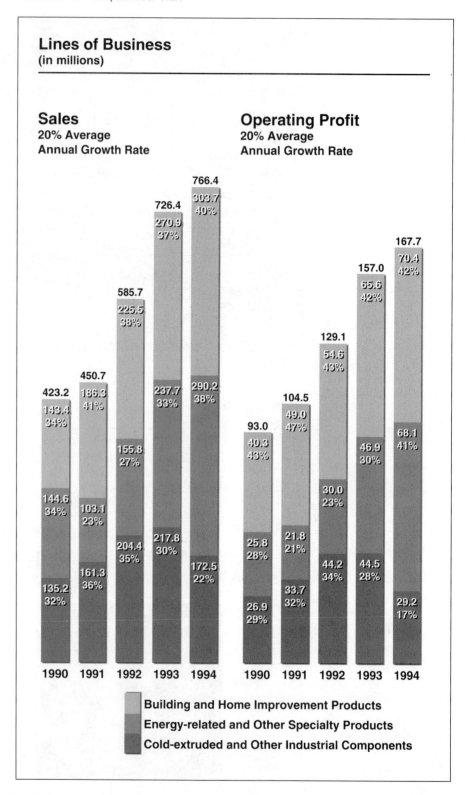

Lines of Business
(in millions)

Sales
20% Average
Annual Growth Rate

Operating Profit
20% Average
Annual Growth Rate

Building and Home Improvement Products
Energy-related and Other Specialty Products
Cold-extruded and Other Industrial Components

RATIO CHARTS

Ratio charts compare growth trends.

For comparisons of growth, *ratio charts* are often appropriate. These charts are drawn on semilogarithmic paper. For example, on an ordinary chart a change in one nation's reserve strength from 3,000 to 30,000 and another nation's reserve strength from 10,000 to 100,000 would be difficult to represent. The major change in the second nation's figure might force line or bar designations off the chart completely. The same figures can be represented more compactly on a ratio chart, which telescopes quantity. Because the scale is based on percentages instead of on absolute units, comparisons of growth rates or percentage increases can be made. The chart in Figure 17–14 shows that the each nation's reserves grew at exactly the same rate, each increasing by ten times.

ORGANIZATIONAL CHARTS

Organizational charts depict the company hierarchy.

Many organizations are so complex that it is sometimes difficult for employees to have a clear understanding of who reports to whom. An *organizational chart* depicts employees' positions within the company, exactly who is their supervisor, and who is their supervisor's supervisor.

Most common of the several kinds of organizational charts is the vertical chart (shown in Figure 17–15), which reads from top to bottom. There are also horizontal charts, which read from left to right, and circle charts, which show

FIGURE 17–14 Ratio Chart

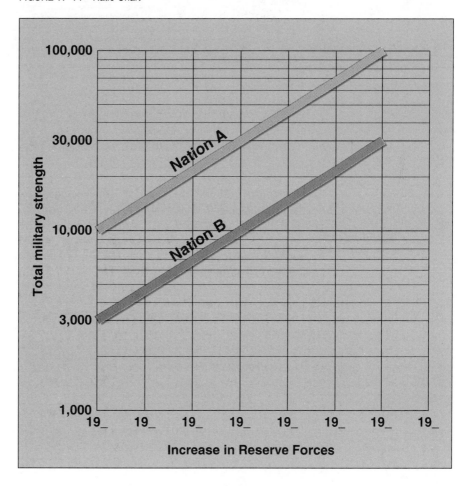

FIGURE 17–15   Vertical Organizational Chart

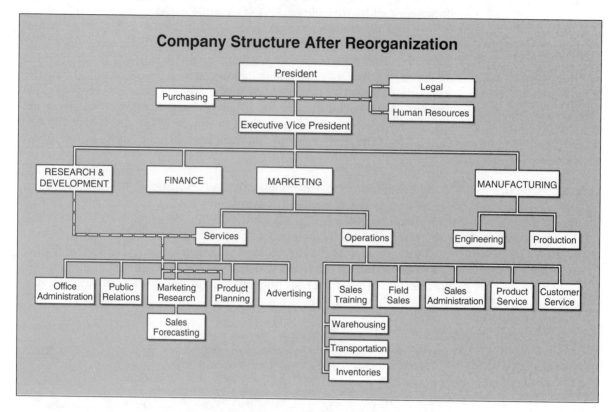

authority emanating from the center. A variation of the circle chart is the bee-hive chart. In most organizational charts, solid lines indicate direct relation-ships; broken lines indicate indirect relationships.

FLOWCHARTS

Flowcharts depict the history of a product or process.

Flowcharts indicate the direction of movement of a product or a process from the initial stages to completion. Sometimes simplified drawings or symbols are used to represent stages, with arrows to indicate direction. The flowchart, flow sheet, or routing diagram can be valuable to the new employee or anyone who needs to quickly become familiar with the sequence of activity in a process (see Figure 17–16 on page 407).

FIGURE 17–16 Flowchart

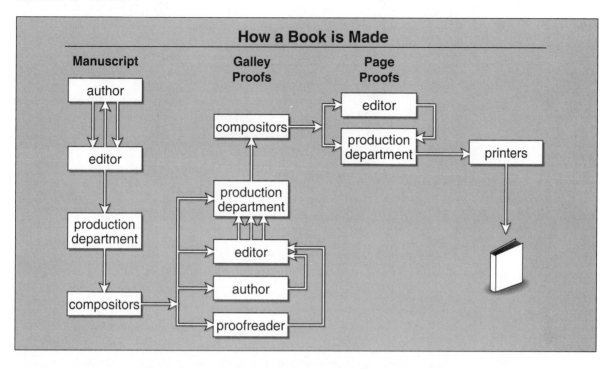

PICTOGRAMS, OR PICTORIAL CHARTS

Pictograms represent concepts symbolically.

The *pictogram* (see Figure 17–17) is ideal for readers who are in a hurry or who are disinclined to interpret a six-line curve chart. They can quickly see, for example, that the cost of living has gone up if market baskets are shown marching up a chart, or that more office buildings were constructed this year than last year if five additional skyscrapers are shown.

The symbols, such as dollar signs, autos, homes, planes, tires, are usually of uniform appearance and size. (Sometimes, as in Figure 17–17, the size of symbols suggests relative importance or quantity.) Each usually represents the same quantity or dimension. The symbols should be simple and so representative that it would be almost impossible for two readers to interpret them differently.

Only a limited amount of uncomplicated information can be presented in a pictogram. For data having several facets and requiring thoughtful interpretation, other visual aids are preferable.

FIGURE 17–17   Pictogram

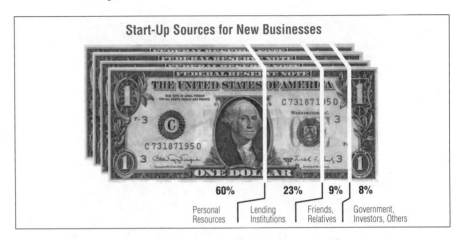

Start-Up Sources for New Businesses

60%   23%   9%   8%

Personal   Lending   Friends,   Government,
Resources   Institutions   Relatives   Investors, Others

MAP CHARTS

Map charts show locations and spatial relationships.

For representation that depends on geographical or spatial relationships, *map charts* are excellent (see Figure 17–18). Symbols (trees, oil wells, people, livestock, and so on) can designate quantities, and their position on the map can indicate location.

FIGURE 17–18   Map Chart

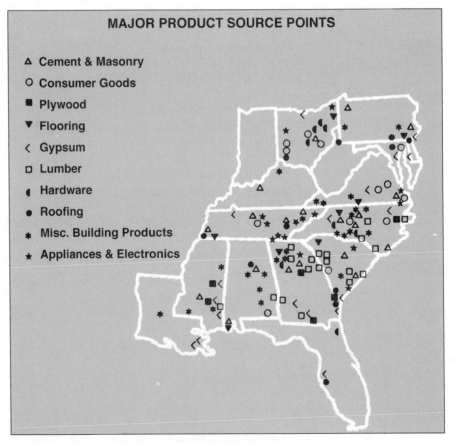

MAJOR PRODUCT SOURCE POINTS

△ Cement & Masonry
○ Consumer Goods
■ Plywood
▼ Flooring
< Gypsum
□ Lumber
◖ Hardware
● Roofing
✳ Misc. Building Products
★ Appliances & Electronics

Courtesy of the Lowes Company, North Wilkesboro, North Carolina

FIGURE 17–19   Cutaway Diagram

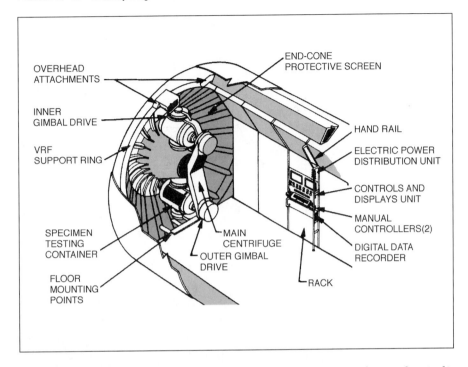

A map drawn out of proportion to its true land areas can be used to indicate the disparate characteristics of various areas of the nation. For example, a map of the United States depicting manufacturing output will have the eastern and midwestern states drawn so that they appear much larger than other states.

CUTAWAY AND EXPLODED DRAWINGS

Cutaway drawings show the inner workings of a part or product.

Exploded diagrams show how the pieces of a part or product fit together.

Cutaway and exploded sketches or photographs are excellent for showing the reader the component parts of a piece of equipment, as well as subsurface areas. They are usually arranged to give a perspective view. A *cutaway drawing,* such as the one in Figure 17–19, can often convey a much clearer picture of the interior working parts of a complex mechanical device than could a complicated description.

An *exploded diagram,* such as the one shown in Figure 17–20, presents the component parts of a device. Each piece is drawn to show how it fits into, or next to, a contiguous piece. If it is a piece part, for example, each of its segments is exploded. Dotted lines are sometimes used to illustrate how the entire unit is attached to the larger mechanism.

Cutaway and exploded diagrams are common in technical reports. They require the services of an artist who can draw with care, precision, and imagination.

PHOTOGRAPHS

Photographs are convincing and quickly produced.

The use of photographs in reports has increased in recent years, and with good reason. They are most persuasive as visual evidence in support of text. If a report writer wants to indicate that a shield does not bend on impact, a picture can be taken at the precise instant of impact. If the writer wants to prove that a

FIGURE 17–20   Exploded Diagram

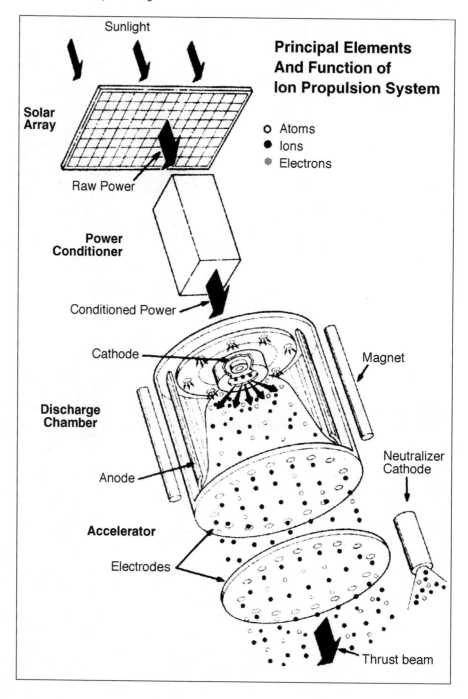

cement support cracked, a photo can prove it. If a potential buyer wants a view of a piece of property, the seller need only snap the picture and pencil on it the width, depth, frontage, or other pertinent data. The contractor need not draw a diagram of a kitchen that is to be remodeled; the room can be photographed from several angles and the dimensions can be written in, saving hours of drafting time.

Another advantage of photographs is the speed with which they can be made. An instant photo can be snapped and printed in minutes, in black and white or color. Photographs are also easier, less time consuming, and less expensive to prepare than charts and graphs, although they are more expensive to reproduce in printed form. If only ten or twenty copies of four or five pictures are needed, an industrial photo lab can supply them at a nominal charge.

PLACING GRAPHIC AIDS IN REPORTS

Place graphic aids near the discussion of the data they clarify.

A table or chart should appear in the text if the material it presents is directly related to the topic under discussion. Any explanation, interpretation, or analysis of it should appear in the body of the report immediately before or after. On the other hand, tables and charts meant only to present material that is related to text information or that amplifies—but is not vital to it—can be placed in an appendix or supplement.

The report writer should keep in mind the obvious danger of placing anything important in an appendix. If readers can refer to a chart easily and quickly, they will use it. If they are required to flip back and forth between the body of the report and charts in the appendix, they may stop referring to the illustrations altogether.

In some instances a table or chart appears in a footnote, but it usually seems out of place there. The footnote area at the bottom of a page is not recommended for illustrations.

USING GRAPHIC AIDS IN ORAL PRESENTATIONS

Graphic aids make oral presentations persuasive.

Many of the graphic aids illustrated in this chapter are powerful tools in oral communication. A number of studies (see the articles listed in Suggested Resources,) demonstrate the importance of using graphic aids in oral presentations. Speakers who include transparencies have been shown to have a better chance of influencing their audience than speakers who have no graphic aids. In addition, audiences tend to judge presenters who show transparencies as more prepared, more professional, and more credible than those who do not. Whether an audience is a single person, a small group, or an auditorium full of professionals, appropriate use of graphic aids can create strong and lasting impressions.

The key, of course, is the suitability of a particular graphic aid to the presenter's purpose, audience, and material. No matter how expertly prepared, no graphic aid in itself is guaranteed to enhance a presentation. Each chart, graph, or drawing used in an oral presentation must be designed and placed meaningfully—just as graphic aids in printed materials must—to clarify, emphasize, or synthesize important points.

Presenters should consider as well whether the audience will be addressed in person or by teleconference. A graphic aid that appears as a full-screen close-up in a teleconference may be less visible to a large audience in an in-person presentation. Similarly, a handout prepared for a large in-person audience may be difficult to use in a teleconference, unless distribution of the handout has been prearranged at teleconference sites.

GUIDELINES FOR
GRAPHIC AIDS IN
ORAL PRESENTATIONS

Almost anything an audience can look at while you are speaking can add visual impact to your presentation. Common forms of graphic aids include slides, transparencies, flip charts, storyboards, and films and videotapes. The following guidelines will help you use various graph forms effectively in oral presentations:

Limit the number and complexity of graphic aids.

Limit the number and complexity of your graphic aids.   Beginning presenters often make the mistake of trying to put everything into their graphics. By contrast, skilled presenters know that graphic aids highlight the story rather than telling it completely. As a general rule, focus each graphic aid on a small number of points, often only one. Transparencies and slides, for example, should be designed for easy understanding by the audience. In preparing such graphics, many presenters limit themselves to no more than five lines of text and seven words per line. When you need to express a complex set of ideas by means of a single graphic, use the *overlay technique:* start with a basic outline of your overall graphic image and add details (by superimposing transparencies or slide images) one at a time. Never add new details until you have explained clearly what is already before your audience.

Base the nature of your graphic aids on the size and make up of your audience.

Use graphic aids that are appropriate for the size and nature of your audience.   The size of an audience often determines what types of graphic aids will be most effective. Every person in large audience may not be able to see some graphic aids such as models, flip charts, and photographs. A small audience (two or three managers, for example) may consider a slide presentation unnecessarily formal or impersonal. Similarly, the nature of the audience may make some graphics more suitable than others. A younger audience may appreciate fast-paced, multimedia graphics such as those seen on MTV. An older audience may respond to less dramatic graphics, including print-based visuals such as handouts and text slides.

Display a graphic aid only when discussing it.

Talk about each graphic aid while displaying it; move it out of sight as you proceed to new topics.   Because graphic aids command attention, you are sure to confuse an audience if you display one visual aid while talking about something else. Presenters fall into this danger most often when using flip charts or posters. Never tack a visual on the wall or display it on a stand before you are ready to discuss it.

Point out the important features of a graphic aid.

Highlight particular points while displaying a graphic aid.   Focus attention on the relevant parts of each graphic aid as you talk your way through it. For example, consider using a piece of paper to cover part of a transparency, gradually revealing each item on the transparency as it occurs in your talk. Or use a pointer or light beam to direct attention to particular portions of a graphic aid.

Ensure that everyone can see the graphic aid.

Make sure that everyone can see your graphic aids.   If you are making a presentation to one or two people, a clear view of your graphic materials is seldom a problem. The group can sit at the same table and look at graphics spread out before them or placed on a convenient chart stand or wall. In larger meetings, however, finding a place to display your visuals can be more complicated. Some presenters make the mistake of positioning themselves between the audience and their graphic aids. The following room arrangements can help you secure visibility:

- Center table arrangement

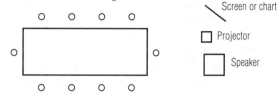

- Conference room with screen at an angle

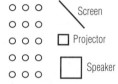

- Theatre or auditorium with two screens

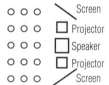

- Table in U arrangement

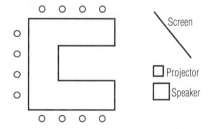

- Small office with two or three people at a desk

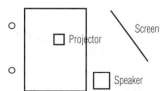

GRAPHIC
REPRESENTATION
OF STATISTICS

*Graphic aids enliven
statistical data.*

Statistics are a powerful means of recording and summarizing information. Rather than describing every item in a production run, statistics can record a 3 percent scrap rate. Rather than recounting the details of hundreds of student records, statistics can show that there is a .49 correlation between GPA and achievement test scores.

These common uses of statistics do summarize large amounts of data in a convenient way. Nevertheless, statistics often fail to present information in a way that is interesting and easy for people to interpret. Properly used, graphic aids can make "cold" numbers come to life by adding in visual emphasis and persuasive appeal.

Statistics that require close examination can be distributed as a handout. Note that highlighting may be used to emphasize the items that matter most to the presenter.

POPULAR GRAPHIC
AIDS FOR ORAL
PRESENTATIONS

*Test projection equipment
and practice using
transparencies before
your presentation.*

Slides continue to be a popular graphic aid, especially now that computer programs such as Harvard Professional Graphics and Quattro have made them easy to produce from a computer screen. Many times text and picture slides can be intermixed effectively in a presentation. Always know the projection equipment well and practice advancing through a slide presentation. Have you ever witnessed the disaster that occurs when a bulb burns out, a slide jams, or a misordered or upside-down slide appears on the screen?

Transparencies (see Figure 17–21) can also be produced easily and inexpensively by means of computer graphics programs or photocopying machines

FIGURE 17–21   Acetate Transparency

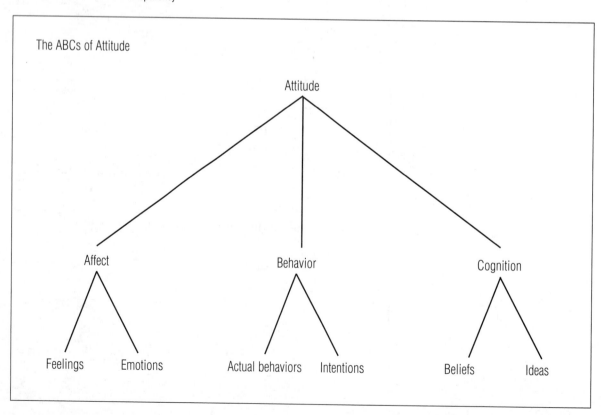

equipped for transparencies. Vary the content of transparencies for the sake of interest and don't merely repeat the words of your presentation on them. Practice using transparencies so that you can avoid awkward interruptions to adjust the placement of a transparency or to focus the overhead projector.

Flip charts give easy access to information.

A flip chart (as shown in Figure 17–22) can be prepared in advance or drawn during the presentation itself. In either case, use a variety of colors to add emphasis and variety to the information contained on the pages of the chart. Information on a flip chart can be accessed and changed more easily than similar information on slides.

Computer programs allow presentation of graphic aids on the computer screen.

Some computer programs (e.g., IBM's Storyboard) allow users to prepare graphic aids for display directly on the computer screen. The term *storyboard*, a term used originally in movies and television, refers to a series of images that "tell a story." Storyboard displays can be static (fixed forms that can't be changed during the presentation) or dynamic (images that can be altered by means of a keyboard or mouse). See Figure 17–23.

Films and videos should not overshadow other parts of a presentation.

Films and videotapes can provide powerful graphic enhancement to a presentation, so long as they do not overpower it. Use these media to support, not replace, the major points of a presentation. Remember, films and videotapes need not be played in their entirety during a presentation. Brief, pertinent clips selected in advance are especially effective as high-interest graphic support for key points.

Taken together, graphic aids can contribute powerfully to the success of oral presentations. Test your own reactions the next time you attend a business or classroom presentation for which the speaker has prepared stimulating graphic aids. Notice how your enjoyment increases your willingness to like the speaker and be persuaded by his or her points. Notice as well the long-lasting impressions and memories left by well-prepared, skillfully used graphic aids. A picture may be worth a thousand words, in part, because it lasts so much longer in our consciousness.

FIGURE 17–22   Flipchart

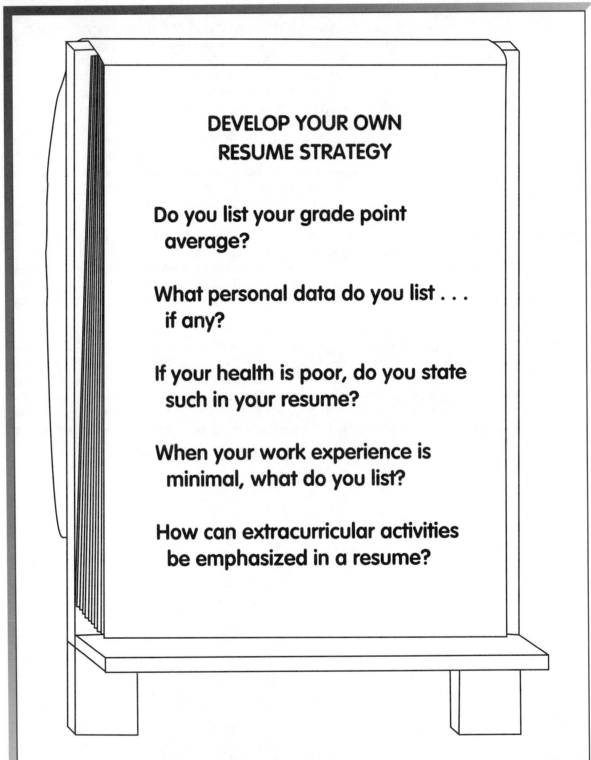

**DEVELOP YOUR OWN
RESUME STRATEGY**

Do you list your grade point
average?

What personal data do you list . . .
if any?

If your health is poor, do you state
such in your resume?

When your work experience is
minimal, what do you list?

How can extracurricular activities
be emphasized in a resume?

FIGURE 17–23   Storyboard

VIDEO: LONG SHOT House on Deserted Highway and Streaking Panther

AUDIO: "Faster than a Speeding Bullet ...Able to leap Tall Buildings in a ..."

SFX/MUSIC: SOUND OF JET TAKING OFF MIXED WITH PANTHER'S ROAR

VIDEO: LONG SHOT House on Deserted Highway

AUDIO: ....

SFX/MUSIC: WIND SOUNDS

**WRITING AND
SPEAKING
EXERCISES**

1. Investigate the growing field of presentation software, which allows computer users to produce increasingly sophisticated visual aids with little or no training. Prepare a short written report that describes some of the more recent examples of this type of software. Provide a sense of similarities and differences as well as features offered.

2. Use one of the software programs you investigated for question 1. Prepare a guide that would allow other students to access that software with as little difficulty as possible.

3. Locate at least three secondary sources that discuss how the use of color visual aids affects the readers of business documents. Prepare a summary of each article, making sure to document each properly. Can you assume it is always better to use color when preparing visual aids?

4. Words must explain their message in linear fashion, one at a time, whereas graphic images communicate more immediately. What advantages or disadvantages do you see in the speed with which graphic aids create impressions?

5. You are to prepare a report that explains the nature of your academic department's curriculum. The report will be presented to high-school juniors (who are unfamiliar with the college), to alumni of your program (who will be familiar with some of the operations of your college), and to parents of current students in the program. Although the substance of the report will be basically the same, how will the visuals change?

6. Collect five graphic aids from recent business magazines. For each, discuss what was done well or poorly in the communication of ideas and statistics.

7. Develop a bar chart representing student enrollment in, for instance, your college, department, or student organization. Besides focusing on the data over a specified period (such as the past eight to ten years), also indicate the changes in the male-female makeup of the total numbers. After you have completed the bar chart, prepare a one-paragraph critique of your work.

8. Find a table in a business document (perhaps from a report in your business library). Write an evaluation of the table based on the checklist for constructing tables in this chapter. Then redesign the table. Use a photocopy of the data to avoid recopying.

9. As a manager of Home Medical Devices, Inc., you've seen profits explode in the past ten years. For your annual report, you must decide on a graphic way of representing the increase. Make up net sales figures for each of the past ten years; then draw up three different graphic representations of the figures. Choose one for your annual report. Explain why you chose it over the others you prepared.

10. Discover what graphic capabilities students can gain access to on your campus. Make use of the facilities to generate one or more of the visual aids described in this chapter. Write a short summary of what is available for student use. If no facilities exist on your campus, suggest how students can generate graphs and charts on their own, without a significant financial expenditure.

11. Find three examples of visual aids in a current business magazine. For

each, evaluate the effectiveness and integrity of the visual in representing data and communicating impressions to readers. Make suggestions for improvements where possible. Remember to cite the source for each visual used.

12. Chart your own academic progress (approximate grade average, perhaps?) beginning with elementary school. Estimate where necessary. Without resorting to trickery, choose a visual mode of representation that puts your academic path in as complimentary a light as possible.

13. Identify the vocation you plan to enter and specify a particular industry you hope to join—perhaps even a particular organization. For your future job, industry, and perhaps company indicate the current status of computer graphics and the potential for using computer graphics.

14. Describe in writing a recent business presentation or college lecture that could have been enhanced by the use of graphic aids. Be specific regarding precisely which graphic aids you think should have been used, where they should have appeared in the presentation, and how the presenter should have used them.

15. Using standard typing paper, create a small flip chart of at least eight pages demonstrating your skill in the creation of this graphic aid. Type or print in the message you would record on the regular flip chart pages.

SUGGESTED RESOURCES

Boyd, Stephen D. "When Visuals Aid in the Presentation." *Canadian Manager* 16 (July 1991):22–23.

Cothran, Tom. "The Value of Visuals." *Training* (July 1989):4–8.

Falvey, Jack. "Does Your Company Need First Aid for Its Visual Aids?" *Sales & Marketing Management* 142 (July 1990):97–99.

Fraser, Winston. "Using Slides in Speeches." *Executive Speeches* 3 (April 1989):33–36.

Johnson, Virginia. "Picture-Perfect Presentations." *Training & Development Journal* 43 (May 1989):45–47.

Kern, Richard. "Making Visual Aids Work for You." *Sales & Marketing Management* 141 (February 1989):45–48.

Nies, Joyce I., and Tas, Richard F. "How to Add Visual Impact to Your Presentation." *Cornell Hotel & Administration Quarterly* 32 (May 1991):46–51.

Sonnenberg, Frank, and Hoff, Ron. "Making Visuals Count in Your Presentations: Common Sense Guide to Presentations." *Executive Excellence* 7 (April 1990):11–14.

REPORTS FOR DECISION MAKING

Accurate data and carefully constructed foundations both give support and integrity: the former to reports; the latter to buildings.

Reports give managers the information on which they base decisions.

An important aspect of every manager's job is decision making. At times, decisions are simple: Shall we hire three more part-time employees or one full-time employee? At other times, decisions are quite complex: Shall we close this 100,000-square-foot plant and move the operation to Websterville? Simple or complex, most decisions are based on reports—daily or weekly reports of sales, periodic reports, detailed analytical reports, and others.

Managers need valid and logically presented information for decision making. That is a fact a young aerospace engineer quickly learned when he attempted to present what he considered to be an excellent idea:

> I discussed it with my boss and his boss at lunch; I talked about it to them at coffee breaks; I mentioned it on the golf course, in the parking lot, and meetings. Nothing seemed to work. They listened politely (and not so politely if they were in a hurry), asked questions, requested that I repeat data, and almost always ended up saying, "Well, let's see something tangible when you get the bugs worked out."
>
> And then I woke up. When they said, "Let's see something," that "something" was a written report or proposal. I sat down and worked on that document off and on for a week. I carefully developed my ideas, included a cost analysis, listed carefully thought-through recommendations, added the substantiating tables and charts, had them carefully typed, and then put them all together. Copies went forward to the four decision makers involved. The letters of transmittal asked for a response in ten days. I received them, and in every case the reply was affirmative. The product that I recommended went into production. It has done extremely well, and so have I. It's all the result of my report-proposal which was read, analyzed, evaluated, and approved!

The report may be simple or complex, formal or informal, internal or external, oral or written, or a combination of several formats. Whatever its length,

Reports should present facts objectively.

the report must be complete, specific, and accurate. The writer must present all necessary facets of the problem, carefully draw all conclusions, and thoroughly substantiate all recommendations.

A report should be a factual, objective presentation of information. Some reports also interpret and evaluate the information given. Others not only present and interpret information, but they also adopt a persuasive tone. When the purpose is other than the objective presentation of data, the writer should state the purpose clearly.

Most reports are part of the decision-making process. Even the short personnel status report issued each Monday eventually plays a role in the quarterly action (decision) of the vice president of human resources. The future of the employees, and often that of the company, depend on the decisions this executive makes. These decisions, in turn, depend on information in reports.

HOW REPORTS FLOW IN AN ORGANIZATION

Reports, which can be formal or informal and verbal or written, travel up, down, and laterally.

A variety of reports travel up to the manager. Some deal with specific problems. Other are turned in by each department head at periodic intervals. The periodic reports are frequently written, but they may be oral, for example, in an interview or a conference. The manager also receives data through informal communication: while waiting in the lunch line, in a casual chat while walking down the corridor, from the attitudes reflected by various people in conversations and at meetings. In addition, the manager receives data reports from the computer: sales volume, personnel turnover, inventory levels, production quantities, and many other facts of an organization's activities. These data, when properly interpreted and evaluated, are enormously helpful to a decision maker.

Reports also travel down, bringing information to every member of an organization. The data contained in these reports help guide employees and give further direction to continuing activities.

Lateral reports indicate that a department is communicating internally in order to function efficiently.

For each department or division to function most efficiently, reports should travel laterally as well. The sales manager profits by being aware of the status of production, the problems of personnel, and the plans of marketing. Such lateral communication operates rather haphazardly in most companies. Many department heads *must* send information up because their superiors require it. Managers *must* send information down if their departments are to function effectively. But managers are often too busy (or think they are too busy) to communicate laterally. Furthermore, managers' interest in other departments is usually minimal, unless something arises unexpectedly that forces them to consult with department heads. For these reasons, lateral communication does not always take place effectively.

HOW REPORTS ARE CLASSIFIED

As you have seen, a *report* is a message (usually objective) that conveys information from one organization (or organizational level) to another to assist in decision making and problem solving. This definition characterizes all reports, but there are many ways of classifying reports.

Elaborate formal reports present vast, complex research findings. Informal reports, such as memos, share routine information.

Formal or informal. The *formal report* often is very elaborate and well organized, with carefully drawn conclusions and thoroughly substantiated recommendations. In most cases, this report is detailed and objective. Formal reports may result from scientific and technical research or investigative business research. An example of an *informal report* is an interoffice memo that transfers relatively routine information from one department to another.

Progress reports update decision makers on the status of assignments.

Informational or other purposes.   Many reports are strictly *informational.* Their primary purpose is to convey information for problem solving or decision making, though some document a policy or problem. Other reports may be analytical, persuasive, comparative, or argumentative. These are usually rather detailed (see Chapter 20 for an expanded discussion).

Periodic reports reflect performance over a given time.

Internal or external.   When we look inside an organization, we find reports called *progress,* or *status, reports.* These reports usually permit a superior to know the progress an individual or team is making on a particular assignment. *Periodic reports* are reports distributed either internally or externally at designated times: daily, weekly, monthly, quarterly, semiannually, and annually. These reports are often quantitative and are used for comparison with previous periods.

External reports provide requested information to people outside the company.

External reports are those sent to an outside organization. The outside organizations usually request the reports. Examples are the various reports requested of an organization by local, state, and federal agencies or the technical reports a prospective purchaser may request from a company on a product or a possible work assignment. Lending institutions may ask for a financial report covering specific areas. Often a company may submit a proposal as a response to a request for proposal (RFP). Though designated as a proposal, this document is a type of external report that gives the details of how a proposed activity will be completed, by whom, and at what cost.

Computers can analyze data and generate reports quickly.

Computer generated.   With the increased processing power of silicon chips and programming advances spawned by artificial intelligence (AI) research, many reports can now be generated by computer. For example, computers can automatically generate monthly sales figures by territory or what-if projections based on inputs of different variables, such as interest rates or prices. It is important that these reports be clearly labeled as computer-generated reports. Readers must understand that selection and interpretation of data within computer reports are only as good as the program that generates them and the data entered.

Reports often serve more than one purpose; therefore, they fall into more than one category.

Functional.   *Functional reports* are issued by a functional department, such as accounting, marketing, or finance. The same "marketing report" may also be called an analytical, formal, or even progress report, depending on its content.

Report classifications are quite arbitrary. Often reports can legitimately fall into more than one classification. Become familiar with the various designations used in business. You will undoubtedly encounter some of the titles discussed here. Remember, however, that what one firm calls a "research report" may be labeled a "marketing report" by another organization or a "formal report" by a third company.

REPORT CONTROL

*Report control—
determining which reports
to keep and which to
eliminate—helps control
company costs.*

The management of every company must place report control high on its list of cost-saving exercises. Report requirements, including those from the computer, should be reviewed periodically to eliminate some reports, combine some, and initiate new ones.

Many firms find that it is efficient to conduct a *report inventory* each year to judge which reports should be continued and which dropped. Eliminating a report is difficult without the support of top management. Therefore, the person responsible for report control must possess adequate authority. Some people in the organization will be unhappy when their reports are eliminated or incorporated into existing ones. Part of their work responsibility has been dropped, and they are likely to feel that their importance has been lessened. Nevertheless, once an inventory policy is announced, supported, and carried through a few times, the task becomes routine and—more importantly—valuable to the firm.

Conducting a report inventory is not easy. Employees responsible for this task must first list all reports issued in a department or the organization. They must then visit all receivers on the report distribution list to find out if those recipients found a given report to be of no value, of some value, or very valuable. After evaluating the responses, a senior person decides to retain, eliminate, or combine reports.

Keep in mind that the task is difficult. Eliminating a report is sometimes viewed as eliminating "good old Marty's job." Of almost equal importance is the report authors' identification with the report and their own ego involvement. Despite the difficulties, report control is a critical function in today's business world.

REPORT SECURITY

*Report security ensures
that sensitive information
does not fall into the
hands of competitors.*

A ten-page report can cost a company thousands of dollars in labor and overhead to produce, but that report in the wrong hands can cost the company millions. Because reports contain new-product information, market projections, personnel assessments, strategy formulations, and other matters of proprietary interest, they are a popular target for industrial theft and espionage.

Increasingly, therefore, companies are limiting the hard copy distribution of sensitive reports to only the most trusted readers. Channels of distribution, similarly, are guarded: hand-picked couriers within the company may be the only people besides readers to have physical possession of the document. "For Your Eyes Only" is often marked at the beginning of the report, indicating that any photocopying of its pages is strictly against company policy.

Shredding also plays a part in report security. When reports have served their communication purpose, all copies—usually numbered for inventory— are routinely gathered and shredded. Reference copies are retained in company vaults and in protected computer files.

Mechanical security devices of all types are now available to protect reports stored on computers. Passwords and encryption (coding) are quite common. Equipment, file, and keyboard locks and locking devices are available. Some computer systems have keys to activate or deactivate a power source, the mouse, or the keyboard.

The best way to select a computer security system is to first determine your needs. Exactly what is most important to protect—the hardware, the software, or both? Then refer to a listing of the devices available and their manufacturers. A 1992 article, for example, lists eight different companies that have hardware security products for sale and twelve others that specialize in software security devices.

When you work in an office setting day after day, you will become very familiar with the content of your project, the data you use, and the sources you consult. Your familiarity may lead you to think that the material is well known, which may not be true. As a result, you may not protect your report. Others (including visitors) may review your material when you leave for lunch or are out for a day or two. In addition, your work can be copied, borrowed, or even eliminated. One author on computer security states it well: " . . . the final success of a security system depends on its administrators and users. So if you think about safety last, that's probably what you'll get."[2]

KNOWING WHAT TO REPORT

Determine what to report by understanding what the requestor wants. Together, decide the report's purpose so that the requestor gets the right kind of report.

Sometimes a report does not fulfill the desired purpose because the purpose was not clearly defined or the report requestor and author had different perceptions of the problem to be addressed. For example, a department store chain has received a large number of letters regarding "poor service." If the president (to whom most of the letters were addressed) simply requests a report on poor service from the customer services director, the finished report may have little or no value, because the request is much too broad. Will the report cover clerical service, delivery service, cashier service, or telephone service, or even a comparison of some facet of the organization's service in comparison with a competitor's?

Knowing what to report starts with a specific request, in writing, that identifies a specific problem, the purpose the report is to serve (informational or analytical), whether or not recommendations are to be presented, and other guidelines. Reports should be factual and impersonal with adequate data and supporting materials so that decisions may be made. An initial and one follow-up meeting between the requestor and report writer will help ensure that all involved are moving in the same direction.

WRITING THE REPORT

Long or short, simple or complex, most reports follow a basic pattern. When you carry through a procedure, whether it is changing the tire on your car or getting ready to use your computer, you follow a specific a series of steps. In many instances, the procedure becomes almost automatic. In some cases, however, you recognize, because of a particular situation, that specific tasks may be skipped or shortened. When you write reports, you will find that following a procedure, with perhaps some deviations from time to time, is also wise.

In carrying through the report process, various tasks can be assigned to seven steps.

First, determine the problem and purpose and identify the reader.

Step 1: *Define the problem, establish the purpose, and identify the reader.* (See Chapter 6, "The Writing Process," for details.) Often the report writer and the individual for whom the report is being written haven't communicated adequately. They need to be in complete agreement on exactly what the problem is, what precisely is the purpose of the report, and for which specific group of readers the report is being written. Each of these three sub-areas (problem, purpose, readers) should be identified in clear, written statements. In addition, the concerned parties must accept the statements *before* the next step is taken.

Second, narrow your focus, start a working outline, and decide how much development individual parts require.

Step 2: *Limit the topic, design a tentative outline, and determine the depth of the report's segments.* (See Chapter 6, "The Writing Process" for details.) Again, the principals involved (the requestor and the writer) must agree on the boundaries of the topic. Whether the report is "Marketing to Consumers" or "Sources of Capital for the Start-Up Entrepreneur," boundaries must be set. If not, the finished report may be too general to be of value or it may cover areas not desired.

In the case of "Marketing to Consumers," here are just a few questions you as the report writer must answer before going further: Marketing what types of products? autos? foodstuffs? athletic events? Marketing to which groups of consumers? Elderly? Middle-aged? Teenagers? Children? Are you marketing to all ethnic groups or to just to specific groups? Which groups? Where do your prospective consumers live? Throughout the United States? Internationally? The west coast? Eastern seaboard? Southwest? Once decisions are made on questions like these, you and the report receiver have limited the topic.

The next substep is to draw up a tentative outline that covers the limited parameters of the topic. The outline must be logical and coherent. Give all headings and the points under them roughly equal weight in the report. To apportion 15 subtopics under one heading and 3 under another will result in an unbalanced final report. The reader might wonder if the more detailed topic should have been a separate report and the other one dropped. You need not treat each topic in equal depth; on the other hand, the treatment should not be widely disproportionate.

Third, formulate your research plan and conduct primary and secondary research.

Step 3: *Formulate the research plan and then conduct the primary and secondary research.* (See Chapter 16, "The Research Process" for details.) Formulating the depth, the sophistication, and the methods of research (the plan for the report) will largely depend on the human resources, funding, and research sources available. If the question to be researched is relatively simple, there is no need to employ a large staff, send out thousands of questionnaires, conduct hundreds of interviews, or search countless sources. If, however, you are dealing with a topic that requires accuracy and precision (such as the effectiveness of a medication), then in-depth research is absolutely necessary.

After you have decided on what type and how much research is required, begin your research with secondary sources. Establish a design to accurately record material from secondary sources. Next, move to primary research—with a plan and procedure—to establish the quality of the questionnaire or interview instruments, the sample size, the sample selection, and the accuracy of sample distribution.

Step 4: *Evaluate, edit, tabulate, and interpret the material.* You will probably begin by examining the information you have acquired to determine what

Fourth, decide how best to use your research data.

to use and how to use it. Which data are valid and which are not? Are secondary source materials based on solid evidence? Have the authors substantiated their comments? Are the writers individuals whose opinions are respected and accepted?

What about the qualitative and quantitative data gathered from primary sources? Certainly, responses from individuals must be edited and checked for accuracy. Should some questionnaire responses be discarded because they are obviously not serious responses or they make no sense? The job of editing is a vital one if you are to rely on your research material.

Once you feel you have material that you can rely on, then you can interpret it. What does it all mean? Here you must be careful not to let your biases influence you as you try to reach meaningful interpretations. Also, just because the data indicate the respondents did not prefer red or green, you must be careful not to assume they preferred blue. There are many other colors (or conclusions) even though *you* prefer blue.

You now have material from a variety of secondary sources and information and data from primary sources, and you have evaluated, tabulated, and edited all this. However, you do not yet have a finished product. In some respects you have all the ingredients on the table, but you don't have a cake. Now, put it all together to achieve a valuable end product: a completed report.

Fifth, expand your outline into a rough draft.

Step 5:   *Create a detailed outline and a rough draft.* From an outline you can write a rough draft, insert tables, charts, photos, and any other illustrative material needed, and determine what supplements or appendices to add. Drawing up the final outline should not be difficult. You have a tentative outline from which to work, plus you have the familiarity that comes from researching a topic for days or weeks.

Once the detailed outline is acceptable to you and the report requestor, begin writing. As noted earlier in this book, writing should move quickly. Your primary purpose at this point is to cover the topics and get ideas on paper. Don't worry about a perfect synonym, an illuminating example, or an unforgettable quotation.

After you finish the rough draft, you can insert tables, charts, visuals, and supplementary materials. Some may displace a paragraph or two already written, others may require the expansion of a section to ensure accurate interpretation for the reader, and still others may indicate that an appendix or supplement should be added.

Sixth, edit and draft into final form.

Step 6:   *Edit the rough draft and turn it into a final paper or report.* This is the step you have probably anticipated for too long a period. However, if you attempt to edit the rough draft the day after you have spent the previous two weeks (or two months) living, breathing, and dreaming about the material, you may not be successful.

Give yourself a breather. Step away from the rough draft for several days. Return refreshed and edit with a vengeance. Cut out every unnecessary word, phrase, and sentence. Search for the exact word. Find the perfect illustrative quotation and check the accuracy of all data. You will find tremendous pleasure, even exhilaration, in writing the final draft. You know what you have is solid and will be the basis for important and accurate decision making.

Seventh, decide how best to present the final report so that it receives the recognition it deserves.

Step 7:   Formulate your presentation strategy. Now that you have the finished project, how should it best be presented so that everyone benefits? Sometimes the work of days or weeks is handed to the decision maker's secretary. It may sit in an in-basket for days or be buried under other material for a week. Worse, you may be asked to "Summarize your findings as long as we still have five minutes left in our meeting."

You have expended much time, effort, and company funds on your assignment. Your report is important and should be presented with the dignity it deserves. Make an appointment with the report requestor so you can explain the purpose, the findings, and perhaps the implications of your written report. Perhaps you may find it more beneficial to request 20 minutes at the next department meeting where you may give a briefing together with substantiating data on slides or overhead transparencies. A 70-person orchestra would hardly give a ten-minute performance for three people. It deserves better, and so do you.

These seven steps should be carried out for every report. Actually, many of the steps become almost mechanical for the efficient writer. You may even skip a few steps if the nature of the report or the situation permits. Always keep in mind that following a logical series of steps is key to producing an excellent report.

Chapters 6 and 7 described steps 1 and 2 of writing the report in detail. So let's assume here that you have defined the problem, established the purpose, and identified the reader (step 1) and limited the topic, designed a tentative outline, and determined the depth of the report's segments (step 2). Now you are ready to collect data and information for your report (step 3).

RESEARCH DESIGN AND HYPOTHESIS

The best research design serves your needs at the least possible cost of time and money.

In researching a topic, be careful not to collect a truckload of material. It is pointless to send out thousands of questionnaires, conduct dozens of interviews, examine hundreds of company documents, and evaluate the contents of scores of articles, bulletins, reports, and pamphlets if you don't need all that information. The question to ask is, What research design will best serve our needs and at the same time conserve our time and funds? You may decide, in a particular case, that your research design should include these elements:

> A search of company records
> An evaluation of secondary sources
>> Magazines
>> Journals
>> Newspapers
> A check of government publications
>> Technical reports
>> Translations
> A series of 20 interviews with company production managers

After you get into the research, you may have to modify your design. Perhaps the material in the journals doesn't fill your needs, you want to emphasize interviews more. Perhaps the findings presented in the government reports are so complete and up-to-date that you don't need the interviews. But you can't be sure until you begin to evaluate the research materials.

The Fatal Ills in Business Writing . . . and the Medications to Cure Them

1. **Vapid verbs** (is, are, was, were, seems to be)
   NOT: *It seems to be indicated that we should sell the building.*
   BUT: *We will sell the building.*
2. **Passive poopout** (passive construction)
   NOT: *The ball was thrown carelessly by Tom.*
   BUT: *Tom threw the ball carelessly.*
3. **Misplaced emphasis** (unnecessary words dissipate emphasis)
   NOT: *It would seem that we can plan production quite soon.*
   BUT: *Production can begin almost immediately.*
4. **And the beat goes on and on and on** and . . . (overly long sentences)
   NOT: *It was determined that some executive training might be in order to complement what has been found to be productive in training, which is our management training and to almost the same degree our supervisory training.*
   BUT: *Executive training will strongly complement our present management and supervisory training.*
5. **Overweight nouns** (elongated nouns when shorter ones will do)
   NOT: *To maximize the accountability of personnel as well as the marketability, profitability, and acceptability of our product, we should consider the decreasability of our retail price.*
   BUT: *Cutting the price of our product will increase sales.*
6. **Monotonous rhythms** (lack of sentence structure variety)
   NOT: *We agree to examine sales, to evaluate markets, and to review shipping.*
   BUT: *Our sales, markets, and shipping will be evaluated.*
7. **Nonstop nouns** (too many nouns in a row)
   NOT: *Please evaluate and make a recommendation on our management personnel Keystone benefits program.*
   BUT: *Evaluate the Keystone benefits proposal.*
8. **Sleep-inducing repetition** (unnecessary repetition)
   NOT: *We received and evaluated the new marketing program. The marketing program, which is new, will target . . .*
   BUT: *The new marketing plan, which we have evaluated, will target . . .*
9. **Write to express, not to impress** (choosing long or unfamiliar words when shorter, more familiar words will do)
   NOT: *The president, in a situational and controversial impasse, hypothesized that further effort would only exacerbate . . .*
   BUT: *The president felt that further effort would only make the situation worse.*
10. **Paunchy paragraphs**
    Avoid the one-paragraph-to-a-page appearance and even pages with two *"fat"* paragraphs on them. They are overwhelming to the eye. Use six- to four-line paragraphs and from time to time one or just a couple of sentences.

Use a hypothesis to direct your research.

To help give direction to the research, formulate a hypothesis. A *hypothesis* is a statement that may be proved or disproved as a result of research findings. For example, you may wonder if premiums will increase the sales of the company's Sunshine Cake Mix by 10 percent per month, as measured against monthly sales last year. Your hypothesis might then be formulated as follows: Sales of Sunshine Cake Mix will rise 10 percent during 19__ as compared to 19__ when Kitchen Brite premiums are given with the product. This is a positive hypothesis whose validity can be tested through research.

Because of the importance of research to the business manager, Chapter 16 focuses on that topic. The research supplement at the end of that chapter lists guides and indexes to information sources, including computerized information systems.

DOCUMENTATION OF SOURCE MATERIALS

Cite sources of information used in your report.

In reports and presentations, you will frequently use the research, concepts, ideas, and data secured by someone else. Readers rely on footnotes and bibliographic references as substantiation for points made in the report and as resources for further investigation. When you use other sources, give credit in appropriate documentation or in a citation. If you do not, and state or imply that the data comes from your own research, you may be accused of unethical conduct or plagiarism.

To avoid such a serious accusation, follow the basic rules of documentation noted in this section. Information that is common knowledge need not be documented. You can assume that a statement such as "the number of homicides due to gang violence has increased steadily since 1988 in major urban centers" is well known and thus requires no citation. If, however, you present information that is not generally known or relies heavily on the work of others, reference that information in a footnote and, where appropriate, a bibliographic entry.

In addition to serving as a citation of a source, footnotes can assist you in the presentation of materials. For example, you can use footnotes:

- To cite data or other references in support of statements made in the presentation
- To cite other points of view
- To refer to information that is related but not vital or thoroughly relevant to the basic presentation. To include such information in the report may upset the continuity or coherence of the report. Noted in a footnote, however, it may be valuable to the reader.
- To note differences among authorities in the field
- To offer critical evaluations of major sources. For example, a comment on the sample used, the type of survey employed, inaccuracies in the source, or any appropriate statement that may be valuable or interesting to the reader can be noted in a footnote.

Citations can appear at the bottom of the page (hence the term footnotes) or as endnotes. Endnotes may appear at the end of a chapter or section of the report. Still another method is to make the citation within the material itself. Here is an example of this method:

```
In discussing the qualities of leadership, Warren
Bennis states, "The first test is knowing what you
want, knowing your abilities and capacities, and recog-
nizing the difference between the two" (123).
```

Internal documentation allows you to place parenthetical references within the text, thus avoiding the need for footnotes or endnotes.

This example of internal documentation is in the format recommended by the Modern Language Association (MLA). The reader would find the complete documentation by referring to the Bennis entry in the bibliography. The page number is noted after the quotation. Some writers number each entry in their bibliography and use the corresponding number in parenthesis after the citation to refer the reader to the source list.

The three most common reference methods are those favored by the MLA, American Psychological Association (APA), and *The Chicago Manual of Style* (published by the University of Chicago Press).

APA internal documentation gives the author's last name and date of publication in parentheses in the text. If the author's name is used in the narrative, only the date is listed in parentheses. The full entry appears in the bibliography. Bibliographic entries are listed alphabetically by the last names of the authors.

```
"The three critical factors determining the success
of the communication are the message content, the
receiver's bias, and the receiver's perceptions"
(Weston, 1991).
```

The MLA format, in internal documentation, gives the author's last name and page number in parentheses in the text. If the text cites the author's name (as in the Bennis example above), only the page number is listed in parentheses. The bibliography supplies full bibliographic information arranged alphabetically by the authors' last names.

The Chicago Manual of Style uses superscript numbers within the narrative but full-size reference numbers in the footnotes. In the bibliography, all references are listed alphabetically by authors' last names. Notice that the "Notes" and "Suggested Resources" sections of this book follow *The Chicago Manual of Style*.

NARRATIVE IN THE REPORT

```
In discussing the qualities of leadership, Warren
Bennis states, "The first test is knowing what you
want, knowing your abilities and capacities, and recog-
nizing the difference between the two."[1]
```

FOOTNOTE ENTRY

```
1. Warren Bennis, On Becoming a Leader (Reading, Mass.:
   Addison-Wesley Publishing Company, Inc., 1989): 123.
```

BIBLIOGRAPHIC ENTRY

```
Bennis, Warren. On Becoming a Leader. Reading, Mass.:
   Addison-Wesley Publishing Company, Inc., 1989.
```

Some Latin abbreviations still appear in citations, although that method is not now used very frequently. Three terms still used are ibid (from the Latin *ibidem* meaning "in the same place."), op. cit. (from the Latin *opere citato* meaning "in the work cited") and et al. (from the Latin *et alii* meaning "and others"). When ibid is used, it means the citation is exactly like the one immediately preceding it. If the reference is ibid, p. 37, the reference is the same as the one preceding except for a different page number. Op. cit. refers to a work previously cited but not immediately preceding it. Et al. is used in listing several authors of one work: "Winston Roman et al. "instead of Winston Roman, Frank Mayberry, and John Jacobs. Sometimes these Latin abbreviations appear in italic type.

INDIRECT QUOTES

Paraphrasing enables you to quote indirectly.

By quoting *indirectly* in the text, you can avoid a report that is saturated with quotation marks. You still use the author's information *and* acknowledge the source. Here's an example of how to change a direct quotation into an indirect one:

DIRECT QUOTE

```
Ashkan (1989) comments, "The trend is toward better-
paid marketing managers who possess increased respon-
sibility and have a larger staff under them than in
the past" (p. 18).
```

INDIRECT QUOTE

```
Ashkan (1989) comments that the trend in management
today is toward better-paid marketing managers who have
more responsibility and manage a larger staff than in
the past.
```

Notice that approximately every fifth word is edited to avoid exact repetition of the sentences.

PROPER CREDIT

Give proper credit whenever you use a source.

To give credit to an author, cite the author's name and date every time you use information from that source—even if practically every sentence in the paragraph ends with a citation. Also, always introduce every *direct* quote you use by telling who said it: Brown asserts that " . . . " But avoid overuse of direct quotations. You don't need a quotation in every paragraph.

SUGGESTED FOOTNOTE FORMS

Use the same style of documentation format throughout a report.

Select one form or style for footnotes and use it throughout your report. Whichever style you prefer (MLA, APA, or the *The Chicago Manual of Style),* be consistent in all details: titles, authors' names, dates, punctuation, page numbers, and so forth. The MLA pattern is followed in the following examples; however, your organization or school may prefer its own style or one that is popularly used.

SINGLE BOOK AUTHOR

```
A. H. Bell, Business Communication: Toward 2000
   (Cincinnati: South-Western Publishing Co., 1992) 67.
```

TWO OR MORE BOOK AUTHORS

```
Thomas First and Laura Canby, Management Techniques for
   Japan (Chicago: Pan-Pacific Press, 1993) 37.
```

EDITED BOOKS

```
E. Raymond Corey, ed., MBA Field Studies (Boston: Harvard
   Business School Publishing Division, 1990) 21.
```

JOURNAL OR MAGAZINE ARTICLE
```
Janet Barnard, "The Information Environment of New
   Managers," The Journal of Business Communication,
   28 (1991): 312.
```

LATER REFERENCES
```
Bell, p. 230.            (If you cite more than one book by Bell, refer
                         also to the appropriate title.)
Velasquez, p. 399.       (Note that for multiauthor books and articles,
                         you only need to cite the first author.)
```

ARTICLES WITHOUT NAMED AUTHORS
```
The Wall St. Journal, Jan. 24, 1992, p. 34.
```
(Titles of articles should be cited, if relevant, and are included before the
name of the journal or newspaper.)

SUGGESTED BIBLIOGRAPHY FORMS

Placed at the end of a report after endnotes, a bibliography differs from footnotes primarily in that it gathers together not only works referenced in the report but also works that the reader may wish to consult for further reading. Bibliographic items appear in alphabetical order, not order of appearance in the text. When books, articles, and other sources are grouped separately, items within each group are alphabetized. Note that the author's last name appears first.

```
Bell, A. H. Business Communication: Toward 2000.
   Cincinnati: South-Western Publishing Co., 1992.
Barnard, J. "The Information Environments of New Man-
   agers," The Journal of Business Communication, 28.4
   (1991): 312.
First, Thomas and Laura Canby, Management Techniques
   for Japan. Chicago: Pan-Pacific Press, 1993.
The Wall St. Journal. Jan. 24, 1992, p. 34.
```

For other reference situations, consult the MLA *Stylesheet*, the APA *Publication Manual*, *The Chicago Manual of Style*, or another standard reference.

ALTERNATIVE DOCUMENTATION STYLES

Most technical documents and some business documents use the APA style for documentation. Note the differences particularly in placement of date and use of abbreviated author citation. The following examples are in the style of the APA *Publication Manual*.

BOOK—ONE AUTHOR
```
Ober, S. (1992). Contemporary Business Communication.
   Boston: Houghton Mifflin Company.
```

BOOK—TWO AUTHORS
```
Lesikar, R. & Pettit, J. D. (1989). Business Communica-
   tion. Homewood, Illinois: R. Irwin, Inc.
```

JOURNAL—ONE AUTHOR
```
Beason, L. (1991). Strategies for Establishing an
   Effective Persona: An Analysis of Appeals to Ethics
   in Business Speeches, The Journal of Business Commu-
   nication, 28, 4, 327.
```

SHORT QUOTATION

Lyons asserts that "feedback from the listener may determine understanding but it is often unreliable" (Lyons, 1993, p. 21).

LONG QUOTATIONS—SEVERAL LINES (WITHIN A REPORT)

Lyons (1993) asserts the following:

Feedback from the listener may determine understanding but it is often unreliable. This may be due to several factors: the listener may believe he/she understands but really does not; the listener's ego may motivate him/her to indicate understanding; and not infrequently, the listener may understand part but not all of the message.

The APA style does not use the title of the work within the citation, but includes it for reference in the endnotes.

THE FINAL PAPER

At this point, let's skip a few stages. Assume that you have finished your research, evaluated the data, interpreted the findings, drawn up a final outline, selected the visuals, and written and edited the draft of the report.[3] With the final draft in mind, you recognize that other writers will be competing for the reader's attention. Every busy person has too much material to read and digest effectively. You must try to make your material so attractive, complete, and interesting that the reader will turn to it in preference to competing material.

The best way to achieve this goal, of course, is to have something important to say and to say it effectively. Some rather mechanical procedures will do a great deal to increase the attractiveness of a report: clear topic heads; ample white space; useful supplements; and an effective strategy of presentation.

TOPIC HEADS

Topic headings act as signposts to direct the reader through the report and to save time.

Mountains of words can be frightening. It is certainly disheartening to open a report and find 14 pages of type staring at us—paragraph after paragraph after paragraph. We need help penetrating it. Assimilation is so much easier when writers put a few signposts along the way. "Here," they might say, "is a section on supervisory training, and here is another dealing with management training, and over here is a third section covering cost of training."

When these signposts, or topic heads, are placed throughout the report, they give the reader a sense of direction. They also save time. Perhaps the vice president wishes to review only the segment on participants' evaluation of training. If topic heads appear throughout the report, the vice president can find that section easily. If someone pulls the report from the file two years from today to look only at the data on the cost of sales training, the reader can find this information quickly.

Place topic heads along the left-hand margin of typed material. By using uppercase letters, boldface type, and a combination of uppercase and lowercase, you can communicate major and minor headings. Centered topic headings and italic type give a further indication of level of importance.

BARRIERS TO COMMUNICATION

Interpersonal Barriers
Emotions
Personality
Bias

Environmental Barriers
Noise
Odors
Physical Obstacles

The wording in the headings should be as parallel as possible, and the material treated under each heading should balance in importance the material discussed under similar headings.

Note in Figure 18–1A the heavy block paragraphs. These overwhelm most readers, who will most likely decide to skip the material. In contrast, Figure 18–1B look attractive, easy to read, and easy to assimilate. In addition, the topic headings tell the reader what to expect in the material and serve as guide to the subject material. There can be no doubt that good formatting makes the communication of ideas easier.

WHITE SPACE

Use white space generously to prevent bulky text from "putting off" your reader.

Generous use of white space and careful arrangement of the material will enhance the appearance of any page. Report pages solidly typed from top to bottom and side to side, with narrow margins and heavy, block paragraphs can look overwhelming to a reader. Keep your paragraphs short and your margins wide (see Figure 18–2).

APPENDICES
AND SUPPLEMENTS

Place relevant supplemental material in an easily located appendix.

Some report writers will examine a segment of their material and conclude that, though it isn't relevant to the subject at hand, it's really too good to discard. So it goes into an appendix. Sometimes, conversely, the report writer has important information that ends up in an appendix instead of the body of the report.

Both approaches are unwise. If the material isn't useful, discard it. If it supplements the text data and may be of value to the reader, place it in an appendix. If you do place material in an appendix, be sure to introduce it in the report. If material is vital to the understanding of the report, then put it in the body.

When you use appendices and supplements, make them as easy as possible to find. Use color dividers or separators, so the reader can turn to the correct supplement easily. A color- or number-coding system may help.

STRATEGY OF
PRESENTATION

All too often, writers spend six weeks gathering information, a week evaluating it, three days writing, and, alas, only five minutes making the presentation. Without a strategy of presentation, a report may not receive the attention it and you, the report writer, deserve. It is not unusual, in a busy business environment, for your report to get buried under the papers that came to the secretary's or decision maker's desk. Or the report may be read without the proper background or introductory setting. When either scenario occurs, not only does the report writer lose, but so does the individual and the organization for whom the report was written.

FIGURE 18–1A ORIGINAL ROUTINE REPORT. The reader has difficulty picking out key ideas and statistics because they are not well formatted or clearly expressed.

To: Wilson Reilly, Director, Company Operations
From: Maria Cabrera, Real Estate Specialist
Date: February 6, 19__
Subject: On-site Inspection of City Ice House

You were essentially right in your intuition, expressed to me on January 10 in our meeting in your office, that the company might find advantageous use for the old "Ice House" building now subject to demolition by the city. We discussed other matters that day, but you may recall that you wanted me to look into the structural and locational factors pertaining to the building and get back to you as soon as possible. I hope this memo is soon enough to serve your decision-making processes, and I will certainly be happy to answer any questions you may have as a result of reading my evaluation of the subject property. You can contact me most mornings at my office extension (3923); in the afternoons I'm usually in the field, but of course can be reached by beeper. I try to respond to all beeper calls within ten minutes, so feel free to reach me this way (and try, if possible, to be near a phone yourself for ten minutes following your call so I can call you back).

Dense, unattractive paragraphs generally contain poorly focused ideas that waste the reader's time.

Well, getting back to the Ice House, here's the situation. The timbers inside are essentially sound, without much dry rot or termite damage. This fact amazed me, since some of the structural beams are probably 60 years old. One of the caretakers at the building told me the beams had been prepared in a special way to withstand the moisture of the ice-making process. The electrical system is another story entirely. It is the old "fuse" system, not breakers, and will need to be replaced almost entirely. Heating in the building is by oil furnace. The unit was inspected by Central Heating, Inc., and is said to be in good shape. The roof needs immediate repair. It is rolled composite asphalt that has not been maintained since the 1970s. Estimates run between $16,000 and $20,000 to strip off the old roofing material and replace it with new material. The estimate for the new electrical system, by the way, was $26,000 for a 400-amp, 60-breaker panel and new copper wiring throughout the building.

As for location, I don't see a problem. The area around the Ice House is undergoing a "yuppie revolution," with older buildings being renovated for upscale apartments and restaurants. The police told me the area was considered very safe at all hours. We should have no particular problems with vandalism during construction or later during leasing and maintenance. Insurance is relatively cheap in the area.

I hope these observations have answered your questions about the building. Feel free to contact me if I can be of further help.

FIGURE 18–1B   REVISED ROUTINE REPORT. White space, indentation, numbering, and clear, specific points make the memo easy to read and understand.

To: Wilson Reilly, Director, Company Operations

From: Maria Cabrera, Real Estate Specialist

Date: February 6, 19__

Subject: On-site Inspection of City Ice House, with Recommendations

Background

On January 10, 19__, you instructed me to inspect the old city Ice House and to prepare an evaluation of its suitability for conversion into ten boutique shops. I visited the building three times (January 12, January 28, and February 1). The findings summarized below are supported by a photo record, which I will be happy to provide if you request.

Observations

On January 12, I inspected the Ice House for structural soundness with the assistance of Martha Victors, city building inspector, with the following result:

1. Main rafters and joists are in good condition and can be retained in renovation.

2. Approximately 30 percent of bracing and spanning lumber has been attacked by termites and/or dry rot and will need to be replaced. Estimate: $6,000.

3. Roofing is composite asphalt and in need of immediate replacement. Estimate: $16,000.

On January 28, I returned to the site with Milton Grift, electrical engineer. We inspected all electrical circuits, with these findings:

1. The present system is outdated and cannot be retained within current building codes. Grift recommends conversion to a 400-amp, 60-breaker system with new copper wiring (Romex, #12) throughout the building. Estimate: $26,000.

Topic headings suggest a well-organized set of ideas and make the reader's task easier.

Lists clearly enumerate and draw attention to specific points.

Wilson Reilly
February 6, 19__
page 2

2. Fixtures cannot be reused without extensive repair. Since many are desirable as antiques, you may want to sell them. Estimated income from sale: $10,000. Estimated expense for new fixtures: $14,000.

On February 1, I visited the site to inspect the area for eight blocks in all directions:

1. Within the boundaries of this area, 80 percent of available commercial space is currently rented (primarily as professional offices, shops, and art studios).

2. Approximately 6,000 people live within the area (walking distance to the Ice House), with a median family income of $42,000.

3. Six building renovations are now underway within the area, with two more in the permit stage. These are condominium projects intended to sell to young professionals in the $90,000 to $160,000 range.

4. Police records show a dropping crime rate, comparable to that measured in outlying suburban areas.

Recommendations

Based on these findings, I recommend proceeding with the Ice House project in three steps:

1. Enter into an escrow on the building with contingencies for undiscovered damage.

2. Put major repair items out to bid with both union and nonunion contractors.

3. Work with marketing to develop an initial "early lease" program to attract precompletion tenants.

Contact me at 3923 if you have immediate questions. I look forward to working with you on this project.

White space between points make the reader's job easier. Refer to Figure 18–1A where many points appear within a single block of text. Which memo would you prefer to read?

FIGURE 18–2   Poor Use of White Space vs. Effective Use. The page on the right appears easier to read, and is, because of the added white space.

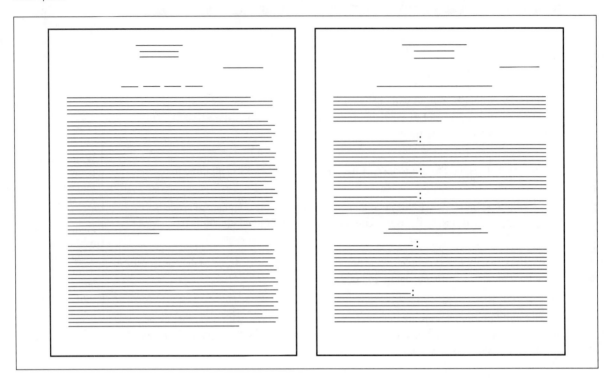

<table>
<tr><td>TIMING YOUR REPORT PRESENTATION

Present the report to the requestor at the right time.</td><td>When you are ready to present the report, oral or written, secure a block of time for the purpose—not just any time, either, but the right time. Make sure that the climate is such that the report will receive the attention it deserves. There is a right time and a right climate for explaining the purpose of the report, what it accomplishes, and what it does not accomplish. Plan the presentation with the following considerations in mind:</td></tr>
</table>

- Who should be present when I submit the report?
- What should I say or explain when I submit the report?
- What visual aids should I use when submitting the report?
- What advance work should I do, and with whom, before I submit the report?

The one basic principle to remember is that the end of the project is as important as the beginning. Never submit a report that has been requested for a special purpose without planning the strategy behind the presentation.[4]

**WRITING
AND SPEAKING
EXERCISES**

1. You notice with some surprise that your boss has instructed you to issue your routine monthly report only on a quarterly basis from now on. Discuss possible reasons for this change.

2. You have decided to research this topic: "A Comparison of Ethical Business Practices: Great Britain and the United States, 1980–1990." Prior to beginning your research, design a hypothesis for this topic which may be either proved or disproved.

3. "Writing good business documents just involves following common sense." Test this assertion by making a list, in order, of the steps you would follow in preparing a report for an executive audience on the importance to your company of upward communication. Then compare your list with the steps suggested in this chapter. Discuss in writing any steps you overlooked or combined.

4. Write down the presentation strategy you would use in delivering the report prepared in the exercise above. Assume that you are delivering the report to Millicent Brady, a busy 55-year-old vice president in charge of human resources. She knows that you are preparing the report, but she did not order its preparation.

5. Explain why a report writer should hold conferences during the entire process of the report writing. Explain why only one meeting generally will not be enough.

6. Report discipline: Is the discipline in the report or in the report writer? Explain.

7. The Cortex Corporation is a typical organization; that is, it has good upward communication, adequate downward flows, and horrid lateral transfer of information. As an example, in the Human Resource Division there are six departments; and although they are literally within a few feet of one another, they might as well be located on different planets. As head of the division, what would you do to improve the information flow, especially of reports, among these units?

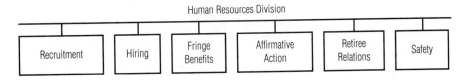

Human Resources Division

| Recruitment | Hiring | Fringe Benefits | Affirmative Action | Retiree Relations | Safety |

8. As assistant to the human resources director in the organization cited in problem 7, you are to make a presentation two weeks from today. The presentation, to be made to the director and the heads of Recruiting, Fringe Benefits, and Affirmative Action, concerns how clearly written brochures may assist the activities of the division. You have finished your report. What can you do to set the stage properly so that you will receive a fair hearing—perhaps even an enthusiastic response—to the ideas you will want to share?

9. Using a ruler, measure the white space on a page that, in your opinion, uses white space well. From your measurements, estimate the proportion of the page that is white space. Apply the standard you develop to a page that uses white space poorly. In general, what percent of a page should be devoted to white space?

10. One step in the process of developing a report is limiting the topic. Limit each of the following broad topics to one on which you could carry through research and present a valuable report: taxes, employee benefits, company goals, and qualities of company leaders.

SUGGESTED
RESOURCES

Haughey, C.F. "Ban Unreadable Reports." *Business Insurance* 25 (July 29, 1991).

Jackson, J., and Hall, B. "Some Ways to Perk Up Your Paperwork." *Supervisory Management* 36 (March 1991).

Maidment, R. "Seven Steps to Better Reports." *Management Solutions* 33 (September 1988).

McTague, M. "How to Write Effective Reports and Proposals." *Training and Development Journal* 42 (November 1988).

O'Connell, S. "Designing Management Reports." *HR Magazine* 36 (May 1991).

Shields, C. "Managing Your Writing." *Management World* 20 (Winter 1992).

Suchan, J., and Colucci, R. "The High Cost of Bureaucratic Written Communications." *Business Horizons* 34 (March-April 1991).

Von Diether, B. "Righting Rotten Writing." *Training* 29 (April 1992).

ENDNOTES

1. Gregory Wasson, "Crime Stoppers," *MacUser* (March 1992):113–126.
2. *Ibid,* p. 122.
3. Suggestions for effective writing may be found in Chapters 6 and 7, and the use of visuals in Chapter 17.
4. V. A. McClelland, "Upward Communication: Is Anyone Listening?" *Personnel Journal* 67 (June 1988).

19

ROUTINE AND SHORT REPORTS

Data and information are **not** communication.   —P. Drucker

The previous chapter explained the importance of reports in organizations. They are vital for providing information, analyzing a problem, and offering recommendations—all factors that are important to decision makers. In this chapter we focus on specific types of reports, their purpose and make up.

A good report turns the spotlight on the topic and frequently secures action. It may start production lines rolling, halt expenditures for TV advertising, or even bring about the merger of two huge organizations.

Let's examine, in this chapter and the next two, the types of reports used most frequently in U.S. companies. Although their purposes may differ, the principles of effective reports are found in all.

MEMO REPORTS

Although a memo is sometimes referred to as a memo report, in this book we treated the memo as a brief written communication issued frequently. As such, the memo is described in detail in Chapter 9.

LETTER REPORTS

For those accustomed to writing business letters, completing a report in letter form is convenient and easy. Be aware, however, the business letter and the *letter report* differ in important ways.

Letter reports present the complicated material usually associated with long formal reports in letter format.

The tone of the letter report is usually quite formal and objective. The writing style is factual, and tables and charts may be used to present substantiating data. The typical inside address, salutation, and complimentary close are often included. Topic headings and subheadings are common. Like the business letter, the letter report is presented on letterhead stationery.

The letter report illustrated in Figure 19-1 reflects significant data. They data are presented for easy assimilation and understanding under relevant topic headings.

FIGURE 19-1   Letter Report with Inside Address, Salutations, Topic Headings, and Signature

Central Computing Supply
3928 Frederick Highway
Fredericksburg, Virginia 22401   Letterhead stationery

May 1, 19__

Mr. George Loesing
Loesing Business Consultants   Inside address
98 Sixth Street
Macon, Georgia 31201

Dear Mr. Loesing: Salutation

In response to your request, we have listed our observations and recommendations on
the inventory level of computer products which you maintain.

Inadequate Inventory of Essential Software   Topic headings
Your current inventory levels of such basic software programs as WordStar, WordPerfect, Lotus 1,2,3, Symphony, Fastback, Xtree, and other standard products should be
raised by 40 percent. At your present pace of retail sales, you will find yourself out of
stock on many of these items during the expected summer peak in computer sales.
Reorder time is now 10 to 15 days — too long to suit your potential customers, who
may choose to shop elsewhere.

Inadequate Inventory of Laptop Computers
In your region, laptop computers for both personal and business use are increasing in
sales more than 39 percent each month. At the same time, laptop manufacturers are
experiencing difficulty filling mounting backorders. We recommend that you increase
inventory of laptop computers by 60 units to last through the summer.

Adequate Inventory of Printers
You now have on hand a good retail stock level of both dot-matrix and letter-quality
printers. You may, however, wish to stock 10 more units of the Okidata laser printer.

I have enclosed a partially completed order form for your review and signature. Again,
thank you for the confidence you've shown in Central Computing Supply. We look
forward to providing you with the best advice, the best products, and the best prices.

Sincerely,

Nancy Springfield   Signature
Nancy Springfield
Sales Manager

COMPUTER REPORTS

Two of the computer's most significant contributions to business have been generation of data for purely informational purposes and generation of data that are vital in the decision making process.

Computer technology can generate volumes of data quickly and easily in the form of computer reports.

Reports can be produced almost automatically through the miracle of computer programming by simply requesting data from the computer's storage devices. No longer is it necessary for a manager to review, analyze, tabulate, and record dozens of pieces of information concerning product sales, personnel changes, advertising expenses, shipping completions, and other items to produce a report. The manager can use a program that makes the computer do all the work, and the printer provides the manager with a good-looking report.

For example, most major grocery stores now use scanners. The check-out clerk passes each item over a glass screen, exposing a series of vertical lines printed on each item. The number and width of these lines vary according to a predetermined standard called the Universal Product Code. The code is "read" and immediately decoded on the screen as well as on the sales slip: six cans of Coke, $2.59; 1.5 pounds of bananas, 50¢ lb., 75¢; and so on. The sales slip is a familiar way that the consumer receives information electronically.

Let's see how the supermarket's managers can use the same data for decision making. Because all scanners record information at a central terminal, the managers can determine sales of not only each store but also of individual check-out lines, the speed with which each checker works, the average number of items purchased per consumer, the rate of returns, and the use of coupons per store or check-out line. In addition, determining which items are selling and which aren't is simplified. Because of the computer's capacity to keep a running score, the managers can monitor each product's inventory level and easily decide when to reorder. Alternatively, the computer can be programmed to generate a reorder form when certain products reach a designated reorder level. If the computer inventory level doesn't match the actual level, the managers have some indication of level of pilfered products ("shrinkage") or those misplaced or shipped in error. Figure 19-2 shows a computer-generated inventory report.

Computers are useful tools, but they are incapable of independently analyzing the vast amounts of data they store.

Many routine reports that are highly dependent on quantitative data no longer require laborious hand recording or tabulation. Many of these functions are now computer generated—daily, monthly, or at the flick of a switch. Keep in mind that computers do not analyze data, they don't write the prose that tells the reader or decision maker what the increase or decrease may indicate. Of course, if the computer has been programmed to print a message (such as, "Time to reorder") when the stock level hits 3, it will do that. However, there was no analysis or interpretation connected with that statement. It was only a command generated by the number 3. Only the report writer can turn the computer reports into meaningful statements on which the decision maker can take action.

Inundating people with computer printouts might cause them to stop taking all of your written messages seriously.

Some individuals become so enamored of their ability to generate computer data easily, they may overwhelm the recipient with pages of "computer printouts." The danger is that either the sender of receiver may feel communication is taking place, when in reality, only data are being transmitted. The end result of inundating others with too much data is the breakdown of effective communication between the parties. Nevertheless, computer reports, when properly generated and used, can supply us with enormous amounts of vital information.

FIGURE 19-2 COMPUTER-GENERATED INVENTORY REPORT

MIDWEST MUSIC SUPPLY, INC.

Wednesday, January 16, 19__   Inventory Report   No. 6
Note: covers all transactions through January 14, 19__

STOCK ON HAND

Item	Quantity	Serial Number	Wholesale	Retail
Bundy	4	29384	$178	$275
Trumpet		29385	178	285
		39284	195	320
		39824	295	455
Selmer	2	48A670	302	486
Flute		46B392	340	505
King	1	J2943	485	675
Trombone				
Victor	3	39243	138	245
Clarinet		38592	184	299
		39853	295	405
Armstrong	1	AC392	507	785
Tuba				
Brandford	2	ZZex44	605	940
Cello		ZXff98	640	975
Rickami	4	29853	495	786
Violin		29834	495	786
		29385	520	820
		48923	730	990

ON ORDER

Item	Quantity	Order Date	Purchase Order	Unit Cost
Czylo	6	10/5/9_	#39205	$98.00
Cymbals				
Basco	24	11/8/9_	#39235	$ 5.50
Reeds				
Comston	24	11/12/9_	#39240	$ 2.12
Valve Oil				

Raw data arranged
for quick reference

A major factor to consider when using computers to generate reports is the maintenance of confidentiality and security. This topic is discussed briefly in Chapter 18.

ROUTINE REPORTS

The many kinds of routine reports should follow basic principles of effective communication.

Among the most routine reports submitted in organizations are periodic reports and progress reports. Both are primarily designed to transmit information, either simply to inform or to be used as the basis for decision making. In many firms, routine reports may carry other designations: justification report, monthly accounting (or marketing or personnel) report, recommendation report, and sales report are just a few. For all of these, the basic principles of good business communication should be kept in mind.

- The prose should be clear and concise
- Adequate quantitative data should be included
- Dramatic changes (within a period or comparatively between periods) should always be explained
- Quantitative differences between periods should be noted numerically and as percentages
- Questions about data should be anticipated and answered
- Data should be complete
- Recommendations should be substantiated
- The design and format should be attractive and readable[1]

THE PERIODIC REPORT

One of the most widely written reports in industry is the *periodic report of activities.* Bank cashiers prepare daily reports. Factory supervisors write weekly reports. Department managers write weekly or monthly reports to their supervisors. Corporations send out annual reports to their stockholders. Often routine computer-generated data are regular components of periodic reports.

Periodic reports summarize activity over a given time.

Standard elements.   Reports are generally composed of certain standard elements: the opening; the various sections, each with an appropriate topic heading; and the signature or initials of the writer at the end. The periodic report invariably begins with a summary of activities for the period covered. This summary is followed by a fairly detailed discussion of the primary topic (sales and sales volume, for example, if sent out by the sales manager; production accomplishments and problems if done by the production manager; numbers of employees, attrition, and employee additions if written by the human resources manager). The periodic report frequently ends with two sections: conclusions and recommendations.

The primary discussion is supported by facts and figures, which almost always include data for a previous period or periods so that current performance can be compared with past performance. The amount and depth of this information depends on what the company wants. For the monthly sales analysis, some companies will want only data on sales; others will require data on sales personnel, sales advertising, competition, sales problems, and perhaps other data. In the monthly personnel report, one firm may be satisfied with data covering the present employee level, the number added, the number dismissed, and the number who left voluntarily. Another firm will want more—perhaps a careful presentation of compensation levels, training, safety, union-management relations, and so on. Figure 19-3 is an example of a typical periodic report. Note in the report that any situation that is somewhat unusual, as compared to the previous month, is explained. See, for example, the section devoted to Group V sales. Also note that the recommendations appear at the end.

Figure 19-4 presents a different format. Here, the various recommendations are noted from time to time throughout the body of the report. The method used, whether as in Figure 19-3 or 19-4, depends on the complexity of the material, the reader's identity, and the company's preferred format.

Firms that rely heavily on periodic reports (usually monthly) would be wise to study the feasibility of (1) using a standard format to be completed by all people in the job category and (2) developing a program that permits the computer to generate data in a useable form at specific time periods.

Use of forms for periodic reports. Some companies develop a standard form for the periodic report; the report writer need only fill in the blank spaces. A standard form has obvious advantages: it is concise, it elicits the exact data desired, and it lessens the work of the department head. It also ensures that the various managers reporting, who may be stationed in different cities throughout the country, will all send in about the same quantity and level of information. Of course, a standard form may also inhibit discussion and expression of ideas on the part of the writer.

Each firm can develop its own forms. The form illustrated in Figure 19-5 is used by a relatively small organization in all its divisions (sales, production, personnel, finance, advertising, and administrative).

THE PROGRESS REPORT

Progress reports let managers know how a project is evolving.

By studying previous progress reports, managers can anticipate and avoid recurring problems.

Managers have to supervise several activities simultaneously. A single department may have four people doing research on the premises, five others engaged in a government project 800 miles away, and four attempting to install a new operation in a customer's plastic division. Managers must know what progress employees are making on each assignment, what problems they have encountered, and when they will complete the jobs. *Progress reports* help managers maintain control by keeping them informed as a project progresses.[2]

Progress reports have a further value. A review of progress reports filed on projects in the past assists managers in planning and working up cost and time estimates for similar operations contemplated for the future. The reports may tell where problem areas existed, what to avoid, and where to focus attention. Thus they act as a reference guide.

Every project has a beginning, a work period, and an end. Progress reports conform to this arrangement. They consist of an initial report, continuing reports, and a terminal statement.

The initial report should cite the background of the project, along with its purpose, specific goals, and sponsor. In addition, it should review the progress made on the assignment in the period covered by the report. Continuing reports merely recount the activities of the period, and the terminal report presents a final summary and analysis.

Most managers prefer progress reports that provide a brief background of the situation, a detailed summary of the period covered, and a statement of the work to be completed during the next time block. Problems and obstacles encountered are usually noted in some detail with recommendations for solutions. (See Figure 19-6).

FIGURE 19-3 PERIODIC REPORT. Note explanation of visuals in report and Recommendations at end of report.

Hawthorne Toy Corporation
Newtonville, New York 12128

Monthly Sales Report
May, 19__

TO: Robert T. Montgomery, Executive Vice President
FROM: Beth Steiner, Sales Manager
DATE: June 5, 19__

Summary

Sales for the month of May have proved to be somewhat heavier than anticipated, and almost 10 percent above those of May last year.

All items in Group II (metal-mechanical) and Group III (packaged games) have sold as expected. Group IV (plastic items) has moved up to a very satisfactory level. Group V (bicycles) has declined.

Sales of all groups are up 15 percent as compared to the same period last year.

Sales expenses have risen again this month in spite of new efforts to achieve economies.

Sales personnel and advertising expenditures have remained static.

Sales

Although The Toy Manufacturers Monthly for April indicated that overall toy sales should be expected to rise approximately 7 percent in May over last year's figures, our sales reflect about a 10 percent increase. Our Sales Incentive Program as well as our introduction of five new items in May may account for the increase.

Group V figures are a cause for concern. Certainly sales in this category should reflect, as they traditionally have, increases in May over April. The reasons for our decline are not clear. However, there may be two important contributing factors:

1. Our higher price to the dealer for our entire bicycle line (as compared to our competitors).
2. Increase in advertising on the part of competitors. Hi-Flyer, for example, has purchased large blocks of TV time.

Situations that are unusual compared to previous periods are explained in periodic reports.

Robert T. Montgomery
June 5, 19__
page 2

SALES VOLUME MAY, 19__ (IN DOZENS)			
ITEM	MAY 19__	APRIL 19__	MAY (previous year)
GROUP I (misc.)			
A 100	5750	5700	5200
A 101	6500	6400	5800
B 300	9750	9500	8800
GROUP II			
M 101	3150	3100	2800
M 102	2500	2500	2200
M 103	2300	2100	2000
M 104	2400	2300	2100
GROUP III			
G 405	8500	8450	7800
G 407	7500	7300	6500
G 408	7000	7100	8200
GROUP IV			
P 600-5	21,000	20,000	23,000
P 610-5	23,500	24,000	26,000
GROUP V (in single units)			
Whippet			
Girls'	8500	9300	9000
Boys'	12,500	14,000	14,500
Hi-Ride			
Girls'	16,000	16,000	16,500
Boys'	19,000	21,000	20,500
Speedsters			
Girls'	12,500	14,000	13,900
Boys'	16,500	17,500	18,500

Facts and figures presented visually substantiate the observations made in the text of the periodic reports.

Robert T. Montgomery
June 5, 19__
page 3

Advertising Expenditures
According to Bob Carlton, advertising manager, expenditures for magazine and newspaper ads were 5 percent above May of last year. However, he indicated that we will, for the first time, use TV spot commercials during the summer months. An initial expenditure of $45,000 for TV will be made in two carefully selected areas on the east and west coasts. Sales will be observed carefully and correlations, if any, drawn.

Sales Personnel
The number of employees, with the exception of trainees, has remained stable. This number rises and falls periodically and is no cause for concern or action.

SALES PERSONNEL

	MAY 19__	APRIL 19__	MAY (previous year)
Sales Personnel			
Area I	40	38	39
Area II	20	20	22
Area III	25	23	23
Trainees			
Area I	6	3	0
Area II	3	0	0
Area III	3	1	0

Recommendations
1. Do an immediate cost analysis to determine if wholesale prices on the Group V line can be cut 10 percent to meet competition. If this can be done, our market share will certainly rise.
2. Gain additional savings by using plastic instead of rubber handle grips, drop battery-powered road light (as standard equipment), and apply two (instead of three) coats of enamel to the bike frame.
3. Cut all prices in Group II 15 percent when purchases are made in gross lots.

Often, a periodic report ends with recommendations.

FIGURE 19-4   Periodic Report with Recommendations Appearing Throughout

MONTHLY SALES REPORT
MARCH, 19__

To: Mei-ling Chien, General Manager
From: Harold Palmer, Sales Manager
Date: April 5, 19__

SUMMARY

Sales are up 1.2 percent from last month and 10.7 percent from the same period of a year ago. Net profits are up a corresponding amount in spite of added advertising expenditures and increased personnel costs. High unit margins have enabled us to maintain our net return on sales.

While the overall sales picture looks good, the outlook for individual product lines varies from "terrible" to "tremendous." We are passing up opportunities with great growth potential; yet at the same time, we continue to carry some product lines that should have been dropped long ago. Inventories have taken a significant jump (4.6 percent) from last month, but this is largely attributable to the change in accounting procedure. Our monthly inventory turnover ratio has improved from .70 for March 19__ to .74 for March 19__.

SALES VOLUME

Sales volume data are presented below. Items with an asterisk are discussed below.

Sales Volume

Product Line	March 19__	February 19__	March 19__	% Change 3/__ - 3/__
Group One				
*Air Conditioners	102,000	100,000	85,000	20.0
*Sun Roof Conv. Kits	23,000	24,000	37,000	(38.0)
	$125,000	$124,000	$122,000	
Group Two				
Chrome Tailpipe Extensions	22,000	22,000	25,000	(12.0)
Headlamp & Door Trim	20,000	20,000	25,000	(20.0)
Mirrors	21,000	20,000	15,000	40.0
*Ski Racks	4,000	4,000	28,000	(50.0)
Miscellaneous	13,000	14,000	10,000	(30.0)
	$80,000	$80,000	$103,000	

Mei-ling Chien
April 5, 19___
page 2

Group Three

*Stereo Tape Players	104,000	100,000	50,500	105.9
Radios	83,000	82,000	80,000	3.8
Clocks	15,000	14,000	10,000	50.0
	$202,000	$196,000	$140,500	
Total Dollar Sales	$407,000	$400,000	$365,500	

PRODUCT LINES

I. Air Conditioners. Sales forecasts continued to be very bright.

Recommendations:
1. We should continue our heavy emphasis on this line.
2. Truck "camper" market for air conditioners should be investigated.

II. Sun Roofs. Sales of auto sun roof conversion kits are showing a downward trend. Analysis of past sales records indicates that this decline has continued for the past five years. Automotive industry statistics on cars sold without sun roofs as original equipment point out a far greater decline than our own sales drop. As automotive sun roof sales and our kits have always shown a direct positive correlation—but with a three-year lag—we appear to be headed for real trouble in this area.

Our sales personnel report repeated inquiries about bicycle racks for truck "campers." This appears to be an excellent market.

Recommendations:
We should drop standard auto sun roof conversion kits from our sales line. To replace this item, we should consider developing a sturdy lock-type bicycle rack for "campers." Growth potential appears great in this field.

III. Ski Racks. Sales have dropped 50 percent this year. This decline is due to the heavy competition from the new rubber-plastic Hi Snow model. For the foreseeable future, we will not be able to manufacture a similar item because of our production limitations.

Recommendation:
We should drop this product line as soon as possible.

When a periodic report deals with multiple products, projects, or problems, separate recommendations can appear throughout the text.

Mei-ling Chien
April 5, 19__
page 3

IV. Stereo tape players. Sales increases in this area have been fantastic. But we are merely holding our share of the market! This is our big opportunity to push American Automotive Accessories into a period of rapid and profitable expansion.

Evidence continues to support the popularity of the cassette player, particularly in the secondary equipment market. We should continue our policy of specialization on the cassette models.

Recommendations:
1. In spite of sales gains, we should *increase* our efforts on this product line. Increased market penetration is important. Innovation, quality, and availability of product should be of prime concern. Continue heavy advertising.
2. We should strongly consider stocking a tape library as an addition to our product line.

ADVERTISING

Our first-quarter increases in advertising expenditures appear to have paid off well in added sales and profits. However, our Accounting Department feels we should cut back advertising "now that we're rolling." I'm strongly opposed to this. Coca-Cola tried cutting back advertising a few years ago—with highly negative results.

Recommendation:
We should not only maintain but expand our advertising program.

PERSONNEL

While our sales have increased 10.7 percent from one year ago, our sales staff has increased 25.0 percent for this same period. This situation is puzzling, but I'm delaying staff reduction pending (1) developments in our stereo and air conditioning lines and (2) the results of our sales training program.

Recommendation:
Sales personnel strength should be maintained another 90 days. The personnel situation will be reevaluated at that time.

FIGURE 19-5   Periodic Report Form Used by a Small Company

TO:
FROM:
DATE:
TIME PERIOD COVERED:

Number of Employees Entered on Payroll
    Unit A   _____
    Unit B   _____
    Unit C   _____

Total Regular Rate Hours Paid
    Unit A   _____
    Unit B   _____
    Unit C   _____

Total Overtime Rate Hours Paid
    Unit A   _____
    Unit B   _____
    Unit C   _____

Sick Leave Hours Taken (if any employee exceeds 16 hours, attach employee name, work I.D. number, and brief statement of circumstances to this report)
    Unit A   _____
    Unit B   _____
    Unit C   _____

Personal Leave Hours Taken (if any employee exceeds 8 hours, attach employee name, work I.D. number, and brief statement of circumstances to this report)
    Unit A   _____
    Unit B   _____
    Unit C   _____

Unaccounted Absence Hours (attach employee name, work I.D. number, and brief of circumstances and action taken by manager)
    Unit A   _____
    Unit B   _____
    Unit C   _____

Additional Information or Recommendations:
_____

(signature)
_____

(date)

Companies benefit from using a standard format for frequent routine reports.

FIGURE 19-6 Progress Report

Progress Report #4

Period: January 1 — April 30, 19__
Date: May 5, 19__
From: Rachel Thomas, Sales Supervisor
Subject: HumidAir Direct Mail Promotion

Overview:

As created by Jenkins, Williams and Todd Agency, Inc., the HumidAir direct-mail campaign seeks to develop customer leads for the sale of HumidAir 607 units (humidifiers which attach to both gas and oil furnaces).

In a progress report, provide a brief background to the situation.

Activities This Period:

63,000 homes in Sector C received the "Dry Air and Your Health" mailing by January 30. A total of 570 information request cards were returned by March 1, and an additional 54 cards from the original mailing by April 30 (a response rate of 3.8 percent).

These lead cards were distributed as they arrived to sales representatives according to area.

Results of Sales Calls from Lead Cards

	Total Leads	Calls Made	Contracts Signed	Follow-Ups	Contracts Signed from Follow-Ups
Area 7	120	98	31	15	3
Area 8	114	95	32	20	5
Area 9	130	109	35	25	3
Area 10	131	106	41	19	3
Area 11	129	115	30	20	5
Totals	624	523	169	99	19

Summarize the present period's activities thoroughly using specific facts and figures.

Comments on Activities:

Sales representatives for Areas 7 and 8 completed training on December 15, and, therefore, have been assigned lighter client load for their first quarter. We were pleased to see that both of these new salespeople achieved a 33 percent contract-to-call ratio. Based on those results, we will balance the distribution of leads as evenly as possible in future quarters.

Planning for Next Period:

We anticipate the new HumidAir incentive mailing in late April to produce comparable results to the January mailing, assuming that temperatures remain cold through the early spring. Our "May in Milan" drawing should yield an increase in information cards received. Jenkins, Williams, and Todd Agency will monitor contract-to-card ratios to evaluate the cost-effectiveness of the vacation trip incentive approach.

Explain what should happen during the next period.

The progress report may also be prepared by filling out a standard form. When a firm has several teams in the field, each working on a different project, a standard form can be valuable and assures uniformity.

WRITING AND SPEAKING EXERCISES

1. Interview someone at a local business about computer reports the company uses regularly. In an oral or written report, describe what computer reports the company typically issues and why. Describe how such information had to be produced prior to computerization.

2. List the specific areas that are usually covered in an *initial* progress report.

3. Imagine that you own and manage Bristol Auto Supply. Each item in your large inventory is computer-coded. When an item sells, the computer takes note of what it was, how long it sat on the shelf, and how many other like items remain in stock. What kind of computer report would you, as manager, like to receive? How often? What information should the report contain? How will you use the information?

4. Assume that your CEO has given you the task of shortening company reports. Develop a list of guidelines to help company writers report information in fewer words.

5. You're in charge of developing a new product line for the company. You want to receive progress reports from your development team. Make up a product line. Then describe in detail each progress report you want to receive from the project start to finish.

6. Imagine that you are chief developer of a new office tower. Your funding agencies have requested regular progress reports from you. List six stages at which you plan to send progress reports. (Your first report could be submitted after land acquisition.)

7. Use the following facts as the basis for a short progress report directed to Ms. Harriet Conway, executive director, Publications Division, Western Enterprises, Inc.

   Facts: You recently conducted a survey to determine who reads what in the monthly company magazine, *Western Worlds.* On February 6, the current issue was mailed to the home addresses of 2,804 company employees. February 25 telephone interviews with 200 employees chosen at random gave these results:

   • Twenty-four percent did not know if the February issue had arrived at their homes.
   • Fifty-five percent had not looked at the issue.
   • Among those who had at least looked through the magazine, 26 percent could recall no single detail, article title, picture, or advertisement from the issue; 74 percent had fairly good recall of various items.

   The magazines costs the company $1.86 per issue delivered to an employee's home. Total publication costs are escalating at 17 percent per year.

   As director of communications for the company, you have assumed responsibility for publishing and distributing the magazine.

   During the past three months, you have spent $16,500 making the magazine look more professional. You have three unsolicited letters from employees praising the "new look" of the February issue. In addition, you have received one scorching letter condemning the February issue as "more company money spent on frills when it could be spent on salaries."

The company is trying to decide whether the magazine should be expanded, cut back, or dissolved. No statistics exist for determining how readers responded to the magazine at an earlier period. Ms. Conway has asked you to sum up in a progress report how employees are reacting to your efforts to improve the magazine. Make any reasonable assumptions you wish.

8. Four months have passed since you submitted your progress report to Ms. Conway in problem 7. She has asked you for monthy periodic reports, detailing the essential facts about that month's issue of *Western Worlds:*

- Number of pages
- Cost per issue delivered
- Number delivered to employees
- Standard features
- Use of company contributors
- Use of freelance writers
- Number of photographs
- Number of full-time employee hours spent in editing, production, and distribution
- Percentage of your work time spent on *Western Worlds*
- Number of unsolicited letters received within 14 days of delivery
  Number of complaints, written or oral, received within 14 days of delivery

She has told you that your periodic reports will help establish a suitable budget for the magazine at the end of the current fiscal year. Prepare a periodic report that satisfies the director's criteria. Design and submit a report that can be filled in each month and submitted to Ms. Conway.

9. Frequently you find yourself short of time. Prepare a periodic report detailing your activities and time expended on each. You may wish to break your activities into classes, recreational activities, study periods, meals, sleeping, transportation, personal time, social affairs, and so forth. From your analysis of time spent, consider offering yourself conclusions and recommendations for future activities.

10. In what ways does a letter report differ from a business letter?

CASES

Complete the following assignments from the Cases for Discussion section at the back of this book:

1. The Jim Cantonelli case—Assignment 3
2. Hostile Takeover case—Assignment 4
3. The Sun Fresh case—Assignment 4
4. Was This Really Fraud? case—Assignment 4

**SUGGESTED
RESOURCES**

Bredin, J. "Say It Simply: Eschew Obfuscation." *Industry Week* 240 (July 15, 1991).

Geddie, T. "Write Face to Face." *Communication World* 7 (September 1990).

Gilbert, J. "Watch Your Language." *Management Quarterly* 32 (Summer 1991).

Gladis, S. "Talk It Out: How to Write Collaboratively." *Public Relations Quarterly* 36 (Summer 1991).

Gold, R. "Reader Friendly Writing." *Supervisory Management* 34 (January 1989).

Wayne, F., and Scriven, J. "Problem and Purpose Statements: Are They Synonymous Terms in Writing Reports for Business?" *Bulletin of the Association for Business Communication* 54 (March 1991).

ENDNOTES

1. J. Gilbert, "Watch Your Language." *Management Quarterly* 32 (Summer 1991): 28.
2. I.I. Varner, *Contemporary Business Report Writing* (Chicago: The Dryden Press, 1991): 168.

FORMAL AND ANNUAL REPORTS

Effective report: vital key to decision making.

Perhaps one of the most important documents written in industry is the long formal report. It may be composed internally, or by an outside consulting group, or by a financial institution having a major stake in an organization's future. Frequently, a formal report deals with a major problem: a merger, a company restructuring, the introduction and production of a new product, the acquisition of another firm, the construction of a new facility, a change in location of the organization, the opening of a foreign subsidiary, or other important and costly ventures.

In every situation, data must be gathered, analyzed, interpreted, and presented together with carefully drawn conclusions and thoroughly substantiated recommendations. Such a project may require an examination of population trends and growth, economic conditions, sales potential, cultural factors, ethnic considerations, financial requirements, national and international affairs, long-term considerations, government requirements, or other contributing factors.

The annual report is a type of formal report. The Securities and Exchange Commission (SEC) requires all publicly held companies to issue a yearly report detailing the organization's financial status. Most of these reports also include other topics such as: the organization's goals; background information on its officers, products, and research; the corporation's social and environmental concerns; a vision and/or mission statement; and other subjects.

OBJECTIVES OF A FORMAL REPORT

Formal reports persuade, inform, or analyze.

The objective of a formal report may be one or more of the following: to persuade, to inform, or to analyze.

THE PERSUASIVE REPORT

Suppose you want to convince your readers that a new 48-story apartment building to be constructed next year should be heated and air-conditioned with natural gas. You will aim your arguments at several groups: the architects, the

Formal persuasive reports use evidence to convince readers to follow a recommended course of action.

financiers, the contractor, and probably the firm that will operate or sponsor the building. Because these are all intelligent, analytical readers, you must buttress the report with statistical data and information at every point, and with a good deal of logical reasoning. Your purpose is to demonstrate why the building's heating and cooling system, as well as its kitchen equipment, should be gas rather than electric. The persuasive report must persuade through the logic of its arguments and the strength of its substantiating data and should avoid an overly emphatic and hard-sell approach.

THE INFORMATIONAL REPORT

Formal informational reports offer data rather than recommendations.

As the name suggests, the *informational report* serves only to present data to use as a record or as the basis for decision making. Perhaps the most frequent fault of such reports is overkill: they smother the reader with too much information. The scope and limitations of the topic should be carefully defined. The informational report is sometimes referred to as an *investigative* report or *research* report.

THE ANALYTICAL REPORT

Formal analytical reports compare alternatives.

The purpose of the *analytical report* is to analyze data in order to recommend a course of action among the available alternatives. For example, you may want to examine the future of your industry in relation to your company's growth and expansion in the next five years. State your firm's goals and objectives and suggest strategies for reaching them. Your report should examine all supportive activities within the firm, such as human resources, finance, manufacturing, marketing, production, distribution, and research and development. It should also analyze the external environment: the market, consumerism, raw material supply, life-styles and values, legal and legislative forces, energy, and so on.

An analytical report is extremely valuable in a situation where a comparison must be made between or among alternatives. Perhaps two or more products, sales plans, building designs, or production layouts need to be completed. An analytical report carefully compares and analyzes the respective strong and weak points of each product, design, or method for the reader. Invariably, the analytical report concludes with recommendations for a specific course of action.

PLANNING A FORMAL REPORT

Usually, a great deal more time, effort, and funding go into the analysis, research, and execution of the formal report than of most short reports. Because a formal report is a major effort, care must be taken to ensure, every step of the way, that everyone involved is on the right track. Nothing is as devastating for the report requestor and the report writer than to end up with a formal report that does not fulfill the correct objective. The cause of the failure may be a misunderstanding or no understanding of the problem to be investigated, the purpose to be achieved, the audience to analyze, the depth to be investigated, or the limits to recognize.

Plan and adjust the report's purpose and scope by frequently communicating with others involved in the process.

The best way to achieve the desired result is to check at every step during the process. That checking should be carried out by the report requestor *and* you, the writer. If you are not involved with another person, you must check yourself to be sure you have chosen the correct problem, purpose, limitations, research parameters, and so on. Carefully review each of these steps (discussed in Chapter 18) as you plan, develop, research, and write the formal report.

COMPONENTS OF A FORMAL REPORT

The components of a formal report help readers assimilate complex or lengthy information.

When a clearly written report runs to six pages or longer, it probably covers a fairly wide area and includes a good deal of information. At this point you should begin to think of helping the reader assimilate the material by including a title page, a table of contents, a summary, and perhaps an appendix for statistical and/or reference data.

Some of the specific sections of the long report, in the order in which they appear, are discussed in the pages that follow. Few reports contain all the divisions listed. Most long reports do carry a letter of transmittal, title page, table of contents, and executive summary, in addition to the basic body. As you read the next few pages, refer to the sample formal report illustrated later in the chapter. Keep in mind that the report is fictionalized and designed simply as an example.

PRELIMINARIES

The letter of transmittal identifies the audience for and the purpose of the report.

Letter of transmittal. A letter of transmittal should accompany the formal report to set the stage for the readers so they will understand why and for whom the report was prepared. Placed at the top of the report or clipped to the title page, the letter usually covers the following items (see Figure 20-1, p. 464):

- Authorization for research
- Purpose of the project
- Limitations of the report, noting legal restrictions and the boundaries of time and funds. This section can be of great help because it tells the reader what to expect and what not to expect.
- Listing of certain key sources
- Reference to any finding in the report that is of particular importance or interest to the reader. Recommendations and/or acknowledgments of assistance may be included in the letter of transmittal.

A foreword or preface may replace a letter of transmittal; however, that is not typical for long reports.

Title page. The title page should carry the report title; the name of the person, group, or organization for whom the report is written; the author's name; the name of the group or company issuing the report; and the date (see Figure 20-1, p. 465).

Avoid cute titles such as "Pressing Problems: Parker Garment Co." Make yours informative and interesting, for example, "Back to School: Manager's Needs for Continuing Education in International Relations." An aircraft company issued a report titled "Flying High: A Survey of Supersonic Aircraft."

Effective titles encapsulate report contents and stimulate the reader's interest.

Good titles can be difficult to create. Remember that what you want is a title that (1) clearly conveys the subject matter of the document and (2) is phrased to attract the reader's interest. Perhaps the best way to secure a title that measures up to those criteria is to write in steps. First, write a title that is adequately descriptive of the contents of the report. That will probably produce a title that is relatively long. Next, shorten it so that the essential element remains, then add an intriguing word or two. Phrasing the title as a question also does the job.

> **Version 1:** "An Analysis of the Marketability of a New Breakfast Cereal: Bountiful Bran Breakfast Flakes"
> **Version 2:** "An Analysis of the Sales Potential of Bountiful Bran Breakfast Flakes"
> **Version 3:** "Bountiful Bran Breakfast Flakes: Will They Sell?"

Table of contents. The table of contents (see Figure 20-1, p. 466) is prepared after the report has been typed. It lists chapter or section titles and subdivisions, if desired, with page numbers indicated for each. Headings should agree with those in the final outline. Lists of illustrations and tables may also be included (see Figure 20-1, p. 467).

Executive Summary. The *executive summary* has become an almost integral part of reports—especially those reports that are extensive or detailed. Basically, it gives the reader a summary, a synopsis, or an abstract of the entire report. The executive summary is valuable for at least two types of readers: (1) executive decision makers who wish an overview of the long reports they must read in order to take action, and (2) top-level executives who want to keep abreast of what is going on in the divisions within their corporate structure but who do not have the time or inclination to read extensive reports on which they do not make decisions.

The executive summary saves valuable time by giving decision makers a brief yet complete overview of a report.

The executive summary routinely includes these elements:

- Subject of the report or the problem of concern
- Purpose of the report
- Scope of the investigation and research on which the report is based.
- Key ideas presented in the report
- Conclusions reached
- Recommendations made

Although the executive summary follows no precise rule for length, it usually takes less than a typewritten page. Here is an example of an executive summary of a report on the advisability of moving from a rather informal newsletter to an employee magazine for a firm of 21,000 employees.

EXECUTIVE SUMMARY

The executive summary . . . gives necessary background on the origin of the report

As approved by the Executive Committee of the company, a research project was undertaken to determine whether it would be advisable to move from our monthly newsletter, *HiLights at Harper,* to a monthly 32-page employee magazine. A consultant from our advertising agency assisted in the make up and design of a questionnaire and an interview schedule.

. . . identifies research methods

A carefully selected sample of 10 percent of our employees was surveyed with a mail questionnaire. A 70 percent response was received. One percent of the total work force was interviewed. Both sample were carefully selected and the results judged 90 percent reliable (with a plus 2 or minus 2 error).

. . . reports research results

The results indicated the employees desire:

1. more information about company sales, profits, new products, and so forth, not now available in the newsletter.
2. more information about employee contributions to company advances.
3. opportunities available to employees for training and advancement (also not consistently available now).

The approximate increase in yearly cost for a news magazine has already been communicated and approved by the Executive Committee.

... states conclusions

The conclusion the report reaches is that employees desire a monthly employee news magazine and that such a publication would be a wise investment.

The recommendations, based on research, and the conclusions reached are as follows:

... recommends
appropriate actions

1. Publish an employee news magazine (title to be determined).
2. Publish the first issue four months from the first of this month and bimonthly thereafter.
3. Continue *HiLights at Harper* until two weeks prior to the first issue of the magazine.
4. Limit the news magazine to 32 pages and two colors.
5. Hire a full-time employee to assist the present newsletter editor.

BODY

The body of most reports can be divided into three major sections: introduction, discussion, and conclusions and recommendations.

The introduction
elaborates on relevant
background information.

Introduction. If the report has a letter of transmittal, an executive summary, or other prefatory sections, probably most of the introduction has already been presented. In any event, the introduction should give the reader sufficient background to fully understand the report (see Figure 20-1, pp. 463-479).

In the introduction, you may include a history of the situation and a clear statement of the problem to be solved or examined. Note limitations of the investigation and state the purpose of the report. Explain the research methods used as well as how validity or reliability of the survey was secured. If specific definitions are important to the clear understanding of the report, present them at this time.

The introduction should explain the plan of presentation of the report. Telling readers that all statistical data may be found in the appendix, that sample questionnaires are in the body, and that this report is based on the initial study dated March 15, 19__ will orient them to the report.

The discussion presents,
analyzes, and interprets
the evidence on which the
author bases conclusions
and recommendations.

Discussion. The discussion is the vital part of the report and makes up 75 to 85 percent of the total length. In the discussion the investigator presents, analyzes, and interprets the information and points out significant facts and relationships among the data.

Throughout the discussion, assist the reader by being clear in your presentation. To this end, use topic and subtopic headings and present some of the data in easy-to-analyze tables, charts, and graphs, if appropriate.

Conclusions and
recommendations lead
the reader to choose a
specific course of action
in light of the evidence.

Conclusions and recommendations. Conclusions and recommendations are given in most types of reports. Be sure that each conclusion or recommendation is thoroughly substantiated in the body of the report. At no time should the reader of the report ask, "Well, where is the evidence for this?" The evidence should be in the discussion section of the report.

Lately, there has been a trend toward placing the conclusions and recommendations immediately after the executive summary or introduction rather than at the end of the report. This makes sense. Top executives receive reports from every division and department of the organization. These reports are vital if they are to know about all the firm's activities and to appreciate the big picture.

FIGURE 20-1 A FORMAL REPORT

 HUMAN RESOURCE RESEARCH CO.
1400 West Franklin Road
Cincinnati, OH 45206

April 15, 19__

Ms. Joan M. Jenkins, Human Resource Director
Tory Manufacturing Corporation
2762 Fulton Street
San Francisco CA 94111

Dear Ms. Jenkins:

The attached report is the result of the research project that you requested in your letter of January 20, 19__. It is a study of corporate listening training programs, combined with an analysis of top human resources administrators' opinions regarding the importance of listening in industry. You will find our conclusions and recommendations included in this report.

The purposes of the study were to determine
1. How extensively corporations are utilizing listening training programs.
2. How listening as a skill is viewed by human resource administrators.
3. How HR administrators rate the listening ability of employees and managers.

Primary research was limited to a questionnaire mailed to human resource administrators of 98 randomly selected corporations that were members of the 19__ Fortune 500 Corporations in the U.S. Several articles drawn from journals and magazines were used for secondary research.

This project was both a challenging and rewarding undertaking. We believe that our findings will aid you and other human resource administrators in understanding corporate listening training programs. If you have any questions, please call.

Cordially yours,

Juanita Sanchez
Research Associate

Attachment

The letter of transmittal explains the report's origin, purpose, research methods and invites the reader's response.

LISTENING TRAINING PROGRAMS FOR INDUSTRY: A KEY TO PROFITS

Presented to

Joan M. Jenkins
Human Resource Director

Tory Manufacturing Corporation

Submitted by

Juanita Sanchez
Research Associate

Human Resource Research Co.

      April 15, 19__

The title page includes the report's title, audience, author, and date.

TABLE OF CONTENTS

The table of contents lists the beginnings of major sections and subsections.

i

LIST OF TABLES

The list of tables or illustrations locates important graphic aids within the text.

ii

EXECUTIVE SUMMARY

Most people have had courses in reading, writing, and speaking. However, listening, the communication skill used most often, is not usually a part of the U.S. educational system. In this report, we show the importance industry places on listening as a communication skill and the extent to which it has implemented listening training programs.

The report is based on a nationwide mail questionnaire sent to randomly chosen members of the Fortune 500 Largest Industrial Corporations in the United States. It is also based on secondary research from magazine and journal articles.

The results of the survey indicated that top human resource administrators consider listening to be an important communication skill. A slight majority of corporations are utilizing listening training programs: These have proved to be effective.

Because our research indicates that listening is an important and valuable skill, we recommend that the Tory Manufacturing Corporation implement listening training programs for its employees in order to increase productivity and the efficiency of operations.

The executive summary gives decision makers an overview of the report.

CONCLUSIONS

1. Top human resource administrators consider listening one of the most important communication skills for employees in industry.

2. Currently, a significant number of major corporations utilize listening training programs.

3. Top human resource administrators feel that both their employees and other managers are not listening at optimum levels.

4. Corporations that encourage their employees to give feedback to their superiors report higher levels of listening efficiency among both employees and managers.

5. Corporations that have implemented listening programs have been able to measure an improvement in employee morale and an increase in productivity.

Placing conclusions and recommendations before the discussion saves the reader time and clarifies the author's purpose.

RECOMMENDATIONS

1. Tory should implement listening training programs to increase productivity, efficiency, and morale.

2. Tory should encourage its employees to give feedback to their supervisors in order to increase levels of listening efficiency among both employees and managers.

-1-

INTRODUCTION

Background Information

Miscommunication due to poor listening costs industry billions of dollars every year (Choi, 1991). The importance of good listening skills in business today cannot be emphasized enough. People in business today spend more than 50% of their work time in listening-based activities (Winowski, 1990). Even though listening is so vital in business, it is the least-taught communication skill in the U.S. educational system. This is a major problem facing U.S. industry today. Many companies are battling it by using special listening training programs and techniques of their own.

Purpose of the Report

The purpose of this report is (1) to discover how listening as a communication skill is viewed by top human resource administrators, (2) to determine the extent to which corporations are utilizing listening training programs and techniques, and (3) to discover how top human resource administrators rate the listening ability of both their employees and other managers.

Hypothesis

Listening is a vital communication skill in industry that can be significantly improved by utilizing training programs.

Scope and Depth of the Project

The object of this report is to give human resource administrators a general idea of the importance of listening as a communication skill in industry and to urge them to study further the beneficial impact that implementing a listening training program and listening techniques might have on the corporation.

The primary source of this information was a mail questionnaire (see Appendices I and II). The secondary sources, such as journal and magazine articles, were found in various libraries in the San Francisco area.

QUANTUM'S LISTENING TRAINING PROGRAM

One of the leading companies implementing a listening training program is the Quantum Corporation. Quantum began its program in mid-1987. This company has not only increased the efficiency and productivity of its corporate operations, but it has also improved the morale of a large percentage of its employees.

Quantum started by using seminars to train its 700 most senior U.S. and European managers. After the training became well known, demand for the seminar from employees at all levels virtually exploded.

-2-

Specific heading titles organize the arrangement of evidence in the discussion.

Because of the enormous number of requests for the listening seminars, more practical methods of presenting listening material had to be implemented. Quantum's next step was to produce a videotape that explained why listening was important, followed by a cassette tape covering the basics of good vs. bad listening, and a booklet on good listening techniques, which was sent to all of its 45,000 U.S. employees' homes (Tanaka, 1991). By the fall of 1989, a staggering 8,000 employees attended the formal listening seminars.

When asked if he could specifically point out any losses due to poor listening in his company, Quantum's CEO, Verne Patel, replied, "How about $600,000?" Apparently a customer asked for a quote on a large order. Here is what happened, according to Mr. Patel:

> Apparently our employee did not listen and no action was taken. The customer called and made the same request of the same employee. The customer was sent information on the wrong product because of faulty listening. The account would do what you or I would do . . . he went elsewhere and so did a $600,000 order (Tanaka, 1991). This is only one example of dozens Verne Patel said he could cite.

This example clearly demonstrates that good listening skills are invaluable in order to conduct business successfully in today's world.

CORPORATE LISTENING TECHNIQUES

The implications of good listening skills are not only external, but also internal. Poor management-employee relations can lead to high employee turnover, which is expensive. Employees must feel that they can approach management to discuss not only on-the-job problems, but also personal problems. According to Dr. Williams, consultant to the pharmaceutical firm of Jamestown and Whicker:

> Perhaps the best way to secure the excellent ideas which employees have for increasing production, cutting costs, and improving morales is for managers to listen carefully to the members of the work force. The manager who is willing to listen will find the exercise satisfying and profitable (Tanaka, 1991).

Expert testimony from secondary research helps build a convincing case.

Maintaining good management-employee relations and keeping employees happy add to the unity of the corporation, resulting in reduced employee turnover.

Techniques used to listen to employees vary from company to company. A good example of how a large corporation undertakes this task is U.S. Aircraft. Even though this corporation has 67,000 employees, it has outstanding management-employee relations.

-3-

One of U.S. Aircraft's techniques is employee surveys. These are used to reveal the moods and attitudes of its employees toward management, benefits, their salaries, their jobs, their image of the company, and other job-related concerns. The company surveys a cross-section of its employees every six months, keeping the questions basically the same in order to spot changes in employee opinion and see trends. With this constant influx of information, management is able to recognize potential problems and react accordingly.

Surveys are but one of U.S. Aircraft's methods of listening to its employees. Others include an employee assistance department, where employees can contact officers confidentially for assistance with a problem; "Let's Talk," a formal six-step employee problem-solving procedure; and "Open Gate," a system that provides employees a channel to make anonymous inquiries of company officials and receive answers within ten days.

Baker Life Insurance Company's method of listening to its employees is called "Listening Posts." These "posts" are various methods by which management receives feedback from employees. These include surveys, exit interviews, an employees' advisory panel, and a grievance procedure. All of these programs " . . . are vital in any effort to remain alert to potential problems and keep management from isolating itself" (Winowski, 1990).

Incorporating multiple sources indicates thorough preparation.

HOW GOOD LISTENING PRODUCES RESULTS

Listening to employees has not only increased the efficiency of operations, but also has helped firms restructure operations for the better. Employees on the line are the first to discover if there is a better way of getting work done. Historically, this precious information has been suppressed because of the dictatorial structure of antiquated management styles. Managers must listen well to their employees.

Martin Machine Tool Company is an excellent example of a listening "pay-off." Mike Martin has always listened to employees. Until 1991, he recalled, the company had used an assembly line arrangement which seemed efficient for its products. However, in March of that year, an employee committee suggested to Mike Martin that the assembly lines be scrapped and that the employees develop their own production structure.

Autonomous work groups were established, with each group responsible for its own production levels, quality control, and problem solving. In the 18 months this system has been in effect, production has increased 20 %, absenteeism has dropped by 50%, and morale has improved dramatically. Mike Martin said, "It's a good thing I'm a good listener" (Fletcher, 1992).

-4-

SURVEY METHOD

The specific survey of human resource administrators was conducted over a 14-day period from March 4 to April 6, 19__.

Sample Size

A random sample of 100 corporations was selected from the 1992 Fortune 500 Largest Industrial Corporations in the United States. Questionnaires were mailed to the top human resource administrators of 98 of the corporations selected, making an effective sample size of 98.

Analysis of Questionnaire

The questionnaire was formulated to assess four general issues:

Explain the rationale behind your primary research methods.

1. How top human resource administrators valued the importance of listening as a communication skill for their industry

2. What percentage of major industrial corporations were using listening training programs

3. How top human resource administrators rated the ability of their employees and other managers to listen to them

4. Whether or not these same administrators felt there was some correlation between management listening skills and improved production and morale

SURVEY RESULTS

The results on the following pages are separated into five sections. The first section deals with questionnaire returns. The other sections cover the general issues just described, along with several results extrapolated from the comparative results of different combinations of questions. Appendix I is a copy of the cover letter to the mailed questionnaire. Appendix II is the copy of the questionnaire with all responses tabulated on it.

Provide copies of your primary research tools in appendices, but refer to these appendices in the text.

Response to Questionnaire

The response rate by the cutoff date was 28 returns of the effective sample of 98, or 28.69%. Six members of the sample population returned unusable answers. Four corporations sent letters of refusal, and two returned questionnaires containing incomprehensible data.

The Importance of Listening

When asked to rate the two most important communication skills from a list of five, the greatest number of respondents, 42.8%, selected listening as the most important. The skill chosen by most respondents as the second most important, by a slight margin, was speaking (see Table A). According to the responses, the respondents view listening as a critical skill for both managers and employees. On a 10-point scale, listening as an employee skill received a mean score of 8.11, while listening as a management skill received a mean of 8.50. The rating most frequently given for both managers and employees was 10 (out of 10). These results tend to indicate that while listening is regarded as very important for both managers and employees, it is crucial for managers to listen well. Interestingly, not a single respondent selected a value of less than 5, or "important," for this question.

TABLE A
The Importance of Listening

Rate these communication skills in order of importance for your industry.						
Choice	Reading	Writing	Listening	Speaking	Nonverbal	Total
First	6	2	12	8	0	28
Second	5	6	7	8	2	28

These results indicate that top human resource administrators viewed listening as the most important communication skill, with speaking the second most important.

The Utilization of Listening Training Programs

A majority, 57.14% of the respondents, indicated that they do, in fact, use listening training programs. When asked why they implemented the programs, the overwhelming majority, 75% selected the answer "other." No respondents selected "low employee morale," and only 12.5% each selected "labor inefficiency" and "misunderstood orders" (see Table B).

Respondents were also asked, "If your company has been using a listening training program, how long has it been in effect?" To this question, 26.27% answered "one year or less," and 33.33% answered "more than five years."

Of the 42.68% of the respondents who do not have a listening training program, only one out of eleven had plans to implement a new program.

-6-

Emphasize the implications of research results.

Tables and other graphic aids give the clearest possible summaries of statistical and numeric data, but they should supplement rather than overshadow your interpretation of the data.

When asked, "How valuable would a listening training program be to your company?" the respondents averaged a score of 6.92 on a 10-point scale. This number is somewhat lower than the mean for question 2, regarding the importance of listening. Presumably, a number of firms see listening as an important skill, but feel that implementing a listening program would not be worthwhile.

TABLE B
Reasons for Implementing Listening Training

If your company uses a listening training program, what prompted this action?

Low Employee Morale	Labor Inefficiency	Misunderstood Orders	Other	Total
0	2	2	12	16

These results indicate that our assumptions as to why listening training programs were introduced were not accurate. See Schedule A for explanations from respondents who selected "other."

The Ability of Management and Employees to Listen

When asked, "How well do your employees listen to you?" respondents indicated a mean score of 6.74 out of 10. However, when managers were asked the same question, the mean score was 7.11. Again, these results are somewhat lower than the mean score indicated for question 2, regarding the importance of listening. Apparently, both management and employees are listening at a somewhat lower level than desired (see Table C). Not a single respondent said that employees listen "very well," or a score of 10.

In response to question 8, "Are your employees encouraged to give feedback to their superiors?" the greatest number of respondents selected "always," or 10 out of 10. The mean score was 7.25.

Extrapolated Results

Eight respondents answered "always" to question 8, regarding employee feedback. When asked question 9 and 10, regarding employee and manager listening ability, these firms responded with a mean score of 7.00 for employees and 8.125 for managers. These are 6.74 and 7.11, respectively (see Table D).

Acknowledging that current research corrects a previous assumption wins the reader's confidence.

-7-

A significantly lower result was obtained for questions 9 and 10 from respondents who answer 4.00 or 5.00 to question 8. For this group, the mean for question 9 was 5.25 and the mean for question 10 was 5.875. Also, none of the respondents in this group answered any higher than 7.00 on question 10, while in the other group, none answered lower than 7.00 on question 10.

TABLE C
Actual Listening vs. Importance of Listening

Responses for question 2	Responses for questions 9 and 10
A. Management Average = 8.0	A. Question 10 Average = 7.11
B. Employees' Average = 8.11	B. Question 9 Average = 6.74

These results indicate that the attained levels on the right do not meet the levels of importance given for listening on the left.

TABLE D
How Employee Feedback Affects Listening

Group	Feedback always encouraged	Feedback often encouraged
Managers	Mean listening score = 8.125	Mean listening score = 5.875
Employees	Mean listening score = 7.00	Mean listening score = 5.25

These results indicate that when feedback from employees to their superiors is encouraged, the listening efficiency of both managers and employees increases correspondingly.

The general trend shown here is that corporations that encourage employees to give feedback to their superiors also employ people who are better listeners than those employed by firms that do not encourage feedback.

An interesting pattern was discovered when the data for question 6, "If your company has been using a listening program, how long has it been in effect?" were correlated with those of questions 9 and 10. For the 26.67% of respondents who answered "one year or less" to question 6, the mean responses for questions 9 and 10 were 6.00 and 6.25, respectively. As the duration of the training program increased, the level of listening ability moved correspondingly. For those firms with programs in effect more than five years, the mean score for the listening ability of employees and managers were 8.25 and 8.00 out of 10 (see Table E).

Thoughtful, detailed analysis establishes credibility and gains clients.

-8-

These results demonstrate that as listening training programs were implemented and utilized, they did, in fact, aid personnel at both the management and employee levels in improving their listening ability. Presumably, the longer the program had been in effect, the more it had contributed to improving listening within the company.

TABLE E
Length of Program and Listening Level

Group	Age of Program		
	One year or less	*Two to five years*	*More than five*
Managers	Mean = 6.25	Mean = 6.83	Mean = 8.00
Employees	Mean = 6.00	Mean = 7.67	Mean = 8.20

Mean = mean of scores attained when rated for ability to listen

These results indicate that as listening training programs have more time to take effect, they do improve the listening ability of both management and employees.

The questionnaire also provided a space for comments and suggested such areas as quality, productivity, employee morale, cost-effectiveness, and value of listening on the part of the managers. Every respondent made some comment, with the majority noting an increase in both production and morale in his/her organization as a direct result of effective management listening.

APPENDIX I: COVER LETTER TO QUESTIONNAIRE

March 24, 19__

Human Resource Administrator's Name
Company Name
Address
Location

Dear Human Resource Administrator:

We would appreciate your help in determining to what extent major corporations are utilizing listening training programs, and what effect these programs have on business. We are surveying 100 top human resource administrators from around the nation regarding the state of corporate listening techniques and training programs today.

Because you are a highly respected leader in the industry, your opinions are valuable to the success of this survey. The results of this survey will assist organizations such as yours in deciding if listening techniques and training programs are profitable investments.

Please take a few minutes from your busy schedule to complete the enclosed questionnaire. Because of our carefully selected and limited sample size, every response is vital. So that we may have the results available as soon as possible, please return the completed questionnaire on or before April 5, 19__. For your convenience, a stamped, self-addressed envelope is provided. Please respond today.

Thank you for your cooperation. If you would like a summary of our survey, please contact us at the above address after May 10, 19__.

Very sincerely yours,

Juanita Sanchez

Juanita Sanchez
Research Associate

-10-

Appended copies of your research tools give the reader a chance to evaluate your research methods. Strive for objectivity and thoroughness.

APPENDIX II: QUESTIONNAIRE

28 responses from a sample of 98 (28.69% return)

Listening Programs Questionnaire

1. Rate these communication skills in order of importance for your industry. Please indicate #1 (most important) and #2 (second most important) in the spaces provided.

   _3_ Reading *21.43%*
   _4_ Writing *7.14%*
   _1_ Listening *42.86%*
   _2_ Speaking *28.57%*
   _5_ Nonverbal *0*

2. Rate listening as a management and employee skill. Check the appropriate box for each.

Management

Not important / Very important

1	2	3	4	5	6	7	8	9	10
0	0	0	0	2	2	4	3	6	11

Employees

Not important / Very important

1	2	3	4	5	6	7	8	9	10
0	0	0	0	1	5	4	6	4	8

3. Does your company utilize an established listening training program?

   Yes _16_   No _12_
       57.14%   *42.86%*

4. If so, what prompted this action? Check appropriate box or explain other.

   Low employee morale _0_
   Labor inefficiency _2_ *12.5%*
   Misunderstood orders _2_ *12.5%*
   Other: _____ *12   75%* _____

5. If your company does not utilize a listening training program, does it plan to in the future?

   Yes _1_   No _10_
       9.09%   *90.9%*

-11-

6. If your company has been using a listening training program, how long has it been in effect?

1 year or less __4__ 26.27%
2-3 years __3__ 20.00%
4-5 years __3__ 20.00%
More than 5 __5__ 33.33%

7. How valuable would a listening training program be to your company? Check appropriate box.

Not valuable				Valuable					Very Valuable
1	2	3	4	5	6	7	8	9	10
0	0	1	1	6	3	5	4	2	4
		3.85%	3.85%	23.08%	11.54%	19.25%	15.39%	7.69%	15.39%

8. Are your employees encouraged to give feedback to their superiors? Check appropriate box.

Never				Often					Always
1	2	3	4	5	6	7	8	9	10
0	1	0	4	4	2	1	6	2	8
	3.57%		14.29%	14.29%	7.14%	3.57%	21.43%	7.14%	28.57%

9. How well do your employees listen to you? Check appropriate box.

Not well				Fairly well					Very well
1	2	3	4	5	6	7	8	9	10
0	0	1	2	5	3	4	8	4	0
		3.7%	7.41%	18.52%	11.11%	14.81%	29.63%	14.8%	

10. How well do other managers listen to you? Check appropriate box.

Not well				Fairly well					Very well
1	2	3	4	5	6	7	8	9	10
0	0	0	0	6	3	6	7	4	1
				22.22%	11.11%	22.22%	25.93%	14.82%	3.7%

PLEASE RETURN THIS QUESTIONNAIRE NO LATER THAN APRIL 5, 19__
THANK YOU

-12-

SCHEDULE A

Explanations for the selection of "other" in response to question 4 ("If your company does utilize an established listening training program, what prompted this action?)

"An effort to improve skills"

"Job content structuring"

"Recognition as integral training skill"

"General need to be an effective listener"

"Belief in importance of improving total communication"

"We realized the importance of listening in the communication process."

"Needs analysis"

"Listening is a basic communication skill necessary for conducting business"

"Realization of the need to maintain skills at high level"

"Recognition of employee development needs"

"Communication enhanced"

"Company survey of employees"

BIBLIOGRAPHY

Choi, B. (1991). Techniques of Listening for Managers. Baltimore: Worny Press.

Fletcher, M.M. (1992). Listening Pays Off. Journal of Management Skills, 27, 1, 27-32.

Tanaka, T. (1991). The New Management Vision. Chicago: Management Publishing Co.

Winowski, T. (Ed.) (1990). New Management Techniques. Cincinnati: Frontier Press.

The bibliography documents sources for further information.

-13-

They don't need to know all the details, but they should be familiar with each division's broad plans. If they can get that information from the executive summary, conclusions, and recommendations sections, then they need not plow through the entire text.

ADDENDA

Addenda include supplemental materials that clarify the author's arguments and research methods.

Following the body of the report are the appendices and various supplements, such as copies of questionnaires, interview schedules, diagrams, statistics, maps, and any other information related to the subject of the report that may interest the reader. Make sure you refer within the body of the report to all appended items.

THE CORPORATE ANNUAL REPORT

Perhaps the best-known example of a long report is the once-a-year summary of company activities that is issued by thousands of corporations: the *corporate annual report.*

Shareholders want to know how "their" company is being managed. Their desire for a clear, concise, and complete picture, coupled with management's awareness of its public responsibility, have contributed to better and more complete reports.

The corporate annual report is no longer a drab summary statement of company activities. Today, it is usually a well-written document divided into narrative and financial sections and enhanced by attractive colors, excellent visual aids, and appealing format.

Although most financial analysts would agree that the annual report is a good way for companies (both public and private) to communicate with their diverse publics or readers, they would not usually recommend basing a heavy financial investment on the report alone. More and more critical readers are requesting the firm's 10-K, which is the report that must be filed with the SEC. This report contains far more detailed financial data than does the annual report. Now a few firms issue to their stockholders the 10-K rather than the annual report. However, most companies feel the stockholder enjoys the color and the photos of the annual report. If they can retain these qualities while improving clarity, adding vital detail, and increasing candor, they can achieve a complete yet attractive combination of the 10-K and annual report.

PURPOSES OF THE ANNUAL REPORT

The corporate annual report relates the company's financial activities, significant achievements, and problems over the previous year.

The primary purpose of the annual report is to present an informative summary of company activities to stockholders. Each stockholder owns a share of the company and is interested in learning about the progress the firm has made during the previous year, its financial structure, its profits, its union-management relations, its expansion of facilities, its new-product development, its relationship with government agencies, its long-range objectives, and so on. The company treats these topics with discretion, so that competitors are not given a marketing or financial edge.

Even the cover of the annual report is designed to convey a message about the organization: its stability, its products or services, and perhaps its position of strength. The cover depicted in Figure 20-2 accomplished those goals for Baker Hughes Incorporated, a world leader in the manufacture of oil drilling and related equipment.

FIGURE 20-2 Cover of an Annual Report

Reprinted by permission of
Baker Hughes Incorporated

*Imaginative covers
communicate important
feelings about
the company's
product and attitude.*

But the modern annual report has still another purpose. It attempts to build goodwill among its shareholders and sell its products, stock, and company image to others. To accomplish these other goals, corporations distribute many more reports than they have stockholders. The additional copies go to employees, educators, suppliers, government agencies, libraries, securities analysts, brokerage firms, banks, foundations, financial institutions, insurance firms, university endowment officers, financial editors of newspapers and magazines, legislators, and many others.

With this wide readership, the writer of an annual report is confronted with a major problem in composition. How should style, word choice, financial data, complexity of charts, and overall content be adjusted to the variety of reader levels and interests?

To do a good job, the writer must weigh every word, examine every sentence, check every graph, and evaluate every page to make sure that all readers will find the report interesting and valuable. It *is* possible to write an annual report with these qualities for two different readerships: the company shareholder and the security analyst. Of course, success requires consummate skill, but a good writer can discuss the necessary activities and select and explain financial data that will prove acceptable to both technical and nontechnical readers.

**CONTENT AND
MAKEUP OF THE
ANNUAL REPORT**

*The letter of transmittal
that accompanies an
annual report primarily
seeks to build goodwill.*

Writers usually divide annual reports into three major sections: the introductory section (letter of transmittal and table of contents), narrative portion, and financial information.

The president's or chairperson's letter to the stockholder, or letter of transmittal, is usually an upbeat summary of the highlights of the year's activities (see Figure 20-3). It gives the reader an overview of the entire report and serves a purpose similar to that of the letter of transmittal in the typical formal report.

FIGURE 20-3 Letter to Stockholders with Annual Report

To Our Stockholders

Fiscal year 1991 demonstrated once again the volatility of the worldwide oil and gas markets. An all out war in the Middle East caused a significant, but temporary, upward spike in the price of oil. Oil prices then fell and remained remarkably stable in the post-war period. At the same time, expectations were for a continuing gradual improvement in U.S. natural gas prices, but another abnormally warm North American winter, a decrease in industrial gas demand and gas on gas competition led to a collapse in gas prices. These unexpected developments have led to an unusual environment for the oilfield service industry. Outside of the U.S., the predominantly oil-driven markets continue to grow. Within the U.S., activity is depressed as evidenced by operator and service company lay-offs and consolidations. Our Process Technologies group experienced significant year-to-year revenue growth as a result of the acquisition of the instrumentation units of Tracor Holdings in the prior year, but profitability was impacted by the recessionary conditions in the global economy. Against this backdrop, Baker Hughes generated revenues in fiscal year 1991 of $2.83 billion, an 8% increase from 1990. Net income rose to $173.5 million, a 22% increase, and earnings per share improved from $1.06 to $1.26, a 19% increase.

Given an overall decline in the average worldwide rig count of 3%, from 2,029 in fiscal year 1990 to 1,974 in fiscal year 1991, our improved operating performance demonstrates our success in identifying and exploiting profitable market niches. This contributed to growth and margin enhancement opportunities in an overall activity environment that has been flat to down over the past several years.

In fiscal year 1991, we again made a number of acquisitions and divestitures designed to further strengthen our array of products and services in the oilfield and process industries. Having accomplished many of our major acquisition objectives in prior years, opportunities to enhance our oilfield operations further will likely be on a smaller scale as the entire service industry continues the consolidation process begun in earnest in 1987. Smaller, strategic acquisitions can and will have a meaningful impact as we go forward.

In October of 1990, we completed the acquisition of ChemLink for $136 million in cash. By combining ChemLink with Baker Performance Chemicals, we now are the largest U.S. oilfield chemical company and rank second on a worldwide basis. We also completed several relatively small acquisitions during the year to strengthen our product lines.

On the divestiture side, we sold the balance of our holdings in BJ Services for $95 million, sold our TOTCO division to Varco International Inc. for $40 million in cash and stock and, in October of 1991, sold our Vecto Services subsidiary to Tuboscope for $75 million in cash and stock.

Within Baker Hughes, several strategic decisions were implemented during fiscal year 1991 that will positively impact future results. In February we announced the formation of Baker Hughes Integrated Engineering Services (IES). IES provides a vehicle for the Baker Hughes companies to pursue the developing market for the delivery of an integrated suite of products and services to the operator on a performance or incentive basis working toward mutually determined goals.

The market leading Baker Hughes companies are unsurpassed in the industry in their ability to offer a complete performance drilling package virtually anywhere in the world.

In 1991, we also began a major effort to develop a modular state of the art MWD system that will set the industry standard for reliability. We currently occupy a small but important position in this market; the product delivery capability inherent in Eastman

Christensen and Exlog for the full range of MWD services however are the best in the business. We strongly believe that our efforts in this area will be rewarded and will allow us to increase market share in a segment that is among the fastest growing in the oilfield service business.

Our Process Technology companies had a challenging year in 1991 with several major customer projects being delayed as a result of worldwide economic conditions and the Middle East war. As the recovery from the recession progresses and our markets in the rapidly growing environmental businesses increase, we should see improved results in fiscal 1992, particularly in the latter half of the year.

The progress we have made in our operating performance has also been matched with improvements in our balance sheet and leverage ratios. In fiscal year 1991, total debt increased only slightly to $646.9 million from $640.2 million, and we ended the year with a debt to equity ration of .419, the lowest level since the merger of Baker and Hughes. In recognition of this performance, Moody's and Duff & Phelps both saw fit to raise our senior debt

ratings to an A– level. BHI was one of the few industrial companies to receive a ratings upgrade in the face of a worldwide recessionary environment.

Outlook

The fundamental forces for a less volatile marketplace based on stable to improving prices for oil and gas are slowly but surely moving into place. The oil side of the equation appears firm from a supply and demand standpoint and we anticipate that oil prices will likely improve by at least the rate of inflation in the coming years. Natural gas prices in North America may have passed their low point but will require time to achieve a level that is conducive to increased drilling activity. With our Process Technologies business likely to improve in the coming year, we are confident that we can produce operating results which will generate a performance ranking competitive within our peer group.

Focus on People

Any corporation's rise or fall is largely based on its ability to manage three basic variables— strategies, technologies and people. In past letters and in last year's annual report we devoted considerable time in describing BHI's strategic objectives and its approach to technologies through the research and development process. In the remainder of this Annual Report, we feature what is Baker Hughes' single most valuable asset—its people. The past decade has been a time of considerable adversity for the industries we serve. Baker Hughes has emerged from that decade of adversity in a position clearly superior in virtually all respects to where it was a decade ago. Our ability to be in that enviable position is attributable to the years of hard work and dedicated effort by the remarkable people—21,000 strong—of Baker Hughes. I sincerely thank them and I am pleased to share a brief cross-section of their talents with you. Additionally, I must regretfully announce the retirement of our director, Robert H. Quenon. We thank Bob Quenon for his many years of guidance and advice.

The People of Baker Hughes

Baker Hughes' mission is to generate increasing value for its stockholders, customers and employees through its role as a leading worldwide supplier of quality goods and services. The primary strategy for our employees is to provide a challenging and rewarding environment that creates an opportunity to realize their full potential while contributing to the Company and their community.

At September 30, 1991, Baker Hughes employed 21,300 people; 11,200 in the United States and 10,100 in over 50 other countries. A large majority of our non-U.S. work force is comprised of citizens of these countries. The Company recognizes the value of its diverse work force and endeavors to provide an environment where the employees can achieve optimal productivity. In addition to modern, well-equipped facilities, the Company provided established policies and programs and an environment in which our employees can satisfy individual goals, while collectively meeting the Company's objectives.

In all aspects of our business, whether in the design and manufacture of products or the delivery of services, people are considered to be our most valued resource. Much of our success in hiring, motivating and retaining our employees is related to a belief in participative management and team building. Also, the organizational structure of Baker Hughes, with its highly autonomous divisions organized along product lines, recognizes the entrepreneurial value of individual initiative and performance.

J.D. Woods
Chairman, President and Chief Executive Officer

Source: Baker Hughes Incorporated Annual Report, 1991. Reprinted by permission.

This letter should be friendly and written from the stockholder's point of view. A stiff, formal, "boardroom" tone will make few friends among stockholders. This letter *is* the corporation to many; it is vital that it build goodwill.

The narrative portion of the report discusses the company in relation to topics such as these:

- Products and services: Stockholders want to know about the specific products the company handles and what services it makes available to its customers. The annual report usually includes a discussion of new products contemplated, future markets, advertising and marketing programs, the reactions of customers, and other areas related to the firm's products.
- Plants and equipment: The report reviews present operations and notes future acquisition of plants and equipment, together with projected capital costs and return on investments. It also discusses investments in foreign plants and equipment, together with possible implications.
- Employees: The report describes how many employees the firm has, the benefits extended to them, payroll information, educational activities, affirmative action programs, employee participation in community affairs, employee health and safety records, and so on.
- Labor relations: The report should present a clear and frank discussion of company relations with unions. If the firm has had labor problems, strikes, or disagreements during the year, the report should discuss them objectively. Stockholders will have learned of the firm's problems from newspaper articles; they deserve a clear and honest explanation of them in the report.
- Stockholders: How many stockholders does the company have? How and where are they distributed? What are their interests?
- Government: What percentage of the firm's production goes to the government? What are the trends likely to be? What interest do federal agencies have in the company? Have investigations been completed? Are investigations contemplated?
- Community: The report should comment on the firm's relations with and contributions to the community. Have employees held public office? What recognition or complaints have been directed to the company?
- Research and development: Where is the firm going? Does it contemplate expanding its product line? It is going to diversify? Will it merge with other firms?
- Social issues: More and more firms are indicating their views on various social issues, such as involvement or noninvolvement in political activities, medical costs, day care, gender equity, and contributions of money and supplies to areas or nations hit by natural disasters.
- Legal issues: Because of the enormous growth in government regulations, plus a strong trend toward a more litigious society, firms are frequently involved in court suits. Many firms comment on pending suits and their probable financial impact on the firm, along with the firm's perception of its liability.
- Environmental issues: Every company wishes to be a good citizen in regard to conservation, recycling, toxic waste disposal, and concern

for the environment. In recent years, environmental issues have received more and more attention in annual reports.

Most readers of annual reports are stockholders or potential investors who care about company finances.

These are only some of the areas that can be included in the annual report. There are many others.

The financial information in the annual report is vital to most readers. It should be complete, objective, and presented in a style that is easily understood by the average stockholder.

Inclusions of a comprehensive balance sheet permits comparison with previous years' records. As for the narrative text, the American Management Association considers it almost as important as the figures themselves. The text can serve to amplify the statistics, to explain certain conditions, to qualify various items, and, in general terms, to throw additional light on the firm's financial picture.

Presenting financial figures for the previous five or ten years is now commonplace; longer periods are not unusual. This span is vital for the serious reader who wishes to follow financial trends in the firm.

The guidelines set down by the American Management Association for good reporting are excellent: the report must be complete, it must be interesting, and it must possess clarity of expression.

DEALING WITH COMPANY PROBLEMS

Ethics demand that companies disclose problems to stockholders. Effective annual reports maintain trust and confidence while meeting this demand.

The annual report provides a way for management to speak directly to investor worries. Such concerns are often addressed in the introductory letter from the president and/or chairperson of the board. Topics that may be dealt with are a major decline in sales, a reduction in demand for specific company products, lawsuits pending, a government investigation of an aspect of company operations, a disaster or crisis situation, consumer opinions or demands, plant closings, and similar events. Whether or not every stockholder is aware of a problematic situation (from reading the daily papers), ethical management requires that some discussion of the topic be made in the annual report.

PRODUCTION AND DISTRIBUTION

Producing and distributing the annual report is a complex, time-sensitive task best managed by a single individual who has superior organizational skills.

Collecting information from various divisions or subsidiaries of a large corporation, securing high-quality photographs, and amassing accurate statistical data are major tasks in themselves. Wrapping up everything clearly and concisely in a limited number of pages—to the satisfaction of the company's officers and stockholders—requires creative planning.

For these reasons, most firms make one competent person responsible for the production of the annual report. The wise employee prepares a timetable and holds to it: narrative explanation of the following areas is due on this date; financial data on that date; selection of photographs and drawings of graphs must be completed by this time; and presses to roll on this date. The lack of a timetable often means that information will trickle in, changes will be made constantly, and confusion will result.

A careful plan for the distribution of the annual reports should also be followed. Of course every stockholder receives a copy, but many other people and groups should be considered, for, as noted earlier, the annual report can be a potent builder of goodwill.

Because the annual report sells an image, it is vital to a company.

With stock ownership so widespread in the United States, a company that does not produce an outstanding annual report may lose the competition for investors. May firms have found that a report helps their stock sales and improves their public image.

1. A student group of which you are a member has completed a formal report on the advantages of placing computer games in a special room in the student center. Prepare three different title pages for the report. Give considerable attention to the report title. The report is to be presented to the director of the center.

2. For the report in exercise 1, write a letter of transmittal. As chairperson of the group, you will want to recognize the contributions of the group members and also of Mary Lee Sunquist, assistant to the student center director, and Bob Lee, manager of Video and Electronic Games (VEG), a company that distributes games like the ones you are proposing for the center.

3. For the situation in exercise 1, explain some potential addenda that could be added to your formal report.

4. Make a list of visual elements, including a balanced title page, that can add to the positive effect of a long formal report.

5. Find a formal report that lacks a summary or synopsis. Prepare this part of the report and keep it to one page. Submit the report with the summary you write. The report may be one that another student has written, a document you discover in the records of an organization, or a government report on file in the library.

6. Obtain an annual report from a business that interests you. Prepare an evaluation of the content of the document, noting both strengths and weaknesses. Pay particular attention to ways in which the document slants its material toward special readers. What is intended to appeal to stockholders? What will catch the eye of company employees? What seems designed to attract potential major investors, such as insurance corporations, unions, mutual fund organizations, and banks? What would attract the "small" investor who purchases 10 to 100 shares? Do not attempt to evaluate the format, typography, and printing details. Concentrate specifically on the writing.

7. How would you communicate in a formal report to alumni of your college or university? Describe the sections you would include in the report and any recommendations.

8. Organizations besides profit-making companies often produce annual reports. Select a nonprofit organization with which you are familiar.
   (a) Name and explain the group, summarizing its purpose.
   (b) In some detail, outline what could be included in the annual report.
   (c) Indicate the categories of people and organizations that might receive this annual report.

9. Select a real company and assume you are to make recommendations to this firm about the content and presentation of its annual report. Prepare a memo in which you make your recommendations. Also, to illustrate your ideas, select two annual reports—one good and one bad. Append these reports to your memo so that the reader can actually see favorable and unfavorable attributes of annual reports. (You may secure copies

from your local chamber of commerce or your business library. Determine if either source can give or lend you two reports.)

10. The 10-K report is an important document to businesspeople. Obtain a 10-K report on a company. Then prepare a memo in which you explain the purpose and data of the 10-K report to a person who is unfamiliar with 10-Ks.

11. As CEO of Alpha Industries, Inc., you're aware of the large investment it took to produce 10,000 copies of your annual report. You have only 3,000 stockholders and 400 employees. Develop a distribution plan for the remaining reports.

12. Consider the following facts about Beta Engineering, Inc.:

   - For the first time since 1980, annual earnings per share have sunk below the $1.00 mark ($.77 per share in 1993).
   - The company faces an infringement of patent lawsuit ($38 million) that will probably not reach court until 1995.
   - The research and development funds invested in teleconferencing devices show no sign of recovery within the current fiscal year.
   - Company real estate holdings have increased in value by 12 percent since 1984.
   - Long-term company debt ($178 million), while not being reduced, has not been increased during the year.
   - The Machinists' Union has formally threatened a strike against the company if current wage demands are not met.
   - The company has won a major proposal competition for a $22-million Navy contract, due to begin midyear.
   - The number of employees has declined by 9 percent. Most of the people who left were technically trained.
   - Two former employees have filed "unlawful work termination" suits against the company.
   - Two small companies were purchased in the past eight months: Eaton Electronics ($2,750,000) and Charter Chips ($3,150,000). Management felt that the addition of these two firms would give Alpha a strong professional edge over the competition.

   Use these facts and others of your own creation to write the president's letter of transmittal for inclusion in the company's annual report.

13. Complete a formal report on any one of the following topics. In an effort to keep the length of the report to a reasonable minimum, limit your report to a one- or two-year span, the specific area or topic you cover, the reader(s) to whom the report is addressed, and the goal or purpose of the investigation. Before you plunge into your research, hold a conference with your instructor and secure approval for the topic, the purpose, the intended audience, the type(s) and depth of the secondary and primary research required, and the due date of the report

   - A Comparison of the U.S., Canadian, and British health care systems
   - Why Japan Will (Will Not) Be a World Economic Leader in the Years 1995–2000
   - Opportunities for the Business School Graduate in the Expanding Field of U.S. Health Care
   - An Analysis of the Commercial U.S. Aerospace Manufacturing Industry, 1992–1995

- The Multibillion Dollar Pharmaceutical Manufacturing Industry: Are the Companies Involved "Good Guys" or "Bad Guys"?
- A topic of your choice (agreed to by your instructor).

CASES

Complete the following assignments from the Cases for Discussion section at the back of this book:

1. The Barney Burton case—Assignment 3
2. But Talking Isn't Working case—Assignment 3
3. Whose Perception Is Correct? case—Assignment 3
4. Bill Webster's Ethical Dilemma case—Assignment 3

SUGGESTED RESOURCES

Blunn, R. "1990 Reports More Serious: In Line with Economic Climate." *Financial Post,* May 4, 1991: 17.

Goldstein, L. "High Impact Reports." *Internal Auditor* 48 (December 1991).

Howard, E. "Preparing Annual Reports in the 1990s." *Public Relations Journal* 47 (May 1991).

Longhurst, J. "Report Design: Handle With Care." *Accountancy* 107 (April 1991).

Otterbourg, R. "Annual Report Copy: Banishing the Boredom." *Public Relations Journal* 46 (July 1990).

Pettet, N. "Creating an Annual Report That's on the Money." *Across the Board* 27 (June 1990).

Steele, E. "Ten Ways to Get More From an Annual Report." *Public Relations Quarterly* 35 (Fall 1990).

LEGAL CONSIDERATIONS
REPORTS AND
THE LAW

Of the many common business reports, one type is especially significant from a legal perspective. Companies devote considerable effort and expense to producing "stakeholder" reports for both internal and external audiences. (A stakeholder is anyone who has an interest or "stake" in the company, including employees, members of the community, and suppliers.) Management must provide stockholders and owners with sufficient information to permit them to make intelligent decisions on company issues and to evaluate the stock. The Securities and Exchange Commission (SEC) administers the relationship between management and the owners. The SEC directs how and when management is to communicate with its stakeholders. It also regulates what may not be communicated. For example, "inside" information (information that may influence the price of the stock) may give some the opportunity to profit unfairly. During the 1980s and 1990s some notable Wall Street and corporate figures were fined or jailed for either releasing or acting on such privileged information.

Consider this case. As a director of a company, you participate firsthand at the board meeting in a decision to split company stock 3 for 1. The decision will almost certainly cause the stock to rise substantially. But how and when must that information be released? To your best friends in the company first? To your brother-in-law, to whom you owe a "tip"? All such handling of the stock information would be deemed illegal by the SEC, which specifically defines the timetable and channels for the release of potentially influential information.

Even the language of such reports is monitored closely be regulatory agencies and the courts. No longer can companies hope to hide deleterious information from the public by ambiguous "bureaucratese" or obscure jargon. In reports, as in warranties and contracts, the language used must be clear to stand up to legal tests.

21

PROPOSALS, BUSINESS PLANS AND OTHER MANAGERIAL COMMUNICATIONS

In earlier days when businesses needed a product or financing, they simply approached a manufacturer or a lending institution. Today, with competition keen and a fraction of a percent in profit or loss sometimes determining success or failure, firms make choices more carefully. Now firms often make major buying decisions by selecting a specific proposal from among several. To obtain financing, they submit a business plan to a lending institution.

PROPOSALS

Business customers "shop" for the highest quality at the lowest cost.

Given the level of expertise that exists in almost every field, firms or government agencies that need a very expensive product manufactured, a four-story building completed, a sophisticated aircraft produced, or a dam constructed can "shop" among suppliers for the best product at the lowest price. Some shopping in the world today is done globally.

The request for proposal is an invitation to bid on a project.

Whether the project is enormous or relatively simple, the sponsoring organization usually requests, announces, or advertises a request for proposal (RFP). In some instances city, county, state, and federal agencies *require* that any expenditure over a specific sum can only be made after evaluating several proposals. The purpose of this requirement is to avoid favoritism in awarding contracts and to obtain the best product or service at the lowest price.

All proposals share a single goal: convincing the reader to respond affirmatively.

Probably the two principal preparers of proposals are companies competing for government contracts and colleges, universities, and research organization seeking funding for projects. Proposals are also prepared within organizations and submitted to management or to committees. Whether intended for an in-house audience or an external review panel, all proposals have one common element: they seek an affirmative response.

WHAT IS A PROPOSAL?

Successful proposals convince readers that they have a need and that the proposed action best meets that need.

In essence, a *proposal* is a reasoned request for action, and it can be as short as a single page or as long as several bound volumes. By logic and persuasion, the writer tries to convince the readers that they have a significant need and the proposed action contained in the document best meets their need. Effective execution of both elements is crucial for proposal success. Many proposals have fallen flat because they have not directly addressed the reader's perceived need: "You may have a good idea, but it certainly doesn't meet our needs." Also, a proposal writer can err by supplying too few specific details about the recommended action: "You understand our need, but we can't figure out what you plan to do about it."

These elementary considerations can spell success or failure. Winning a major aerospace contract can send a company's stock zooming and create jobs. On the other hand, losing an important proposal can result in massive layoffs. Successful proposal writers must squarely confront two business realities:

1. Competition is stiff. Simply possessing the organization, the personnel, the facilities, the experience, and the creativity to secure the contract isn't enough. The proposal defining and describing all these assets must *communicate* with such excellence that readers sitting miles away will examine it and conclude, "The proposal award goes here."

2. Funding agencies do not always know exactly what they want. Proposals must often educate the readers about their own need. A city, for example, may seek proposals to alleviate a summer swarm of mosquitoes, but where and why mosquitoes are breeding may not be common knowledge or immediately apparent. The proposal writer who clarifies and defines the reader's need has a huge advantage when it comes time to develop plans to meet that need.

REQUESTS FOR PROPOSALS

Proposals must be responsive to needs the customer advertises in the RFP and in the SOW.

Although proposals may run from thousands of pages (a plane based on an aircraft carrier) to a few pages (drinking fountains for three new buildings), all must satisfy the reader's requirements. Governmental agencies usually issue an RFP. RFPs are usually very precise, formal documents that list specifications for the product or service, due date, delivery schedule, testing procedure, guarantees required, performance minimums, and so on. Some elements may be included in a separate document called *statement of work* (SOW). This document specifies the product, a list of regulations or references to them, forms to certify compliance, a contract for the supplier to sign, and other details.

Firms planning to submit a proposal should study the RFP and SOW carefully. They must answer every item clearly and honestly. To bypass one of the requirements, regardless of how minor, or to indicate the firm's inability to handle even one item, make the proposal nonresponsive. A nonresponsive proposal is a sure loser.

STEPS IN PLANNING THE PROPOSAL

Know your customer's needs.

The first step, then, is to be sure you have a clear idea of the customer's *needs*. If the city planners want 40 drinking fountains installed, exactly what do they want? Should the fountains be stainless steel or white vitreous china? Are they to stand alone or be recessed in a simple wall dispenser? Should some be designed for children or disabled people? Must the water be iced or just cold from the line's tap? These are just a few questions to ask.

*Analyze your company's
ability to meet the
customer's needs and
consider your competition.*

The next step is to clearly analyze how your organization's *capabilities* fill those needs: your equipment, experience, facilities, personnel, finances, and so forth. Once you have matched your abilities with the customer's needs, look at the competition. The purpose is not to mention the competition in your proposal but to recognize your comparative strengths and weaknesses so you can deal with them intelligently.

*Prepare detailed
descriptions of your
facilities, equipment,
and personnel.*

In most cases, the RFP requests a detailed response in the areas of facilities, equipment, and personnel. In addition, it requests information concerning schedule dates (start-up, production, and delivery), funding, training, subcontracting (if necessary), guarantees, replacement parts, technical manuals to accompany the product, and other related items. An important factor is whether you already have sufficient facilities and equipment or must add more. However, a firm that lacks adequate facilities or immediately available equipment should not drop out of the competition. In some cases, the contract generator pays for such expenditures. Also, it is quite possible that competitors may be in the same position as you are.

*Include detailed resumes
of team members assigned
to work with the customer.*

One of the most important sections of any proposal is the list of people who will be involved in the assignment. Include resumes of key people; give clear descriptions of their experience, education, and awards.

Proposals for complex projects, such as a new type of helicopter, or a computer-based inertial aircraft guidance system, require a team effort. No one person can be expert enough to submit detailed plans, drawings, and schedules for what goes into that helicopter and into the many peripheral areas involved. Thus, the proposal requires input from individuals with expertise in such areas as engineering, manufacturing, production, computer information systems, design, avionics, finance, and testing. Also, the timeframe for submitting a proposal is usually too short for one person to do all the work. A team leader and a proposal writing expert are usually responsible for consolidating the entire work. In the final analysis, though, a major proposal must be a collaborative effort (see Chapter 8).

Although the outline of major proposals will differ, on the whole the organizational pattern will probably be close to the following:

1. Introduction
2. Definition of the problem
3. Proposed solution
4. Description of facilities available
5. Description of equipment available
6. Description of key personnel
7. Overall work design to include manufacturing and production plan
8. Manufacturing, production, and delivery dates
9. Financial data to include pricing
10. Concluding statements

Other aspects that may be included under any of the above headings or as appendices are evaluation, testing, quality control, replacement parts, contract details, guarantees, audit intervals, performance standards, schedules for segment and total completion, handling, storage, labeling, packaging, and environmental regulations and compliance.

As is true of the formal report (see Chapter 20), the proposal contains a preliminary section (letter of transmittal, title page, table of contents, table of illustrations, executive summary, the body (introduction, discussion, conclusions and recommendations), and addenda.

THE SHORT PROPOSAL

The short proposal, running from five to twenty pages, is similar to the long proposal. Again, the proposal writer must recognize and respond to the customer's needs. As shown in Figure 21-1, the short proposal condenses the various parts of the organizational pattern listed for proposals in general. The description of available facilities, for example, may take only a paragraph in a short report, whereas the same topic may occupy most of a volume in an extended proposal.

Short proposals do not, however, leave out any major portions of the proposal argument. A carefully worded description of the problem, the plan, equipment, facilities, and personnel still is vital and must be handled with thoroughness and integrity.

In Figure 21-1, the writer (an independent analyst/trainer) tries to "sell" Economart Corporation on a retraining program for employees in the gardening department. Note that the writer does not make the case solely on the grounds that "training is good," or "I'm quite capable," though both assertions may well be true. Instead, the writer grounds the proposal solidly in the *specific needs* of the company: the gardening personnel must be retrained and relocated to save the company money.

PERSUASION IN PROPOSALS

Just how do proposals go about persuading their readers to say "yes"? Consider the influence of logical order, psychological order, and solid evidence.

Logical order. Business writers arrange the parts of a proposal to appeal to an audience's sense of reason. When one point logically follows from a previous point, we feel reassured that the writer has thought through the proposal with care. When at last the writer asks us to make a decision on the proposal, we feel it is only natural to continue the chain of logic that has been established. We forge the final link by saying yes.

Logical order links ideas in an unbreakable chain that leads the customer to buy a proposal as a matter of good sense.

Notice in the following illustrations how logic snares us. The proposal writer creates a series of links similar to this circular chain. The proposal need only one more link to be complete. Because the pattern has been worked out with such care, we feel an almost irresistible urge to complete it, to finish the circle by saying "yes."

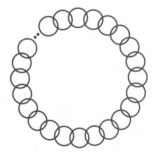

For example, observe the development of a logical train of thought in the following propositions (briefly summarized) from a consultant's proposal:

FIGURE 21-1 Short Proposal

**PROPOSAL TO RETRAIN
ECONOMART GARDENING PERSONNEL**

submitted to

Ms. Morgan Henderson Baillison
Vice President, Retail Sales
Economart Corporation

by

Patricia C. McKay, Ph.D.
Director, Training Specialists, Inc.

May 16, 19__

*Short proposals
list the title,
the customer,
the author,
and the date
on a separate
title page.*

PROPOSAL OVERVIEW

At your request, this proposal examines the problems Economart Corporation faces in its retail gardening sector and suggests how Training Specialists, Inc., can help to solve those problems efficiently.

Background

In 19__, Economart opened the doors of its 17 departments for the first time. Success came at different rates for different departments, but within a year all sectors of the store showed healthy profits. Based on that success, the company decided in February 19__ to add a large outdoor addition to the store: the gardening department.

In the past two years, the gardening sector has shown substantial losses for each quarter, with no significant potential for a turnaround. This proposal will argue that the company risks further, more serious losses by continuing the operation. The key, however, to a smooth phaseout of the gardening sector lies in a retraining plan for gardening employees.

PROBLEM ANALYSIS

The financial problems of the gardening operation have been apparent to management since late spring 19__.

The Record

Except for a brief sales peak during the initial Grand Opening month (February 19___), the record of gross receipts vs. expenses clearly demonstrates the worsening financial situation of the operation (see Graph I).

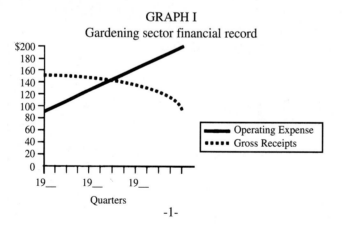

GRAPH I
Gardening sector financial record

-1-

Begin with an overview that states the proposal's purpose and the customer's needs.

Base the argument on specific figures that are summarized in graphic aids.

Observe that expenses (including facility overhead, salaries, merchandise, supplies, and losses) have risen almost 100% during the past two years. During that same period, gross receipts from the gardening sector have fallen 24%.

Reasons for unprofitability

The gardening operation has proven unsuccessful for internal and external reasons:

1. Product waste. Because Economart has no facility for restoring or treating damaged plants, an average of 18% of all plants displayed for sale each month end up in the trash. These rejects include plants damaged by customers or insects, by improper feeding or watering, and by moving and storage.

2. Rising labor expenses. Because each plant must be cared for while on display, the gardening operation requires a full-time staff of 16 gardeners and salespeople to maintain the department. As Graph II indicates, both the number of employees and the total cost of salaries/benefits have risen dramatically in the last eight quarters.

Use list format to organize and emphasize important points.

GRAPH II

Gardening sector employee census and compensation

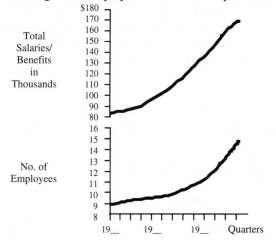

Observe that the total salary/benefits cost has risen more rapidly than the expansion of the gardening staff because of the unionization of workers beginning January 19__. Given present union demands for salary/benefit increases, we can expect the trends illustrated in Graph II to continue into the foreseeable future.

Analyze and explain causes that produce observed effects.

3. Competition. The market area served by Economart now has three retail nurseries, all larger than Economart's gardening department. One of these nurseries,
Kwai Gardens, is able to charge significantly less for plants than Economart
because of the family nature of the Kwai organization. Prices charged by the
other two nurseries are roughly equal to those of Economart, and these competitors also offer attractive delivery and consultation services.

EVALUATION

Because of waste, labor expenses, and competition, the Economart gardening
department stands little chance of reversing its record of unprofitability. Although
one of these factors—waste—could be lessened by the purchase of a company plant
farm, the expense involved outweighs benefits to be achieved.

The problem can also be evaluated by considering profits in relation to each
square foot of floor space in the Economart store. Excluding the 6,800 square feet of
interior floor space now used by the gardening department, the store's remaining
24,000 square feet produce an average of $3.20 profit per square foot each month.
By contrast, the gardening operation produces a loss per square foot of $.43.

We can conclude, therefore, that the interior space now used by the gardening
department might be more profitably occupied by another product line. Several
departments have long-standing requests to management for expansion. The majority
of these requests present statistically persuasive arguments that additional floor space
will produce additional profits at or above the rate already established in the current
department.

*State
conclusions
clearly.*

PROPOSAL SPECIFICS

Economart management should phase out the gardening operation by dealing
effectively with three factors:

1. Labor retraining and relocation. Present labor relation make it unwise for management to simply dismiss the workers now employed in the gardening department.
While legally such a dismissal might be upheld, Economart would no doubt be
the target of boycotts, picket lines, and unfavorable advertising in the coming
months. Management may, therefore, decide to retrain the present nursery workers for jobs as stock clerks, shipping clerks, and floor staff.
2. Stock reduction. Current inventory in the nursery now totals $204,000 retail
value. Assuming that the loss factor of 18% will remain accurate during the
coming months, the company should reduce inventory as quickly as possible.

*Make recom-
mendations
that move the
customer to
take specific
actions in
light of the
conclusions.*

-3-

With spring and summer gardening seasons upon us, management may authorize a 15%-off sale on all gardening merchandise. In the highly competitive gardening field, this price break will significantly undercut the prices of other nurseries. If the sale prices bring quick reduction of stock, the store may actually make a greater profit per month because less merchandise is lost to the 18% waste factor.

3. Store image. Management will not want customers to perceive the closing of the gardening operation as a failure on the part of Economart. Hence, the 15% sale referred to may be cast as a "Remodeling Sale," an event marking the transition from a gardening operation to a Patio and Outdoor Furniture operation, or whatever retail line is chosen for the gardening floorspace.

In summary, management should act quickly to relocate staff, reduce inventory, and redirect advertising to put the best face possible on the closing of the nursery.

Proposed retraining

Training Specialists, Inc., will retrain the 16 workers now employed in the gardening department. For each employee Economart management can select a retraining route:

1. Stock clerk
2. Shipping clerk
3. Floor staff

Training location

All training will be conducted on Economart premises during regular business hours. Our trainers will use your Conference Room A or a similar room of your choice.

Training time

Each employee will receive ten hours of training, divided into four 2.5-hour session spread over four consecutive days. Thus, all employees will finish training within four work days. Scheduling will be arranged so that ordinary work patterns within the gardening department are not significantly compromised during the training period.

Training personnel

Sessions will be conducted by personnel with extensive experience in training and a successful history of training with Economart personnel:

Patricia C. McKay, Ph.D. (specialist in training program development)
Andrew Ortega, M.A. (specialist in sales/marketing training)

Sell your proposed service or product as the tool the customer needs to take the required action.

Discuss the proposal's recommendation before stating your fee.

Training costs

Total expense to Economart for employee retraining is $4,480, including all materials and personnel supplied by Training Specialists, Inc. Here is a breakdown of specific expenses: 16 workers * 10 hours of training (Economart premises) * $28 per hour training cost = $4,480.

CONCLUSION

Training Specialists, Inc., trusts that you will find this problem analysis and proposal helpful in your planning for continued corporate success. We look forward to working with you on the project described in this document. We certainly welcome your questions or comments on the action we propose.

Thank you for the confidence you have shown in Training Specialists, Inc. in the past and for inviting our proposal in this case.

End by looking forward to serving your customer's needs.

Ensign Engineering has determined that it can save $2,800 per day by leasing a mainframe computer costing $800 per day. The company leased the computer.

Unfortunately, Ensign Engineers is presently able to use the computer to only 20 percent of its capacity due to a lack of programming and hardware knowledge. Hence the company is saving only $560 per day (20 percent of $2,800), though the computer still costs $800 per day.

By consulting for Ensign Engineers for one month, I can ensure 100 percent use of computer capacity through my knowledge.

The company now loses $2,240 per day. My consulting fee is $300 per day for one month.

To save money, hire me. I'm worth it.

WITHOUT CONSULTANT

A	*B*	*C*
Computer Cost/Day	*Theoretical Savings*	*Actual Net Savings*
$800	*$2,800*	*20 percent of $2,800*
		minus $800 = –$240

WITH CONSULTANT

A	*B*	*C*
Computer Cost/Day	*Theoretical Savings*	*Actual Net Savings*
$800	*$2,800*	*$1,700*
+ 300 (consultant)		*(B – A = C)*
$1,100		

Before considering the logic of the argument, the proposal's readers may have cringed at the thought of spending $9,000 (30 days times $300) for a consultant. But although the fee is substantial, company officials may conclude that hiring the consultant is reasonable in the light of logic.

Illogical order fails to command the customer's reason.

Too often, however, logic goes astray and the proposal fails. Faulty logic may be compared to scattered links of a chain. We feel no attraction to fulfill an inevitable pattern of any kind when faced by the chaos of an illogical argument.

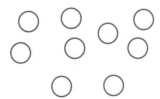

Be on guard for these logical disasters in business proposals you write and read:

- Hasty generalization: a conclusion based on little evidence
  Buy my product because it worked last year for your sister's roommate.
- Circular reasoning: a purported explanation that turns out to be a mere restatement
  We require employee contributions to the retirement fund because it is the policy of this company to fund retirement benefits by means of deductions from employee wages.

- Personal bias: using personal judgments as the standard for evaluating ideas
  Kim's a good chap. Why would you want to oppose his plan for a stock split?
- Non sequitur: a conclusion that does not follow from the evidence
  Tracy's clients love her jokes. Make her sales manager.
- Either/or thinking: two alternatives posed as the only alternatives
  Either we raise prices or go bankrupt.
- Straw man: setting up a fake target as if it were a true target for your argument
  The whole question comes down to personalities. Fire Jenkins and the entire company will turn around.
- False cause: incorrectly taking an earlier event as the cause of a later event
  Jenkins came aboard at the beginning of 1991. Nine employees quit that year. That must show you what kind of president Jenkins has been.
- Stacking the argument: piling up biased evidence while ignoring other valid evidence
  The Rolls Royce Silver Shadow has only fair acceleration, gets poor gas mileage, and cost too much to repair. I think I've made my case: the Silver Shadow is an overrated automobile.
- Faulty syllogism (a syllogism is a pattern of thought): drawing incorrect conclusions from correct assumptions.
  All managers arrive at 8 A.M. I arrive at 8 A.M. Therefore, I must be a manager. (The correct version: All managers arrive at 8A.M. I am a manager. Therefore, I arrive at 8 A.M.)

Although these faulty arguments may stand out clearly here, they hide themselves cleverly in many business proposals and other documents. Can you spot the logical errors in these assertions?

EXAMPLE 1: *Benson Lamination's profits soared 42 percent higher within nine months of their purchase of the new Quadrex computer-driven plywood press. We here at Star Lumber can expect similar results by purchasing a Quadrex press.*

EXAMPLE 2: *For years, all of the best life insurance companies in the United Stated offered double indemnity policies in case of accidental death. Miller Farm Insurance has just announced its policy of double indemnity for accidental death. In so doing, Miller Farm proves itself to be one of the best life insurance companies in the United States.*

In the first example, the error is false cause. Benson Lamination's profits soared *after,* not necessarily *because of* the purchase of a Quadrex press. In the second example, the error is faulty syllogism. The argument asserts that all A have B characteristics; C has B characteristics; therefore, C must equal A. If this was true, then we could argue that, "All toads have warts; Fred has warts; therefore, Fred is a toad."

Such logical slips tend to emerge in less humorous ways in multimillion-dollar proposals. Too often, faulty arguments go unnoticed until, in the final stages of proposal review, an alert executive adjusts his or her glasses and says, "Wait just a minute. Am I to understand that . . . ?" Like a castle of cards built on shifting ground, the whole proposal can collapse due to flawed logic.

Psychological order plays on emotions rather than appealing to reason.

Psychological order. The best business proposals move both our minds and our wills. We develop not only thoughts about the merits of the plan, but strong feelings as well. Proposal writers manage our feelings by carefully timing the length and placement of bad news and good news.

Placement of bad news. In some cases, such as a business letter, bad news usually follows the solution (or good news) to a problem. For example, a customer request 24 Excello units. You no longer carry them but you do stock the Superior. It is less costly, completely fireproof, guaranteed for ten years, and available in one of four colors to match other office furniture. Thus, you open your letter by acknowledging the customer's order, then you list the Superior and its major selling points, and *finally* relate the bad news: "For those reasons you can see why we no longer handle the Excello."

Beginning a proposal with bad news about the severity of the problem may make the customer eager for the good news of the proposed solution.

The proposal, however, does not usually offer an alternate product or service; it attempts to sell a solution to a problem. Sometimes, therefore, it is wise to open the proposal with a discreet discussion of the problem (the bad news) and then offer the solution or proposal (good news) that solves the problem.

Why would a proposal writer ever want to mention bad news? For the same reason, perhaps, that fire-and-brimstone preachers begin a sermon with vivid descriptions of hell's hot agonies: to prepare the audience for later rescue. The skillful use of bad news creates a need for an answer or solution—a need felt emotionally by the reader. When later in the proposal the writer presents *good news*—the solution, the proposed idea—the reader welcomes it with satisfaction and some relief. Bad news should never be so overwhelming or negative, though, that is colors the entire proposal and causes it to be rejected.

The writer of a good proposal makes sure that readers will appreciate the good news by setting the stage with well-chosen items of bad news. Placing negative aspects effectively has the additional advantage of anticipating any questions and objections that may occur to the reader. Such anticipation reduces the negative effects of these questions and objections. Whatever negative influence remains can be overcome by the good news suggested in the proposal.

Customers will not buy good news that seems improbable. Ground the proposed solution in evidence and analysis.

Placement of good news. When turning to the good news of a proposal, a business writer must show that the benefits of the proposed idea are not only *possible* but *probable*. The readers of most business proposals, after all, stopped wishful thinking long ago; they know the ways of the business world, with its hard-earned rewards and its ready disappointments. These readers are suspicious of proposals that naively broadcast the good news of a proposal without also examining accompanying risks, resistances, and liabilities.

Consider, for example, the good news promised in a "Proposal to Substitute Look-alike Plastic for Genuine Leather in Lejax Wallets." The proposal writer set forth three items of good news for the Lejax Company:

1. Plastic costs 75 percent less than leather.
2. By using plastic, Lejax can rid itself of the bothersome regulation and inspection entailed in the use of leather.
3. Unlike irregular pieces of leather, premeasured sheets of plastic can be machine-fed into pattern-cutting machines. Waste is cut by 40 percent.

The proposal writers feel that their good news is unassailable and that the company's approval of their proposal is certain. They simply can't believe that a high-level management committee has returned the proposal for more extensive analysis: "Haven't we spelled out the advantages to the company?" they ask. "Yes," a vice president tells them. "Now make them real."

In order to demonstrate, the vice president plays devil's advocate to each item of good news offered by the proposal writers:

GOOD NEWS	DEVIL'S ADVOCATE
Plastic is cheaper than leather.	Of course. But we built our reputation on the feel and smell of real leather. Convince me that plastic won't destroy our image.
Goodbye to government inspection.	Government inspection keeps leather wallets made in other countries out of the market here. Will inspectors still be around to shield us from competition after we've gone to plastic?
We can mechanize production.	We're a union shop through and through. Prove to me that plastic won't invite massive labor problems.

The art of delivering good news, then , is not simply a matter of listing bright, desirable ideas. In fact, the challenge of writing good proposals lies in another direction entirely: showing how a bright idea can surmount obstacles. The bright idea earns its right to persuade us by conquering real-world objection.

Influence of solid evidence. Persuasion depends on the use of examples (termed *evidence* when used to prove a point). Proposal writers often steer a middle course between general and specific evidence.

Persuasive proposal writers know where to place statistical evidence that illustrates general truth and where to place specific evidence that makes an emotional appeal.

General Evidence ("The world's oceans are warmer this year") is composed of a great number of examples gathered together (generalized) in the form of a statement, mathematical measurement, or illustrative chart. *Specific evidence* ("The water off Pierce Pier in San Diego on May 9, 199x, was 73 degrees") focuses on the precise details that make up generalized evidence. Both general and specific evidence can strengthen or weaken a proposal.

Notice in the following example that general evidence can support a point well, but in a clinical, aloof way. Even though we may agree with a point supported by general evidence, we are seldom moved:

Grocery store managers are prone to health problems. In a recent survey of 900 managers, 37 percent had chronic symptoms of stress-related illness.

What is the strength of this bit of general evidence? We grant the weight of the fact that 900 men and women were polled. But this statistic is one like the many other numbers that clutter our lives. Hundreds of grocers may be suffering, but not a single one suffers before our mind's eye.

By contrast, consider a brief sample of specific evidence:

Grocery store managers are prone to health problems. Blaston, Pennsylvania, has three large supermarkets. The managers of each, all in their 30s, began work in the mid-1980s. Today, one suffers from ulcers, one

*works half-time owing to acute hypertension, and the third doesn't work
at all: he suffered a fatal heart attach at age 36.*

In this case, we *feel* the impact of the words. The suffering grocers appear to
us visually in imagination. Words like *ulcer* and *heart attack* strike us more
powerfully than percentages.

The weakness of specific evidence, of course, is its severe limitation of sampling. Do the illnesses of three sick store managers really prove whether grocery store managers are more or less prone to stress-related illness? No. Only
broad, quantified studies can prove broad assertions.

Skilled proposal writers steer a middle course between the strengths and
weaknesses of general and specific evidence. They try to bring out the general
truth of statistical evidence without sacrificing the emotional appeal of specific
evidence. Notice how the following statement combines the best of general and
specific evidence:

*Grocery managers are prone to health problems. In a nationwide survey
of 900 of them, 37 percent were found to suffer from such stress-related
illnesses as ulcer, hypertension, skin rashes, and heart irregularities. In
some communities like Blaston, Pennsylvania, virtually all supermarket
managers in town are chronically sick.*

To sum up, persuasion in a proposal has little to do with fast talking or
tricks. Proposal writers *earn* influence over their readers by constructing tight,
logical arguments, psychologically effective patterns of good news and bad
news, and convincing demonstrations of general and specific evidence.

APPEARANCE OF PROPOSALS

*A physically attractive
proposal gains an
important psychological
advantage over
the competition.*

Because proposals are often judged competitively, they must win attention and
respect by how they *look* as well as by what they have to *say*. Wandering margins, heavy block paragraphs, bleary type, and smudged graphics all say "unpro-
fessional" and "unreliable" to an evaluator who wants value for money invested.
Here are six ways to give your proposals a crisp, professional appearance:

1. Use a laser printer rather than a dot-matrix printer or typewriter.
   If you must use a typewriter, install a new carbon ribbon.
2. If a variety of type fonts are available to you, choose a nontypewriter
   font for the body and a larger font size for headings. Make heading
   progression clear by using the largest or most prominent font for the
   first-level headings and progressively smaller or less prominent fonts
   for subheading levels.
3. Use heavy bond white paper. Beware of pastel shades, especially if
   your plan to photocopy the work.
4. Abide by strict margins on all sides of the page. Word processing
   software makes right-justified margins possible without typesetting.
5. Decide if the effect of your proposal will be more powerful if it is
   bound with a vinyl or heavy paper cover rather than unbound. Do not
   bind proposals of just a page or two. Most photocopy and fast-print
   businesses can bind your work for a few dollars per copy.
6. Make sure that photocopied versions of your proposal, are in clarity
   and crispness, comparable to your original. If you used a computer,
   print out multiple originals rather than photocopy. If you must photocopy, try to use a machine that will copy on your white bond paper.

Desktop publishing. *Desktop publishing* is advanced software that gives writers the ability to control most aspects of the appearance of documents generated on personal computer systems. Desktop publishing stems from word processing, but it goes far beyond the typewriter or word processor by enabling users to manipulate text and graphics.

Desktop publishing allows writers to experiment with design and layout to create visually impressive proposals.

When you use desktop publishing, you can vary your proposal's appearance through different text styles, sizes, and even colors. You can move text around easily, "import" text segments from documents prepared with other software, and insert unusual and attractive lettering and illustrations. You create illustrations—tables, charts, graphs, drawings—and place them almost anywhere in your proposal. Desktop publishing is different from word processing because it includes the ability to manipulate such visuals.

By using the capabilities of desktop publishing in creative ways, you function like a publisher in many (but not all) ways. The line between desktop publishing and word processing, however, is becoming more difficult to distinguish as word processing programs become more sophisticated. So, too, is the line between desktop publishing and the visual elements of traditional publishing becoming narrower.

Refer to Figures 21-1 and 21-2 for examples of the results of desktop publishing. Note especially Figure 21-2; how attractive and how closely related to traditionally published documents these pages appear: photos, graphs, varied type styles and sizes, even boxing in of important items. Desktop publishing software, such as Aldus Pagemaker, Quark XPress, and Ventura Publisher can give your proposals, reports, and business plans a typeset appearance.[1]

HINTS FOR WINNING PROPOSALS

We have discussed how to make proposals persuasive (through logical order, psychological factors, and solid evidence) and attractive (through the variety offered by desktop publishing). Finally, let us consider a few hints, final touches, to help create winning proposals.

- Use topic headings and inset material freely. Judge for yourself the difference in effect as depicted in Figure 21-3 on page 510.
- Never bury crucial information in appendices or footnotes. If the reader needs to know a fact to make sense of your proposal, include that fact in the text itself. If necessary, state the fact briefly in the text and elaborate elsewhere in a footnote or appendix. Never, however, should the reader simply be told "see footnote 34" for important information.
- Be direct and specific, rather than vague and general.

VAGUE, GENERAL (a proposal to remodel the floor plan of a factory): *Production has been hampered by the physical separation of related work units.*

DIRECT, SPECIFIC: *The company loses $400 per day in lost time as employees from the graphics and word processing units walk the 700-yard path between their two related work areas.*

VAGUE, GENERAL (a proposal to market a new perfume): *In the past, our company has had success marketing floral fragrances.*

FIGURE 21-2 Example of Desktop Publishing

Office of Management Development in Health Care   Winter 1992

 The MANAGER'S EDGE *in Health Care*

Winter Executive Program Scheduled by Office of Management Development

Phil Rapa, Director of the Office of Management Development in Health Care, announced a new open program for 1993: the Executive Institute Program in Health Care.

The one week session will be held in Palm Springs, January 24-29, 1993, at the beautiful Marriott Las Palmas and Annenberg Center at the Eisenhower Hospital complex.

The program will emphasize Total Quality Management, will be staffed by top level faculty and will be conducted in intensive sessions. Time will be provided, however, for recreation and relaxation.

The total program is primarily designed for executives and managers approaching executive level appointments, or those already in upper level management positions in health care.

For maximum value to the participants, enrollment will be limited. Please call (213)342-1364 for more information, a descriptive folder, and an application blank.

New Approach to Employee Health Care

In an effort to save money and bypass intermediary organizations such as insurance firms and HMO's, corporations are now moving in the direction of dealing directly with health care providers.

Among those firms that have instituted direct relationships with health care providers are Digital Equipment, Savannah Business Group, Baxter International, John Deere and Southern California Edison.

Fed up with skyrocketing employee health care costs, high insurance company charges and extensive delays in paper processing, corporations are now dealing directly with physicians and hospitals.

In the case of Southern California Edison, Dr. Jacque Sokolov (a member of the Advisory Board of the USC Office of Management Development) reported a corporate savings of $38 million for 1989 and 1990. To accomplish this, Southern California Edison

owns 10 clinics staffed with company-paid doctors and manages a network of 7,500 physicians, 85 hospitals and 155 pharmacies. Dr. Sokolov, Vice President and Medical Director at Southern California Edison, says he walked into one hospital and said, "We spend over $1 million each year here. How can we do business?"

It is this company-to-provider direct relationship that is saving money and drawing more and more attention in corporate America as a partial solution to health care costs.

Wall Street Journal, August 19, 1991

Those candidates for the Dual Degree PharmD/MBA program, who have just completed their MBA Core work. (Left to right) Cynthia Rich, Daniel C. Powers, Julia E. Kyle. Standing behind the students: Phil Rapa, Coordinator, PharmD/MBA Dual Degree Program.

Source: N.B. Sigband (Ed.) *The Manager's Edge in Health Care* (Winter 1992). University of Southern California.

Power of a Minute Programs Draw Rave Reviews

It is estimated that almost 60 percent of prescriptions are not complied with in one way or another: medications not taken, taken improperly, course of treatment not completed, etc. Of even greater interest is the fact that some 10-12 percent of hospital admissions are due to "drug interactions."

As a result, California has joined over 20 other states on January 1, 1992, in requiring the pharmacist to counsel every patient who receives a new prescription or a prescription requiring a change in dosage or strength. The following January 1, the same statute will be put in place by the Federal government for every state receiving Medicaid funds.

The USC School of Pharmacy has responded with a four-hour seminar/workshop designed to sharpen the skills of pharmacists to counsel patients effectively. Speed and excellence are emphasized in the program to assure a high level of pharmacy productivity while building patient goodwill and sales.

The program was funded with a generous $40,000 grant from the Whitmire Distribution Company, one of the nation's leading organizations in pharmaceutical distribution.

The USC program provides each participant with a 110-page reference manual and the opportunity to view a 21-minute color video. In addition, each participant has an opportunity to participate in pharmacist-patient counseling role-plays, critique ongoing situations and receive valuable pointers on how to handle impatient and emotionally upset patients, as well as those who are non-English speaking.

Dr. Norman Sigband, Distinguished Emeritus Professor in the USC School of Pharmacy, wrote the manual and video script and heads up the program.

Call Phil Rapa, Director, Office of Management Development in Health

▼ Care Programs, at (213)342-1364 for information on how your pharmacists can take advantage of this program and at the same time receive Continuing Education credit.

Professor André Van Niekerk conducting a Strategic Planning session during October 1991 open enrollment program.

Demographics in Los Angeles Will Change Health Care Demands

Everyone living in an urban center has certainly noted the dramatic changes in the last decade in population make-up. Los Angeles is probably the leading example of that in the nation. The number of whites in Los Angeles dropped from a 52.9% figure in 1980 to 40.8% in 1990, while Hispanics increased from 27.6% in 1980 to 37.8% in 1990. Other changes among Asians and Blacks have been almost as dramatic.

These figures will surely be important to all health care personnel in planning for the acquisition of personnel, office and clinic locations, language training and other factors.

L.A. Business Journal, November 4, 1991.

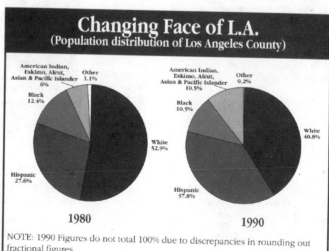

Changing Face of L.A.
(Population distribution of Los Angeles County)

1980

American Indian, Eskimo, Aleut, Asian & Pacific Islander 6%
Other 1.1%
Black 12.4%
White 52.9%
Hispanic 27.6%

1990

American Indian, Eskimo, Aleut, Asian & Pacific Islander 10.5%
Other 0.2%
Black 10.5%
White 40.8%
Hispanic 37.8%

NOTE: 1990 Figures do not total 100% due to discrepancies in rounding out fractional figures
Source: California Department of Finance

2

Team of participants making their case analysis presentation to the "Corporate Board Members" and to fellow program participants in the National Wholesale Druggists' Association/Merck Sharp Dohme/USC Program held during December 1991.

Alcohol and Heart Disease

Researchers at Harvard's School of Public Health, as part of a continuing study, looked at 44,000 men (between 40 and 75 years old) over a two-year period. Those who drank light to moderate amounts of alcohol had a 25 to 40 percent lower chance of developing heart disease. Moderate drinking is defined as one-two drinks per day, a standard drink being 12 ounces of beer, 4 ounces of wine or 1.5 ounces of 80-proof spirits. On the other hand, the government estimates that alcohol is responsible for over 100,000 deaths per year! Surely a controversial topic.

"Wellness Letter," University of California at Berkeley, November 1991.

Passive Smoking:#3 Killer in U.S.

Experts now rank "passive smoking" (breathing another's cigarette smoke) as the nation's third leading cause of preventable deaths in the U.S., exceeded only by active smoking and alcohol. Some 46,000 to 54,500 nonsmoking Americans die each year from passive smoking.

This is obviously a great reason to have your spouse or someone you spend a great deal of time with, give up the noxious weed. It could save you or your children from an early illness or death.

"Wellness Letter," University of California at Berkeley, October 1991.

Guns and Death

Would you believe there are about as many guns in homes as there are people in the United States? More than 200 million firearms may be found in half of all the homes in America.

It's a bit frightening to think that when one of your children visits a neighbor, there's a 50-50 chance that a gun will be in that home.

The National Center for Health Statistics reports about eight fatalities each day among children and teenagers and about five times that number of injuries due to firearms.

Although most people buy guns for self-protection, a study in the state of Washington determined that there were two fatalities involving criminal intruders and 333 domestic fatalities (usually family members, relatives, or friends) in a single given period.

Caution: If you have a gun in the house, lock it up securely and keep it unloaded. If you don't have a gun, think twice (or five times) about the advisability of buying one.

"Wellness Letter," University of California at Berkeley, Oct. 1991.

4

FIGURE 21-3 Visual Effects of Headings and Inset Material vs. Solid Type

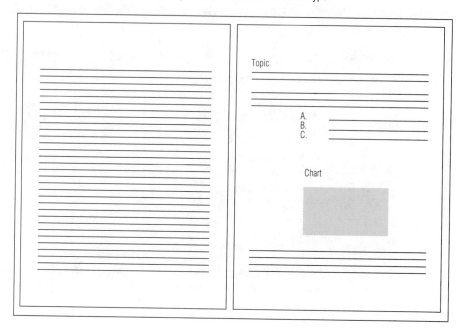

DIRECT, SPECIFIC:

Since 1990, our company has marketed "Orchid Memories," "Gardenias in May," and "Roses are Red." Each of these flower fragrances produced a quick profit margin of well over 50 percent in the first nine months of sales.

Proposals are the primary means by which business asks for work to do, for money to earn. Long or short, the proposal requires a writer's sharpest writing skills.

BUSINESS PLANS

The business plan seeks funding for an entrepreneurial idea.

Inevitably, some individuals have excellent ideas for various entrepreneurial ventures but are short of cash to fund such efforts. The business of venture capital organizations is to provide financial resources to fund development of new ideas into marketable products. How to bring together venture capitalists and entrepreneurs—for the benefit of both parties—is basically a matter of communication, and the communication vehicle is usually a business plan.

Many more plans are written than are accepted and funded. The fault at times is not necessarily in the entrepreneurial idea itself, but in the faulty written document that requests funding to implement the idea. One Boston venture capital firm received 1,200 business plans during a period of several months. Of these, 600 were read, 45 were researched, and only 14 funded.[2]

Venture capital experts indicate that many business plans are too long. They include data and information that are not vital, gloss over areas that are critical, and sometimes completely ignore central issues such as the competition, marketing steps, and the experience of the key personnel involved.

THE VIEW OF
VENTURE CAPITAL
ORGANIZATIONS[3]

Persuasive business plans give details about the proposed product or service, personnel qualifications, market conditions, competitors, manufacturing and distribution plans, and projected goals.

Funding new, unproven ventures is a high risk business. To lessen the risk, venture capitalists take every precaution to ensure that their investments will provide a viable return. For that reason, the investors want to know as much as possible about the product or service being offered, who will manage the organization (background, expertise, experience, knowledge, commitment), the market and the marketing plan, the competition, the manufacturing plan and process, the distribution network, and long-range goals. All of these elements should (and must) be explained clearly, concisely, and completely in a business plan.

WRITING THE
BUSINESS PLAN[4]

Find out exactly what your investor wants to know.

Perhaps the first step in writing the business plan is to determine what topics the venture capitalist wants covered and in what depth. You can usually determine the appropriate topics and depth through a conference with the funding firm or from a guide booklet or form the firm has prepared. The requirements will vary based on whether capital is for a product or for a service; whether the funding amount requested is $5 thousand or $5 million; whether the business is cyclical or ongoing; and whether the market is local, national, or international.

Consult the following checklist, which briefly outlines the format of most business plans.

The executive summary sells the plan's marketability by highlighting key information.

Section 1: an executive summary. In the executive summary include a brief description of the product and service, why it is marketable, possible future demands for the product or service, and an overview of the present position of the company and personnel involved.

Section 2: products and services. Fully describe the product or service: where it stands in its life cycle (e.g., is it a new product, or one that because of attractive innovations will compete with one that is now in the marketplace), the present status of patents or copyrights, and future plans for product research.

Section 3: Manufacturing and Distribution. Describe the manufacturing process in this section: how complex the operations are and what logistics are required, what the production capacity of the present organization is, and at what percentage (of 100 percent production) is the present level. In addition, spell out the distribution system required along with how complete (or incomplete) it is at the present time.

A complete marketing plan is the business plan's most important feature.

Section 4: Marketing Plan. The marketing plan is a critical segment of the business plan. Cite facts on the industry in which the product is competing and the present sales trends. What are the short- and long-term profit potentials?

In addition, a specific marketing plan should identify the market segment(s) targeted. Include a customer profile as well as an analysis of market needs, market segments, sales by geographical areas, and how these areas will change with the passage of time, increased competition, and environmental, social, and economic changes. Also include in the marketing section a brief analysis on how and why this marketing plan is not only different but also superior to that of competitors.

Section 5: Financial Information. Include a financial statement for the current year, the previous three years (if possible), and the next three to five years. These projections should cover sales, cost of sales, cash flow, *pro forma* balance sheets, and key statistics (current ratio, debt-equity ratio, and inventory turnovers).

Include in this section, or perhaps a separate one, a comment on pending lawsuits by or against the organization, the potential for liability, insurance coverage in force or needed, and related areas.

Section 6: Management Personnel. List the key management people with a summary of their personal backgrounds, work experiences, education, community activities, and memberships.

The business plan should inform investors about the company's current financial status.

In essence, the business plan is a type of proposal.[5] It is directed to an organization for the primary purpose of selling the company presenting the plan. If the effort is successful, the venture capitalist will lend funds to develop the new concept or idea into a saleable product or service. Those who assume the risk of advancing their funds and those of *their* investors are critical individuals. Not only must they be convinced of the potential market for the product or service, but also every detail of the enterprise must be substantiated and explained to their satisfaction. Preparing a complete and convincing document is the task of the successful business plan writer.

PROCEDURE MANUALS

Procedure manuals ensure that changes do not disrupt company operations and assist in the training of new or reassigned employees.

Procedure documentation can vary, depending on the audience for whom the procedures are intended. For example, procedure X, for shipping a new line of TV sets internationally, has been changed. A new procedure must be written for the shipping departments for six warehouse locations. Note, however, that one set of procedures must be written for the line employees, one for managers (to include all new documentation instructions concerning bills of lading, government forms, tariff regulations, computer entry, etc.), and one for company management to appreciate the various steps and implications. Most procedures reflect the following steps to a greater or lesser degree:

1. Introduction: why the procedure has been instituted together with background needed to understand the reason for performing the procedure
2. Description of major steps and functions
3. Specific step-by-step instructions, using short, clear sentences together with explanatory visuals
4. Conclusion recapitulating major procedural steps, with an added statement of why the work is vital and how it fits into the company's overall goal

JOB DESCRIPTIONS

Job descriptions flow naturally from procedure statements. Nevertheless, many organizations have either manuals of job descriptions and no procedure manuals, or procedure manuals and no job descriptions. In any event, job descriptions are designed for job classes in which a number of employees carry out the same or similar tasks.

FIGURE 21-4 Job Descriptions

SENIOR PUBLIC COMMUNICATIONS ADMINISTRATOR (DIRECTOR OF PUBLICATION AND PERIODICALS) - REQ. 27863 - PUBLIC RELATIONS/PERIODICALS — A professional in public communications is being sought to direct the University's publications program, which includes staff supervision, budget development and administration and strategic planning. This individual will be responsible for editing and publishing "Transcript," the weekly faculty/staff newspaper, and other publications including "USC at a Glance," a map and visitors guide, and monthly "Fact Files." Duties will also include: developing and managing the graphic identity program; developing relationships with other publishing entities on campus; encouraging high standards and conformance with policies; offering consultation and support; and overseeing recruitment, hiring, orientation, training and supervision of staff. Min. Req. - Five years experience in college or university publications management. Knowledge of design and production; familiarity with Macintosh desktop publishing equipment and software, particularly Microsoft Word and Quark XPress. Demonstrated ability to write and edit news and feature stories, and manage creative staff. Ability to work comfortably with faculty, administrators, staff, writers and designers. Knowledge and understanding of the environment of a large, complex, private research university. (Grade 11)

ACCOUNTING TECHNICIAN - REQ. 31406 & 31407 - SPONSORED PROJECTS ACCOUNTING — The Accounting Technician is responsible for second-line supervision, management of sponsored accounts receivable and accountability for contracts and grants. Duties will also include: preparing annual, quarterly and monthly expense reports to recover allowable program funds expended in accordance with contract or grant agreements; preparing financial analysis for accounts when award terminates and conducting close-out audit of total program expenditures; providing account reconciliation assistance; reviewing and interpreting grant and contract agreements; analyzing program budgets; and reviewing budget changes for allowance and availability. Min. Req. - Bachelor's degree in accounting or equivalent experience. One to two years experience with sponsored contracts and grants administration and FASB accounting principles. Fund accounting experience is desirable. (Grade 7)

Effective job descriptions give employees a clear understanding of how to perform assigned tasks.

Job descriptions give employees a detailed step-by-step description of what they should do to accomplish a specific assignment. Often, the steps are numbered; the language is concise and clear; and almost invariably the words are supplemented by visual aids. One successful method is to divide the steps of the job description into two columns. The left-hand column describes what must be done. An adjacent right-hand column describes the result of the action.

5. Tighten wing bolt B to maximum . . . .

5. Yellow heat bar should now protrude from side approximately 2 inches.

6. Attach identification number to *smooth* surface of yellow heat bar . . . .

6. Identification number should be directly above imprinting "Garrison Corporation" in metal frame.

The language of job descriptions must conform to the technical and educational level of the reader. Because of the influx of foreign workers into the United States, many job descriptions are now written in other languages, among them Spanish, Korean, Vietnamese, and Chinese.

Job descriptions for administrative positions are usually much more general than those written for routine or production-line work. It is assumed that if the job description states, "Competence in handling accounts receivable" or "preparation of documentation for express and overnight mail," those descriptive phrases imply the skills needed so those attributes do not have to be listed. Figure 21-4 presents two brief job descriptions.

WRITING AND SPEAKING EXERCISES

1. As a manager of a small neighborhood grocery store, your are concerned about the frequent bickering among your four employees over who does what. List and describe four duties for each of the four employees.

2. You've invented "Lopside," a board game for children and adults. A wealthy friend shows interest in backing your developmental efforts, but first requires a proposal from you. In no more than three pages, propose your plans to the prospective investor.

3. Create an RFP for some improvement that needs to be made at your campus or workplace.

4. Western Ways Mail Order Company is interested in including your handmade Christmas decorations in an upcoming catalog. The company requests that you sum up in a brief proposal what you will do for them and what you expect in return. Do so in not more than three pages.

5. As office supervisor, you're tired of repeated questions about common office procedures. Choose an office activity or procedure and then write a clear description of the process, as if for a process manual.

6. Assume that you plan to set up a mail order business (operating from your home initially) to sell gift packaging and all related products to a consumer market. You estimate that you will need an initial investment of $175,000 for inventory, catalog design and printing, mailing, packaging, miscellaneous advertising, samples, legal fees, and so on. Your bank would like to see your business plan. Develop your plan.

7. Select a business in which you would like to work. Name the product or service, market niche, and basic details for your reader. Then draw up a business plan to secure financing for your project.

8. Interview a teaching assistant at your school about his or her duties. From what you learn, write a job description that might be used by the department chair when there is a need to fill the same position in the future.

9. Duplicate assignment 8 with a different teaching assistant. However, this time also record the perceptions of the teaching assistant's instructor as to the teaching assistant's duties. Now write a short report on the differences in duties each has listed and your analysis of why you think the perceptions differ. Submit all three parts to your instructor.

10. Identify the following with one of the designations for illogical statements listed in the discussion of "Logical Order."

    (a) The school's football and basketball teams finished last out of the top 25 in their respective leagues, three fraternities were placed on probation, and undergraduate enrollment dropped 4 percent last year. You can see why I called it a third-rate school.

    (b) It seems to me that we have only two choices: we either support his suggestions or we ask him to leave.

(c) Carol Ching is an attractive and personable young woman; she will surely make an excellent TV news announcer.

(d) Tim Nozawa has a laugh like a donkey; how can you possibly think he would make a good production supervisor?

11. Nine possible errors in logical thinking were described in this chapter. Any one of these may give your reader a negative view of your proposal. Write an example of a hasty generalization and personal bias.

12. Repeat the assignment, but this time write an example of a false cause and a straw man.

13. Assume you would like to rent one of the vacant stores at the Westlake Mall to sell Tasty Flavors Ice Cream and Frozen Yogurt. At present, there are no competing outlets of this type in the mall. The mall is five years old and has extremely heavy traffic, and overall sales have increased 8 to 14 percent in each of the years following the opening year. Make all necessary assumptions concerning start-up expenses and projected sales. Prepare a brief business plan to submit to a venture capital organization. You would like initial funding of $125,000.00. You may make any reasonable assumptions.

CASES

Complete the following assignment from the Cases for Discussion section at the back of this book:

1. Hostile Takeover case—Assignment 5

READINGS

See "High-Tech Guru Steven Burrill on High-Tech Start-ups" in the Readings section at the back of this book.

SUGGESTED RESOURCES

Anser, M. "Creating a Winning Proposal." *Business Quarterly* 55 (Winter 1991).

Beck, C., and Wagner, K. "Toward a Rhetoric of Technical Proposals, Ethos and Audience Analysis." *Technical Communication* 39 (February 1992).

Bermar, A. "Strong Business Plans Can Make or Break Startups." *EDN* 35 (January 11, 1990).

Blankenhorn, R., and del Valle, H. "A Network for Writing and Publishing Proposals." *Technical Communication* 39 (February 1992).

Bowman, J., and Brandchaw, B. *How to Write Proposals That Produce.* Phoenix, Ariz: Oryx Press, 1992.

Crawford-Lucas, P.A. "Providing Business Plan Assistance to Small Manufacturing Companies." *Economic Development Review* 10 (Winter 1992).

Fraser, W. "To Buy or Not to Buy." *Management Accounting* 71 (December 1989).

Gaines, L. "Joselyn: Small Details in Win Proposals." *Travel Weeekly* 51 (March 30, 1992).

Hardwick, M., and Kantin, R. "Making Your Sales Proposals More Effective." *Sales and Marketing Management* 144 (July 1992).

Holtz, H. *The Consultant's Guide to Proposal Writing,* 2nd ed. New York: John Wiley & Sons, 1990.

"How to Devise a Winning Business Plan." (Interview with CEO B. Charles Ames). *Journal of Business Strategy* 10 (May-June 1989).

Miner, L. and Griffith, J. *Proposal Planning and Writing.* Phoenix, Az: Oryx Press, 1993.

Rutberg, S., Moin, D., and Friedman, A. "Macy's Business Plan Seen Helping Image." *WWD* 162 (September 2, 1992).

Sandy, W. "Link Your Business Plan to a Performance Plan." *Journal of Business Strategy* 11 (November-December 1990).

Stephenson, M. "Completing the Picture: The Business Plan." *Fund Raising Management* 22 (November 1991).

Wyckham, R., and Wedley, W. "Factors Related to Venture Feasibility Analysis and Business Plan Preparation." *Journal of Small Business Management* 28 (October 1990).

ENDNOTES

1. Much of the information on desktop publishing was contributed by Rod Faccio, coordinator, University of Southern California Medical Illustrations and Graphics and Howard L. Berman, associate director, Biomedical Communications, USC School of Medicine.

2. *The Wall Street Journal,* May 15, 1987: 36D.

3. *William M. Fraser, "To Buy or Not to Buy?,"* Management Accounting 71 (December 1989): 34–37.

4. William Sandy, "Link Your Business Plan to a Performance Plan," *Journal of Business Strategy* 11 (November-December 1990).

5. B. Charles Ames, "How to Devise a Winning Business Plan." *Journal of Business Strategy* 10 (May-June 1989).

P A R T **6**

PROFESSIONAL
SPEAKING
AND LISTENING

John T. Fay, Jr., Ph.D. retired from Bergen Brunswig Corporation in 1992. As Vice President and Corporate Secretary, he participated in Bergen's decade of growth in sales from $1.1 billion to $5 billion. He continues to provide occasional service as a specialist in business communication.

A former Washington representative for the National Wholesale Druggists' Association, the American Pharmaceutical Association and Foremost-McKesson, Inc., Dr. Fay is now Corporate Editor of *Wholesale Drugs Magazine* and an adjunct faculty member at Chapman University School of Management.

Bergen Brunswig Corporation

4000 Metropolitan Drive, Orange, CA 92668   (714) 385-4000

John T. Fay, Jr., Ph.D.
Vice President, Corporate Affairs
and Secretary

AN OPEN LETTER TO <u>INTERESTED READERS</u>

Clear, effective oral communication appears to be a simple task for some people and a major difficulty for others. Why is that? All of us can talk. We do it every day. Some of us talk too much. Others provoke boredom or confusion whenever they open their mouths. Ordinarily, this is because the brain is not engaged before the mouth is opened.

A careful review of the principles involved is a useful exercise. The next segment of this readable book should remind you how important preparatory thought can be. We communicate best after an investment of time in <u>thinking</u> about speaking, writing, and recording exactly what we want to convey.

Meaningful progress in business and innovation in any activity depends in large part upon the concise, clear expression of original thought. The convincing speaker enjoys a genuine competitive edge. Personal effort applied to the sharpening of communication skills will yield solid results.

Think about it.

John T. Fay, Jr.

22

PRINCIPLES OF ORAL COMMUNICATION

What and how you communicate often determine what you are to the world.

Oral presentations are opportunities to express your communication skills.

Businesspeople are called upon to speak frequently in a variety of formal and semiformal situations. Some occasions involve a 20 minute presentation to a group of prospective customers, visitors to the plant, or security analysts. At other times businesspeople express ideas at meetings and conferences. Panel presentations; recruiting, appraisal, and counseling interviews; and many other situations call for oral communication skills. Each of these is an opportunity—an opportunity to express yourself and impress others not only with your knowledge of the topic, but also with your ability to convey that knowledge.

An interesting aspect of speaking is the correlation listeners frequently draw between the effectiveness of presentations and the ability of speakers in their field. The speakers may be outstanding accountants, engineers, or financial analysts, but if they speak inarticulately or fumble, the listener's perception of their ability may suffer. Such an evaluation may be unfair, but that negative evaluation—fair or not—remains.

Even though you recognize the importance of making effective oral presentations, do you face the task with some fear and trepidation? You are not alone. When Americans are asked about their greatest fears, they frequently list "speaking before a group" as a situation they fear more than heights, accidents, insects, financial problems, and even death.

You can follow a variety of steps to lessen that fear and eventually overcome it. Those steps, such as preparation and knowledge of the topic and the audience, plus others, are discussed in this chapter.

TYPES OF PRESENTATIONS

Oral communication can be persuasive, informative, or entertaining. Whether a presentation is long or short, taking place in an interview, a panel, or at a meeting, it usually falls into one of these three categories.

THE PERSUASIVE TALK

Successful persuasive presentations result in action by the listeners.

The persuasive presentation aims to gain the listener's acceptance or approval. One method of gaining acceptance is to follow a logical order of development that involves four elements.

Arousing interest. Capture the audience's interest by making a startling statement, telling a story with which the members of the audience can identify, demonstrating an activity, holding up a sample, or carrying through any action that will cause the audience to become alert and receptive to your message.

> *Perhaps you saw this morning's headline: "Drought Threatens Planned Housing Development." The accompanying news story would have you believe that the fate of this important civic project depends solely on increased rainfall. I want to tell you the full story . . .*

Describing and explaining. Make your description clear enough that listeners can easily understand your ideas. Also, make your explanation revolve around the benefits for the listeners: the fulfillment of their needs, their hopes, their desires.

> *Three out of five senior citizens in the United States are financially unprepared for major illness. Consider what that statistic means. Before they can qualify for Medicaid assistance, seniors must usually spend all their assets, including their equity in their homes and retirement savings. For such seniors, the stress of falling seriously ill is compounded by the stress of becoming financially destitute.*

Proving and visualizing. Substantiate your claims by citing past experiences, testimonials from others, or some guarantees that the members of the audience will find acceptable and believable. Statements that help visualize results are also important in persuading others:

> *You will therefore be able to dispose of eight out of ten filing cabinets now in use.*

> *Picture the added work space available to you.*

> *This equipment will increase your production-line speed by almost 40 percent. The increased speed should almost double your output, thus making a sizable contribution to your profit margin.*

Moving to action or approval. After you capture attention, describe the idea, concept, product, or service, explain the need for it, and prove its value. Then ask for approval. The request for approval should be specific and positive.

> *Now that you have the facts, an accurate evaluation of the return on investment we will receive, and the overall benefits to our company, please send me your written approval for the project by May 15.*

THE INFORMATIVE TALK

An effective outline keeps the presentation organized.

In an informative talk, it is vital that the audience clearly understand the concept presented. For that reason, pay special attention to clarity, organization, and coherence in the presentation. In other words, develop an outline that will assist both the speaker and listener.

Good visual aids contribute significantly in most informative speeches by helping the audience see as well as hear how important points are related. Consider, for example, the following outline of an informative speech. Notice how the graphic aids indicated in the outline contribute to the informative purpose of the presentation.

I. Current Minority Enrollment in U.S. Business Schools (Pie chart: percentage of minority business majors)
II. Trends in Minority Enrollment 1980–19__
   (Line graph: steady rise in minority enrollment)
III. Factors Favoring Further Rises in Minority Enrollment
   (Bulleted text chart: favorable factors)
IV. Future Prospects for Minority Enrollments
   (Bar chart projections: anticipated future minority enrollment)

THE ENTERTAINING SPEECH

Use humor appropriately and remember that your main job is to inform or persuade.

The entertaining speech may have as its basis humor, description, picturesque language, drama, mystery, or a combination of these. Certainly, audience interest level must be kept high. Remember that although humor may be one attribute of the entertaining speech, it is not the only one.

Few business speakers, of course, are asked to give an entire presentation with the sole purpose of entertaining the audience. More often, entertaining elements of a presentation blend with informative or persuasive elements. A luncheon presentation, for example, might begin with one or two jokes or humorous stories and then proceed to more serious material of interest to the audience.

ORGANIZING THE SPEECH

The work of organizing a presentation begins by gathering key concepts and supportive details appropriate to your audience and purpose. Apply the principles of audience analysis and the purpose analysis discussed in the next section ("Qualities of the Effective Speaker") to this development stage of your presentation.

From the outset, speakers must also consider what graphic aids are available to support the presentation. Both development time and financial resources may play a role in deciding which and how many graphics to use. The guidelines set forth on pages 527–528 provide reasons for using graphics and suggestions for their placement. Often speakers feel that once they have selected their key concepts, completed their research, and arranged their visual aids, they are ready to give their speech. However, there are other steps in organizing a presentation: the design of the introduction, the body, and the conclusion.

INTRODUCTION

The introduction sets the tone of the entire speech.

The introduction is vital because it often determines the overall reaction of the audience to the speech. The saying, "We never have a second chance to make a good first impression," has much merit.

Good introductions result from careful planning. They may involve beginning with an unusual statement or story, referring to the audience or a problem or situation with which they can identify, posing a rhetorical question, or injecting humor associated with the topic. Beginnings such as the following are sure to lose or alienate the audience:

Well, I'm not sure why Mr. Baxter selected me to address you, but here goes anyway . . .

I really have little or nothing to add to what has already been said on the topic, but . . .

Instead, consider these more positive and assertive openings:

I deeply appreciated Mr. Baxter's invitation to speak to you.

I have a unique perspective to share with you on the topic of . . .

BODY

Focus all elements of the presentation on a central theme you want the audience to remember.

The body of the speech usually accounts for 70 to 80 percent of the presentation time. It is the heart of the presentation. In organizing the body, select and write out the central theme, main ideas, and supporting ideas.

The central theme is what the speaker wants the audience to remember, even if all or most of the other ideas are forgotten. State the central theme in one sentence. Make the sentence distinctive, if possible. After selecting the theme, choose a series of main ideas to buttress that concept. Normally, listeners will be able to retain four or five such main ideas, but not more.

Then bring in supporting ideas to the main ideas. Their primary function is to substantiate, prove, and reinforce the main ideas. Statistics, analogies, examples, and quotations often serve as support materials.

After selecting the central theme and main and supporting ideas, take the time to arrange them in a consistent and logical order of development. Choose one or more of these methods of developing a presentation: chronological sequence, spatial sequence, causal sequence, deductive sequence, inductive sequence, or problem-solution sequence.

Chronological sequence relates the history of events.

The *chronological sequence* organizes material on the basis of time, usually from past to present to future. For example, a presentation on space travel might recount developments from early satellite launches to present space-shuttle successes to future plans for a permanent space station.

Spatial sequence organizes material according to relationships in space.

The *spatial sequence* organizes material according to location. Most common are far-to-near and near-to-far spatial patterns. A presentation on voter registration, for example, could begin with registration in the speaker's hometown (near), proceed to registration within the county (farther), and end with the situation in the state or region (farthest).

Causal sequence relates the causes of events.

Causal sequence arranges material according to the principle of causality—the causes responsible for certain occurrences. A presenter using this pattern could, for example, discuss urban poverty and joblessness as root causes for social unrest in some U.S. cities.

In deductive sequence, a general observation is followed by specific examples.

Deductive sequence begins by setting forth a major principle, which is then applied to specific cases and conclusions. For example, a political speaker begins by asserting the major principle that only those who have served in the armed forces are truly qualified to hold elective office. Based on this assumption, the speaker goes on to deduce that certain candidates are better qualified than others in an upcoming election. The deductive pattern of argumentation surfaces commonly in presidential elections as one party tries to promote its candidate over another party's.

Inductive sequence moves from specific examples to a general observation.

Inductive sequence occurs when specific cases are cited in an effort to arrive at a general statement or principle. A securities regulator, for example, cites ten examples of unfair business practices on the part of a stock broker and reaches the general conclusion that the broker is dishonest. (See"Critical Thinking Concepts" on page 173 for more information on deductive and inductive analysis.)

Problem-solution sequence poses a problem or question and then offers a solution or answer.

The *problem-solution sequence* involves material organized into a problem (or question) and a solution (or answer). The topic of illegal immigration, for example, could be treated as a problem (such as stress on the job market due to the influx of illegal immigrants) and a solution (such as stricter controls on borders).

Speakers need not feel bound to any one pattern of development. No matter which pattern or combination of patterns they select, the goal remains the same: to present material effectively for the audience and purpose at hand.

CONCLUSION

The conclusion should drive home the main point memorably.

The conclusion should "fix" the central theme in the minds of the audience and serve as a closure. You may wish to summarize the main points, suggest a specific course of action, propose a solution, or request approval. At times, a quotation from an authority will tie in perfectly with your theme and serve as an effective conclusion.

Here, for example, is an example of an effective conclusion. Notice how the speaker returns to the main themes of the presentation and draws them to a final, memorable call to action:

> *In the past 20 minutes, I've described to you the cultural, financial, and marketing challenges we face in bringing our product to Japan. Culturally, we must remember to enter Japan as a guest, not a conqueror. Financially, we must look for innovative partnerships with Japanese banks. As for our marketing efforts, we must look to native Japanese marketing experts for successful advertising campaigns. In achieving our cultural, financial, and marketing goals, we also achieve our business mission. Let me therefore call on each of you for your commitment to the kind of sensitivity, openness, and tolerance that will make our company truly a welcome business guest in Japan.*

QUALITIES OF THE EFFECTIVE SPEAKER

The members of the audience to which the manager speaks—in business, industry, and government—do not expect or demand a spellbinding presentation. However, they do expect the speaker to be *knowledgeable, prepared, well organized,* and *honest.* If, in addition, speakers deliver their comments with impressive gestures, careful enunciation, and excellent inflection, and remember to maintain good eye contact, so much the better. But at the least, a speaker must do an effective job with the "formidable four."

Knowledgeable speakers do their homework.

Be knowledgeable. As a speaker, you should possess excellent background knowledge of both the audience and the topic. Make sure your research is complete and your information sufficiently thorough so that you can anticipate questions, comments,and objections.

Know something about areas related to the topic as well as ideas that oppose your own. With knowledge on this level, you will be able to handle rebuttals as well as answers to questions with confidence.

Prepare an outline and practice using graphic aids.

Be prepared. Be prepared in several ways. In organizing your speech, make sure you write a thorough outline of the presentation (as described in the following section on organization). Develop meaningful graphic aids well in advance of the presentation so that you have time to practice using them. Prepare notes if you need them, but keep them simple. Notes should never be so detailed that they require word-by-word reading. (The exception to this general rule is the presentation that deals with sensitive or extremely important topics. In this case, a carefully prepared manuscript may have to be read verbatim to avoid misstatement.)

Organize the speech by sticking to the central theme.

Be well organized. Effective organization requires that you clearly state your central theme and develop it persuasively. Make your main ideas and supportive evidence appear to be distinct, yet related, much like chapters in a book. Use guiding language, or signposts, often to remind the audience of what you have said or to tell them what you are about to say. Include transitions between parts of the presentation to keep the audience oriented and focused. The structure of a presentation, in other words, should be clear to the speaker and to the audience at all times.

Be honest when making your presentation and fielding questions.

Be honest. Probably no activity reveals a person more completely than speaking. An ancient philosopher said, "Speak that I may know you."

Somehow, people's personalities, knowledge, truthfulness, emotions, and self are revealed when they speak. Because speech is so revealing, do not pretend to be something you are not. The audience will recognize deception.

Be honest in your presentation—in action and in statements—if you wish to maintain the goodwill of your audience. Also respect your audience, and recognize the value of a straightforward, "I'm sorry, I really don't know the answer to that question."

DELIVERING THE SPEECH

Your nervousness will be much more apparent to you than to your audience.

If the steps leading up to a speech (research, preparation, organization, and honesty) are well handled, the speech will probably be effective. Nevertheless, do not discount the importance of delivery. It isn't quite enough to just give a speech, even if you do have the "formidable four" well in hand.

If you are like most people, your emotional state will contribute to your presentation. Your pulse rate will probably be higher than usual; your breathing may be shallow and rapid; and your stomach and mouth will not feel the way they usually do. But this condition, you may be sure, will be much more apparent to you than to the audience. In fact, nervousness may give you a slight edge because you are so alert and sensitive to the climate in which you are involved.

The best way to handle nervousness is to prepare thoroughly.

To some extent, ways of coping with speaker's nerves are highly individual. Some speakers find it helpful to meet and greet audience members as they enter the room. Feeling secure with the audience, such speakers reason, breeds assuredness and relaxation for the presenter. Other speakers find comfort in simply accepting their nervousness, knowing that it will dissipate quickly within the first minute or two of the presentation. Common to virtually all speakers, however, is the calming effect of thorough preparation. If you know your presentation well, you will be less likely to worry about getting stuck or going blank. Focusing your attention on the presentation itself rather than on nervous symptoms plays a powerful role in reducing the uncomfortable feelings of speech anxiety.

FACTORS IN THE DELIVERY OF THE SPEECH

Your audience probably won't demand that the delivery of your speech be accomplished with the perfection of a first-rate orator. They will appreciate, however, care on your part concerning basic principles of word selection, enunciation, eye contact, use of graphic aids, and the like.

CHOICE OF WORDS AND WORD USAGE

Base word choice on your audience's knowledge of the material.

A primary purpose of communication is to transfer ideas. Ideas are made up of words. Therefore, the more extensive your vocabulary is, the easier is the task of selecting the exact word for your meaning. Then ideas can be expressed with precision, force, and clarity.

Your choice of words must be based on the audience. Try not to be so deeply involved in your own area of specialization that you forget that your technical terms are not known to everyone. Remember, too, that certain words arouse emotional reactions that increase prejudice, build support, or evoke opposition. Words such as *strike, scab, delinquent,* or *radical* may cause a strong reaction among listeners. It is one thing to choose emotionally charged words intentionally to better convey ideas, but be aware that a careless choice of such words may cause listeners to tune you out.

ENUNCIATION OF WORDS

Speak clearly.

Take care to enunciate clearly the words you choose. Careless or sloppy enunciation is usually the result of simple laziness in the use of mouth, tongue, and lips. A "yeah" for a "yes," "dontchathink" for "don't you think," and "we're gonna" for "we are going to" neither help present ideas nor enhance your image to the audience.

INFLECTION

A change in your voice can emphasize an idea.

At times it is vital to give specific inflection to ideas as you speak. That change in tone, emphasis, and volume often reflects, better than the words, feelings of emotion, anger, enthusiasm, humor, or support. If you do not permit your voice to reflect feelings, you will miss an important factor in oral communication.

VOLUME

Speak loudly enough for all to hear you and vary the volume to keep your listeners interested.

The audience must be able to hear you easily before it can accept your ideas. If members of the group strain to hear you, they will eventually find the effort too taxing and give up. On the other hand, if your voice is too loud or scratchy, or pitched too high, the audience may find that an irritation, and again you will lose. Make the effort to determine and maintain the proper volume and pitch.

One of the most important factors in volume is variation. A monotone or one-level presentation becomes monotonous. Vary the volume, but not in a way that sounds mechanical or affected. Changes in volume should be related to the ideas being presented. A speaker's volume often rises to signal a key idea or a crucial statistic. The volume then falls for more subsidiary matters. This general pattern can occasionally be reversed for variety and emphasis; the main idea can be whispered, somewhat intimately, into a microphone almost as a secret might be told.

RATE OF DELIVERY

Base the rate of delivery on your audience's needs and your personality.

Changes in the rate of delivery, like changes in volume, help arouse audience interest and dispel monotony. If you deliver the speech too rapidly, the audience will have trouble following it. Even if an audience does comprehend easily, it is taxing for most people to stay with someone who speaks rapidly for more than 30 minutes. On the other hand, if your words come out at a snail's pace, the audience will become bored, inattentive, and even irritated. Always adjust your rate of delivery to the subject matter, the audience, and your personality.

GESTURES AND POSTURE

Use natural gestures to convey emphasis, and take care that your posture is straight.

Freely motivated and natural gestures can add to the communication of ideas. Effective nonverbal communication by means of the torso, hands, head, face, and eyes all help convey your message, mood, and attitude. But your gestures must be spontaneous and natural; they should not look artificial.

Also, watch your posture. If you slouch or drape yourself on the lectern, the audience may think that your ideas are as slovenly as your posture. A speaker who stands erect and is vigorous commands the attention of the audience.

EYE CONTACT

Eye contact ensures the interest and participation of listeners.

Eye contact, carefully and naturally maintained, helps keep the audience involved. One way to maintain good eye contact is to pick several individuals in the audience and speak directly to them. Then pick others and focus on them. Soon, most members of the audience begin to feel involved with you and with what you are saying.

Do you recall speakers or teachers who stared out the window or at the floor or glued their eyes to their notes? Those speakers lost directness, and their audiences lost interest. In contrast, the speaker who looks at the listeners arouses their interest and captures their attention.

AUDIENCE FEEDBACK

Watch for audience feedback to determine how your speech is being received and make adjustments accordingly.

Be alert to the feedback you receive from the audience while you speak. Often, you must adjust the content, depth of analysis, organization, use of humor, and other factors according to the response.

Effective speakers are not tied to notes and outlines. On the contrary, alert speakers quickly become aware of the questions on the faces of people in the audience and add another example. They immediately sense when a point has been covered adequately. To continue would be to belabor the point and lose many of the group; therefore, they move on quickly.

Good speakers "feel" the audience and respond accordingly.

GRAPHIC AIDS

The nature of graphic aids for oral presentations is described in Chapter 17. Remember these important do's and don'ts when including graphic aids in an oral presentation.

Do vary your graphic aids. Don't bore your audience with a succession of similar graphic aids. Perhaps you have had the experience of almost nodding off

Include a variety of graphic aids to maintain audience interest.

during a slide presentation, particularly one depicting the most recent vacation of a relative. Your sleepiness was probably due to the repetition of the slide format itself rather than the content of the pictures. Similarly, as a business presenter vary the types of graphic aids you use. The wide variety available is described in Chapter 17.

Point out why a graphic aid is significant.

Do show interest in your own graphic aids. Don't expect your audience to find interest that you do not. Too many presenters apparently feel they have fulfilled their purpose once they press the slide button or flip on the overhead projector. Such speakers show little or no interest in what appears on the screen; they, after all, have seen it before. This kind of lackadaisical attitude toward graphic aids is contagious! As a speaker, keep your audience interested. Look at and even point to portions of particular graphics with the same high level of interest that you expect from the audience.

Make effective transitions between graphic aids.

Do lead into and lead out of graphic aids. Do not drop graphic aids into your presentation without explanation. Skilled speakers say a few words to introduce each of their graphics and to exit from each graphic to the next topic. For example, a speaker could introduce a line graph in this way:

> *We can see the dramatic rise in food prices [flips on overhead to show line graph] for the past five years in this graph.*

The speaker can eventually leave the discussion of the graph by referring again to its central content:

> *But what have these steep price increases [flips off projector] meant to the average consumer? First, . . .*

Make sure your listeners can hear you despite noise in the room.

Do vary your volume to account for projection noise. Don't be drowned out by your equipment. Slide projectors, movie projectors, and overhead projectors produce significant noise in the form of whirring fans and raspy motors. Speakers are often unaware that when the projector goes on, their speaking effectiveness goes off, if the audience cannot hear well. Test the clarity and carrying power of your voice above the noise of a projector by practicing your speech in the room in which it will be given. Ask a friend to sit in the back of the room and to tell you honestly if your words are obscured by projector noise. If so, increase your volume and sharpen your enunciation. For larger rooms and audiences, consider using a microphone.

The problem of projector noise has been resolved, in part, by computer-controlled visual aids. Presentation software (such as Harvard Graphics and Storyboard) allow you to call up predesigned computer images to a large-screen monitor without the whir of a slide projector. Depending on the sophistication of the software, these images can be fixed (much like slides) or dynamic, that is, with moving text or pictures and interactive features.

WRITING AND SPEAKING EXERCISES

1. Form a group of four students. As a group, determine the information you would include on visual aids prepared for an oral presentation on the topic of "The Effective Speaker." Once you've reached a consensus, let each group member present one form of visual aid: chalkboard, flip

chart, slides, or transparencies. Present each visual aid to the entire group and discuss the strengths and weaknesses of each presentation. Next, work as a group to develop one final visual aid which incorporates the group's discussion. Present this visual aid to the class for feedback.

2. Relying on secondary research, discuss how nonverbal communication skills affect oral presentations. How important is nonverbal communication to effective speaking? Can anything be done to enhance credibility through managing nonverbal techniques? Prepare a memo to your instructor that addresses these questions.

3. Discuss, in memo format, the proposition that it is impossible for effective oral communication to be too interesting for its own good. Use personal experiences and library research to support your thesis.

4. You are to give an oral presentation to a group of high school seniors. The topic is "Your College Campus." Select three different organizational sequences and outline each.

5. Research the sales letter and then report (orally or in writing) on the similarities between that type of message and the persuasive presentation.

6. Some gestures command attention and others detract from the presentation. Select a recognized television personality and list the gestures he or she uses that command attention. Then list the gestures that are distracting. Be specific in identifying and explaining the items you list.

7. Listen to an extended address by a politician, religious figure, or other personality (perhaps on television or radio). Discover where the speaker routinely pauses; then develop a short speech of your own, placing pauses in similar locations. Assess the influence of such pauses on your effectiveness as a speaker.

8. It sometimes appears that we are becoming slovenly in the way we speak our language or substitute inappropriate words for correct English. Besides the examples cited in the chapter, list ten words you frequently hear that are enunciated poorly or are slang terms.

9. Study the speaking habits and techniques of two TV newscasters. Then, using at least six categories of comparison, write down their similarities and differences as speakers. Decide which, in your view, is the most effective speaker.

10. Using a tape recorder, conduct the following experiment. Choose a long paragraph in this text (or another) and read it slowly and distinctly into the tape recorder. Then read the same passage again into the recorder, this time very quickly. Listen to the two versions. For each, write down the impression you gain about the speaker based on the pace of speech. (Does a fast pace, for example, make the speaker sound ill-at-ease and impatient? Or does the speaker sound more compelling?)

11. There are at least three types of presentations: informative, entertaining, and persuasive. Besides being types of speeches, the elements of information, entertainment, and persuasion can be parts of a total speech. You are a concerned student who feels that the academic standards of your institution have declined. You have met with the dean to explain your feelings and after several discussions the dean said, "I want you to make a seven- to ten-minute presentation to a faculty group." The purpose of your speech is to convince the audience to increase the institution's academic standards. To achieve your purpose you want to inform them and include some appropriate humor along the way. Outline your

presentation and specifically identify the elements of information, entertainment, and persuasion in the outline.

12. As one of the better speakers in your company, you've been assigned as a personal speech coach to help a company vice president overcome "speaker's nerves." You have two weeks to help this executive before an important presentation must be given. Describe the steps you would take to lead this person to confident speaking.

13. Thirty minutes before a business meeting your boss tells you to say a few words about the history of the company for the benfit of guests at the meeting. In that amount of time, what information must you gather? What personal preparation and planning must you make?

14. Many student presentations in classes can be represented in one word: dull. You are to make an oral presentation in a class; other students in the class will be making speeches on the same topic. You want to differentiate yourself from the others by gaining the attention of the audience immediately. Write the introduction on a sheet of paper and explain what you will be doing to gain the audience's attention. Select one of these classes and topics:

COURSE TOPIC

Basic Accounting	Why Accountants Must be Precise
Secretarial Studies	Men Enter the Secretarial Profession
Human Resources	Fringe Benefits of the Future
Finance	Changes in Banking Regulations
Marketing Sales	Salesmen Aren't Necessarily Men Anymore

15. Locate a public figure reputed to be honest and sincere in his or her speaking manner. List specific verbal and nonverbal techniques (whether conscious or unconscious) used by the speaker in creating this impression.

CASES

Complete the following assignment from the Cases for Discussion section at the back of this book:

1. The Sun Fresh case—Assignment 5

READINGS

See "Six Rules to Get Your Messages Across" in the Readings section at the back of this book.

SUGGESTED RESOURCES

Ailes, Roger et al. "Public Speaking Survival Strategies: How to Make an Audience Love You." *Working Woman* 15 (November 1990):118–122.

Bell, Arthur H., and Skopec, Eric. *The Speaker's Edge.* New York: Asher Gallant, 1989.

Boyd, Stephen D. "Writing for the Ear." *Canadian Manager* 15 (September 1990):24–25.

Brown, Lillian. *Your Public Best: The Complete Guide to Making Successful Public Appearances in the Meeting Room, on the Platform, and on TV.* New York: Newmarket Press, 1989.

Burns, Robert Edward. "Combating Speech Anxiety." *Public Relations Journal* 47 (March 1991):28-30.

Calabrese, Ric. "Designing and Delivering Presentations and Workshops." *Bulletin of the Association for Business Communication* 52 (June 1989):26–32.

Cosnett, Gary et al. "A Survival Guide to Public Speaking." *Training & Development Journal* 44 (September 1990):15–26.

Decker, Bart. "So You're Giving a Speech: How to Involve Your Audience." *Supervisory Management* 36 (July 1991):5–8.

Klepper, Michael. "What Are You Talking About?" *Communication World* 7 (October 1990):20–22.

Sheppard, D.J. "Poised for Confidence." *Canadian Manager* 16 (March 1991): 28–30.

23

SHORT AND LONG PRESENTATIONS

Memorable words can produce memorable results.

Many situations in business require oral presentations. It is important for a brief talk to be as effective as a long, formal one.

As a businessperson, you may have to give short presentations before employees, community members, business and professional organizations, and government representatives. You may be the only speaker or you may be participating as a panel representative or a committee member at a meeting. Among the occasions that require short, oral presentations are these:

- The informational talk to a small group or an individual
- Introductions of individuals, projects, or concepts to an audience
- Recognition of individuals or groups for their contributions
- Welcoming visitors or others on behalf of an organization
- Luncheon or dinner presentations
- Briefings on technical or semitechnical projects to those who need to know about the project

At the same time, important business opportunities occur for the longer presentation, including the following:

- Convention, conference, and major-meeting addresses
- Presentations to financial and regulatory audiences
- Extended informational and persuasive speeches to company and civic audiences

As we will see later in this chapter, speakers face special obstacles in keeping the audience's attention during long presentations. We turn first, however, to the challenges of short presentations.

SHORT PRESENTATIONS

THE INFORMATIONAL TALK

Many business situations call for an informational talk. You may be called on to inform employees about new rules or procedures. Or you may wish to inform students, community members, or stockholders about your firm, its activities, products, or organization. You may wish to give customers information about a new sales allowance or a new product.

Informative talks give listeners new information.

The primary purpose of the informative talk is to provide listeners with information they did not previously possess. Members of the group usually have little knowledge of the topic, but you must still determine their level of knowledge so that you do not speak above or below their heads.

Visual aids often serve a useful purpose in this type of talk. A chart, cut-away drawing, model of a piece of equipment, or diagram can assist in the transfer of information.

THE INTRODUCTORY TALK

The purpose of an introduction is to motivate the audience to want to hear the speaker—not the introducer. For that reason, introductions should be short and attention catching. They should make the speaker feel welcome, yet not embarrass him or her by being too effusive, humorous, or long. Introductions that state, "This individual needs no introduction," "I really don't know what I can tell you about our speaker that you don't already know," or "Last, but not least . . ." are trite and only make the speaker's job more difficult.

Introductory talks peak the audience's interest in the speaker.

The introduction can (1)emphasize the accomplishments of the speaker, (2)concentrate on the topic, (3)examine both, or (4)discuss the speaker and the topic and their relationship to the audience. In most cases, following this last suggestion arouses the greatest audience interest.

As an introducer, learn as much as possible about the speaker as well as the interests of the audience. Attempt to find a common ground that can be used to heighten audience interest. If the speaker is a corporate officer of a food manufacturer and is scheduled to address 2,000 chain-store managers, you may point out that the speaker herself was a store manager 18 years ago: "Her knowledge and appreciation of the daily problems you face are derived from hard work and experience, not reports read in a walnut-panelled office."

Another technique is to cite names of several members of the audience and their relationship to the speaker. At times, a relevant quotation can arouse interest, for instance, a statement made about the speaker by a national authority. Or perhaps you can link the speaker or the topic to a quotation from a major source such as the Congressional Record, Shakespeare, or *The New York Times.* Quoting the section of the Bible concerned with the Tower of Babel was an interesting and effective method one introducer used in presenting a speaker in the field of communications.

Emphasize how the audience can benefit from the speaker's presentation.

The key is to learn about the speaker and the audience. Then draw interesting elements from the backgrounds of each to serve the mutual interests of all concerned.

In introducing concepts or projects, the same key holds true. What in the concept or project will be of significance to *this* particular audience? Once you know what to select concerning the project or concept, you can bring those factors into focus for a specific audience. Perhaps a firm is introducing a new product to its sales force. Some members of the sales force call on distributors, others on chain-store buyers, still others on independent retail outlets, and others on government agencies. The key device in this case may be to have several short presentations, each made by someone who is familiar with one of those groups. Credibility rises because everyone recognizes that no one can be an expert in *every* area. The audience will accept the fact that certain individuals have a better feel for the needs and desires of a particular group than others have.

THE RECOGNITION SPEECH

Recognition speeches honor the recipient of an award.

Sometime in your career you will be asked to present an award to an individual or a group. The audience has gathered, of course, to honor the recipient—not the presenter. Remember to comment on the award, the achievement of the recipient or recipients that prompted the award, and the honor or significance of the recognition.

Most people who work hard or perform beyond the call of duty appreciate recognition as much as financial payment. For that reason the recognition is important, but be careful to avoid embarrassing the person honored. The words chosen and the method of presentation or recognition are most important, and the place and manner in which the ceremony is held should be planned with care.

Often you can determine the appropriateness of the place and manner of recognition simply by discussing your plans with the intended recipient. By verbal and nonverbal signals, he or she will probably indicate feelings about your plans—feelings that can guide you in revising those plans as necessary. If the recognition is intended as a surprise, work closely with someone who knows the recipient well to ensure that your expression of appreciation fits the personality and circumstances of the recipient.

In the speech of recognition or presentation, keep the following advice in mind:

- Be brief. Give honest and sincere recognition. Don't make the statement a eulogy, however, or so long as to be boring to the recipient or the audience.
- Identify the award or gift or read the certificate. Many in the audience may have contributed money for the purchase of the award, or they may simply want to hear the words describing the recipient's accomplishments.
- Conclude the comments with the presentation of the gift or certificate.

In a busy society of giant organizations, accomplishments of individuals are often overlooked or not handled well. When there is recognition, therefore, it should be accomplished with care, good taste, discretion, and professionalism. After an individual is recognized, both the person honored and the audience should feel a real glow of inner satisfaction.

THE WELCOME SPEECH

Welcome speeches greet visitors to a facility or institution.

Often individuals or groups visit plants, offices, schools, or other facilities. In almost all instances, someone should welcome them with brief and sincere statements.

In a speech of welcome, note the accomplishments of the visitors and add that you hope they will gain from their visit. Perhaps the key in this brief presentation is mentioning what the visiting group or individual has accomplished or achieved. Noting accomplishments of the astronaut who visits an aerospace firm would not be difficult, but what about a high school computer club that is touring the data processing division of a large corporation? In that instance, you might commend the group for its conscientious efforts and the students' desire to learn more by making the visit.

Sometimes the welcome must include some specific information regarding safety, such as wearing a hard hat or safety goggles in certain areas, prohibiting picture taking or interrupting a worker's assignment, or returning to a designated point at a specific time. Handle information in a positive, courteous way and from the point of view that you are making such suggestions for the visitors' benefit and safety.

In almost all instances, the welcoming speech (1)should be brief, (2)should recognize the accomplishments or position of the visitor or group, (3)should contain a little humor or "light" reference, (4)should offer the goodwill and assistance of the host organization, and (5)should list any rules that should be observed.

THE AFTER-MEAL SPEECH

Because the groups to which an after-meal speech is delivered can vary so much, it is difficult to suggest any one pattern to follow. Some groups appreciate a brief, humorous presentation. Others want to learn and come prepared to ask penetrating questions. Because these two kinds of groups have such tremendously different objectives, it is vital for you as the speaker to determine in advance what type of presentation is expected.

Light after-meal speeches stick to a central theme but are intended to amuse.

The "light" after-meal speech has a theme running through it, but it also has a fair amount of humor. Keep stories in good taste and associated with the theme. If appropriate, introduce a memorable quotation or short poem that applies to the occasion.

Serious after-meal speeches offer important information.

The serious after-meal speech (to a professional accounting, dental, or financial organization, for example) should not be overly long. Here, however, your goal is to leave a message, introduce a new concept, or ensure that some learning takes place. Therefore, it is vital not only to present the necessary ideas but also to reinforce them through a story, a little humor, a demonstration, or the use of visual aids. A flip board with large-sized lettering might prove appropriate, but to turn down the lights and use slides is to take a calculated risk. People who have been working and have enjoyed a big meal might find a nap more attractive than your presentation.

Whether your after-meal speech is light or serious, make it comparatively brief, word it carefully, and, to a greater or lesser degree, make it humorous. A quotable phrase or two can help the audience retain a key idea.

In almost all instances, the toastmaster plays a vital role in helping make the after-meal speech successful. The introduction of the speaker should be light and humorous and give an indication of the topic to be discussed. The comments afterward should not only reflect appreciation but also reinforce (very briefly) the key ideas.

THE BRIEFING

Briefings summarize the current status of a complicated project or activity.

The oral briefing is precisely what the name implies. It is a *brief* presentation of a complex topic designed to inform the listeners of a planned or ongoing project or activity. A nuclear engineer may present a briefing to a group of physicians on a new medical-nuclear piece of equipment. A shop manager may explain the functions of a new machine to the maintenance crew. An office manager may inform the company board of directors on the functions of the new mainframe computer. In every case, the presentation must be brief and not too detailed, and both words and ideas must be easily understandable to those who listen.

Informational briefings make ideas easily understandable.

The *information briefing* presents ideas in easy-to-understand terms and attempts to list concepts for easy retention. Use charts or handouts to make sure the key ideas are not only *heard* but *seen*. This reinforcement can help convey basic information on what might be a complex operation.

Instructional briefings teach listeners how to do something.

The *instructional briefing* is designed to *teach* listeners how to operate or carry through a practice or a procedure. Here again, present the basic ideas, not detailed or complex concepts.

In the instructional briefing give the listeners, if at all possible, an opportunity for a hands-on application. If they can actually handle, closely observe, or even participate in working with the item being discussed, they are more likely to understand.

Although individuals usually give briefings, a team briefing is not unusual. A team may present a briefing to the new members of a board of directors. One person briefs the group on the organization's financing, the next on production, the next on marketing, and the last on personnel activities. Each is limited to his or her topic and by time. The briefing team leader usually coordinates the presentation with opening and closing comments.

OPPORTUNITIES TO PRACTICE THE SHORT PRESENTATION

Practice giving short presentations whenever possible to perfect this vital communication skill.

Because practice is vital to becoming a good speaker, seize every opportunity to make an oral presentation. The next time your conference leader asks for a volunteer to present "a brief report on the new benefit program," raise your hand. When your association, fraternity, sorority, or club director is looking for someone to preside at the annual convention, push your arm up. When your boss requests an employee to visit the "upcoming conference and represent us," be the first to say, "I'll do it." The more times you practice, the more confident you'll become. Evaluate your performances and improve your weak areas.

Better than self-evaluation, at times, is the constructive criticism of colleagues and peers. One effective method for obtaining criticism is to involve yourself in ongoing speaking activities. Some organizations exist primarily to promote such activity. One effective organization that is easily available to most individuals in the United States is Toastmasters International. It has representative chapters in thousands of companies, corporations, hospitals, government agencies, and other organizations in the public and private sectors. Each chapter holds weekly, semimonthly, or monthly meetings. All members have frequent opportunities to speak and receive the constructive comments.

Organizations that provide speaking opportunities for their members have grown rapidly during the past 20 years. Toastmasters, for example, has grown from approximately 50,000 members in 3,000 chapters worldwide in 1975 to 135,000 members in 6,000 chapters in 47 countries.

LONG PRESENTATIONS

Long presentations require special preparation.

The presenter's task would be much simpler if a long presentation were no more than an extended short presentation. In reality, the long speech—one taking more than 20 minutes to deliver—involves content factors, delivery strategies, and purposes that require special attention.

CONTENT FACTORS AND DELIVERY STRATEGIES

The ideas are complex.

Ideas. The ideas presented in the long speech are almost always more complex than those in the short talk. The long presentation may analyze the financial, marketing, and manufacturing aspects of a product, or it may build a series of ideas designed to persuade the audience to take specific action.

The speaking time is greater.

Length. The time required to make a long presentation may vary from ten minutes to an hour instead of the three to five minutes usually required for the short talk.

Visual aids are a must.

Use of visuals. Whereas the short talk sometimes includes the use of visual aids, the long presentation almost requires them. Charts, graphs, samples, cutaways, handouts, and similar items that help communicate an idea are commonplace in the long presentation.

Listeners ask questions and offer comments.

Exchange-involvement. The long presentation permits the interaction of ideas between members of the audience and the speaker. Exchange and involvement provide opportunities for ideas to be explored, questions to raised, clarification to be offered, and concepts to be reviewed.

TYPES OF LONG PRESENTATIONS

Long presentations are distinguished primarily by the purpose they set for themselves—to persuade, inform, exchange, compare, or analyze.

Persuasive. A plant manager makes a presentation to the firm's executive council in which he attempts to have the council approve the purchase of a new piece of automated manufacturing equipment. Not only must the manager describe the equipment, he must analyze the effect it will have on productivity and review its financial implications as well.

Informative. The executive vice president makes a presentation to all department heads. Her purpose is to inform the department leaders of changes in government regulations concerning the hiring of minority personnel, the completion of documents, and guidelines for job interviews.

Technical exchange. A marketing representative addresses production and manufacturing personnel. In this case an "exchange" is required so that the marketing representative may explain what the potential buyer will or will not purchase. The technical representatives can then present the manufacturing constraints under which they must operate. Through this exchange or sharing, problems can be explored and solutions found.

Comparative. A presentation is made to explain and discuss two or more products, concepts, policies, or activities. The primary purpose is to present all the facts to the audience so that a decision concerning a specific course of action may be made. Careful substantiation and objective analysis of data are vital in this situation.

Analytical. A controller makes a presentation to the firm's financial committee regarding the possible acquisition of a small company. The controller analyzes the present financial position of the firm being considered, its potential for increased sales, its debt structure, and other facets that will influence the committee's decision. In every area careful analysis is vital if the decision is to be accurate. This type of analytical presentation may be used by people from various areas of the company in many different situations, but typically it is part of a persuasive presentation.

SIX STEPS FOR A SUCCESSFUL LONG SPEECH

Almost any activity requires a specific plan, system, or series of steps. That is certainly true for an effective long report or speech. Six steps are involved: (1)select the purpose and objectives; (2)plan the presentation; (3)analyze the audience; (4)select a presentation method; (5)use visual aids effectively, and (6)select a strategy to secure desired results.

STEP 1: SELECT THE PURPOSE AND OBJECTIVES

Have you ever had the rather disturbing experience of listening to someone for 15 or 20 minutes and then not knowing what to do when the speaker finished? Did the speaker intend merely to inform? Did he or she want you to vote? Or was the intention to motivate you to ask questions? Or was the speaker's hope that you now go out and buy the product or service? The error of leaving an audience confused about the purpose of a speech is probably more serious than the error of delivering it poorly. People are busy; they need specific direction. Of course, they will make their own decisions, but the material upon which their decisions are made must be clear, concise, and well organized.

Know your purpose and objectives so that you can tell the audience the specific action you want them to take.

Specify your purpose, whether it is to inform, to persuade, or to compare. For example, indicate clearly that you are going to "list the four alternate fuel systems available to our firm and show why solar power will prove to be the most advantageous."

Selecting the purpose of the presentation and the objectives you hope to achieve is your first step. Write out the purpose and your objectives so you can examine them critically and evaluate every word to be sure you have selected words that convey exactly what you mean in your statement of purpose. Once the purpose or purposes have been selected to your satisfaction, you may wish to transfer them to flip charts (or other visuals) for use at the most appropriate time during your presentation.

Knowing precisely what your purpose and objectives are will assist your audience in evaluating and acting in response to your speech, and it will help you plan every segment of your presentation.

STEP 2: PLAN THE PRESENTATION

Planning the presentation is simply organizing the talk for the most effective results. First, write a tentative outline and evaluate it to determine if it covers your purpose and objectives. After completing the outline, gather facts, figures, and details. Company records, questionnaires, interviews, journal articles, reports, and many other sources are possibilities. During the course of research, edit, revise, and restructure the outline so the speech can have its greatest impact. Out of this process comes a final outline for the actual presentation.

Plan by preparing an outline, researching the topic, anticipating questions, designing visual aids, and checking the location and equipment.

Planning also includes anticipating logical questions, objections, and requests for information from the audience. You should have the answers or information ready, even if you may not use them.

Designing the proper visuals and selecting the meeting site also are part of planning. The type and complexity of the visuals depend on such factors as the makeup of the audience, the nature of the topic, and the room size.

The meeting place plays an important role in the success of a presentation. Attempting to speak before 40 people jammed into a tiny room or before 9 people seated in an auditorium can prove disastrous.

In preparing or planning, remember to check the visual aid equipment, microphone, light switches, and other mechanical items. All too often, if something can go wrong, it will! But if you plan well, the odds are usually in your favor.

STEP 3: ANALYZE THE AUDIENCE

Try to know the makeup of your audience.

If your presentation is to be delivered within your firm, you have a better opportunity to know the makeup of the group. How many in the audience are from engineering? From finance? From marketing? If you are speaking to an external group, you may know only that the audience consists of community residents, members of a particular association, or elementary school teachers. But knowing just that, and exploiting that knowledge, can help you.

Not only should you know the makeup of the audience by background or vocation, but you should also know something about their attitudes, biases, sympathies, or opinions. In addition, are there specific cliques or factions in the audience that agree or disagree with each other?

Another major factor in audience analysis involves knowing what knowledge they already possess and what knowledge they *should* possess. If you cover material with which the audience is familiar, you may bore them and, in effect, lose some of their support. If, on the other hand, you assume they possess knowledge which in fact they do not, the results can be equally harmful.

Find out what audience members already know, what they should know, and what they want to know.

Your analysis should also determine what the audience wishes to know. If you are aware that most members would react favorably to a 6 percent increase in prices and you intend to request 9 percent, that knowledge may assist you in planning. If you are aware that most members of the audience want thorough substantiating data plus proof before they will accept a recommendation to purchase an $80,000 piece of equipment, again you can plan accordingly. Without that knowledge, you might not have possessed adequate data to win your point.

If possible, determine who the "influentials" are in the audience and their points of view. Consider whether it would be to your advantage to elicit a comment from such an individual either early or late in your presentation.

STEP 4: SELECT A PRESENTATION METHOD

Choose the right kind of notes for you.

For the long presentation, it is almost imperative to have some materials, such as notes, for reference. Such data will keep you on the topic, prevent digressions, and remind you to "make points 3 and 4." Also, if you wish to read an important statement or quote an authority, having the precise words in front of you is critical.

What format should the notes for a long presentation take? Consider what makes you comfortable and the type of speech you are making.

Read your speech word for word only when misstatement would seriously damage you or the firm. Make sure the manuscript is easy to read, and practice reading in a natural voice.

Manuscript. For an important talk in which specific wording is critical, it may be wise to read your speech. In that case, make the type large and clear and arrange the body of the text with plenty of white space. Double or triple spacing with very wide margins can make reading easier. Add side notes in color: "pause," "emphasize this point," "repeat name," "look up and smile," "gesture toward head table," "wait for slide," and "indicate cost data on flip chart." Always prepare the manuscript with enough white space to permit notes, changes in content, and additions.

You can imagine the boredom that could occur from listening to an entire long presentation read solely from manuscript. If you choose to read from a manuscript, therefore, practice so thoroughly that you seem to be speaking naturally from notes rather than actually reading from a manuscript.

Note cards effectively organize main points.

Note cards. The use of note cards (5- by 8-inch; not 3- by 5-inch, which are too small) can be helpful. Usually, an outline of your presentation plus a quote or two are about all you need on cards. Such an arrangement keeps you on track and permits you to read a key statement or quotation. Remember to number your cards consecutively in the event that the packet is inadvertently dropped.

Hidden notes make a speech seem extemporaneous.

Hidden notes. If you wish to have your long presentation appear extemporaneous, or if it actually is, assist yourself by placing key ideas in hidden notes. For example, list in large, heavy print on the flip chart your three key methods for cost reduction. Under each pencil in, in small print, your substantiating ideas. These notes are effectively hidden from the audience but not from you. Or simply present, on a transparency, your five key points, each listed as one word. That "outline" and those five words clearly remind you of everything you intend to discuss concerning the five areas. Or, add more detailed notes on the cardboard frame that holds your transparency.

STEP 5: USE VISUAL AIDS EFFECTIVELY

Visual aids are critical in maintaining audience interest throughout a long presentation.

Most long oral presentations contain some financial, production, manufacturing, or development data that are not simple to assimilate. The listener often finds the task of assimilation easier if the oral message is supplemented and complemented by a visual aid.

Many people find it difficult to follow a presentation of 30 to 45 minutes. However, a good visual aid helps retain the attention of the audience, brings variety to the message, and clarifies the message.

Refer to Chapters 17 and 22 to review the various visual aids used to accompany a speech: handouts, reports, chalkboards, slides, flip charts, transparencies, table flip charts, computer-controlled graphics, and overhead projectors. The complexity of the topic, nature of the audience, type and size of room, purpose of visual aid (to introduce, to clarity, to reinforce) all play important roles in the selection process. Keep these basic principles in mind: All visuals should complement, clarify, or reinforce the idea presented orally; be easy to see; and be easy to assimilate.

The effective speaker always spends a little time not only preparing the visual aid but also preparing for its use. Do you know where the light switches are? Can you change a projector bulb quickly? Are the markers at the podium dry or will they write? Will the cord on the projector extend far enough to reach the electrical outlet? Can the flip chart be seen from all parts of the room? Are the pages of the handout in correct order? This preparation requires only a few minutes, but they are minutes well spent.

As a general rule, the following visual aids are common and effective in long presentations:

- Slides, overhead transparencies, and brief film or video clips are popular and successful in conference, convention, and large-meeting presentations.
- Flip charts, handouts, models, photographs, and handouts are often used effectively in long presentations to smaller audiences. Slides,

computer-controlled graphics, and transparencies are also good for these audiences.

STEP 6: SELECT A STRATEGY TO SECURE DESIRED RESULTS

The usual purpose of the long presentation is to secure some desired action or result. It may be the sale of a product, approval of a proposal, or understanding of a concept. Getting that precise response often depends on the strategy of the presentation, which may involve several factors.

Time and timing. In a perfect world, business speakers would always have the amount of time they need, no more and no less, to make effective presentations. Unfortunately, many speaking situations require last minute adjustments in presentation plans. For example, a previous presentation may run long and you may be forced to select key points from your presentation that fit into the time remaining. In another situation it may even be necessary to request a postponement of your presentation entirely if it cannot be delivered satisfactorily in the time available. As an alternative to postponement, some speakers choose to pass out their speech in written form and present only highlights orally.

Research the situation to determine the best timing for your speech.

Timing, as actors know, can make or break a performance—including a presentation performance. You must judge the appropriate timing for your presentation. Let's say, for example, you learn your firm will show a $600,000 loss this year. You must assess in advance, as much as possible, whether that fact will prove to be an asset or liability as you make your presentation today. Don't simply guess. Treat the question of timing as a research question. Take time to ask those who will later be in your audience what they think. Also get advice from those who won't be attending your presentation. The information you receive will help you decide whether to speak before or after another speaker, such as the sales manager; what persuasive strategies to use to overcome audience resistance to your ideas; and perhaps what audience members to recognize to build allies for your position.

Base the order of presentation development on analysis of your audience.

Order of development. Based on careful analysis of your audience and purpose, you must settle on a developmental strategy to achieve your presentation goals. (Refer to Chapter 22 for a discussion of methods of developing a presentation.) If your audience is relatively unacquainted with your topic, you may decide to use the chronological development pattern so you can show past, present, and future perspectives on the topic. If your audience has a parochial view of your topic, you may want to follow the spatial development pattern to widen their frame of reference. A worried or hostile audience may be approached best by moving directly to a causal analysis of the problem and likely solutions. A suspicious audience may be convinced more easily by the inductive pattern of development, which takes them through a series of specific cases toward a general conclusion. In making all such strategic decisions, consider your knowledge of what your audience knows, feels, and wants.

Establish rapport and interest by asking your listeners for input.

Involvement and participation. Often an excellent strategy is to first present the fundamentals and then invite audience participation for the purpose of decision making. People are more likely to accept and support a decision which they have had a hand in shaping than a decision proposed by someone else.

Participation is usually a plus. Confident speakers who can remain in control usually make audience participation to serve their own advantage.

Recognize your listeners' individual and collective viewpoints.

Recognition of audience makeup. How far you can or should go in pushing for a desired response depends on who is in the audience. If the audience is composed of many supporters of your idea, you will follow one plan; if there are opposing or unsympathetic cliques, you probably will follow another.

No speaker should approach an audience without knowing its makeup. Just as the politician first determines if the audience favors or disapproves of price supports, or whether they are conservative or liberal Republicans or Democrats, so should you first determine the attitudes and perceptions of your audience.

Decide how best to move your audience to act.

Calling for action. Experienced salespeople know they should press for the sale, ask for the sale, or let the prospect do it. Good presenters also know how to prompt the audience to take the desired action.

At times it is strategically wise to tell the audience specifically what action to follow; at other times it is best to suggest. In some instances, it is preferable to let the audience come to its own conclusion.

HANDLING QUESTIONS

The question period offers an excellent opportunity to clarify and reemphasize ideas.

Too many speakers act as if presentations end with the last item of their notes. In fact, a complete presentation often includes a period of questions from the audience. These final moments are crucial in achieving your communication goals. You have a last chance to clear up misunderstandings, address specific audience concerns, and reemphasize ideas.

The question period is no less important for the audience. Members of the audience gain an opportunity to see how the presenter acts and speaks apart from prepared notes or manuscript. They can ask the speaker to elaborate on points or clear up confusing statements.

The following six guidelines can help you, as a presenter, handle the question period skillfully:

1. Be sure you understand the question before attempting to answer it. If you do not hear or grasp the entire question, politely ask the audience member to repeat it.
2. Ensure that all audience members hear and understand the question before you begin your answer. Particularly when fielding questions from large audiences, a speaker may have to repeat the question into the microphone so that the entire audience hears it. Without such repetition, even the best answer may seem confusing.
3. Answer questions as naturally and forthrightly as possible. Audiences appreciate a speaker who can get right to the point of a question without elaborate background or explanatory prefaces.
4. Answer questions as fully as your audience wishes in keeping with the time available. If you anticipate several questions from the audience, do not devote so much time to one question that you have none left for others.
5. Handle difficult or complex questions by restating them in manageable or divided form. Then begin your answer with the part of the question you can answer best. After hearing a complex question, for example, a speaker might rephrase its content as follows:

I've been asked how my economic plan will affect minimum-wage workers, particularly those with child- or elder-care responsibilities. Let me answer that question by talking first about those most at risk, those minimum-wage workers who are single parents. Then I'll discuss more general effects of my economic plan.

6. Face up to questions you cannot or do not wish to answer. For example, if a question involves personnel data you cannot divulge, simply say so. Do not try to fake a reply.

PARTS OF THE LONG PRESENTATION

Like every speech, the long one is made up of an introduction, body, and conclusion. Each segment has several purposes, and the speaker should determine what these are in the planning phase of the presentation.

INTRODUCTION

The introduction accomplishes several objectives: indicating the topic, defining terms, and establishing rapport.

In the introduction tell listeners what you will talk about, define terms and constraints, and establish rapport.

Indicating the topic. Some members of the audience may not know what you are going to talk about. Make sure that everyone in the room knows precisely what you are covering and why. For example, two of the managers who were invited could not attend today's session and sent substitutes. These alternates may not be aware of the agenda, so take a minute or two to set the stage.

Defining terms. Because the long presentation is often complex, begin with a definition of technical terms as you will use them, or indicate certain parameters or constraints that you will observe.

Establishing rapport. In many instances the audience will not be familiar with you or your ideas, and it is important for you to establish a good relationship immediately. Various factors can help you achieve rapport, but the most important are sincerity and honesty.

If you sincerely feel that what you are saying is important and in the best interests of the listeners, that feeling will be transmitted to them. Conversely, if your intent is to manipulate, that intent, too, will be conveyed. Consider voicing some of the concerns you know members of the audience have. Maybe refer by name to some of those in the audience.

A smile is certainly an asset, as is an approach that makes people feel you are talking *with* (instead of *at*) them. Also, a bit of humor, in good taste, tends to relax a group.

Be confident, convinced that you have an important message to deliver, and in control. Do not begin with a statement that invites disaster:

NOT: *If you will go along with me for a moment, I'll get on the track and probably convince you . . .*

INSTEAD: *Let's pause for a moment to discuss a specific case. Then we'll return to our main theme . . .*

NOT: *Many of you, I'm sure, know more about this than I, but it was my misfortune to be sitting in front of Ms. Ruiz when she was looking for a speaker . . .*

INSTEAD: *I consider it an honor to be asked by Ms. Ruiz to speak to you today . . .*

The introduction is a vital part of the long presentation. Plan it carefully. The introduction contributes significantly to the listener's first impression of the speaker.

BODY

Organize the body around a controlling theme by using appropriate strategies. Maintain interest through visual aids and audience participation.

The body is the heart of the presentation. Clarity and conciseness are vital. In planning the body of the presentation, give special attention to the following elements:

- Organization: Considering the audience, what is the best organizational plan? Should you present the financial aspects first and then the marketing plan or vice versa? Questions such as these, as well as those concerned with the method of development, must be answered.
- Visuals: What kind and when should you use visuals? Are you better off with charts, handouts, slides, cutaways, or samples of the actual items?
- Audience involvement: Should you encourage participation or involvement during the presentation?

The body of the presentation may use 80 percent of the time of your speech. How you handle that time depends on the many factors already discussed: content, knowledge, organization, delivery, visual aids, strategy, and others.

CONCLUSION

Restate the theme or recommend a course of action in the conclusion.

Consider the conclusion, an integral part of any speech, a critical factor in the strategic planning of your presentation. To end by saying, "Well, I guess that does it," or, "That brings me to my last note, but if anyone has any questions . . ." or, "I'm sorry I took longer than anticipated, but I didn't think you folks would mind sitting a few extra minutes," is to invite a negative response.

In your conclusion, you may wish to recapitulate key points. As teachers are often told: "First you tell them what you're going to tell them [Introduction], then you tell them [Body], then you tell them what you told them [Conclusion]."

If the long business presentation is other than informative, it usually contains conclusions and recommendations. Conclusions should be thoroughly substantiated by material presented in the body and the recommendations completely justified by the facts.

Because recommendations (to buy, to sell, to construct, to change, or to take some other course) are the key to action, consider listing them on a visual aid and reviewing them to fix the recommendations in the minds of the audience and motivate them to take the action you desire.

CAREER HINT

Long presentations contribute importantly to the advancement of business careers. Seize opportunities to give them, and when you do so, be sure they are so well organized, so clear, so concise, and so impressive that every person in the audience will, remember you gave them and want you to receive the credit the presentation's merit.

**WRITING
AND SPEAKING
EXERCISES**

1. Organizations such as colleges and universities are known for their policies, procedures, and rules. People know the restrictions but often do not know why they exist. Identify a restriction that students on your campus would know. Outline the explanatory short talk you could give that would present the "why."

2. Present a briefing of your last class to a group of other students. Assume none were present for the session.

3. You are to give a welcoming talk to a group of college students from another state who are visiting your campus for the weekend. What items of specific information do they need to know and must be included in the welcome in addition to a sincere greeting?

4. We live in an era of technological explosions. Each day we learn of new technology applicable to our profession. Identify your profession and outline a short informative speech that reports on a new technology (or new application of an existing technology) for your profession. Plan the speech for a group of people who have the same professional interests as you have.

5. Break into groups of three. Person A interviews person B on the topic of "What I Want from a Career." Person C records the results, then organizes them into a short speech of introduction. As time allows, people may switch roles so that all have a chance to interview, be interviewed, and speak.

6. Imagine that you are being introduced to a business audience. Write a short introduction you would like to hear about yourself. Study it as a potential model for the kind of introductions others probably want to hear about themselves.

7. You are to make a short recognition speech at the college's Honors Day Program. Select one of the following situations and prepare your recognition speech. Work with another student in developing the data; that is, use information about your colleague in preparing your presentation. Give the speech and have the person being recognized (who will receive a plaque) standing near you. Be sure you establish appropriate eye contact with the recipient and the audience.

   Student with Highest GPA in the Department
   The Most Likely to Succeed Award
   Leadership Aware to Student Making Contributions to the College
   Kindness Award to Student Considerate of Others
   Award to Student Getting the Highest Test Scores on Statistics Examinations in the College

8. Develop a visual aid to be used with a hypothetical informative talk. Create a checklist of at least six points you will want to consider in using the aid. (For example, when should it be shown to the audience?)

9. For your profession and for the specific job you hope to assume, identify a common kind of "technical exchange" that would take place.
   (a) Specifically indicate the parties involved in the exchange.
   (b) Indicate the elementary gaps in their knowledge or information bases.
   (c) Create concrete suggestions on how you could attempt to bridge the gaps in your long oral presentation.
10. Assume that you will be speaking to the local Rotary Club, a group composed of businesspeople. Choose your own topic. Describe in specific ways what you would like to know about your audience prior to speaking and how you could find that information.
11. Interview a manager who holds the kind of job you hope to attain eventually. You want to find out from the manager how long presentations are used in the organization and what the manager thinks are the major pitfalls in the long presentations he or she must sit through. Prepare a three-minute speech in which you report your findings.
12. What is rapport? Make a list of specific ways in which you would attempt to establish rapport with an audience unsympathetic to your point of view (You may invent details to make this situation as realistic as possible.)
13. Observe your own attention span while listening to a presentation (perhaps a lecture) more than ten minutes long. Report to the class on how often your mind wandered and what the speaker did (or could have done) to regain your attention.
14. Watch a business or political interview on television. Evaluate the interviewee's use of facial expressions. What do they communicate? Whom do they influence? For your own use, make up a guide sheet regarding the use of facial expressions during interviews.
15. Give an eight- to ten-minute presentation to managers, owners of a company, college administrators, a board of directors, or any group that has authority to accept or reject the proposal you will make to them. Your persuasive presentation may involve a change in policy, purchase of a piece of equipment, acceptance of a new regulation, or any item of your choice. You are required to use visual aids to accompany your presentation.
16. Give an eight- to ten-minute presentation that is explanatory/informative to a group. Identify the makeup of the group. You may explain how to carry through a procedure, process, or activity. You are required to use visual aids to accompany your presentation.

READINGS

See "Use Creativity to Educate Your Benefits Audience" in the Readings section at the back of this book.

SUGGESTED RESOURCES

Hayes, Lynn. "Beating the Paranoia of Presentations." *Lodging Hospitality* 47 (October 1991):38–40.

Koehler, Kenneth G. "How to Make an Effective Presentation."
  CMA Magazine 65 (February 1991):25–28.
Mayfield, Lee A. "Presentations: How to Do It Wrong." *Sales & Marketing
  Management* 142 (July 1990):79–81.
Palca, Jeffrey A. "How to Give a Great Speech." *Insurance Review* 52
  (May 1991):41–43,
Parachin, Victor. "Ten Tips for Powerful Presentations." *Training* 27
  (July 1990):58–60.
Snyder, Elaine. *Persuasive Business Speaking.* New York: AMACOM, 1990.
Walton, Donald. "How to Make the Pitch They Can't Resist." *Working
  Woman* (December 1989):102–105.
Zaremba, Alan. "Q and A: The Other Part of Your Presentation." *Manage-
  ment World* 18 (January—February 1989):8–10.

LISTENING SKILLS

We have two ears and one mouth and should use them in that proportion.

—Epictetus

Managers who are effective listeners give employees a greater sense of self-worth, which in turn leads to improved job performance.

"It's amazing how quickly you can gain a reputation for being a great conversationalist when you begin to listen carefully to others." That quotation, from a recent TV show, certainly contains a strong element of truth. We like people to listen to us. When others really listen to us, our ego needs are partially satisfied; we feel respected. We feel knowledgeable, and we like the attention we receive. Good listening also improves relationships, job performance, and creativity.

Now the obvious questions arise: If listening is so effective and important, why don't more of us do it? Why don't we do it effectively? The answers are not easy, but one is our lack of training in *how* to listen. Most of us were involved in an educational system that included practice and review of how to read and write from first grade to twelfth. When we reached college, we continued to take courses in composition and perhaps one or two in oral communication. Indeed, we spent considerable time on reading, writing, and even speaking. But how much time did we spend improving our ability to listen?

Listening and hearing are very different activities.

It's difficult to understand why we haven't spent more time improving our ability to listen. Perhaps the primary reason is that society in general has always assumed that hearing and listening are the same. However, even with training to improve our ability to listen, it's still a hard task. Formidable barriers, coupled with lack of training and the acceptance that hearing is listening make effective listening difficult to achieve.[1]

HEARING IS NOT LISTENING

Managers spend approximately 60 to 70 percent of their working hours in some form of communication. Of that percentage, 65 percent is spent—not in talking, writing, or reading–but in listening. Yet only an average of six to eight managers of a hundred have had any formal instruction on how to listen effectively. Fortunately, that number is increasing steadily.

One reason for that increase is the fact that more and more individuals are becoming aware that hearing is not listening. Hearing is an almost automatic,

Hearing is a passive physiological function. Listening is an active choice of the conscious will.

physiological function that occurs with little or no conscious reaction. When you drive your car, you hear a horn blaring, a child shouting, a truck roaring, a jet flying. But you don't *listen* to them. Hearing requires almost no effort. Listening does.

Listening requires both physical and mental effort to overcome the barriers in your environment as well as those in yourself. You can't really listen with full effectiveness if you completely relax, slouch in your chair, and stare in the general direction of the speaker. You may be "hearing," but that is not "listening." Listening requires as much effort on the part of the receiver as speaking effectively does on the part of the sender.

BARRIERS TO EFFECTIVE LISTENING

Each listener has the ability to receive many more words per minute than a speaker can send.

Perhaps the most important barrier to effective listening results from the fact that most of us talk at about 125 to 150 words per minute, while we can listen to and comprehend some 600 to 800 words per minute. Obviously, if senders talk at 125 words per minute and receivers listen at 600, receivers are left with a good deal of time to think about matters other than the message; and they do: illness, bills, cars, the baseball game score, what's for dinner tonight, and so on. These mental distractions represent *internal competition* for attention.

External noise competes for the mind's attention and prevents effective listening.

However, *external competition* to effective listening also exists. Outside distractions come from ringing telephones, noisy production lines, heated arguments, intriguing smells, captivating sights, and other factors we encounter in a complex society.

We lack sufficient time to take in the many messages that bombard us in this age of information.

Time, or more accurately, the lack of it, also contributes to inefficient listening. As the supply of information increases, the availability of time to listen seems to decrease. How well do you "listen" to the increasing load of mail that you receive, the added volume of journals, newspapers, and magazines, and the growing number of channels on TV and radio. Add to this voice mail, increased telephone calls, fax messages, and computer disks. The answer, some say, is simple: "Just turn them off." But that answer is too simplistic. To do your job, to keep up with your profession, to be informed, you *must* tune in. But the misguided solution for many is to tune in but not to listen.

If you are to profit from all the information around you, the answer is to listen *selectively* and learn how to listen more effectively.

"The most prevalent mistake that people make about listening is to regard it as passively receiving rather than as actively participating."
—Mortimer Adler

Some individuals require more time than others when they are speaking to you. If you are, or appear to be, impatient, they will either not express themselves fully or will simply demand more time than usual. Yet, you as the listener possess a limited amount of time. In addition, some people monopolize *all* of your listening time. If you begin to listen to such a person at noon, you could still be listening at 3 p.m. You must turn off an individual like this as tactfully as possible.

In contrast, there are others with whom you work or live that you should listen to with undivided attention. Remember, if you don't listen to them, they will always find someone who will. If employees feel their supervisor won't listen to them, they will find other employees or the union representative who will. If young people feel their parents won't or don't listen to them, they may find friends, gang members, or people whose influence might be detrimental.

If customers feel a supplier really isn't listening, they will find a competitor to the supplier who will. Communication doesn't take place in a vacuum.

Many listeners are conditioned to tune out information that contradicts or upsets them.

Conditioning is another factor that contributes to poor listening. Many of us have conditioned ourselves not to listen to messages that do not agree with our philosophy or that irritate, upset, or anger us. TV and radio play a role in this conditioning. If the program we see or hear doesn't entertain or intrigue us, we have been conditioned to simply change channels or stations, and we carry this habit of tuning out a message into our daily listening activities.

Listeners who are quick to evaluate a speaker's meaning and plan their response may fail to comprehend the complete message.

Evaluating what we hear may constitute still another barrier. Often we listen and immediately evaluate and reject the idea before it is completely voiced. Or we listen and then detour mentally while the individual is still talking. Of course, it is impossible not to evaluate, but we should continue to listen after evaluating. The problem is that most of us tune out as soon as we hear an idea or point of view that does not agree with ours.

High emotions inhibit effective listening.

Emotions, if colored or at a high level, may also get in the way of effective listening. Surely if you hear ideas that are counter to yours, or if you are involved in a confrontation or are emotionally upset because of fear, anger, or happiness, effective listening becomes very difficult.

Preconditioned perceptions cause listeners to hear what they want to hear or to refuse to listen at all.

Perceptions that we bring to the listening task may form a barrier. Because we frequently perceive what we wish to perceive or are conditioned to perceive, we may sometimes not even listen to specific individuals or topics.

At other times, we may listen to a message and perceive what we wish to perceive, even if that perception completely disagrees with what the speaker had in mind. An example is the statement that the speaker feels (perceives) was fair, positive, and direct but that the listener perceives as dogmatic, abrasive, rude, and tactless. Another example is the comment we feel is complimentary while another interprets it as fawning, insincere, and self-serving. Our perceptions, along with our conditioning and tendency to evaluate, can be a strong deterrent to effective listening.

Education stresses reading, writing, and speaking without giving equal training in the most time-consuming communication activity—listening.

Lack of training on how to listen is still another barrier. Most of us have received much instruction on how to write more concisely and clearly, read more efficiently and rapidly, and speak more forcefully and effectively. But few of us have ever received any instruction on how to listen. Perhaps this flaw in our educational system stems from the belief on the part of many educators that if people hear, they are listening. The fact remains that more effective listening can be taught. Fortunately, increasing numbers of schools, including universities, today are teaching students how to listen more effectively.

Lack of training in how to listen might explain the absence of concentration that transforms effective speakers and writers into poor listeners.

Failure to concentrate is another barrier to effective listening. Lack of concentration may result because many of us have not been taught how to listen or because we don't work at listening.

Look around the room at the next meeting you attend. Note how many people are sitting in a sprawled posture; some may even have their feet stretched out on the chair next to them or on top of the meeting table or desk. How can anyone really work at listening while in a completely relaxed posture? And even if the individual does listen well in that position, think of what that posture conveys nonverbally to the speaker!

There are many reasons why we don't listen well that could be added to the list. Some might overlap those already noted: distractions, disruptions, bias, lack of interest, and certainly the fact that many of us just don't *work* at listening. However, more important than this list of reasons is how we can become good listeners.

TYPES OF LISTENING

Listening can be categorized into four types: (1) casual or social listening, (2) attentive or critical listening, (3) empathetic listening, and (4) active listening.

CASUAL, OR SOCIAL, LISTENING.

Casual, or social, listening occurs in relaxed situations where people can afford to tune out information that does not interest them.

Casual, or social, listening is the way most of us listen at parties, coffee breaks, or ball games. It is also the manner in which most of us listen to music or news reports as we drive to school or work. Because we have become *selective listeners,* we have trained ourselves to listen in these situations at a level which we feel is satisfactory. The same holds true when we are in a hotel ballroom with 600 other attendees. We may be talking or listening while the band plays, announcements are made, and friends dance by. Certainly we miss a few words, but we have retained the gist of the comment, and that is sufficient. This is casual listening and is quite adequate for the situation.

ATTENTIVE, OR CRITICAL, LISTENING

Attentive, or critical, listeners analyze messages and retain information that they intend to use again.

Attentive, or critical, listening is the type of listening most of us employ when we are in class, in a fact-finding interview, or at an important business briefing. In this type of listening the receiver analyzes, interprets, evaluates, and weighs information. A conscious effort is made to accept some portions of the message for further retention and processing and to also determine what to discard, usually on the basis of previously received data. This type of listening requires concentration and effort.

Critical listening is enhanced when there are opportunities for questioning, interaction, visual observation, and feedback. Sometimes, however, the number and speed with which we receive facts makes them difficult to retain. How can we become more efficient at the task of retaining facts?

If you are a student, you have probably experienced missing an important class. If you are a manager, you have occasionally missed a meeting. The problem is playing "catch up." For example, you approach Mitchell and ask about Monday's class and what you've missed. If Mitchell can tell you little more than it was "an interesting class and I really thought the financial analysis of the case was OK," he probably is not very efficient in his attentive listening for facts. If you continue to press him, he may go on to say, "It was a great case," or, "It emphasized financial aspects of a major corporation." Then you surely know that he doesn't listen very well (or attentively) for facts.

On the other hand, you may find Pat's response to the same question on the same class quite different. "Yes," says Pat, "it was a very interesting class. First, Professor Maxwell set the stage by indicating we would look at three aspects of high interest rates and the problem of getting residential mortgages: the trend in home sales, the cost of mortgage money, and the tax benefits secured by the residential purchaser." Pat may then go on to list the specific subpoints under the three items noted and even give you Professor Maxwell's summary statement.

What is the difference between Mitchell's ability to listen for facts and Pat's ability? To some extent, Mitchell has not used his class time very well and will surely spend much more time reviewing for his final exam than Pat will. The real pity is that his store of knowledge doesn't grow as quickly or as efficiently as Pat's. Pat listens and retains facts; Mitchell does not. How do you listen? Like Pat or like Mitchell?

Fortunately, you can improve your attentive listening skills by following a few guidelines:

Attentive listeners remember important ideas by associating them with key words.

Catalog key words. In almost every discussion, several key ideas are presented. You can retain these ideas by remembering a key word associated with each key idea. In the example, Pat probably remembered "home sales," "cost of money," and "tax benefits." Remembering these key words made Pat able to discuss intelligently the concepts presented during the class.

Make a conscious effort to resist distractions when listening for important ideas.

Resist distractions. Many distractions take place while you listen. Whether you are in a group listening to a speaker or having a conversation with one other person, distractions occur. There are the external ones such as heat and humidity, noise and smell, and competing activities. Internally, there are the tendencies to daydream, evaluate, and think of other important matters as well as your emotions, values, and the speaker's personality.

But you must resist these distractions and focus on the key concepts and words. Listening requires effort, but the task is made easier if you assume a posture of attentiveness and mentally force yourself to pay attention. Many people find that taking notes during the presentation assists them in resisting distractions. Our friend Pat may have taken notes during the class in question and underlined the key words.

Using free time to review key ideas keeps your attention focused and prepares you for more critical listening.

Review key ideas. In the course of Professor Maxwell's lecture, both Mitchell and Pat had a good deal of free time. Professor Maxwell spoke at an average pace of about 140 words per minute. Both Mitchell and Pat comprehend approximately 600 to 800 words per minute. Mitchell used the "extra time" to think about last night's dinner date. Pat, on the other hand, used the "extra time" to review the evidence Professor Maxwell cited in relation to home sales, cost of money, and tax benefits. Learning is a constant search for key ideas.

Keeping an open mind and listening attentively lets you judge ideas fairly.

Be open and flexible. "Don't bother me with the facts, my mind is made up." Humorous, but true for many people. Their biases are so strong that they may prefer not to listen. Or perhaps their instant assessment of the speaker's clothes, ethnic background, hair style, or accent, is enough for them to fix their opinions.

Obviously, such an attitude is an injustice not only to the speaker but to the listener as well. It is true that Mitchell had an unhappy experience in a real estate transaction last year. But is that any reason for him not to listen to Professor Maxwell today?

Listen to whatever is being directed to you. Be flexible and receptive. No one suggests that you must *accept* the ideas and concepts presented by others. You should, however, listen to them.

Keep listening even if you disagree.

Evaluate but don't tune out. Closely associated with being open and flexible is this suggestion: evaluate but don't tune out. If your evaluation results in rejection of a concept or idea, that is perfectly acceptable. But don't immediately tune out. The information that follows may place new light on the matter; if you don't even listen to those subsequent ideas, you may be the loser. Or it is possible that the subsequent material may introduce a completely new topic. If you are still tuned out from the previous one, you may miss important data. The point is, disagree with what you hear if you feel disagreement is correct, but continue to listen.

Like other forms of communication, listening demands hard work.

Work at listening. Effective speaking, writing, and reading require the expenditure of energy. That energy is applied to planning, organizing, and assimilating. Effective listening is no different. It requires effort to concentrate, to sit up attentively, to review ideas, to remain open, to resist distractions, and to remain alert mentally and physically while someone else is talking. And that person may well be talking and presenting ideas with which you disagree.

Still, you have an obligation to listen. In fact, when you elected to sit in that classroom, in that office, or in that easy chair, you made—in effect—a contract that the other person would talk and you would listen.

If you are a student and you have the ability to listen effectively for facts, you will not only assimilate more knowledge but will find great satisfaction as you watch your grade level rise. If you are a manager, you will find your decision-making ability increased as your body of facts expands. The greatest satisfaction will come, however, in the knowledge that you are using your time more efficiently.

EMPATHETIC LISTENING

Empathetic listeners respond to the speaker's feelings rather than to the speaker's words.

We are employing empathetic listening when we make an effort to understand the feelings in the speaker's words. While we must also be aware of and retain the facts (attentive listening), our response to the "unspoken" message is vital to understanding. We must be sensitive, in empathetic listening, to hear the fear, hurt, anger, love, pride, frustration, hopelessness, joy, and a hundred other emotions, and then to respond. Some typical reasons might be similar to these:

I really appreciate how you feel. I've been in a similar situation and didn't know where to turn.

You must be really pleased with how well the project came out. You put a lot of work into it.

Something like that would devastate anyone; you are handling it better than most, but I know it must be very difficult. Perhaps I can help by . . .

"The most important thing in communication is to hear what isn't being said."
—Peter Drucker

For example, Chief Nurse Higgins just walked on the floor at 7 a.m. The first person she encounters is Registered Nurse Ben Chen, who looks frazzled, exhausted, upset, and concerned. Before Ms. Higgins can even offer a "good morning," Mr. Chen blurts out:

What a night! Two of our staff didn't show up for work, we had three emergencies, and both John Baxter and Mrs. Cox had terrible problems. In fact I thought we would lose Cox when she began hemorrhaging again, but we saved her.

And then you wanted me to complete the monthly status report in my free time, which I did, but even though I began my shift two hours early, it was a job that proved almost impossible. And if I never have another night like this last one, it will be too soon.

If Chief Nurse Higgins now says, "Well, take off now, get a good rest; I'll see you tomorrow," then it is obvious that she hasn't listened to what Nurse Chen did not say! What was Nurse Chen *really* saying? If Ms. Higgins was listening empathetically, she might have heard one or more of these messages:

I deserve some praise.

I worked beyond the call of duty.

You were unreasonable to ask me to complete the status report.

I'm an exceptional nurse.

I should really be paid for at least two hours of overtime.

Which of the above *possible* messages should Ms. Higgins respond to? She can't ask Nurse Chen what he was really saying; if Nurse Chen could have really said what he meant, he would have said it. However, Ms. Higgins could make a rather neutral statement such as, "You really must have had a difficult night," or "You must certainly be exhausted." or Ms. Higgins may paraphrase what Nurse Chen said. In response, Nurse Chen may say what is in his heart. Or it is even possible that Ms. Higgins knows Nurse Chen so well she can select the correct response to make from the five alternatives listed. Certainly people who work together for many years know what the other individual is really saying in what he or she is not saying. That ability results when individuals listen empathetically; when they listen for feelings; when they listen sensitively.

How effectively do you listen to the feelings of others? Consider the following suggestions.

Ask the speaker if your perception is correct to indicate that you are making an effort to understand.

Listen with the speaker. Listen with the speaker's emotions, hopes, desires, perceptions, point of view, values, age level, and so on. You need not agree or even accept that perception, point of view, or value structure, but make an effort to *understand* it. To check your understanding, paraphrase to the speaker your perception of his or her meaning.[2]

Interpret word connotations from the speaker's viewpoint.

Appreciate the speaker's meaning for the words used. Words have different meanings for different people. Try to appreciate the speaker's connotation for the words he or she uses. What does the speaker mean by the words *immediately, costly, responsible, early*? In our fast-changing world there are often differences in meaning for the same word between a 48-year-old parent and a 16-year-old son; a 50-year-old teacher and 21-year-old student. Words even take on new meanings that the communicating parties may not understand the same way.

Nonverbal messages often convey feelings and ideas more truthfully than do words.

Listen for nonverbal communication. Hand gestures, drumming fingers, tapping heels, voice inflections, worried glances, facial expressions, perspiration, cracking knuckles, voice level and intensity, and body tension are just a few nonverbal messages that may constitute an important part of the message conveyed. Watch, listen, and evaluate carefully every part of the message directed to you. Listening with your eyes (that is, observing the nonverbal messages) can sometimes be as important as listening with your ears. Although there has been much written on interpreting body language, be cautious. A specific mannerism doesn't always mean XYZ, although some authors would have you believe it does. You must always interpret body language as well as other nonverbal communication within the context and cultural norms of the situation and according to the personal style of the individual.

Paralanguage exposes disparity between stated words and unspoken feelings.

Be aware of *paralanguage,* which includes the tone and quality of the voice, sounds such as a sigh or a grunt, pauses, and the length of silences. Any one of these may reinforce or contradict the verbal message. If you are alert to them, they will help you listen effectively.

Empathetic listeners who respond to the feelings hidden in words know how to keep communication channels open and how to close them.

Listen and respond to what is said within what isn't. In many instances, when you listen empathetically, it is relatively simple to respond to what isn't said within what is. Such a response will assist the communication to continue or it will close the loop. What is the speaker really saying with the comment, "Since I took over the department, production is up over 60 percent," or "it's almost too hot to fix dinner tonight," or "I guess I was lucky winning three sets in a row"?

If it is appropriate and you are empathetic to the feelings expressed, you can respond to what wasn't said in the above messages. Doing so assists the communication process. However, you must also recognize that you should not always respond, even when the speaker hopes you will. For example, Bob says, "Boy, I really worked 28 hours yesterday to have that report ready for you today at noon." Because you know Bob, you also know that this is his oblique way of saying, "Give me a pat on the back; tell me what a great job I did." But Bob doesn't deserve a pat on the back; he has had a month to finish the report. Had he planned carefully, he would not have had to work" 28 hours yesterday.

In such cases, it may be perfectly acceptable not to reply to what wasn't said. However, the "loop" should be closed in the most appropriate and tactful way under the circumstances. In this case, a simple, "Thanks for the report, Bob," may be the best reply.

Admitting your own biases helps you maintain an open mind.

Listen with an open mind. To listen empathetically to another person, you must recognize your own biases on the topic under discussion. You need not change your point of view, but you should be able to weigh and recognize it in relationship to the views of the other person. Poor listeners often hear the first few sentences and reach a decision of agreement, friendliness, hostility, or indifference. Instead, listen to the message, appreciate the speaker's viewpoints, and then weigh the facts and analyze carefully before making a judgment. Don't jump to conclusions or give up your ideas. Just listen with an open mind.

Whenever possible, anticipate distractions and postpone discussion until the time and place are right for effective listening.

Select, if possible, the right time and/or place. At times you may really want to listen to the other person, but if adequate time is not available or the place is too noisy, how can you? There is nothing wrong in saying, "This is really important to both of us, but I have a class in five minutes, and it just isn't fair to you if we begin to discuss this and I'm required to rush off. When would be a convenient time for us to get together?"

ACTIVE LISTENING

Active listeners show interest without passing judgment and encourage speakers to continue sharing ideas.

Active listening requires that we listen attentively and empathetically and then take another step: listening without judging or evaluating. We simply listen in a way that permits the speaker to present his or her feelings, to voice some inner ideas, to even suggest possible solutions to his or her own problems. The listener may not (or should not) offer a positive or negative response, for once such a stand is taken, the speaker will most probably become silent. Why continue to speak when the listener has already made a judgment or decision?

Active listening is the type of listening that is practiced by not only psychiatrists, psychotherapists, counselors, religious leaders, and other professionals, but also every sensitive individual when the need arises.

In an outstanding presentation in the Benjamin Rush Award Lecture to the American Psychiatric Association in May 1991, S.W. Jackson, M.D., made the point that active listening is nothing new; it can be traced to the Bible. Dr.

Jackson cited: "Hear my prayer, O Lord, and let my cry come unto thee . . . incline thy ear unto me." (Psalms 102); "Lord, I cry unto thee: make haste unto me; give ear unto my voice, when I cry unto thee." (Psalm 141). In this same presentation, Dr. Jackson cited works published in the 1940s and 1950s that became the foundation for most of the present day writings in this area of communication.[3]

One of the most frequently quoted sources in this field is Carl Rogers, who stated, "It is called 'active' because the listener has a very definite responsibility. He does not passively absorb the words which are spoken to him. He actively tries to grasp the facts and feelings which he hears. . . . " Rogers goes on to say:

> Active listening is an important way to bring about changes in people. Despite the popular notion that listening is a passive approach, clinical and research evidence clearly shows that sensitive listening is a most effective agent for individual personality change and group development.
>
> When people are listened to sensitively, they tend to listen to themselves with more care and make clear exactly what they are feeling and thinking. Group members tend to listen more to each other, become less argumentative, more ready to incorporate other points of view. Because listening reduces the threat of having one's ideas criticized, the person is better able to see them for what they are, and more likely to feel that his contributions are worthwhile.
>
> Not the least important result of listening is the change that takes place within the listener himself. Besides the fact that listening provides more information than any other activity, it builds deep, positive relationships and tends to alter constructively the attitudes of the listener. Listening is a growth experience. . . .[4]

Paraphrase the speaker to ensure that you are receiving the intended message.

Nonjudgmental comments such as these will encourage a speaker to respond in greater depth: "You sound upset; please tell me more." "Can you expand on that so I can understand your feelings more completely?" "Perhaps you could tell me exactly how you feel when that happens; I really want to help." Active listening requires probing, seeking more information from the speaker, and an effort to have the speaker "open up" to the listener. Paraphrasing also assists in the listening process by attempting to confirm if the message the listener heard is really what the speaker said (or meant): "Now if I have interpreted you correctly, you feel that Luis is not at all sensitive to your situation and you don't understand why he shouldn't be. Is that correct, Ana, or am I off base?"

THE VALUE OF EFFECTIVE LISTENING

Up to this point, we have reviewed the factors that cause inefficient listening, differentiated the types of listening, and considered how to improve listening ability. Perhaps you are asking, "Why make the effort? What do I gain?" The gains are significant and can strongly influence your work relationships, personal life, and almost every other facet of your daily activities.

Effective listeners are able to gather accurate information on which to base decisions.

Information. Attentive listening gives you data, facts, and figures in your classes, work situations, and personal activities. The added information assists you in decision making, learning, and dealing with problems.

Ideas or concepts. Effective listening often gives you another way of conceptualizing that will help you advance on the job, deal with others, or earn a better

Listening to how others formulate ideas yields insights into your own conceptual processes.

Effective listening leads to greater understanding of people. Understanding people gives you the power to persuade and motivate them.

By setting the example, effective listeners are often listened to more effectively.

grade in a class. It is amazing how many new ideas are available to you if you only listen for them.

Understanding. Empathetic listening provides you with insight and understanding about those around you. You come to understand that Mariko has difficulty saying what she really means, that Kevin requires a great deal of praise, that Jose is an extrovert and Chris an introvert. When you understand what motivates, drives, inhibits, or turns others off or on, you can communicate more effectively with them.

Cooperation and improved listening on their part. When individuals feel that you are listening attentively and empathetically to them, they may listen more effectively to you! People do not necessarily want you to agree with them. They do, however, want you to listen. Your full, open effort to listen and understand them may motivate *them* to cooperate and listen to you.

MAKING THE LISTENING EFFORT

In a world of communication overload—where too many people, media, institutions, and organizations are shouting louder and louder to be heard—effective, attentive, and empathetic listening is not commonplace. But it should be.

Everyone's listening can be improved if the effort is made. Programs, books, articles, and videos are available that offer instruction on how to become a better listener. If as much attention were given to the subject of listening as is presently given to reading and writing, most students' scholastic efforts and careers would improve significantly.

**WRITING
AND SPEAKING
EXERCISES**

1. Identify and explain a situation in which you have conditioned yourself *not* to listen.
2. Ask five of your classmates if you may see their lecture notes after they have all attended the same class. Analyze their notes in relation to the topic of "Attentive Listening."
3. Examine your relationship with your girlfriend, boyfriend, mother, boss (select one from this group—or any other person). Determine a specific major listening barrier that you encounter in this relationship and attempt to explain why it exists and on whose part.
4. Conduct a listening experiment: turn the contrast or brightness control on your television so that no picture shows. Listen to a news or informational program for 15 minutes. Make a check mark on a score sheet each time you catch your attention wandering from the program. Then repeat the activity, this time with full picture and sound. Again, make a check mark on your score sheet when your attention wanders. Based on your results, write an evaluation of the importance of sight and sound to listening effectiveness.
5. Work at listening! It is easy to say and difficult to do. Take a few moments and evaluate your listening skills and habits. Then in a concise

list, indicate what you need to do to improve your ability to "work at listening."

6. "Appreciate the speaker's meaning for the words used." Discuss this quotation in relation to semantics broadly and word connotation and denotation specifically.

7. How can an effective listening program for all the employees of Webster Electronic Corporation have an effect on the company's bottom line?

8. Ask a classmate to speak to you about some topic for three to five minutes. Next, try to sum up and repeat back the major points to the satisfaction of the speaker. Then switch roles and repeat the experiment. Finally, write an evaluation of this activity as an aid to training in listening.

9. Managers spend a considerable amount of their time involved in some aspect of communication—talking, reading, writing, and listening. There are a variety of estimates on how the manager's total time is spent communicating and how time breaks down among the four activities. Find a cooperative manager in the profession you plan to pursue and ask to observe his or her normal work routine for a specified period of time (e.g., two hours or a half day). During that time be a silent observer and carefully audit how the manager's communication time is allocated. Specifically identify these elements:

   • The time spent speaking, reading, writing, and listening
   • How your figures (percentages) compare to those given in this chapter
   • The listening environment
   • What could be changed in the physical placement of people and things and in individual habits to improve the quality of listening

10. As an employee known for good listening skills, you've been assigned confidentially to help Hugh Melton, a company vice president and notoriously poor listener, to improve his listening skills. You'll have four two-hour sessions with Melton. Sketch out how you'll use the time.

11. What are the signs that tell if someone has truly listened to what you have said? Make a list of the specific symptoms that tell you whether a person is really listening.

12. Draw up a list of five irritating listening habits you have observed in these people: your present or past boss, an instructor you now have or have had, your girlfriend, boyfriend, wife, husband, friend, mother, and so on.

CASES   Complete the following assignments from the Cases for Discussion section at the back of this book:

1. The Jim Cantonelli case—Assignments 1 and 2

SUGGESTED RESOURCES

Conley, C. "What To Do When Someone's Yelling." *Supervisory Management* 35 (February 1990).

De La Garza, A. "Sculpting the Spatio-Temporal Scene: Steps to Successful Communication." *American Salesmen* 36 (February 1991).

Hamilton, B. "Hearing, Analyzing, Empathizing and Succeeding in Management." *Training and Development Journal* 44 (August 1990).

Lewis, M., and Reinsch, N. "Listening in Organizational Environments." *Journal of Business Communication* 25 (Summer 1988).

Sigband, N. *Patient-Pharmacist Consultation Program.* Los Angeles:University of Southern California School of Pharmacy, 1992.

Sigband, N. "Listening: A Key to Problem Solving." 2nd ed. Video (color), 28 minutes. Chatsworth, Calif.:AIMS Media, 1992.

Szmczak, J., and Cuthrell, S. "Communication Improves with Listening, Observing." *Business First of Buffalo* 7 (March 25, 1991).

ENDNOTES

1. See *Listening: A Key to Problem Solving,* 1993, Norman B. Sigband, consultant. Paramount Pictures. Available from AIMS Media, 9710 De Soto, Chatsworth, CA 91311-4409. Based on The Jim Cantonelli Case, which appears in the Cases for Discussion at the end of this book.

2. Beatrice Hamilton, "Hearing, Analyzing, Empathizing, and Succeeding in Management," *Training and Development Journal* 44 (August 1990): 16.

3. Stanley W. Jackson, "The Listening Healer in the History of Psychological Healing," *American Journal of Psychiatry* 149 (December 1992): 1624.

4. Carl R. Rogers and F.J. Roethlisberger, "Barriers and Gateways to Communication" *Harvard Business Review* November-December 1991.

25

INTERVIEWS AND MEETINGS

To conduct excellent interviews and meetings, practice listening—not talking.

When businesspeople sit down together for an interview or a meeting, no natural instincts or abilities guarantee that their interaction will be productive. As with other communication skills, the ability to make the most of interviews and meetings must be learned and practiced. And much is at stake in such interpersonal communications. Through selection interviews, the company renews itself by evaluating and hiring new employees. Through exit interviews, the company learns what department employees liked and disliked about the company. In technical and sales interviews, the company develops and promotes its products. Meetings, of course, play a key role in decision making throughout the company.

Although meetings and interviews occur frequently and provide vital channels for internal communication, they often present difficulties for managers who lack proper training.

Despite the frequency with which meetings and interviews are held, probably no two other communications activities are carried on so inefficiently. Surprisingly, few managers have been trained to conduct interviews and meetings effectively, yet almost every manager must do so frequently.

Interviews and meetings are vital activities for the exchange of information and for reaching the solutions to problems. They are as important in the small retail store as they are in the huge corporate headquarters.

THE INTERVIEW IN GENERAL

The interview usually is a one-on-one exchange of information.

The *interview* is basically a one-on-one interaction. Although it is possible for more than one individual to act in the capacity of interviewer or interviewee, the most typical interview situation involves two people.

The purposes of the interview are many. In general, the interview is an effective communication method for these tasks:

- Sending and receiving information
- Gaining understanding and the acceptance of ideas
- Developing and changing attitudes and behavior
- Motivating others to work for a common goal

There are also many specific types of interviews. Those held most frequently are discussed in the pages that follow.

Every interview varies, depending on the purpose, the personalities involved, the emotions of the participants, and the complexity of the topic. The

Interviews succeed when both parties work to receive as well as send information.

successful interview is a two-way process. Each of the parties must be an adept listener (receiver) as well as sender; each person must be sensitive to the other's needs and be able to listen actively. In all cases, the successful interview is planned, with objectives carefully defined.

Although many think the interview is simply a situation involving two people—one asking questions and the other answering—it is much more. The interview is an *exchange* of thoughts, feelings, and attitudes in which ideas, goodwill, and understanding can grow between the individuals.

MAJOR CATEGORIES OF INTERVIEWS

Sometimes the different types of interviews overlap. The information interview is part of an appraisal interview, selection interview, and all other types of interviews. Also, the disciplinary interview has aspects of the persuasive interview in it. Nevertheless, let's look at each category individually.

SELECTION INTERVIEW

Managers conduct selection interviews to choose new employees.

The selection interview is an information-gathering process used for choosing new employees. The interviewee attempts to get as much information as possible about the organization, the benefit package, the job responsibilities, and so on. The interviewer attempts to get as much data as possible about the qualifications, personality, potential, and background of the applicant. Both must plan carefully and design a series of cogent questions prior to the interview if they are to achieve their objectives.

To avoid embarrassing word choices that might result from nervousness, employment candidates should prepare and practice their questions in advance.

Because word choice is vital, both applicant and interviewer should write out each question to make sure they don't use the wrong word. For example, it is perfectly acceptable for the prospective employee to ask about promotion, but to use that precise word even before he or she has been hired may seem presumptuous. So the applicant may wish to phrase the question in writing this way and test it: "Assuming hard work and excellent performance, what is your firm's policy on moving employees up?" That sounds better than, "When can I expect a promotion?" Interviewees must do an outstanding job in the selection interview. Otherwise, they may not get another opportunity.

The interviewer also should prepare in advance, taking care to avoid legally impermissible topics.

Today, it is probably more true than ever that the prospective employer should also prepare a list of questions. Given the many government regulations, such as the rules of fair employment practices legislation and equal employment opportunity guidelines, it is imperative that the interviewer only ask questions that are acceptable. A long list of questions concerning age, marital status, race, religion, and so on can, if asked, be the basis for legal action.

ORIENTATION INTERVIEW

Managers conduct orientation interviews to inform employees about company policies and practices and to learn about the employees.

The interaction in the orientation interview orients new and old employees to organizational policies and practices or changes made in them. Employees can, of course, be given an orientation by means of a presentation. But presentations tend to be one-way forms of communication that focus on what the company has to offer, not what the employee seeks. The orientation interview, by contrast, involves the employee in the process of "finding a fit" in the communication of company information. A typical orientation interview begins with inquiries into the employee's interests and experiences. The result is mutual orientation; the employee knows what the company is all about, as viewed from his or her point of view, and the company knows a great deal about the employee's attitudes and background.

The training interview instructs employees in new skills, attitudes, or company practices. The attention span of even the most intelligent trainee is remarkably short when information is presented by the lecture method. But that same trainee can be attentive and tuned in for hours at a time when training occurs by more interactive means, such as in the training interview. Let's say, for example, that you want to upgrade a report writer in the company from word processing skills to desktop publishing skills. Instead of simply presenting desktop publishing techniques, you could use the interview format in which you inquire about what worked and what didn't for the person in using word processing. As the shortcomings of word processing have uncovered, you can present information about the advantages of desktop publishing. In this way, trainees feel they are part of the training process. They feel motivated to learn because they recognize how new skills and abilities can help them.

The appraisal interview is used for evaluating and reviewing job performance, establishing objectives, and designing and agreeing on future objectives. Unfortunately, employees seem to complain more about company appraisals than almost anything else. Many managers let the interviews for which they are responsible "accumulate." One day they look at their calendar and say, "Wow; all appraisal interviews are due tomorrow and I haven't even begun mine yet! If I space them ten minutes apart beginning at 8 a.m. tomorrow, I should be done by noon."

That is certainly no way to hold effective appraisal interviews. How can objectives be established thoughtfully; how can the workload be reviewed; how can plans be made for further professional training; how can mutual goals be developed? All these elements require open discussion and time.

The primary purpose of the appraisal interview is to have the manager and subordinate employee *mutually* evaluate the latter's performance in such areas as production, efficiency, responsibility, creativity, initiative, judgment, delegation, and professional growth. In addition, it is an opportunity for them to determine how well previously stated goals have been achieved and to design new ones for the future. In some organizations that operate on a management-by-objectives basis, these goals are noted and accepted by both parties by initialing or signing the interview form (or contract). It is important for the discussion to be open; mutual trust is vital. The goal is to have reasonable and obtainable employee objectives established for the next work period.

The one-on-one situation of the problem-solving interview allows departmental or company problems to be discussed by the people who are likely to have the answers. When they function as they are supposed to, these sessions can produce results (though too often meetings devolve into lecture sessions). In a problem-solving interview, both parties usually come to the occasion aware that there is a problem. The business of the interview is to define the nature of the problem, review attempts to solve the problem, discuss barriers in the path of that solution, and develop new approaches that will prove more successful. For example, the communications director of a corporation may interview a senior manager with the goal of removing blocks in the company's communication channels.

DISCIPLINARY INTERVIEW

The goal of the disciplinary interview is to correct a behavioral problem while maintaining goodwill.

Disciplinary interviews deal with behavioral problems. In a typical situation, the manager, parent, or teacher hopes to correct the situation while retaining the goodwill of the interviewee. Because there is so much potential for a confrontation, this interview is not easy to conduct.

An important point to keep in mind in the disciplinary interview is to criticize the *action* and not the individual. The interviewer, for example, should criticize the *action of smoking* by the employee who was handling highly sensitive gauges rather than the employee. In another instance, the manager may evaluate the result of missing meetings but not the person who missed them.

In a disciplinary interview, select words carefully. Negative, tactless expressions can arouse antagonism. Rather than saying, "You neglected to complete . . . " it might be more effective to say, "When you complete . . . " Instead of saying, "I was dismayed to find that your work was unsatisfactory," it is better to say, "I will be extremely pleased when your satisfactory efforts . . . "

In certain disciplinary interviews, it may be appropriate to "come on strong." If you have stated your point of view carefully, tactfully, and diplomatically on more than one occasion without results, it may be time to be forceful and direct. Some individuals respond to that style only. Remember, however, the successful disciplinary interview is one that brings problems into focus, suggests solutions, and maintains goodwill and an open line of communication.

COUNSELING INTERVIEW

To avoid inappropriate, awkward, and dangerous situations, managers should refer employees to a psychologist who is qualified to offer personal advice.

One of the tasks of the manager is to assist subordinates by offering suggestions and advice. A manager may wish to counsel a worker on how to improve productivity, mediate a problem, deal with suppliers or vendors, establish goals, solve a specific problem, cut costs, reschedule an operation or develop a new process. At other times, a supervisor may find it appropriate to listen to a subordinate discuss a personal problem. However, in the case of personal counseling, it is almost always inappropriate for a manager to become involved in the areas of marital affairs, alcoholism, drug abuse, and financial problems. Because the manager is not a qualified psychologist, offering advice may do more harm than good. For that reason many firms retain a professional staff to work with employees in sensitive, personal areas.

EXIT INTERVIEW

In exit interviews, individuals who are leaving the company are consulted in an effort to learn about employee attitudes toward jobs.

Management personnel conduct exit interviews with employees who are leaving the company. The purpose of the exit interview is to profit from the input of someone who has been on a job for many years and can supply the organization with valuable information. However, such meetings often become sessions with unhappy employees disparaging (whether true or not) former supervisors and colleagues but never themselves. Perhaps they are trying simply to relieve their own guilt. When employees who are leaving the firm voluntarily or involuntarily are questioned carefully, the information they supply can prove valuable for future operations.

The exit interview should be conducted by an objective individual in an impersonal and professional manner. In almost no instance should the employee's former supervisor conduct the interview. A well-thought-out series of questions should be covered; personalities should not. The focus should be on the manufacturing process, the production procedure, the office routine, or whatever primary activity was of concern to the employee. What actually took place? What flaws did you observe? What interrelations existed? What specific barriers arose? What changes in procedures do you suggest? How should they be implemented?

PLANNING THE INTERVIEW PROCESS

Three basic elements contribute to an interview: preparation for the interview, the interview itself, and the follow-up to the interview.

PREPARING FOR THE INTERVIEW

Although there are many different types of interviews, they all require the same seven preparatory steps:

1. Establish goals and objectives for the meeting. Because this step is so important, it is advisable to write these out. Only when you set down the objectives in black and white can you properly evaluate them to determine if they precisely express what you hope to accomplish.
2. Obtain necessary background data. You may need background on the problem to be discussed, on the individual with whom the discussion will take place, on factors that might impinge on the solution, or on other related areas.
3. Formulate critical questions. Here again, set these down in black and white before the meeting. Because one carelessly chosen word can result in problems in an interview, the thought involved in the writing-out procedure pays major dividends.
4. Determine the interviewee's needs, personality, and attitudes, and attempt to adapt to them.
5. Determine possible solutions, courses of action, or even appropriate reactions to items that may arise during the interview.
6. Secure data or other items that will be needed during the interview. These may include reports, samples, or company records.
7. Select an appropriate interview site. Although this point may seem minor, it is really quite important. Nothing will destroy the climate of an interview more quickly than a noisy interview site. Check to see that the site is quiet, comfortable, private, well-equipped with chairs, and adequately illuminated.

CONDUCTING THE INTERVIEW

You hope to secure specific information from the interviewee during the course of the interview and attain the objectives you established. Here again, guidelines are helpful:

1. Establish a comfortable climate. Begin with a cordial and sincere greeting, start the interview at the time scheduled, and have adequate reference sources and information available.
2. Prepare and ask key questions of the interviewee. Note questions beforehand so that none is forgotten. At the same time, anticipate

questions and topics about which the interviewee will probably inquire.

3. Observe, evaluate, and note the interviewee's verbal and nonverbal communications and reactions. Remember, nonverbal behaviors may prove more valuable to the alert interviewer than verbal ones.

4. Be alert to crucial junctures (or crucial periods) in the conversation. These key moments may be vital signals for closure, new directions, counternegotiations, agreements, or compromise.

5. Establish key actions and a schedule for follow-up. Write down key actions agreed on in the interview and give a copy to the interviewee immediately or within 24 hours. Key action statements should fix responsibility on specific individuals (most usually, the interviewer or interviewee) for completing specific tasks by specific dates.

6. Terminate the interview in a thoughtful, appreciative manner. The interviewee who finds the conversation brought to an abrupt halt as a result of the interviewer's jangling telephone has every right to be resentful.

In addition to following these guidelines, remember that the most important factor for both parties is to listen attentively and empathetically. Effective listening ensures effective participation.

Take the time to prepare for the interview and to anticipate the interviewee's concerns.

Good interviews don't just happen; they require careful preparation and follow-through. Both parties must take into consideration not only the guidelines noted, but also the personalities involved, the type of problem or situation under discussion, the objectives of both individuals, and the environment in which the interview is taking place.

ACTING AFTER THE INTERVIEW

Follow-up is essential to the ultimate success of the interview.

Participating in a well-prepared interview is not the final step. If the "transaction" is to be successful, the parties have further obligations. The agreements made and the decisions reached must be completed. Too often, the parties concerned complete an interview, shake hands, and go on to their respective tasks. Somehow the items each person was to follow up on fall between the cracks. Here are several guidelines the interviewer should follow after the interview:

1. Follow through on all key actions that have been designated as the interviewer's responsibility.

2. Assist the interviewee in those key actions designated as the interviewee's responsibility.

3. Supply the interviewee with all items promised: brochures, application blanks, reports, and so on.

4. Maintain contact with the interviewee if you agreed to such an action.

5. Be available to the interviewee for follow-up questions or to supply data not available at the time of the discussion.

The interview is a vital communication activity that occurs frequently. In activities at work, at home, or at leisure, you are involved in one-to-one (interview) situations. These are held for the purpose of solving problems, reaching decisions, setting goals, exchanging information, and for simple day-to-day relationships. Each has the potential for building goodwill and assisting both parties in achieving their objectives.

Of course, every interview will be different because people are involved and people are different. Sometimes the guidelines listed here will fit perfectly. At other times you will need to design your own.

To be proficient in playing the role of interviewer or interviewee, practice the suggestions made here. Above all, remember to listen. The interview is a communication situation where receiving ideas, feelings, and attitudes may be more important than sending them.

MEETINGS IN GENERAL

Meetings give a group of problem solvers the opportunity to exchange ideas.

A *meeting* is a gathering of a group of individuals who pool ideas and experiences to solve, in a democratic and open manner, common and individual problems. Its further purpose is to create the will to work together to achieve mutual goals. In some instances a meeting may be called to disseminate complex or detailed information. However, in most of these cases a memorandum containing the information sent to the interested parties will suffice.

Perhaps there is no corporate activity that is blamed for wasting more time and creating more antagonism than the meeting. Yet it need not be so. An unorganized, unplanned, bickering meeting results in frustration, antagonism, and confusion. And a complex mathematical formula isn't necessary to determine how costly it is to confine 16 people in a room every Tuesday afternoon from 1:00 to 3:30. At a rate of approximately $50 per hour per person (salary plus overhead), one two-and-a-half-hour meeting can "cost" an organization $2,000.

But meetings should not waste money. They should not create hard feelings. They should not result in confusion.

On the contrary, meetings can and should produce acceptable plans, worthwhile goals, profit-making decisions, and a climate that establishes the will to work together. All that is required is the formulation of a philosophy for meetings and attention to a three-step system for organizing them. If you are ever a meeting leader or a meeting participant (and almost everyone in business is at one time or another), you have a responsibility to help make every meeting you attend a success.

MANAGEMENT POLICIES FOR MEETINGS

Companies that believe in participative management must establish policies that result in productive meetings.

If the top personnel in the firm really believe in participative management, then a basic fact must become part of management philosophy: group meetings, where plans are made, objectives established, and decisions reached, are an integral and vital part of the company's decision-making process. Once that concept is accepted, the firm's meetings are on their way to success.

Meetings are more likely to succeed if management establishes, announces, and supports a list of meeting policies such as these:

1. Hold only meetings for which there is a demonstrated need. In many organizations so much activity occurs that a weekly or biweekly meeting is justified. Regular staff meetings can bring department members up-to-date. But under no circumstances should a meeting be held every Monday or the third Wednesday of every month on the expectation that "we will surely have some items to review."

2. State a purpose and objectives for every meeting in writing. In most cases the purpose will be rather broad: "to discuss," "to evaluate," or

"to compare." The objectives will be narrower: "to purchase Brand A or Brand B," "to construct a $40,000 addition to the plating room or not."

Meetings called to exchange ideas may not result in any conclusions. A meeting purely for brainstorming is acceptable provided the brainstorming has a specific purpose with stated objectives.

3. Send a written memo to all meeting participants a reasonable length of time prior to the session. The memo should include the date, time, place, and list of meeting participants. It may be part of the meeting agenda or be sent with it.
4. Invite only individuals who can make a positive contribution. People should not be invited because of protocol, politics, or fear of offending someone.
5. Prepare and distribute an agenda before every meeting. In the case of emergency meetings called on short notice, the meeting leader may post the agenda in the meeting room on a flipchart, whiteboard, or blackboard prior to the start of discussion.
6. Begin and end meetings precisely at the times scheduled on the agenda sheet.
7. Distribute a set of minutes or a recapitulation of the meeting within 24 hours of the close of the session. The minutes should list decisions reached and key actions with completion dates and the name of the individual responsible for each action.

WHAT MAKES A SUCCESSFUL BUSINESS MEETING?

An effective meeting is a forum where knowledgeable individuals come together to solve organizational problems through open and participative communication. It is a place where the will to work together is developed. An effective meeting is also a group session that participants find exciting and provocative; it's one where every member who has something to say is heard; it's one where everyone is on an equal level; it's one where decisions are reached.

The background to a successful meeting involves two factors: (1) the fact that a meeting is an important, worthwhile activity, and (2) management's commitment that the ideas, suggestions, and decisions reached at such meetings *will* be put into practice as soon as is reasonably possible. Once this philosophy is established, following the three-step plan to achieve a successful meeting becomes almost a matter of mechanics.

THREE-STEP PLAN FOR SUCCESSFUL MEETINGS

STEP 1: THE PREMEETING PERIOD

Key personnel must decide if a meeting is necessary.

Establish the need. The pre-meeting period requires a brief discussion among key personnel in which the need for the meeting is clearly established. Too many meetings are called simply because "we always meet on Tuesdays at 1 p.m." If no useful purpose can be accomplished, a meeting should not be called.

State the problem or discussion topic clearly and in writing.

Define the problem or topic for discussion. A clear statement of the problem or discussion topic must be agreed to and set down on paper. All too often the meeting leader and participants have only vague ideas about the meeting's subject. Discussion then goes in circles, and decisions are difficult to reach. Let's not look into "Fringe Benefits with Special Attention to a Profit-sharing Program." Instead, let's be specific: "An Analysis of Profit-sharing Programs in

Companies Similar to Ours," or "Cost of a Profit-sharing Program to the Jono Company," or "Should the Jono Company Adopt a Profit-sharing Program?"

Defining a problem or selecting a topic usually requires careful analysis. Be careful not to designate a *symptom* of a problem as the problem. It is true that production has slowed down, but installing faster punch presses will not solve the problem. The slowdown is only a symptom of the real problem, which may be low morale among people in the production department. That is the issue with which the meeting should deal—not the possible acquisition of newer and faster punch presses.

Decide which meeting type—information, problem solving, training, or brainstorming— would best serve the group's needs.

Determine the type of meeting. Once the need for the meeting has been established, the next step is to decide what type of meeting will best serve the immediate situation. The *information meeting* provides information in the same way at the same time to everyone concerned. Questions may be answered and facts explored.

In the *problem-solving meeting,* questions or problems are dealt with and people concerned with them are expected to help work out solutions. This is the type of meeting where solutions are sought, not past positions defended.

Only people directly responsible for solving the problem should participate in the meeting.

Training meetings explain specific skills, concepts, or ideas. These sometimes include demonstrations and question-answer periods.

In *brainstorming meetings,* almost anything goes as long as it has to do with solving or exploring the topic or problem under discussion. This type of meeting is also valuable for the presentation and discussion of unusual ideas for new products, procedures, or customs.

The difficulty that frequently arises involves a meeting leader who tries to combine all four of the preceding types in one meeting. It is almost impossible to disseminate information, solve problems, train, and brainstorm in one session!

Select participants. Invite only those individuals who are clearly concerned with the topic. People should not be asked "just to keep them informed." There are easier and less time-consuming methods of informing people. Also, do not invite individuals just because their feelings might be hurt if they are not asked.

It is important that the company policy on meetings clearly state that only those directly concerned, or who have knowledge or experience to contribute, will be asked to meetings.

Choose a leader who is able to motivate all participants to contribute.

Designate the meeting leader. A meeting often flies or falls because of the leader. Actually the term *leader* is a misnomer, for the best leader is one who doesn't formally lead but who acts as a catalyst, a stimulator, a moderator, a facilitator, or an arbitrator. The leader who talks least and stimulates most usually does the best job.

There is good reason to advise that the highest ranking member of the group *not* be designated as the leader. When that person is in the position of leader, too often he or she can't forget who's boss, nor can the participants. Why not ask one of the knowledgeable people in the group to serve as the leader? Or— an idea that is gaining some popularity—have the assistant to the president of the company serve as leader. Also consider rotating leaders so that a different individual from the group presides at each session.

In all situations, an effort should be made to select a leader who possesses the following characteristics:

Ability to think quickly and clearly
Analytical mind
Impersonal attitude
Unbiased position
Patience
Tact
Poise
Self-restraint
Ability to express ideas easily
A good sense of humor
Understanding of problem-solving techniques

And where is that saint with all these qualities to be found? Perhaps nowhere, but there is no reason why the leader can't attempt to strive for these qualities.

Organize the meeting by designating topic areas that relate to the problem.

Designate topic area. Once the main topic is set, divide the topic into sub-areas for discussion. Choose sub-areas with care, keeping in mind the complexity or simplicity of each point, how much discussion may be needed, and the overall time allowed for the meeting. To list more topics than can reasonably be discussed in the time scheduled is frustrating, because it means that discussion of some of them will have to be cut short.

Announce the meeting agenda well in advance and encourage participants to prepare.

Distribute the conference announcement agenda. The announcement/agenda should be sent out to everyone concerned approximately three to seven days before the meeting. Provide the following information:

- Date, time, and place of meeting
- Topic(s) for discussion with approximate times allotted
- Sub-areas for discussion
- List of participants
- If applicable, materials to be reviewed prior to the meeting

Figure 25–1 is an example of a satisfactory announcement/agenda form. Think of the many advantages in distributing such an announcement. First, participants who wish to prepare for the meeting may do so. No one can say later, "If I had known we were going to discuss this, I could have brought tons of statistics!"

Second, digressions can be easily and tactfully curbed by the meeting leader: "That's a good point, Jeff, but I think we will defer it until later. At the moment we are trying to tie up point number 2 on the agenda, so let's turn to Suzanne who has a comment on that area."

Third, all participants know who has been invited, and thus they can plan their strategies, if necessary.

Finally, the leader (who makes up the agenda) is forced to *plan* and prepare for the session.

Confirm the availability and appropriateness of the meeting place.

Prepare physical facilities. The mechanical aspects of the meeting always seem so obvious, yet breakdowns in this area have ruined countless meetings. What's the good of having 12 people congregate in front of the meeting room at the appointed time only to find it occupied or locked and the key in the possession of somebody who is on a coffee break? Irritation and confusion are certain to follow as some make their way to the substitute meeting room while others

FIGURE 25–1   Announcement/Agenda Form

JONO COMPANY

DATE: February 2, 19__

TO: Roger Carter, Production Manager

FROM: Jean Kean, Vice President

SUBJECT: Meeting, February 15, 19__
                        1 p.m., Lounge #2

Topic for Discussion:
Should the Jono Company establish a physical fitness program?

Specific Items for Discussion:
1. Advantages and disadvantages of a physical fitness program for all employees
   a. Advantages and disadvantages to company (cost, absenteeism, space)
   b. Advantages and disadvantages to employees (cost, improved health, time)
2. Physical fitness staff required
   a. Professional
   b. Company paramedical staff
3. Medical considerations
   a. Cost of supervising physician
   b. Qualified personnel on staff or brought in
4. Legal considerations
   a. Potential liabilities
   b. Insurance coverage
5. Cost (first three years)
   a. Space
   b. Personnel
   c. Equipment
   d. Insurance
6. Other business

Distribution:

Jane Berg	Tom Mace	Christine Burton
Larry Strong	Amanda Foreman	Terry Green
Emilio Garro	Juanita Hernandez	Joe Cox
Barbara Chin	Roger Carter	Yoko Kishiwara

The meeting announcement identifies the meeting time and place.

The meeting announcement clearly identifies the problem and related topics.

The meeting announcement lists meeting participants.

drift back to their desks. To avoid such problems, prepare a checklist on the physical arrangements:

1. Room setup: Reservations for room made? Enough chairs? Podium needed?
2. Audiovisual materials: Projectors? Flip charts? Microphones? Display materials? Tape recorders?
3. Handout materials: Adequate number of copies for distribution?
4. Refreshments: Coffee? Fruit juice? Sandwiches?
5. Miscellaneous materials: Pads? Paper? Pencils? Marking pens? Name cards?

You are now ready for the meeting itself.

STEP 2: THE MEETING PERIOD

Companies need to accept this basic concept: Various aspects of the management of the firm, and of management development, can and should be built into the meeting. Let's make this point by looking at a typical situation.

Of the six reports presented at today's meeting, three focused strongly on customer dissatisfaction with the carrier we are now using. One of the young women present, with a degree in marketing, made some thoughtful remarks on the advantages of using commercial carriers. Several of the old-timers wondered if we shouldn't transfer our entire delivery operations to a third party. The meeting leader turned back to the young woman, who volunteered to complete a study on this important issue for the next meeting. A final decision on the problem is expected to be made at that time.

Certainly more than discussion just took place. Management of the firm occurred and, in the case of the young woman, personnel development.

Meeting leaders must establish a participative climate and manage time so that all important points are covered.

If the meeting is to go well, the leader must set the right climate. He or she must know the participants and watch the time. Care must be taken not to march down the list from first point to last, pushing discussion here, cutting off comments there. Rather, discussion must be stimulated so that the topics are covered while at the same time the participants feel they have made significant contributions.

Developing the technique for doing this is not really difficult. It requires a sincere feeling on the part of the leader that the participants, taken together, are smarter than any one individual, possess a wealth of experience, and are as eager to solve the problem before the group as the leader is.

The meeting should begin on a positive note in which the leader communicates, verbally and nonverbally, respect for each person in the room. The climate that is set in the first few minutes will either motivate the participants to contribute actively and effectively or cause them to retreat into their shells.

Designate someone to take notes.

Note-taking. Someone should take notes. It may be a participant who is respected by the group (Not someone who says, "I'm invited only because I write fast") and is impartial. Or a secretary can help; however, discussion may be inhibited if some of the participants feel that the secretary is not discreet.

In the past, the general procedure was for a secretary to take notes on a notepad. These were later transcribed and a set of minutes issued. The problem with this procedure is that the secretary records what she or he heard. If that is incorrect, many days can pass before the record is set straight.

A trend today is to have a secretary (who may very well be a participating group member) record brief notes on a flip chart. In that way, if the secretary records his or her perception of what was discussed, said, or voted on, and if that is incorrect, everyone in the room has the opportunity to make that fact known immediately.

If a flip chart is used, the recorder may wish to also record key actions on another flip chart page. This list should include the action, the name of the individual designated to carry it out, and the due date for completion. Usually actions consist of assignments to secure specific data, complete tasks, carry out a negotiation, and so forth (see Figure 25–2).

Begin and end the meeting on schedule.

Time management. The meeting leader should begin and end at the times scheduled. No one has enough time these days, and if the leader doesn't begin the meeting until 20 minutes after the time scheduled or holds the group an extra 20 minutes at the close, he or she will surely encounter antagonism.

Effective leaders empower rather than dominate participants.

Leading the meeting. The meeting leader should be careful not to dominate the meeting physically. A leader standing at a podium that is separated from the conference table conveys the feeling, "I'm in charge." If the leader sits in front of the group with space to the left and right (as in a U arrangement), this, too, suggests that the leader is in charge. In most situations an unbroken rectangular or oval arrangement is preferable. The leader need not sit at the head; discussion may flow more easily if he or she takes a seat as part of the team. Perhaps the most important point for the meeting leader to keep in mind is not to dominate the meeting. The less you, the leader, talk and the more the participants contribute, the more successful you will be in attaining your objectives.

The leader should prepare questions to stimulate further discussion if participation wanes.

Encouraging participation. As a meeting leader, prepare a few pertinent questions for each topic on the agenda. Then if discussion slackens, you can toss a question to the group. Sometimes a leading question can be fed to someone who has much to contribute but for some reason prefers to remain silent.

Also, step in at an appropriate moment to summarize discussion on a topic and move the group on to the next point. Avoid talking a topic to death.

The leader should consider each group member's personality and develop strategies for transforming problem individuals into productive contributors.

The participants. Most meeting participants are eager to contribute, cooperate, and assist the total effort toward the group's objectives. However, some occasionally cause problems, and one of them may be sitting at your next meeting.

- *Nonstop Norbert* is invariably hypnotized with the beauty of his voice and the brilliance of his comments. A tactful interjection, *"We'll pursue that excellent point later, but let's get back to agenda item 4 right now,"* is usually adequate to stop him (even though it may only be temporary).
- *Obstinate Ollie* immediately says "white" if you say "black" or "yes" if you say "no." Don't try to argue with him; simply ask the other participants to react to his point of view. For the leader to "take him on" may psychologically divide the meeting into two groups: those who agree with the leader and those who side with the opposition.
- *Silent Sally* says little or nothing but does have an idea to contribute. Often she may be brought out by a carefully worded question that doesn't put her on the spot but simply seeks information. Once that is accomplished, she's on her way to making other contributions.

FIGURE 25–2   Minutes of a Meeting

JONO COMPANY

MINUTES OF THE MEETING

DATE: February 15, 19__

TO: Roger Carter, Production Manager

FROM: Jean Kean, Vice President

SUBJECT: Minutes of Meeting
                 February 15, 19__, 1 p.m., Lounge #2

Present: Jane Berg, Larry Strong, Emilio Garro, Barbara Chin, Tom Mace,
                 Amanda Foreman, Juanita Hernandez, Roger Carter, Christine
                 Burton, Terry Green, Joe Cox and Yoko Kishiwara.

*Minutes
. . . identify
participants*

Summary of Discussion:
Item 1:   Companywide physical fitness program
Item 2:   Employee participation in election campaigns
Item 3:   Conversion of employee lounge #3 to a conference room

*. . . tell what
they discussed*

Decisions Reached:
1. Physical fitness program discussion continued to April meeting
2. Employee participation in municipal elections not approved
3. Conversion of lounge #3 approved

*. . . record the
decisions they
reached*

Key Actions:

Item No.	Task	Individual Responsible	Completion Date
1	Investigation of physical fitness program in other companies	J. Berg	April 5,19__
2	Legal ramifications of physical program	B. Chin	April 5,19__
3	Medical department input on physical fitness program	J. Hernandez	April 5,19__

*. . . suggest
what should be
done next*

- *Tardy Terri* may be a supervisor or a vice president. Walking in late is simply her style whether for a lunch date, a dinner, or a meeting. The solution is simple: always begin and end meetings at the time the meeting announcement lists.
- *Ali Astronomer* finds the clouds outdoors or the ceiling above simply fascinating. He often responds to the same technique as Silent Sally. Be careful in both cases not to draw them into the discussion if they have little to contribute and would be embarrassed. Participation purely to participate is of little value.
- *Fumbling Felicia* really has something to say but the truth of the matter is that she does not express herself well. Be patient; let her finish and then *very* tactfully feed back to her as part of your discussion, the point you think she tried to make. If she accepts your rephrasing of her idea, she has made an important contribution to the meeting.
- *H. A. Harry* comes to the meeting with a hidden agenda, and regardless of how alert the leader is, Hidden Agenda Harry will get his comment out. What he has to say is designed only to impress the president who is present or deprecate a colleague. One thing is certain: H. A. Harry made the comment for a reason, and because of that, you must deal with it. At times, deal with the comment at that moment, even though to do so causes a digression in the discussion. At other times, do not focus the spotlight on the statement during the session; instead, discuss Harry's comment with him after the meeting.

Can you think of others who sometimes make a meeting problematic? Basically, however, courtesy, tact, patience, and restraint on the part of the leader will be effective in securing a successful meeting.

The leader should conclude the meeting by summing up outcomes, identifying areas of consensus, and advocating collaboration or compromise in areas of disagreement.

Meeting tie-up. Everyone who leaves a meeting should feel that something has been accomplished. Often, that feeling can be guaranteed if the last minutes of the session are handled properly. During that time the leader should summarize the discussion and key issues. If adequate time has been given to the topics listed, and they are the type that call for a decision, the leader should determine if consensus has been reached. The leader's action in this regard is much more low-key than asking the participants to raise their hands for a count of those for and those opposed. Obviously, not everyone can be satisfied, but most will be glad to see matters brought to a conclusion and decisions made.

The astute leader can also bring about a decision by carefully suggesting or permitting the group to accept a *compromise* solution. Another method is to demonstrate how *collaboration* or even *cooperation* can result in all parties securing most, if not all, of their goals. The leader should not permit a concluding situation (if at all possible) where some of the participants view themselves as "winners" on the basis of the decision reached and others as "losers."

Skill on the part of the leader will help him or her avoid driving for a decision. Instead, let the request for a decision come from the group. As a leader, you have done a good job if the worst thing any of the participants say as they walk back to their desks is, "Well, I wasn't in complete agreement with the decision, but we *did* accomplish something."

Much else is involved in the conduct of a meeting: the effective use of visual aids and report presentations, methods of handling debate, the participation of

Much has been made, in the past decade, of the impact women's presence in the workforce on communication among colleagues. Locker-room humor, sexual innuendo, even sports talk as a way to break the ice has passed from natural parts of work life to serious issues of environment quality and equal opportunity for success.

Do men and women approach communication differently? If so, is one approach better suited to the workplace than the other? These two questions have dominated discussions of men, women, and communication at work, and while it appears that the answer to the first one is an unequivocal "yes," the answer to the second is still under debate.

At first glance, it appears that "male vs. female" communication patterns are assymetrical, with one oriented toward control and the other toward the pursuit of human closeness. This difference results in the potential for power imbalance; that is, the control orientation dominates interaction when paired with the orientation seeking intimacy. A second look, however, through the lens of group communication theory, suggests the assymetry may be condition for complementarity: men and women each bringing to the table half of the whole range of communication strategies needed to make a meeting work.

We know from socialization theorists that as they grow up, boys and girls receive powerful messages about appropriate gender behavior. Boys get the message early that they will work throughout their lives and are conditioned to achieve, attain status and power, and accumulate material wealth. Girls, on the other hand, are cued early to their future roles as mommies, and the emphasis for them is on human interaction, care giving, the development of relationships, and interpersonal intimacy. They receive increasingly strong career messages, too, these days, but evidence suggests that "girls are nurturers." That

remains the strongest signal throughout the growing up years.

How do these conditioning differences translate into communication patterns? Georgetown sociolinguist Deborah Tannen characterizes the situation as negotiation, with men bargaining for control and women pursuing closeness. Another way to frame the situation is in terms of what happens in mixed-sex conversation: men appear to assert their right to dominate the conversation and women seem to collaborate in letting them.

Looking at two elements of conversation, declarative statements and turn taking, illuminates the differences in men's and women's talk and shows the potential for male-dominant and female-submissive communication in work meetings. Women are far more likely than men to add verbiage that has the impact of softening, or making more tentative, their declarative statements. This happens in three ways:

1. Tag questions: Two to three words "tagged on the end of a declarative sentence have the effect of turning it into something in between a statement and a question.

   This really could make the difference for this department, couldn't it?

   The format would look better if it was justified on both margins, don't you think?

2. Qualifiers: These words, attached to the beginning of a declarative sentence, have the effect of softening the "punch" in a statement.

   Perhaps you shouldn't do that (vs. You shouldn't do that!)

   It seems to me that's superfluous. (vs. That's superfluous!)

   I wonder if you're seeing that correctly? (vs. You're seeing it all wrong!)

   Well, no. (vs. No!)

CULTURAL DIVERSITY IN COMMUNICATION

Women and Men in Working Meetings: Cross-cultural Impasse or Opportunity for Symmetry?

———

Carol Shuherk
University of
Southern California

3. Disclaimers: These are "mitigator" devices, phrases that precede a declarative statement and have the effect of hedging or apologizing for what the speaker is about to say.

I know this sounds silly but . . .

This may strike you as odd, but . . .

Well, I'm no expert, but . . .

These are positive communication strategies in that they invite others to have input, allow for the possibility of alternative points of view, and acknowledge the incompleteness of any one person's perspective. On the other hand, they can be viewed as relinquishing control or authority if used to excess and cause a speaker to seem unsure or short on confidence.

The difference in the two styles can be seen in this set of instructions as delivered first by a man and then by a woman.

Next! Put your pencil on the bottom left corner of the square. This will be the midpoint of a line you'll draw. Draw your line at a 45-degree angle to the left side and the bottom side of the square. Now get this! This line is the top side of a second square. Remember! I said the corner intersects the top. Don't get if off center or you'll blow the whole thing.

Then I'd like you to construct another box just below the first one, all right? Only this time, try to arrange it so the left point of the first box touches the top of the second box in the middle.

When men and women are talking to each other, the pattern of control and concession is striking. It appears, from research conducted since the mid-1970s, that women tend to work harder than men to keep a conversation going by listening passively with head nods and um-hms and by allowing themselves to be interrupted. These turn-taking issues characterize mixed-gender conversation in three ways:

1. Interruptions: In mixed-sex conversations, men commit 96 percent of interruptions.
2. Overlaps: An overlap occurs when two people speak at once, with the original speaker's sentence being completed by the second speaker or the second speaker responding to the first's statement before it is complete. Virtually 100 percent of overlaps in mixed-sex conversation are committed by men.
3. Delayed minimal response: An "um" following a two- to three-second silence after a speaker's statement has the effect of ending the discussion. Men do this three times more often to women than vice versa.

Taken together, these behaviors had the effect of stopping 64 percent of the attempts by women in the study to initiate topics. Not surprisingly, the men in the groups talked at greater length than women, with their length of input ranging from 10.66 to 17.07 seconds per remark compared to 3 to 10 seconds for women.

Expecting that by the late 1980s highly intelligent, highly educated women would talk as much or more than men in meetings, Amherst College psychology professor Elizabeth Aries recorded conversations of college men and women in small groups. She found that women did talk more, but that there was a distinct difference in what men and women talked about. The men tended to set the meeting agenda, giving opinions on how to proceed, and providing information and suggestions for solving problems or for taking action. The women tended to react, either agreeing or disagreeing with someone else's input. This observation corresponds with the theory that men assert control and women tend relationships. On the surface, it also seems to bode ill for women who want to have impact in meetings. In fact, however, these two distinct communication styles have long been cited as equally necessary to effectively working in groups.

Group theorists argue that two primary communication patterns are required to accomplish work in a meeting and keep meeting participants committed to the group as well as the task at hand. They call the two patterns *task* communication and *maintenance* communication. As the names imply, task communication moves the group through the rational process required to accomplish the work at hand. It includes any communication that acts to diagnose the situation, set goals, propose actions, seek and obtain information, respond to fluctuating conditions, or plan for implementation. Maintenance communication, on the other hand, seeks to develop harmonious working relationships among meeting members. It is listening, soliciting opinions, resolving conflicts, introducing levity in tense moments, agreeing with good points, acknowledging hard work, and striving for full participation by all members. In sum, task communication tackles the job at hand and maintenance communication attends to the human process to maximize the contribution of all involved.

Women tend to go into meetings with an emphasis on developing a working process that provides individual satisfaction for the people at the table. Men, on the other hand, tend to view meetings as opportunities to get organized, to put together a winning plan of attack. Communication in the meeting itself tends to lean more toward task communication in the case of men and maintenance communication for women. Is one more effective than the other? In large part, it depends on how you define meeting leadership. If you see meetings as decision making among equals, with a functional leader to set priorities and then facilitate broad participation until group goals are met, women lead better meetings. If, on the other hand, you view meetings hierarchically, with each member understanding his or her specific role and status and the leader functioning to set the agenda, define priorities, and solicit input as deemed appropriate, then men make better meeting leaders.

A better strategy might be to view meeting participation from the nongendered point of view of the group theorists. Although there may very well be a biological predilection for men to be action takers and women to be nurturers, communication patterns themselves are all learned. As such they can be unlearned, and new patterns can be substituted in their place. The effective meeting participant or leader, whether woman or man, will consciously select the appropriate communication strategies based on the expectations of the meeting participants and the task at hand. And the two seemingly asymmetrical approaches to communication can be built into a complementary pattern that serves the best interests of all.

consultants, and the handling of the president who has "just dropped in to listen quietly." But common sense, based on the principles cited, will usually provide workable techniques.

STEP 3: THE POSTMEETING PERIOD

Follow-up is essential to the success of meetings.

The meeting has been held, but it is not over. The meeting's basic purpose was to hammer out another link in the chain of successful management. Fastening of that new link to the others in the chain takes place in the postmeeting period.

Evaluation of the meeting. Now it is time for those who called the meeting to sit together for a few minutes to determine what the session accomplished, how

Identify accomplishments and discuss ways of improving future meetings.

the results or findings fit into overall company plans, and how the next meeting can be improved.

Minutes provide a permanent record of the meeting topics, votes, and decisions.

Distribution of the minutes. The *minutes,* a recapitulation of the meeting, should be sent to each participant as quickly as possible. The form should cover the topics discussed, votes taken, and decisions reached (see Figure 25–2). The advantages of distributing such a form are many. First, everyone receives the same summary of what took place. If anyone thinks he or she heard anything different from what is reported in the summary, those views can be made known to the recorder immediately.

Next, there can be no confusion as to who was assigned to do what. The minutes state names and spell out assignments in the section on key actions. This prevents someone from saying three weeks after the meeting, "Well, I didn't know *I* was supposed to do that. I remember there was a suggestion that I gather statistics, but I sure don't have them for tomorrow's meeting."

In addition, no confusion will exist on the decisions reached and the votes taken. They will be clearly stated in black and white. Here again, someone can hardly say three weeks later, "Well, I don't remember the vote going *that* way; I thought we agreed to wait until the next meeting before a final vote was taken on that item."

Finally, the minutes become a matter of record. They can be referred to by those who were absent and reviewed by those who were present.

The postmeeting period is as important as the other two parts of the meeting plan. It helps tie the package together and completes the job that was begun when someone said, just five weeks ago, "We ought to get some additional input on this, kick it around, and then decide which way to go."

ADVANTAGE OF THE THREE-STEP PLAN

There are those who feel that the structured approach of this three-step plan has a decided disadvantage. What happens if a participant has a brilliant idea he or she wishes to discuss, but which has not been included on the agenda (is not part of the preplanned structure)? Will that idea be lost forever? Certainly not! All that is necessary is that the agenda carry an item called "other business." The leader must then be sure that time is always saved to cover that point. In this way, the advantages of both the structured and the unstructured meeting may be retained.

The meeting decides which way to go—by common agreement. Voices are heard, ideas pursued, and personnel developed. A meeting that is well run and allows democratic participation is an outstanding communication vehicle.

USE AND MISUSE OF MEETINGS

Meetings represent one of the most useful communication tools in an organization. They bring about decision making through the democratic process; they build a team concept that engenders loyalty and commitment; they provide a forum for the exposure of divergent ideas; and they give young employees an opportunity to be seen and heard.

Managers should not use meetings to review basics, to hide their responsibility, or to pass the buck.

On the other hand, a few negative aspects have become increasingly apparent in meeting conduct. Meetings should not be called for the discussion of basic information, new procedures, or changes in regulations. On the whole, most items of this nature can be handled by a well-written announcement or bulletin. Some complex items may require a meeting to discuss detailed points so that all those affected have a similar understanding of the data.

In addition meetings should not be called to avoid decision-making responsibility. Such meetings are usually concerned with relatively inconsequential items. "Should we change the coffee break time?" "Should we move the copy machine?" "Should plants be added to the office reception area?" All such items should be settled by a manager making a decision. If the meeting is called for such trivial items, considerable time and money will be wasted. Even more important, it will send a signal to other managers that holding meetings for minor purposes is acceptable.

Sometimes managers call meetings simply to "cover themselves." If the decision doesn't work out in practice, they can say, "But it wasn't my decision; I only followed the recommendations of the people who attended the meeting of May 10!" If managers have the authority and responsibility for making decisions in designated instances, then calling a meeting to "cover themselves" is completely unacceptable.

The best way for an organization to avoid holding unnecessary meetings is to have a brief statement about meetings (e.g., "Meeting Policies for the Baxter Corporation"). When such a policy statement is endorsed and *followed* by top management, it becomes a "way of life" for meeting conduct.

**WRITING
AND SPEAKING
EXERCISES**

1. Assume that you manage a large production facility. Employee turnover is low, but still common. Invent details as to what kind of business you conduct. Then develop a set of questions to be asked of exiting employees. For each question, indicate in writing what information you hope to gain by the query.

2. Exchange with another student some of the graded assignments you have received in this course. Study your colleague's work and then conduct an appraisal interview with him or her.

3. Sit in, as an observer, on a meeting of a campus group or some other organization. Afterwards, evaluate the effectiveness of meeting participants in achieving their apparent goals. If the group members show interest in your evaluation, share it with them in a tactful way.

4. Recall an interview situation in which you felt uncomfortable. Analyze your discomfort. Who or what caused it? List several ways in which the interview could be restructured or reconsidered to reduce such discomfort.

5. You have noted that a group that you belong to (e.g., a student group) seems to waste considerable time in meetings. The group has several of the classic problems: lack of preparation, the wrong people in attendance, and little or no follow-up after the meetings. For such a group, prepare a policy statement on meetings.

6. Some people see meetings as their opportunity to set up a soap box. The meeting is not to be a replication of Sunday morning in London's Hyde Park. Sometimes, however, a meeting chairperson must verbally restrain one individual so the group can move forward and solve the problem at

hand. Be prepared. Develop a list of ten optional statements (increasing in lack of tact) to derail the nonstop talker and keep the meeting on track.

7. The membership of your student organization has been on a steady decline, and the executive committee of the group has decided to meet in two weeks to discuss, "What Is Wrong with Our Group." In reviewing good meeting procedures, you feel the the topic is too big and will not lead to profitable discussion. Defining the appropriate problem is crucial if a solution is to be found. With this in mind, develop three alternative titles for the coming meeting that will aid the committee in accomplishing beneficial results.

8. Recently you were advanced to the position of manager of parts promotion for the Amco Tractor Co. In ten days you are to conduct your first interview with a prospective employee. You will be on your own, and the decision will be your responsibility alone. Because the firm has had some previous problems concerning fair employment practices, the company has a procedure for you to follow. Managers who are going through the interviewing process for the first time must submit potential questions in writing to the human resources office for approval. In a memo to Jane Deer in the human resources office, list 12 questions you may ask the prospective employee. The interviewee is a recent college graduate from Belmore College. She has a double major in marketing and technology. (In preparing your materials you may want to review the legal implications of interviewing noted in Chapter 15).

9. You're an assistant manager at Beta Video Productions. You find yourself conducting a sales meeting at which no one seems to have much to say. Although you're reluctant to be an overly dominant meeting leader, you're afraid that if you stop talking, an embarrassing silence will fall. Consider your dilemma. Then list four ways to get others to participate freely in the meeting. List your suggestions in the order in which you would try them.

10. The head of your academic department has decided it would be beneficial for someone in the department to hold exit interviews with a sample of students graduating each year. Exit interviews don't just happen, and if they are to be beneficial, they must be more than gripe sessions. Assume you are assistant to the department head and you have been asked to outline policies, procedures, and implementation requisites for exit interviews. Place your materials in memo form and be thorough in your analysis and statement of procedures.

11. The business department at your college is going to host a group of businesspeople for one day on campus. The meeting is scheduled for two months from now. You have been placed in charge of one session in the meeting. You are to make all the pre-session arrangements for a roundtable discussion between students and the business representatives on "What Business Wants in Today's Business Student." The head of the business department has asked you to prepare a memo that outlines the actions needed to get the session organized. Be very precise in detailing your pre-session responsibilities.

12. You are the director of human resources at Federated Utilities. You're concerned about the high turnover rate among employees (less than 18 months of service per employee, on the average). You prepare for an

extensive series of exit interviews by drawing up questions you hope will get to the heart of the matter. You want to avoid leading questions such as, "Did you want more money?" (Of course employees want more money.) List at least six questions you could use in such exit interviews.

13. Draw up a set of meeting policies for an organization of which you are a member.

CASES

Complete the following assignments from the Cases for Discussion section at the back of this book:

1. Hostile Takeover case—Assignments 1 and 2
2. Brooks-Martinez case—Assignments 2 and 5
3. The Sun Fresh case—Assignment 6
4. But Talking Isn't Working case—Assignment 6
5. Was This Really Fraud case—Assignment 5

SUGGESTED READINGS

Ambash, Joseph W. "Knowing Your Limits: How Far Can You Go When Checking an Applicant's Background?" *Management World* (March—April 1990):9–11.

Bell, Arthur H. *The Complete Manager's Guide to Interviewing.* Homewood, Ill.: Business One Irwin, 1989.

Bell, Arthur H. *Extraviewing: Innovative Ways to Hire the Best.* Homewood, Ill.: Business One Irwin, 1992.

Bell, Arthur H. *Mastering the Meeting Maze.* Reading, Mass.: Addison-Wesley, 1991.

Berry, U. "Making a Contribution to Meetings." *Management Solutions* 33 (September 1988).

Blits, Jan H., and Gottfredson, Linda S. "Employment Testing and Job Performance." *Public Interest* (Winter 1990):18–24.

Caernaraven-Smith, P. "You Don't Really Have to Be at This Meeting." *Technical Communication* 38 (April 1991).

Erb, L. "How to Make an Interview Come Alive." *Public Relations Quarterly* 35 (Fall 1990).

Fenton, James W. "Recruitment: Negligent Hiring/Retention Adds to Human Resources Woes. *Personnel Journal* (April 1990):66–68.

Ferguson, Julia, and Fletcher, Clive. "An Investigation of Some Cognitive Factors Involved in Person-Perception During Selection Interviews." *Psychological Reports* 64(1989):735–742.

Graves, Laura M. "College Recruitment: Removing Personal Bias from Selection Decisions." *Personnel* (March 1989):48–60.

LaBarbara, Barbara L. "Recruiting and Interviewing: the Trump Card of the Personnel Game." *Supervision* (December 1988):14–28.

Martin, Christopher L., and Nagao, Dennis H. "Some Effects of Computerized Interviewing on Job Applicant Responses." *Journal of Applied Psychology* 74(1989):72–90.

Mitchell, Brooks. "Interviewing Face-to-Interface.:" *Personnel* (January 1990):24–40.

Meyer, Gary. "New Program Conducts Exit Interviews." *HR Magazine* (January 1991):27–29.

Phillips, Amanda Peek, and Dipboye, Robert L. "Correlational Tests of Predictions from a Process Model of the Interview." *Journal of Applied Psychology* 74(1989):41–60.

Riggio, Ronald E., and Throckmorton, Barbara. "The Relative Effects of Verbal and Nonverbal Behavior, Appearance, and Social Skills on Evaluations Made in Hiring Interview." *Journal of Applied Social Psychology* 18(1988):341–360.

Robertson, Ivan T. "The Validity of Situational Interviews for Administrative Jobs." *Journal of Organizational Behavior* (January 1990):69–80.

Sandwich, P. "Better Meetings for Better Communication." *Training and Development Journal* 46 (January 1992).

Sigband, N. "Meet If You Have To, But Do It Efficiently." *Los Angeles Business Journal* (September 25, 1989).

Simpsen, D. "Meetings that Work." *Training and Development Journal* 43 (December 1989).

Van Holm, B. "Interviewing Techniques." *Journal of Property Management* 56 (July-August 1991).

LEGAL CONSIDERATIONS
EMPLOYEE COMMUNICATION AND THE LAW

The most common audience for managers is the employee audience. The manager's freedom to communicate is limited in personnel matters, conditions and circumstances of employment, and labor relations.

Evolving from civil rights activities of the 1960s, laws and regulations were instituted that directly affect employment practices of many public and private organizations. The government directed its agencies to institute nondiscriminatory hiring, promotion, and retention procedures. It also directed most private firms doing business with the government to do likewise. The following acts contain the central legislation to date in these areas:

- Equal Pay Act 1963
- Civil Rights Act 1964, Title VII
- Age Discrimination Act 1967
- Equal Employment Opportunities Act 1972
- Vocational Rehabilitation Act 1973

By these acts, employers are generally prohibited from discriminating with regard to compensation and other aspects of employment or potential employment on the basis of race, creed, color, sex, national origin, disability, or age. Court interpretations of these acts have extended that list to include sexual practice.

For managers, therefore, it is important in all kinds of employee-related communications to avoid mentioning explicit or implicit consideration of decisions premised on the factors listed here. This prohibition includes handwritten notes, as in the following case. Roger Henry, supervisor of administrative services at Fashion Frames' Midwest office in Evanston, Illinois, knows his company's regulations with regard to discrimination. He also values his frank, honest relationship with his subordinates. When a job announcement at a sister store in New Mexico is circulated among his employees, Ms. Joan Alred, in Accounts Receivable, expresses interest in the position. Henry, though he finds Alred's work record quite satisfactory, passes her over for someone else. In an effort to soothe her disappointment, he makes a serious mistake. He "explains" in terms that are clearly discriminatory:

"As you are married and have children starting school this fall, I didn't recommend you for this position; also, I understand that it could be difficult for your husband to find employment in Albuquerque—but I'm keeping you in mind for an advancement."

Putting the best construction on Henry's words, he was trying to be honest about his evaluation process. He sincerely felt that Joan Alred wouldn't have the time necessary to devote to this new, demanding job.

But his written words, as viewed by the Equal Employment Opportunity Commission, seemed clearly discriminatory. Alred apparently was not being judged on her performance but instead on her sex and circumstances. In such situations, employees frequently sue not only for the position they sought but also for back pay and punitive damages. When written records such as Roger Henry's handwritten note exist, employees usually win their cases.

Labor Communications

It is illegal for employers to threaten employees (e.g., "I'll fire you if you join the union.") Over the long history of labor relations law, the thrust of legislation is that the company (including its agents) may not intimidate employees over how they might vote on establishing a union. The employer does, however, have the right to communicate with employees on the issue. Companies do often ask their managers to intervene when a union tries to organize. But the written and spoken message of the company cannot threaten the individual employee nor offer a benefit for a vote. The company's communications during such periods are governed by strict (and changing) regulation from the National Labor Relations Board.

Interviewing Candidates

In spite of the employer's desire to know as much about potential employees as possible, many interview questions are prohibited by law. For example, the employer cannot explicitly ask, "Do you intend to have children?" "Will you submit a photo with your application?" "What is your religious affiliation?" "Where were your parents born?" These and other questions bearing upon race, religion, political preference, national origin, age, and sexual practice are ruled out of bounds by the Equal Employment Opportunity Commission.

Affirmative Action

Affirmative action plans developed since the Civil Rights Act of 1966 call for (1) reviewing how the firm currently employs women and minorities, (2) comparing the numbers of people in various ethnic and sexual categories in the firm to the numbers available in the recruiting area, (3) establishing goals to correct inequities, (4) developing plans to accomplish the goals, and (5) auditing the flow of applicants and reporting periodically to the government. Communication concerning hiring and promotion of employees, especially where affirmative action is involved, must be done with the utmost care. To blatantly justify hiring an employee simply because of race or sex is as discriminatory as firing an employee on similar grounds. Employees passed over for the position may file reverse discrimination suits in such cases.

The most prominent job discrimination case in recent years is Ford Motor Company's $13 million damage settlement with the Equal Employment Opportunity Commission, which accused Ford of discriminating against minorities and women in hiring and advancement programs. In an investigation that spanned the period 1973 to 1980, the EEOC investigated employee complaints of discrimination. Ford agreed to divide the $13 million among 14,000 people allegedly discriminated against and to spend an additional $10 million to recruit and train minority-group and women workers.

26

COMMUNICATION DURING CRISIS AND CHANGE

As more and more attention is given to conservation, food and drug purity, toxic wastes, and consumer and worker health and safety, we can only look at crisis management as a "growth" industry.

In this rapidly changing world, new products, services, and procedures are announced daily. In many instances they advance our way of life dramatically. Some change modes of transportation, others save or extend lives, others bring new fuels, a few save time, others introduce new methods of leisure, learning, or investing. Sometimes the plans for these changes do not proceed smoothly. Problems arise, expectations are not met, failures occur. In most cases, developers make corrections and adjustments. In others, however, an error impinges, in one way or another, on the lives of thousands. Individuals die, the environment is polluted, the health of many is in danger, and serious problems appear imminent.

DISASTERS AND THE MEDIA RESPONSE

Technology enables the news media to report a crisis rapidly and globally. As a result, companies in crisis can lose credibility and assets overnight.

Whenever disasters occur, news channels communicate the news rapidly to the world. A serious oil spill that occurred at 1 p.m. is known around the world by 4 p.m. An organization that has spent years and millions of dollars building an image of its product or service to reflect quality, dependability, integrity, and excellence may have that image shattered overnight. In the few hours between a consumer's complaint or an event's occurrence, and the print media's headline on page 1, the TV evening news announcement, and the journalist's radio interview, a firm's carefully polished image cracks, crumbles, and may even collapse.

Consider the disasters that have occurred in the past decade:

- Seven people died as a result of alleged product tampering with Tylenol.
- Twenty-one men, women, and children were killed by one man's random gunfire at a McDonald's restaurant.
- Procter & Gamble's Rely tampons were linked to the deaths of several women from toxic shock syndrome.

- Northrup and Hughes Aircraft companies were alleged to have falsified various test results for Department of Defense products.
- A gas leak in a Union Carbide plant in Bhopal, India, caused thousands of deaths and injuries.
- Chrysler Corporation was accused of selling as "new" (with odometers turned back to zero) cars that had been driven by employees and other vehicles that had been damaged in accidents.
- Dow Corning's silicone breast implants caused severe health problems for an untold number of women.
- Perrier's bottled water carried traces of benzene.

The list goes on: Heinz in Great Britain, the Ford Pinto affair, the defective Shiley heart valve, Star-Kist tuna, SmithKline Beckman's cold medicine (Contact), Ashland Oil's ruptured fuel tank.

Companies can successfully manage a crisis by using news media to secure greater exposure, present their side of their story, and apologize and accept responsibility.

In every instance, instant-communication news media presented the facts that were available, which is proper. The public should know about situations that affect them, their environment, their health, and their finances. These are crisis situations and crises are newsworthy. In fact, because crises almost always involve public health, the environment, or the government, the media have an *obligation* to report the events. Not infrequently, however, the headline may be an eye-catching, negative statement (see Figures 26–1 and 26–5).

In situations that have received wide media exposure, the involved company often uses the press, TV, and radio to (1) secure greater exposure, (2) present their side of the story and their perception, and (3) to apologize and promise to do better in the future. Let's look at two examples.

In the AT&T letter shown in Figure 26–2, the president of the company apologizes quickly and completely for inconvenience caused by service disruption to customers. No ifs, ands, and buts appear. "We made a mistake and we will correct it" comes through loud and clear.

The Jack in the Box letter deals with the much more serious issue of tainted food.[1] Three deaths and the illness of more than 450 people occurred as the result of tainted food. In Figure 26–3 the chairman apologizes for the situation and attempts to build goodwill. Because of the potential for costly litigation, the chairman is careful not to indicate the responsibility of his firm. Note the statement, "an outbreak of food-related illness in the Pacific Northwest." It does *not* state, "in Jack in the Box outlets."

Companies should have a crisis management plan in place before disaster strikes.

Organizations that have contributed products, services, and money with care and concern for years should not be ruined in a few days when a problem has been unintentional and is correctable. In such situations, an organization's carefully thought-through crisis management plan comes into operation. That plan's purpose should never be to cover up a flaw that the company was aware of prior to its exposure. A *crisis management plan* should be designed to bring thoughtful appraisal and reasoned judgment to all parties concerned with a problem so that no one is penalized beyond what is reasonable as the result of an honest error. An organization may not be able to avoid losing millions of dollars as a result of outside forces (such as product tampering). But it does not have to handle a crisis (for which it may not be responsible) so inadequately as to completely lose customer confidence and as a result find itself in a position from which it cannot recover.[2]

FIGURE 26–1   The Perrier Promise[1]

The Promise.

The problem has been fixed.

It was never a health or safety problem. But for a product known for purity, it was definitely a mistake.

It has been identified and corrected.

The spring water itself was never at issue. It's still as pure as it has been for thousands of years.

But to insure the good name of Perrier, we have recalled all of the product currently in the market. Future bottles will carry the "nouvelle production" labels pictured below. This will be your assurance of quality.

Unfortunately for all of our loyal customers we have created a bigger problem. We won't be able to totally resupply the country for some time. In some areas, maybe even several months.

But we make you this promise: we'll be back as soon as we possibly can. If you have any questions, call us toll-free at 1-800-937-2002.

The Proof.

The Perrier you've always loved. Same pure spring water. Same green bottle. Coming soon to the same restaurants, hotels and grocery stores you've always found us in before.

Perrier. Worth waiting for.

Source: The Perrier Group of America, Inc.

FIGURE 26–2 Crisis Communication That Accepts Responsibility[2]

Robert E. Allen
Chairman of the Board

550 Madison Avenue
New York, NY 10022
212 644-1000

Dear AT&T Customer:

AT&T had a major service disruption last Monday. We didn't live up to our own standards of quality, and we didn't live up to yours.

It's as simple as that. And that's not acceptable to us. Or to you.

Once we discovered the problem, we responded within minutes with every resource at our disposal. By late evening, normal service was restored. Ironically, the problem resulted from a glitch in software designed to provide back-up in a new signaling system we were installing to bring even greater reliability to our network. It has now been fixed.

We understand how much people have come to depend upon AT&T service, so our AT&T Bell Laboratories scientists and our network engineers are doing everything possible to guard against a recurrence.

We know there's no way to make up for the inconvenience this problem may have caused you. But in an effort to underscore how much we value our relationship with you, we've filed with the FCC to offer a special day of calling discounts on Valentine's Day, Wednesday, February 14.

> Discounts all-day for residence and business customers on most out-of-state calls made on the AT&T public network throughout the U.S., and on international calls to all 158 direct-dial countries.

We've also extended the provisions of our AT&T 800 Assurance Policy to cover this extraordinary situation.

For more than 100 years, we've built our reputation on superior quality, reliability and technological innovation. Our goal is to ensure that you <u>always</u> regard us that way.

Sincerely,

R.E. Allen
Chairman

An immediate apology appeals to the public's goodwill.

A convincing explanation satisfies the public's need to know.

Offering restitution maintains customer loyalty.

Source: *Los Angeles Times*, January 19, 1990.

FIGURE 26–3 Crisis Communication That Carefully Avoids Accepting Legal Liability[3]

9330 Balboa Avenue
San Diego, CA 92132-1516
Mailing Address: P.O. Box 783
San Diego, CA 92112-4126

A Message from the Chairman of JACK IN THE BOX

As you may know, there has recently been an outbreak of food-related illness in the Pacific Northwest. All of us at JACK IN THE BOX extend our prayers for a complete and speedy recovery to everyone who has experienced this illness.

Company responsibility can be acknowledged tactfully.

Since we first learned of the problem, we have taken several steps.

We immediately recalled all hamburger meat suspected of contamination and we are no longer having hamburger meat processed by our former meat supplier.

We increased our hamburger cooking times to levels above state and federal standards. In addition, the company has retrained all food preparation staff to ensure that all new and existing cooking procedures are followed.

Enumerating specific steps the company has taken to correct the problem regains trust.

At the same time, we have increased our testing procedures on all hamburger meat now being processed so that we will perform seven separate quality control checks before it ever gets to our restaurants.

We are confident that all of the food we are serving in our restaurants is safe and wholesome. JACK IN THE BOX has been a part of this community for many years, and we will do everything in our power to keep your trust.

If you have any questions, please call toll free (800) 695-8225.

Jack Goodall
Chairman
JACK IN THE BOX

Source: Los Angeles Times, February 7, 1993.

PLANNING FOR CRISIS MANAGEMENT

A recent newspaper article reported that Mary Woodell, director of crisis management and risk communications at Arthur D. Little, identified the following problems that many companies encounter when a crisis arises:[4]

Paralysis
Lack of clear leadership
Lack of information
Strained relations between headquarters and crisis site
Strained relations among crisis management team members
Insufficient infrastructure to handle crisis
Bunker mentality
Denial
Inflexibility

Because of these problems, every organization needs a concrete, workable plan in place to deal with a crisis.

A crisis plan should not be set down in a 200-page policy manual. There is no time for such depth. Nevertheless, the plan should be clear and at a minimum it should take these actions:

- Preassign responsibilities at three levels: policy, strategy, and execution.
- House decision makers for those three areas in one location for rapid and face-to-face interaction.
- Designate specific organization spokespeople. No other personnel should respond to the media.
- Assign specific roles to only a few executive-level personnel.
- Put specific plans and policies in place for several potential crisis instances.
- Keep adequate funds in reserve for immediate release to handle potential crisis situations.

A firm can respond more quickly to a crisis if it already has a broad crisis-management plan in place. The plan itself should be based on input from senior staff members and should be familiar to all management personnel. Plans will differ widely in depth and length according to the size of the company (50 employees v. 50,000), level of risk to the industry (commercial aviation vs. manufacturing of jeans), and location (major urban center vs. rural area).

An example of a crisis communication plan is illustrated in Figure 26–4. Although designed for a school district, it reflects elements that should be included in all plans.

Perhaps the best reason for crisis planning is to minimize the risk of a change in the organization's image. A second reason is simply "the times." Instant communication worldwide means any incident—major or minor—can become a crisis, instantly known everywhere. In contrast, 75 years ago the same incident may have been classified as a local tragedy or accident.

COPING WITH THE MEDIA

With the increase in government regulations, more vocal consumer and activist groups, and a more inquiring radio, TV, and press, chief executive officers and

FIGURE 26-4   Crisis Communication Plan[5]

Westside Community Schools
Omaha, Nebraska

CRISIS COMMUNICATIONS PLAN
Guidelines for News Media Relations in Emergency Situations

This plan is intended to supplement other administrative procedures and guidelines for dealing with emergency situations. It should be reviewed on an annual basis, and should be distributed to all members of the District who could be affected.

Emergency Situations

It is always to the District's advantage to cooperate with news media, but never more so than during a crisis situation. Our schools are always open to public scrutiny, and that includes the media. But not all news is good news. But no news often has a far more negative effect on the public, so we will try to provide information in a timely fashion at all times. This plan is intended to be used in situations which, because of their scope or seriousness, become the focus of much media attention. The 1975 tornado is a case in point. The actual implementation of the plan should be determined by the size and nature of the emergency.

A crisis management plan . . . clearly defines what constitutes an emergency.

Situations can include:

- Serious accidents involving students or staff

- Acts of violence involving staff or students and/or non-district persons

- Natural disasters striking any district property

- Fires, explosions

- Strikes

Before an Emergency

- Designate an Emergency Communications Coordinator (ECC) and an alternate ECC. The Coordinator should not be directly involved in efforts to resolve the emergency situation itself, e.g., the superintendent, but should be someone who is familiar with working with the news media on a regular basis. (In most situations, the Director of Communications may be designated.) A back-up person should be selected to act when the ECC is unavailable. Technical or other experts may be designated as spokespersons as well. *All employees should know that the ECC, alternate, and designates are the only employees authorized to speak with the media.*

. . . prepares for an emergency by establishing procedures that will guide the staff's actions throughout the crisis.

Source: Laurence Barton, *Crisis in Organizations: Managing and Communicating in the Heat of Chaos* (Cincinnati: South Western Publishing Co., 1993).

- Members of the EC Team will hold organizational and review meetings.
- Select one primary and one or two secondary locations to be emergency newsrooms (point of assembly for reporters), apart from the area designed for dealing with the crisis itself. The room(s) designated should be able to accommodate news conferences, with multiple telephones, electrical outlets and typewriters, and even refreshments. (The Board Rooms of the ABC Building are obvious first choices. Other locations should be designated in the event that those rooms are made unaccessible by the emergency.)
- News media identification badges should be made available for distribution by the ECC.
- A brief version of the plan should be distributed to all area news media.

During an Emergency
- The emergency should be reported at once to the superintendent who will inform the ECC, who will activate the plan. The ECC will inform the other members of the team of the nature of the emergency. The superintendent will notify the Board of Education members and keep them up-to-date on a timely basis (they may be sought out for interviews).

. . . tells what to do while the emergency is occurring.

- Employees should refer all news media inquiries to the ECC. Reporters should be directed to the Emergency Newsroom. Reports will be issued at the newsroom. Interviews will be arranged and updates gathered by the ECC and EC team.
- All members of the team should be helpful and courteous at all times to the news media, but should refer all questions to the ECC. Depending on the situation, persons other than the ECC (e.g., the principal of the school where the emergency occurred) may be designated as spokespersons, and should then respond to all questions to the best of their ability. Answer honestly, but do not speculate or guess. If you don't know, say so . . .then get the answer as soon as possible. Be prompt in your dealings with the media; they have pressing deadlines. Always call the media back when you say you will, usually immediately after you have gathered the facts. Don't use educational jargon. Do not speak "off the record." Do not ask to see the story before it is used. Always inform the ECC or Communications Department when you have talked with a reporter. This eliminates possible contradictory statements. Do not give "exclusives" to members of the media. All should have an equal chance for gathering information, which is a key reason for having a media center and news conferences.

- The media should be provided with the following information:
  Facts—no speculation, and no cover-ups. In laymen's terms, tell the key facts who, what, when, where, why, and how:
  - What happened? When? And Where?
  - How and Why did it happen? (Do not speculate if you don't know; say so.)
  - Who was involved?
    Provide names only after next of kin have been notified of death or injury, and only according to the District's other policy on releasing confidential information.
  - Extent and nature of injuries, property damage (no dollar amounts), continuing damage, and insurance coverage.

- Photographers (and others) should not be allowed at the scene if there is still danger in the area, but should be allowed in when the immediate danger has passed. They should be provided with stills of the facilities for the Crisis Plan Preparedness file.

- Employees should be informed of the details of the situation as soon as possible, by the fastest means possible.

- Key community and political leaders should also be informed as soon as possible on an individual basis by designated personnel if the situation is serious enough to warrant it.

After the Emergency

- If the situation warrants it, make arrangements for the media to be personally escorted to the site.

- Arrange for other photographs if confidentiality prevents photographing the scene or people.

- Release to the news media, as soon as possible, company decisions relating to the incident, whenever it is deemed necessary. Where appropriate, express gratitude to the community, police and fire departments, emergency crews, and employees for their help. This places a positive ending on what could have been a negative story.

- The ECC or delegate should follow up by compiling a file of clippings and a summary of how the Crisis Plan operated during the emergency, and what might improve the Plan. This should be accomplished within two weeks, while the information is fresh.

. . . tells what to do after the emergency has ended.

As company spokespeople, managers must communicate cautiously to protect company interests while satisfying the public's right to know.

managers are required to speak more freely and more frankly when involved in sensitive issues than they did just 10 to 15 years ago. Whether modern managers like it or not, they have become corporate spokespeople. A carelessly conducted press conference can result in "bad press" and cost the company millions in loss of goodwill and reputation. An angry retort to a reporter, a careless statement that implies possible company negligence, or a comment that can be used as backup for "unlawful termination" may all be read back later in a court of law. Given regulations by the dozen, court awards running into astronomical amounts, and a society involved in thousands of lawsuits, executives must be very careful with their communications. Even the timeliness of their communications will be scrutinized. For example, read about the problems Dow Corning caused itself by delaying disclosure of negative information (Figure 26–5).

What can management do to achieve the best possible return when appearing before representatives of the media and special-interest groups in sensitive and controversial situations? The first step is to recognize the obligation *they* have to make the results of the interview as unbiased and as factual as possible. Managers should view appearing before an investigative group as an opportunity to build the reputation of the organization, rather than an adversarial situation to be feared.

ESTABLISH POLICIES OF COMMUNICATION

Before we even discuss what to say and how to say it, we must recognize the need for a company policy on communication to various publics concerning sensitive issues. Such a policy must be drawn up, published, and distributed to company managers. It should list company rules on precisely who in the company is permitted to talk to outside organizations or individuals regarding catastrophic, sensitive, and unusual or highly negative situations.

Preestablished communication policies indicate who should talk on the company's behalf, what should be said, and to whom.

Guidelines should be developed about what may be said and to whom and the legal implications involved in explaining the accidental death or injury of an employee or visitor. The policy should also include statements on terminations, layoffs, plant closures, labor problems, product quality, consumer complaints, environmental issues, and so forth. Of course, every contingency cannot be noted. But everyone in the organization should clearly understand that only designated people may respond in critical situations. When everyone companywide knows this, the danger of an unauthorized employee responding to an inquiring reporter—and saying the wrong thing—is diminished.

PREPARE: THE KEY TO WINNING

As a spokesperson prepare specific answers, avoid words that convey negative feelings, and stress words that convey the company's positive, caring attitude.

In an interview itself, whether it is with print media, radio, television, special interest groups, or employee groups, preparation is the key. As company spokesperson, you must prepare answers to almost every possible question. A wise plan involves preparing specific answers to be sure that the words come out correctly. Rather than stating, "We haven't had any serious accidents in five years . . ." it is better to say, "Our safety record in the industry is outstanding; as a matter of fact, last year we received an award . . ."

In your preparation, include recognition of terms and phrases to be avoided:

Negligence
Death
Accidents
Discrimination

FIGURE 26–5   Slow Disclosure Can Damage a Company's Image[6]

Dow Corning: Harsh Lesson in Crisis Management

To Dow Corning, a $1.8-billion-a-year high-tech corporation, breast implants are a tiny part of its business—a money loser. Even before the current controversy over their safety, the product was something of an embarrassment to scientists and managers who develop the space-age silicone materials for the aerospace and electronics industries that make up the bulk of the company's business.

Now, some corporate ethicists and public relations specialists say, Dow Corning's failure to move quickly to disclose—and take responsibility for—problems with implants threatens the health of the entire company, and is causing headaches for its huge parents, Dow Chemical and Corning Inc.

These experts say they are surprised Dow Corning did not take heed of the lessons learned by other major corporations that have faced serious problems with their products or business practices.

Circumstances can vary widely, and companies must be able to adjust their public response to a crisis, depending on the nature of the problem and the potential long-term repercussions for shareholders and the public.

Still, most experts interviewed Tuesday agreed that the basic lesson usually is the same. The earlier bad news is revealed, the better. While a company will naturally want to avoid legal liability by admitting a problem with one of its products, trying to keep it secret usually doesn't work.

Consultants in crisis managements say full disclosure, combined with a commitment to put things right, most often will help save a company's reputation. In addition, such a posture may lower the size of punitive damages juries are willing to award and help save a company's bottom line.

What seems to ratchet up punitive jury awards is not so much a defective product as a perception that a company was not forthcoming about a problem, experts say. "The smartest thing is to come out as quickly as possible with the information," said Henry Cheeseman, clinical professor of business law at the USC Graduate School of Management. "It's a circle: Once you haven't disclosed the problem for a while, then by human nature you won't disclose it until you have to. But if it comes out in a trial you knew something and did not warn people, then you're in big trouble."

Dow Corning was badly hurt by its release of documents Monday showing that it has known for 20 years that some silicone gel would seep out of the implants' envelopes, but officials did not believe that the leakage would cause health problems.

But the company's replacement of its chief executive with Keith R. McKennon, who was widely praised for his handling of Dow Chemical's problems with Agent Orange, the defoliant associated with serious health problems in Vietnam veterans, reassured many observers.

McKennon on Tuesday set a new empathetic tone by saying that his "overriding responsibility is to the women using silicone" implants. He added that his chief concern is not "damage control" for the company.

(Article continued but not reproduced here.)

Source: "Dow Corning: Harsh Lessons in Crisis Management" by Susan Moffat, February 12, 1992. Copyright, 1992, *Los Angeles Times*. Reprinted by permission.

Fired
Catastrophe
Layoffs
Probably could happen . . .

Similarly, recognize those that should be stressed:

Safety
Care
Concern
Employment opportunities
Long record of excellent relations
Equal opportunities
Satisfactory

You can also prepare by requesting that media representatives give you a list of questions before your meeting. Although some journalists may tend not to do so, there are situations in which this request may work.

As a spokesperson preparing answers to possible questions, make every effort to secure strong substantiating information, dates, facts, and statistics. These all give authority and credence to your answers. Keep such data at hand. Don't hesitate to refer to a few note cards that contain facts, figures, and numbers.

APPRECIATE YOUR RELATIONSHIP WITH THE INTERVIEWER

Showing respect for the interviewer and for the public's right to know can win the support of the people who will question you as the crisis unfolds.

If possible, learn the name and identify of the interviewer (e.g., whether he or she is a media person or a special-interest group representative). Use the individual's last name with respect and sincerity. If he or she addresses you as "Mr., Ms.," or "Miss," follow suit and use the interviewer's last name.

Interviewers have a job to do. And, with rare exceptions, they are trying to do it honestly. If you remember this, you will welcome the media and set the tone for an honest and open exchange. Media representatives are professionals who want to do a professional job. They represent the public and feel the public has a right to know. Certainly, no one can argue with that. Make your replies reflect your *appreciation* of the public's point of view. You may disagree with that point of view or consider it unacceptable under the circumstances, but you must begin by appreciating it.

LEARN HOW TO HANDLE QUESTIONS

Spokespeople who field questions professionally and respond accurately protect company interests.

How well you handle questions will usually determine how effectively you come through the interview. Here are six critical concepts to keep in mind:

1. Welcome the interviewer, reporter, or group.
2. Answer questions concisely and directly. Don't get involved in a discussion that may take you far afield or even into quicksand. Simply reply and stop.
3. Never repeat an incorrect statement made by the reporter. You may be quoted, and if your statement is taken out of context, it will appear that you accept or agree with the misstatement. A wiser policy is simply to say:

That is incorrect. The precise situation is this: . . .

4. Have facts, data, figures readily at hand, if possible, to lend weight to your answers. Your interviewer will appreciate a reply based on proof. It makes strong copy and places you in a position of authority.

5. Learn how to *bridge*—a technique of taking a question, answering it, and then moving to a comment, usually related to the topic, which reflects credit on your firm.

> *Yes, I imagine that is a possibility in handling toxic wastes. However, in the ten years our firm has been involved with the XYZ product, I am happy to state that we have been successful in . . .*
>
> *It is also important to note that at our St. Louis facility, 98 percent of our workforce rated company safety programs as either "excellent" or "superior." As a matter of fact, our firm received the Railroad Association's award for "Outstanding Safety Measures" last year and for the three previous years.*

6. Turn a negative into a positive. If an interviewer phrases a question or a statement negatively, don't pick up on it or repeat it. Answer it, but rephrase it or state your reference to it positively.

> **QUESTION:**
> *Isn't it possible that some employees could be killed or seriously injured in a situation like that?*
>
> **ANSWER:**
> *I really can't speak to that. Our safety experience is outstanding. Not one of our employees at this facility has ever been involved in a reportable accident in the past 12 months. This is surely due to the attention given to safety procedures and concern for employee welfare in our organization.*
>
> **QUESTION:**
> *Although your bank has some thirty-five vice presidents, how do you explain the fact that only 5 are women?*
>
> **ANSWER:**
> *All appointments to vice president are made on the basis of board selection and an examination. Every opening is posted and any employee of the appropriate grade is eligible to apply.*
>
> *In the past three years, we have had nine openings for vice present. Ten women took the examination and two were appointed. In the same period, thirty men took the examination and seven were appointed. Thus 20 percent of the women and 23 percent of the men taking the exam were appointed. I would say that we had a similar level of treatment and equality in both cases, wouldn't you?*

CONSIDER NONVERBAL ASPECTS OF THE INTERVIEW

Nonverbal communication is a highly important area, especially if you are being taped for a television broadcast or you are appearing on live television. Your attire is important, however, whether or not you are being videotaped. Those present at the interview will certainly be influenced by your dress. All you need do is to use common sense. For men, a dark suit, calf-length socks, light blue or white shirt, and a conservative tie should be worn. For women, a conservative suit with a plain white blouse, or a tailored dark-hued dress, is appropriate.

When communicating about the crisis, dress to reflect the seriousness of the situation.

Think ahead of time about what gestures will best convey the image for which you are striving. If you appear before a group, either stand behind a rostrum or be seated behind a table. Choose whatever feels most comfortable to you. Some speakers feel that a standing position, offering a downward view of a seated audience, gives them a certain psychological advantage. Others prefer to sit with notes carefully arranged in front of them on a table top or on a podium. Regardless of the method, *you* should make the selection. It is your show, and you have the right to call the shots. If you are appearing on live television, the choice should still be yours as to how, where, and in which surroundings or situation you wish to be photographed or taped.

Maintain eye contact with the individual who asked the question.

Whether you appear "live" on camera or in front of a group, be careful of your eye contact, hand and body gestures, and facial expressions. Maintain direct eye contact with the individual who asked the question. Look for response in his or her eyes or face and react appropriately. When presenting a prepared statement to a group, avoid reading it. Use notes and look directly at people in the group who are to your left, right, and straight ahead. Don't look at areas; select people and look directly at them. If you are aware of the influential members of the group, address your remarks directly to them.

Avoid making nervous gestures.

Pay attention to your hand and body gestures to avoid conveying nervousness or defensiveness. Don't drum on the table or podium, inch nervously back and forth in your seat, or slouch defensively or discourteously in your chair.

Maintain positive, sincere facial expressions.

Finally, and perhaps most importantly, be conscious of your facial expressions. The value of a smile or a pleasant expression can't be overestimated. A smile, sincerely made at an appropriate moment, can be invaluable in conveying honesty and believability.

Speak with your audience in a helpful, composed manner.

Make the audience feel you're speaking *with* them, not *at* them. Use your head and face to show agreement with a statement made. Let your features reflect "that's a good question; I'm glad you asked it." Try not to exhibit anger, irritation, fear, or shock. The best way to avoid such expressions is to maintain a frame of mind of desiring to work with those who are interviewing you.

Maintain control

Controlling your emotions helps you control the information and the perceptions that the media report to the public.

Maintaining control can sometimes make or break you in an interview. Remember, in the interview situation, *you* are in charge; *you* can accept a question or pass on it; *you* can answer or not answer; *you* can make the points *you* wish to make. Respond with firmness, courtesy, tact, and, when possible, a smile. Never, never get angry, nasty, sarcastic or "lose your cool." You are in control; maintain that control in a firm, participative, cooperative, democratic manner.

Several specific ground rules will assist you in maintaining control:

Use the best space and position. Do not permit yourself to be interviewed or videotaped in the middle of a noisy crowd, on a busy factory floor, or surrounded by a crowd of reporters, bystanders, or employees (unless you feel that is to your advantage).

You select the interview site. If you feel more comfortable standing behind a rostrum with the interviewers seated in front of you, request that arrangement. If you feel more comfortable sitting behind a table or desk, with or without a small, table top podium, specify that arrangement. If you prefer to have the interview take place in your office or in the company conference room, schedule the discussion for that site.

Make vital statements. Because you are in charge, don't hesitate to state what you feel must be said. This can be an opening statement or an add-on to one of your answers. Don't feel constrained to simply answer questions. You have a vital point to make or an issue to address. Make that statement, and if an interviewer breaks in on you, override the interruption and complete your comment.

Choose questions and questioners. In many cases you will be aware of who the professional journalists in the group are or the reasonable individuals among the special interest representatives. Call on those people for questions. You will probably also be aware of the rabble-rousers. Ignore them if possible.

Keep in mind that you don't have to recognize the individual who shouts loudest or jumps up most vigorously. Of course, such a person may attract the most attention, but you can always say, "Thank you. I know you have an important question, but there were two hands on this side of the room that I have yet to call on. I'll try to get to you in a minute."

Use time advantageously. You may wish to announce at the beginning of the interview that, "Because of meetings (other obligations, the need to work on this problem, etc.), I will take just 15 minutes at this time to answer your questions." Keep in mind that if it is not convenient for you to be interviewed "now" (because you are not prepared, aren't completely familiar with all necessary details, lack vital statistics or data, etc.), there is no reason for you not to say, "I will be happy to meet with you at 3 p.m. today." You need not give an answer at the convenience of the interviewer. Granted, time is vital to the media, but be wary of answering too quickly in a highly sensitive situation where all the facts may not be at your disposal.

In addition, you should control the length of an interview. If you feel you have done your part and nothing further may be gained (or an advantage may be lost) by fielding more questions, call a halt to the session. Remember to add a courteous, "Thank you for attending," or "I'll be happy to meet with you again if you feel that would be valuable."

Adopt a positive attitude. Your mental approach to the interview can also prove to be an important factor in handling the session successfully. Remember, you are in charge; you are in control; and you are honest. If you are in a position to accept these three statements in what you say (or what you don't say), you will have the advantage.

Go into the interview with a cooperative attitude and the knowledge that you have the option of answering those questions you wish to answer and the authority to make the statements you wish to make. When you walk in and face your questioners, simply say to yourself, "I am in charge; I am in control."

Make a strong closing. Your opening and closing statements can often be the most critical ones. Naturally, you will prepare the opening to set the stage to your best advantage. But remember that the closing can be equally important.

Distill vital points in a strong closing statement. Make it clear that what you said was indeed a closing statement. Don't let your ideas be diluted by further questions or digressions. After you finish your statement, the interview should end.

COMMUNICATING TO EMPLOYEES IN TIMES OF CRISIS

In a crisis, quickly communicating facts to employees preserves morale and loyalty.

The focus of this chapter has been on the timely and effective communication with external groups, such as the media, community and activist groups, unions, and others, following a crisis. However, there are other important groups, which may be designated as "internal," with whom communication is just as necessary.

Employees should be told as quickly as possible about the details of a crisis. Almost nothing undercuts morale among employees more than learning of a serious company event from a neighbor or a newspaper article. When employees feel they are the last to know, their trust and loyalty, even though previously carefully nurtured, will drop significantly. Another result of lack of communication is their heightened curiosity and probably anxiety. A crisis is fertile ground for the grapevine to grow—sometimes with extremely harmful results. Upper management should convey to employees, in a timely manner, at least as much as is given to external groups. These statements should be followed with the promise to convey more "as soon as further details are available."

The communication to employees should be as factual as possible and transmitted at the same time or earlier than that relayed to the media. If additional details can be given to the employees without doing harm to the organization, that should be done also.

Share facts with clients and others who have professional ties to the company.

Others who need to receive the same level of information as employees are steady suppliers and vendors. Creditors should also be informed as well as professionals and groups serving the company: consultants, financing agencies, insurers (health, liability, and others), and accounting and advertising firms working with the organization.

Give information to shareholders in a timely manner to maintain their trust.

Another large group of stakeholders are the shareholders. Some debate exists about how quickly shareholders should be informed. Some analysts believe that if 20,000 letters are sent to shareholders on the day of the event (or immediately after), the organization's stock price may drop precipitously as a result of a selling "run." Others feel quite the opposite. Shareholders are intelligent and will learn of the event quickly under any conditions. Consider informing them by mail, if the event is serious enough, on the day the information is given to the media.

ACTING MEANS OVERCOMING THE CRISIS

By accepting responsibility and taking corrective action, companies can almost always overcome a crisis.

Nothing we have said in this chapter should be construed as attempting to "win" a bad situation when the fault is certainly the organization's. In every instance where an organization has responded immediately and accepted responsibility, that firm has emerged a winner. Johnson & Johnson immediately pulled Tylenol off the shelf, and recovered; its sales today are stronger than ever. Perrier did the same with thousands of its bottles of water, and the results were again positive. Ashland Oil immediately accepted blame for a tank rupture and recovered. In every case where an immediate, truthful answer was given, the response from the public was favorable.

Being interviewed on a sensitive or controversial issue or a crisis may not be the most enjoyable way for a company spokesperson to spend a morning. On the other hand, as that spokesperson, you may well turn the session into an advantage for you and your organization. As is true of any venture, being prepared and playing the game professionally are vital factors in achieving your goals.

WRITING AND SPEAKING EXERCISES

1. Visit five corporations and interview members of top management in each. Determine, through a carefully formulated questionnaire, what steps or policies they have for handling the media in a crisis should such action be necessary. Report on your findings.

2. Determine in your above interviews if any of the firms have been involved in a crisis. If so, what action was taken, and what were the results?

3. Watch a television interview of a prominent individual being questioned by a skilled interviewer. What did the interviewee do right or wrong? How could he or she have improved his or her position?

4. Design a policy statement that you feel leading newspapers and TV networks should issue to personnel to ensure equitable and responsible interviewing of news subjects.

5. Collect five manuals on handling crises issued by five different corporations. Report to your class, and explain the manuals' distribution (who in the organization receives them) and their individual strong and weak points.

6. Break into groups of ten. Each person should assume he or she is a CEO of an organization. Select one topic from among the six listed below, and prepare and make a four- to five-minute statement. Then accept questions from the other nine individuals. These nine will play the role of media representatives (such as reporters and newscasters) or members of a special-interest group concerned with such issues as the environment, the rights of minority groups, religious groups, and toxic wastes. The "CEO" and the "reporters" should play their roles as authentically as possible according to real-life situations. At the conclusion of each exercise, hold a five-minute debriefing to explain to the "CEO" what he or she did correctly and what could be improved and how.

   - One of your firm's trucks badly injured a 6-year-old in a school zone just two hours ago. The driver involved has an excellent record and maintains that the youngster unexpectedly dashed into the street after a ball. Apparently, there are witnesses who have stated that the truck was exceeding the speed limit (15 mph) by at least 20 mph. Unfortunately, one of your trucks was involved in a similar situation (in the same school zone) five years ago. At that time, damages of $100,000 were levied against your firm.

   - The League of African-American Citizens has voiced its concern over the fact that among 15 company officers and 55 managers there are only two African-Americans. Why? Is this blatant discrimination?

   - Fred Kochinsky, one of your vice presidents, just resigned. There has been some question concerning the way he handled company funds and the possible misappropriation of significant amounts. However, the company has not brought legal charges against Mr. Kochinsky. Interestingly enough, Mr. Kochinsky is also a member of the city council. This group must act frequently on your company's requests for zoning variations, change in ordinances, and so on. Is there a connection?

- The special-interest group "Equity for Women" is concerned. Your firm professes to be an equal opportunity employer with a policy of promotion from within among present employees, but EFW doesn't agree. Although your firm has 145 individuals in Grade 4 and up (department head and higher), only 2 women have been promoted to Grade 4 as contrasted to 16 men in the last 12 months. Why?

- Your firm has manufactured dry cereals for almost 90 years. Yesterday, a child choked to death on a foreign object, which the family claims was ingested as the child ate one of your cereals. "The object was definitely in the box of cereal and that is what caused her death," the mother told the press. All of your products go through two careful checks before packaging to eliminate all foreign objects. At this time, you have no other information. Talk to the reporters who want to know precisely what happened and have asked this question: "Why is your firm permitting dangerous items to get into your products?"

- Determine your own topic. Explain it briefly to your group and then make a four- to five-minute presentation.

7. If employees are aware a disturbing situation has taken place in relationship to the organization for which they work, but no official explanation has been given to them, what is likely to occur?

8. In the case in question 7, what is likely to occur if the employees read about the incident in their local papers, but they still have received no explanation from management?

9. Examine the Jack in the Box letter (Figure 26–3). Although the letter could have easily been placed in a quarter-page space, the firm purchased a full newspaper page. Do you think this decision was a wise expenditure of company funds? Explain.

SUGGESTED RESOURCES

Barton, L. *Crisis in Organizations: Managing and Communicating in the Heat of Chaos.* Cincinnati: South-Western Publishing Co., 1993.

Braverman, M. "Can Firms Afford Not to Have Crisis Intervention?" *Boston Business Journal* (January 29, 1990).

Fisher, L., and Briggs, W. "Communicating with Employees during a Time of Tragedy." *Communication World* 32 (February 1989).

Lamkin, L., and Carmain, F. "Crisis Communication at Georgia Power." *Personnel Journal* 70 (January 1991).

Light, L. "Killing a Rumor Before It Kills a Company." *Business Week* (December 24, 1990).

Lipman, J. "Sudafed Maker Faulted for Failing to Follow Through After Recall." *The Wall Street Journal* March 11, 1991.

Saunders, M. "Eastern's Employee Communication Crisis: A Case Study." *Public Relations Review* 14 (Summer 1988).

Schultz, D. "Toxic Chemical Disclosure." *Public Relations Journal* (January 1989).

Taylor, A. "CEO's in the Slammer or What To Do While Your Boss Does Time." *Communication World* 7 (May-June 1990).

Toyne, P. "Communicating the Crisis." *Communication World* 8 (February 1991).

Wisenbilt, J. "Crisis Management Planning among U.S. Corporations: Empirical Evidence and Proposed Framework." *Advanced Management Journal* 35 (Spring 1989).

ENDNOTES

1. "Child Dies from Bacteria; Parents Had Voiced an Appeal to Clinton," *Los Angeles Times*, February 21, 1993.
2. See these cases at the end of this book: "Bill Webster's Ethical Dilemma" and "Was This Really Fraud?"
3. *Los Angeles Times*, July 10, 1991.
4. Phillip Toyne, "Communicating the Crisis," *Communication World* 8 (February 1991):13.
5. Laurence Barton, Crisis in Organizations. *Managing and Communicating in the Heat of Chaos* (Cincinnati: South-Western Publishing Col, 1993).
6. Susan Moffat, *Los Angeles Times*, February 12, 1992.
7. The Perrier Group of America, Inc.
8. *Los Angeles Times*, January 19, 1990.
9. *Los Angeles Times*, February 7, 1993.

CASES FOR DISCUSSION

1. THE MARK TELLER CASE
2. THE JIM CANTONELLI CASE
3. HOSTILE TAKEOVER
4. BROOKS-MARTINEZ CASE
5. WHEN EAST DOESN'T MEET WEST
6. THE SUN FRESH CASE
7. THE BARNEY BURTON CASE
8. BUT TALKING ISN'T WORKING
9. WHOSE PERCEPTION IS CORRECT?
10. BILL WEBSTER'S ETHICAL DILEMMA
11. WAS THIS REALLY FRAUD?

The cases in this section have been adapted from real-life situations, although the names are fictitious. As you read the cases, you will likely say, "I saw a similar situation when I worked at the Blank Company three years ago."

The cases reflect interpersonal and organizational communication situations. In some instances, potential problems are just beginning to emerge; in other situations, problems are in sharp focus.

One of the major objectives of studying these cases is to improve your abilities to analyze, solve problems, and make decisions. What do *you* see as the problem in the case as compared to your colleague's perception? What action do you suggest? How would you handle the interview? the report? the directive?

Don't look for a "textbook" solution. In most instances, no one right answer exists, because the cases are very brief, and many variables (the people, companies, situations, economic conditions, and so forth) are not given. The value is not in finding one answer, but in analyzing and recognizing that your colleagues may perceive the situation very differently from the way you do.

Keep in mind there may be more than one way to solve a problem. And it is quite possible that the "correct" way may not be yours. Try to develop abilities for careful analysis, critical thinking, problem solving, and an appreciation for different perceptions, so that you can complete your decision making logically.

HOW TO USE THE CASES

Each case has the potential for an almost infinite number of communication exercises. You may decide to design some of your own. The following sections list several possibilities:

GROUP ANALYSIS AND DISCUSSION

Groups of four to five people may wish to analyze and discuss the case. Each group selects a spokesperson who tells the other groups the important points identified and the solutions reached by his or her group members.

Each paragraph in the cases is numbered to facilitate reference and identification in group discussions.

WRITTEN EXERCISES

Your instructor or group leader may request:

> Reports
> Letters
> Memos
> Proposals
> Written case analyses
> Summaries

Any one of these can be drawn from the case. Individuals named in the case may address letters or memos to each other, request a report, or issue a proposal.

ORAL EXERCISES

Your instructor or group leader may request that you and one or more of your colleagues hold an interview or meeting or give an oral report. In these situations you will probably be asked to participate in a role-playing situation and to assume the identity of someone described in a case.

When the exercise has been concluded, an unbiased individual(s) should give you constructive feedback on the content and delivery of your presentation. In the case of interview role plays, you probably should ask one person to act as an "observer." (Your instructor has an Observer Evaluation Checklist.)

In all situations, whether you are holding a discussion, conducting an interview, or writing a report, assume the case is a real-life incident and you are the involved manager or employee.

CASE 1

THE MARK TELLER CASE

1. Mark Teller has been with the Pembroke Company for nine months, but he hasn't done as well as you expected. Prior to coming to Pembroke, he had a successful career as a sales representative for three different firms, one in recreational and school equipment, one in commercial real estate, and one in printing.

2. He is 36 years old, married for the second time (now separated), and evidently likes to live well. He is a bit overweight, jovial, and apparently always in good spirits. He is well liked by his fellow workers, usually insists on picking up the tab, and is always good for a lively joke.

3. Mark has participated in several sales-training programs, both on his own and under company sponsorship. He invariably takes a very active part, knows the answers, and contributes materially to the success of such meetings. He has a fine grasp of sales principles, reads extensively in the professional sales journals, and has undoubtedly retained much of what he learned about marketing at the University of Michigan, which he attended for almost three years.

4. Despite all of this, the sales in his territory have been declining—not seriously, but steadily. This worries you for two reasons: (1) His areas have excellent potential, and sales should be twice what he now has because of a boom in industrial and retail business firms. (2) Mark's record is far less than you expected. Of course, this is a blow to your own ego, for you confidently told your partner that, in your judgment, Teller was a "real comer." This statement is now beginning to bounce back on you.

5. In an effort to find some answers, you have gone out on the road with Mark on several occasions. He is always greeted by industrial accounts as a long-lost brother. There is much good-natured ribbing, back slapping, and coffee drinking. Mark's supply of jokes is inexhaustible, and his faculty for remembering names is remarkable.

6. He is a fluent and easy talker, and you envy his steady line of chatter. He is never at a loss for an answer, a word, or a phrase.

7. You have made several stops among Mark's prospects, and everyone feels he's a great guy. Mr. Kelly said, "Without Mark, I'd be a flop; he keeps me supplied with jokes." Goren feels he's a good man, but "he has a terrible time giving me the information I want. He changes his quotes and prices from day to day."

8. Only Ms. Kimball has complained directly about Teller. Kimball has been a major customer and should be a good long-term account. She recently said, "I feel business is business, and there is a limit to horsing around. Teller could get his calls done here in 15 minutes if he knew what he was doing. He wastes his time and ours."

9. Back at the office, you check Mark's files and you find that many of the problems in his transactions have arisen purely as a result of his carelessness and negligence in making notations, reporting, and entering quotes.

10. The ironic thing about this is that Mark seems to have every attribute that makes for a good sales representative, and yet his sales are declining. There is a special sales-training program scheduled for July by the San Diego Sales Association. Maybe you should send him to that.

11. What are the major problems? What communication barriers exist? What action should be taken now? What should have been done in the past? By whom?

ASSIGNMENTS

1. GROUP DISCUSSION

Break into small groups and discuss the case. Your first step should be to review the situation. The purpose of this review is to determine that all participants in each group have a similar perception of the incidents described in the case.

Next, analyze the case. What is the major problem? What are the contributing problems? What specific communication barriers are evident? Who is responsible? How can the major and minor problems be solved? What action should be taken now?

After 10 to 15 minutes of private discussion among the members of each group, open the case to the entire class. Do this by having the spokespersons of four or five groups report their group's findings to the class. Permit class members to respond or ask questions after each spokesperson reports.

2. INTERVIEW ROLE PLAY

Break into groups of three. Have one person play the boss; one, Mark Teller; and one, the observer (ask your instructor about the Observer Evaluation Checklist). Act out a five- to eight-minute interview between the boss and Mark Teller in which an attempt is made to resolve the situation described. At the conclusion of the interview, have the observer report his or her reactions.

Change roles and repeat the role playing to get another person's approach to the same problem.

3. MEMOS

(a) Assume you are the boss. Write a memo to Mark Teller in which you attempt to alleviate or correct the situation described.

(b) Assume you are the boss. Write a memo to your partner, describing the situation and the action you intend to take to solve the problem(s).

4. LETTER

Assume you are the boss. Write a goodwill letter to Ms. Kimball. Make any logical assumptions you consider valid.

| C A S E | 2 |

THE JIM CANTONELLI CASE*

1. For some time, Southern California Utilities Director of Finance Bob Baker had been looking for a competent individual to take over Section Two, Employee Disbursements. Unfortunately, Ken Carpenter, who headed up Section Two for three years, was leaving to take over a family business in the Midwest. Baker had thought about Marty Martin, who had been one of Ken's assistants for two years. However, Baker wondered about Martin, inasmuch as the latter was attending an MBA program

*In conjunction with this case, you may wish to view the video (based on this case) by Norman B. Sigband, *Listening: Key to Problem Solving*, 2nd Edition, 1993. It is available from AIMS Media, 9710 De Soto, Chatsworth, CA 91311.

at night, trying to pay for a Porsche, and leading a very active social life.

2. Baker also talked to Jim Cantonelli, about whom he had always received very favorable reports. Cantonelli had been in Section One (Accounts Payable) for three years and had done a good job programming many routine functions on the computer. Although Baker and Jim had a favorable initial chat, Jim seemed reluctant to pursue the discussion.

3. Before 1985, Jim worked for an aerospace firm, and before that, at an electronics corporation. He had completed an engineering/computer education in Europe to what would equal our junior-college level. However, he could not continue because he was called up for army service.

4. Jim has proven to be one of the hardest working and most conscientious employees in the Finance Division of Southern California Utilities. He has never complained about assignments, has frequently stayed after hours and worked Saturdays "on his own." No job seems too difficult for him. He has completed not only regular tasks, but also extra ones willingly. And there were dozens of extra ones in 1993 when the new IBM equipment was installed.

5. Jim's relationship with other company employees is minimal. He rarely participates in employee affairs and doesn't trade chitchat to any great degree with other workers. Nevertheless, he seems respected, if not well liked, by his associates.

6. When Jim was approached about becoming the chief of Section Two, he was reluctant. He noted his slight foreign accent, his lack of formal education in this country, and the trouble he has in writing up his weekly reports. But when Baker pointed out, in three discussions, the extra compensation he would receive, his new job title, his experience in computers, the seniority level he was in, and the confidence Baker and other officers had in him, he still had some misgivings, but Baker overrode them.

7. During the first two months of Section Two's operations under Jim, all seemed to go quite well, although Baker understood that Jim had two or three rather severe arguments with Marty Martin. Baker also suggested to Jim that it wasn't necessary for him to stay late so many nights, that if he would just let his subordinates take over on assignments, they would probably fulfill them to his satisfaction. It was true that payroll activities worked in a very cyclical way, but no one should work until mid-night night after night.

8. Last month Marty Martin left his position. He told Baker it was for a better job in industry. However, others have indicated that he left because of utter frustration in never being permitted by Jim to handle a complete assignment or to take over full responsibility for a major project.

9. When Baker questioned Jim about this, he said, "That guy has school and women on his mind; besides, he's about as slow and lazy as every other worker in this unit." Of course, he backed up after a few minutes, probably because Baker appeared so surprised by his remark.

10. In the past few weeks, Baker has visited Jim's area almost every day. Jim usually appears agitated. In the past three weeks, Baker has received several informal complaints from the personnel of Jim's section. Jim himself seems more upset than ever, perhaps because of several computer-related problems and comments concerning errors. Also of major concern is the quality (or lack of it) of the work produced by his section. There have been several kickbacks, and Baker's vice president told Baker he isn't overjoyed with the operation of Section Two. The heads of other sections with whom Jim must work have also complained (rather quietly) about Jim's grouchiness and lack of cooperation.

11. Two weeks ago, Jane Albermarle, who worked under Jim, quit, saying, "I can't work with that nut, Cantonelli." Yesterday, Bob Carter and Art Phillips, both excellent employees, caught Baker on the way out of his office and asked for transfers to Section Three. When Baker questioned them, Carter and Phillips said something about people in Section Three being in their car pool. However, a couple of others who work under Jim said, "I guess he's OK. All bosses are the same. He's new and nervous . . . but he should settle down."

12. It's obvious Baker must do something about Jim Cantonelli. But today when Baker questioned him in general terms, Jim said that he's just about got everything under control, "and in another month, if I can get these idiot employees to do a day's work, we'll be running as smooth as silk."

13. But Baker is upset and so is management. Perhaps that seminar next month at State University on "New Techniques in Computer Payroll Methods" sponsored by the Western Finance Officers Association might be just the thing for Jim. The reg-

istration fee is nominal.

14. What are the communication problems between Baker and Cantonelli? Between Cantonelli and his people? What do you think should have been done in the past? What should be done now?

ASSIGNMENTS

1. GROUP DISCUSSION

Break into groups of four or five and discuss the case. Your first step should be to review the situation presented in order to determine that all participants in each group have a similar perception of the incidents described.

Next, analyze the case. What is the major problem? The contributing problems? What specific communication barriers are evident? Who is responsible? How can the major and minor problems be solved? What action should be taken now?

After 10 to 15 minutes of discussion by the groups within themselves, open the case to the entire class. Do this by having the spokespeople of four or five groups report their groups' findings to the class. Permit class members to respond or ask questions, or both, after each representative speaks.

2. INTERVIEW ROLE PLAY

(a) Break into groups of three. Have one person play Mr. Baker; one, Jim Cantonelli; and one, the observer (ask your instructor about the Observer Evaluation Checklist). Act out a five- to eight-minute interview between Mr. Baker and Jim Cantonelli (after paragraph 13) in which an attempt is made to alleviate or correct the situation described. At the conclusion of the interview, have the observer report his or her reactions.

(b) Change roles and repeat the role playing to see another person's approach to the same problem.

(c) Break into groups of three. Have one person play Bob Baker; one, Art Phillips; and one, the observer (see paragraph 11). Repeat as above.

3. REPORT

Assume you are an outsider who has just reviewed the situation existing under Mr. Baker. Submit a report to Mr. Baker's boss on your findings, conclusions, and recommendations. Remember that you are an unbiased and objective consultant.

4. MEMOS

(a) Assume you are Bob Carter. Send a memo to Mr. Baker through your boss, Jim Cantonelli, in which you request a transfer to Section Three (see paragraph 11).

(b) Assume you are the vice president to whom Bob Baker reports. Send a memo to Bob Baker concerning the situation in Section Three (see paragraph 10).

5. LETTERS

(a) As the director of training of Jim Cantonelli's company, send a letter of inquiry to the Western Finance Officers Association asking for details (content, fee, prerequisites, length) of the seminar "New Techniques in Computer Payroll Methods" (see paragraph 13).

(b) As the human resources director of Jim Cantonelli's company, send a letter to Marty Martin, inviting him to an exit interview with you at his convenience (see paragraph 8).

CASE   3

HOSTILE TAKEOVER

1. Susan Underwood, a senior manager in charge of company publications, first read of the takeover attempt in *The Wall Street Journal.* She saw her shares of company stock soar, then plummet, as news broke, pro and con, about the takeover. Her emotions rose and fell as well. After 16 years with Lever Electronics, she felt considerable loyalty to the goals, methods, and overall culture of the company. It had been her home.

2. She feared that a takeover, even if it didn't cost her job, might change her work environment drastically. Would she be told to manage in a new way? Would she be given an impossible workload? Would her authority be ripped away from her by putting her in a subordinate reporting position, no matter what her title? At 41, Susan wasn't eager for a job change.

3. H. Richard Galloway, financier, was indeed in the process of taking over Lever Electronics through a carefully staged program of buying company stock. He now owned enough to sway board deci-

sions, and soon would control the board completely. Lever Electronics seemed powerless against Galloway's invasion, as stockholders one by one sold out to his inflated offers for company stock.

4. Galloway's announced goal was to "trim" Lever Electronics of its cash-rich, asset-rich business base—in short, to mortgage it to the hilt. He would carry away the proceeds from new loans, sales, and stock offerings as his booty for a successful takeover. In fact, he stood to make more than $30 million from the 12-week business venture.

5. On the very day that Galloway successfully installed a new chairperson of the board, Susan Underwood began receiving new instructions for company publications. The first came in a terse memo from Galloway himself:

> Design and submit a program of communications, reassuring company employees that, while changes will take place, every effort will be made to assure their positions, with some adjustments in compensation made necessary by our transition period.

Susan was being asked—told—to "sell" the takeover through the publications she managed.

6. Since she was in large part responsible for assigning all and writing many of the articles in the company magazine and newsletter, Susan felt an ethical and professional dilemma. Could she in good conscience ask her coworkers to trust new management that might well prove untrustworthy? How should she use the bond of trust that had developed over the years between her and her readers?

ASSIGNMENTS

1. GROUP DISCUSSION

With class members playing the roles of company employees, enact an off-site meeting of "old" company employees. They can speak freely and off the record about their concerns.

After the discussion, decide what makes the difference between a general gripe session and a meeting that leads to constructive action. Once you have decided how the group can settle upon action goals, reenact the meeting, this time redirecting discussion toward a goal of some sort—something employees can do about their situation.

2. INTERVIEW ROLE PLAY

A student should take on the role of Susan as she

interviews Galloway about his plans for the company. The interview ostensibly serves the purpose of gathering information for articles; its hidden agenda, however, is for Susan to feel out Galloway's real motives and plans.

3. MEMOS

(a) Write a memo from Susan to one of her staff writers, instructing the writer to prepare some articles, in keeping with Galloway's directive. Go on to instruct the writer how the article should be researched. Bear in mind Susan's strong ethical commitment to telling her readers the truth.

(b) Write a memo from Susan to Galloway. In the memo, develop some means of finding out more about his plans for the company. You could, for example, ask a series of direct questions. Or you could request a meeting, with suggestions for agenda items. If you deem it wise, you might write a frank memo expressing your personal ambivalence and misgivings.

4. REPORT

Draw up the report requested by Galloway. Show what communications employees will receive, how such messages will be written, and where they will appear. In your report, cover as many employee subgroups as possible.

5. PROPOSAL

Draw up a short proposal to circulate, privately, among Lever employees. The proposal should show a practical way by which employees themselves could take over ownership of the company and forestall Galloway's takeover. Remember that good proposals demonstrate not only solutions but also a clear understanding and exposition of the problems.

6. LETTERS

(a) On behalf of employees, write an open letter to Galloway. Express the personal and professional concerns of employees. Ask for a meeting or series of meetings in which these concerns can be discussed directly with the new CEO.

(b) In the role of Galloway, write an open letter to employees. Before beginning your letter, decide whether you are going to "play it tough"

or give in to employee requests for meetings, reassurances, and compromises.

CASE 4

BROOKS-MARTINEZ CASE

1. Joe Green has been in charge of the drafting department of the Belleville Plant for about 18 months. He has always enjoyed his job, the security of the position, the elimination of traveling, and the friends he has in Belleville.

2. Joe did encounter a problem recently when one of the five supervisors under him resigned. Green's superior, Sandra O'Brien, asked Green to designate a replacement. This was not an easy task for Green because the individual who he thought was most competent, Georgia Brooks, was an employee with whom he had a good many differences of opinion. Another employee in the same unit, Carlos Martinez, was also considered seriously by Green. However, Carlos has had a series of absences, and because of a strong accent, he sometimes has difficulty making himself understood. But he is a very competent employee and has excellent training. Both Georgia Brooks and Carlos Martinez are "leadpeople" (a position just below supervisor) in their groups.

3. Green knew that if he chose Georgia, some people would say that he was forced into it by his superior because of Georgia's competence. If Green did *not* select her, he would be accused of being jealous of Georgia's ability.

4. If he selected Carlos, it would appear that he was just avoiding the competition Georgia might give him. If he did *not* choose Carlos, there was sure to be talk of discrimination on his part, and accusations of bias from the Hispanic workforce.

5. Green discussed this whole affair with his supervisor, Sandra O'Brien, who listened carefully to Green, examined all aspects of the situation with him, but would not commit herself. "You must work with this person," she said, "and you're the only one who can make the decision."

6. After a good deal of thought, some soul-searching, and a few sleepless nights, Joe Green designated Georgia Brooks as the supervisor.

7. It's been about two months since Georgia has been on the job, and things have gone from bad to worse. Green now feels his decision was not wise, but he's sure that had he selected Carlos, things would not have turned out any better.

8. Carlos has not worked well since Georgia's appointment; comments have drifted back to Joe Green and Sandra O'Brien in the cafeteria and elsewhere about prejudice against Hispanics, and production and efficiency in the Green's workforce has declined.

9. Although Green thought Georgia Brooks would really begin to work with him, the situation between Green and Brooks is now worse than ever. Because things aren't going too well (errors in production, confusion in priorities, work pile-up, and so on.), Brooks has accused Green of trying to make her look bad. Her appointment, she insists, was against Green's recommendation and was forced on him because of her competence.

10. Brooks has also changed Green's orders on certain procedures on at least two occasions, causing confusion in the unit. Brooks claimed it was to speed things up and avoid red tape.

11. Sandra O'Brien has tried to counsel Joe Green on a couple of occasions. She has even suggested that Green stop "being so hard" on Brooks. At that suggestion, Green almost exploded. But more and more, O'Brien seems to be upset with Green . . . and vice versa.

12. Green has hesitated to ask another manager to take Brooks. First of all, there don't seem to be any openings elsewhere in the plant; second, it will cause Green to lose a great deal of face; and of even more importance, everyone has heard of the problem and would prefer not to get involved.

13. "This dissension as well as the low morale in your unit must end and productivity must increase. The company's internal auditing team has selected the Belleville Plant for total review next month," O'Brien tells Green. Then she goes on, "And I want your section humming smoothly in two weeks or else!"

14. Green wonders what he can or should do. Just a few weeks ago he was delighted with his job. Now he's miserable. He'd like to quit himself, but he's got nine years with the company and a family that depends on him.

15. What communication problems brought all this on? Who was at fault? Green? Brooks? O'Brien? What plan of action do you suggest for Green? What should be done with Carlos?

ASSIGNMENTS

1. GROUP DISCUSSION

Break into groups of four or five and discuss the case. Your first step should be to review the situation presented in order to determine that all participants in each group have a similar perception of the incidents described.

Next, analyze the case. What is the major problem? What are the contributing problems? What specific communication barriers are evident? Who is responsible? How can the major and minor problems be solved? What action should be taken now?

After 10 to 15 minutes of discussion by the groups within themselves, open the case to the entire class. Do this by having the spokespeople of four or five groups report their group's findings to the class. Permit class members to respond or ask questions after each spokesperson reports.

2. INTERVIEW ROLE PLAY

(a) Break into groups of three. Have one person play Joe Green; one, Georgia Brooks; and one, the observer (ask your instructor about the Observer Evaluation Checklist). Act out a five- to eight-minute interview between Georgia Brooks and Joe Green (after paragraph 14). After the interview, have the observer report his or her reactions.

Change rolls and repeat the role playing to experience another approach to the same problem.

(b) Break into groups of three. Have one individual play Joe Green; one, Carlos Martinez; and one, the observer. Hold the interview with Carlos *after* Georgia Brooks has been appointed supervisor (after paragraph 6). Repeat as above.

3. MEMOS

(a) In the capacity of Manager Joe Green, send a memo to Georgia Brooks, appointing her supervisor. Add any special instructions you feel are necessary.

(b) In the capacity of Manager Joe Green, send Carlos Martinez a memo, thanking him for his interest in the opening for supervisor, commenting on the discussion you had with him regarding the job, and telling him that Georgia Brooks has been designated for the position.

(c) In the capacity of Sandra O'Brien, send a memo to Joe Green, noting the production and morale decline in Green's unit and the fact that the company's internal auditing team will be visiting the plant next week (after paragraph 13).

4. LETTER

In the capacity of Sandra O'Brien, send a letter of congratulations to Georgia Brooks on her appointment as supervisor of Section Three (after paragraph 6).

5. MEETING

Break into groups of six. In the capacity of Joe Green, call a meeting of your five supervisors to prepare for the visit next week of the company's internal auditing committee. The committee will want to check productivity, morale, housekeeping (cleanliness), attitudes, safety, training, and related factors.

Hold the meeting for 20 minutes. At the conclusion of the meeting, spend 15 minutes evaluating the conduct of the meeting leader, participants, progress, visual aids, and related factors.

CASE 5

WHEN EAST DOESN'T MEET WEST

1. Maria Sanchez is an entrepreneur-professional businessperson. She is alert, progressive, conscientious, and honest. All these qualities paid off for her. Five years ago she purchased Crown Drugs. At that time it was owned and operated by Steven Crown, who served as pharmacist, clerk, manager, bookkeeper, and in just about every other necessary capacity in a small operation. Each day for 20 years, Steven opened and closed his 3,000-square-foot operation. Then with a good offer from Sanchez, he sold out.

2. Sanchez, with a doctor of pharmacy degree, four years of chain store experience, and great expectations, had big plans for Crown Drugs. Now, just three years after the store's purchase, it is really a different operation. Sanchez knocked down the side walls and expanded the store's area fourfold; closed off and refurbished the pharmacy section, giving it a very professional air; purchased $10,000 worth of new display fixtures; and expanded the

over-the-counter areas significantly. Patient records were computerized, marketing and sales promotion efforts increased, and all customer services expanded.

3. Sales at Crown Drugs have climbed steadily and the profit margin has kept up. Obviously this is no longer a one-person operation. Sanchez has four store clerks now, one of whom is part-time. Chances are good that she will need at least two more full-time clerks for the Thanksgiving /Christmas period, perhaps even as permanent employees. The most dramatic improvement has come in the pharmacy section. Sanchez has visited all the physicians in the area and is now well known among them. She has addressed many community groups on everything from "New Medications for the Cardiac Patient" to "Drugs and the Teenager." She has cooperated in different ways with church and local fund-raising groups. The result has been more prescriptions filled in the last year than Steven Crown filled in five.

4. But all is not sweetness and light at Crown Drugs. There are problems in the pharmacy which don't have to do with sales, inventory, or dispensing. There are people problems *behind* the counter, not in front of it.

5. John Webster and Barbara Choi are both full-time, experienced registered pharmacists. John is outgoing, popular with the individuals who bring prescriptions in to be filled, excellent on the telephone with doctors and their staffs, and a competent employee. Barbara Choi is quite different. She is extremely knowledgeable and will always come up with an answer when John cannot. However, Barbara is quiet, reserved, and would prefer not to get involved with customer relations and counseling or phone calls, especially when a physician's prescription must be questioned. But Barbara is a genius when it comes to technical matters.

6. On the surface, these two should make a great team, but they do not! They seem to bicker constantly. Because Maria Sanchez has not only been spending more time on community affairs but also searching for a possible second store location, she isn't around to arbitrate between Webster and Choi.

7. Webster feels that Choi doesn't do her share of the work at the counter, with customers, or on the phone. Choi, on the other hand, says she does much more work than Webster because she fills most of

the incoming prescriptions. Furthermore, says Choi, because she is quiet and polite, Webster plays the "big boss" and orders her around as well as the clerks. The fact is, Choi continues, Webster is not as knowledgeable as he should be on patients' questions about some of the new drugs, is not fully aware of obvious drug problems and trends, and on the whole, "is a big bag of wind."

8. The result of all this bickering is that the clerks are confused, neither Webster nor Choi speaks to each other except for essential discussion, customers sense a tense and charged atmosphere, and quite a few sales have been lost.

9. Choi had a brief discussion with Sanchez just a few minutes ago as the latter was leaving the store on her way to inspect a possible new store location. Choi complained (for the tenth time) about Webster and said that she would probably have to leave at the end of the month.

10. As far as Sanchez is concerned, that would be disastrous. It is imperative, she feels, that both Webster and Choi stay. They are both good employees and should constitute an excellent team. But all they are doing now is losing sales for Crown Drugs.

11. Maria Sanchez is in the middle of her expansion effort and would hate to make changes at this time. She's got to turn this around, and she's sure that neither money nor fear of termination will prove to be effective motivating factors with Webster or Choi. Thus, she's left with communication to solve her dilemma.

12. What specifically should Sanchez do with Barbara Choi and John Webster? Be precise in your recommendations as to the place, type of statements to be used, and the near-term objectives. Also, be practical.

ASSIGNMENTS

1. GROUP DISCUSSION

Break into groups of five or six individuals and analyze the case. What action should Maria Sanchez follow with Barbara Choi and John Webster? Do you suggest training? counseling? termination? discussion? Be specific in your suggestions.

Have one spokesperson from each group offer suggestions. Invite comments on the suggested course of action.

2. INTERVIEW ROLE PLAY

(a) Have one student take the role of Barbara Choi and another the role of Maria Sanchez. Role-play an interview. Sanchez wants to solve the problem in the case.

Have a third student act as the observer (ask your instructor about the Observer Evaluation Checklist). The observer should offer constructive criticism after the interview.

(b) Conduct the role play with different students—except have one student in the role of John Webster, one as Maria Sanchez, and one as the observer.

(c) Have a neutral individual (perhaps the president of the local pharmacists' association) interview both Choi and Webster (together) in an effort to solve the problem. Have several students act as observers/evaluators of the interview. A student should role-play the pharmacy association president.

3. MEMOS

(a) As Maria Sanchez, write a memo to Barbara Choi in which you attempt to motivate her to work more cooperatively with John Webster.

(b) As Maria Sanchez, write a memo to Barbara Choi in which you attempt to change her mind about leaving at the end of the month.

4. Letter

(a) Write a letter to a customer who complained to you (Maria Sanchez) because she received two different opinions (one from Choi and one from Webster) concerning how to take one specific medication.

(b) As Maria Sanchez, write a goodwill letter to a physician who has just set up practice in the neighborhood. You will, of course, point out that Crown Drugs will be happy to fill his prescriptions as well as take care of the various pharmaceutical-related needs in his practice.

(c) A new chain of convalescent care facilities has recently begun operations in your city. Write a letter to the head administrator offering to fill all pharmaceutical needs for all her facilities. You can offer competitive prices, delivery service 18 hours each day, and patient records. Offer any other services which you feel are reasonable.

(d) Write a letter to all patients now on your mailing list. Offer them free and accurate blood pressure tests during the week of June 21–28.

CASE 6

THE SUN FRESH CASE*

1. Bill Hillman is the operations manager of the Sun Fresh Food chain located in the Midwest. This is a strong organization, founded in 1966 and now made up of 82 stores in Illinois and Wisconsin. Most of the stores cluster around the greater Chicago area.

2. The chain has had its ups and downs over the years, but some of its greatest changes have taken place since 1990.

3. In that year, a large Eastern food manufacturer, Jackson and Trent, purchased Sun Fresh, supplied funds, and gave the green light to expansion. Up to that date, everyone seemed to know everyone else at Sun Fresh. Of course, Sun Fresh only had 38 stores at that time, and promotions and changes in personnel always occurred from within. As a matter of fact, this has always been a well-known company policy and practice: advancements and promotions from within.

4. However, in 1992 the company opened 22 new stores, and the chain (or Bill Hillman) just couldn't find enough competent store managers in Sun Fresh to take over. The company had to go outside, and as a result about 16 of the new store managers came from other firms in the area or simply as a result of recruiting: newspaper ads, recommendations from friends in the food industry, and so forth.

5. Bill Hillman doesn't seem to be concerned one way or another about this source for new managers. However, he is slowly becoming aware that his "old-line" employees resent this deeply. As he travels around with Rob, a company officer, he notes that store managers and even district supervisors comment on the new policy. Bill and top management have talked about putting out a bulletin or having all district and store managers in for a two-day meeting to explain growth, company goals, policies, and new directions. But they agreed that a printed bulletin wouldn't do the job, and Bill felt strongly that it would be extremely costly to hold

*In conjunction with this case, you may wish to view the film by Norman B. Sigband, *Communication: The Company Grapevine* (based on this case). View it *after* the case has been discussed and a role-play exercise completed. It is available from: AIMS Media, 9710 De Soto, Chatsworth, CA 91311.

such a meeting, even if time were available (which it isn't). Largely due to Bill's strong feelings, such a companywide meeting of store managers was not held.

6. The comments Rob and Bill receive are biting; they rise above the humor level and give clear indication of fear and antagonism. "So the brass is sweeping all us old hands out, I see." "It looks like my 16 years with Sun Fresh will soon be tossed in the trash can." "Now that we've helped make the firm, it looks like our usefulness has come to an end and we're being replaced." These are the types of statements they heard.

7. Of course, Rob and Bill try to counter these individual comments, for replacement of seasoned employees is not a company policy at all. But it is evident that the managers don't really believe the statements from top management. On top of this, four store managers have been replaced since the first of July. They had each been promoted from within and had been with Sun Fresh (prior to promotion) for many years. But Kelly left Sun Fresh to join a family-owned business, Ferris and Martinez proved incompetent, and the other manager asked to be relieved when he complained that the responsibility was too much for him. Purely by chance, outsiders replaced each of the four.

8. These four cases are frequently cited to Bill Hillman (and certainly to many others) as clear evidence of the new policy. Bill has also noted a lack of enthusiasm and evidence, perhaps, of poor morale in the stores. There just doesn't seem to be the old banter, good-humored kidding, and "let's set another sales record this week" attitude, which always seemed to exist in the past. This attitude change is obvious among the store managers, produce and meat department supervisors, and almost everywhere else in the company. Sales are also down and employee pilferage is up (on a percentage basis) throughout the chain.

9. Today, Bill encountered the most serious problem. Three store managers, including Hugh Purcell at Oakdale, are leaving Sun Fresh as of September 1 and are going to work for the competing chain, SavMor, or themselves. Bill has spent two hours with two district supervisors, and they told him that the three are among the very best store managers in Sun Fresh. They are seasoned veterans, and they each said, in so many words, "As long as the company is going to bounce us in the near future, we might as well leave while we have an opportunity to make a good connection." In addition, three department supervisors, such as Joanne, produce manager at Oakdale, have also resigned.

10. The employees' perceptions about bringing in outsiders is not accurate. But Bill realizes he must—somehow—communicate the truth to all the Sun Fresh employees. Yet he just can't send out a bulletin and say, "We aren't replacing our old-line employees," for that is just about what everyone will then believe.

11. What communication problems exist? Between whom do they exist? What barriers exist? What channels of communication are being used and why? What should have been done in the past? What should be done now?

ASSIGNMENTS

1. GROUP DISCUSSION
Break into groups of four or five and discuss the case. Your first step should be to review the situation presented in order to determine that all participants in each group have a similar perception of the incidents described.

Next, analyze the case. What is the major problem? What are the contributing problems? What specific communication barriers are evident? Who is responsible? How can the major and minor problems be solved? What action should be taken now?

After 10 to 15 minutes of discussion by the groups within themselves, open the case to the entire class. Do this by having the spokespeople of four or five groups report their group's findings to the class. Permit class members to respond or ask questions, or both, after each representative speaks.

2. INTERVIEW ROLE PLAY
(a) Break into groups of three. Have one person play Bill Hillman; one, the store manager, Hugh Purcell, who has indicated he will leave Sun Fresh as of September 1 (see paragraph 9); and one, the observer (ask your instructor about the Observer Evaluation Checklist). Act out a five- to eight-minute interview between Bill Hillman and Hugh Purcell (after paragraph 10). At the conclusion of the interview, have the observer report his or her reactions.

Change roles and repeat the role playing to experience another approach to the problem.

(b) Break into groups of three. Have one individual play Bill Hillman; one, District Supervisor Mark Webster who has ten Sun Fresh stores under his supervision; and one, the observer (ask your instructor about the Observer Evaluation Checklist). Act out a five- to eight-minute interview between Bill Hillman and District Supervisor Mark Webster (after paragraph 10). At the conclusion of the interview, have the observer report his or her reactions.

Change roles and repeat the role playing to get another approach to the problem.

3. Memos
(a) In the capacity of Bill Hillman, send a memo to the editor of the Sun Fresh employee monthly magazine, *Sun Up.* Ask him to run a story: "Promotion Opportunities to Store Manager Positions Now Available." Enclose with your memo a copy of page 4 of the *Sun Fresh Policy Manual,* which states eligibility requirements for the job.

(b) In the capacity of Bill Hillman, send a memo to each of the store managers who has indicated his or her desire to resign as of September 1 (see paragraph 9). Attempt to have each call you for an interview during which you will attempt to retain the individual as a Sun Fresh Manager.

4. REPORT
Send a report to corporate president Claire Campbell, who has requested a review of the personnel problems you are encountering in the area.

Make any reasonable assumptions you feel are necessary (personnel, sales, turnover, construction, training, etc.).

5. ORAL REPORT
After you have completed the written report, give an oral presentation to the firm's board of directors based on the material in the report. Be prepared to answer questions from the board members.

Ask your colleagues for constructive criticism at the end of your oral report.

6. MEETING
In the capacity of Bill Hillman, call a meeting of the eight Sun Fresh district supervisors. Your purpose is to discuss and determine which method of communication should be used to eliminate the rumors (after paragraph 10) and improve employee morale.

Hold a ten-minute evaluation of the meeting form, content, leader, and participants.

CASE **7**

THE BARNEY BURTON CASE

1. The Goldberg Corporation has been manufacturing helicopters in its Southern California facilities since 1965. Beginning in 1989, however, it began to use some of its surplus funds to diversify.
2. Various areas, some complementary to aerospace and some not, were acquired. Some units were integrated while others were spun off in the period from 1989 to 1992. For the past year or so, a point of stability has been reached and Goldberg now seems to be concentrating on several specific lines: helicopters, small consumer power units (mowers, snowmobiles, power water skis, chain saws, etc.), dental chairs and X-ray equipment, electrical and power equipment for medical scanning, and space and satellite components as well as naval heavy-ordinance controls.
3. On the surface, the company seems to produce a very mixed bag of items; on the other hand, there are enough similarities among the product lines to make things mesh quite well.
4. But the company's problems are not in securing contracts, a labor force, facilities, financing, or markets. The headaches seem to come from people.
5. A problem that has surfaced recently—and seems enormous—involves Barney Burton, or Dr. B. Burton as he signs all his memos (which, by the way, fly from his desk like snowflakes in a Minneapolis storm).
6. Because of the acquisition of new companies in the past few years, it seemed reasonable to set up divisions that concentrate on certain functions and that serve all other divisions of the organization. These are called functional support units (FSUs). For example, all divisions turn to a plastic unit for the design of plastic components whether they are for mowers or helicopters; a motors unit for motors to power various items, whether it is a rotating gun mount or a flexible piece of X-ray equipment; and an electrical cables and connectors unit for consumer items such as a snowmobile or a space vehicle.
7. The FSUs seem to work quite well with the strategic business units (SBUs), which were orga-

nized at the same time. For example, there are SBUs for consumers items, helicopters, medical equipment, and defense.
8. The cables and connectors FSU is headed by Barney Burton, a Ph.D. in electrical engineering from the Massachusetts Institute of Technology, a fact known far and wide in the Goldberg Corporation. For the past few months, however, Dr. Burton has turned out to be a space-sized problem to many managers at Goldberg.
9. There is no denying that Burton is creative, knowledgeable, and at times, brilliant. Some of his items, especially his flat, flexible, plastic-encased printed cable devices have been awarded patents. He has also solved electrical ribbon cable and connector problems for consumer devices that have to withstand extremely hard usage and for intricate and sophisticated cable and connectors destined for uninterrupted operation for a guaranteed ten-year period in satellite components.
10. Burton's relationship with the people under him seems to be excellent. Morale is high and most of his supervisors believe he is as brilliant as *he* thinks he is. He represents them well and works hard to secure increases in pay for them as well as better facilities and promotions.
11. However, every manager at his level, almost anywhere in the organization, views Burton as an adversary. Why? It's his complete lack of cooperation. If he is asked to design a new flexible printed circuit device, he will start by trying to redesign the entire product, whatever it is, and all its components for the SBU involved. In the final analysis, there is no compromise with Burton. It's either his way or no way, or if not his way, his design comes in 40 days after the last possible deadline.
12. Two SBU managers, both long-term and valuable employees, Mike Michelson and Cathy Conover, have actually contracted with outside electrical engineering groups to solve their problems. They secured the flexible cables they wanted in record time, the cost was nominal, and the results were more than satisfactory. However, if the head of every SBU did that rather than using a Goldberg FSU that is available, the internal organizational structure of Goldberg would suffer a serious blow.
13. Several attempts to solve the Burton problem have been tried. Both the president and executive vice president have had diplomatic sessions with Barney Burton on the need for his support and

cooperation with the SBUs. "I couldn't agree more," he stated. "They need my unit, and I'm prepared to go 100 percent and work with them. But when I see something wrong in one of their components, it's my duty to correct it so we don't build a potential problem into the system. You can be sure I'll cooperate."

14. But when it comes down to a one-on-one situation, Burton doesn't change.

15. Just two months ago, a meeting was held of the heads of the nine SBUs and five FSUs, ostensibly to consider business ethics. However, the hidden agenda was "how can we build a better climate and improve cooperation among the units." Believe it or not, Burton made some significant contributions to the discussion.

16. But, once again, Burton didn't change when it came down to one-on-one situations.

17. Right now, Goldberg's President Martinville and Executive Vice President Rawlins are meeting to discuss and make a decision on Barney Burton.

18. What suggestions, if any, do you have to offer? Martinville and Rawlins have been debating whether the Stanford Program in November on "Executive Planning in a Turbulent Society" might be something in which to enroll Burton. Or would that simply take Burton out of his office for three weeks at a tuition cost of $5,000 . . . and not solve the problem of having someone who apparently believes he is a team player but really is not?

ASSIGNMENTS

1. GROUP DISCUSSION

Break into groups of four or five and discuss the case. Your first step should be to review the situation presented in order to determine that all participants in each group have a similar perception of the incidents described.

Next, analyze the case. What is the major problem? What are the contributing problems? What specific communication barriers are evident? Who is responsible? How can the major and minor problems be solved? What action should be taken now?

After 10 to 15 minutes of discussion by the groups within themselves, open the case to the entire class. Do this by having the spokespeople of four or five groups report their group's findings to the class. Permit class members to respond or ask questions, or both, after each representative speaks.

2. INTERVIEW ROLE PLAY

(a) Break into groups of three: Have one person play Dr. Burton; one, Executive Vice president Rawlins; and one, the observer (ask your instructor about the Observer Evaluation Checklist). Act out a five- to eight-minute interview between Burton and Rawlins (after paragraph 17) in which an attempt is made to alleviate or correct the situation described. At the conclusion of the interview, have the observer report his or her reactions.

(b) Change roles and repeat the role play to appreciate another person's approach to the same problem.

3. REPORT

Assume you are an outside consultant to the Goldberg Corporation and that you have reviewed the Barney Burton situation. You have interviewed Burton and several of his colleagues as well as four department heads. Submit a report on your findings to Goldberg's President Martinville on your findings, conclusions, and recommendations.

4. MEMOS

(a) Assume you are Barney Burton. Write a memo to Cathy Conover in which you ask why she went outside the company to secure the services of electrical engineering firms and did not use your group. Offer to be of assistance in the future.

(b) As Cathy Conover, reply to the above memo but make no commitments that you will work with Barney in the future.

5. LETTER

As Ms. Nicole Jameson of the Franklin Corporation, write a letter to Dr. Burton and ask for details on how the Goldberg Corporation uses FSUs and SBUs. The Franklin Corporation may adopt a similar system.

CASE   **8**

BUT TALKING ISN'T WORKING

1. Randy Takashita is the pharmacy manager of store 75 of the Sun Fresh Supermarket Chain. He began work as a pharmacist with Sun Fresh almost ten years ago and retained that position for five years without a change in status. In 1983 he received his first promotion; then he was transferred from one store to another until, in 1988, he became pharmacy manager of store 34 in San Diego.

2. Subsequently, Randy has been moved to two different stores, and in June 1989, he was transferred to store 75 located in Westlake Village, California. Since 1980, the community of Westlake Village has held tremendous potential for a "complete supermarket" because of its almost explosive growth in population and housing. Auto dealerships, small and large entrepreneurial businesses, chain operations, and professional offices of all types have absolutely mushroomed in Westlake Village. Unfortunately, this growth has not been reflected in the pharmacy operations of store 75. However, the other departments of that same store have experienced tremendous increases in sales.

3. The chain's pharmacy vice president is concerned because store 75 was targeted as a real growth unit for 1990–1993 along with eight other locations. Extra effort, dollars, and marketing materials were allocated to these nine operations. Eight responded with significant increases, but not the pharmacy unit in store 75.

4. The regional manager, Donna Frigozi, has been out to see Randy Takashita on several occasions. She has been concerned because Randy has not spent the amount of time with the community warranted by the growth and demographics of Westlake Village. Randy maintains that there is so much to do in the pharmacy that he must remain inside.

5. "But what takes so much of your time, Randy?" Donna asked. "Well, I have staff meetings three days a week where I pass on needed information—especially that received from Regional. Then I spend a lot of time training and counseling our clerks, technicians, and even store personnel on what a pharmacist is all about. I need time to write the reports which go along with the computer printouts or those that simply stand alone. Recently, I've spent time on the new furniture and fixtures at the pharmacy, and then I had to do something about improving the record system here."

6. "But Randy," Donna interjected, "we don't need reports to accompany the computer printouts. Those are complete in themselves. The clerks have all completed our part-time clerks' training pro-

gram and are certified as competent to work independently; we have a decorating and design division to handle furniture and fixtures; and as for the files and records department, last year's audit said store 75 was fine on that score. What we need to work on is the source and growth of our business, Randy."

7. "I know, I know," replied Randy. "It's just that I can't do everything. But, I do have ten appointments scheduled for next week with various physicians, health care units, and community organizations in the area. I'm also having special meetings with staff to tell them to be more sales-oriented at the counter and in dealing with patients." "Good," said Donna, "let's hope you score high on those and others."

8. But Randy did not. The "positives" turned into "possibles," the "possibles" into "maybes," and the "maybes" into "dismals" insofar as an increase in sales and accounts was concerned. As for the visits that Randy planned to make to physicians and others . . . almost all seemed to fall through. The rain was too heavy one day, doctors were not available on Wednesdays, and unexpected absences of regular staff at the store "just didn't permit me to leave . . . "

9. Six days ago Donna met again with Randy and even visited store 62 with him in Ventura on the pretext that she wanted to show Randy the new operation in Ventura. The real purpose was to have Randy meet and watch Juan Martinez, the Ventura pharmacy manager.

10. On the way back to Westlake Village, Donna said, "What did you think of Juan and his store operations?" "OK, I guess," replied Randy. "Of course Martinez has it made. Everyone up there is Hispanic and he just talks a blue streak in Spanish to them, but I don't have any Japanese in Westlake to talk Japanese to, even if I could talk Japanese, which I can't. Besides he's a talker and I don't like to waste my time yakking. I just tell people what must be done, or answer their questions, and then get back to work." Donna protested, "But talking is part of a manager's job!" Answered Randy, "Well, maybe it is for Martinez, but I'd rather work at my trained profession."

11. Donna dropped Randy off at Westlake and then drove to the regional office, feeling pretty dejected. She's going to see Randy again a week from tomorrow and she's not sure how to structure the meeting. Do you have some suggestions? What specific barriers do you see? What goals would you establish for yourself in relation to Randy? How should you handle Randy at this point?

ASSIGNMENTS

1. GROUP DISCUSSION
Break into groups of four or five and discuss the case. Your first step should be to review the situation presented in order to determine that all participants in each group have a similar perception of the incidents described.

Next, analyze the case. What is the major problem? What are the contributing problems? What specific communication barriers are evident? Who is responsible? How can the major and minor problems be solved? What action should be taken now?

After 10 to 15 minutes of discussion by the groups within themselves, open the case to the entire class. Do this by having the spokespeople of four or five groups report their group's findings to the class. Permit class members to respond or ask questions, or both, after each representative speaks.

2. INTERVIEW ROLE PLAY
(a) Break into groups of three. Have one person play Randy Takashita; one, Donna Frigozi; and one, the observer (ask your instructor about the Observer Evaluation Checklist). Act out a three- to five-minute interview between Randy Takashita and Donna Frigozi (after paragraph 11) in which an attempt is made to alleviate or correct the situation described. At the conclusion of the interview, have the observer report his or her reactions.

(b) Change roles and repeat the role play to appreciate another person's approach to the same problem.

3. REPORT
The chain's pharmacy vice president is concerned about store 75 and has requested a report from Donna Frigozi about the situation. Write such a report (after paragraph 11) to include your analysis, conclusions, and recommendations.

4. MEMOS
(a) As the chain's pharmacy vice president, write a brief memo (after paragraph 3) to Donna Frigozi, indicating that of the nine outlets targeted for increased growth in 1990–1993, eight have responded positively but not store 75 (Randy Takashita's store). Ask Donna if she can account for the low response from store 75.

(b) As Donna Frigozi, send a memo to Randy (after paragraph 3), noting the vice president's concern. You may also request a reply from Randy.

5. LETTERS
As Donna Frigozi, send a letter (after paragraph 11) to your former pharmacy school professor, whom you respect highly, explaining the Randy Takashita case to her (in general terms) and asking for her counsel and suggestions on how to turn it around.

6. MEETINGS
The Sun Fresh regional managers hold their own meeting once a month. As Donna Frigozi, conduct a 15-minute segment of one of those meetings around the Randy Takashita situation. Attempt to secure feedback and solutions from your seven colleagues on how to turn Randy from a liability into an asset as a store manager.

CASE   **9**

WHOSE PERCEPTION IS CORRECT?

1. Maya Dawson graduated with a degree in engineering in 1982 and went to work for Lockheed. Two years later, she took a more demanding position at McDonnell Douglas. She remained there for four years and then accepted an offer made by Harmon Aircraft.

2. Maya, who is now about 38 years old, is married, has two children, and has a mortgage and the usual set of responsibilities and bills. She frequently attends technical lectures, appears on engineering programs occasionally, and is a candidate for a master's degree. Her university tuition is being underwritten by Harmon's educational reimbursement program. She certainly seems to be a dedicated employee.

3. Her relationship with other employees is good. She seems well liked, though she is not particularly respected for outstanding leadership or technical innovation and creativity. Her strongest point seems to be personal attributes. Customers, suppliers, and Department of Defense representatives think "Maya is a great person and a barrel of fun at dinner." Secretaries like Maya, work hard for her, and always provide cakes for her birthday.

4. However, Jim Jervakis, her supervisor, doesn't see Maya quite that way. Jim became Maya's supervisor in 1993 and almost immediately began to evaluate Maya. Jim found that Maya was great on delegation of project duties, but she rarely followed up. Nor did Maya really get involved with her subordinates in the assignments given them. When Jim questioned several of Maya's subordinates, he found them working on assignments that should have been finished (according to Jim) some time ago. When asked about the amount of time expended, some of her subordinates said: "Well, we don't see her after she's given us a job. Sure we like to be on our own, but some direction from the boss is needed from time to time." But several others said they liked the autonomy.

5. Jim spoke to Maya about her relationship with her subordinates and her policy. "It's simple," said Maya. "I like to delegate jobs and then get out of the way so the employees can do it their way without a lot of interference from management."

6. "But your projects often fall behind schedule," said Jim.

7. "That may be true," replied Maya, "But that's because the project requires more time, not because of my leadership style. Besides, I can show you a hundred projects at Harmon Aircraft that have fallen behind schedule."

8. The discussion between them continued but did not seem to resolve any of the differences in perception that each had.

9. In January 1994, Jim completed an evaluation on Maya. The rating was below average and was supported by comments relating to Maya's lack of follow-up on project assignments and Maya's inadequate coordination on project responsibilities.

10. On the basis of this evaluation, and the guidelines which were issued in 1991, Maya was given a low salary increase in March. Nevertheless, her pay level was still average for her classification and level of job performance.

11. When Maya was told of the increase she received in March, she immediately made an appointment with her supervisor, Jim Jervakis.

They met, talked, and argued a bit, but nothing was resolved.

12. The same day Maya filed a complaint with the Employee Relations Department. She indicated that (1) her evaluation from Jim was the first one she had since 1990, even though company policy states that annual evaluations should normally be held, (2) she had no idea that any of her supervisors perceived her work as less than excellent, (3) there are no disciplinary or negative documents in her file, and (4) Jim Jervakis is merely trying to make an example of her.

13. Jim immediately followed up, and to his surprise, he found that there were no evaluations of record on Maya for 1988–1992. He then called two of Maya's former supervisors. One said he counseled Maya about better follow-up on assignments at least twice and orally indicated project responsibility deficiencies on other occasions. The other supervisor said she had completed at least one evaluation on Maya, indicating that Maya handled responsibilities in a less than satisfactory manner. The supervisor did not remember if the evaluation was written or oral.

14. Both supervisors indicated, however, that their oral comments, suggestions, and complaints to Maya were never documented.

15. Jim Jervakis has decided to talk to Maya Dawson about the situation before it goes further. What do you feel his approach should be? What are the communication barriers which you see? How can they be resolved now? What should have been done in the past? Do you feel this conflict situation can be resolved? How?

ASSIGNMENTS

1. GROUP DISCUSSION

Break into groups of four or five and discuss the case. Your first step should be to review the situation presented in order to determine that all participants in each group have a similar perception of the incidents described.

Next, analyze the case. What is the major problem? What are the contributing problems? What specific communication barriers are evident? Who is responsible? How can the major and minor problems be solved? What action should be taken now?

After 10 to 15 minutes of discussion by the groups within themselves, open the case to the entire class. Do this by having the spokespeople of four or five groups report their group's findings to the class. Permit class members to respond or ask questions, or both, after each representative speaks.

2. INTERVIEW ROLE PLAY

(a) Break into groups of three. Have one person play the role of Maya Dawson; one, Jim Jervakis; and one, the observer (ask your instructor about the Observer Evaluation Checklist). Act out a five- to eight-minute interview between Jim Jervakis and Maya Dawson (after paragraph 15) in which an attempt is made to alleviate or correct the situation described. At the conclusion of the interview, have the observer report his or her reactions.

(b) Change roles and repeat the role play to appreciate another person's approach to the same problem.

3. REPORT

As Supervisor Jim Jervakis, write a recommendation report to the executive vice president, recommending that all managers in the organization complete a work appraisal report on each subordinate every six months. Furthermore, recommend that the appraisal reports be signed by both the supervisor and subordinate, dated, and a copy filed for documentation purposes. You may wish to do some library research and include substantiation of your recommendations by citing actual sources.

4. MEMOS

(a) As Jim Jervakis, write a memo to Maya Dawson (after paragraph 8) in which you record the substance of your interview (paragraphs 5, 6, 7, and 8) and suggest some changes in Maya's relationship with her associates.

(b) As Maya Dawson, try to appreciate her perception and reply to Jim's memo (also after paragraph 8).

(c) Write the memo Maya would have completed when she filed her complaint with the Employee Relations Department (paragraph 12). The memo should serve as the complaint.

CASE **10**

BILL WEBSTER'S ETHICAL DILEMMA

1. The Webster Pharmaceutical Distribution Company is a relatively small firm with 80 percent of its accounts on the West Coast. Like most pharmaceutical distribution firms, it acts as the intermediary between manufacturers and independent pharmacies, chain drugstores, hospital pharmacies, home health organizations, and many small mail-order pharmacy organizations.

2. Bill Webster established the firm in 1986 with headquarters in San Francisco. It has been a struggle, but he has managed to slowly grow despite the giant distributors. Because he can't beat them on price, he has emphasized service in a meaningful way. One method is his computer system, which is tied in to each of his accounts. Outlets that did not have computer capability were supplied with a computer for only a $100 fee and a promise to be a customer for at least a year.

3. Bill has also worked on twice-a-day delivery, where needed, for 80 percent of his accounts. In addition, he has emphasized face-to-face relationships, a valuable biweekly newsletter, and a delivery system that is efficient, fast, and made up of courteous and competent drivers.

4. As a result, Webster now has distribution centers in Seattle, Portland, San Diego, and Los Angeles as well as San Francisco.

5. All of these initiatives have stretched Webster rather thin, but there was no problem until mid-1990 when fires broke out in two major distribution centers: San Francisco and Los Angeles. It was obviously arson (never solved) but the incident proved to be a catastrophe for Webster Pharmaceutical Distribution Company. Orders were delayed, computer records were scrambled, and confusion reigned. It was almost two weeks before the Los Angeles and San Francisco accounts could be properly serviced through a variety of makeshift arrangements.

6. As a result, 20 percent of Webster's accounts switched to other distributors, several drivers quit to join competitors, pilferage rose, and absenteeism increased.

7. Bill almost threw in the towel, but he did hang on, slowly came back, and even forged ahead. But it was a struggle to regain accounts and rebuild con-

fidence. Everything was doing quite well until today . . .

8. On the 6 A.M. news Bill Webster heard that consumers in San Jose, Seattle, and San Diego were *possibly* poisoned by a substance in the common cold medication, Flu-Gone. He immediately called the manufacturer, the FDA, and another distributor for information. None of them had any verification, information, or even advice except to say the Flu-Gone packets (that are allegedly involved) came from Lot A202. Bill checked and found that was the same identification number (among several other lots) of Flu-Gone in all his distribution centers.

9. All his trucks leave at 7:15 A.M. and begin deliveries. He can't pull Flu-Gone from the orders to several hundred accounts; all he can do is stop deliveries to everyone and pull the product. If he does that, deliveries will be delayed by 24 hours, and when they are made, none of the accounts will receive the Flu-Gone ordered.

10. Should Bill halt deliveries and cause ill-will if the scare is unfounded? Should he let the deliveries go, assuming this is another of ten similar unfounded rumors in the past year. What about his liability now that he knows the lot number? If someone *is* poisoned, and Bill was aware of the lot number, he will surely lose every asset he has.

11. What decision do you suggest to Bill Webster, considering the ethics involved and the background and development of the Webster Pharmaceutical Distribution Company?

ASSIGNMENTS

1. GROUP DISCUSSION

Break into groups of four or five and discuss the case. Your first step should be to review the situation presented in order to determine that all participants in each group have a similar perception of the incidents described.

Next analyze the case. What is (are) the major ethical problem(s)? What are the contributing problems? What specific communication barriers are evident? Who is responsible? How can the major and minor problems be solved? What action should be taken now?

After 10 to 15 minutes of discussion by the groups within themselves, open the case to the entire class. Do this by having the spokespeople of four or five groups report their group's findings to the class. Permit class members to respond or ask questions, or both, after each representative speaks.

2. INTERVIEW ROLE PLAY

(a) Break into groups of three. Have one person play Bill Webster; one, his immediate subordinate; and one, the observer (ask your instructor about the Observer Evaluation Checklist). Act out a five- to eight-minute interview between Bill Webster and his subordinate (after paragraph 11) in which they discuss alternative courses of action to alleviate or solve the problem. At the conclusion of the interview, have the observer report his or her reactions and the reasons why he or she selected one solution over another.

(b) Change roles and repeat the role play to appreciate another person's approach to the same problem.

3. REPORT

Assume you are an outside consultant. Write a report on this case which is to be submitted to the Ethics Committee of the National Wholesale Drug Distributors Association. Indicate the situation that you found plus the conclusions and recommendations you made to Bill Webster. Make any assumptions you feel are reasonable and necessary.

4. MEMO

As Bill Webster, assume this case has been taken care of (one way or another) about three weeks ago. Write a memo to your four department heads in which you lay out concise instructions on how similar situations should be handled in the future.

5. LETTER

As the outside consultant in assignment 3, write a cover letter to the ethics committee to accompany your report.

C A S E **11**

WAS THIS REALLY FRAUD?

1. Betty Wagner had been employed for several

years as a social worker with the Bureau of Public Welfare in the city of St. Louis. Just three months ago, she was relieved of some of her cases and assigned to the Fraud and Ethics Committee. This moved Betty up a pay grade and increased her monthly compensation. In her department, this assignment was looked on as a bit of a plum and an indication of possible additional advances. Betty, however, still enjoyed her assignment as a case worker.

2. Betty, in the fourth month of her new dual role, enjoyed the work. Because she felt so strongly about cheaters who received welfare and did not really qualify, she received special satisfaction from her Fraud and Ethics Committee work. She pointed out, in no uncertain terms, that such cases cut down on funds available (even through millions were allocated each year to her department), that deserving people were deprived of a higher allotment, and that all taxpayers suffered.

3. Today, however, Betty is in a dilemma. She has just come from the tiny apartment of Wilma Perkowski, a 77-year-old welfare recipient who has obviously committed fraud.

4. Betty determined, after spending over an hour in an interview with the welfare recipient that (1) Mrs. Perkowski receives $100 each month in food stamps, (2) Mrs. Perkowski is more than a little confused and really has no idea what is legal and what is illegal in connection with food stamps, and (3) Mrs. Perkowski did indeed sell $80 of her March food stamps to a stronger for $30. There is no doubt that if this situation is evaluated and Mrs. Perkowski appears before the Fraud and Ethics Committee, it will ask her to refund $80 to the city and it will also disqualify her for food stamps (and other welfare assistance) for 12 months.

5. In her interview with Mrs. Perkowski, Betty learned that late in February, Mrs. Perkowski came down with a bad case of flu. With no one to care for her, Mrs. Perkowski took the bus to her sister's home 200 miles away. She remained there almost four weeks, recovered, and returned home on March 28. In fact, she showed Betty her bus tickets.

6. On March 29 she took all her March food stamps with her when she went shopping. Waiting in the check-out line, she explained to the woman behind her that it was a pity that she would only be able to use about $20 of her $100 March allotment before the month ended. (On April 1, the

March stamps became invalid.) The woman promptly offered to buy Mrs. Perkowski's surplus stamps for $30.

7. Because Mrs. Perkowski had spent most of her small Social Security check on the bus tickets and gifts for her sister's children, she really needed some additional money to buy her April medications. As a result, she told Betty, she was happy to get the $30.

8. Betty was absolutely convinced that Mrs. Perkowski did not purposely defraud. Nevertheless, what she did do was illegal. Betty wondered if she should report Mrs. Perkowski or assume that the admonition she administered would take care of things. On the other hand, Betty isn't convinced that Mrs. Perkowski understands—even now— that what she did was wrong. If one of the division inspectors uncovered the whole affair (a very good possibility), Betty was sure to be disciplined if not terminated. Betty would find it difficult to secure another good job in the currently depressed job market. Furthermore, she would have no basis for fighting such a termination because fraud and one of her clients were involved. In addition, Betty is convinced that Mrs. Perkowski would not hesitate to discuss this incident openly with almost anyone at any time. If Betty did nothing today, the incident may still come out in six months, a year, or even longer from today.

9. What decision should Betty make, in your opinion?

ASSIGNMENTS

1. GROUP DISCUSSION

Break into groups of four or five and discuss the case. Your first step should be to review the situation presented in order to determine that all participants in each group have a similar perception of the incidents described.

Next, analyze the case. What is (are) the major ethical problem(s)? What are the contributing problems? What specific communication barriers are evident? Who is responsible? How can the major and minor problems be solved? What action should be taken now?

After 10 to 15 minutes of discussion by the groups within themselves, open the case to the entire class. Do this by having the spokespeople of four or five groups report their group's findings to the class. Permit class members to respond or ask questions, or both, after each representative speaks.

2. INTERVIEW ROLE PLAY

(a) Break into groups of three. Have one person play Betty Wagner; one, Mrs. Perkowski; and one, the observer (ask your instructor about the Observer Evaluation Checklist). Act out a five-to eight-minute interview (after paragraph 7) in which Betty attempts to convey to Mrs. Perkowski the seriousness of the situation. At the conclusion of the interview, have the observer report his or her reactions on the success (or lack of success) of Betty Wagner's discussion with Mrs. Perkowski.

(b) In this role play, have Betty Wagner talk with her superior, who is now in full possession of all the facts. Have the observer report back as to the success (or lack of success) of Betty's discussion with her superior. Naturally, Betty will try to make a strong case for everyone to overlook Mrs. Perkowski's unintentional but illegal action.

(c) Have one person play the role of Betty; one, the inspector for the Bureau of Public Welfare; and one, the observer (ask your instructor about the Observer Evaluation Checklist). The interview should be held after paragraph 8 and on the assumption that the inspector knows all the facts and has spoken to Mrs. Perkowski. Here again, Betty will try to make a strong case for everyone to overlook the entire situation and Mrs. Perkowski's unintentional but illegal act.

3. MEMO

Assume you are Betty Wagner. Write a memo to file with a copy to Mrs. Perkowski (after paragraph 7). Your intent is to explain to Mrs. Perkowski that her action was illegal. Your secondary purpose is to protect yourself in the event of future action against you.

4. REPORT

As the inspector from the Bureau of Public Welfare of the city of St. Louis who has investigated this case, write a report to the director of the bureau. You are now in possession of all the facts and you have interviewed both Betty Wagner and Mrs. Perkowski. Remember to include your conclusions and recommendations. Make any assumptions you feel are reasonable.

5. MEETING

As the chairperson of the Commission of the Bureau of Public Welfare (all nonsalaried citizens), call a meeting of six to ten people. Your objective is to reach a decision on how similar cases (to the one described) should be handled in the future.

READINGS

READING 1

THE CASE OF THE TEAM-SPIRIT TAILSPIN

R. Daniel Foster

Century Airlines had made it—so far. In the decade following airline deregulation, every month seemed to usher in a new crisis—whether over the availability of landing slots and gates or over the cost of equipment leases and fuel. But under the skillful leadership of its long-time president and CEO, the $300 million regional carrier struggled through.

In 1989, Century's battle-weary leader retired and handed the reins to his protégé, Richard Johnson. Johnson's appointment was no surprise within the company, nor was it a disappointment. Johnson knew the airline industry inside and out. He had helped negotiate a partnership to feed the hub of a large domestic carrier, and he had been instrumental in winning the cooperation of Century's unions.

Johnson knew that Century's continued survival depended on consistently high levels of customer service and that service excellence in turn required the commitment of the work force. He also knew that employees had made many sacrifices—wages and hiring had been frozen for two years—and that morale had suffered as workers complained of being asked to do more work for less pay. To build commitment and boost morale, he enlisted the help of the unions, middle management, and the human resources department to develop what he called the Century Spirit program.

Johnson announced the Spirit program in a letter to employees. The letter described his goal of creating a positive work environment in which teamwork, creativity, and change could flourish. The program consisted of four mechanisms: cross-functional task forces, open communication, recognition committees, and individual initiative. "The effectiveness of these mechanisms and the success of the program." he wrote, "depends on you. Your spirit and mine—a Century Spirit—will pull us through."

By December 1990, the Spirit program was well under way. Two task forces had completed their training and were about to begin their meetings; the recognition committee had given awards to all employees for achieving performance targets companywide; and the *Plane Truth,* a biweekly newspaper a group of flight attendants had started, was beginning its second year in print.

But while the Spirit program showed signs of lifting morale, outside forces were undermining it. As fuel costs soared in the wake of Iraq's invasion of Kuwait and passenger miles slumped in the face of a business downturn, management cut back worker's hours and set ever-higher quality goals. Anxious to preserve their jobs, employees agreed to management's requests, but tensions mounted. When the employee newspaper—one of the individual initiatives Johnson had explicitly encouraged—began to publish articles critical of the company, it was hard to tell whether the newspaper was venting workers' frustration and reinforcing team spirit or was stirring up old animosities and bringing the whole company down.

"And please return your seats to their upright position."

Chris Gulden hung up the microphone and strapped herself in for the landing, then turned to her coworker Bob Rodriguez, who was seated beside her. "Have you seen the latest *Plane Truth*? she asked.

"I read it in the lounge this morning. That *Ask Myra* column is pretty funny."

"Sometimes it is. That one about what people did with those little service awards—you know, those miniature silver-plated DC-9s we all got—was kind of clever. Seven percent played war games with other employees, 12% leased it to Ridgeway Air, 42% gave it to their kids, who lost it right away."

"That's why I like it. It's not afraid to be irreverent. And you have to respect management for encouraging something like this."

"But some of the articles are so critical. It makes you wonder if we're doing anything right. That's not what we need to hear right now—and apparently management agrees. My friend Pat works in the executive offices, and she says Johnson is pretty mad about the whole thing."

"The paper's not that critical. It's just meant to be funny. Why should it bother Mr. Johnson so much? He seems to have a good sense of humor."

"It's like giving somebody's kid a fifth of whiskey. Richard Johnson's Spirit program is near and dear to his heart, and he thinks that it's being corrupted."

"He should just ignore the paper. It's not meant for management. Besides, nobody takes that stuff seriously."

"The people writing it sure do."

Richard Johnson had summoned Joan Raffin, Century's director of human resources, to his office. Raffin knocked on Johnson's open door and walked in. Even before she had pulled up a chair, Johnson started.

"One of our board members stopped by my office this morning. He handed me a copy of the *Plane Truth*. Somebody left it in first class on a crowded morning flight, and he picked it up. Damn good thing he did. Have you been monitoring this? Nothing but satire and half-truths. This paper is dangerous. Can you imagine what customers would think if they got their hands on it? Our own employees complaining about slow turnarounds and lost luggage!"

"I understand what you're saying. Some of the articles touch on some sensitive issues. But the newspaper is very popular, even with the pilots and machinists. I myself wrote an article that explained our new insurance procedures, and I've gotten some useful feedback from the letters to the ed—"

"We can't have this," Johnson shot back. "I don't know who's responsible. Frankly, I don't care. I want this stopped. We can't let one drop of vinegar turn the whole company sour."

"When you say stopped, do you mean you want to cancel the newspaper completely?" Raffin asked uneasily. "We should talk about that. It's true that people are uncomfortable with the tone and don't want to keep reading about problems. But I've also heard people say, 'We never would have seen this before Richard Johnson took over.' For some, the newspaper is symbolic. I'm worried that if we come down too hard—"

"You know what I worry about? Team spirit. Fuel costs have doubled in the past six months. Passenger miles are down 10%. We'll have to post another loss this quarter. The only way we'll pull through is to run more efficiently—boost our yields, cut fuel usage. Most of all, we need to make customers happy: improve our turnaround and on-times, provide a quality experience. We need positive thinking! Don't worry about coming down too hard. What you're really doing is coming down on the side of team spirit. That's what we need to make the Spirit program work."

When Raffin returned to her office, her secretary reminded her of a lunch meeting with Helen Wein, president of the United Federation of Flight Attendants (UFFA) local. Raffin dashed down to the company cafeteria, where Wein was waiting. They worked their way through the buffet line, cleared a table in the corner, and sat down to eat.

Wein started. "Joan, you and I have been through a lot together, and you know I've always been a peaceful person. So you should be among the first to know that I'm no longer opposed to violence—as long as it's directed at Al Jacoby in technical operations!"

"I thought you and Al had a friendly antagonism."

"Most of the time he's just having fun, but lately it hasn't been very amusing. He's always lording his power over somebody, especially when his cherished machinists are on the ropes. Now that their hours have been cut back like everybody else's, some of the more vocal members have been complaining to Al since he's the shop steward. So Al's been looking for a scapegoat, and he thinks he's found one in UFFA."

"What's he blaming you for?"

"He comes nosing around here saying we don't have team spirit and accusing us of undermining Johnson's Spirit program. That's ludicrous. We've been supporting the program from the beginning. Why wouldn't we? We helped create it."

"What triggered all this?" Raffin asked."You want the plain truth? That damn newspaper. Everyone knows that flight attendants publish it. So Al assumes it's some kind of official organ of UFFA. He knows better, but he plays dumb."

"So he's mad about what's in the newspaper?" Raffin asked.

"He's furious. He thinks UFFA is intentionally trying to weaken the machinists' credibility by writing articles implying that the machinists are lazy and take too many breaks. He says that they're not getting enough credit for their work, that it doesn't show up in the turnaround figures because the fleet is so old. He's got a point, but he should leave us out of it."

"I just talked with Al yesterday," Raffin said. "He didn't discuss any of that with me."

"That's because he doesn't want to advertise the fact that he's struggling to keep his group together. Some of the machinists are mad about cutting their hours—especially now that no one is getting any profit sharing. As if they're the only ones feeling overworked and underappreciated. They don't even trust the recognition committee because they think the flight attendants and pilots get all the glory."

"Al seemed to understand the philosophy when we set those targets. Shared responsibility and shared rewards—that's the whole point."

"Frankly, things aren't as bad as Al thinks. You'll always have a handful of people who complain. We have them in UFFA. The difference between Al and me is that I'm facing up to it. I'm willing to confront the complainers, while Al's afraid of losing votes in the next election."

"What do you propose we do?" Raffin asked.

"The solution is easy. Since my complainers are stirring up his complainers, we can kill two birds with one stone if we stop publishing that newspaper. Otherwise, all the talk about openness and teamwork will be a big joke."

Flight attendant Angie Palazzo waited nervously outside Joan Raffin's office. When Raffin returned from lunch, Palazzo rose quickly to greet her.

"I don't have an appointment, but I was hoping I could talk to you."

"Of course, come in." Raffin gestured for Palazzo to sit in one of her upholstered chairs. She closed the door and sat in the chair beside her. "You seem upset. What can I do?"

"I suppose you know that I've done some writing for the *Plane Truth.*"

"Actually, I didn't know that," Raffin responded cheerfully.

'Palazzo started to relax. "I'm new at it, as a lot of the contributors are. It's probably pretty obvious."

"No. It's been terrific to see how talented some of our flight attendants are."

Palazzo smiled, then her face grew serious. "I heard that management wants to stop the newspaper. That's what I came here to talk to you about. Everybody used to hold it up as a model. Even Mr. Johnson. Now all of a sudden UFFA doesn't like it, and we're getting pressure to stop publishing it."

Raffin wasn't prepared to make Johnson's decision public, especially since she wasn't sure she agreed with it. "I don't know where you're getting pressure from, but I can tell you that Mr. Johnson hasn't made any decisions yet. We're aware of some problems, but why don't you tell me your thoughts about it."

"I think it would be a big mistake to cancel it. Maybe I'm off base, but it really bothers me," Palazzo said.

"What bothers you?"

"The hypocrisy. I mean, I really believe in teamwork. Flight attendants have always had to work together. That's how we're trained, and that's probably why we're publishing the paper and not the pilots or the machinists or the baggage handlers. They can't cooperate on anything. So here we thought we were setting an example. And we felt pretty good about that. But now everybody wants us to stop."

"Who's everybody? Do you mean the union?"

"Mostly UFFA," Palazzo responded. "Some of the machinists are giving the flight attendants a hard time too. But this morning, everyone's saying that management is going to tell us to stop. It's just a matter of time until we get the memo saying forget it."

"To be honest, I've heard some complaints about the newspaper too," Raffin said. "But I'd like to hear what people have said to you."

"That it's nothing but a lot of complaining. That it goes against company goals. Everybody wants to pretend that we're one big, happy family. But we're not. We've got a lot of problems, problems we'll never solve if we keep our heads in the sand. If people are upset about the *Plane Truth,* it's because they can't face up to what's really going on."

"I think the fact that you name names is what a lot of people find so disconcerting," Raffin interjected.

"If it hits too close to home, maybe people ought to think about why. Maybe the machinists see a little too much truth in the reports that they take long breaks and cover for each other. That's not a reason to cancel the paper. That's a reason to continue it! And so are the letters we get from people who never would have said anything before. Even the pilots and machinists are writing."

"No one seems to object to the *idea* of the newspaper," Raffin responded. "The issue seems to be whether there's been too much criticism. As you know, people are struggling to keep a positive attitude."

"Right," Palazzo agreed, "and part of feeling positive is believing that we're doing the right things—and not denying that things aren't perfect. And having a little fun. What's Mr. Johnson's idea of open communication, 'Free Kitten to Good Home'? I thought that was the point of the Spirit program. What's going to happen with the task forces? Are *they* going to be too negative?"

"There's also concern about what customers would think if they saw the paper," Raffin said.

"Customers know when employees are miserable. It comes through in everything. If we lose this newspaper, it will be one more blow for employees. It's bound to show up in the work."

Raffin was sympathetic, but she didn't want to be too encouraging. "I'm not quite sure what I can say to make you feel better, Angie, except that I want to see us overcome this problem. It took a lot for you to come up here and have this conversation. I appreciate that."

Joan Raffin replayed the day's conversations over and over in her mind. Why was she so con-fused about what to do? She knew that she was supposed to carry out Richard Johnson's wishes, yet she didn't want to act until she was sure he had thought the matter through. True, the *Plane Truth* could be very damaging in customers' hands. But losing it might undermine the Spirit program; the paper was, after all, the kind of individual initiative the program encouraged. The newspaper was creating tension, but it was also creating unity. And while some people found the negativity dispiriting, others found the humor uplifting. Raffin could see the logic on both sides and found herself standing alone in the middle.

Reprinted by permission of *Harvard Business Review.*
"The Case of the Team-Spirit Tailspin" by R. Daniel Foster, January-February 1991. Copyright © 1991 by the President and Fellows of Harvard College; all rights reserved.

How to Use Electronic Mail Successfully

Roger Nall

You can't discuss organizational change today without discussing the impact of new technology. And because of its growing popularity in the workplace, one technological development worthy of note is electronic or "E-mail."

Electronic mail is a unique way of communicating. E-mail is information provided without such cues as body language or voice tone to clarify the intent of the message. And if managers are to make the most of it, it's important they remember this fact. If it is to have the impact it promises on productivity and organizational effectiveness, then managers have to be especially conscious of how people may read the messages sent via E-mail.

A CASE IN POINT

To illustrate, a note might read, "Don't you think you should look at this possibility?" How the message is interpreted depends on many factors, including the receiver's professional relationship with the sender, the general "climate" and stress levels at work, perhaps even the receiver's mood at the time. The sender's level of responsibility in the company also may determine the receiver's reaction.

If the same manager said the same thing in person in a conversation, or perhaps made the same comment in a larger formal memo, the receiver might see the message as a way of the manager showing support to the receiver or receiver's project by offering an option that might not have otherwise been considered. Another, equally possible interpretation is that the recipient of the message is being asked to support some project of the sender of the message. But when one sees such a message on a screen, one could assume that someone thinks the receiver of the message has been negligent in his or her responsibilities or that the sender is being patronizing.

Another uniqueness of electronic mail is its immediacy, and this, too, can create problems. We've all seen cases when a note written and sent in the heat of the moment has damaged a long-term working relationship. E-mail sent in haste can have the same effect, and unknowingly so, since the sender has no such cues as facial expression, body language, or tone of voice to determine the receiver's response to the message.

Electronic mail does not allow receiver feedback.

SENDING E-MAIL

Given these aspects of E-mail, what can you as a manager do to make your messages via E-mail most successful?

- Always read what you have written before you send it. Put yourself in the receiver's shoes. Read the note as if you were him or her.
- Never write anything when you are irritated or upset about something. Walk away from the screen and relax or calm down, then return and reflect on the note before possibly doing any damage by sending it.
- Write complete messages, not just a few phrases or words. A complete message shows more interest in and respect for the receiver.
- Use the spell check and formatting processes, if they are available, to enhance the readability of the note.
- Remember to use words like "please" and "thank you" to soften the message.

- Use E-mail sparingly for negative news. Sincere, positive notes can strengthen professional relationships with your colleagues.
- Use at least as much tact on electronic notes as would be required on a similar note on paper. Always remember that a note might be received by accident by the wrong person or that the receiver might send the note to another individual.

READING **3**

LEARNING FROM JAPAN

Kevin Kelly, Otis Port, James Treece, Gail DeGeorge, and Zachary Schiller

Like countless suppliers before him, James J. Lohman was seething as he left a 1985 meeting in Detroit. Three years earlier he had mortgaged his company, Excel Industries Inc. in Elkhart, Ind., to develop a better way to make car windows. His innovations promised to help Ford Motor Co., Excel's top customer, slice inventory and assembly costs. Yet now, Ford was planning to bring the technology in-house—a move that would ravage Excel.

Lohman still recalls with satisfaction what happened next: Ford couldn't master Excel's process. So, in a humbling rapprochement, America's No. 2 auto maker proposed a sweet deal. For $18 million, Excel would buy Ford's window factory in Fulton, Ky. Then, to keep some control, Ford would acquire 40% of Excel for $25 million. Ford also agreed to buy 70% of its windows from Excel through 1993. By last year, the smaller company's sales had hit $350 million, nearly four times its 1985 revenues, and Ford had saved millions. Emboldened, Excel has plowed $4 million into better manufacturing systems. Today, it can equip new Ford models a year faster than before, helping Ford shorten its new-product cycle. Declares Dennis F. Wilke, general manager of Ford's glass division: "There's a spirit of trust. We're both trying to find the most efficient solutions."

Besides making sense, the Ford-Excel deal speaks volumes about U.S. frustration at being overtaken by Japan. For a decade, American companies have been altering their game to play Japanese-style, streamlining their lumbering corporate hierarchies to focus on teamwork, quality, and speed. But no matter what they tried, most fell further behind. "It's like we're still playing single-wing football, while they've found the forward pass," says Marshall C. Phelps Jr., director of governmental programs at IBM.

LEVELING THE FIELD

Well, the contest isn't over yet. In the past six years, hundreds of companies, from big IBM to little Excel, in industries as diverse as computers, semiconductors, autos, farm implements, and motorcycles, have shared Ford's revelation. They, too, are revamping their cultures and recasting their investment practices to form cooperative links both vertically, down their supply lines, and horizontally, with universities, research labs, and their peers. Encouraged by the Bush Administration's leniency toward antitrust, even direct competitors are slipping between the sheets. The most astonishing deal may be the one last June between IBM and archrival Apple Computer Inc. to jointly develop personal computers and software.

These ventures may do more than any presidential mission to help level the playing field with Japan. Indeed, says David E. Cole, director of the University of Michigan's Office for the Study of Automotive Transportation, U.S. industries finally are learning to compete in the same league with the monoliths the Japanese call *keiretsu,* or business groups. Cole sees a new U.S. industrial pattern emerging. He calls it "an American-style *keiretsu.*"

Such a comparison can't be taken too literally, of course. U.S. laws enacted during the 1930s broke up huge multicompany trusts such as the powerful House of Morgan, which included banking, steel, railroad, and shipping companies. Fiefdoms like that were probably America's closest counterpart to Japan's horizontal *keiretsu.* These giants are collections of dozens of major companies spanning several industries and held together by cross-shareholdings, old-boy networks, and a compulsion to hammer rival groups. At the hub of each is a bank or cash-rich company that provides low-cost, patient capital. Together, the Sumitomo, Sanwa, Mitsui, Mitsubishi, Fuyo, and Dai Ichi Kangyo groups account for roughly one-fourth of Japan's total business assets and revenues.

PYRAMIDS

Nor would Western culture tolerate vertical *keiretsu,* Japan's other variety. These are pyramids of companies that serve a single master. Every large manufacturer, whether it belongs to a horizontal group or not, dictates virtually everything—including prices it will pay—to hundreds of suppliers that are often prohibited from doing business outside the *keiretsu.* At the pyramid's bottom is a swarm of job shops and family ventures with primitive working conditions and subsistence-level pay and profits.

But if pure *keiretsu* are un-American, the U.S. can still learn from them. The horizontal groups provide security and stability to promote the risk-taking and long-term investment often shunned by U.S. companies. And by collaborating on research and production, *keiretsu* members regularly deliver new products ahead of lone-wolf rivals. Toyota Motor Corp., one of 24 companies in the Mitsui Group, drives its new-car designs into showrooms in four years, vs. five to eight for Detroit and Europe. And even the pyramids of indentured companies, with their emphasis on continual cost reduction and quick response, prove the value of having close supplier ties.

U.S. companies can no longer ignore these advantages, say experts such as Lester C. Thurow, dean of Massachusetts Institute of Technology's Sloan School of Management. Across the spectrum of industrial technology, from advanced materials to next-generation semiconductors and futuristic "agile" factories that ultimately may turn out customized cars in a few days, the costs of research and development are soaring—at accelerating rates. Tomorrow's keystone technologies are so expensive to nurture, says Deborah L. Wince-Smith, Assistant Commerce Secretary for technology policy, that U.S. companies "cannot commercialize them" with out banding together and sharing the risks. This is especially true given the compressed time frames within which new products must get to market.

In short, there's a pressing need for U.S. manufacturers to develop something similar to *keiretsu.* What they're building could even be better:

alliances where collaboration reinforces capitalism at all levels. American suppliers, more than their Japanese counterparts, provide many of the advances that drive innovation. Elevate their role, and some executives believe that America can build an industrial system that is technologically stronger and swifter afoot than Japan's. Three years ago, for instance, Digital Equipment Corp. acquired a 5% stake in MIPS Computer Systems Inc., which is 25% owned by Japan's Kubota Corp. Then, DEC used a MIPS chip for new workstations instead of designing a chip of its own. Because of such moves, "we're more efficient as a technology organization than ever before," says Henry A. Crouse, DEC's vice-president for strategic relations.

Despite such assessments, there's plenty of skepticism whether a keiretsu-style approach will work in the U.S. Many large manufacturers still treat suppliers like disposable diapers, changing them frequently to get the best price. And playing suppliers off against each other—which even Ford still does—keeps them short of capital to modernize. That's one reason U.S. factories have more outmoded equipment than the plants of other industrialized countries: The average age of the U.S. equipment is around 14 years, which experts believe is double the figures for Japan and Europe. Contentious tactics also spawn distrust, which may help explain the lackluster record, so far, of the 250-odd R&D consortiums formed in the U.S. since 1982. Still, TRW Inc. Chairman Joseph T. Gorman, who accompanied President Bush on his recent trip to Japan, thinks keiretsu experiments are a must. "Unless we move in that direction, we don't stand a chance against the Japanese," he says.

GOING HOME

Such sentiment is richly ironic. People forget that Henry Ford started out totally reliant on suppliers, notes Susan Helper, assistant professor of economics at Case Western Reserve University in Cleveland. All Ford did was bolt on a body and wheels. The chassis, engine, gearbox, and other parts were built by suppliers and assembled by Dodge Bros. But by the 1930s, Ford was vertically integrated down to its own steel plant, partly because its suppliers couldn't make quality parts.

Now, Ford and others are returning to their roots. Building on the Excel deal, Ford in late 1990 paid $100 million for 10.8% of Cummins Engine Co., which next fall will supply low-pollution diesel engines for Ford medium trucks. Ford thus avoided a $300 million investment to do the work itself. And Cummins got much-needed cash to fund key R&D for its flagship product, big diesel-truck engines. Over the past few years, Ford has also passed the peace pipe to General Motors Corp. and Chrysler Corp. so the Big Three don't waste money on duplicate research in such "precompetitive" technologies as new materials and electric car batteries.

But the company with the strongest keiretsu leanings may be IBM. Prodded by growing competition from Japan, fear of losing an independent supplier base, and a need to cap its spiraling research costs, Big Blue has been dismantling the fence of insularity and self-sufficiency that once surrounded it. In fact, in what President Jack D. Kuehler terms its "reach-out phase," IBM is helping buttress the infrastructure of the entire U.S. electronic industry. The company's restructuring plans should accelerate the process.

For example, IBM was instrumental in organizing America's first stab at emulating Japanese-style corporate collaboration: the granddaddy of R&D consortiums, Microelectronics & Computer Technology Corp., which does basic research in computer technologies. IBM attended quietly at MCC's 1982 birth, leery that the Justice Dept. might otherwise scuttle MCC on antitrust grounds. By 1987, the antitrust climate had changed, and IBM publicly backed Sematech Inc., the consortium aimed at restoring U.S. leadership in semiconductor-making equipment. IBM became a member and furnished the first chief operating officer for Sematech, which is expected to get a new lease on life, with $100 million a year in federal funding when its charter expires this year. IBM's cajoling has also gotten officials from Sematech and Jessi, Europe's better-funded counterpart, to explore potential collaborations.

Beyond such leadership, IBM is doing plenty of deals. In the past 10 years, it has plowed $1 billion of patient capital into more than 200 companies in Japan, Europe, and the U.S., studiously taking minority stakes in U.S. firms so as not to muddle their entrepreneurial culture. The computer maker also has forked over millions to troubled suppliers as advance payments on future orders or contract research. And IBM can virtually assure the success of a startup by forming a strategic partnership and giving its products a seal of approval. Unlike traditional venture capitalists, "IBM doesn't care much about quick returns on equity," says a former executive of a company that IBM bankrolled. "It wants technology for the long haul."

LOW TECH

Lately, this strategy has involved bigger partners. On the heels of the IBM-Apple agreement came a July deal that shatters more precedents: IBM is teaming up with Germany's Siemens, a competitor, to launch joint production of the next generation of memory chips, 16-megabit dynamic random-access memories (DRAMs), in an IBM plant. Siemens will sell the chips in Europe, the first time IBM chips will have been sold on the open market. Later, Siemens will transfer the technology to its plants.

Dumbfounding as this may seem it's almost anticlimactic in light of the string of shockers IBM uncorked in 1989 and 1990: It took the once-unthinkable step of licensing its crown-jewel DRAM technology to Idaho's Micron Technology Inc. It signed up Siemens to jointly design the 64-megabit memory chips that will replace 16-meg designs around 1994. And it invited Motorola Inc. to send engineers to IBM's hush-hush Advanced Semiconductor Technology Center in East Fishkill, N.Y., to help develop a new chipmaking technique for use at the turn of the century. "These are things we never would have considered in the past," says one IBM manager.

But there's a strong motive now: fear. That has been mounting since 1981, when IBM began doing "technology audits" of the competitiveness of its suppliers vs. their Japanese rivals. IBM was stunned by its findings. In the U.S. and Europe, its handpicked vendors "were becoming less competitive—at an alarming rate," recalls Kuehler. If the trend continues, IBM and the U.S. electronics industry will be dependent on the Japanese not only for DRAMs but also for critical chipmaking equipment. And since most Japanese suppliers are connected to Japan's giant computer builders, that seems a prescription for reducing IBM to a colony of Japanese business.

INTO THE BREACH

Thus, when Perkin-Elmer Corp. put its microlith-ography operations up for sale two years ago, IBM leapt into the breach. Lithography machines are the cornerstone of chipmaking: They "print" the complex circuitry that turns silicon wafers into computer chips. During the 1980s, the Japanese all but drove the U.S. from this business. To preserve an American role, IBM helped underwrite a management buyout of one Perkin-Elmer division and lined up California's Silicon Valley Group Inc.to take the other. IBM also guaranteed SVG's instant success, chipping in $20 million to continue research and ordering enough machines to keep SVG's new unit busy for two years. "IBM was determined to do this for the long term," says Vahe A. Sarkissian, president of SVG Lithography Systems Inc.

Joining Big Blue's circle is not without risk. Sources close to Image Business Systems Corp. (IBS), a three-year-old pioneer in systems that handle documents as graphic images rather than as computer text, say that IBM forced founder David E.Y. Sarna to resign when the New York company ran over budget on development work. IBM had just a 10% IBS stake, worth $6 million, so it couldn't demand Sarna's resignation. But it hinted that it wouldn't aggressively market IBS's product if Sarna stayed on. IBM denies this scenario. And such reports aren't deterring other companies from seeking a place at IBM's table: Big Blue says it can't begin to handle them all.

Manufacturers must be careful about whom they invite because of the commitment it takes to get suppliers up to snuff, then teach them how to continually shorten design times, cut costs, and improve quality. In the mid-1980s, when Harley-Davidson Inc. cut its supplier roster from 320 to 120, it held classes for the survivors in just-in-time inventory management, so they could cut their own costs. "We buy 50% of the dollar value of our motorcycles from suppliers," says Gary E. Kirkham, Harley's manufacturing manager. "So improvements we made [internally] only got us half way."

Such handholding severely tests the engineering and management expertise of the lead company. Both partners also have to build bridges for exchanging information and nurturing trust, which usually means dealing face-to-face. All this can only work if manufacturers use a lot fewer suppliers. And that usually tilts the buyer-supplier relationship. The buyers are still boss—but are compelled by their increased dependence on suppliers to be an ally and partner.

In return for comfy, long-term contracts, suppliers have to jump when they're told to. "We won't do business with them otherwise," declares Cummins Engine President James A. Henderson. And increasingly, suppliers are being asked to open their books to ensure that profits aren't too fat. Excel does this for Ford. "They know every cost we incur," says Excel CEO Lohman.

Still, when the relationship is built on respect as well as price, "both parities win," says Rodney Spear, director of quality assurance at TTI Inc., a Fort Worth company that produces electronic components for Harris Corp., a $3 billion electronics company. TTI was a survivor when Harris' Electronic Systems Sector winnowed its supplier list from 2,500 to 270 in 1989 and 1990. Now, "we get to think long-term," says Spear, and to make investments that will boost quality and productivity.

Harley shows where this can lead. When the motorcycle maker tried drawing up long-term agreements with its remaining suppliers in 1987, its lawyers produced a 40-page book that codified every detail of performance. At that point, says James H. Paterson, a Harley executive vice president, "we threw the lawyers out." Harley produced a brief document outlining goals for suppliers and a way to resolve disputes. "We no longer wage war one against the other," says Kirkham. Instead, Harley battles Honda Motor Co. And it has upped its U.S. share of big-bike sales by 39 points since 1983, to 62%. "It's understandable why the Japanese are doing so well," adds TTI's Spear. "They started implementing these concepts 40 years ago."

USED TOOLS

Financing gets easier when a partnership blossoms. Morton Metalcraft Co., which makes parts for Caterpillar Inc., can't afford the newest machine tools. So, Caterpillar often sells the Morton (Ill.) company used ones—cheap, says CEO William Morton. Novellus Systems Inc. in San Jose, Calif., sometimes equips suppliers, too.

Design also goes smoother with a *keiretsu* approach, as farm-machinery giant Deere & Co., has found. Deere jointly designed its combine cabs with McLaughlin Body Co. in Moline, Ill., and has handed responsibility for their production to McLaughlin, which also makes cabs for Ford and Caterpillar. Says combine factory General Manager Richard E. Kleine: "They knew how to get the noise reduction and increased visibility we needed."

One element still missing from the U.S. approach is the patient capital a *keiretsu* provides. A Bush Administration bank-reform package, debated in the Senate last year, proposed letting manufacturers buy banks, and vice versa. But this idea is all the more controversial because of banking's problems and won't get by Congress soon. That hasn't kept Ford, for one, from making plans for what it would do with a bank. So, says MIT's Thurow, it isn't implausible to imagine, someday, a Ford Group replete with a bank and parts and vehicle makers, tied together by interlocking ownership. "The only question," Thurow adds, "is how soon?"

Skeptics still say that it can't happen here, that cooperation cuts against U.S. individualism. But "look at team sports," notes Michael L. Dertouzos, chairman of the Commission on Industrial Productivity at MIT. Even within companies teamwork is more often the rule than not. "The U.S. is extremely good at blending cooperation and individualism," adds Dertouzos. So, a hybrid that combines a *keiretsu's* strengths with Yankee ingenuity might be a formidable competitor.

Two years ago, Hiroshi Kashiwagi, director general of Japan's most prestigious research lab, the Ministry of International Trade & Industry's Electrotechnical Laboratory, told *Business Week* that if U.S. giants started making better use of their vast storehouse of technology, "we would not be able to compete with them." Today, many companies are embarking on a transformation that may prove him right. It will be a decade or so before the answer is in. But this much is clear. The *keiretsu* approach is one Japanese import that many U.S. companies like.

Source: Reprinted from January 27, 1992 issue of *Business Week* by special permission, copyright © 1992 by McGraw-Hill, Inc.

READING 4

HANDLING SEXUAL HARASSMENT IN THE WORKPLACE

Jeffrey P. Englander

Perhaps the single most important legacy of the confirmation hearings over Judge Clarence Thomas' appointment to the U.S. Supreme Court is that not since passage of the Civil Rights Act of 1964 has the nation's consciousness regarding sexual harassment in the workplace been so abruptly and pervasively raised. Long after the bitter debate over Judge Thomas' fitness has subsided, we will all remain aware that sexual harassment in the workplace is unlawful and need not be tolerated by its victims.

As a practitioner in the area of employment discrimination, I view this as a most important time for businesses (1) to assess their awareness of the legal precepts underlying a viable claim of sexual harassment, (2) to inquire whether they have promulgated written policies on the subject, (3) to scrutinize the legal and practical effectiveness of these policies, and (4) to ensure their proper enforcement.

IS SEXUAL HARASSMENT IN THE WORKPLACE A PROBLEM?

It has become increasingly clear since enactment of Title VII of the Civil Rights Act of 1964 ("Title VII") that "sexual harassment in the workplace is among the most offensive and demeaning torments an employee can undergo." The impact upon victims of sexual discrimination is partly summarized in a 1988 study conducted by the U.S. Merit Systems Protection Board as follows:

> Victims pay all the intangible emotional costs inflicted by anger, humiliation, frustration, withdrawal, dysfunctional family and other damages that can be sexual harassment's aftermath. Victims of the most severe forms of harassment, including rape, can face not only severe emotional consequences, but even the possibility of a life-threatening disease. Some victims may leave jobs for one with a poorer career path, to escape the sexual harassment.

The same study concluded that the cost to the federal government resulting from sexual harassment was devastating as well—over a two-year period, the cost in lost productivity, as well as use of sick leave and job turnover, was $267.3 million.

There is ample evidence to conclude that the problem is at least as widespread and destructive in the private sector. A more recent study concluded that approximately 40% of all working women in both the public and private sectors have, on at least one occasion during their careers, been

the object of sexual advances, propositions, or unwanted sexual discussions from men who supervise or could otherwise affect their positions at work. Given the ever increasing percentage of the total work force in this country who are women (i.e., from 29.6% in 1950 to 45.3% in 1990), the percentage of women who perceive themselves to be the victims of sexual harassment in the workplace translates into a problem of significant magnitude. It also underscores that American employers have been largely unsuccessful in raising corporate consciousness and awareness of the issues and in combatting the root causes of the problem. Thus, while a variety of surveys continue to suggest that only an exceedingly small percentage of women who consider themselves to be victims of sexual harassment actually make formal complaints—either through internal employer grievance mechanisms or with administrative agencies—neither these statistics, nor a belief that the odds make it unlikely that a particular employer will be faced with a formal charge of sexual harassment, should deter a prudent employer from taking all necessary steps to minimize the possibility that it will be compelled to defend such a claim in the future.

WHAT IS SEXUAL HARASSMENT?

As the law has evolved, there are two separate and distinct types of conduct which have been found to constitute sexual harassment in violation of Title VII.

Tangible Job Benefit. The first type, first identified in 1977, is the so-called "tangible job benefit" type, also known as "quid pro quo" harassment. As the name suggests, this form of sexual harassment is found to exist where an employee's career path is directly impacted by a supervisor's unwelcome request for sexual favors or other sexual advances and where the employee's decision ultimately results in a tangible job benefit or detriment or otherwise forms the basis for employment decisions. Specific examples of quid pro quo harassment include: (1) requiring submission to a supervisor's request for sexual favors as a condition of continued employment; (2) granting specific job benefits such as a salary increase or promotion in exchange for sexual favors; and (3) withholding job benefits, such as a wage increase or promotion, or assigning more onerous tasks to an employee who has rejected a supervisor's request for sexual favors. A refusal to hire a job applicant or outright termination of employment would, of course, also be actionable in this context. By extension, it has also been held that an employee who has not been the subject of direct sexual harassment has a viable claim against her employer where another, less qualified employee received a promotion or other job benefit instead of the complainant based upon the other's submission to a superior's request for sexual favors.

Hostile Work Environment. More recently, the U.S. Supreme Court formally recognized a second type of sexual harassment, referred to as "hostile work environment" harassment. Unlike quid pro quo harassment, hostile work environment harassment is actionable even in the absence of any economic effect upon an employee's job status or employment. Employer conduct which is actionable under this type of harassment has been characterized in a variety of ways, perhaps most succinctly in the guidelines of the EEOC promulgated in 1980:

> Unwelcome sexual advances, requests for sexual favors and other verbal or physical conduct of a sexual nature constitutes sexual harassment when . . . such conduct has the purpose or effect of unreasonably interfering with an individual's work performance or creating an intimidating, hostile or offensive working environment.

State courts as well as federal courts have given great deference to these administrative guidelines.

Adopting these guidelines almost verbatim, the Connecticut state legislature has, in Connecticut's Human Rights and Opportunities Act, effective October 1, 1991, expressly defined and outlawed hostile work environment sexual harassment and has thus become one of the more progressive jurisdictions in treating this issue. A similar type of explicit codification of hostile work environment sexual harassment has been proposed in New Jersey (as part of New Jersey's Law Against Discrimination) but, as of this writing, has not been enacted.

The elements necessary of proof in a hostile work environment sexual harassment claim have been enumerated as follows by a New York State court:[1]

> A person would have to show that (1) he or she belongs to a protected group [i.e., female[2] or minority group]; (2) he or she was subject to unwelcome sexual harassment as defined above; (3) the harass-

ment complained of was based upon his or her membership in the protected class; and (4) the harassment complained of affected the terms, conditions or privileges of his or her employment.

Needless to say, the creation of a hostile work environment in violation of Title VII can occur in a multitude of ways depending upon the specific dynamics of an employer's workplace, the size and demographics of the workforce, and, perhaps most importantly, the predisposition of the employer's owners, corporate officers, managerial and supervisory employees, i.e., their sensitivity to sexual harassment-type issues and their collective willingness to do whatever is necessary to prevent the creation (or maintenance) of a hostile work environment. Thus, "firm culture" and the employer's amenability to preserving or changing it is of utmost importance.

STUDIES AND TRENDS

A rather graphic example of an unlawfully hostile work environment was recently described in an opinion of the U.S. District Court for the Northern District of Illinois wherein a female employee's supervisor, under the guise of increasing productivity, yelled at the complainant regularly, called her insulting names such as "syphilis," hit, pinched, and pushed her, made rude and boorish comments and asked her offensive questions. The court held the employer liable, finding that it knew of the supervisor's egregious conduct but condoned it because the supervisor, by engaging in the conduct complained of, substantially increased the employer's profitability. The court awarded the employee both compensatory and punitive damages. It is interesting to note here that part of the court's factual findings revealed that the supervisor did not treat his male subordinate employees anywhere near as badly as he did the plaintiff.

Far more passive employer conduct has also been held in violation of Title VII if it constitutes or contributes to a hostile or offensive work environment. Thus, a federal court has held an employer liable under Title VII for its refusal to remove "girly pin-ups" from its dispatcher's office after newly hired female dispatchers complained. The court ordered that the objectionable material be removed notwithstanding evidence that the practice had been in place for almost 20 years.

The judiciary's increasing sensitivity to claims

of hostile work environment sexual harassment is clearly illustrated by a recent decision of the U.S. Court of Appeals for the Ninth Circuit which promulgated a "reasonable woman" test in order to overcome what it perceived to be the male bias associated with the prior, "reasonable person" test. In that case the court upheld a female employee's claim that she was subjected to a hostile work environment when her employer refused to discipline a male coworker who sent her love letters and engaged in other conduct which she found to be "bizarre and frightening."

The broad scope of situations in which courts have come to the aid of employees who have claimed to be victims of sexual harassment in the workplace is clearly illustrated by a recent case in which a New York court concluded that the plaintiff, who had appeared in a Penthouse magazine centerfold, had cohabited with the magazine's owner and publisher over a period of several years and had, according to her testimony, been coerced to engage in sexual relations with several of the publisher's business associates over a period of 18 months, was made to endure a hostile work environment in violation of the New York Human Rights Law, thus entitling her to punitive damages in the sum of $4 million. That case has been appealed to the Appellate Division on a variety of issues, including the question of a plaintiff's entitlement to punitive damages in connection with a successful claim of sexual harassment brought under New York's Human Rights Law (i.e., New York State's analog to Title VII).

REMEDIES TO VICTIMS OF SEXUAL HARASSMENT

Generally, relief under Title VII is limited to equitable relief, sometimes described as a "make whole" remedy. Such relief is normally limited to an award of back pay. Injunctive relief, i.e., a judicial order requiring an employer to cease and desist from continuing an unlawful practice, is also available. Neither compensatory damages, (i.e., for mental anguish, pain and suffering, etc.) nor punitive damages are normally available in such cases. However, victims of sexual harassment and other employment discrimination who are represented by competent practitioners normally allege tort claims (e.g., intentional infliction of emotional distress, etc.) in the same acton as a Title VII claim which, if substantiated, could result in an award of compensatory and/or punitive damages.

Remedies at the state and local level may be more expansive than under federal law. For example, under New York State's Human Rights Law, a successful litigant may be entitled to a "make whole" remedy and an award to compensate him or her for mental anguish. The same is true under Connecticut's Human Rights and Opportunities Act. New Jersey's Law Against Discrimination goes further by expressly authorizing the N.J. Division on Civil Rights to award treble damages where warranted to provide appropriate redress to harassment victims and to provide a powerful deterrent to employer recidivism. While punitive damages are not available in New York through administrative complaints, it is unclear whether punitive damages are recoverable if a sexual harassment plaintiff chooses to bring his or her claim directly in state court, as is his or her right under Sec. 297 of the Human Rights Law, rather than before the Human Rights Division.

NEW AMENDMENTS TO NEW YORK CITY ADMINISTRATIVE CODE PROVIDE GREATER EMPLOYER PITFALLS

Until recently, the rights of sexual harassment plaintiffs who made claims under New York State's Human Rights Law or the Administrative Code of the City of New York (the "Code") were almost identical. With passage of "Intro 465-A," effective on September 16, 1991, a victim of proven sexual harassment who brings his or her case under the Code, as amended, has substantially greater rights. Intro 465-A, which represents a comprehensive revision of New York City's Human Rights Law, now provides for injunctions in employment discrimination and sexual harassment cases, enables a successful litigant to recover both compensatory and punitive damages as well as attorney's fees, and provides for civil penalties up to $100,000 for offenders. Another newly enacted provision of the Code permits victims of sexual harassment to sue not only their employer but the individual supervisor(s) at whose hands the unlawful conduct occurred. Finally, the new Code provisions permit an aggrieved employee to bring his or her action in the State Supreme Court in the first instance without first filing an administrative claim and suffering the red tape and time lag entailed in that process.

PREVENTION AND REMEDIES

Armed with a basic understanding of the laws which prohibit sexual harassment in the workplace and the evolution of the case law pertinent to those laws, we now come to the individual employer's most important question: What can I do most effectively to insulate my business from the type of environment which foments such claims? This is indeed a critical question in light of (1) the well-documented prevalence of sexual harassment in the workplace and (2) the possibility that an employer will, at one or more times during its existence, be compelled to defend sexual harassment claims regardless of whether they be meritorious or truly devoid of merit. Proper preparation, such as promulgation of thorough policies and procedures for dealing with such claims, will be invaluable in an employer's efforts to withstand claims that are totally devoid of merit as well as those which may be somewhat less clear cut. First, one should know who will be held accountable and under what circumstances.

TANGIBLE JOB BENEFIT HARASSMENT
In cases of tangible job benefit sexual harassment, an employer will be held strictly liable. The principles of agency will apply and an employer will thus be held liable for the unlawful acts of its supervisors or agents. An employer may nonetheless successfully mitigate its damages or even avoid a finding of liability altogether if it promptly and effectively makes the aggrieved employee whole for his or her loss and takes appropriate action to ensure that there can or will be no repetition of the conduct complained of.

HOSTILE WORK ENVIRONMENT HARASSMENT
Employer liability for hostile work environment sexual harassment is not so clear. It is dependent upon the status of the individual(s) who are responsible for creating the allegedly offensive work environment, the ability of the employer to discover its existence and the employer's prompt and forthright attempts to correct or eradicate the problem once knowledge of it has been acquired.

Clearly, the more authority possessed by the supervisory-type employee, the more easily it will be found that he or she speaks for and binds the employer by his or her acts. Thus, an employer may be bound by the harassing acts of a supervisor more

readily than by those of a victim's non-supervisory co-worker. However, it should be noted that there may even be instances in which an employer will be found liable for unlawful sexual harassment perpetrated not by its own employee, but by a non-employee third party. This may occur more readily in a service-type business in which a patron or client of the employer is the individual responsible for creating a hostile or offensive work environment.

CONDONATION
In those situations in which an employer's liability for the creation of a hostile work environment is premised upon acts of low-level supervisors, co-workers, or non-employees, the crucial questions in determining whether liability will attach are:

- Did I as the employer know what was going on?
- If I didn't, should I have?
- Now that I know about it, what am I going to do about it?

EEOC guidelines suggest that where an employer knew or should have known about the conduct underlying the hostile work environment and did nothing to correct it or acted too slowly to correct it or acted insincerely, liability is likely to attach. Employer condonation of a hostile or offensive work environment is thus the single most important element in assessing an employer's exposure both in terms of liability and damages. Fortunately, it is also the element which an employer has most within its power to change.

THE STEPS TO TAKE

A SEXUAL HARASSMENT POLICY
The first step to take and the one in many instances which will make it clear to your workforce that you mean business is to promulgate a formal, written sexual harassment policy that should be disseminated to all employees, either in the form of inclusion in your personnel policy manual, as a posting on employee bulletin boards or as a circular to be periodically included along with employees' paychecks or other pertinent documents. The text of the policy will, of course, vary based upon the particular industry, the general educational background of the staff, firm or workplace culture, etc. In essence, the policy should briefly define unlawful sexual harassment and state that any employee

conduct which falls within that definition—or arguably may be characterized as such—will not be tolerated and that those employees who, notwithstanding the policy, engage in such conduct or activities will be disciplined up to and including discharge.

A GRIEVANCE PROCEDURE

It is of equal importance that a grievance mechanism be established in order that employees who perceive themselves to be the objects of sexual harassment have a comfortable, efficient and effective process to obtain redress. The policy must unambiguously provide a mechanism for addressing an employee's sexual harassment claims. It is crucial that where such claims involve the affected employee's supervisor, he or she be permitted to address his or her concerns to higher-level management in strict confidentiality. If the employer's infrastructure permits, a right of further appeal is useful.

The policy must also provide for a thorough investigation of the allegations—usually within a specified and relatively short time frame. The policy must make it clear that resort to the procedure will not be ground for retaliation against a complaining employee and that retaliation by the employee accused of sexual harassment or other employer representatives will be treated in the same fashion as the unlawful sexual harassment itself: discipline up to and including discharge.

ENFORCE YOUR POLICIES

Mere adoption of these policies, while helpful, will not in itself insulate an employer from liability. Quite to the contrary, an employer that promulgates such policies and then proceeds to ignore them or to apply them unevenly or in a perfunctory fashion will be found to have condoned the unlawful activity in the same way as an employer that has no written policies in effect.

Employer investigations must be undertaken in earnest. This means that any witness to the events in question should be interrogated. Merely asking the alleged offender for his or her version without taking further steps as may be necessary to get to the heart of the matter will not suffice.

The reasons for this are two-fold: (1) most employers *do* want to know what is happening in the workplace and how to eradicate unlawful conduct, and (2) an employer's ability adequately to redress a complainant will hinge largely upon how seriously he or she perceives the employer is in responding to his or her complaint. You can show that you are serious by conducting a real investigation of the allegations giving rise to the complaint and by taking appropriate remedial action.

REMEDIAL ACTION

If the investigation reveals merit in the complainant's allegations, you should acknowledge this fact and take appropriate corrective action. Corrective action should not only include discipline for the offender(s), but should also encompass employer efforts to correct the hostile or offensive work environment. This may take the form of a transfer (i.e., assigning the supervisor to different duties or, in appropriate and non-retaliatory circumstances, transferring the complainant to other or more comfortable duties). Even where you conclude that no specific corrective action is necessary, it may be appropriate to recirculate your written anti-discrimination policy. While institution of these policies and appropriate efforts to enforce them will go far to insulate your workplace from the root causes of sexual harassment as well as from the claims of employees who fall victim to sex discrimination, obviously each case must be handled with sensitivity and on its own merits.

DON'T RETALIATE

It is important to remember that employer retaliation against an employee for seeking to enforce his or her rights, either through an internal grievance mechanism or through institution of a charge or complaint of employment discrimination with an administrative agency, is as unlawful as sex discrimination. Title VII as well as virtually all state and local anti-discrimination laws provide a separate and distinct cause of action for employees who are victims of retaliation for grieving sex discrimination, filing charges alleging such discrimination or testifying in support of such charges. Moreover, while an employee may have a difficult task to satisfy his or her burden of proving the underlying sexual harassment, the burden of proving retaliation based upon the exercise of his or her rights is usually far easier. The point to remember is don't engage in any conduct that may arguably be viewed as retaliation no matter how angry, upset or frustrated you may be over the filing of the charge. Forms of conduct which may be characterized as retaliation are termination of employment on a pretextual basis, demotion, involuntary transfer or any other job action that seeks to punish or may be construed as punishment for the exercise of statutory rights.

Perhaps the one question that I have fielded most often in my years of practice in this area has been "do you mean I can't even tell my secretary that she's wearing a pretty dress?" The answer to this question, as with many others in this area of the law, boils down to the basic question of sensitivity.

- Will such a statement embarrass her?
- Will the compliment, if made in a group setting, result in untoward inferences being drawn?
- Would you like your spouse to be required to endure similar treatment from her boss?

Honest answers to each of these questions will probably provide the right answer to the initial inquiry.

[1] A federal court sitting in New Jersey, suggesting an appropriate formulation to be adopted by the New Jersey state courts, has alternately constructed a five-prong test for establishing a sexual harassment claim as follows:
"(1) the employees suffered intentional discrimination because of their sex; (2) the discrimination was pervasive and regular; (3) the discrimination would detrimentally affect the [employee]; (4) the discrimination would detrimentally affect a reasonable person of the same sex in that position; and (5) the existence of respondeat superior liability."

[2] Although the vast majority of complaints alleging sexual harassment are brought by female employees against male harassers, the law also protects aggrieved males. In a recent study, the New York State Division of Human Rights reported that of 1,349 verified complaints of sexual harassment filed between April 1, 1984, and October 31, 1989—a shockingly small number—approximately 10% of them were filed by men.

Source: Reprinted with permission from *The CPA Journal*, February 1992, copyright 1992.

MISHANDLED INQUIRIES ARE LOST OPPORTUNITIES

Howard Feiertag

There is no way to know how much business we lose because of mishandled inquiries. We can't track or follow up if we never get the calls or the information from the inquirer.

Here's a typical example of how we lose business: In preparation for a training session I was conducting, I called eight hotels to inquire about holding a reunion. On the positive side, seven of the calls were answered within two rings, with pleasant greetings announcing the names of the properties. Six of the calls were routed to the catering department. This was expected since I had asked to speak to someone about a party for a family reunion.

ASSISTANCE WAS SPOTTY

On two of the calls, I was asked for a name and fax number so the hotels could send me information right away. One hotel followed up with a fax; the other did not. One contact asked about the use of sleeping rooms. Only one contact sounded interested and enthusiastic about the reunion I was planning. All asked about the dates and proceeded to check availability. I finally hung up on one contact because I had to wait far too long for someone to come back to the telephone.

Let's look at what was learned from this experiment:

- Telephones need to be answered promptly at all times. Four rings or more can lose a prospect.
- Routing the call to the correct department is a must. Someone in that department than must answer the phone promptly.
- All persons answering phones must do so enthusiastically and with smiles.
- Name of caller, company, address and telephone number should always be taken immediately upon contact.
- Get to understand the purpose of the inquiry, what is needed and when it is needed.
- Do not keep prospects on hold while checking availability. You can always get back to them later on this. It is amazing how often prospects will switch dates if space is not available when they want it. Of course, the prospects have to feel you are the right person to deal with and the property is the right site.
- Keep discussing the event in a positive way and provide consultation. Suggest how the event may be accomplished at your property.

- Do less talking and more listening. Ask open-ended questions.
- Steer away from offering rates and prices until the entire picture is developed.
- Be alert for tips on what the caller likes or dislikes.
- Discuss benefits rather than features when relating to prospect's needs.
- Try to close the deal, or at least offer to hold space.
- If you can't close the deal, then find out when a decision will be made and by whom. Find out when it would be appropriate to follow up, and then be sure you do.
- Get the inquirer to visit the property for an inspection. This is your time to make a sales presentation. This tactic works if the caller is local or if he is planning a conference and would expect to make a site inspection.
- Be sure to thank the caller for the inquiry.
- Immediately provide appropriate written communication by fax or overnight mail. If a fax is sent, then also send the communication by regular mail.
- Create a file and trace card.

How does your operation stack up when telephone inquiries are made? Are you losing any good, hot prospects?

Source: Hotel and Motel Management, March 23, 1992, p. 17. Reprinted with permission.

READING 6

FINDING SOLID GROUND IN A SHAKY JOB MARKET

Joel Russell

Interviews with headhunters and corporate recruiters from coast to coast turned up one hard fact: it's not just a recession we're seeing. It's a whole new business economy forming. America's companies are reorganizing to prepare for a competitive global marketplace, and the professionals who'll land on their feet are the ones who can figure out the new set of rules first.

Often, being bilingual will be a rule. Companies are looking for employees with a little something extra, such as Spanish language ability or international experience. For example, says Ana Riojas, owner of Able Employment Inc. in Kansas City, she has placed more than 40 bilingual Hispanics recently in the telecommunications industry. For many U.S.-born career shoppers, these opportunities mean taking courses in Spanish, since as Ms. Riojas points out, "many of the jobs are now going to candidates from Mexico and South America" who are more fluent.

Companies "are looking for people who are bilingual and bicultural in anticipation of the North American free trade agreement," says Earnesto Fresquez, president of the diversity recruiting firm Fresquez & Associates in Oakland, California. Mr. Fresquez sees bilingual workers providing enhanced services for companies "on both sides of the border."

But that bilingual bargaining chip won't go far without the right training and job skills. "Corporations want candidates who can, for example, go to Mexico, collect information in Spanish, and then present it in English," Mr. Fresquez notes. For the companies he works with, the degrees or skills that most often fit the bill are in marketing, public relations work, and accounting.

At the executive level especially, this unfolding field of opportunity includes not just Mexico but all of Latin America. As executive recruiter Korn/Ferry International concluded in a recent report, there is "a surge of executive demand in Latin America," while the rest of the world languishes. Fueling this new interest, the report says, is the privatization of many state-owned enterprises in much of the Latin world.

Basically, international "companies have been disappointed with results in Europe," says Korn/Ferry Partner Mercedes Mestre, calling from her New York office. "We're very busy helping companies establish a presence in Latin America . . . I get one or two phone calls each week about Mexico too . . . and I'm also recruiting for Latin American companies that can now enter the United States. There's business going in both directions."

These international placement requests, Ms. Mestre calculates, are most concentrated in the fields of health, investment banking and other banking services, computer marketing, home construction, and chemicals.

Louis Laguardia, SVP human resources of American Express's large Travel Related Services Company, is a bit more reserved in assessing international opportunity. He sees personnel officers putting positions that open up "on hold" when they can, although he expects things to loosen up "in the middle of 1992" as the European Community unifies and the GATT negotiations continue.

Meanwhile the U.S. workplace and market continues to diversify. Whether through visionary planning or hard necessity, companies one after the other are realizing they need professionals who can manage diversity—preferably bilingual. It's no accident that courses in "corporate anthropology" and "diversity management" are popping up everywhere.

Diversity recruiter Mr. Fresquez emphasizes that there is "a big shift toward manufacturing" firms looking to diversify their work force. Other areas where he's seeing strong interest in ethnic variety for management are healthcare, consumer products, and accounting firms.

Overall, it's one job arena where the current extraordinary glut of job hunting corporate middle managers isn't a big factor. These mid-level executives, currently the prime target of cost cutters, are primarily male and mainstream, and make up about 98 percent of all the applicants Able Employment's Ms. Riojas has been seeing.

Seemingly good news for college students is that many companies are trying to achieve diversity cheaply by favoring new graduates over experienced managers. "Although workers with three to five years are a proven commodity, they are more expensive, require relocation expenses, etc.," comments Wendy Musto, head of the new Chicago-based minority headhunting firm Musto & Associates Inc.

SOME ADVICE FOR THE HUNT

1. If you have a job and can avoid moving now, don't. It's a market for the employer, not the employee, so sit tight until the economy thaws. At a minimum, don't leave your job until you have something else signed on the dotted line.
2. By the same token, even if you're happy where you are, explore the opportunity if a headhunter should call with a lead. Ask qualifying questions. Some opportunities are unique.
3. Attend professional organizations and chamber of commerce events, check professional journals, contact your college alumni organization, and submit your resume to resume database services like HispanData (sponsored by Hispanic Business Inc.) for consideration by corporations and agencies seeking qualified Hispanic professionals.
4. While looking for permanent work in line with your career goal, take any job. Depending on your profession, temporary work or freelance jobs can be a smart move. Many employers will find a position for someone they've come to respect, and "temping" gives them a chance to see what you can do.
5. Improve and update your skills. Take a computer course, obtain experience or education that you couldn't get while working full-time. Or offer to work for less where there's also an opportunity to learn a new skill. The idea candidate for today's "streamlining" companies is someone with diverse skills in three or four areas.
6. Also consider going back to school full-time. Look for financial help for minorities. According to the executive recruiters, hot degrees for bilinguals now include the CPA, MBA, and Master of Public Health. The odds of a successful career switch—e.g., from accounting to marketing, or technical to sales—are not good without special training.
7. Pick target companies carefully: research their future needs, and focus on those where you can highlight a match with your own strengths.
8. Contact target firms regularly. Because of unsettled conditions, the wind can change fast for any company, and those with no intention of hiring yesterday may suddenly need people ASAP. Make sure your name and resume are constantly fresh in their minds.
9. Keep your resume current and tailor it as needed. Chronological resumes remain the easiest to understand, but define what it all adds up to. List accomplishments for each position: money saved, sales figures, special projects, etc.
10. During interviews, remember that the company wants someone to come in and solve a problem, and you must be the solution. Ask questions as necessary to find out what the company wants.

Source: Hispanic Business (February 1992).

11. Be flexible on salary and your own requirements, since it's an employer's market. Be
willing to give on income to get benefits.

THE KNOWLEDGE-CREATING COMPANY

Ikujiro Nonaka

In an economy where the only certainty is uncertainty, the one sure source of lasting competitive
advantage is knowledge. When markets shift, technologies proliferate, competitors multiply, and
products become obsolete almost overnight, successful companies are those that consistently create
new knowledge, disseminate it widely throughout
the organization, and quickly embody it in new
technologies and products. These activities define
the "knowledge-creating" company, whose sole
business is continuous innovation.

And yet, despite all the talk about "brain-
power" and "intellectual capital," few managers
grasp the true nature of the knowledge-creating
company—let alone know how to manage it. The
reason: they misunderstand what knowledge is and
what companies must do to exploit it.

Deeply ingrained in the traditions of Western
management, from Frederick Taylor to Herbert
Simon, is a view of the organization as a machine
for "information processing." According to this
view, the only useful knowledge is formal and systematic—hard (read: quantifiable) data, codified
procedures, universal principles. And the key met-
rics for measuring the value of new knowledge are
similarly hard and quantifiable—increased efficiency, lower costs, improved return on investment.

But there is another way to think about knowledge and its role in business organizations. It is
found most commonly at highly successful Japanese competitors like Honda, Canon, Matsushita,
NEC, Sharp, and Kao. These companies have
become famous for their ability to respond quickly
to customers, create new markets, rapidly develop
new products, and dominate emergent technologies. The secret of their success is their unique
approach to managing the creation of new knowledge.

To Western managers, the Japanese approach
often seems odd or even incomprehensible. Consider the following examples:

- How is the slogan "Theory of Automobile
Evolution" a meaningful design concept for a
new car? And yet, this phrase led to the creation of the Honda City, Honda's innovative
urban car.
- Why is a beer can a useful analogy for a personal copier? Just such an analogy caused a
fundamental breakthrough in the design of
Canon's revolutionary mini-copier, a product
that created the personal copier market and
has led Canon's successful migration from its
stagnating camera business to the more lucra-
tive field of office automation.
- What possible concrete sense of direction can
a made-up word such as "optoelectronics"
provide a company's product-development
engineers? Under this rubric, however, Sharp
has developed a reputation for creating "first
products" that define new technologies and
markets, making Sharp a major player in
businesses ranging from color televisions to
liquid crystal displays to customized
integrated circuits.

In each of these cases, cryptic slogans that to a
Western manager sound just plain silly—appropriate for an advertising campaign perhaps but certainly not for running a company—are in fact
highly effective tools for creating new knowledge.
Managers everywhere recognize the serendipitous
quality of innovation. Executives at these Japanese
companies are *managing* that serendipity to
the benefit of the company, its employees, and its
customers.

The centerpiece of the Japanese approach is the
recognition that creating new knowledge is not
simply a matter of "processing" objective information. Rather, it depends on tapping the tacit and
often highly subjective insights, intuitions, and
hunches of individual employees and making
those insights available for testing and use by the
company as a whole. The key to this process is personal commitment, the employees' sense of identity with the enterprise and its mission. Mobilizing
that commitment and embodying tacit knowledge
in actual technologies and products require managers who are as comfortable with images and symbols—slogans such as Theory of Automobile

Evolution, analogies like that between a personal copier and a beer can, metaphors such as "opto-electronics"—as they are with hard numbers measuring market share, productivity, or ROI.

The more holistic approach to knowledge at many Japanese companies is also founded on another fundamental insight. A company is not a machine but a living organism. Much like an individual, it can have a collective sense of identity and fundamental purpose. This is the organizational equivalent of self-knowledge—a shared understanding of what the company stands for, where it is going, what kind of world it wants to live in, and, most important, how to make that world a reality

In this respect, the knowledge-creating company is as much about ideals as it is about ideas. And that fact fuels innovation. The essence of innovation is to re-create the world according to a particular vision or ideal. To create new knowledge means quite literally to re-create the company and everyone in it in a nonstop process of personal and organizational self-renewal. In the knowledge-creating company, inventing new knowledge is not a specialized activity—the province of the R&D department or marketing or strategic planning. It is a way of behaving, indeed a way of being, in which everyone is a knowledge worker—that is to say, an entrepreneur.

The reasons why Japanese companies seem especially good at this kind of continuous innovation and self-renewal are complicated. But the key lesson for managers is quite simple: much as manufacturers around the world have learned from Japanese manufacturing techniques, any company that wants to compete on knowledge must also learn from Japanese techniques of knowledge creation. The experiences of the Japanese companies discussed below suggest a fresh way to think about managerial roles and responsibilities, organizational design, and business practices in the knowledge-creating company. It is an approach that puts knowledge creation exactly where it belongs: at the very center of a company's human resources strategy.

THE SPIRAL OF KNOWLEDGE

New knowledge always begins with the individual. A brilliant researcher has an insight that leads to a new patent. A middle manager's intuitive sense of market trends becomes the catalyst for an impor-

tant new product concept. A shop-floor worker draws on years of experience to come up with a new process innovation. In each case, an individual's personal knowledge is transformed into organizational knowledge valuable to the company as a whole.

Making personal knowledge available to others is the central activity of the knowledge-creating company. It takes place continuously and at all levels of the organization. And as the following example suggests, sometimes it can take unexpected forms.

In 1985, product developers at the Osaka-based Matsushita Electric Company were hard at work on a new home bread-making machine. But they were having trouble getting the machine to knead dough correctly. Despite their efforts, the crust of the bread was overcooked while the inside was hardly done at all. Employees exhaustively analyzed the problem. They even compared X rays of dough kneaded by the machine and dough kneaded by professional bakers. But they were unable to obtain any meaningful data.

Finally, software developer Ikuko Tanaka proposed a creative solution. The Osaka International Hotel had a reputation for making the best bread in Osaka. Why not use it as a model? Tanaka trained with the hotel's head baker to study his kneading technique. She observed that the baker had a distinctive way of stretching the dough. After a year of trial and error, working closely with the project's engineers, Tanaka came up with the product specifications—including the addition of special ribs inside the machine—that successfully reproduced the baker's stretching technique and the quality of the bread she had learned to make at the hotel. The result: Matsushita's unique "twist dough" method and a product that in its first year set a record for sales of a new kitchen appliance.

Ikuko Tanaka's innovation illustrates a movement between two very different types of knowledge. The end point of that movement is "explicit" knowledge: the product specifications for the bread-making machine. Explicit knowledge is formal and systematic. For this reason, it can be easily communicated and shared, in product specifications or a scientific formula or a computer program.

But the starting point of Tanaka's innovation is another kind of knowledge that is not so easily expressible: "tacit" knowledge like that possessed by the chief baker at the Osaka International Hotel. Tacit knowledge is highly personal. It is hard to formalize and, therefore, difficult to communicate to others. Or in the words of the philosopher Michael Polanyi, "We can know more than we can tell." Tacit knowledge is also deeply rooted in action and in an individual's commitment to a specific context—a craft or profession, a particular technology or product market, or the activities of a work group or team.

Tacit knowledge consists partly of technical skills—the kind of informal, hard-to-pin-down skills captured in the term "know-how." A master craftsman after years of experience develops a wealth of expertise "at his fingertips." But he is often unable to articulate the scientific or technical principles behind what he knows.

At the same time, tacit knowledge has an important cognitive dimension. It consists of mental models, beliefs, and perspectives so ingrained that we take them for granted, and therefore cannot easily articulate them. For this very reason, these implicit models profoundly shape how we perceive the world around us.

The distinction between tacit and explicit knowledge suggests four basic patterns for creating knowledge in any organization:

1. From Tacit to Tacit. Sometimes, one individual shares tacit knowledge directly with another. For example, when Ikuko Tanaka apprentices herself to the head baker at the Osaka International Hotel, she learns his tacit skills through observation, imitation, and practice. They become part of her own tacit knowledge base. Put another way, she is "socialized" into the craft.

But on its own, socialization is a rather limited form of knowledge creation. True, the apprentice learns the master's skills. But neither the apprentice nor the master gain any systematic insight into their craft knowledge. Because their knowledge never becomes explicit, it cannot easily be leveraged by the organization as a whole.

2. From Explicit to Explicit. An individual can also combine discrete pieces of explicit knowledge into a new whole. For example, when a comptroller of a company collects information from throughout the organization and puts it together in a financial report, that report is new knowledge in the sense that it synthesizes information from many different sources. But this combination does not really extend the company's existing knowledge base either.

But when tacit and explicit knowledge interact, as in the Matsushita example, something powerful happens. It is precisely this exchange *between* tacit and explicit knowledge that Japanese companies are especially good at developing.

3. From Tacit to Explicit. When Ikuko Tanaka is able to articulate the foundations of her tacit knowledge of bread making, she converts it into explicit knowledge, thus allowing it to be shared with her project-development team. Another example might be the comptroller who, instead of merely compiling a conventional financial plan for his company, develops an innovative new approach to budgetary control based on his own tacit knowledge developed over years in the job.

4. From Explicit to Tacit. What's more, as new explicit knowledge is shared throughout an organization, other employees begin to internalize it—that is, they use it to broaden, extend, and reframe their own tacit knowledge. The comptroller's proposal causes a revision of the company's financial control system. Other employees use the innovation and eventually come to take it for granted as part of the background of tools and resources necessary to do their jobs.

In the knowledge-creating company, all four of these patterns exist in dynamic interaction, a kind of spiral of knowledge. Think back to Matsushita's Ikuko Tanaka:

1. First, she learns the tacit secrets of the Osaka International Hotel baker (socialization).
2. Next, she translates these secrets into explicit knowledge that she can communicate to her team members and others at Matsushita (articulation).
3. The team then standardizes this knowledge, putting it together into a manual or workbook and embodying it in a product (combination).
4. Finally, through the experience of creating a new product, Tanaka and her team members enrich their own tacit knowledge base (internalization). In particular, they come to understand in an extremely intuitive way that products like the home bread-making machine

can provide genuine quality. That is, the machine must make bread that is as good as that of a professional baker.

This starts the spiral of knowledge all over again, but this time at a higher level. The new tacit insight about genuine quality developed in designing the home bread-making machine is informally conveyed to other Matsushita employees. They use it to formulate equivalent quality standards for other new Matsushita products—whether kitchen appliances, audiovisual equipment, or white goods. In this way, the organization's knowledge base grows ever broader.

Articulation (converting tacit knowledge into explicit knowledge) and internalization (using that explicit knowledge to extend one's own tacit knowledge base) are the critical steps in this spiral of knowledge. The reason is that both require the active involvement of the self—that is, personal commitment. Ikuko Tanaka's decision to apprentice herself to a master baker is one example of this commitment. Similarly, when the comptroller articulates his tacit knowledge and embodies it in a new innovation, his personal identity is directly involved in a way it is not when he merely "crunches" the numbers of a conventional financial plan.

Indeed, because tacit knowledge includes mental models and beliefs in addition to know-how, moving from the tacit to the explicit is really a process of articulating one's vision of the world—what it is and what it ought to be. When employees invent new knowledge, they are also reinventing themselves, the company, and even the world.

When the managers grasp this, they realize that the appropriate tools for managing the knowledge-creating company look very different from those found at most Western companies.

READING 8

HIGH-TECH GURU STEVEN BURRILL ON HIGH-TECH START-UPS

G Steven Burrill is Head of the High Technology Group of Ernst & Young, the New York-based mega-accountancy. He has been advising high-tech corporations, including Apple Computer, Intel, Genentech, and Cetus for 20 years. A graduate of the University of Wisconsin, Madison, with a B.B.A. in accounting, he co-authored the firm's "Guide to Venture Capital." Mr. Burrill was interviewed in his San Francisco office by *High Technology Business* editorial consultant Mel Mandell.

HT Business: What is the biggest mistake made by entrepreneurs in setting up a new high-tech business?

BURRILL: They often make big mistakes, such as neglecting to formulate a marketing plan. But their initial major failing is not recognizing that the way they finance at their earliest stages drives their strategies. They like to think that they first figure out what business they're going be in and then go about financing it. In fact, your strategy is driven by where you get your funding: from venture capitalists, a corporate partner, or "an angel"—some large private investor who just gets emotionally involved. Or, if a public offering is possible, by going to the public. Entrepreneurs assume that all they need is capital; they're indifferent to where it comes from. In fact, because the capital strategy frequently dictates the business strategy, the company they end up with is other than the company they had originally planned.

HT Business: Can you give an example of a company that evolved in a way management didn't anticipate because of the financing method?

BURRILL: Let me start with a hypothetical example. You and I form a company and we get backing from a venture capitalist. He believes that by putting money in today, his mentorship, and helping things happen he can get his money out relatively quickly—three to five years, five to seven years, surely in less than ten years—and that his return will be high enough to compensate him for the high risk he has taken. He must also believe that investing in us is better than other investment alternatives. That's his agenda. So he invests in us and then drives our strategy as a company to meet his end objective. One alternate to going after venture capital is the public equity markets.

HT Business: Tell us more about the public-offering alternative.
BURRILL: Suppose there is a strong market for initial public issues. Now we end up with a strategy that has to meet the demands of the public, which expects quarter-to-quarter growth and consistent earnings. So we end up with a business strategy that is quite different than the one we would develop if we had been backed by venture capitalists. We'll end up with a strategy oriented toward a short-term market win, a high-performance profile, and consistent growth. And we will end up with a different product portfolio—in essence, a completely different business strategy.

HT Business: How about a real example?
BURRILL: Cetus Corp., in Emeryville, Calif. Until this bioscience operation went public in 1981, it was able to focus on long-term opportunities and still satisfy its private investors. As soon as it went public, investors' expectations for quarter-to-quarter growth were somewhat in conflict with Cetus' long-term plans. The result was that Cetus' stock has not performed well at all, and Wall Street has been disappointed. This situation has forced Cetus' management to continually reevaluate its business plan to meet investor expectations and business realities. In contrast, privately held Triton Biosciences Inc., in Alameda, Calif., which is largely funded by Shell Chemical Co., has been able to focus efforts better on long-term opportunities without being distracted by Wall Street.

HT Business: When should a high-tech firm go public?
BURRILL: When the business is mature enough to meet the pressure of public investors.

HT Business: What other funding alternatives are there?
BURRILL: We could approach an angel or a large corporation.

HT Business: With regard to that last alternative, are you ever involved in "intrapreneuring" situations, where corporations like Kodak or General Electric fund their own entrepreneurial employees in a start-up?
BURRILL: We do a tremendous amount of that today. But it has not been very successful—as I will explain. But, whether it's a strategic alliance, intrapreneurship, a wealthy private investor, a limited partnership, the public, or venture capitalists, the source of capital dictates a very different agenda. And when that agenda does not square with management's agenda, management's agenda is often forced out. In effect, the two parties get divorced much as in a failed marriage. And that's very painful. Because of such divorces, the venture capitalists have been painted as heavies when they aren't. Venture capitalists are superbly skilled at what they do. Entrepreneurs don't understand the venture capitalists will enough.

HT Business: Many would-be entrepreneurs have some notion that if they hold 51 percent of the stock, they're in control.
BURRILL: That's crazy, absolutely crazy. Remember the golden rule: "If you need my money, I'm in charge." Entrepreneurs get very focused on the 51 percent question. It's a silly issue. In essence, if you are going to build a successful company over time you are going to end up with a lot less than 51 percent. It's highly unlikely you will always be able to finance so that you retain more than 51 percent. Generally, we see that in the first round of financing for high-tech start-ups, early capital takes 40 percent to 60 percent of it [stock]. In the next round of financing, another 25 percent will go, and after three or four rounds of financing, the founding group is down under 20 percent, with CEO/founder frequently holding no more than 5 percent to 10 percent. Getting over the "51 percent question" early on is helpful. Then you can concentrate on building the company.

HT Business: Earlier, you referred to the intrapreneurial approach, where professionals within a company develop an advanced technology that is mismatched to the company, but which the company decides is viable and funds a start-up. Kodak does this.
BURRILL: There are a lot of companies that end up in businesses they shouldn't be in. They also end up with a lot of opportunities that are better met by development by a specialized team with its own capital structure. Two scenarios result. The new

business either spins out, which is especially true in Silicon Valley, or the founding company follows the intrapreneurial model by forming an inside group it funds entirely and hopes to profit from. Generally, intrapreneurship hasn't worked, and there's a strong reason why. If you're the lead guy at Kodak in that particular technology, the economic opportunities for you to benefit from it outside the company are dramatic. You are also faced with extremely jealous colleagues who were not offered, or who can't create, similar opportunities. Also, in a large corporation, some decision processes are different than those in an independent company, which is really fighting for survival and is very reactive to its markets. In the intrapreneurial model, some decisions tend to be dictated more from the top. The large corporate parent isn't quite as comfortable with its offspring going in unexpected directions. When the history of all this is written some years from now, we'll find that the entrepreneurial experience will be seen as a far more successful model than the intrapreneurial model.

HT Business: What is the role of patents in start-up situations?
BURRILL: Some people are very concerned about patents, but I don't think patents are the real issue. The real issue is the barriers to entry. For example, in certain categories of software, the barriers to entry are relatively low. You and I punch out a little piece of software. Then we have it duplicated, and we're in the market place this afternoon.

HT *Business: Is that good?*
BURRILL: Yes, if you are trying to get into the software business. But if you're trying to cure cancer, the barrier to entry is much higher.

HT *Business: Aren't high barriers to entry sometimes desirable, because that means the next start-up has to overcome barriers?*
BURRILL: True. If you're trying to achieve high-tech success, you will generally try to be in a business where the barriers to entry are high, so that you are protected. Most barriers are somewhat intangible; for example, that you just happen to know more about this [technology] than anybody else. Patenting it may give the barrier away. It may write the recipe so others can learn what you know. Publication may also destroy barriers. The scientific

community has to learn to protect what it has. It needs to focus on what's critically different, what we call in the trade the "unfair advantage" or the "distinct competence." What is it that makes you stand apart from the rest? Maybe it's the intangible in your head. But as soon as you get a patent, everybody knows it.

HT *Business: Isn't it often true that when a company gains a lead it fails to maintain it, and some other company comes along and takes over its market?*
BURRILL: More companies fail tactically than strategically. They either don't get enough money and get caught in a financing squeeze when capital isn't available, such as when the stock market crashed in October 1987. Or, they lose control because they didn't put together a sound financial control system, or they didn't understand costing. Then there was Osborne Computer, where management didn't understand product transition. There's an analogy I relish that compares a rosebush with a tulip. The technology companies that win are rosebushes—they have multiple buds that open at different points and times on different branches, creating continuity. But the tulip sends up one beautiful flower that blooms in great grandeur and then it's over. A lot of technology companies start as tulips. They have this one product that's going to make it, but they never make the transition to multiple products.

HT *Business: But isn't it also dangerous for a smaller company to try to do too many things at once?*
BURRILL: True. But what I'm referring to is a succession of successful products. The goal should not be to make just one thing that has its day in the sun. It's being able to build a company around it. And one of the things that our venture friends have learned the hard way is that there's real difference between a product and a company. Some products should merely be licensed or partnered away. The trick is building high-tech companies, and that calls for an understanding of the market served by a series of products.

HT *Business: It is difficult to create continuity in the marketplace?*
BURRILL: Very, and it's getting more so. We have these shortening product lives because of the acceleration of technology. Coping calls for an ability to

know how and when to change your product and how to deal with product progression. Some high-tech companies need to focus on vertical markets and serve those markets well. High-tech operations naturally start off with a high technical component, particularly if the founders came out of the academic world where the technology is really important. But the business of the technology is a different world. Some entrepreneurs handle the transition well. The biotech industry is an example. It has done a very good job of advancing from its technological phase, through its clinical phase, into its commercial phase. This has not taken place without pain and suffering. Many observers think biotech is in trouble. In fact, biotech has never been in better shape. It is in the midst of its commercial phase. The problem is that in the commercial phase, companies must deal with earnings per share, price-earnings ratios, and so forth, whereas before they were dealing with the perception of technology and market opportunities. We American are very short-term oriented.

HT *Business: Can you cite some examples of companies that made the transition successfully? How about Apple Computer?*
BURRILL: Apple's board knew the company had to move beyond its spiritual leader, Steven Jobs, to professional management that understood products, consumer marketing, and where the business was going. They ended up with a superb guy in John Sculley. The tactical transition was very painful for everybody, including the company. But that transition finally came about. It was important for that transition to happen in that company.

HT *Business: Apple is now a $6 billion company. Is it doing well?*
BURRILL: Yes. If you stand back and look at success factors, what you'll find is it's not technological success that really drives these high-tech companies, although that's a big piece of it.

HT *Business: How do you feel about American firms taking on Japanese partners, particularly at the start-up level?*
BURRILL: There's a lot of that happening.

HT *Business: Obviously, the Japanese want more than profit; they want the technology as well.*
BURRILL: And they're getting the technology. But

they don't need to own the company to gain that technology.

Source: High Technology Business (November-December 1989).

READING **9**

SIX RULES TO GET YOUR MESSAGES ACROSS

Michael McTague

"She speaks yet she says nothing," Romeo says of Juliet. If you have ever feared that your employees thought this about you, here are some simple pointers to get your message across when talking one-on-one or in group sessions.

ONE-ON-ONE

Speaking one-on-one is the most effective but also the most difficult type of communication. After talking to you, an employee may be motivated or angry and confused. These three pointers will improve your chances for success:

Say exactly what you expect. Tell the employee *what* he or she should do, *when* it should be done, and *how* to report back to you. If nothing else is communicated, these points should be.

Have the employee restate what you expect. Instead of asking "Do you understand what has to be done?" ask, "How are you going to accomplish this task?" A thoughtful answer to this assures you that your message has gotten across.

Anticipate the employee's reactions. You want to ensure that the employee leaves the discussion ready to act. Allow the employee a chance to ask questions and to elicit your support. Before the meeting, think about how to respond to questions and objections. For example, a typical reaction is, "I just don't have time to do it." Another is, "I need help from two other people. Is this a high priority for them?" By knowing how to answer questions of this sort, you avoid the need to meet again or waste time until an answer is found.

GROUP COMMUNICATION

When you direct your remarks to a larger group,

you reduce the impact you would have with one-on-one communication. The three tips for one-on-one communication will help with group meetings as well. But here are three other tips specifically to improve group communication.

Use a flip chart to maintain focus. No matter how clear you are, someone in the group will need clarification of your key points. The simplest means of keeping everyone on track is to list your points on a flip chart. If the group is made up of 20 or more individuals, then you will need to use an overhead projector, but know that an overhead will lower the feeling of personal contact an easel or flip chart provides.

Use the Five-Minute Rule. Don't talk for more than five minutes without some break in the action. Writing on the flip chart is one way to avoid verbal overload. Encouraging group participation is another. The most manageable form of participation is to ask a specific question that furthers the discussion: "Has anyone seen this type of problem? or "Who is not familiar with this part of the operation?" rather than "Does everybody agree with this?"

Tight, purposeful questions allow a controlled discussion with responses that can be put on a flip chart.

Use a past success as a motivator. You want to motivate the group and one way to do this is to appeal to a well-known group achievement. Pick something everyone knows about, participated in, and feels proud of. State the achievement. Tell them that you are proud of them. Indicate that the current situation is no more difficult.

In a famous quip, President Truman, following Eisenhower's election, said, "He'll sit here and he'll say, 'Do this! Do that!' And nothing will happen." Use the six suggestions here to avoid the possibility of your employees doing nothing.

Source: Reprinted, by permission of the publisher, from *Supervisory Management*, August/1991 © 1991. American Management Association, New York. All rights reserved.

USE CREATIVITY TO EDUCATE YOUR BENEFITS AUDIENCE

Although this looks like the set of the Oprah Winfrey show, it's actually New York Life Insurance Co.'s newest high-tech way to communicate benefits to its employees.

The firm's new flex benefits were announced to employees through a *telemeeting* broadcast to 23 of the organization's 250 U.S. offices last year. What's so unique about this communications approach is that it's probably the first use of satellite technology by a company to communicate its benefits program to employees, and it demonstrates how far human resources has come in the use of modern technology. It's one small step for HR directors, and one giant leap for employees.

Television, interactive computer software, automated voice response systems and video productions all are high-tech communication tools being used today with increasing frequency to tell employees about their benefits plans. As benefits have become more complex because of increased choices, the tools that HR and benefits managers have used to communicate those benefits also have had to change just to keep pace.

More organizations now are shifting the responsibility of choosing benefits to workers, through flex and cafeteria-style health plans. Employers no longer simply hand employees a one-size-fits-all plan, but actually allow them to choose their own coverages. Helping employees adjust to this idea is a communication challenge with which HR managers are grappling, say the experts.

The most difficult part of benefits communication seems to be how to describe the roll-out of a completely new benefits plan. "Thirty years ago, a company provided a benefits package—period. It wasn't even take it or leave it; you just got it," says Pam Cook, a partner with Kwasha Lipton, an employee benefits consulting firm based in Fort Lee, New Jersey. Employers used to do no more than explain to employees verbally what their plan was, or give them a benefits "laundry list"; then they answered any questions they might have had afterward.

A big concern for management these days, after all the layoffs that have occurred over this past year, is the "general aura of anxiety" now hovering over those employees who remain, says Cook. "Companies are trying to offset that anxiety with good, solid, honest, two-way communication, because the worst thing that can happen is that the people who *have* jobs become unproductive because they're paralyzed by the fear of everything that's going on around them."

HR and benefits managers with whom she's talked lately aren't cutting down on communications, especially in the area of benefits. In a recent survey conducted by her firm, 600 HR directors were asked if they think it's difficult to justify spending money on communicating benefits. More than 73% of them said it wasn't difficult, and only 21.3% said it was. Interestingly, 82.5% of that group also believe that it's difficult to justify spending more than currently is spent on benefits (only 9.6% disagreed).

It's clear, however, that informative communication about the benefits employers *do* offer is crucial to employee morale. The same survey also indicated that 94.5% think frequent communication is an important element in establishing and maintaining high employee morale. Only 1.5% of those surveyed think it doesn't help.

"I don't see companies retreating from communicating. In fact, they now have a harder job and more to communicate," says Cook. Although most of those surveyed agree that communication is important, some employers are concerned about the perceived costs of the communication pieces they create, she says. "They're saying, 'We have an important message to get out, but let's make sure that it doesn't look too expensive,'" she notes. If a company is laying off employees at the same time it's spending thousands of dollars on benefits communication, the remaining employees may be wondering what's wrong with this picture. "It's very hard in an environment in which companies are asking employees to be concerned about production costs and expenses, to come out then with some real fancy communication pieces," says Cook.

"One really positive outcome of a fairly dismal economy is greater commitment to dialogue than I've ever seen before," Cook adds. "There's less the feeling that management knows best. I've seen a number of companies going to some lengths to ask people what they think about everything from plan designs to communication styles."

Asking for employee input often takes the form of focus groups—an increasingly popular method of gathering data before designing a benefits communications approach, she says. Cook cautions benefits plan designers, however, to understand that focus groups need to be given clear goals at the outset.

It's important to identify what you want to accomplish with the groups. "Sometimes people put the cart before the horse. They decide to use focus groups and *then* try to figure out what they were trying to accomplish with them," explains Cook. Instead, it's better to give people specific questions to answer, rather than ask for information as vague as what type of communication is most meaningful to them. It's more important to ask for such specifics as: "Do you understand information through pictures or words, video or brochures, live presentations or audiotapes?"

Focus groups were an important part of New York Life's new benefits communication plan design, says George Trapp, senior VP of human resources for the New York City-based organization. By asking for employee's input, their needs are more likely to be met.

"As today's work force becomes increasingly diverse, and health care costs continue to rise, employers are becoming more creative and flexible in their benefit plans," says Trapp. "There really is no such thing as a typical employee anymore, so a one-size-fits-all benefit plan no longer is appropriate," he explains. And helping employees to understand their flexible benefit options is crucial to the plan's success, he says.

Interestingly, Trapp's 14-year background in public relations at the company before moving into human resources three years ago, helped him quickly assess the need for a creative communications approach when it came time to revamp the benefits plan.

Because the company paid out 498 million ($11,000 per employee) on all employee benefit programs in 1990, the topic clearly was important to New York Life, and human resources needed to communicate that message effectively to workers.

After many meetings with individuals from senior management, Hewitt Associates (a Lincolnshire, Illinois-based benefits consulting group), his own human resources department and other departments, such as communications, systems, public relations and the controller's office, Trapp had the basic outline of the communications program he wanted to implement. He then called together about a dozen focus groups of employees who were demographically similar, such as professional staff, higher-level managers, recent college graduates, non-college graduates, home office employees and field employees.

As a result of the feedback he received from those carefully orchestrated meetings, Trapp knew the benefits education program was on the right track. He also received other valuable data.

Interestingly, half of the employees surveyed in these focus groups indicated that they thought benefits were "as important as pay," but they didn't fully understand the benefits they already had, admits Trapp. Although the organization's business is selling and providing life, group and disability insurance products (in addition to managed health care and a variety of financial services), not all its employees are experts on those subjects.

"We realized that we have big differences in levels of understanding about benefits," explains Trapp. "We have some people who do this for a living (design and sell benefit plans) but we also have other people who are looking at benefits, not as experts, but as consumers." Added to the challenge of educating people who have various levels of knowledge about benefits, Trapp also discovered from the focus groups that people understand information better through varying types of media. "Some people like to analyze things to death by seeing a lot of detail and written material, some want a broad overview, some learn by hearing and seeing and some learn just by asking questions," explains Trapp. "So we built all of those different elements into the package."

The firm's new benefits communications program, titled "Directions," came out of this data and was launched officially on January 1, 1992. Under the new plan, New York Life employees receive specific amounts of flex dollars toward the purchase of eight types of benefits.

Communication about the program began in August 1991, which included a printed enrollment kit, a computer software program called DecisionDisk, a telephone hot line, newsletters and the telemeeting.

The special two-hour teleconference aired on September 27 and was broadcast to 23 of the company's 250 offices from a studio near the company's home office. Employees from more than 50 offices travelled to the studio. To accommodate the time

difference between the East and West coasts, the program began at 1:45 p.m. (EDT).

The telemeeting was designed to explain the program in an interesting, entertaining way. It consisted of live presentations, such as showing one employee using the DecisionDisk onstage, as well as pretaped vignettes or commercial-type segments, such as a pinball machine talking about flexible spending accounts and a creative take-off on a popular soap opera "As Your Benefits Turn." Even the comedy team of Penn and Teller provided an entertaining segment on understanding benefits.

Trapp was a co-host of the "show," along with Gwen Kelly, a consultant who helped with telemeeting production planning.

In addition, viewers participated in call-in segments with questions answered by the HR staff. The meeting was taped and edited for use in other benefits orientation sessions held in the home office and other field offices from October 7 to 18. Human resources managers travelled to field offices to answer questions at these additional meetings.

Part of the reasoning behind using a live broadcast was that the company already had the beginnings of a TV network operated by the company's public relations department. The network has been used for the past 2 1/2 years on a monthly basis, mostly to broadcast new information to the firm's sales staff.

Because he wanted to accommodate a larger home office viewing audience than usual, Trapp decided to rent a studio a few miles away instead of using the company's own facility in-house.

The message was transmitted via satellite on a special frequency that only New York Life offices could pick up using a decoder. No new equipment had to be purchased for this broadcast, and the only costs incurred were the price of the production itself, a rental fee for the use of the satellite, freelance technicians and duplication of the video.

The total bill was about $150,000, says Trapp. He agrees that this seems like a lot of money to spend on one part of a benefits communication program. Analyzing alternative costs, however, which would include training an entire staff to deliver the benefits message, then paying for their transportation costs, made the television broadcast a more viable option.

Why use a videoconference instead of sending HR managers out to every office? "Consistency of information," explains Chris Hugg, corporate vice president of new York Life's public relations department, which helped coordinate the event. "Conducting the telemeeting and reusing it in other benefit communications sessions helped us convey the same message to all of our employees regarding what the plan means for them," says Huff.

New York Life Insurance Co. doesn't have a personnel staff member in each of its U.S. locations. "We don't have a network like that, so we had to think of something that would communicate, not only to the 4,000 people or so based here in New York, but also to the 4,000 or so based around the country," says Trapp.

Advantages of the telemeeting included:

- Communicating with employees in geographically diverse areas
- Reduced number of trips made by the HR staff
- Spending less time on training HR staff by using the telemeeting tape.

In addition to the television broadcast, New York Life's HR staff also developed (in conjunction with Hewitt Associates) a computer diskette that allows employees to choose their benefits through a step-by-step, online planning process. Trapp says that in the future he wants to enable employees actually to enter their choices onto the diskette, then send it to the home office's HR department, where the data could be electronically entered and stored on the department's mainframe computer.

This year, however, employees had to write their choices on paper, mostly because Trapp didn't want to run the risk in the first year of totally confusing everyone. "Once we have people used to the notion of making the decisions, by the second or third year, we'll hand everybody a disk, give them access to a PC and let them make their decisions that way," explains Trapp.

There are two basic advantages to using diskette. "Not only do you save a forest of paper, but you also cut down on administrative time and expense," explains Trapp. He says that the basic programming for the diskette cost close to $100,000.

A response card was included with the enrollment kit. Results tabulated from that survey indicate that 70% of employees used the diskette. Of those who used it, 92% said that it was *very helpful.* "So our suspicions were confirmed, we had a real winner in that," says Trapp.

The kickoff for the communications process

was a fold-out teaser, which was set out on each employee's desk, that said "Why? Because you're an individual." That was followed by a letter and a green enrollment folder.

The outside of the envelope in which the enrollment kit came informed employees of what they would find inside:

- Enrollment booklet
- Personal report
- Enrollment worksheet
- Enrollment form
- Beneficiary form
- Return envelope for forms
- Directions survey card.

The back of the envelope also gave employees information about the Directions DecisionDisk, in addition to the hot line number and available times and dates. Daily tabulation of calls to the hot line indicated that about 37% (about 3,000) of employees made use of it.

The hot line phones were set up in an area just outside the home office's main lobby and also included a walk-in service center. A basic skeleton staff of HR employees answered questions from 8 A.M. to 6 P.M. EST. A voice mail system even recorded messages when staff members weren't there and all voice mail calls were returned the same day whenever possible.

Response to the program has been amazingly positive, says Trapp. A total of 8,286 survey cards were sent out with the enrollment materials, and about 6,400 people returned the cards—a 77% response rate. "I've done surveys for 20 years, and I've never seen a response like that. Even 50% is phenomenal," he says.

"When it all came together, it was a rousing success," says Trapp, although he admits that the benefits communications approach was unusual. "We aren't always large, dull and conservative," says Trapp. "We decided to take a risk on this one."

Decisions that remain to be made next year will include whether to allow employees to make their benefits choices through a diskette or by touch-tone phone. As far as the communications process goes, Trapp says that he doesn't think they need to take the same broad-based approach as last year, because they now have put the basic ideas across. "It probably doesn't mean that we need to re-create this every year, but some form of enrollment book and explanatory material will be necessary," he says.

Another company that recently faced a benefits communication challenge is American Express' Information Services Corp. (ISC). A reorganization in 1989 joined nine separate business units, each having its own different culture and style, and each having its own existing benefits plan and human resources staff.

Wayne Olson, now president of another American Express division called Integrated Marketing Services, became ISC's corporate human resources director during the reorganization and was responsible for updating the benefits plan and pulling together a creative communications plan to announce it to 15,000 employees, primarily second-wage earners (mostly women) working in five different states.

When Olson took the HR position, he discovered, among other things, that there were 11 pension plans. "ISC was spending $25 million dollars on health care benefits, and it wasn't obvious to me that anybody, other than the financial fraternity, was aware of the financial impact which that was having on the organization," explains Olson.

He formed a coalition of human resources officers from the various operating units, and also sought assistance from Stamford, Connecticut-based TPF&C benefits consultants and Hewitt Associates, to develop a new benefits plan. The committee decided on a flex plan, a first for all of the businesses, and that was implemented on January 1, 1991. Not only could employees choose from a variety of benefits, but each operating unit also could adjust the plan to fit its own cost and benefits structure.

"It was a whole movement to begin to empower the work force and to put across the message that we really were changing the way we do business as a company, in dealing with our people—that they have a choice," says Olson.

After the flex plan decision, the next challenge was preparing a communications plan. Stamford, Connecticut-based TPF&C coached Olson on the best ways to approach the ISC audience. Through much discussion, they decided to produce an innovative video and slide show, in addition to an announcement flyer, enrollment booklet, and posters. The theme for the program was "Flex Expressions," which played on the word "express"—part of the company's name, "American Express." The title also emphasized that employees could "express" their individuality and needs through their choices.

The enrollment booklet was designed to look like a popular television programming guide, complete with such benefits information as medical, long-term care and legal assistance. It even contained mini-feature articles such as "Alzheimer's Disease: One Woman's Struggle," and "Ask the Doctor." A benefits crossword puzzle at the back of the guide challenges readers to test their benefits knowledge.

The most creative of all the communication elements was the 11-minute video. Instead of one continuous production, the tape is split into five separate "commercial-like" segments. The first fast-paced portion titled "Can Benefits Meetings Be Fun?" features quick interviews with children and adults as they emerge form a mock benefits meeting. The second segment "How Flex Works" is a comic look at the philosophy behind flex, using old movie footage, such as Charlie Chaplin being strangled by a fellow actor. This segment leads directly into a traditional slide presentation, during which each business unit describes its specific plan in detail to employees.

The third segment "A Brief Recap" is a spoof on how most meeting leaders deliver information. A straight-faced HR manager spews out strings of numbers and information so fast that no human could possibly understand her. When she asks if anyone has questions, four puzzled participants all raise their hands.

The fourth segment "Enrollment" depicts the "horror" of enrollment. Scenes from such old movie classics as "The Creeping Horror" and "From Space Beyond Outer Space" show screaming actresses and actors who gasp in ultimate fright as they see the flex expressions booklet emerge from the depths of darkness. This segment played on the horror that the HR department thought the employees would feel when they saw all the forms and information they were about to sift through. By poking fun at the process, they hoped to make it less intimidating.

The last segment "Rockin' Benehits" scrolls a medley of benefits songs, such as "Gimme Tax Shelter" by the Rolling Stones and "Stock in the Name of Love" by the Supremes, while bikini-clad go-go dancers and other '60s images humorously entice viewers into thinking that benefits are fun after all.

The humorous video was a risky approach, says Olson, but management really needed to get employees to sit up and take notice. "If you're a new company, you're in a formative state, so you aren't breaking any barriers," says Olson. "Also, you're talking about a work force that's young—the MTV generation."

The meetings were conducted in the fall of '90 with groups of 20 to 30 employees at a time. They even were served popcorn during the meetings to give a feeling of enjoyment and fun.

"We were trying to be tongue-in-cheek on everything," says Diana Salesky, a principal at TPF&C who helped ISC to develop the communications program. "American Express is really unusual because it's willing to make fun of itself and to take the perceptions that people come into meetings with—that they're boring—and to say, "We know how you feel."

In developing the video, the company also recognized proven marketing techniques, such as commercials shouldn't last more than a minute or so, because you'll lose people's attention, says Salesky. Results of the communications program showed that 90% of all employees enrolled on time, exceeding the 80% figure that HR hoped to obtain.

Although benefits communications can be successful in the end, many HR managers emphasize that a lot of thought needs to go into them at the front end.

"It's a big project, but it's really worth the effort," says Ursula Fairbairn, senior vice president of human resources for Bethlehem, Pennsylvania-based Union Pacific Corp. Her organization introduced utilization review and pre-certification into its health care plan several years ago. It than added a preferred provider option last year and is implementing a flexible-spending account (FSA) plan for 9,000 of its 50,000 workers this year.

"You almost can't overestimate the amount of time it takes to communicate effectively a benefits plan such as this," cautions Fairbairn. "The value is that our employees understand their benefits far better than they ever have in the past, because in having to make choices, they first had to educate themselves about what their current benefits are," she says.

To determine how to communicate these benefits changes, the HR department sought input from senior management, a benefits consulting firm, and employees in the form of focus groups. Based on information from them, the company's human resources managers decided to put together a new

benefits information folder and also use an automated voice response (AVR) enrollment system to document employees' choices. The AVR system was new to Union Pacific employees, but Fairbairn says it has worked amazingly well for them.

Benefits folders were mailed to employee's homes, one piece at a time, beginning with a cover letter, and the basic folder that described the core and optional benefits. Ten days later, four booklets followed that were more descriptive. Those included information on financial security, flexible spending accounts, health plans and an enrollment guide. "There's a lot to absorb, and we wanted to spread it out so employees could absorb it more easily," says Fairbairn.

She says that she spent slightly more than usual on benefits communication this year, but thinks the added cost is worth it. "I think it was a wise investment to communicate this program effectively," she says.

Although the comments from employees so far are positive, Fairbairn explains she plans to conduct formal surveys next year to document specific reactions to the benefits communications effort.

Another interesting application of video was used by Dallas, Texas-based Dresser Industries, which produced a special videotape with the help of William M. Mercer Inc. to tell about the company's mental health benfits that were just introduced into the flex plan in April last year.

"Mental health is a very sensitive topic," says D. Mark Schumann, a principal at William M. Mercer's Dallas office. There are three barriers for most employees, he says. The first is: They think they don't need it, even when they do. Barrier number two is: It's a "shrink" and you climb up on a couch. Barrier number three is: It won't help.

The 13-minute production, which was shown during employee benefits meetings, shows "John," an employee (really an actor) talking to an off-camera therapist, whom viewers hear, but never see. In four "sessions," viewers watch John gradually learn to overcome his fear of failing as a husband and father, and increase his self-confidence through the therapy.

"I think video application like this used to be unusual, but I think it's becoming less unusual. There are different levels of belief in what video can accomplish," says Schumann.

"The value of the tape is that the long-term

impact has been strong because it really taught people how to use that service," says Schumann.

Other innovations, such as payroll processing systems, also have helped companies in communicating the extent of benefits to employees.

Bob Rivenburgh, assistant vice president of human resources for the U.S. offices of the German Dresdner Bank recently did a bottom-up review of his company's benefits plan, starting with the company's philosophy statement. With the consent of senior management, he upgraded both the philosophy and the benefits to support the philosophy, says Rivenburgh, who works in the bank's New York City branch.

"The idea of that philosophy was that we were going to educate employees and give them a greater sense of the value of the programs that we have," he says. In the process, Dresdner changed insurance carriers and decided to go with one that also offered benefits communication support. The insurance carrier had generic printed materials that the bank was able to customize for its own program at a cost less than that of producing from scratch.

Dresdner employees received "For Your Benefit," a three-ring binder of information, including an updated employee handbook. Personalized employee benefits statements were produced in-house using a mainframe compatible payroll program designed by Control Data Corp., whose headquarters is in Minneapolis. The program is called Signature™ and allows HR or benefits directors to print any or all benefits information on a single form.

The statements include a consolidated list of all benefits information. "On it we published the value of employees' benefits in terms of a percentage of their pay and what the bank was contributing to costs," says Rivenburgh.

William Beaumont Hospital, located in Royal Oak, Michigan, is another employer that uses the Signature payroll processing system to print benefits information right on its payroll checks. "It's saved time," says John Liston, assistant hospital director for the medical center, which currently employs 10,000 people.

"Because employees have that information communicated directly to them, they ask fewer questions of both the payroll staff and the human resources staff." The information helps employees with their tax planning, because it has their current tax status on the checks. It also gives such data as vacation and sick time.

"In health care, the nursing shortage and shortage of clinical personnel in general, has required hospitals to be very competitive in the benefits arena, and in order to do that, you have to have a method to communicate that to employees," explains Liston. "It's good for employees, and although there's a cost to the company, that's just the price of doing business."

This type of system wasn't even possible until last year, says Mike Ritonia, a Control Data marketing manager. "It really wasn't reasonable to do until we had laser printing and that's what brought the whole piece together," he says.

More information can be included than ever before. For example, there's now room to list about 25 after-tax deductions and about 43 pre-tax deductions. Where technology previously put a limitation on the number of lines that could be printed on a single statement, such limitations no longer apply.

By using such recent technological breakthroughs as expanded earnings statements, videos and satellite telemeetings, human resources professionals not only can do a better job of getting their benefits messages across, their jobs may even become redefined in the process.

"I think the '90s are really going to be years in which HR is going to have to be recognized as a service function," says Rivenburgh. "We'll have to get out there among employees and demonstrate our value. Education and communication really are going to be important because we don't have a lot of dollars anymore. The best thing we're going to be able to do is provide employee service."

Source: "Use Creativity to Educate Your Benefits Audience" by Jennifer J. Laabs, copyright February 1992. Reprinted with the permission of *Personnel Journal*, Costa Mesa, California; all rights reserved.

GUIDE TO PUNCTUATION AND GRAMMAR

In preparing a speech, writing a report, or composing a letter, you may, from time to time, have to stop and check the correctness of a punctuation mark, the spelling of a word, or the grammar of a sentence.

Use this appendix as a quick reference guide. Many excellent texts and handbooks offer a more comprehensive discussion of punctuation and grammar.

The following guidelines correspond to those specified in *The Chicago Manual of Style,* 13th ed. (Chicago: University of Chicago Press, 1982).

PUNCTUATION

USE A COMMA

1. to set off an introductory phrase or subordinate clause from the independent clause.

   Lacking the proper tools to complete the job, the carpenter decided to return the following day.

   When I entered the crowded assembly hall, I immediately noted the presence of armed guards in the gallery overlooking the stage.

2. before the coordinating conjunction (*and, or, but, for, yet,* or *nor*) linking two independent clauses. If the independent clauses are very short, the comma may be omitted.

   Key managers in the organization should be carefully selected, and all managers should be informed of their responsibilities.

   Barry shouted and Betsy turned.

3. to set off nonrestrictive (or nonessential) phrases, clauses, or appositives.

   The holiday, coming as it does on a Thursday, will probably delay deliveries scheduled for Friday.

   The president of the company, as you may or may not know, began as a clerk with this firm 41 years ago.

   Ms. Spear, fashion director for Century Clothes, was elected treasurer of the Designers' Association.

4. to set off a name directly addressed.

    If you will write me at your earliest convenience, Mr. Barclay, I'll arrange a tour for your group.

5. to set off a mild interjection.

    Oh, I didn't want you to purchase a new one.

6. to separate adjectives in a series when they modify the same noun.

    They were young, promising, enthusiastic athletes.

7. to separate words or short phrases in a series..

    The sofa was clean and uncluttered, inexpensive but not cheap, and colorful but not garish.

    The final comma before *and* in a series may be omitted. If you decide to do so, follow this pattern consistently throughout a document

    She gathered the disks, contracts, and file folders she needed for the meeting.

    [or]

    She gathered the disks, contracts and file folders she needed for the meeting.

8. to set off a quotation from the reference source in a sentence.

    "I will arrive in Los Angeles before midnight," said Mrs. Kelley.

9. to indicate the omission of a word or words (usually a verbal form).

    Buckingham Way has been renamed Washington Street; Devonshire Place, Adams Avenue; and Kavenaugh Way, Jefferson Street.

10. to avoid confusion in interpretation or to assist in reading a sentence correctly.

    Whatever is, is right.

USE A SEMICOLON

1. between coordinate, independent clauses not joined by a conjunction.

    Ms. Spear submitted her monthly report; it was accepted without comment.

2. before a conjunctive adverb (*hence, however, therefore, consequently, inasmuch as*) joining two coordinate clauses.

    The students enjoyed their vacation; however, their funds were badly depleted by the end of the second week.

3. before a coordinating conjunction joining two independent clauses if the clauses are very long or have commas in them.

```
When the race, which has been held every year since
1925, was scheduled, we had 22 contestants; but 5 addi-
tional entrants paid their fees to the official regis-
trar, who immediately issued a verified certificate.
```

USE A COLON

1. to introduce a list, a statement, a question, a series of statements, a quotation, and in some cases, a word. Note that the colon should be used only after an independent clause.

```
Each person should bring the following equipment: one
sleeping bag, hiking boots, rainwear, a small shovel,
and heavy outdoor clothes.
```

2. before or after a specific illustration of a general statement.

```
In the first week he broke a turning rod, dropped a
glass test kit, and tore a rubber protection sheet: he
was an extremely negligent worker.
```

```
Winter arrived with a sudden fury: the temperature
dropped to 15° below zero, 6 inches of snow fell, and
the wind howled violently.
```

3. following the salutation in a business letter.

```
Dear Mr. Anderson:
```

USE A DASH

1. to set off—and emphasize—parenthetical material.

```
Rolsted—you know he had worked for us since the 1960s—
retired in June.
```

2. to precede a summarizing statement at the end of a sentence.

```
Magazines were everywhere,the record player was on,
clothes were tossed helter-skelter, food disappeared
like magic, laughter filled the air—the kids were home
for the weekend.
```

USE PARENTHESES

1. to enclose ideas not directly related to the main thought of the sentence.

```
Compton's periodic reports (following the format recom-
mended by the National Trade Council) were submitted by
all department managers.
```

2. to enclose a numerical designation of a verbal statement. This use sometimes occurs in legal documentation.

```
The escrow deposit of five hundred dollars ($500) will
not be refunded except through court order.
```

USE BRACKETS

1. to enclose an explanatory comment within a quotation or to insert a correction into quoted material.

> In her article on political upsets, Sarah stated, "Martin was defeated in the election of 1956 [he was defeated in 1952], and this marked the end of 36 years of Democratic treasurers in Wade County."

USE ITALICS (DESIGNATED IN TYPING BY UNDERLINING)

1. to indicate the titles of books, plays, journals, long financial documents and reports, movies, and newspapers.

> We read <u>Theories of Management</u> before seeing the film <u>Listening: A Key to Problem Solving</u>.

> One article in the <u>Los Angeles Times</u> referred to the E.P.A. report, <u>Hazardous Waste Removal Techniques</u>.

2. to identify some foreign words and phrases.

> We simply could not say <u>adieu</u> as the French say it.

3. to give words and phrases special emphasis.

> On the contrary, I instructed you <u>not</u> to reveal the ingredients of our product before testing was completed.

4. to call attention to words as words.

> Your letter uses <u>I</u> more often than <u>you</u> and <u>me</u>.

USE QUOTATION MARKS

1. to enclose direct quotations.

> Maria said, "People don't change; their basic characteristics remain the same throughout their lives."

> "I don't agree," said Marty.

2. at the beginning of each paragraph and the end of the last paragraph in a quoted passage.

> "This sentence begins paragraph one. This sentence concludes it.

> "This sentence begins paragraph two. This sentence concludes it.

> "This sentence begins the last paragraph of the quoted passage. This sentence concludes the passage."

3. to enclose a quotation within a quotation. The initial quotation is enclosed in double quotation marks, and the quotation within the quotation is enclosed in single quotation marks.

> Stevenson said, "If we are to live in peace, we must,

as the Israeli representative has indicated, 'Appreciate the dignity of all people at all times.'"

4. to enclose titles of articles, chapters in a book, or any part of a whole
unit such as an opera, play, book, or magazine.

Thomas Carton wrote the article, "The Problems of
International Finance," which recently appeared in
The Financial Quarterly.

5. to enclose a question mark or exclamation point if it refers to the quotation. Place the question mark or exclamation point outside the last quotation mark if it applies to the statement as a whole.

Dr. Steinberg asked, "Isn't that their usual performance?"

Did Dr. Jameson say, "The students completed work at a
very high level"?

Dr. Cho asked, "Did you write the article, 'Communication and Decision Making'?"

Kelly replied, "No, I did not, but I did submit one to
The Journal of Communication titled, 'Is There a Relationship between War and Words?'"

Note regarding quotation marks with other punctuation.   In using punctuation marks with quotations or quoted words or statements, remember

1. that commas and periods are almost invariably placed *within* quotation marks.
2. that semicolons and colons are almost invariably placed *outside*
quotation marks.
3. that question marks, exclamation points, and dashes are placed
within the quotation marks when they apply to the quoted material
but *outside* when they refer to the whole statement.

USE A HYPHEN

1. to divide a word at the end of a line.

If the word caption fell at the end of a
line in such a way that the entire word would
not fit, the word would be hyphenated as caption, with the first part of the word appearing
at the end of the line and the last part appearing
at the beginning of the following line.

2. to form compound nouns, verbs, and adjectives. Note, however, that
hyphens should not be used to join adverbs to other words.

She was highly motivated. (No hyphen is placed after
the adverb.)

Mrs. Lyons is Steve's mother-in-law.

The assignment included five double-spaced letters.

USE AN ELLIPSIS

1. to indicate the omission of a part of a sentence within a quote. Use three periods if the omission is within the sentence. If the omission is at the end of the sentence, use four periods.

   ```
   "The transaction was completed . . . and provided for
   Garzon to receive the car plus miscellaneous items. . . ."
   ```

USE AN EXCLAMATION POINT

1. After statements of very strong or sudden emotion.

   ```
   "I will not!" she almost shouted.
   ```

   ```
   Stop that noise!
   ```

   (See also the section on quotation marks for placement of this mark.)

USE A QUESTION MARK

1. after a direct, but not an indirect, question.

   ```
   Have you completed your analysis of the Compton Company
   case?
   ```

   ```
   He asked if we were coming.
   ```

   Note. A question mark is not followed by a comma, period, or semicolon when used in a quotation.

   ```
   Glenn said, "Will you drive or should I?"
   ```

   (See also the section on quotation marks for placement of this mark.)

USE A PERIOD

1. after a complete declarative or imperative sentence.

   ```
   Effective communication is a vital management tool.
   ```

2. to indicate an abbreviation.

   ```
   She worked for Kingston, Inc. for more than ten years.
   ```

USE AN APOSTROPHE

1. to indicate the omission of one or more letters in a contraction or one or more digits in a numeral.

   ```
   He hasn't been home since he graduated in '70.
   ```

2. to indicate the plural of letters, figures, or words. (Usage varies. The apostrophe is often omitted where there is no chance of confusion.)

   ```
   Betsy received three A's and two B's on her report
   card.
   ```

   ```
   His essay contained one sentence with three and's in it
   (or ands).
   ```

   ```
   Her l's always looked like t's.
   ```

   ```
   The program reviewed the '60's (or '60s).
   ```

3. to form the possessive case of nouns. To form a singular possessive, the apostrophe and *s* are placed after the singular form (boy's). To form a plural possessive, the apostrophe is placed after the plural form (boys', children's), with an *s* added after the apostrophe only if the plural form does not already end with an *s*.

```
The three boys' jackets were red.

He purchased a dollar's worth of candy.

That was my aunt's coat.

The men's tools were left behind.
```

Note. On the whole it is best to avoid the use of possessives with inanimate objects; e.g., *sink's top, lamp's cord,* or *chair's leg. Sink top, lamp cord,* and *chair leg* are standard.

ADDITIONAL USES OF THE APOSTROPHE TO INDICATE POSSESSION

1. If two or more people or objects own one item, possession is indicated on the last name only. If the writer wishes to indicate individual possession, an apostrophe is used with each name or object.

```
Robin and Shelley's car (Robin and Shelley own one car
in partnership.)

Robin and Shelley's cars (Robin and Shelley own more
than one car in partnership.

Robin's and Shelley's cars (Robin and Shelley each own
one or more cars individually.)
```

2. In compound words, an apostrophe is added to the secondary or last word to indicate possession.

```
My brother-in-law's car was damaged in the accident
(singular possessive).

My brothers-in-law's cars were all parked in front of
the house (plural possessive).
```

3. Certain phrases involving time that seem to express possession use the apostrophe.

```
A month's pay was granted.

Three hours' time is not adequate for the job.

His dream was to take four weeks' vacation in Hawaii.
(or a four-week vacation)
```

4. The apostrophe is used to indicate possession with indefinite pronouns.

```
One's thoughts are sometimes private.

Anybody's ideas are acceptable in this brainstorming
session.
```

5. Where an appositive is used, possession is indicated on the appositive, rather than on the basic word.

   `That is Mr. Carson, the janitor's, responsibility.`

6. Possession is indicated on the junior or senior.

   `Martin Kelly, Jr.'s, coat was a plaid.`

   `Thomas Kale, Sr.'s, store was sold.`

7. When one-syllable words, especially names, end in s, an 's should be added to show possession. If the basic word has more than one syllable and ends in s, usage varies. Either 's or simply an apostrophe can be added.

   `Mr. Jones's car is new.`

   `Charles' (or Charles's) coat is lost.`

8. Pronouns in the possessive case do not use the apostrophe to indicate ownership; such words are already possessive.

   `The radio is hers.`

   `The chair is yours, but the table is ours.`

   `Its surface was scratched, but it's (this is a contraction of it is, not the possessive pronoun) really not important.`

PRONOUNS

Pronouns take the place of nouns and help you avoid constant repetition.

1. Pronouns agree in person, number, and gender with the word to which they refer (antecedent).

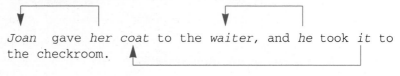

Joan gave *her coat* to the *waiter,* and *he* took *it* to the checkroom.

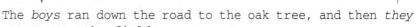

The *boys* ran down the road to the oak tree, and then *they* cut across the field.

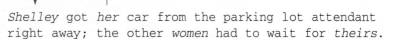

Shelley got *her* car from the parking lot attendant right away; the other *women* had to wait for *theirs.*

2. Use a singular pronoun for antecedents connected by *or* or *nor*. Note that the pronoun refers to one or the other antecedent singly, not to both collectively.

```
Kate or Lei will give you her key if you arrive before
noon.

A rake or a hoe will serve no purpose if its handle is
broken.

Neither Mr. Carleton nor Mr. Rodriguez will give you
his advice without an assurance of confidentiality.
```

3. The pronoun should be plural if the antecedents are connected by *and*.

```
The car and the train blew their horns simultaneously.

Barnes and Blackwell gave their briefcases to the
messenger.
```

4. When two antecedents are simply different names for the same person, the pronoun is singular.

```
The professor and conference leader received a scroll
for her efforts.
```

5. When two antecedents refer to different people, the pronoun is plural. Usually the second reference is preceded by *the*.

```
The professor and the conference leader received
scrolls for their efforts.
```

6. When two or more antecedents are closely associated by usage or practice, a singular pronoun is used.

```
Tea and toast has its place in a convalescent's diet.
```

7. Antecedent nouns take either a singular or plural pronoun, according to the sense of the sentence or the idea to be conveyed.

```
The jury reached its verdict. (one verdict coming from one jury)

The jury put on their hats and coats and left
for home. (Here, the jury is treated as a collection of individuals.)
```

8. The words that follow, when used as antecedents, should take singular pronouns. More and more frequently, however, many of them are being interpreted as plural.

anybody	someone	nobody
neither	none	any
either	everyone	one
each	somebody	another
everybody		

```
Neither of the men paid his bill.

Everybody in the room has his or her own opinion.
```

None of the women had <u>her</u> paper completed.

(or)

None of the women had <u>their</u> papers completed.

The sentences above really say, *Neither one of the men; Every single body in the room; Not one of the women.*

9. To avoid gender bias, the personal pronouns *he* and *she* (or *his* and *her* or *him* and *her*) should both be specified when referring to an antecedent shared by both genders.

A surgeon must wash his or her hands before operating.

When this practice becomes stylistically awkward, a business writer can often substitute the plural form of the antecedent and pronouns.

Surgeons must wash their hands before operating.

PERSONAL PRONOUNS
The choice between *I* and *me, she* and *her, they* and *them* sometimes causes confusion. Each of the following explanations includes the standard grammar rule as well as an easy test to help you decide which case to use. To begin, let us review the pronouns in the objective and subjective cases.

	SINGULAR	**PLURAL**
Subjective or nominative case	*I, you, he, she, it*	*we, you, they*
Objective case	*me, you, him her, it*	*us, you, them*

Nominative case

1. A pronoun takes the nominative case when it serves as the subject of a sentence or a clause.

Beth, Lisa, and I (not *me*) have made arrangements for the party.

Test: Would you say, "*I* have made arrangements" or "*me* have made arrangements"? Certainly you would choose the former.

Mr. Kelly and I (not *me*) were selected.

Test: Would you say, "*I* was selected," or "*me* was selected"? Certainly you would choose "*I* was selected."

2. A pronoun completing the meaning of a connective verb or predicate complement (*am, is, are, was, were, be, been,* or *will be*) should be in the nominative case.

It was *he* who was selected.

I believe it is *she* who should receive the award.

3. When the pronoun is the subject of an implied verb, the nominative case should be used.

`He is quicker than I.` (not me)

Test: Would you say, "He is quicker than *me* am quick," or "He is quicker than *I* am quick"?

`He did more for the church than they.` (not them)

Test: Would you say, "He did more for the church than *they* did for the church" or "He did more for the church than *them* did for the church"?

Objective case. A pronoun in the objective case is chosen when it is the object of a verb or a preposition or when it serves as an indirect object.

`He mailed the books to Sarah, John, and me.` (not I)

Test: Would you say, "He mailed the books to *I*" or "He mailed the books to *me*"?

`He called Ms. Johnson, Miss Short, and me.` (not I)

Test: Would you say, "He called *I*" or "He called *me*"?

RELATIVE PRONOUNS

Some of the more frequently used relative pronouns are *who, whom, which, what,* and *that.* The two that are often confused are *who* and *whom.* However, informal usage seems to be accepting *who* for *whom* more and more.

Nominative case—who. *Who,* like personal pronouns in the nominative case, is used as the subject of a sentence or a clause.

`Ms. Costello is someone who` (not whom) `I am sure will do well.`
Test: Would you say, "I am sure *she* will do well" or "I am sure *her* will do well"? Because "*she* will do well" is correct, choose the relative pronoun in the same case as she: who.

`Ms. Costello is someone who I am sure will do well."`

Objective case—whom. *Whom,* like the personal pronouns in the objective case, is used as the object of the verb or preposition or an indirect object.

`The soldier whom` (not who) `she loved has been sent overseas.`

Test: Would you say, "She loved he" or She loved him"? Because "she loved him" is correct, choose whom because it is in the same case as him.

`Mrs. Colgate is the person to whom` (not who) `we gave the award.`
Test: Would you say, "We gave the award to *she*" or "We gave the award to *her*"? Because *her* and *whom* are both in the objective case, the sentence must be "Mrs. Colgate is the person to whom we gave the award."

Whoever and whomever. *Whoever* is in the nominative case and *whomever* is the objective case. Their use follows the same principles as for *who* and *whom*.

```
The company will award contracts to whomever
```
(not whoever)
```
they find acceptable.
```
Test: Would you prefer "They find *they* acceptable" or "They find *them* acceptable"? The second choice is better, and because *them* and *whomever* are in the same case, the sentence must be "The company will award contracts to *whomever* they find acceptable."

```
Sam, Manuel, and whoever
```
(not whomever)
```
else is selected
will vacation in England.
```
Test: Would you say, "He is selected" or "Him is selected"? Because "he is selected" is correct and he and whoever are in the same case, the sentence must be "Sam, Manuel, and whoever else is selected will vacation in England."

PLURALS

Form the plural of most nouns by adding *s:*

report	reports
page	pages
Mr. and Mrs. Brown	the Browns
editor-in-chief	editors-in-chief

Nouns ending in *f* or *fe* change their final letters to *ve* before adding the *s:*

leaf	leaves
life	lives

Nouns ending in *y* after a consonant change their final letter to an *i* before adding *es:*

lady	ladies
buddy	buddies

Nouns ending in *o* form their plural by adding *es.* In some cases, such nouns add only *s.* Check a dictionary when in doubt.

hero	heroes
solo	solos
auto	autos
veto	vetoes
memo	memos
zero	zeros/zeroes

Some nouns form irregular plurals:

ox	oxen
goose	geese
alga	algae
child	children
thesis	theses
fungus	fungi

Lowercase letters and abbreviations form the plural by adding an apostrophe and then an *s:*

```
c's                          R.F.P.'s
```

When the practice causes no confusion, the plural of such letters and abbreviations often omits the apostrophe:

```
three Bs                     the VIPs
```

CAPITALIZATION

1. Capitalize the first letter in the opening word in a sentence or a direct quotation.

```
He was an outstanding student.

Ms. Boynton said, "Effective communication is the exec-
utive's primary management tool."
```

2. Titles that precede names are capitalized.

```
Senator Birmingham      Aunt Anna
President Adams         Commissioner Baxter
```

3. Names of national groups, races, languages, or similar designations are capitalized.

```
French      Israelis      Canadians      English
```

4. Names of holidays, days of the week, holy days, and months of the year begin with a capital letter.

```
Veterans Day            Rosh Hashanah
Wednesday               June
Good Friday
```

5. Capitalize the first letter in words which designate names of historical periods, treaties, laws, government departments, conferences, commissions, and so on.

```
Renaissance             United States Supreme Court
Clayton Act             Bill of Rights
```

6. Capitalize the first letter of a noun referring to a deity, a Bible, or other religious reference sources.

```
The Bible,the Koran,and the Torah
Allah
the Congregation of the Missions
God,Lord,and the Almighty
```

Capitalize pronouns referring to a deity only in biblical extracts or to avoid ambiguity.

```
God in His mercy
```

7. The first letter of each important word is capitalized in titles of magazines, books, essays, plays, and so on. Short prepositions, articles, and adverbs in such titles are not, except as first word.

   Journal of Business Communication
   An Analysis of Government Taxation
   The Decline and Fall of the Roman Empire
   The Taming of the Shrew
   My Fair Lady

8. Capitalize a general term that is part of a name.

   ```
   Santa Fe Railroad
   Southern College of Arts and Sciences
   New Horizons Psychedelic Temple
   Baptist Church
   Hudson River
   ```

9. Although words that refer to directions are not capitalized, words derived from directional terms are. Names of geographical areas or directional terms that refer to parts of a nation or the world are also capitalized.

   ```
   a path directly northwest of the tower
   Far East      Wild West      Orient      a Southerner
   ```

MODIFICATION

In English, it is customary to place modifiers (words or phrases that add extra meaning) next to or near the words or phrases they modify. When this practice is not followed, the result can be a misplaced modifier.

> Error: `She looked out at the large audience trembling with fear.` (The misplacement of *trembling with fear* suggests that the audience is afraid, not the speaker.)

> Correction: `Trembling with fear, she looked out at the large audience.`

Sometimes a modifier can be ambiguous. In such cases, revise the sentence for clear meaning.

> Error: `She promised in June to mail the tickets.`
> (The ambiguity lies in whether she promised in June or mailed the tickets in June.)

> Correction: `In June, she promised to mail the tickets.`

> (or)

> `She promised to mail the tickets in June.`

The key is to keep modifiers next to or close to the words or phrases they modify.

EXPRESSING NUMBERS

Should numbers be expressed in figures or words in written communication? To help solve this question, a number of general rules have been established.

1. When several numbers are used in one sentence and they are all above ten, use figures. If they are ten or below, write them out. If a sentence begins with a number, write it out. However, usually try to revise the sentence to avoid beginning the sentence with a number.

   ```
   We shipped 75 chairs, 90 tables, 32 lamps, and 32
   pictures.

   You have requested two rugs, three TV sets, and eight
   area rugs.

   Seventy-five chairs, 90 tables, 32 lamps, and 32
   pictures were shipped on December 3.

   On December 3 we shipped 75 chairs, 90 tables,
   32 lamps, and 32 pictures.
   ```

2. When some numbers above ten and some below are used in one sentence, follow one pattern for consistency. Round numbers over ten are usually written out.

   ```
   She owned three shares of AT&T, seven shares of Sears,
   and fifty-five shares of Zenith.

   The Scouts consumed 8 pies, 7 chickens, 8 quarts of
   milk, and 32 bottles of soda.

   He made two great throws, one of sixty feet and the
   other of fifty-five.
   ```

3. If the context of one number requires that it be written out (as in "thirty-person team"), other numbers not in that context in the sentence may be expressed in numerals (as in "50,000 homes").

   ```
   The thirty-person team canvassed more than 50,000
   homes.
   ```

4. When one number immediately follows another, express the smaller in words and the larger in numerals.

   ```
   He purchased five 59-cent notebooks for use in his
   spring quarter classes.
   ```

5. Place a comma between two unrelated numbers when they immediately follow each other.

   ```
   In 1975, 95 supersonic aircraft were available for com-
   mercial use.
   ```

DATES

1. Write out the month when expressing a date. In less formal documents, the month is often abbreviated.

   ```
   June 27, 1993
   ```

   ```
   27 June 1993
   ```

   Although U.S. custom is to place the month first and then the day, the reverse is true in many other countries.

   ```
   Preferred in United States: January 4, 1992
   ```

   ```
   Preferred in many other countries: 7 March 1992
   ```

2. Only use nd, rd, st, or th with the day of the month when that day precedes the months or stands by itself.

   ```
   She finished her thesis on the 4th of January.
   ```

   ```
   Please mail your check by March 28.
   ```

ADDRESSES

1. Street numbers should always be expressed as numerals except the number *one,* which should be written out.

   ```
   One East Wilshire
   ```

   ```
   10 North Roscomare Road
   ```

   ```
   2157 South Topeka Avenue
   ```

2. Use words for streets from one through ten; use numerals after ten. The letters nd, rd, st, or th may be used with numerals.

   ```
   2115 West Fifth Avenue
   ```

   ```
   210 North 19th Street
   ```

3. When a number is used as a street name, use a dash to separate it from the street number only if a street direction is not included.

   ```
   210—10th Street
   ```

   ```
   205 North 41st Street
   ```

AMOUNTS OF MONEY

1. All sums of money, domestic or foreign, should be presented in figures.

   ```
   Johnson paid $155.60 for the merchandise.
   ```

   ```
   It is difficult for me to convert £275 into dollars.
   ```

2. For sums of less than a dollar, follow the figure with the word cents or the cent sign (¢); an alternative is to use the dollar sign with a decimal point.

   ```
   It cost 25 cents.
   ```

   ```
   It wasn't worth 65¢.
   ```

   ```
   Tom paid $.75 for the ball.
   ```

3. When expressing even or round sums of money, omit the decimal and zeros.

```
Her payment was $275.
```

4. In legal statements the numerals should be enclosed by parentheses and the sum written out.

```
A firm offer for the car of seven thousand one hundred
dollars ($7,100) is hereby made.
```

**DECIMALS
AND FRACTIONS**

1. When a decimal fraction begins with a zero, do not place a zero before the decimal. If the decimal fraction begins with a whole number, precede the decimal with a zero.

```
.04683    0.1746
```

2. Simple fractions are written out. When whole numbers and fractions make up one unit, a decimal is used only for fractions in decimal notation.

```
It took him one-half hour.

It was 25.5 feet long.

It was 25 1/2 feet long.
```

Fractions that are written out (such as *one-half*) should have a hyphen when they act as a compound adjective (as in *one-half hour*). When the fraction acts as a noun, however, no hyphen should be used: *one half of an hour.*

**MISCELLANEOUS
QUANTITIES, UNITS,
AND MEASUREMENTS**

1. Distance: Use numbers unless the amount is less than a mile.

```
We were one third of a mile from the house.

It is 9 miles to Kingston and 350 miles from there
to Prampton.
```

2. Financial quotations: Use numerals.

```
IBM stock hit 56 7/8 this afternoon.
```

3. Arithmetic expressions: Use numerals.

```
Multiply 70 by 44 and you will have the area of the
house in square feet.
```

4. Measurement: Use numerals.

```
He quickly found that 15 kilometers did not equal
16 yards.
```

5. Specific numbers: Use numerals.

   ```
   The engine number was 4638147.

   Write for Training Manual 255.
   ```

6. Time: Use numerals for specific times except when the word *o'clock* is used.

   ```
   The plane leaves at 7:17 P.M.

   She is due to arrive at ten o'clock.
   ```

7. Dimensions: Use numerals with either x or *by.*

   ```
   The room measured 10 x 15 feet.

   The trim size of the annual report was 8 1/2 by 11
   inches.
   ```

8. Age: Use numerals except where approximations are used.

   ```
   She became 21 and graduated on the same day.

   I would say that he's about seventy years old.

   For your information, Juan is exactly 3 years and 6
   months old today.
   ```

9. Government units: Write out such expressions as congressional units or districts.

   ```
   She served in the Eighty-seventh Congress and repre-
   sented the Tenth Congressional District of the state.
   ```

10. Book or magazine references: Major units or divisions are indicated by Roman numerals; minor units, by Arabic numbers.

    ```
    He found the reference in Volume XX, number 4, of the
    Journal of Communication.

    You will find Figure 4 next to Table 7 on page 83.
    ```

WORDS FREQUENTLY CONFUSED

Accede: to comply with
Exceed: to go beyond

Accent: to stress or emphasize; a regional manner of speaking
Ascent: a rising or going up
Assent: to agree; agreement

Accept: to receive; to give an affirmative answer to
Except: to exclude; to leave out; to omit

Access: admittance or admission
Excess: surplus or more than necessary

Accidentally: by accident; not according to plan
Incidentally: by chance; in an inconsequential manner
    In both cases, the *-ly* ending is added to the adjective forms, *accidental*
    and *incidental,* and not the noun forms (*accident* and *incident*).

Ad: abbreviation for advertisement
Add: to join; unite; to sum

Adapt: to accustom oneself to a situation
Adept: proficient or competent in performing a task
Adopt: to take by choice; to put into practice

Advice: counsel; a recommendation (noun)
Advise: to suggest; to recommend (verb)

Affect: to influence (verb)
Effect: result or consequence (noun)
Effect: to bring about (verb)

Aggravate: to increase; to intensify; to make more severe
Irritate: to exasperate or bother

Allot: to distribute
A lot: much or many

All ready: prepared
Already: previously

All right: completely right
Alright: an incorrect usage of *all right*

Allusion: a reference to something familiar
Illusion: an *image* of an object; a false impression
Delusion: a false belief

Almost: nearly; only a little less than
Most: an informal use of *almost*; correctly, it means greatest in quantity or
    the majority of

Altar: a place to worship or pray
Alter: to change

Altogether: completely or thoroughly
All together: in a group; in unison

Alumnus(sing.): male graduate
Alumni(pl.)
Alumna(sing.): female graduate
Alumnae(pl.)

Among: refers to three or more
Between: refers to two only

Amount: quantity without reference to individual units
Number: a total of counted units

Anxious: upset; concerned about a serious occurrence
Eager: very desirous; anticipating a favorable event

Anyone: any person in general
Any one: a specific person or item

Assay: to evaluate
Essay: to try to attempt
Essay: a literary composition

Balance: as an accounting term, an amount owed or a difference between debit and credit sums
Remainder: that which is left over; a surplus

Bank on: informal expression for "rely on"

Bazaar: an establishment that sells merchandise
Bizarre: eccentric in style or mode

Being as, being that: should not be used for *since* or *because*

Beside: by the side of
Besides: in addition to

Biannually: two times a year (also, *semiannually*)
Biennially: every two years

Borne: past participle of *bear* (to carry, to produce)
Born: brought into existence

Breach: an opening; an infraction of a law; a broken promise
Breech: part of a firearm

Calculate: to determine by mathematical process; dialect for "think" or "expect"

Callous: not sympathetic, hardened
Callus: hardened area of skin

Can: refers to ability or capability
May: refers to permission

Canvas: a coarse type of cloth
Canvass: to solicit; survey

Cannon: large gun
Canon: a law; church official

Capital: a seat of government; money invested; a form of a letter
Capitol: a government building

Carat: unit of weight generally applied to gem stones
Caret: mark showing omission
Carrot: vegetable
Karat: indication of gold content

Cease: to halt or stop
Seize: to grasp or take possession

Censer: an incense pot
Censor: a critic
Sensor: An electronic device
Censure: to find fault with or to blame
Criticize: to evaluate; to examine

Cereal: any grain
Serial: arranged in successive order

Cite: to quote from a source
Sight: act of seeing; object or scene observed
Site: a place, such as "building site"

Coarse: composed of large particles; unrefined
Course: a direction of progress or series of studies

Collision: a clashing of objects
Collusion: a conspiracy or fraud

Command: to direct or order; an order
Commend: to praise or laud

Complement: that which completes or supplements
Compliment: flattery or praise

Confidant: one who may be confided in
Confident: positive or sure

Consensus of opinion: redundant; *consensus* means "general opinion"

Continual: taking place in close succession; frequently repeated
Continuous: no break or letup

Council: an assembly of persons
Counsel: to advise; advice; an attorney
Consul: a resident representative of a foreign state
Councillor: a member of a council
Counselor: a lawyer or adviser

Core: a center
Corps: a body of troops; a group of persons in association
Corpse: a dead body

Credible: believable or acceptable
Creditable: praiseworthy or meritorious
Credulous: gullible

Critic: one who evaluates
Critique: an analytical examination of
Criticism: an evaluation

Currant: fruit
Current: timely; motion of air or water

Data: factual information
Criteria: standards on which decisions are based
Phenomena: observable facts or events
  The plural forms of *datum, criterion,* and *phenomenon. Data* is some-
  times used as a singular, collective noun.

Deal: informal use for a business transaction; use instead *sale, agreement,*
  plan

Deceased: dead
Diseased: infected

Decent: correct; proper
Descent: going from high to low
Dissent: disagreement

Decree: a proclamation of law
Degree: difference in grade; an academic award

Defer: to delay or put off
Differ: to disagree

Deference: respect
Difference: unlikeness

Depot: a storehouse for merchandise or goods
Station: a place for passengers; a regular stopping place

Deprecate: to express disapproval of
Depreciate: to lessen in value because of use and/or time; to belittle

Desert: a reward or punishment
Desert: to abandon
Desert: a barren geographical area
Dessert: a course at the end of a meal

Device: a mechanism
Devise: to formulate a plan

Different from:
Different than: either may be used, although U.S. usage prefers "different from."
Differ from: to stand apart because of unlikeness
Differ with: to disagree

Disapprove: not to accept
Disprove: to prove wrong

Disburse: to make payments;to allot
Disperse: to scatter

Discomfit: to frustrate; to disconcert (verb)
Discomfort: distress; not comfortable (noun)

Discreet: prudent; good judgment in conduct
Discrete: separate entity; individual

Disinterested: neutral; not biased
Uninterested: not concerned with; lacking interest

Disorganized: disordered
Unorganized: not organized or planned

Dual: double or two
Duel: a contest between two antagonists

Dying: in the process of losing life or function
Dyeing: changing the color of

Each other: refers to two
One another: Refers to more than two

Either:
Neither: Refers to one or the other of two. With *Either* use *or;* with *neither* use *nor.*

Elicit: to draw forth, usually a comment
Illicit: unlawful; illegal

Eligible: acceptable; approved
Illegible: impossible to read or decipher

Elusive: difficult to catch
Illusive: deceptive

Emerge: to come out
Immerge: to plunge into; immerse

Emigrate: to travel out of one country to live in another
Immigrate: to come into a country
Migrate: to travel from place to place periodically

Eminent: outstanding; prominent
Imminent: impending, very near, or threatening
Immanent: inherent

Envelope: container for a communication
Envelop: to surround; cover over or enfold

Erotic: sexually arousing
Erratic: unpredictable, irregular
Exotic: foreign
Esoteric: of interest only to a select few

Exceptional: much better than average; superior
Exceptionable: likely to cause objection; objectionable

Expansive: capable of extension or expansion
Expensive: costly

Expect: informal use of *suppose* or *think*

Extant: living or in existence
Extent: an area or a measure

Extinct: no longer living or existing
Distinct: clear, sharply defined

Facet: a small surface of a cut gem stone; aspect of an object or situation
Faucet: a spigot

Facilitate: to make easier
Felicitate: to greet or congratulate

Faint: to lose consciousness (verb); feeble, weak (adjective)
Feint: to pretend or simulate; a deceptive movement

Farther: refers to geographical or linear distance
Further: more; in addition to

Fate: destiny
Fête: to honor or celebrate (verb); a party (noun)
Feat: an act of unusual skill

Faze: to disturb, discomfit, daunt

Fiancé: the man to whom a woman is engaged to be marred
Fiancés (pl.):
Fiancée: the woman to whom a man is engaged to be married
Fiancées (pl.):

Flair: natural ability
Flare: a signal rocket; a blazing up of a fire

Formally: according to convention
Formerly: previously

Freeze: to turn solid because of low temperature
Frieze: ornamentation along the top edge of a wall, sometimes on hung fabric

Genius: unusual and outstanding ability
Genus: a grouping or classification, usually on a biological basis

Grisly: ghastly; horrible; very bad
Grizzly: a subspecies of bear

Hale: free from defect; healthy
Hail: precipitation that has frozen
Hail: to greet or call out

Healthful: giving or contributing to health
Healthy: having health

Hoard: to collect and keep; a hidden supply
Horde: a huge crowd

Holey: having perforations or holes
Holy: sacred, saintly
Wholly: entirely; completely

Human: pertaining to people
Humane: kindly, considerate

Immunity: safety from infection; exemption from regulation
Impunity: freedom or exemption from punishment

Imply: to hint at or to allude to in speaking or writing
Infer: to draw a conclusion from what has been said or written

In: indicates location within
Into: indicates movement to a location within

Incite: to stir up
Insight: keen understanding; intuition

Incredible: extraordinary; unbelievable
Incredulous: skeptical; not believing

Indignant: angry
Indigenous: native to an area or country
Indigent: needy; poor

Individual: refers to a single item
Party: a festive occasion; legal reference to a group or single person

Ingenious: clever, resourceful
Ingenuous: frank, honest, free from guile

In regards to: incorrect; use *in regard to* or *as regards*

Inside of: informal use for *within* as "inside of five minutes."
Outside of: informal use for *except* or *besides* as "outside of those three
    members . . . "

Irregardless: nonstandard for *regardless*

Its: a possessive singular pronoun
It's: a contraction for *it is*

Later: refers to time; the comparative form of *late*
Latter: refers to the second named of two

Lean: to rest at an angle
Lien: a legal encumbrance

Learn: to acquire knowledge
Teach: to impart knowledge

Less: smaller quantity than, without reference to units
Fewer: a smaller total of units

Let: to permit
Leave: to go away from; to abandon

Lie, lay, lain: to recline
Lay, laid, laid: to place

Likely: probable
Liable: legally responsible
Apt: quick to learn; inclined; relevant

Load: a burden; a pack
Lode: a vein of ore

Loath: reluctant; unwilling
Loathe: to hate; to despise; to detest

Locate: informal for *settle*; "to make one's residence"

Lose: to cease having
Loose: not fastened or attached; to set free

Magnate: a tycoon; important official
Magnet: a device that attracts iron

Marital: used in reference to marriage
Marshal: an official; to arrange
Martial: pertaining to military affairs

Maybe: perhaps (adverb)
May be: indicates possibility (verb)

Medal: a badge of honor
Mettle: spirit or temperament
Metal: a mineral substance
Meddle: to interfere

Miner: an underground laborer or worker
Minor: one who has not attained legal age; of little importance

Moral: a principle, maxim, or lesson (noun); ethical (adjective)
Morale: a state of mind or psychological outlook (noun)

Notable: distinguished
Notorious: unfavorably known

Observance: following or respecting a custom or regulation
Observation: act of seeing; casual remark

Off of: informal use of *off*

Oral: by word of mouth
Verbal: communication in words whether oral or written

Ordinance: a local law
Ordnance: military weapons; munition

Overdo: to do in excess
Overdue: past due

Peak: top of a hill or mountain; topmost point
Peek: a quick look through a small opening
Pique: to arouse anger or interest

Peal: sound of a bell
Peel: to strip off

Pedal: a foot lever
Peddle: to sell

Percent: should be used after a numeral (*20 percent*)
Percentage: for quantity or where numerals are not used (a larger *percentage*)

Persecute: to subject to harsh or unjust treatment
Prosecute: to bring legal action against

Personal: private; not public or general
Personnel: the staff of an organization

Plaintiff: the complaining party in a lawsuit
Plaintive: sorrowful; mournful

Plane: to make smooth; a tool; a surface
Plain: area of level or treeless country; obvious, undecorated

Practical: not theoretical; useful, pragmatic
Practicable: can be put into practice (not used in reference to people)

Precedence: priority
Precedents: cases that have already occurred

Proceed: to begin; to move; to advance
Precede: to go before

Principal: of primary importance (adjective); head of a school; original sum;
    chief or official
Principle: a fundamental truth

Provided: on condition; supplied
Providing: supplying

Quite: almost; entirely; positively
Quiet: without noise

Real: actual, tangible; also slang for *very* or *extremely*

Recent: newly created or developed; near past in time
Resent: to feel indignant

Respectfully: with respect or deference
Respectively: in order named

Resume: to begin again
Résumé: a summing up (commonly used without accents)

Right along: informal for *without interruption* or *continuously*

Rise: to move upward; to ascend (rise, rose, risen)
Raise: to elevate; pick up (raise, raised, raised)

Root: part of a plant
Rout: to defeat
Route: a traveler's plan

Sit: to be seated
Set: to put in position

Shear: to cut
Sheer: thin; steep; altogether

Sometime: at one time or another
Sometimes: occasionally

Spoonfuls, carfuls, shovelfuls: the plural forms of *spoonful, carful, shovelful*

Stationary: not moving; fixed
Stationery: writing paper or writing materials

Statue: a carved or molded three-dimensional reproduction
Stature: height of a person; reputation
Statute: a law

Straight: direct; uninterrupted; not crooked
Strait: narrow strip connecting two bodies of water; a distressing situation

Than: used in comparison (conjunction): "Joe is taller than Tom."
Then: relating to time (adverb): "First, she ran; then, she jumped."

Their: belonging to them (possessive of *they*)
There: in that place (adverb)
They're: a contraction of the two words *they are*

To: preposition: "to the store"
Too: adverb: "too cold"
Two: number: "two apples"

Toward:
Towards: identical in meaning and used interchangeably; *toward* is preferred.

Veracity: truthfulness
Voracity: ravenousness; greed

Vice: wickedness
Vise: a clamp

Waive: to give up; relinquish
Wave: swell of water; a gesture

Ways: procedures; also slang for distance

Weather: climate or atmosphere
Whether: an alternative

Who's: a contraction of the two words *who is*
Whose: possessive of *who*

Your: a pronoun
You're: a contraction of the two words *you are*

TWO HUNDRED FREQUENTLY MISSPELLED WORDS*

About twenty years ago a researcher in the field of English made the claim that 95 percent of the spelling errors made by educated people occur in just 100 words. Our language has undergone many changes in the past two decades, but many of the same words *do* continue to plague us. The list below contains the 100 words in question as well as 100 others that often give trouble.

absence	appropriate	category	definitely
absorption	argument	ceiling	description
accede	asphalt	cemetery	desirable
accessible	assistant	changeable	despair
accommodate	asterisk	clientele	development
accumulate	athletics	collateral	dilemma
achieve	auditor	committee	dilettante
acoustics	bachelor	comparative	disappear
acquittal	balloon	competitor	disappoint
advantageous	bankruptcy	concede	disbursement
affiliated	believable	connoisseur	discrepancy
aggressive	benefited	connotation	discriminate
alignment	bicycle	conscience	dissatisfied
all right	brilliant	consensus	dissipate
aluminum	bulletin	convenient	drunkenness
analyze	calendar	convertible	ecstasy
anoint	campaign	coolly	eligible
apostrophe	canceled	corroborate	embarrassing
apparent	canvass	criticism	endorsement

envelop (verb)   irresistible   pageant   rescind
exaggerate   irritable   panicky   rhythmical
exceed   jewelry   parallel   ridiculous
exhaust   judgment   paralyze   sacrilegious
exhilaration   judicial   pastime   salable
existence   khaki   peaceable   secretary
extraordinary   kindergarten   penicillin   seize
fallacy   labeling   permanent   separate
familiar   legitimate   perseverance   sergeant
flexible   leisure   persistent   sheriff
fluctuation   license   personnel   stationary
forty   likable   persuade   stationery
gesture   litigation   physician   succeed
grammar   loneliness   plagiarism   suddenness
gratuity   loose   plebian   superintendent
grievous   maintenance   possesses   supersede
haphazard   mathematics   potato   surgeon
hemorrhage   mediocre   precede   surprise
holiday   minimum   predictable   tangible
hosiery   misspelling   preferred   tariff
hypocrisy   necessary   privilege   technique
illegible   necessity   procedure   tenant
immigrant   negligence   proceed   tranquilizer
incidentally   negotiable   professor   truly
indelible   newsstand   pronunciation   tyrannize
independent   nickel   psychology   unanimous
indispensable   noticeable   pursue   until
inimitable   occurrence   questionnaire   vacillate
inoculate   omission   receive   vacuum
insistent   opponent   recommend   vicious
intermediary   oscillate   repetition   weird

* This list was compiled by J. Douglas Andrews, University of Southern California.

GUIDE TO MEMO, LETTER, REPORT, AND PROPOSAL FORMATS

MEMO FORMATS

The following conventions apply to memo writing across industries in the United States. In other countries, format conventions for memos, letters, reports, and other documents differ significantly from the guidelines presented here. For such international communication conventions, see the examples of international letters and memos on pages 703-706.

The memo as used in U.S. and Canadian businesses and government follows these conventions:

1. The memo is *not* centered vertically on the page.
2. The use of a title after the name of the sender and recipient is recommended. Should questions arise later involving the memo, it may be important to establish what levels of authority (job titles) were in correspondence.
3. The sender does not sign the memo as if it were a business letter. Instead, the sender signs his or her initials after the "FROM:" information. Such initialing indicates that the sender has approved the typed or printed copy of the memo.
4. Enclosure notations, reference initials, copy notations, and second page headings are used as in business letters.
5. The body of the memo is made up of block paragraphs, the first of which is separated by one blank line from the heading, as illustrated in Figure B–1. (Block memo format is the most common in business. Some corporations and government agencies, however, separate the date from the rest of the heading, beginning the date at the midpoint of the page as in a modified block letter.)
6. Managers who compose their own memos at the computer keyboard usually omit reference initials and handwritten initialing, especially when such memos are transmitted by electronic mail.
7. In many corporate environments, less formal memos omit the titles of the sender and receiver and may, in some cases, bear only the first names of these parties.

FIGURE B–1   Block Memo Form

At least 1 inch

Heading

Body

Reference

MEMORANDUM

TO: Vincent Reynolds, Production Supervisor

FROM: Linda Ortega, Vice President for Manufacturing

DATE: January 8, 19__

SUBJECT: OSHA inspection scheduled for February 10, 19__

I've just been informed by OSHA's Washington office that their inspection team's visit to your work unit will be delayed until March 15, 19__.

Vince, that extra month should give us time to conduct at least two dry run inspections of our own. I'm attaching the latest OSHA safety checklist. Please use it to design a thorough inspection plan that can be carried out with no more than four hours downtime. I would like to receive your plan no later than January 15.

When I have approved the plan, we'll run two unannounced inspections in early February (you and I can settle on the exact dates). If we have less than satisfactory results from those dry runs, we'll still have several weeks to resolve the problems before the OSHA visit.

Thanks for your help with this. Call me if you have questions (ext. 9832).

LO/coe

BUSINESS LETTERS

SECTIONS OF THE
BUSINESS LETTER

The business letter is usually divided into six parts: the heading, which includes the letter head and the date; the inside address; the salutation; the body; the complimentary close; and the signature. These parts are discussed below and illustrated in Figure B–2.

Heading. The heading of the business letter contains the letterhead and the date. Most firms put a great deal of thought into letterhead design because it contributes to the company image.

The date should *not* be typed in numerals, such as 1/4/9_ or 1/4/9_, even in intracompany memos, because the numerals can be misinterpreted. Although most North Americans would read 4/7/9_ as April 7, 199_, most Europeans and Latin Americans would read it as July 4, 199_.

The date should be written out using either of the following methods:

```
January 4, 19__                    4 January 19__
```

Inside address. The information in the inside address should duplicate the address on the envelope. Exact company designations and titles (as they appear in the letterhead) should be followed for the inside address.

The recipient's name in the inside address should be preceded by his or her title—*Ms., Mr., Mrs., Dr., General, Reverend,* and so forth. Both the title and the area of responsibility should be indicated.

```
Dr. Lester Jameson, Director
Medical Research Department
Cicero Clinics
3148 North Cicero Avenue
Chicago, IL 60606
```

If the initials that designate degrees have the same meaning as the person's title, one or the other should be omitted.

INCORRECT	CORRECT
Dr. Robert Clock, M.D.	Dr. Robert Clock Robert Clock, M.D.
Dr. Roberta Mann, Ph.D.	Dr. Roberta Mann Roberta Mann, Ph.D.

Words in the inside address, such as *street, north,* and *avenue,* should not be abbreviated unless the company specifically requires such action. On the whole, do not use abbreviations in the inside address.

Street numbers should always be written in numerals with the exception of *one.* Street names should be written out from First to Tenth streets. After that, numerals should be used. The zip code should follow the state. The following examples illustrate these recommendations.

```
Dr. Alberta Fine, Director    Ms. Joan Star, Manager
Conrad Research Center        Personnel Department
Conrad General Hospital       Foods, Inc.
1007 West 63rd Street         One East 95th Street
Los Angeles, CA 90024         Cincinnati, OH 45216
```

FIGURE B–2 Typical Business Letter

SCHOOL OF HOTEL MANAGEMENT
Midwestern University   Ann Arbor, Michigan 48109   (313) 555-2819

August 3, 19___

Ms. Elaine Cane, Editor
Gourmet Times
1500 East Pine Street
San Francisco, CA 94111

Dear Ms. Cane:

Your December issue of Gourmet Times was absolutely outstanding. The content, layout, four-color photography, and a dozen other details were completed in a most professional manner. In fact, it was all done so well, we want to request a favor of you.

As you probably know, the Division of Hotel Management at this University enjoys an excellent reputation. In addition to our usual classes and degree program in Hotel Management, we conduct two seminars each year for Chefs de Cuisine. Each of these seminars is four weeks long.

The participants in this program receive notebooks of materials. These are reference papers, readings, and a variety of materials which supplement the presentations and demonstrations. We would like to purchase 200 of your last two issues of Gourmet Times to include in the notebooks.

In addition, we would appreciate your participating in each seminar as a guest lecturer for a three-hour period. Of course we would be happy to provide first-class air fare, necessary accommodations, and a modest honorarium of $800 for each presentation.

Please call me collect, Ms. Cane, so we may discuss this, and if at all possible, select dates that you find convenient.

Cordially yours,

Raphael Peterson

Raphael Peterson, Ph.D.,
Associate Dean

RP/bp

Enclosure: Sales Brochure, Chefs de Cuisine Seminars

(Margin labels:) Heading · Inside address · Salutation · Body · Complimentary close · Signature · Enclosure line

Reverend Peter Jackson
Lutheran Central Church
7 South Ninth Avenue
New York, NY 10010

John T. Kasper, Ph.D.
Department of Management
Illinois State University
Springfield, IL 62704

Rabbi Herman Schaalman
Temple Emanuel
5959 North Sheridan Road
Chicago, IL 60626

Juanita Diaz, M.D.
Allerton Medical Center
17 North Bolton Avenue
Columbus, OH 43227

Salutation. Every effort should be made to use the recipient's name in the greeting or salutation. People respond more positively to their names than to *Dear Occupant, Dear Friend, Dear Sir,* or *Dear Purchasing Agent.*

Many firms have expended large sums of money to have a personally typed inside address and/or salutation added to thousands of form letters before mailing. It is felt (usually with reason) that the form letter receives a much better reaction from the reader because of the added personal touch.

When individual letters are typed and the name of the recipient is not known, it is still acceptable but somewhat old-fashioned to use *Dear Sir* or *Dear Madam* in the singular, and *Gentlemen* or *Ladies* in the plural. *My Dear Sirs, Dear Sirs,* and *Mesdames* are all considered obsolete. Today, in an effort not to use one-sex designation over another, neutral titles are strongly suggested by most office managers. *Dear Director, Dear Supervisor, or Dear Owner* are all preferable to *Dear Sir* or *Dear Madam.*

Body. Any discussion of the body of the letter must be concerned with the type of letter (sales, credit, collection, etc.) under consideration. From the point of view of appearance and format, however, the body should be attractively centered, broken into relatively short paragraphs, and surrounded by plenty of white space.

Complimentary close. The standard forms used in most letters are *Sincerely, Sincerely yours, Best regards,* and to a lesser extent, *Cordially* or *Cordially yours.* The complimentary close you choose should always be in keeping with the tone and purpose of the rest of the letter. A warm letter of praise for a business success, for example, might appropriately be closed with *Cordially,* while that same complimentary close would seem out of place in the signature block of a routine informational letter.

Signature. This section of the letter is handled in a variety of ways. In most firms the signature has three or four parts, with the trend toward four. The four-part signature includes the name of the company, the signature of the writer, and his or her typed name and title. If the signature has only three parts, the name of the company (in the letterhead) is omitted.

Yours truly,
CAIN PRODUCTS CO.

Tania Freeman

Tania Freeman
Sales Manger

Sincerely Yours,

Robert Black

Robert Black
Superintendent

```
Truly yours,                    Sincerely yours,

LOOP LAMP COMPANY               BAINE INC.

William Key                     Roberta Baine

William Key, Manager            Roberta Baine
                                Partner
```

Sometimes initials are placed immediately below the signature. This is done when the secretary signs the writer's name and adds his or her own initials. Readers often interpret this practice negatively. A reader may be irritated that the writer apparently could not find 15 seconds to sign the letter, so the writer should make every effort to sign all letters.

Of course it is possible that the writer dictated the letter in the morning and then left on a business trip. In such case, the writer obviously would not have been available to sign the letter when it was ready for a signature. Nevertheless, the fact is most people resent what the initials below a signature imply.

OTHER MECHANICAL FACTORS OF BUSINESS LETTERS

Attention line. Frequently you will find that one person in a company with which you are doing business gives you excellent service. Thus, in order to have Kelly handle your requests, you send your communications to his *attention*. If you send the letter directly to him, and he has left the company, it is very possible that the envelope will be *returned* to you or *forwarded* to him. However, if the letter is sent to his *attention* and he has left the company, the communication will normally be opened and processed by his successor. When a recipient's name is not known, address the letter to the department or position (e.g., Attention: Service Department).

The position of the attention line varies according to the letter style, although it usually appears in one of the following places:

```
Belmont Steel Company
1122 West Ninth Street
Bellmore, Indiana 47830

Dear Ms. Kaminsky:  Attention of Ms. Dana Kaminsky, Treasurer


Belmont Steel Company
1122 West Ninth Street
Bellmore, Indiana 47830

Attention of Ms. Dana Kaminsky, Treasurer

Dear Ms. Kaminsky:


Belmont Steel Company
1122 West Ninth Street
Bellmore, Indiana 47830

            Attention of Ms. Dana Kaminsky, Treasurer

Dear Ms. Kaminsky:
```

Many firms use an abbreviation for *attention*, either *Attn:* or *Att*.

Subject line. The subject line is a device used to speed handling or retrieval of correspondence from files. In addition, it can eliminate much of the first paragraph if it is worded carefully. Its position, like the attention line's, varies according to company preference.

```
Kelvyn Clock Company
1515 West Granby Street
Springville, CA 93265

Dear Purchase agent:           Subject: Your order #2136



Betsy B. Ice Cream
1000 West Nevada Avenue
Boulder, CO 80303

Dear Manager:

Subject: Your invoice #201
```

This subject line, like a *file number* or *in reply refer to file number B318*, can save time and increase office efficiency.

Identifying initials. For many years it was customary to place the dictator's and typist's initials in the lower left-hand section of the business letter. In recent years the trend seems to be toward omitting them.

But many firms still follow the practice, especially when all letters from a department are signed by one individual, even though any one of several people may have done the dictating. In this instance, the dictator's initials are used and, of course, do not match the signature of the department head. The initials identify the person who actually wrote the letter.

Some of the accepted variations in handling identifying initials are shown below. Note that both a slash mark and a colon are acceptable separators.

```
JS/rt              MRL:AO              TTA:bm
```

Enclosure line. The enclosure notation is usually placed immediately below the identifying initials and indicates that some item such as a check, invoice, or reprint has been included in the envelope along with the letter.

Either the word *Enclosure* or the abbreviation *Enc* is used. For only one enclosure, no numeral is used; for more than one, the number is indicated. Some firms and most federal government agencies identify each enclosure so that when one is withdrawn, it can be easily identified.

```
BM:rt                      LSM/rd
Enc                        Enclosures 3

GM/tl                      LM:ML
Enc 3                      Enclosure
  1. Birth certificate
  2. Visa
  3. Letter of reference
```

Carbon copies or photocopies.   If a letter is sent to Mr. Robert Blackstone, a copy of that letter should ordinarily not be forwarded to anyone else; the content of a business letter is a private matter between the writer and addressee. It is easy to understand how offended Mr. Blackstone might become if another person indicated, through a comment or a note, that he or she was aware of information that had been contained in a letter sent by Acme Products to Blackstone.

To avoid such a situation, and because it is also a matter of ethics, Mr. Blackstone is told that a copy of this letter addressed to him was sent to Mrs. Clayton. The device of *cc:* (carbon copy) or *c.* (copy) is used. Now that photocopies have taken the place of carbon paper, the abbreviation *pc* or the word *copy* is as common as *cc*.

```
DM/ts                           LT/sa
cc:Mrs. Clayton                 copy: Mrs. Clayton
[or pc:]                              Credit Department
```

Firms sometimes employ the initials *bc* or *bcc* which stands for *blind copy* or *blind carbon copy.* This is typed only on the copy and not on the original letter and tells the reader of the photocopy that Mr. Blackstone is not aware that a copy has been sent to a second party.

Letterhead.   The design of a letterhead depends on the impression a company is trying to convey. A law firm, for example, may choose classic type fonts and colors (such as black or gray) for its conservative letterhead. By contrast, a high-volume T-shirt distributor may choose a rainbow letterhead that, in type and design, virtually shouts out the company's business mission and sales enthusiasm. Companies usually hire graphic designers to create letterhead designs appropriate for the company, its industry, and its clientele.

Graphic designers and advertising agencies assist businespeople in designing a new letterhead or revising one. Revision is necessary, for styles in letterheads change as does company image. Outmoded type styles or a picture of a 25-year-old car or office machine in the letterhead design will not contribute to the impression of the company that wants to say it is an innovator. *Printer's Ink* magazine had this to say about the letterhead design and the message it conveys:

> In addition to identifying the sender, letterheads convey, both liminally and subliminally, an image of the company. The great mass of mail sent out by the average company gives its letterhead a significant role to perform in its sales-promotion and public-relations programs.

Many of the large paper corporations also assist in letterhead revision. Their staff artists draw up a new letterhead or send out letterhead kits that contain sample designs of letterheads and different grades and colors of stationery, graph paper, and directions for a do-it-yourself approach.

In addition to being attractive, meaningful, and in good taste, the letterhead should tell *who, where,* and *what.* The *who,* of course, is the name of the company, presented exactly as the firm wishes to be identified. This includes the precise abbreviations ("Corp." or "Inc.") and designations ("Furniture Manufacturers" or "Manufacturers of Furniture").

The *where* includes street address, city, state, zip code number, telephone number, fax number, and other items of this nature.

The *what* tells the reader the nature of the company's operations. It is disconcerting to receive a letter from the R. T. Cronin Corporation at 102 East Adams Street in Los Angeles and not be able to determine whether the firm manufactures kitchen appliances or conducts national surveys.

Many firms now use the empty space along the bottom of the page of a letter. A listing of the cities in which the company has outlets or plants, small pictures of the firm's products, or even the company address can be placed at the bottom. The type should be small and distinct, and the layout in balance with the information at the top of the stationery.

If you are writing on paper without a letterhead, place the inside heading, consisting of your street address, city, state, zip code, and date, above the inside address (see Figure B–3).

PUNCTUATION

The terms *open* or *closed* punctuation refer to end-of-line punctuation in the salutation and complimentary close. Open punctuation omits the colon or comma after the salutation and the comma after the complimentary close (see Figure B–4). Closed punctuation provides these punctuation marks (see Figure B–5). Much correspondence today uses open punctuation because it saves typing time and therefore money.

LETTER PLACEMENT
AND FORMAT

The appearance of the letter adds to the reader's image of the organization. A 12-line letter jammed at the top or bottom of the page contributes little to a good impression. A similar reaction on the part of the reader results when the letter or report has two heavy block paragraphs on each page with one 34 lines long and the other 44!

On the other hand, a well-balanced page with plenty of white space, attractive and adequate margins on all four sides, and typing that is centered, provides a positive visual appearance. These factors contribute to the type of image most firms wish to convey.

The most popular letter formats are block, modified block, modified block with indented paragraphs, and AMS simplified style. A *block letter* (Figure B–6) moves all letter elements to the left margin. This arrangement may appear somewhat less balanced on the page than other letter patterns, but it has the advantage of simplicity and efficiency, for the person who prepares the letter and for the reader. A *modified block letter* (Figure B–7) moves the date and the signature block to a point beginning at the vertical midline of the letter. Some writers and readers prefer the more balanced appearance of this letter arrangement on the page. The *modified block letter with indented paragraphs* (Figure B–8) follows the modified block pattern and also indents paragraphs (conventionally five spaces). This letter form is most like business letters written prior to 1960 and may appeal to those who favor traditional forms.

The *AMS simplified style* (Figure B–9) is the newest and most radical of business letter forms. Although less common than the other patterns discussed here, the AMS simplified style is used for marketing letters, announcements, and other communications where a sense of urgency and efficiency take precedence over other considerations. In AMS simplified style, the salutation is replaced by a subject statement. The complimentary close is omitted entirely or included in the last sentence of the letter text.

FIGURE B–3   Heading on Blank Stationery

```
4130 South Nelson Drive
Dallas, TX 75240
April 28, 19__

Mr. Yoshi Akita
Personnel Director
Compton and Compton, Inc.
1000 North Point Drive
Dallas, TX 75242

Dear Mr. Akita:
```

FIGURE B-4   Open Punctuation

```
Mr. Robert T. Scott
Morrell and Company
1515 West Ohio Street
St. Louis, MO 63125

Dear Mr. Scott

_____
_____
_____

Sincerely
```

FIGURE B-5   Closed Punctuation

```
Mr. Robert T. Scott
Morrell and Company
1515 West Ohio Street
St. Louis, MO 63125

Dear Mr. Scott:

_____
_____
_____

Sincerely,
```

FIGURE B–6   Full Block Form

Lyons Laundry Supply   *4880 West Markham Avenue*   *Oklahoma City, Oklahoma 73127*   *(405) 555-3000*

December 3, 19__

Ms. Eleanor Lang
Christ Community Hospital
1200 West Piedmont Ave.
Oklahoma City, OK 73128

Dear Ms. Lang:

Thank you for your inquiry of November 28 concerning the uniforms of your cafeteria and security personnel. Yes, we can certainly handle your request.

If it meets with your schedule, we can arrange to pick up all soiled linen on Monday and Thursday or Tuesday and Friday. All items picked up on Monday will be returned on Thursday; those picked up on Thursday will be returned on Monday. This rapid turnaround service permits you to operate with a minimum number of uniforms in your inventory.

All uniforms are washed in mild detergents, which lengthens the life of your linens. Minor tears or holes are repaired free of charge and areas of heavy stain are carefully hand scrubbed.

You will find our prices are extremely competitive: 55 cents for each shirt, jacket, skirt, or trouser unit. This includes washing and ironing and applies to 100 units or more per pickup. If less than 100 units are picked up, the price is 50 cents each.

We now service Manor Community Hospital, all branches of Franklin Savings and Loan, The Health-Mor Retirement Homes, and many others. We guarantee your complete satisfaction. Please call or visit our installation today, Ms. Lang, and we can begin service tomorrow.

Sincerely yours,

Joan Lyons
Sales Manager

JL/rm

FIGURE B-7 Modified Block Form

CHATEAU BABY TOYS, INC.

2511 State Street • Pecos, New Mexico 87552 • (505) 555-2500

October 12, 19__

Mr. Toby Wren, Senior Buyer
Gale's Department Stores
One North Hampden Road
New York, NY 10024

Dear Ms. Wren:

Although it will require overtime scheduling on our part, we will certainly fill the special order you called in yesterday. Of course we are delighted that our new Charming Toddler Line has been received so favorably by your customers.

As you requested, we will ship Order 2150 to your Lincoln Warehouse, and Order 2151 to your Market Terminal. Both shipments will arrive on October 24. Billing will be on our usual terms plus $450 for the additional labor charge we will incur. As you recall, we agreed on this sum (45 hours at $10 per hour) in our telephone conversation of October 11.

It is always a pleasure to do business with you. I am especially happy we were able to fulfill this emergency request.

Cordially yours,

Fern Maple

Fern Maple
Production Manager

FM/mm

pc: Mgr., Gale Lincoln Warehouse
    Mgr., Gale Market Terminal

FIGURE B–8 Modified Block with Indented Paragraphs

Quality Auto-Parts

1500 West Fulton Street   Philadelphia, Pennsylvania 19102   (215) 555-0550

May 15, 19__

Mr. John Baker, Mgr.
Ford Auto Service Center
100 West Conway Blvd.
Philadelphia, PA 19106

Dear Mr. Baker:

   Thank you for your interest in stocking our complete line of auto radio, stereo, and tape decks. Certainly the Clear Bell product has earned an excellent and well-deserved reputation.

   We discussed with our headquarters your request to stock 200 units on a consignment basis. Since your request would be a departure from our usual COD terms and might cause problems with our other accounts, we feel it is not possible to comply.

   We can, however, offer an alternative. We will ship the order with payment of one half the total on a COD basis and the balance within 90 days. In both instances, our 2 percent discount will apply.

   We do want to work with you in every way possible, Mr. Baker. Please call us collect and all items will be shipped to you within ten days.

Cordially yours,

Martin Cahill

Martin Cahill
Vice President, Sales

MC/bp

FIGURE B-9   AMS Simplified Style Letter

Williams Electronic Supply, Inc.
3892 Breston Place
Ft. Collins, CO 80525-4061
(303) 555-9540

January 7, 199__

Frank Devlin, Manager
Devlin Industrial Wiring, Inc.
55 Leavitt Street
Denver, CO 80112

UPCOMING INDUSTRIAL ARTS FAIR, MAY 15-17, 19__

Your booth at last year's Industrial Arts Fair certainly made a hit, Frank. No doubt your creative staff is already planning surprises for us this year.

Williams Electronic Supply wants to team up with Devlin Industrial Wiring for this year's fair. Together we can put on a fascinating demonstration of recent advances in domestic and industrial uses of electricity. You and I spoke briefly of this possibility at last year's fair. We agreed then that our mutual efforts would be great for the fair and good advertising for our companies.

I'm planning to visit Denver on January 18, 19__. Can we meet to discuss our common interests then? You can reach me weekdays at the number above. If we haven't made connection by January 15, I'll give you a call before my trip to Denver.

Until then, best wishes from all of us at Williams Electronic Supply.

Cindy Galloway

Cindy Galloway
Advertising Director

CG/wol
Enclosure: "Planning for the 199_ Industrial Arts Fair"

**FOLDING A
BUSINESS LETTER**

Distinguish your business correspondence by folding letters precisely. Note that in folding both two-fold and three-fold letters, a one-half inch tab is provided for the reader's convenience in opening the letter.

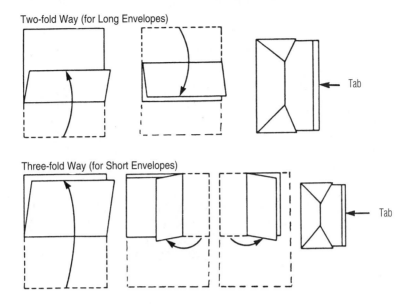

Two-fold Way (for Long Envelopes)

Tab

Three-fold Way (for Short Envelopes)

Tab

**ENVELOPE
CONVENTIONS**

The envelope's balanced, neat appearance influences your reader's attitudes toward your letter, even before he or she has opened it:

RONALD WINTERS
WESTERN INVESTORS INC
396 BRANCHAW BLVD
DALLAS TX 75234

MS BRENDA VICTORS, MANAGER
COGNETICS INC.
33 SEVENTH ST
DALLAS TX 75203

PERSONAL

According to the 1993 *National Five-Digit Zip Code & Post Office Directory,* the U.S. Post Office recommends the following placement of addresses typed in upper case, without optional punctuation (for easier reading by optical character recognition equipment):

Large Envelopes (Number 10)

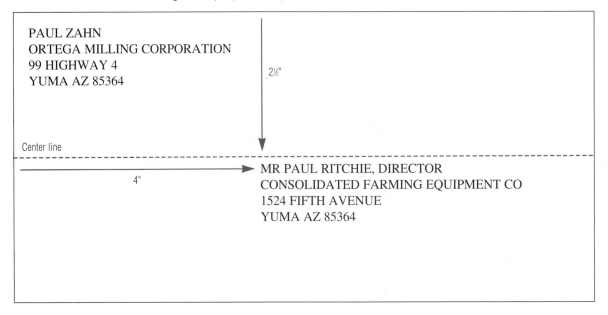

Small Envelopes (Number 6 3/4)

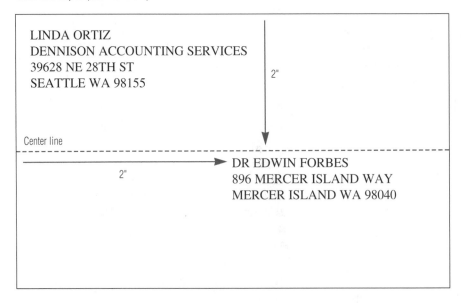

Use the following abbreviations on envelopes for states (without a period that usually accompanies abbreviations):

AL	(Alabama)	LA	(Louisiana)	OK	(Oklahoma)
AK	(Alaska)	ME	(Maine)	OR	(Oregon)
AZ	(Arizona)	MD	(Maryland)	PA	(Pennsylvania
AR	(Arkansas)	MA	(Massachusetts)	PR	(Puerto Rico)
CA	(California)	MI	(Michigan)	RI	(Rhode Island)
CO	(Colorado)	MN	(Minnesota)	SC	(South Carolina)
CT	(Connecticut)	MS	(Mississippi)	SD	(South Dakota)
DE	(Delaware)	MO	(Missouri)	TN	(Tennessee)
DC	(D.C.)	MT	(Montana)	TX	(Texas)
FL	(Florida)	NE	(Nebraska)	UT	(Utah)
GA	(Georgia)	NV	(Nevada)	VT	(Vermont)
HI	(Hawaii)	NH	(New Hampshire)	VA	(Virginia)
ID	(Idaho)	NJ	(New Jersey)	WA	(Washinton)
IL	(Illinois)	NM	(New Mexico)	WV	(West Virginia)
IN	(Indiana)	NY	(New York)	WI	(Wisconsin)
IA	(Iowa)	NC	(North Carolina)	WY	(Wyoming)
KS	(Kansas)	ND	(North Dakota)		
KY	(Kentucky)	OH	(Ohio)		

Additional instructions on envelopes. Business communication texts usually recommend that instructions such as "Confidential," "Personal," or "Time-dated Materials" be placed to the left or the right of the address, and a bit below it:

RACHEL NATHAN
TREVOR COSMETICS INC
702 WEST ST
ST LOUIS MO 63116

                         MS BETTY KONWAY, MANAGER
                         STYLE SETTERS SALON
                         70 BILLINGS ROAD
                         ST LOUIS MO 63137

TIME-DATED MATERIALS

The U.S. Post Office suggests that only instructions intended for the mail deliverer (such as "Special Delivery") be placed on the right of the envelope. Such instructions, the Post Office requests, should be placed four spaces below the stamp.

RICHARD FONG
AVC AUDIO CORPORATION
602 GENSEMER LANE
HARRISBURG PA 17111

CONFIDENTIAL   SPECIAL DELIVERY

                                        TECHNICAL SERVICE DIRECTOR
                                        FREDE COMPUTER PRODUCTS INC
                                        30702 HILL DRIVE
                                        BOULDER CO 80302

FORMATS FOR INTERNATIONAL BUSINESS COMMUNICATION

Other countries use a wide variety of formats for business memos, letters, and other documents. Those presented here are intended to illustrate this variety. As a general rule, a U.S. businessperson writing international memos or letters will be well-served by using standard U.S. memo form and block or modified block form for letters. But international readers may be complimented by a U.S. writer's willingness to use formats (Figures B–10 through B–13) more familiar in their country.

REPORT AND PROPOSAL FORMATS

Formats for reports and proposals differ somewhat from company to company. Some businesses prefer that the body text of these longer documents be double spaced for easier reading and editing. Others specify their own placement for elements on the title page, particularly when the company logo is involved.

The guidelines that follow in Figures B–14 through B–22 are generally accepted in business and government. If the format practices of your company vary from these guidelines, you should follow the established patterns within your organization.

FIGURE B–10 Japanese Memo in Translation

Kyoto Workers' Cooperative   5 October 19__
Messrs. Sun Yee and Hyung Takishi

                              Rising Sun Garment Co.
                              Director, General Manager
                              Karo Yamada (Official seal)

                    Subject: New Hiring Needs

Dear Sirs:

    It has been our pleasure over many years to work with you in filling our labor needs. I would like to take this opportunity to thank you for supporting our business efforts in many ways.

    We have now finalized plans to hire 16 sewing machine operators beginning 1 November 19__. It has been our practice in the past in such matters to rely upon your expertise in providing initial screening of suitable candidates. We hereby authorize you to conduct this activity on our behalf, with terms usual to our business relationship.

    We will appreciate your confirmation of this request as soon as possible.

                              With our best regards.

                    Supplements

          1. Job description
          2. Company employee plan

FIGURE B–11 Chilean Memo in Translation

Memorandum No. 693

Antecedent: Your memorandum
#212, 07, 25, __

Subject: Request for an additional secretary

FROM: FINANCE MANAGER
TO: GENERAL MANAGER

Regarding your memorandum of antecedent, I must regretfully decline your well-supported request for an additional secretary. I sincerely hope that the budget to be approved by the legislature next month will enable all of us to obtain the office help we so desperately need. Until that time, however, no additional employees of Level 3 or lower may be retained.

For your understanding in this difficult matter, I am grateful.

Sincerely yours,

Jose Martinez

FIGURE B–12   Russian Memo in Translation

09.1.9_

Svyatoslav Nikolayevich Kislorodov
Deputy Director of Personnel

Respected Director Kislorodov,

The two agricultural experts you have assigned to my district arrived on 08.20.__ and have already begun to meet with farmers in the area. They have promised a report to me of their initial findings and recommendations no later than 11.1.9_. I will forward a copy of that report to you.

My sincere thanks for your efforts in making the services of these experts available to my district.

With sincere respect,

Boris Ivanovich Boblyubimov
Director, District 7

FIGURE B–13 Brazilian Letter in Translation (Company correspondence from many South American countries begins with a cover sheet bearing the company name and logo. The format in this figure shows the form of the second or following pages.)

19 September 19__

Office of the Director
Government Contracts

Mrs. Maria Ozable
Supervisor of Artisans
Montoya Civic Projects
Montoya, Brazil

My Dear Ms. Ozable,

I am delighted to inform you that your grant application #1908 has been approved by my office. My deputy will be in touch with you within ten days to acquaint you with the accounting and payment procedures used by the Government Contracts Office.

Permit me to congratulate you on your superb achievements in Montoya. We trust that the proceeds of this well-deserved grant will assist you in attaining your future goals.

With sincere respect and best wishes,

Alexandra Ortega
Director

TITLE PAGE

As illustrated in Figure B–14, the title page sets forth the title of your report or proposal, the audience to whom it is directed, the person(s) who wrote the work, and the date of submission (or completion, if so requested). Note how these elements are balanced by centering and spacing to provide an attractive first impression of the document.

TABLE OF CONTENTS

The page (see Figure B–15) lists major headings (and minor headings, if helpful to the reader) with accompanying page numbers. Spaced periods are often used to attach items on the left margin with their page numbers on the right margin. Items in the table of contents are not centered vertically when they do not take up the entire page.

FIRST BODY PAGE AND FOLLOWING BODY PAGES

As illustrated in Figure B–16 this page can begin with the report or proposal title, especially if no title page is used. The body text begins after a double space following the heading (such as Introduction or Overview). The text may be single or double spaced as required by your organization or reader.

Following body pages (see Figure B–17) maintain the spacing chosen for the first page. In no case should a heading appear as the last line on a page.

BIBLIOGRAPHY PAGE

As illustrated in Figure B–18, the word *BIBLIOGRAPHY* appears in uppercase letters centered at the top of the page. Works referred to in the text (or consulted, in the case of a bibliography titled LIST OF WORKS CONSULTED) are listed alphabetically according to consistent bibliographic standards as specified in such guides as the *MLA Style Sheet* or *Publication Manual of the American Psychological Association.*

If notes are place at the end of the report or proposal instead or at the foot of text pages (i.e., instead of as footnotes), a page is placed before the bibliography page and is titled NOTES or ENDNOTES. References are listed sequentially according to their numbered appearance in the text. Again, the guidelines of one style manual should be followed consistently.

ORDER OF PAGES IN REPORTS AND PROPOSALS

Figures B–19 through B–22 specify the usual order of pages within reports and proposals.

FIGURE B–14   Title Page Layout for Report or Proposal

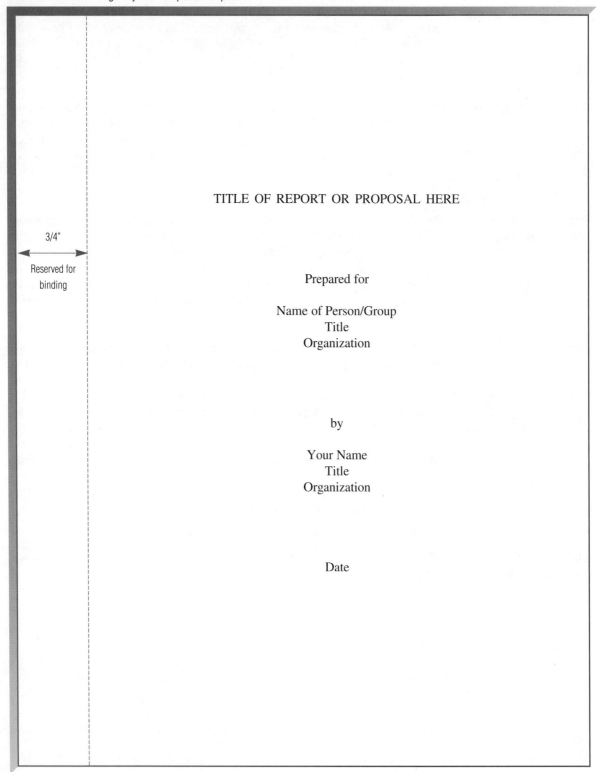

FIGURE B-15 Table of Contents Layout for Proposal or Report

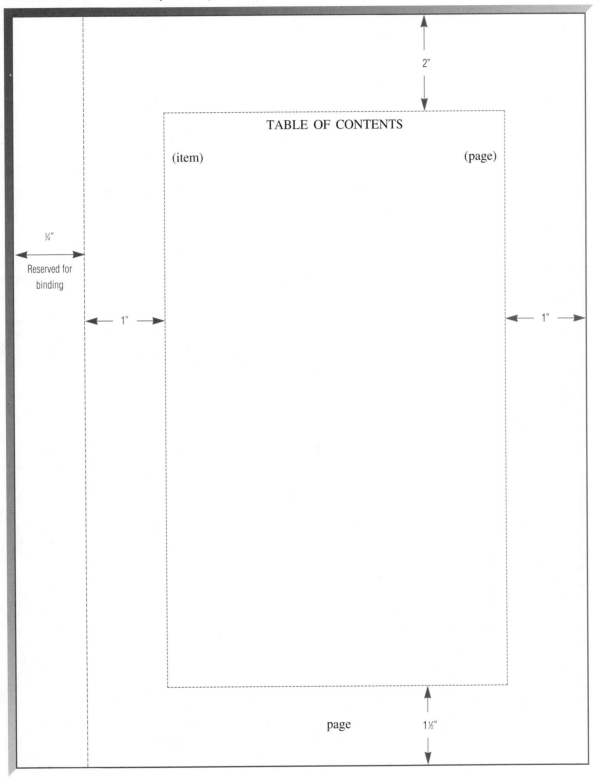

FIGURE B–16   First Page Layout of the Body of a Proposal or Report

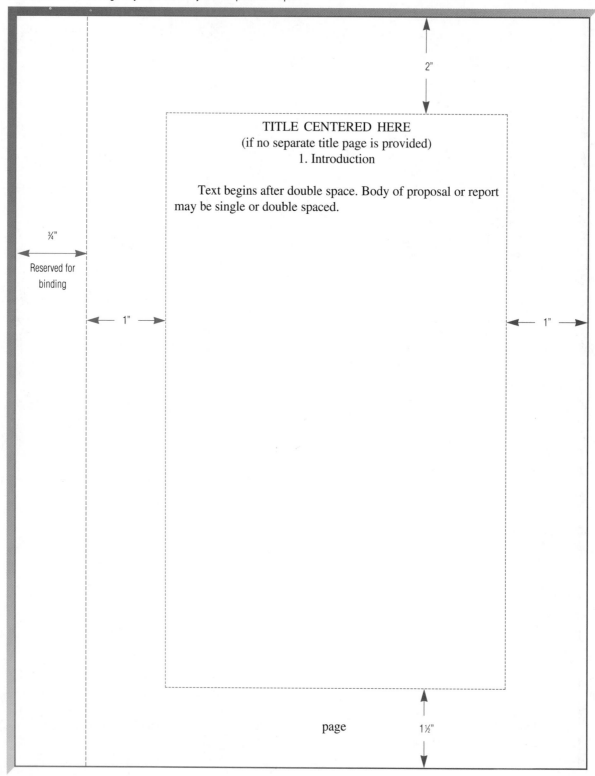

FIGURE B–17   Typical Text Page Layout for Proposal or Report

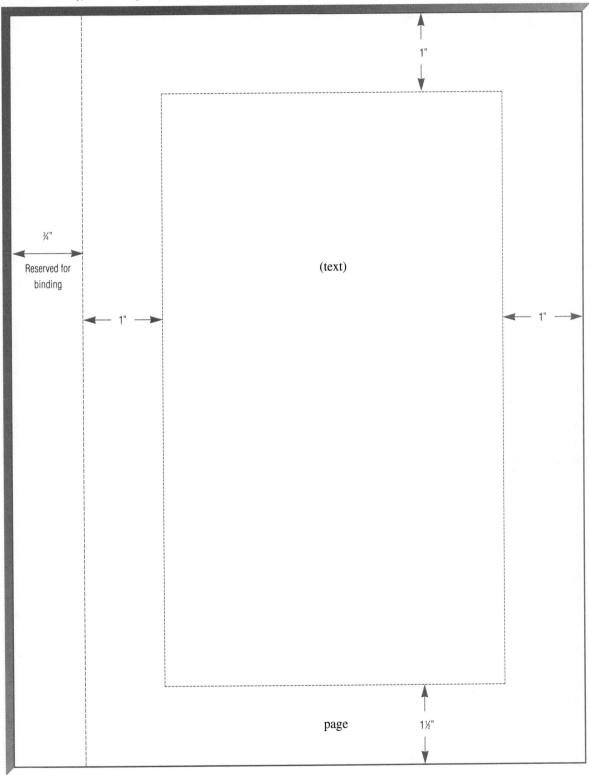

FIGURE B–18   Bibliography Layout for Proposal or Report

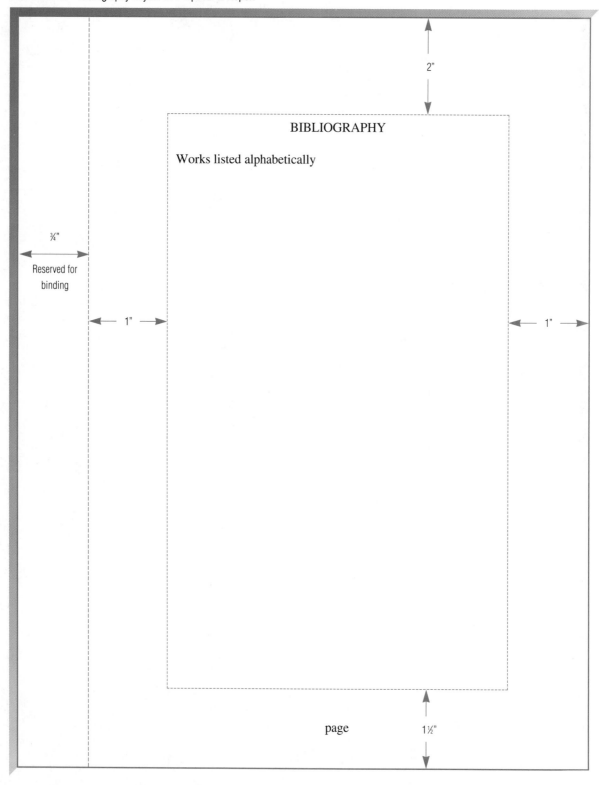

FIGURE B–19 Order of Pages in a Short Report

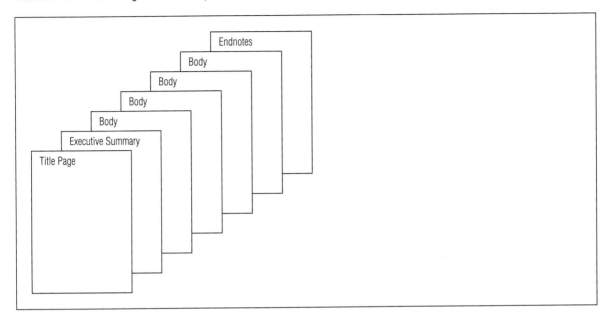

FIGURE B–20 Order of Pages in Formal Report

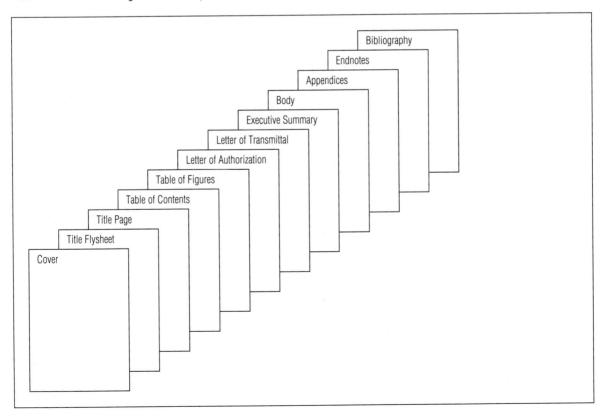

FIGURE B–21   Order of Pages in a Short Proposal

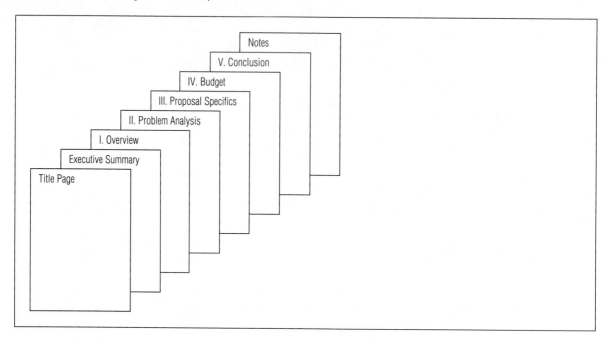

FIGURE B–22   Order of Pages in a Long Proposal

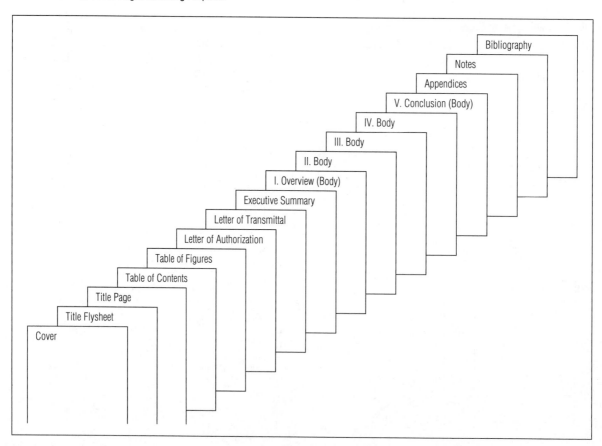

Message
    definition of, 6
    in Mathematical Theory of
        Communication (Shannon and
        Weaver), 50, 51
    perception of, 7
Messaging, 66–67
Metaphor, 157
Minutes
    distribution of after meeting,
        576–577
    of meeting, sample of, 578
Misrepresentation, in facts or graphics,
    103–104, 105
Model, lack of as resistance factor in
    collaborative writing, 171
Modem, 55
Money–back guarantee, as proof in
    effective sales letter, 275
Monitor, flat–screen, for computer
    graphics, 393–394
*Monthly Catalog of United States
    Government Publications*, as
    research tool, 385

National Directory of Newsletters, as
    research tool, 382
*National Minority Business
    Information System: A National
    Directory of Minority– and
    Women–Owned Firms*, as research
    tool, 387
National Newspaper Index, as research
    tool, 384
National Union Catalog, as research
    tool, 381
Need, establishment of for meeting,
    567
Network
    cultural, definition of, 7
    group interaction, definition of, 7
    interpersonal, definition of, 7
Networking, as source for finding job,
    299
Newsearch, as research tool, 384
Newspaper Abstracts, as research tool,
    384–385
Newspaper indexes, guides to, as
    research tool, 384–385
Newspapers
    guides to, as research tool, 382
    as secondary source for research,
        354
Noise, in Mathematical Theory of
    Communication (Shannon and
    Weaver), 50, 51
Nonverbal communication, 83, 86
    barriers to, 11, 14–18
        versus verbal communication
            barriers, 14–18
        during crisis, 598–599

customs and, 88
ethics and, 103–104
listening for, 554
versus verbal communication, 19–20
Norms, importance of in cross–cultural
    communication, 84–87
Notes
    at meeting, 571–572
    use of as presentation method, 540
Numbering, for outline, 131–132

Observation, as survey instrument,
    361
Office systems, integrated, 63–64
Online sources, of indexes, 355
Openings, to attract attention as part of
    effective sales
    letter, 273–274
Openness, as value in United States,
    90
Optical character recognition (OCR),
    54
Oral communication, 66, 520–528
    presentation and, 520–522
Order of development
    of outline in writing process, 130
    as strategy for precise response by
        audience as result of long
        presentation, 541
Orders, 223–233
    acknowledging, 223–227, 228–230
    placing, 223
    refusing, 227, 231–233
    responding to, 223–227
Organization
    beliefs about, 86–87
    poor, causing ineffective
        communication, 17
    as principle of effective
        communication for business
        letter, 209
Organizational chart, as visual aid,
    405–406
Organizational communication, 23–45
    directions of, 23–24
Organizational plan, in writing
    process, 118, 121
Orientation interview, 561–562
Orientation manual, for employees,
    33–34, 35
Outline
    mechanics of, 131–137
    of proposal, 492
    for report, 425, 426
    types of, 135–137
    value of, 129–130
    in writing process, 122–123,
        129–137
Output, definition of, 6
"Outside" agency records, as proof in
    effective sales letter, 275

Paragraph, types of, 151
Paragraph outline, 137
Paragraphs, 151–153
Paralanguage, 554
Parallel development, in outline, 132
Participants
    at meeting, 572–573
    selection of for meeting, 568
Participation, by audience as strategy
    for precise response by audience as
    result of long presentation, 541
Pay envelopes, insertions in for
    employees, 35–36
PC. *See* Personal computer (PC)
Pen plotter, for computer graphics,
    393–394
Perception, 7
    as barrier to effective listening, 550
    differences in causing ineffective
        communication, 14
Periodic report, 422, 445–446
    samples of, 447–453
Periodical indexes, guides to, as
    research tool, 382–383
Periodicals
    guides to, as research tool, 382
    as secondary source for research,
        354
Personal computer (PC), 53–56
    database and, 56
    as file cabinet, 55
    security and, 55–56
    as training tool, 54–55
Personal data, listed in resume, 323
Personal space, 79
Personalities, causing ineffective
    communication, 16
Personnel, description of in business
    plan, 511
Persuasion
    to encourage readers to act, 276,
        277–278
    in proposal, 494, 501–555
Persuasive presentation, 521, 537
Persuasive report, as type of formal
    report, 458–459
Photograph
    as part of effective sales letter, 273
    as visual aid, 409–410
Pictogram, as visual aid, 407–408
Pictorial chart, as visual aid, 407–408
Pie chart, as visual aid, 400–401
Placement office, as source for finding
    job, 297–298
Policy memo, 189, 191
Population
    in research, 357–358
    sample of, 358
    selection of sample of, 358–360
    survey of, 360–361